D1288862

**DOW JONES-IRWIN
GUIDE TO
COMMODITIES TRADING**

Dow Jones-Irwin
guide to
commodities trading.

BRUCE G. GOULD

 1973

DOW JONES-IRWIN, INC. Homewood, Illinois 60430

© DOW JONES–IRWIN, INC., 1973

This publication is designed to provide accurate and
authoritative information in regard to the subject matter
covered. It is sold with the understanding that the
publisher is not engaged in rendering legal, accounting, or
other professional service. If legal advice or other expert
assistance is required, the services of a competent
professional person should be sought.

*From a Declaration of Principles jointly adopted by a Committee
of the American Bar Association and a Committee of Publishers.*

First Printing, August 1973
Second Printing, May 1974

ISBN 0-87094-047-3
Library of Congress Catalog Card No. 72-98126

Printed in the United States of America

PREFACE

I'd rather be right
   and take a profit
Than be wrong
   and take a loss.
     —"100 days" Pomeroy

This is a book about the business of bearing risk, wherein it is suggested that commodities are not stocks and ought not to be traded as though they were. Trading commodities is viewed as a game subject to rational decisions based on real world facts. The price of a stock is based solely on what it will bring; the price of a commodity contract must at all times be the best possible guess of the price at which the actual wheat will be milled, the corn eaten, the silver turned into jewelry and photographs, the platinum into smog control devices. Trading commodities is the last field of speculation in the country which is both rational and legal.

Trading commodities is like playing bridge or poker and the person whose profession requires his immediate interest probably hasn't the time for a second game which will call upon his waking thoughts. Trading commodities doesn't require much direct daily time and isn't even overly risky, properly played, but, like any challenge, it will eat into the thinking time of the player, and any trader looking into commodities ought to see that he has the time to spare. Any college graduate who can point to a bad semester's grades due to playing bridge has already experienced the distraction of a challenge and its effects on what he was supposed to be doing.

I have traded stocks and continue to trade them but for entirely different reasons than I trade commodities. My stock portfolio is designed to complement my life insurance and is made up of blue chipish issues of companies I have been assured will be around long after I am gone. My stocks are dealt with in very somber terms of "estate planning" and accumulating personal wealth. To me, commodities is a game, not an investment, and I do not mix the two in my planning or in my cash accounts. I am a professional speculator, by which I mean I make a significant proportion of my yearly income on the futures exchanges. In 1969 when I was fresh out of law school, in less than seven months I made over $80,000 on a $5,000 investment. I have never turned my back on commodities since. This money is income and, like income coming from my legal practice, I do not mix it with my stock portfolio account money which is used for entirely different purposes.

The book is divided into three parts, starting with a general overview of the market, why it exists, who uses it, how they use it, and the position of the speculator in all of this. I have tried to keep this section as short and to the point as possible with the idea of providing a framework on which the reader can hang as much material as possible. I have tried to organize the data into consistent ideas that form some sort of whole. So doing has inevitably led to some duplication. Any discussion of the commodity contract itself will inevitably border on the people who trade the contracts. So be it. The major problem of the new trader as well as the most experienced, is cataloging in his own mind the data that he finds in all kinds of different sources. Hopefully, material the reader finds in other books, market letters, or the *Wall Street Journal* will fit somewhere in his understanding of the market, even though it is not expressed in the terms I have chosen. The words will be the same and if the ideas are different, the reader ought to be able to interpret them for himself.

The speculator is playing for price appreciation, and Part Two of this book is limited solely to commodity price factors which determine the cash price which in turn determines the price of the futures contract held by the speculator. Random walk, the economists' theory of what is going on, is also discussed. Price is viewed separately as a function of cash fundamentals, again as the vehicle of speculation by the public, and once again as a random fluctuation with characteristics all its own. These three views are not contradictory but they are distinct and have each been given a separate chapter to see that they stay clear. Finally, in Part Two, trading facts about some of the major commodities are given.

Part Three contains specific facts and

trading systems that the speculator will be dealing with. Although the book, as a matter of principle, takes a dim view of predicting the future, the speculator is going to come across prediction systems in his trading if he does not already have his own. Every important forecasting system available is included and tied together through the best economic studies applicable. Chart formations, moving averages, fundamental study, odds, and seasonals all fit into a trader's opinions about the market. Inclusion in this chapter does not necessarily mean recommendation. I have attempted to work them all in so that the newcomer can see in one place what is available and how it fits in with everything else. My own prejudices, I believe, are clear in the text.

Forecasting is a necessary part of any program—the trader does have to choose a commodity and a side to play, long or short. What to do once a position has been chosen, however, will determine a trader's success. Part Three is designed to give the trader a start toward his *own* trading system and a basis for weeding out suggestions that come to him without value, including my own.

My own trading system is outlined in Chapter 15.

In simplifying the book so that the entire market can be understood by a novice without background in commodities, surprisingly little specific data had to be left out. The book does admit to rather distinct limitations, however. Wherever feasible, which was most places, real data has been used to make points and the reader will pick up specific data about three major commodities traded in the United States; soybeans, wheat and corn. But market conditions change and no book can possibly compete with daily, weekly, and monthly periodicals for a "feel" of the current market. Specific aspects of the market are covered in other books on commodities and the trader is encouraged, of course, to use all the material he can get his hands on. A list of periodicals and books is given in the back of this book, and subscribing to a selection of these will give the trader all the data which exists on the various markets. The most significant ones are free from the Department of Agriculture to anyone who puts his name on the automated mailing list.

This book is written from the viewpoint of the speculator and has left out considerable amounts of specific data of use to hedgers. Farmers and processors might find the overview valuable but must be referred to other texts. Traders wishing an academic look at the markets, rather than the pragmatic view given here, are referred to *Economics of Futures Trading* by Thomas A. Hieronymus (New York: Commodity Research Bureau, 1971). This book is of little direct use to the speculator but may be of interest to the serious student. Academics with mathematical backgrounds are referred to advanced theoretical subjects such as the cobweb theorem, random walk, and so on, in the back of Chapter 12. Traders wishing to attempt prediction solely through the study of past chart behavior might try L. Dee Belveal, who believes in such things (*Commodity Speculation with Profits in Mind,* Wilmette, Ill.: Commodities Press, 1967).

Traders of whatever ilk will be well reimbursed for the $18 spent on the *Commodity Yearbook* (New York: Commodity Research Bureau, annual edi-

tion). This is neither a trading book nor a textbook, but a list of charts of commodity statistics (including some that are not traded on futures markets) and is invaluable to the trader who wishes to put the current market in perspective. Chapter 13 of this book presupposes ownership of a copy. Other sources of information are discussed in context. Most are free and the important ones are listed, along with addresses, in the appendix.

Some people can never become successful commodity speculators. Either their open positions (positions which haven't been closed out) take over their entire waking consciousness and ruin their sleep, or they get a taste of success and dive in as though the country were going to give up bread. Commodities is not a Roman Circus, and the successful trader is the actuary who keeps his cool when large masses of money make their move, not the hero who believes soybeans are worth $3.00 a bushel and any other price is un-American.

A good cliche is "sell down to the sleeping point." Keep positions you can live with. If you are strung out in your account to the point where the least reversal will wipe you out, you'll never be around to play the odds and win. Nor will you be in control of your position, for your broker must, by law, close you out.

I am a professional speculator, yet I often have no position at all. Sometimes I see no risk *I wish to take, but more often* I get out for awhile to regain perspective and take a vacation. If you can't get out, you have no business trading commodities. I am biased in favor of commodities speculation; I enjoy it immensely; this book is going to reflect that bias. But at the same time I have no interest in talking anybody into trading.

For those who make it, commodities is the only game in town.

ACKNOWLEDGMENTS

I wish to express my appreciation to the following individuals who have, either directly or indirectly, been responsible for whatever measure of success I have achieved in the world of the commodity markets—Richard G. Jeffers (who will always be Number One in my book), Stephen K. Husby, Donald J. Sankus, Eileen Castello, Harold, Alma, and Mary Ellsperman, Palmer Peterson, Ralph Parks, and Peter H. Pomeroy.

I also wish to express my appreciation to Jack L. Hofer (a scholar in the field of computers and commodities), to Edward J. Mader (my long-time friend and now the Director of Commodity Research for E. F. Hutton & Co. in New York) and to Houston Cox (Commodity Vice President of Reynolds Securities and one of the finest gentlemen I know).

My special thanks go to William Schultz who assisted me in the preparation of this manuscript.

I wish to dedicate this book to Lawrence Douglass Gould—a more understanding father no son ever had—and to Magda F. Pomeroy (may God take good care of her . . . wherever she may be).

July 1973
BRUCE GRANT GOULD

CONTENTS

LIST OF CHARTS

Part one
AN OVERVIEW

1

A WHOLE NEW GAME

After more than 100 years of continuous trading, the nation's commodity futures markets are only now coming into the limelight. In 1972, 18.3 million futures contracts were made on the nation's 13 commodity exchanges, worth $189.4 billion. This figure is up from the year before which saw 14.6 million contracts formed worth $155 billion. (See Figs. 2 and 3, p. 4.)

Since 1960, the growth in commodity futures trading in the United States has been almost phenomenal. In 1960, less than 4 million futures contracts were traded. Twelve years later, the figure had increased to above 18 million contracts, an annual growth rate above 37 percent.

In 1960, the value of the commodities contracted for on the nation's 13 commodity exchanges totaled $30 billion. By 1972 this figure had risen to the $189 billion level. This 1972 figure was an increase of 22 percent from the 1971 level and $42.3 billion *more* than the total value of stocks traded on the New York Stock Exchange during 1971.

Currently, 1972 holds the record for volume on commodity exchanges but it appears as though new records will again be set in 1973. (See Fig. 4, p. 5.)

The Chicago Board of Trade is the equivalent in commodities to the New York Stock Exchange in stocks, normally handling 50 percent of all commodity futures activity. In 1971, the Board of Trade surpassed the New York Stock Exchange in volume with a figure of $88.4 billion. (See Fig. 5, p. 6 and Fig. 1 below.)

FIGURE 1
ESTIMATED MONTHLY VOLUME
(figures in billions of dollars)

	1970	
	July	*August*
New York Stock Exchange	$ 6.90	$ 6.40
American Stock Exchange	.67	.59
Totals	$ 7.57	$ 6.99
Chicago Board of Trade	7.60	7.10
Chicago Mercantile Exchange	4.91	5.56
Totals	$10.10	$ 9.50

Source: Chicago Mercantile Exchange.

The Chicago Mercantile Exchange is the nation's second largest commodity exchange, although far behind the Board of Trade in volume. In the first quarter of 1972, the Merc set new records for the highest volume in any single day and any single month, both in January. The first quarter became the highest volume quarter in the Merc's 52-year history, trading 1,117,000 contracts worth $15.7 billion. This upset the old record set in 1969. (See Fig. 6 on p. 6.)

A new exchange, the West Coast

FIGURE 2
VOLUME OF FUTURES TRADING—1957-72

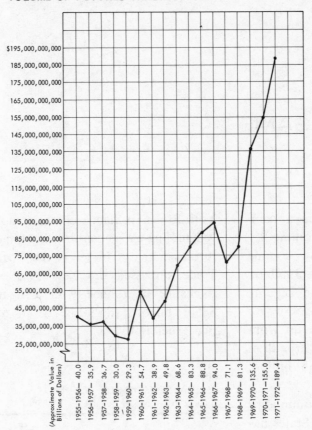

FIGURE 3
ESTIMATED VALUE OF COMMODITIES TRADED—1955-72

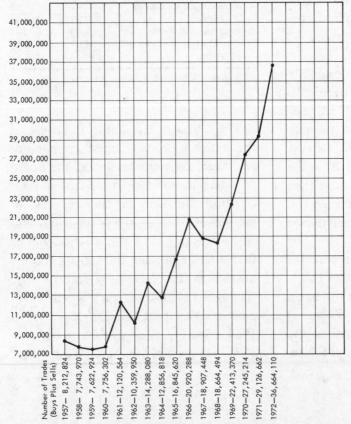

Note: This chart gives total trades, both buys and sells of contracts. To determine the actual number of contracts traded, divide total figure by 2.

FIGURE 4

Commodities

Futures Trading Rose Over 20% to Record; '72 Contract Value Said to Top $200 Billion

By JOSEPH M. WINSKI

Staff Reporter of THE WALL STREET JOURNAL

CHICAGO — Farmers in Aroostook County, Maine, feared their potatoes would freeze in the ground. Feeder cattle were mired in knee-deep Texas mud and couldn't be brought to market. The government in Peru halted fishing for anchovies, and auto makers lined up platinum for use in antipollution devices. Russia jumped into the grain markets.

These diverse events have this in common: They are among the reasons 1972 commodity futures trading surged to a record level by a wide margin. The 1972 trading volume surged more than 20%, hitting 17.5 million to 17.8 million contracts on the nation's 13 commodity exchanges, according to an estimate by John W. Clagett, president of the Association of Commodity Exchange Firms Inc. of New York.

The combination of increased trading and strong price advances in many commodities, Mr. Clagett says, sent the 1972 value of traded contracts to "well over $200 billion," almost triple the value five years ago. The 1971 value was $189.4 billion.

Trading activity in 1972 was triple the level in 1962, says Mr. Clagett, who three years ago predicted futures volume would increase 10% to 15% a year for the foreseeable future. "And I see no reason to change that now," he adds, noting that his forecasts had been conservative.

Market analysts say "the certainty of uncertainty" will continue to build volume among commercial hedgers, who use futures to protect their production and inventories against price drops, and speculators, who assume price risks for the producers in hopes of big profit. They also say that more and more trading is being done by individuals who used to be solely in the securities markets.

"We're getting a continually more sophisticated public and a growing awareness of what commodity markets are," says Henry Hall Wilson, president of the Chicago Board of Trade, the oldest and largest futures exchange in the world. The 1969-70 bear market in stocks may have been a major influence, he says, because "that's when brokerage firms found income from their commodities business was holding up and they beefed up their efforts in commodities."

A concern that has is Merrill Lynch, Pierce Fenner & Smith Inc., which did so much to popularize stock investing. Commodity futures trading has been "the big and dramatically growing segment of our business," says Richard Freeburg, national sales manager of the commodities division. A year ago, Merrill Lynch started its own full-time commodities news wire, and recently it began training commodities brokers for each branch office.

Four years ago, the Board of Trade estimated that 50,000 people were trading commodity futures. The Chicago Mercantile Exchange estimates the number at 500,000 now and predicts it will reach three million by 1980. Even that figure is dwarfed by the 32.5 million people who own stocks, but it represents "the recent explosion of interest" in commodities, says Mr. Clagett, the trade group head.

The Chicago Mercantile Exchange promotes futures trading with a $1.5 million budget (about three times the expenditures of the bigger Board of Trade) as an exciting, profitable investment opportunity. On the other hand, Bache & Co. recently advised its brokers to be extra-careful in screening customers who want to open a commodity trading account with the brokerage firm because of the high degree of risk involved in the fast-moving markets.

But with the risks come potentially big profit, which was the case in 1972 as consumer demand for beef outran supplies, grain exports skyrocketed unexpectedly and other supply-demand variables changed greatly.

The 124-year-old Chicago Board of Trade again accounted for more than half the total United States futures trading because of heavy trading in wheat, soybeans and soybean meal. Board of Trade volume reached about 9.3 million contracts, up from 8.5 million in 1971 and 67.6% higher than 10 years ago. Soybean meal trading was especially heavy late in the year because of higher world demand for protein-rich livestock feed and lower supplies because of the halt in Peruvian fishing for anchovies, which are used to make fish meal, a competing animal feed.

"We're also delighted with the success of silver and plywood," says Board of Trade president Wilson.

The Chicago Mercantile Exchange's volume rebounded to a record of more than 4.5 million contracts, after trading dipped in 1970 and 1971. Pork belly futures trading, which was up 24%, through November, continues to be the volume leader on the 53-year-old Chicago Mercantile. But for the first time since 1964, pork bellies accounted for less than half the exchange volume. That's because activity in cattle futures soared 82% and in live hogs nearly 100%. Prices for these contracts also hit record levels in 1972, along with lumber, milo, Idaho potatoes and feeder cattle. The Chicago Mercantile is the nation's second biggest exchange, with about 25% of total trading.

Trading on the New York Mercantile Exchange increased because of the auto makers' demand for platinum and doubts about the size of the Maine potato crop. Volume on the 100-year-old exchange nearly doubled last year from 1971, to about 475,000 contracts.

Silver and copper trading both set volume records at the Commodity Exchange Inc., in New York, pushing that exchange's contract total to more than one million for the first time.

A spurt in sugar trading, fueled late in the year by reports that Russia was interested in making purchases, helped push trading activity at the New York Coffee and Sugar Exchange to a record of well over 800,000 contracts.

In 1973, the exchanges are looking toward more volume, both from existing and new commodities. A new contract scheduled to start trading soon isn't a commodity: puts and calls, options to buy or sell stocks at a specified price for a certain period, at the Chicago Board of Trade. "Once that market gets moving, people in the stock market will feel compelled to follow it," says Mr. Wilson. "That might be a bridge to their participation in general commodities."

Source: *The Wall Street Journal,* January 2, 1973.

Commodity Exchange, opened in 1970 to service the 200,000 traders in the 11 western states who handle $20 billion worth of commodities a year. The Pacific Coast Commodity Exchange opened in 1972 in San Francisco to help handle the increased volume.

The effect of this growth in trading activity has been to put the commodity markets in about the same position the stock exchanges found themselves 20 years ago. To handle the increased load, the exchanges are expanding their trading areas and information systems so that now commodity quotations can be had in literally any part of the country instantaneously. The Chicago Mercantile Exchange has moved to a new building in order to handle their increased trade activity.

Thirty-two million Americans trade stocks for their own accounts, while public commodities traders number only about 2 million. There are two reasons why the 2 million wield more financial clout than the 32 million. First, futures trading is a very important adjunct to the business planning of companies that deal in the physical commodities and these companies hold positions on the commodity markets worth millions of dollars at any given time. These company

FIGURE 5

Commodity	Cumulative value of trading	
	July-December	
	1972	1971
	Thousand dollars	
Wheat	10,813,715	3,275,952
Corn	9,618,127	5,883,437
Oats	113,220	73,198
Grain sorghums	7,582	22,047
Soybeans	37,657,638	29,409,412
Soybean meal	4,975,212	1,963,255
Soybean oil	3,113,742	6,040,695
Cottonseed oil	27	0
Coconut oil	10,575	---
Cotton	2,651,274	3,528,705
Wool	18,337	5,197
Frozen orange juice	427,206	592,663
Eggs, shell	2,857,498	1,588,708
Eggs, frozen	483	0
Potatoes	300,049	63,859
Cattle	11,346,732	4,858,247
Frozen boneless beef	8,117	10,284
Live hogs	2,662,461	771,079
Frozen pork bellies	13,599,110	8,784,933
Frozen skinned hams	0	1,127
Total	100,181,105	66,872,798

Source: U.S. Department of Agriculture, Commodity Exchange Authority.

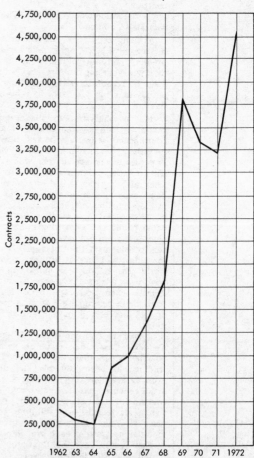

FIGURE 6
COMMODITY VOLUME, 1961-1972

Source: Chicago Mercantile Exchange.

hedgers have no choice but to hedge their needs on the futures exchanges unless they wish to speculate on coming prices for the goods they need to do business (or the goods they must sell, as with the large farmer). The second reason is leverage. In a speculator's margin account, $5,000 will control stocks worth about $7,500 at current margin requirements. In commodities, $5,000 will margin a position worth anywhere from $40,000 in soybeans to $80,000 in corn (the reason for the difference being that soybean prices are more volatile than corn prices and require more margin, lessening leverage).

It is this leverage, ranging from 8x to 16x, that is attracting the new speculator. In any given year, half the commodities traded in futures markets will have price moves sufficient to double a speculator's money. A dozen or so commodities will have moves sufficient to bring back a 500 percent return. A couple will move even more.

In 1972 as a result of Russian purchases and poor weather the wheat market advanced over $1.20 per bushel from the summer low. At the time the advance began wheat margins were $600 per contract. At such a margin rate the commodity trader doubles his money every 12 cents the future moves. Thus on a $1.20 price rise the trader who bought wheat in June of 1972 and sold it six months later would have received a profit of 1,000 percent on his invested capital. By pyramiding his position in even a conservative fashion a trader could have earned from 2,000 percent to 5,000 percent on his capital within a six-month period. (See Fig. 7, p. 8.)

The flaxseed market in Winnipeg was also active in 1972. From a summer low of approximately $2.80 per bushel prices advanced to nearly $5. A trader who entered and exited from the market at somewhere near those levels could have earned from 1,000 percent to 3,000 percent to 5,000 percent on his capital in less than a year. (See Fig. 8, p. 9.)

Sugar futures advanced from 4.5 cents a pound to almost 10 cents a pound. Each 1 cent price advance or decline returns $1,120 profit for each $1,000 invested. Any trader who bought sugar futures at the 5 cent level and sold at the 10 cent level would have earned a return in excess of 500 percent on any capital. This is not to suggest that any trader would have caught the entire advance but merely that the possibilities are widespread. Sugar futures gave back almost the entire advance by August but any long trader had ample time to get out. The return on the short side was nearly 500 percent in sugar on the way back down. Through the use of stops it would be possible for a speculator to have caught both sides of this price movement. (See Fig. 9, p. 10.)

In the spring of 1972, cotton prices started to decline. They declined from 33 cents per pound to almost 28 cents per pound. Each 1 cent price change in cotton yields a $500 return on a $750 margin investment. Thus the trader who netted the 5 cent price decline could have earned 300 percent profit on his capital from the period of May through September.

But by October when rainy weather hit the South and the cotton crop did not look quite as good as it had earlier, prices started to rise. They rose from the 28 cent level to almost 40 cents per pound, a $5,000 profit for every $750

FIGURE 7

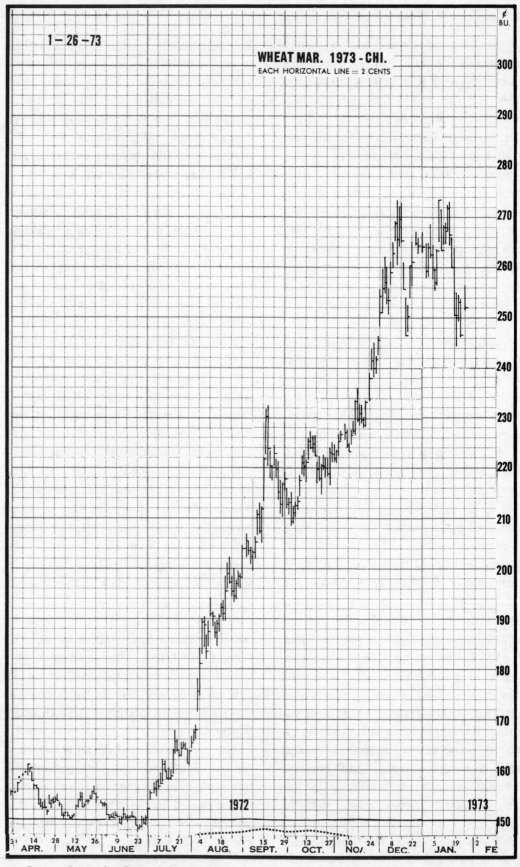

Source: Commodity Research Bureau, Inc.

FIGURE 8

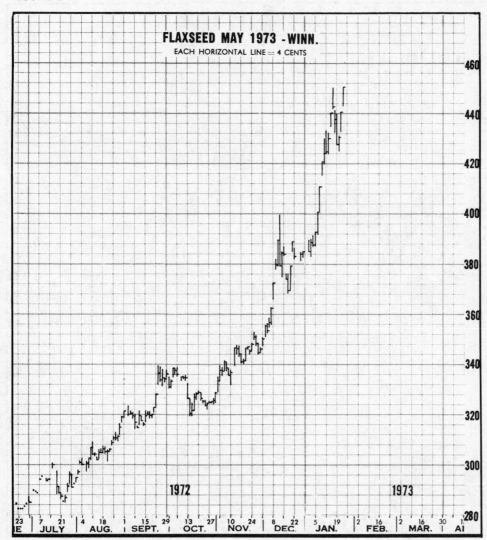

FLAXSEED MAY 1973 - WINN.
EACH HORIZONTAL LINE = 4 CENTS

Source: Commodity Research Bureau, Inc.

FIGURE 9

Source: Commodity Research Bureau, Inc.

10   Dow Jones-Irwin guide to commodities trading

invested within three months. (See Fig. 10, p. 11 and Fig. 11, p. 12.)

The egg market in 1972 traded within a narrow range for several months from a low of the mid-30s to a high of the mid-40s. Then, in the middle of November, cash dealers around the United States started to raise their bids for eggs and prices started to move. Within one month the December future advanced from 36 cents per dozen to 56 cents per dozen, a 20 cent advance within 30 days and one of the sharpest advances in history.

In the egg market a 10 cent price move returns $2,250 for each $600 invested, or approximately 380 percent. Thus within 30 days (without pyramiding) an egg trader could have earned over 700 percent on his capital in less than a month. Had he pyramided he could have earned 2,000 to 3,000 percent on his capital *within* a month. (See Fig. 12, p. 13.)

FIGURE 10

Source: Commodity Research Bureau, Inc.

FIGURE 11

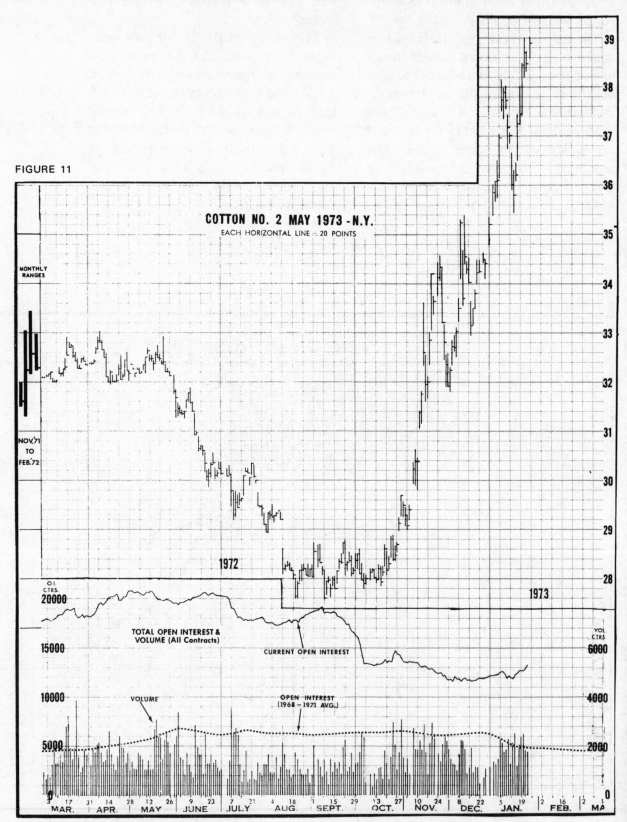

Source: Commodity Research Bureau, Inc.

Orange juice futures were, however, just about the only quiet market in commodities in the year 1972. Even *Business Week* stressed to its conservative business readers the profits which could be earned in the commodity markets (without pyramiding). (See Fig. 13, p. 14.)

The biggest movers of 1972 (the biggest price advances, that is) clearly belong to four major commodities. Plywood led the way, advancing from $100 per 1,000 square feet to over $200 per 1,000 square feet. (See Fig. 14, p. 15.)

Not far behind was soybean meal advancing from the $80 per ton level to a value in excess of $200 on some options. (See Fig. 15, p. 16.)

Soybean futures rose from $3 per bushel to a price of $5 per bushel, the highest price for soybeans in American history. (See Fig. 16, p. 17.)

And cattle prices, as every housewife knows, advanced at the wholesale market from the low 30s to nearly 45 cents a pound. The only people in the United States who did not mind the high price of beef were the futures traders who

FIGURE 12

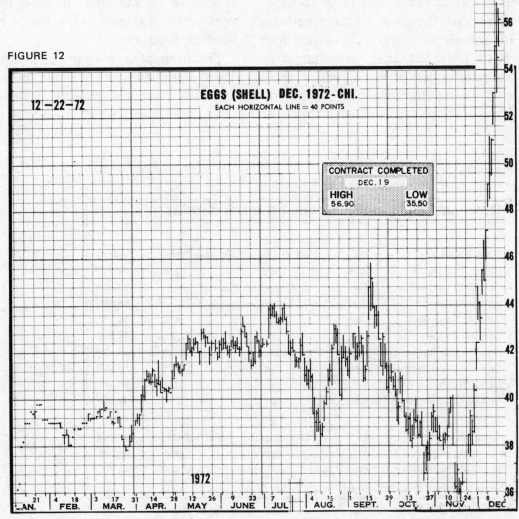

Source: Commodity Research Bureau, Inc.

bought contracts long in mid-March and held on for 500 percent to 4,000 percent profits by the end of January. (See Fig. 17, p. 18.)

When compared to these advances in the commodity market the top New York Stock Exchange Dollar gainers and losers don't compare too well. (See Fig. 18, p. 19.)

Within reason the industry hedger will use the futures market, regardless of price levels, because he is not interested in price movement. He hedges precisely to avoid the risk inherent in commodities handling, and the orange farmer or processor will continue trading the orange futures even though it is a quiet market. The speculator, however, is looking for volatile prices and has the advantage over the industry user of the markets in that he can move from market to market at will. The orange farmer must use the orange futures market, or no market at all, for his futures transactions. The speculator can choose his risks and take only those that suit him. (See Fig. 19, p. 20.)

In order for the speculator to make money in the futures markets he needs just two conditions: (1) a futures market which moves and (2) a position on the right side of the market. The speculator's game breaks down to darting in and out of markets in order to be caught in position for the big moves without getting caught on the wrong side of the market. He expects to guess wrong about as often as not but limits his losses to a tight preset maximum while letting his winnings build up.

Risk assumption is a game of control. The trader doesn't worry about any one trade any more than his insurance com-

FIGURE 13

How you could make money on a commodity

If you bought...	in...	and sold in...	this investment...	*earned
Dec. 1972 cotton	Jan.	Nov.	$800	$4,210
Dec. 1972 flaxseed	May	Dec.	$150	$5,500
Jan. 1973 lumber	July	Oct.	$450	$6,050
Jan. 1973 plywood	Apr.	Oct.	$500	$5,267
Dec. 1972 silver	Jan.	Dec.	$1,000	$5,060
Jan. 1973 soybeans	Jan.	Dec.	$750	$6,400
Dec. 1972 soybean meal	Jan.	Dec.	$500	$10,150
Dec. 1972 wheat	Feb.	Dec.	$600	$6,175
Feb. 1973 porkbellies	Feb.	Dec.	$750	$6,550

If you sold...	in...	and covered in...	this investment ...	*earned
Mar. 1973 sugar	Mar.	July	$800	$3,908
Mar. 1973 British pounds	May	Nov.	$2,500	$15,500

*Based on minimum margin per contract

Data: Commodity Research Bureau, BW   Mario DeVincentis—BW

Source: *Business Week*, December 23, 1972.

FIGURE 14

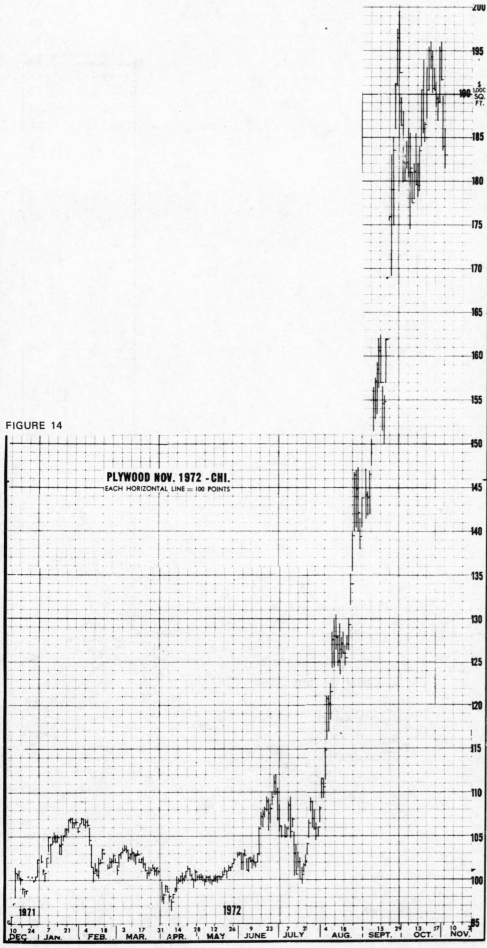

PLYWOOD NOV. 1972 - CHI.
EACH HORIZONTAL LINE = 100 POINTS

$
1,000
SQ.
FT.

1971

1972

10 24 7 21 4 18 3 17 31 14 28 12 26 9 23 7 21 4 18 1 15 29 13 27 10 2
DEC. JAN. FEB. MAR. APR. MAY JUNE JULY AUG. SEPT. OCT. NOV.

Source: Commodity Research Bureau, Inc.

FIGURE 15

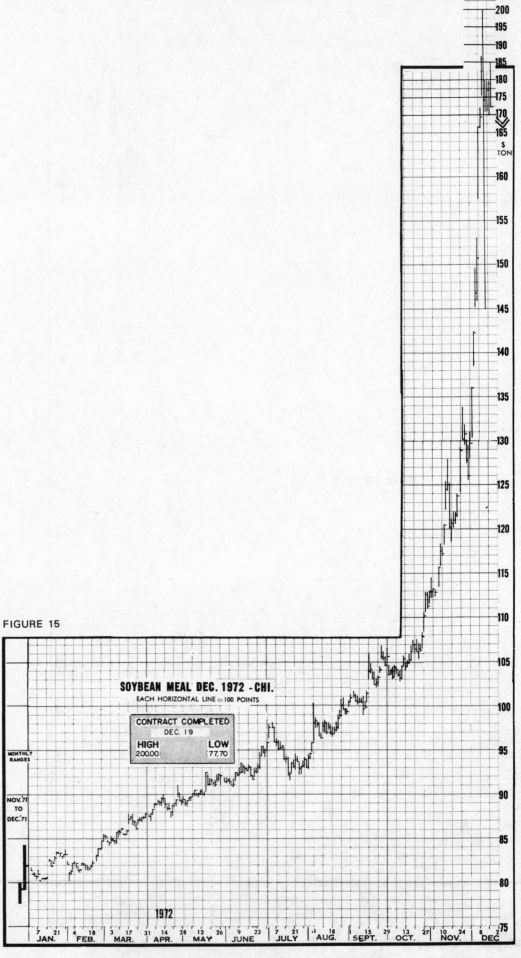

SOYBEAN MEAL DEC. 1972 - CHI.
EACH HORIZONTAL LINE = 100 POINTS

CONTRACT COMPLETED
DEC. 19
HIGH   LOW
200.00   77.70

MONTHLY
RANGES

NOV.'71
TO
DEC.'71

1972

7 21 | 4 18 | 3 17 31 | 14 28 | 12 26 | 9 23 | 7 21 | 4 18 | 15 29 | 13 27 | 10 24 | 8 2
JAN. | FEB. | MAR. | APR. | MAY | JUNE | JULY | AUG. | SEPT. | OCT. | NOV. | DEC

$ TON

Source: Commodity Research Bureau, Inc.

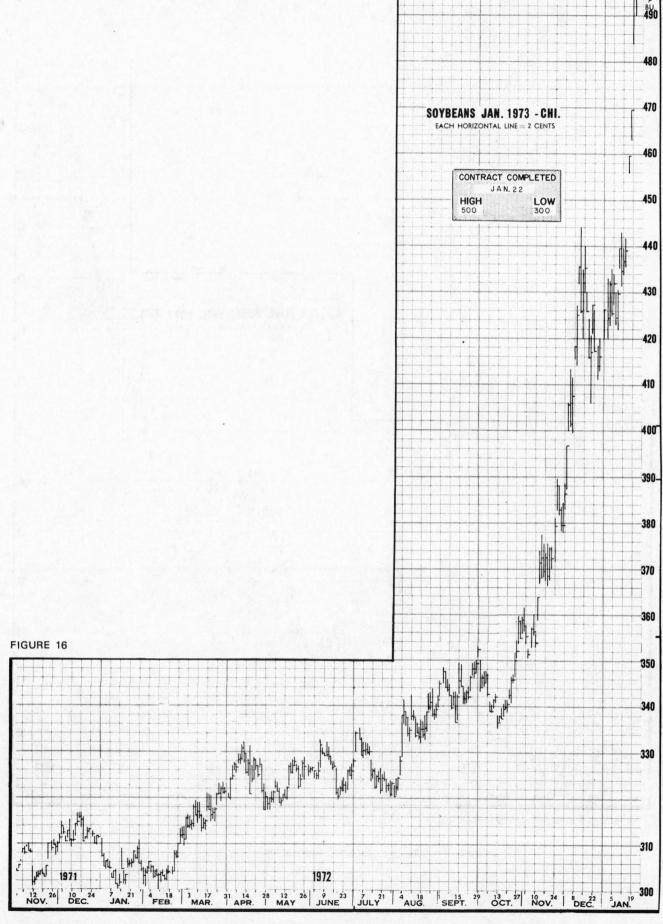

FIGURE 16

SOYBEANS JAN. 1973 - CHI.
EACH HORIZONTAL LINE = 2 CENTS

CONTRACT COMPLETED
JAN. 22
HIGH 500   LOW 300

Source: Commodity Research Bureau, Inc.

FIGURE 17

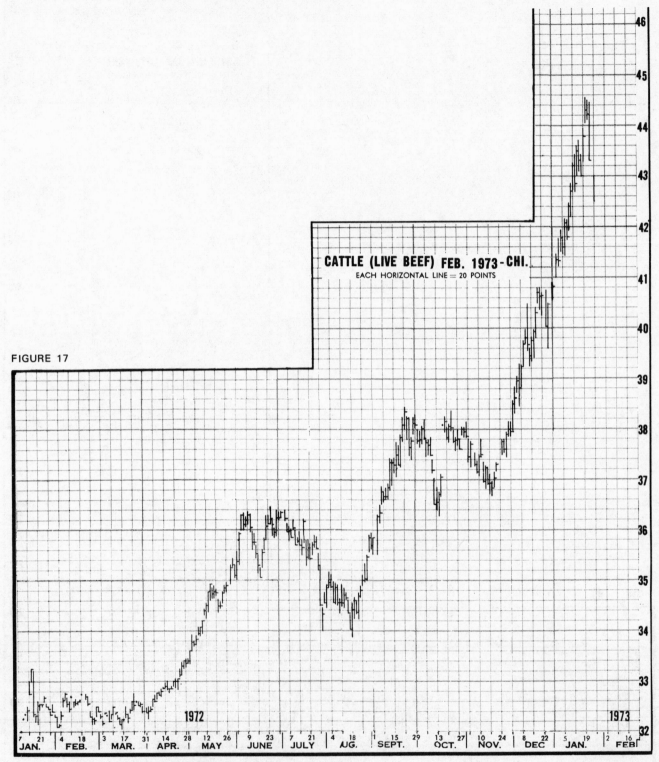

CATTLE (LIVE BEEF) FEB. 1973-CHI.
EACH HORIZONTAL LINE = 20 POINTS

Source: Commodity Research Bureau, Inc.

FIGURE 18

Top NYSE Dollar Gainers and Losers (Ended Dec. 15)

Gainers			Losers		
Name	Close	Dollar Change	Name	Close	Dollar Change
DisneyW	227½	+39⅞	A Medical	36	- 7¼
MtFuel S.	93¾	+39¾	MilesLbs	57¾	- 7⅛
Polaroid	129¾	+18⅜	AmesDS	12	- 7
Ponderosa Sy	80¼	+17½	MorganJ	104¼	- 6⅛
CMI Inv Cp	85¼	+16⅝	SingerCo	74	- 5⅞
Honywll	133	+15½	GrayDrg	23⅜	- 5⅞
Burrghs	225⅝	+15⅜	AetnaLfe	71⅛	- 5⅜
IBM	398⅛	+13⅞	GaPacif	41⅜	- 5¼
MGIC Inv	91½	+13	Cox Bdcst	35	- 5
ThomBet	93	+12⅞	Arctic Entrp	23½	- 5
BakrOilT	73	+12¾	WnUnion	47⅝	- 4⅝
ARA Svc	152½	+12¾	Mallory	28⅝	- 4½
Un Pac Cp	70	+12½	MarionLb	44⅛	- 4⅜
Digital Equip	94⅝	+12	MagicChf	19	- 4⅜
Sony Cp	58¼	+11⅝	Keebler	29½	- 4
Bandag Inc	67	+11⅛	Sangamo	16	- 3⅞
Motorola	131⅞	+11⅛	DeanWtr	17¾	- 3¾
EasKod	149	+11	Nat Airline	34	- 3¾
MercanS	149½	+10½	UnitInns	32⅜	- 3¾
McDonalds	70¾	+10½	Gable Ind	22¾	- 3¾
Avon Pd	138½	+10¼	LynchCSy	13¼	- 3¾
Schlmbg	92¾	+10	CmbEn	61¼	- 3¾
TexasInst	172½	+10	ReynSec	16⅞	- 3⅝
CaroC&Oh	83	+ 9¾	GettyO	91½	- 3⅝
Tropicana	58	+ 9⅝	A Cyan	31⅛	- 3⅝
Hew Pack	79⅜	+ 9⅝	Papercft	31⅜	- 3⅝
Revco DS	54⅝	+ 9⅜	Travelrs	39¾	- 3½
Skyline	50¼	+ 8⅝	HlthTex	50¾	- 3⅜
Smith Intl	47	+ 8½	CIT Finl	50¾	- 3⅜
Collins Rad	25⅝	+ 8¼	HousLP	51⅝	- 3⅜
CorGlW	261½	+ 8	Disston	17¼	- 3¼
Supr Oil	341	+ 8	Rheingld	19	- 3¼
A AirFilt	38	+ 8	A Medicorp	11⅜	- 3¼
Fleet Ent	31⅜	+ 7⅞	GtLkDr	29½	- 3¼
Skelly Oil	62½	+ 7¾	MGM	24¼	- 3¼
Natomas	66⅝	+ 7⅝	FstPenn	48¾	- 3⅛
HouNGas	59⅜	+ 7⅜	FstChrt	31⅛	- 3⅛
SimpPat	55¾	+ 7⅜	ConnMt	26¼	- 3
Pillsbury	53	+ 7¼	Grant W	43½	- 2⅞
OutbMar	44⅞	+ 7⅛	Extendcare	15⅞	- 2⅞

Source: *The Exchange* (NYSE), January 1973.

pany worries about any one car. He worries about the sum total of *all* his trades and how they are averaging out.

The commodity trader knows the market is going to fluctuate for days and months and he knows that his opinion of prices is not any better than average and probably worse. He can admit he was wrong and pull out quickly, and he is willing to take a lot of little losses in order to be in position for the big win. Because he can control many thousands of dollars' worth of commodities for a few hundred dollars in margin he is playing high stakes and even a small percentage movement in price is going to wipe him out or double his money. In July 1970, a trader could have bought or sold corn during the quiet part of 1970 for September delivery at $1.33½ a bushel. When news of the corn blight which threatened to wipe out 10 percent to 20 percent of the crop became known, corn skyrocketed to $1.60. This is an increase of about 20 percent in a month which would have left a stock market trader in no real awe. To the corn trader,

however, this 20 percent overall price increase represented a $1,300 profit in a month on an investment of $600. The trader nearly doubles his money or loses it all for every 10 percent price change in grains.

The commodity trader has two distinct real advantages over the trader in stocks. Futures contract prices are tied to the physical goods in use about the country and are tied to tangible real-world values. Virtually all information of any importance is released by the U.S. Department of Agriculture and is available to all traders at the same time.

Further advantages also make commodity trading rational. There are no new issues of wheat to inspect, and what new commodities do begin trading will have no effect on the other commodities already traded. Six hundred thirty-two firms filed registration in the last half of 1971 asking permission to issue public stock. Fifteen companies went public in seven days in January 1971; 13 of these were profitable and 2 were just getting started. In February, 15 com-

FIGURE 19

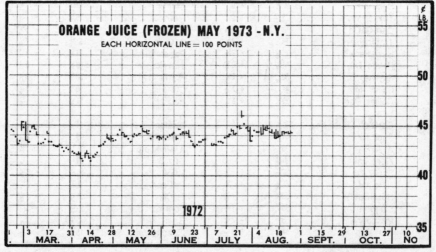

Source: Commodity Research Bureau, Inc.

panies entered their stocks on public exchanges. Ten had some sort of earnings, one was losing money, and four were brand new. How does the stock trader judge the value of these new issues? Nobody knows.

Several new commodity contracts started trading in 1971. None was making money. None had any capital assets. None paid dividends or held proxie battles. They were simply contracts between buyers and sellers to make or take delivery in the future. How does the trader judge the value of a contract in a new commodity future? How? He looks at the cash market for that commodity. Futures contracts generally expire at prices close to that found in the cash markets where the goods are used.

Because futures options generally expire at cash price levels, margin can be set at a low value. Public interest does not inflate the price of futures contracts as it does stocks.

The commodity trader relies on fundamental information about current crop and demand prospects in a manner similar to that used for judging a stock issue. But unlike stock information, commodity fundamentals do not come from a board of directors or an advertising department. Commodity information is released by the Department of Agriculture. There are no insiders. Everyone gets the same information at the same time. When I trade for my own account as a private speculator I do so in Seattle, Washington. There are no active futures exchanges in Seattle but the information is just as good here as it is in Chicago.

Positions of big traders, who are about as close to insiders as there are, are published at the end of each trading month and usually reach the public about two weeks later. A big trader is anyone who holds a position above a certain amount. The amounts vary from exchange to exchange but for the Chicago Board of Trade the figure is set at 200,000 bushels for grains and 25 contracts for soybean oil and soybean meal. In commodities the public trader knows at all times exactly what the big boys think of the news. (See Fig. 20, p. 22.)

As with stocks, any commodity that becomes too volatile will be suspended from trading until the market has a chance to digest the news. In commodities, however, the daily trading limits are specified in advance. Wheat, for instance, cannot drop or rise more than 10 cents in any single session. Potatoes are limited to a $\frac{1}{3}$ cent rise or fall.

Unlike stocks, no speculator can hold a position larger than specified levels in commodities. This position limit is set for most grains at 3 million bushels. Manipulation is therefore much more difficult in commodities than in the stock market. (See Fig. 21, p. 23.)

Unlike stocks, not all traders on the futures exchanges have the same profit goals. The majority of volume on any commodity exchange is the result of hedging. While the speculator is after profits earned on his risk capital, hedgers use the markets distinctly to avoid risk. The truly large positions held by grain companies simply are not in competition with the public speculator for risk profits. This is not true, say, of the Dreyfus Fund in stocks.

There is no such thing in commodities as an overall bull or bear market. Each option will expire close to its cash equivalent, regardless of price activity in other futures markets. The speculator is never in the position in the commodity market of having figured his position correctly and then having the entire market collapse and ruin it as happened in stocks in 1969.

A final advantage to the commodity trader is the rules under which the commission houses are licensed. A stock broker can use margin accounts in his normal business. The certificates held in margined accounts are registered in the name of the broker; he may borrow against them or sell them to pay his operating expenses. Periodically, as happened in 1970, stock commission houses can go bankrupt and for the period of time that its accounts are fouled, before other commission houses can bail it out, the company is like any other bankrupt company. Its assets belong to its creditors, who get whatever percentage on the dollar they can. The stock trader is just another creditor.

Commission houses which trade commodities for public accounts must strict-

FIGURE 20

Section 15.03 <u>Quantities fixed for reporting</u>. The quantities fixed for the purpose of reports filed under Parts 17, 18, and 19 of these regulations are as follows:

<u>Commodity</u>	<u>Quantity</u>
Wheat	200,000 bushels
Corn	200,000 bushels
Oats	200,000 bushels
Rye	200,000 bushels
Barley	200,000 bushels
Flaxseed	200,000 bushels
Soybeans	200,000 bushels
Grain sorghums	11,200,000 pounds
Cotton	5,000 bales
Wool	150,000 pounds[1]/
Wool tops	125,000 pounds
Butter	25 carlots
Eggs - shell	25 carlots
frozen whole	25 contract units
frozen plain whites	25 contract units
frozen plain yolks	25 contract units
Potatoes	25 carlots
Lard	1,000,000 pounds
Tallow	1,000,000 pounds
Cottonseed oil	1,500,000 pounds
Soybean oil	1,500,000 pounds
Cottonseed meal	2,500 tons
Soybean meal	2,500 tons
Millfeeds	1,000 tons
Live cattle	25 contract units
Cattle products	25 contract units
Live hogs	25 contract units
Frozen pork bellies	25 contract units
Frozen skinned hams	25 contract units
Hides	25 contract units
Frozen concentrated orange juice	25 contract units

1/ Clean content.

Section 18.03 <u>Time and place of filing reports</u>.
*   *   *

(b) Reports with respect to transactions in <u>cotton, wool, wool tops, potatoes, cottonseed oil, hides, and frozen concentrated orange juice</u> -- to the Commodity Exchange Authority office in New York, New York, unless otherwise specifically instructed by the Commodity Exchange Authority.

Source: U.S. Department of Agriculture, Commodity Exchange Authority.

ly separate public money from their own assets. No commodity broker can use your money to pay his light bill and no commodity broker can risk account money for his clients. They must do that themselves. No trader has lost money in commodities due to a house failure in 100 years of commodity trading.

Making money in commodities is not an accident. The trader is never lucky in the long run. If he is to win he must make right decisions about what con-

tract to trade, what side to trade it from, and how to manage his account. On the other hand, he has real information to make those decisions. Commodities is not for the indecisive or the man who cannot take a distant view of his game. A plunger will probably get hurt less in stocks. But the trader can make it just as easily on $5,000 as he can on $50,000 if he has the distance and the will power to play the odds.

FIGURE 21

Sec. 150.2 Limits on position and daily trading in cotton for future delivery. It is hereby ordered that the following limits on the amount of speculative trading under contracts of sale of cotton for future delivery, on or subject to the rules of any contract market, which may be done by any person, be, and they are hereby, proclaimed and fixed, to be in full force and effect on and after September 5, 1940:

(*a*) *Position limit.* The limit on the maximum net long or net short position which any person may hold or control in cotton on any one contract market is 30,000 bales in any one future or in all futures combined.

(*b*) *Daily trading limit.* The limit on the maximum amount of cotton which any person may buy, and on the maximum amount which any person may sell, on any one contract market during any one business day is 30,000 bales in any one future.

(*c*) *Bona fide hedging; straddles.* The foregoing limits upon position and upon daily trading shall not be construed to apply to bona fide hedging transactions, as defined in paragraph 3 of section 4a of the Commodity Exchange Act (7 U.S.C., Sup. V, sec. 6a(3)), nor, except during the delivery month, to (1) net positions in any one future to the extent that they are shown to represent straddles between cotton futures or markets, or (2) purchases and sales of cotton which are shown to represent straddles or the closing of straddles between futures or markets.

(*d*) *Manipulation; corners; responsibility of contract market.* Nothing contained herein shall be construed to affect any provisions of the Commodity Exchange Act relating to manipulation or corners, nor to relieve any contract market or its governing board from responsibility under paragraph (d) of section 5 of the Commodity Exchange Act (7 U.S.C., Sup. V, sec. 7(d)) to prevent manipulation and corners.

(*e*) *Definition.* As used in this part, the word "person" imports the plural or singular and includes individuals, associations, partnerships, corporations, and trusts.

Note: Limits are set by law on *all* regulated commodities.
Source: U.S. Department of Agriculture, Commodity Exchange Authority.

2

SOME MYTHS AND SOME TRUTHS
ABOUT COMMODITIES

Futures trading is a new field for the public speculator and like any new field it is surrounded by a good number of myths. Some of these myths are dealt with here, early in the book, with the hope that in so doing it would help clear the air for the fuller, but inevitably slower, text to follow.

Each subject contained in this chapter is handled in the course of the text (although not in the same manner) and any trader who admits to no knowledge whatsoever about commodities, hence no myths, can skip this chapter if he wishes, with the confidence that he hasn't missed anything.

Here then are some of the myths most commonly held by new commodity traders:

MYTH NUMBER 1

Trading commodities is just like trading stocks only a lot faster. This fallacy has cost most speculators more money than all other possible errors put together. Commodities are not at all like stocks and must be played in an entirely different manner. A stock is a tangible item. The investor owns it, he may store it, sell it, give it away, or cover the walls

of his room with the certificates. He buys it at one price either with the expectation of enjoying dividend payments or in the hope that the price will rise so that he can resell it. (See Fig. 22 opposite.)

A commodity contract is an agreement to accept delivery for a long position or to make delivery for a short position at a specified time in the future. The trader must either cover his position before the delivery date or honor the agreement. Commodities is not an investment. It is a speculation. A program of buying and holding simply does not make sense in commodities. The trader can trade either the long or the short side of the market with equal ease.

A commodity trading program must consist of a number of trades, giving emphasis to no single position. A large number of losses is balanced against a smaller number of wins to give a profit or loss for the entire program rather than for a single trade. The commodity speculator makes a large number of plays, testing the water and getting out if profits are not immediately offered. He does this in order to be in *position* when the big profit-making moves occur.

The speculator who selects one commodity as though it were a stock, analyzes it thoroughly, and takes a position is playing the wrong game.

MYTH NUMBER 2

Commodity markets exist to serve gamblers both inside and outside the industry. The majority of trading on any market is made up of hedgers who use the markets precisely to *avoid* gambling on coming cash commodity prices. Once hedged they no longer stand to suffer from a higher (or lower) price for the goods they must use to stay in business. On the Chicago Board of Trade on February 28, 1973 (to choose a date at random), hedgers comprised 63 percent of all open interest in corn, 36 percent in wheat, 31 percent in oats, 55 percent

FIGURE 22

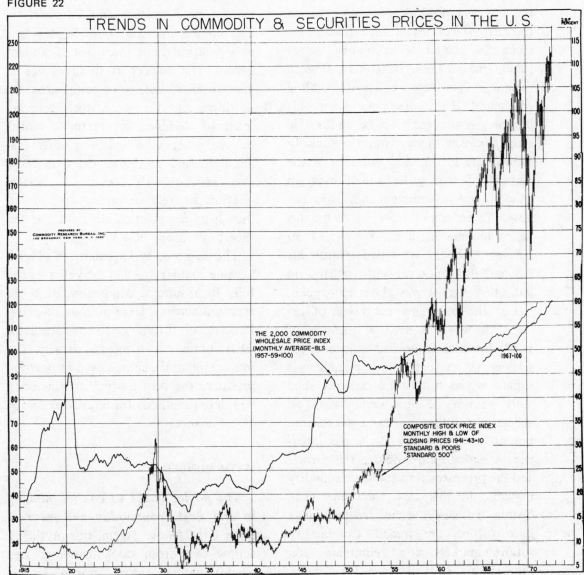

TRENDS IN COMMODITY & SECURITIES PRICES IN THE U.S.

Source: Commodity Research Bureau, Inc.

in soybeans, above 35 percent in bean oil and meal. The percentage of activity by people who wish to avoid risk is even higher on smaller markets which enjoy less speculation.

The winter of 1971 saw contracts, calling for May delivery of orange concentrate, hit a low of 34 cents per pound on January 20th, rocket to 48 cents over the following three weeks due to a freeze in the Florida orange belt, then settle back to 42 cents, at which price the physical product was delivered on the cash markets. Such price shenanigans make the budget of an orange farmer totally meaningless. He cannot finance new land purchases or crop handling equipment if he does not know his income within fairly close limits. He cannot borrow money from the bank. In January he had a solid estimate of the amount of money he would have on hand to run his business and his household. Three weeks later he found his year's income increased by almost 50 percent. Over the next two months his income fell 16 percent with virtually no indication that it was about to happen.

For the unhedged processor of oranges, it was not even a question of year's income. If he had contracts for sales of his product at a set price he was simply wiped out of business. A shoe store cannot be run under such an accounting system, nor can a gas station, nor can a farm. To avoid the risk inherent in agricultural pricing, the farmer and the processor turn to the commodity markets, in this case the New York Cotton Exchange, where frozen orange juice futures are traded. Commodity futures markets don't eliminate risk, they simply shift it from the farmer, who chooses to hedge his bets, to the

person out of the industry who chooses to bear them. The speculator may or may not be more able to afford the gamble but at least he chooses to do so.

MYTH NUMBER 3

You have to be an expert to deal in commodities. Obviously, it helps if you know what you are doing. But what you are doing in commodities is not trying to out figure the U.S. Department of Agriculture or Hershey Foods Corporation. The commodity speculator is playing a mathematical game into a set of random events. The market at all times has an exactly 50-50 chance of going either up or down and the speculator's program must be designed to maximize profits on the random half of his guesses that are right and minimize losses on those that are wrong. He does this by getting out immediately on wrong guesses and increasing his position on right guesses. (See Fig. 23 opposite.)

The commodity speculator is playing a game similar to that played successfully by insurance companies. Risks are averaged across a large number of plays. It makes no difference to the speculator what commodity is moving or why. The movement alone, chosen even at random, produces the profit. Much of this book will detail methods for improving on the 50-50 chance.

MYTH NUMBER 4

The novice ought to confine himself to one single commodity and learn all there is to know. Again, this myth is a follow over from stock handling. You cannot predict futures prices. If this could be done, then General Mills would be doing it, and there would be no need of a futures market, nor the possibility of making a profit from them. General Mills trades the futures market precisely because it does not know what prices are coming. The novice can and ought to play all the markets, each position being considered as only a move in an overall strategy.

MYTH NUMBER 5

Good Lord, the driveway is full of corn and the trucks are still coming! This is one of the most amusing images in commodities. It doesn't happen. Should a long contract holder hang onto

his contracts up to the delivery date, the most he will ever receive is a slip of paper that indicates he now owns so many bushels or pounds of whatever commodity is in a specific warehouse. Ownership registries are supplied by short contract holders in fulfillment of their contracts and given to the oldest standing long in the market. The receiver of the slip can generally mark it "don't want" and it will be passed onto the next oldest long in line. You should be warned, however, that in the case of shell eggs, soybean meal, and a few other commodities the process can sometimes be very complicated and often financially costly. This should be dis-

FIGURE 23

COPPER MAR. 1973-N.Y.
EACH HORIZONTAL LINE = 40 POINTS

Note: Were the label removed from this graph and the graph turned upside down, the profit potential for the speculator would be exactly the same.
Source: Commodity Research Bureau.

cussed with your broker prior to purchasing contracts which may be delivered upon.

Should you hold an open long position to the very last delivery day and be unable to pass the receipt along, your broker will sell the "actuals" for you with little problem, although there is a charge for this extra service. As a general rule, it is a good idea for speculators to stay out of the delivery month as contracts are matched against the actual goods in warehouses. This is a game for processors and warehousemen.

MYTH NUMBER 6

The insiders know it all. Literally all information of any importance whatsoever to the commodity business, both cash and future, is released by the Department of Agriculture as a normal adjunct to their business with the nation's agriculture industry, of which the futures markets form a small part. These reports are assembled behind locked doors with all telephone links to the outside world cut off to assure that no information leaks out before the publication dates. These dates are pre-announced and every effort is made to see that all interested parties get all the information on the same day.

MYTH NUMBER 7

The game is easily rigged. It is unfortunate in a way (a very small way) but the days of the great corners are gone. The 1890s conjure up visions of special trains racing across the country to Chicago in time to meet contract obligations. There was a time when a man could quietly buy up all the wheat in

Chicago warehouses and then go long in the futures market and wait for the screaming shorts to find the grain to meet their contract obligations. But this is no longer possible. Speculators are limited in the size of the position they can hold and these limits are set low enough to ensure that nobody can have an effect on market prices. (See Fig. 24 opposite.)

The last big scandal was in 1963 when Tony de Angeles built a dozen tanks for storing soybean oil and then pumped water and oil back and forth between the tanks to show that they were all full. He just recently got out of jail and claims to have enjoyed his stay and the loss of weight.

MYTH NUMBER 8

In commodities you can come face to face with General Mills. By law a speculator can hold a position in wheat no larger than 3 million bushels. Quite frankly, "the General" couldn't care less what you do with so little wheat. The speculator is not competing with the large grain companies. General Mills, Hershey, Cargil, Continental Grain, all use the markets to secure the goods they will need in the future at a known price, and within reason they will use the markets regardless of price levels. They do this precisely because they do not wish to speculate. Competition between the public speculator and the large grain companies is nil. The hedger is playing the exact opposite game from the speculator. (See Fig. 25, p. 30.)

Holders of the physical commodity (farmers, warehousemen, and so on) have more need of the guaranteed price for their goods than do processors (who can pass any price rise on along with the processed goods), and therefore, hedgers are normally net short on the futures markets, sometimes overwhelmingly so. And yet with the major industries taking the bear side of the market, commodity prices have shown a steady upward bias over the last decade.

As a final check, once a month the Department of Agriculture publishes *Commitments of Traders in Commodity Futures,* outlining the exact position of all large traders in each commodity futures market. In commodities, the speculator knows exactly where he stands against the large institutions. This he cannot know in the stock markets.

MYTH NUMBER 9

The public speculator is normally long in the market because he is more used to buying something than he is to selling short. This fallacy has shown up in print in a number of books on the commodity market. While it is exactly as easy for any trader to go short as it is to go long, the speculator provides a function in the commodity markets by being net long and covering the imbalanced market caused by the net short position of industry hedgers who *have* to sell short. The speculator is not being a nice guy, he is simply buoying up a market that would sag from excess selling pressure and picking up a profit for doing so. (See Fig. 26, p. 31.)

MYTH NUMBER 10

With everyone on low margin it is only a matter of time before the crash. In 1929 when stocks were bought and sold on margins of 10 percent and less, everyone could wield huge fortunes with small amounts of cash. When prices

FIGURE 24

SEC. 9. (a) It shall be a felony punishable by a fine of not more than $10,000 or imprisonment for not more than five years, or both, together with the costs of prosecution, for any futures commission merchant, or any employee or agent thereof, to embezzle, steal, purloin, or with criminal intent convert to his own use or the use of another, any money, securities, or property having a value in excess of $100, which was received by such commission merchant to margin, guarantee, or secure the trades or contracts of any customer of such commission merchant or accruing to such customer as the result of such trades or contracts. The word "value" as used in this paragraph means face, par, or market value, or cost price, either wholesale or retail, whichever is greater.

(b) It shall be a felony punishable by a fine of not more than $10,000 or imprisonment for not more than five years, or both, together with the costs of prosecution, for any person to manipulate or attempt to manipulate the price of any commodity in interstate commerce, or for future delivery on or subject to the rules of any contract market, or to corner or attempt to corner any such commodity, or knowingly to deliver or cause to be delivered for transmission through the mails or in interstate commerce by telegraph, telephone, wireless, or other means of communication false or misleading or knowingly inaccurate reports concerning crop or market information or conditions that affect or tend to affect the price of any commodity in interstate commerce.

Source: U.S. Department of Agriculture, Commodity Exchange Authority.

FIGURE 25   SHELL EGGS, FROZEN PORK BELLY AND LIVE HOG FUTURES

Commitments of traders, Chicago Mercantile Exchange, December 31, 1972

Classification	December 31, 1972		Net change from November 30, 1972	
	Long	Short	Long	Short

SHELL EGGS

LARGE TRADERS	(In carlots)			
Speculative				
Long or short only	1,460	815	+ 763	− 190
Long and short (spreading)	338	338	+ 75	+ 75
Total	1,798	1,153	+ 838	− 115
Hedging	286	1,101	+ 47	+ 712
Total reported by large traders	2,084	2,254	+ 885	+ 597
SMALL TRADERS				
Speculative and hedging	4,150	3,980	− 918	− 630
TOTAL OPEN INTEREST	6,234	6,234	− 33	− 33
Percent held by: Large traders	33.4	36.2	+ 14.3	+ 9.8
Small traders	66.6	63.8	− 14.3	− 9.8

FROZEN PORK BELLIES

LARGE TRADERS	(In contract units of 36,000 pounds)			
Speculative				
Long or short only	2,822	1,828	− 1,132	− 198
Long and short (spreading)	5,138	5,138	+ 689	+ 689
Total	7,960	6,966	− 443	+ 491
Hedging	363	1,088	+ 10	+ 58
Total reported by large traders	8,323	8,054	− 433	+ 549
SMALL TRADERS				
Speculative and hedging	11,493	11,762	− 1,331	− 2,313
TOTAL OPEN INTEREST	19,816	19,816	− 1,764	− 1,764
Percent held by: Large traders	42.0	40.6	+ 1.4	+ 5.8
Small traders	58.0	59.4	− 1.4	− 5.8

LIVE HOGS

LARGE TRADERS	(In contract units of 30,000 pounds)			
Speculative				
Long or short only	2,462	1,696	− 2,324	+ 256
Long and short (spreading)	1,769	1,769	+ 143	+ 143
Total	4,231	3,465	− 2,181	+ 399
Hedging	699	1,371	− 737	+ 222
Total reported by large traders	4,930	4,836	− 2,918	+ 621
SMALL TRADERS				
Speculative and hedging	9,565	9,659	− 171	− 3,710
TOTAL OPEN INTEREST	14,495	14,495	− 3,089	− 3,089
Percent held by: Large traders	34.0	33.4	− 10.6	+ 9.4
Small traders	66.0	66.6	+ 10.6	− 9.4

Source: U.S. Department of Agriculture, Commodity Exchange Authority.

FIGURE 26

WHEAT FUTURES

Commitments of traders, specified markets, December 31, 1972

Classification	December 31, 1972		Net change from November 30, 1972	
	Long	Short	Long	Short

Minneapolis Grain Exchange

	Long	Short	Long	Short
LARGE TRADERS	(In thousand bushels)			
Speculative				
Long or short only	10	10	+ 90	+ 10
Long and short (spreading)	674	219	− 6	+ 209
Total	1,094	229	+ 84	+ 219
Hedging	26,606	18,304	+ 3,827	− 10
Total reported by large traders	27,700	18,533	+ 3,911	+ 209
SMALL TRADERS				
Speculative and hedging	4,756	13,923	+ 1,201	+ 4,903
TOTAL OPEN INTEREST	32,456	32,456	+ 5,112	+ 5,112
Percent held by: Large traders	85.3	57.1	− 1.7	− 9.9
Small traders	14.7	42.9	+ 1.7	+ 9.9

Note: On December 31, 1972, small traders in wheat futures on the Minneapolis Grain Exchange held almost three times the short contracts as they held long. Subsequently the market declined 20 cents a bushel and the small traders earned a substantial profit.
Source: U.S. Department of Agriculture, Commodity Exchange Authority.

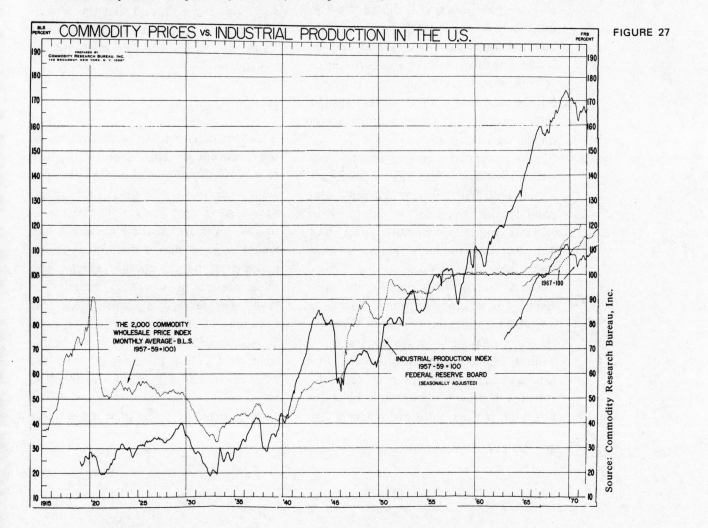

FIGURE 27

dipped, margined account owners were called to put up more cash to cover their positions. If they couldn't do so their stock was sold sending the price spiraling downward. (See Fig. 27, p. 31.)

Current commodity market margins serve the same function as the pre-depression stock markets margins (although they are technically different, being surety bonds rather than down payments). Their function is to cover fluctuation in prices. When price moves against a commodity position, the trader will be asked to put up more cash, but unlike stocks, the value of which is tied only to demand for the certificates, futures prices are tied directly to the physical product which is traded in substantial quantities on many cash markets around the country. The futures price cannot vary much from the price of the actual goods. If it did shorts who must deliver by contract would simply buy the actual commodity and deliver. If the price rose too far above the price of the actual goods in cash markets, longs would simply take delivery against their open positions and sell the goods on the cash market.

In a depression, consumers can very well do without White Sewing Machines and without White Sewing Machine Company stock. They are not going to do without wheat. Corn, oats, silver, and eggs are not suddenly going to find themselves without value.

Open interest—the number of contracts outstanding—normally increases manyfold during the course of the year that a commodity is traded before it expires, as more and more people come into agreement and make new contracts. But this increased interest does not raise prices as it does in stock markets. As more and more people enter the stock markets, prices must necessarily rise, for the newcomers are bidding for a set number of shares. This is not the case in commodities where exactly half the market is long and half short. Volume in commodities has no effect on contract prices. (See Fig. 28 opposite.)

Rather than raising margin requirements because of rapidly increasing public participation, as is standard procedure in stocks, two of the biggest exchanges (the Chicago Board of Trade and the New York Commodity Exchange) have reduced margins on some commodities, including silver. (The Board of Trade deals in 5,000 ounce contracts, Comex in 10,000 ounce contracts.) To buy a silver contract under the new requirements worth over $20,000, a trader need put up only $1,000 as opposed to $1,500 formerly. It was found that the brokerages did not need so much protection as there was little need for retaining the higher margins.

MYTH NUMBER 11

Commodity speculation is little more than gambling. This is quite joyously true. The speculator who plays the best game will make the most money and have a good time doing it. The best odds in Las Vegas are on the blackjack tables where a good player can find a house rake-off of only a couple percent. The odds are much worse in roulette or craps. The racetracks normally rake off between 15 percent and 20 percent. In commodities not only is the game open and going all the time but the odds are actually slightly in favor of the speculator.

It is possible to sit at a poker table

and play one hand and receive four aces—*once;* or place your money on red on the roulette wheel and win—once; or buy corn and watch it go up—once; but it is a one-shot proposition. If the speculator is to make any money over any period of time he must have a program that puts the odds of a risk situation in his favor. It is not the high roller who takes money out of the commodity markets, but the actuary, the man who sticks with his figures. (See Fig. 29, p. 34.)

FIGURE 28

Open Interest

A futures contract is said to be "open" when it has been entered into and not yet liquidated by an offsetting transaction nor fulfilled by delivery. Contracts that are open are referred to as "open interest."

The amount of open interest for each commodity and contract market is obtained each business day by a tabulation of reports made by exchange clearing members. The aggregate of all long open interest reported by clearing members equals the aggregate of all short open interest reported. The open interest figures shown are for one side only, not the long and short sides combined. Annual averages shown in the commodity tables which follow are the average of open interest on the last day of each month of the fiscal year.

Open interest in a commodity reflects the positions of hedgers and longer-term speculative holdings, and thus provides more of a measure of market utilization for merchandising and processing than is afforded by data on volume of trading.

Volume of Trading

Volume of trading is the total of all purchases or of all sales--not of purchases and sales combined. Since there are two parties to every futures contract--the seller and the buyer--the aggregate of all purchases is equal to the aggregate of all sales.

The volume of trading in a commodity is compiled by the Commodity Exchange Authority from data in required daily reports from exchange clearing members. Each clearing member of each contract market makes a daily report of all purchases and sales of commodity futures which it clears. A compilation of these reports gives the volume of trading in each commodity for each market each day.

Source: U.S. Department of Agriculture, Commodity Exchange Authority.

FIGURE 29

AN ANALYSIS OF SPECULATIVE TRADING IN GRAIN FUTURES

SUMMARY

This study is concerned primarily with the trading behavior of small speculators in grain futures, and the results of their trading. Statistics were analyzed on the futures operations of nearly 9,000 traders, extending over a 9-year period (1924–32) and involving more than 400,000 individual futures transactions. This wealth of data, set up on punch cards and processed by machine-tabulation methods, provided comprehensive evidence for the first time on some of the most important questions in the field of futures trading. The study confirms a number of commonly held opinions as to the results of speculative trading; it tends to disprove others which have also been widely accepted.

The first obvious conclusion from the analysis is that the great majority of small speculators lost money in the grain futures market. There were 6,598 speculators in the sample with net losses, compared with 2,184 with net profits, or three times as many loss traders as profit traders. Net losses of speculators were approximately six times net profits, or nearly $12,000,000 of losses, compared with about $2,000,000 of profits. Speculative traders in the sample lost money in each of the four grains traded—wheat, corn, oats, and rye.

Primarily responsible for the high ratio of losses was the small speculator's characteristic hesitation in closing out loss positions. An often-quoted maxim for speculative trading is "Cut your losses and let your profits run." Contrary to this advice, speculators in the sample showed a clear tendency to cut their profits and let their losses run. Futures positions or cycles resulting in losses were held open for consistently longer durations than profit cycles—average losses were larger than average profits—and long cycles were kept open for a greater number of days than short cycles. In wheat futures, for example, the average duration of profit cycles was only 10.5 days, compared with 16.3 days for loss cycles. The average duration of the profit trader in wheat futures was 114.8 days, compared with 182.5 days for the loss trader.

Speculators who did make profits on individual trades were inclined to cut them short. The tendency on individual cycles was to settle for profits which were much smaller on the average than the average loss on trades closed out unprofitably. With this situation, plus the shorter time duration of profit cycles, it is not surprising that there were actually more individual profit cycles than loss cycles.

It has not been possible in this study to explore all the aspects of speculative trading on grain futures markets, nor to answer all the questions which have been raised. A final comment should be made involving a most important question. As already indicated, the losses of traders in the sample were much greater than their profits. If these results are representative of trading by small speculators generally, there must be other groups—large speculators, scalpers, spreaders, or hedgers—which make very large profits.

There is no known empirical study, however, which reveals other groups of traders with net profits sufficient to balance such large losses as those suffered by small speculators in the sample. Yet the nature of futures trading is such that all losses are balanced by profits. This raises the most important question left unanswered by this study. Was the sample in this respect not typical of small speculative traders? There is no apparent reason for pronounced bias in the direction of losses. If the sample is representative, is there another group of traders who consistently make profits large enough to balance the losses of small speculators? There is no convincing evidence that such large profits are made by any class of traders. These are questions which can be answered only by further studies of the results of futures trading.

Source: U.S. Department of Agriculture, *Technical Bulletin No. 1001.*

3

TRADERS

All traders in commodity futures fall into one of two categories, hedgers or speculators. The Department of Agriculture in its monthly analysis of commodity traders adds a third category called "small traders." This is strictly a procedural classification containing traders of whom the department doesn't gather the information to classify as speculators or hedgers. The majority of traders, regardless of classification, trade through brokerage house accounts and have their trades executed by brokerage house employees ("pit traders") on the trading floor (or pit). Other pit traders trade their own accounts on the floors of the exchange. A scalper is a pit trader who deals in eighths and quarters of a cent, helping to keep the flow of offers orderly on the order of a specialist in stocks, who matches buy and sell orders, temporarily taking a position from time to time but closing it before the end of the day. (See Fig. 30, p. 36, and Fig. 30—*Cont.*, p. 37.)

THE HEDGER

Any person who holds a position on the futures exchanges, approximately equal to but opposite to a position he holds in the physical commodity (or must hold in the future), is said to be *hedged*. A man who holds or will harvest 1 million bushels of soybeans is long beans in his cash position. By opening a short position on the Chicago Board of Trade of 1 million bushels, he removes the risk of price deterioration. If the price drops 10 cents on the cash market where he will sell his soybeans he will lose $100,000. He will make the same amount on his winning short position in Chicago. By hedging, the farmer or merchant has helped remove the risk of price loss from his cash operation (hedges aren't perfect). (See Fig. 31, p. 38.)

The soybean crusher or merchant who must buy soybeans is short the cash product. By assuming an equal long position in Chicago he removes the risk of a price rise. Money lost on the cash market, where he must pay more for the soybeans he needs to do business, will be made back on a winning long position on a rising futures market.

The price relationship between futures contracts and cash goods in wholesale markets is called "country basis." "Basis" is the difference between any two commodity prices which are connected but not the same, and so long as the basis between the hedge in Chicago and the cash market price remains constant, neither the short nor the long hedger stands to lose money in his cash dealings due to price deterioration or rise after he

FIGURE 30

AN ANALYSIS OF SPECULATIVE TRADING IN GRAIN FUTURES

TABLE 19.—*Occupational distribution of all traders in sample*

Occupation	Wheat	Corn	Oats	Rye	All grains[1]
	Number	*Number*	*Number*	*Number*	*Number*
Business managers, grain business:					
Country grain business	114	65	33	21	133
Terminal and subterminal grain business	158	107	44	38	183
Total	272	172	77	59	316
Business managers, other:					
Wholesalers	112	44	16	18	131
Retailers	937	452	201	179	1,044
Bankers	16	5	4	3	19
Miscellaneous other than trade	733	364	161	143	824
Real estate, insurance, securities	749	427	178	130	885
Capitalists and financiers	44	19	5	4	50
Business re agriculture	105	73	33	27	134
Total	2,696	1,384	598	504	3,087
Professional:					
Accountants and auditors	80	35	15	10	91
Artists, actors, and musicians	24	11	1	1	26
Clergymen	10	7	4	3	12
Educators	53	30	9	9	58
Dentists	73	26	12	11	77
Engineers and architects	105	55	17	20	120
Lawyers and judges	111	56	20	17	129
Physicians and surgeons	133	82	24	27	152
Professional occupations, n. o. c	88	52	17	16	103
Total	677	354	119	114	768
Semiprofessional:					
Semiprofessional occupations	74	30	12	11	83
Students	15	4	2	3	19
Total	89	34	14	14	102
Clerical:					
Clerical and kindred occupations	225	114	38	41	262
Sales persons and kindred occupations	146	66	25	18	168
Inspectors, estimators, etc	102	50	22	23	119
Municipal and State employees	3	2			3
Federal employees	2	2	1		2
Total	478	234	86	82	554
Farmers:					
Farmers, general	779	365	150	121	900
Farmers, specialty	118	47	19	16	128
Total	897	412	169	137	1,028

[1] The numbers of traders in the "All grains" column generally are not the sums of the figures for the individual grains because many traders traded in more than 1 grain.

Source: U.S. Department of Agriculture, *Technical Bulletin No. 1001.*

FIGURE 30—*Continued*

TECHNICAL BULLETIN 1001, U. S. DEPT. OF AGRICULTURE

TABLE 19.—*Occupational distribution of all traders in sample*—Con.

Occupation	Wheat	Corn	Oats	Rye	All grains[1]
	Number	*Number*	*Number*	*Number*	*Number*
Manual workers:					
Skilled and semiskilled	680	377	134	115	777
Laborers and unskilled	155	75	27	25	171
Total	835	452	161	140	948
Retired:					
Professional	28	13	5	4	32
Semiprofessional	1	-----	-----	-----	1
Clerical	10	7	4	-----	12
Business	292	144	48	37	329
Connected with grain business	44	28	13	11	50
Manual	35	17	4	7	38
Farmers	175	112	43	33	218
Previous connection unknown	222	143	62	46	265
Government employees	8	4	1	3	9
Total	815	468	180	141	954
Unknown:					
Status unascertainable	735	396	176	112	971
Unemployed, former occupation unknown	47	22	6	10	54
Total	782	418	182	122	1,025
Total, nonhedgers	7,541	3,928	1,586	1,313	8,782
Hedgers:					
Processor hedgers	44	15	7	5	47
Grain merchants, terminal	45	22	17	13	49
Grain merchants, subterminal	10	8	3	3	12
Grain merchants, country	23	16	10	6	32
Total	122	61	37	27	140
Total, all traders	7,663	3,989	1,623	1,340	8,922

COMPARATIVE OCCUPATIONAL DISTRIBUTION

One test of the representativeness of the sample is the extent to which the occupational distribution of traders is similar to those found in other studies. There have been several other compilations of futures traders by occupations, but most of them are not closely comparable with the list shown in table 19, because of differences in commodities and dates covered and in the nature of the occupational classifications used. The most nearly comparable tabulation is that given in a study by D. B. Bagnell entitled, "*Analysis of Open Commitments in Wheat and Corn Futures on the Chicago Board of Trade, September 29, 1934.*"[4] This analysis applied to a date 21 months after the final date of the present study, and was a cross

United States Department of Agriculture, *Circular No. 397*.

FIGURE 31

COMMODITY EXCHANGE AUTHORITY

(3) No order issued under paragraph (1) of this section shall apply to transactions or positions which are shown to be bona fide hedging transactions or positions. For the purposes of determining the bona fide hedging transactions or positions of any person under this paragraph (3), they shall mean sales of, or short positions in, any commodity for future delivery on or subject to the rules of any contract market made or held by such person to the extent that such sales or short positions are offset in quantity by the ownership or purchase of the same cash commodity by the same person or, conversely, purchases of, or long positions in, any commodity for future delivery on or subject to the rules of any contract market made or held by such person to the extent that such purchases or long positions are offset by sales of the same cash commodity by the same person. There shall be included in the amount of any commodity which may be hedged by any person—

(A) the amount of such commodity such person is raising, or in good faith intends or expects to raise, within the next twelve months, on land (in the United States or its Territories) which such person owns or leases;

(B) an amount of such commodity the sale of which for future delivery would be a reasonable hedge against the products or byproducts of such commodity owned or purchased by such person, or the purchase of which for future delivery would be a reasonable hedge against the sale of any product or byproduct of such commodity by such person;

(C) an amount of such commodity the purchase of which for future delivery shall not exceed such person's unfilled anticipated requirements for processing or manufacturing during a specified operating period not in excess of one year: *Provided*, That such purchase is made and liquidated in an orderly manner and in accordance with sound commercial practice in conformity with such regulations as the Secretary of Agriculture may prescribe.

Source: U.S. Department of Agriculture, Commodity Exchange Authority, Commodity Exchange Act, Section 4(A)3.

has placed his hedges. If the price on the spot market varies 8 cents from the time the hedger opens his futures position, the Chicago price should also move 8 cents. This "country basis" holds pretty well and the two prices stay within close limits of one another. Once hedged, the hedger stands to lose money only if the basis spreads or narrows before he lifts his hedge. He may make a small windfall profit through basis fluctuation though the amount of the fluctuation may be no more than 1 or 2 cents per bushel. Unhedged he stands to lose many cents per bushel, pound, or other unit, if the cash price moves against him. Because basis is not perfect, a hedge does not totally eliminate risk but it does keep it within tolerable limits.

The feedlot operator in Des Moines, Iowa, who expects to have 1,000 head of choice steers ready for market in July can sell 30 contracts of live beef cattle on the Chicago Mercantile Exchange (30 contracts will approximately equal the herd he will be bringing to the cash markets). The feedlot operator has no intention of shipping his cattle to Chicago; he probably has a local buyer with whom he does business. But if the price of choice steers drops by July, and the feedlot operator is forced to accept a lower price than he had expected from his local buyer, the price of choice steers in Chicago will also drop. The loss that he takes on his cash crop will be closely balanced by the profit he makes on his short contracts in the futures market. Risk is thereby removed from his year's income. Any windfall profit he makes in the form of higher prices on the local cash market for his steers will be eaten up by his hedge. The feedlot operator stands neither to lose nor to gain and has very little interest in price fluctuation once he has placed his hedges.

The breeder has no intention of delivering steers against his short futures position. As he sells his herd, he buys futures contracts until he closes out his short futures position. It makes little difference to the feeder if the contract specifications as to grade, weight, point of delivery, delivery date, and so forth, do not exactly describe the cattle he will be selling, so long as the value of the beef described in the futures contract fluctuates at a constant premium or discount to the grade he has to sell. He could find the price to be 32 cents per pound in Des Moines and 37 cents in Chicago, but if the price drops to 29 cents in Des Moines it will probably drop to 34 cents in Chicago. The prices may never be the same but the movement will be the same on both his local cash market and on his futures position. Three cents made here is lost there.

The hedger, like the speculator, has no intention of delivering to fill his futures contract or accepting delivery. This possibility exists and serves to keep the futures price and the cash price in line so that hedges will work effectively. If cash and futures prices did get out of line, people legally could and would deliver cash goods on the futures markets. In fact, very few contracts are ever filled, probably fewer than 2 percent. The rest are closed by speculators who don't want the goods, and hedgers who do their business on cash markets and lift their hedges as they do so.

Like most things in economics, hedging in practice is not quite as straightforward as in theory. Cash prices in a particular wholesale market, at the time the hedger wishes to buy or sell the actual goods, will be determined to some extent by purely local conditions, which will not affect Chicago prices, and hedging in Chicago will not necessarily cover this local fluctuation. It is largely for this reason that several futures markets often exist for the same commodity in different parts of the country. Futures markets and cash markets will both reflect national conditions and the overall market but country basis will vary according to local price fluctuations which are not reflected in Chicago prices. Hedgers, like any other businessmen, will study local conditions in judging their hedges and act accordingly. While hedgers theoretically will hedge at any price which allows them a profit in their cash operations, the fact is, hedgers rapidly lose interest if they believe the possibility of windfall profit is greater than actual loss on the cash markets. In other words, hedgers speculate on their cash positions by leaving them unhedged if they think this is their most profitable alternative. These complications are of little interest to the speculator who does all his business on one market and has no need of following the country basis between markets.

PIT TRADERS AND SCALPERS

A pit trader may trade his own account, or he may take orders from a brokerage house or hedger not large enough to have his own staff. He is the man who stands physically in the pit and trades contracts by a system of shouting and hand signals. Some pit traders hold fairly large positions for weeks at a time, such as Ed Wilson who is mentioned later in this chapter, but most who trade for their own accounts hold their positions for very short periods of time. The special advantage of being physically in the pit (for any trader who is handling his account) is largely made up of very quick price trades. For normal speculation, holding a position for several days, weeks, or months, being in the pit grants no particular advantage. (See Fig. 32 below.)

The majority of pit traders take advantage of small price fluctuations that occur in any market by buying a temporarily depressed price and selling back a few minutes later when a large buy order comes in slightly raising the price in the pit. These traders are called "scalpers" and serve the same function as the specialist in a stock market. Like the specialist, scalpers trade for their own accounts, although scalpers are not under regulation as are specialists. (See Fig. 33, p. 41.)

Any trader in the pit can quickly "scalp" a price which has dipped and sell the contracts when the price has returned. With such competition for quick one-eighth cent profits, regulation is simply not required. Any trader attempting to distort a price by holding back on trading would quickly find himself undercut by the trader standing behind him.

Scalpers rarely find their profit on a trade to be above a single eighth cent or perhaps a quarter except in extremely rapid moving markets. To hold out for more would be to simply make no trades, because another trader will quickly make the trade if he can find a profit in it. Sometimes a trader can scalp a price instantly, in the confusion, by selling contracts at one corner of the pit and immediately buying them back a little cheaper on the other side. In so doing, the scalper serves to keep prices the same throughout the pit.

Like the stock specialist, the function of the scalper is to provide liquidity to the market by balancing the number of sell offers and buy offers in the pit. An overbalance of buying orders will cause the price to rise. Before it goes too far, scalpers will provide sales, picking up a quick fraction and keeping the buy orders filled. The scalper's position is then closed, often only minutes later, when an excess of selling pressure hits the floor from the ticker rooms of the brokerage firms. Scalpers rarely hold positions overnight and rarely do they alter price trends. They simply help to smooth price out and assure all incoming orders a representative price.

THE PUBLIC SPECULATOR

The Chicago Mercantile Exchange recently took a look at the average commodity speculator and found him to be younger than the average stock specu-

FIGURE 32

(n) *Floor broker.*—This term means any person who, in or surrounding any pit, ring, post, or other place provided by a contract market for the meeting of persons similarly engaged, shall engage in executing for others any order for the purchase or sale of any commodity for future delivery on or subject to the rules of any contract market, and who for such services receives or accepts any commission or other compensation.

Source: U.S. Department of Agriculture, Commodity Exchange Authority.

lator, better educated, in keeping with the general rise in levels of education, and more ambitious with his risk capital. The Merc polled 4,000 speculators at random from those traders holding positions during September, October, and November of 1970. They found the average speculator to be male (56 percent of the sample was male between the ages of 35 and 55). He's a professional man, not yet retired, and earns a healthy income (86 percent earned over $10,000, 39 percent earned in excess of $25,000 per year). On the average, he has a bachelor's degree from college (68 percent of the sample had been to college; of these 60 percent held a bachelor's degree, and 18 percent held graduate degrees).

The traders polled showed a healthy number of new traders (37 percent had been trading fewer than four years) although not new to the investment field (70 percent had securities accounts).

FIGURE 33

Source: Chicago Mercantile Exchange.

The average trader tends to be quite nimble, holding his positions to short terms (85 percent of the poll were holding positions less than a month old, 55 percent held positions less than 10 days old). He also trades in small lots (51 percent of the 4,000 speculators were holding only one or two contracts, 75 percent were holding fewer than five).

It would be possible for a futures market to exist serving only speculators, but in fact, the volume of business done on any of the futures markets directly follows the amount of interest in hedging on the part of industry. Industries with the greatest amount of hedging have the greatest volume of speculation on their futures markets. The speculator is after profit and typically couldn't care less if the contract called for delivery of cotton, corn, or box-top coupons, so long as the price rises if he is long and falls if he is short, granting him a profit. But the speculator must follow the action and the action follows the needs of the industry. Comparatively little corn is held by commercial dealers who might be damaged by adverse price movements, and this fact is reflected by the small amount of hedging compared to the size of the crop (it is the nation's largest). Wheat, on the other hand, is almost entirely held by commercial suppliers, millers, and warehousemen, and is much more heavily hedged. It is no accident that speculation is also normally much greater in wheat than in corn. (In 1970, a corn blight wiped out over 10 percent of the nation's crop, radically increasing both hedger and speculative interest, and putting corn, which is normally third or fourth in volume, on top for the year. Whether or not corn continues to enjoy such volume will depend upon market conditions in the future.) (See Fig. 34 opposite.)

Like the scalper, the speculator serves a function in the futures markets. By looking out for his own profits, he assumes unwanted risk and helps balance the markets. The speculator makes his profit by buying prices which have fallen below a fair and reasonable estimate of the cash price to come in the future, whether because of a large hedging sale or because of improperly discounted information about coming market prices. The speculator profits from selling prices which have risen too far, thereby keeping futures contract prices in line with coming cash prices which are at the price contracts must expire. The question that has never been fully resolved is whether the speculator, in fact, succeeds in performing his function. If he does sell too high prices and buy prices that are too low, he makes a profit and helps level out unwanted price movement, giving a fair price to any who wish to use the markets. He also provides liquidity. (See Fig. 35, p. 44.)

The question is whether the speculator does make profits overall, thereby leveling the market prices, or whether he loses causing unnecessary price aberrations in the process. A study of the onion markets, with and without speculation, indicates that the speculator performs his function very well, and provides a better market while taking his profits. In other markets, speculator stop-loss orders cause irritating price spurts when they are tripped.

If the speculator is doing well, the markets are improved but it is difficult to determine over a market just how well the speculators are doing. Position figures are released by the Department

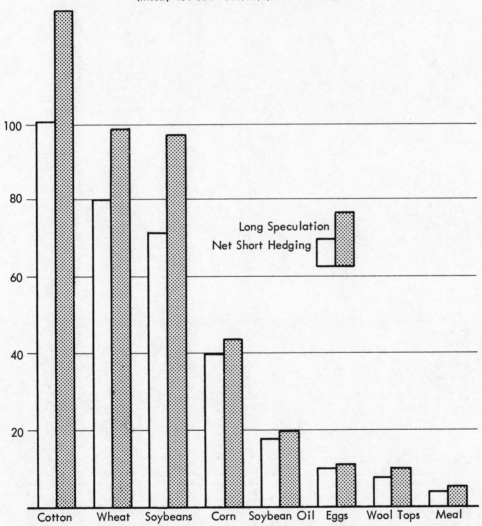

FIGURE 34
ESTIMATED AVERAGE DOLLAR VALUES OF NET SHORT
HEDGING AND LONG SPECULATIVE OPEN CONTRACTS
(mostly 1954/55–1958/59) (million dollars)

Long Speculation
Net Short Hedging

Volume and speculation are greatest on those markets with the greatest hedging interest. Total long speculation is often greater than net short hedging (short minus long hedging). The difference is made up by short speculation.

Source: Holbrook Working, "Speculation on Hedging Markets."

FIGURE 35

AN ANALYSIS OF SPECULATIVE TRADING IN GRAIN FUTURES

TABLE 30.—*Number of speculative traders with profits and with losses, and percent with profits, by grain and major occupational group*

Commodity and occupational group	Traders with—		Total	Percentage with profits
	Profits	Losses		
WHEAT				
Business managers:	*Number*	*Number*	*Number*	*Percent*
Grain business	83	189	272	30. 5
Other	702	1, 993	2, 695	26. 0
Professional	179	498	677	26. 4
Semiprofessional	27	64	91	29. 7
Clerical	130	349	479	27. 1
Farmers	200	697	897	22. 3
Manual workers	214	621	835	25. 6
Retired	240	576	816	29. 4
Unknown	270	509	779	34. 7
Total	2, 045	5, 496	7, 541	27. 1
CORN				
Business managers:				
Grain business	76	96	172	44. 2
Other	577	806	1, 383	41. 7
Professional	133	221	354	37. 6
Semiprofessional	16	20	36	44. 4
Clerical	76	159	235	32. 3
Farmers	151	261	412	36. 7
Manual workers	163	289	452	36. 1
Retired	189	280	469	40. 3
Unknown	144	271	415	34. 7
Total	1, 525	2, 403	3, 928	38. 8
OATS				
Business managers:				
Grain business	23	54	77	29. 9
Other	223	374	597	37. 4
Professional	45	74	119	37. 8
Semiprofessional	7	7	14	50. 0
Clerical	37	50	87	42. 5
Farmers	57	112	169	33. 7
Manual workers	53	108	161	32. 9
Retired	69	111	180	38. 3
Unknown	75	107	182	41. 2
Total	589	997	1, 586	37. 1
RYE				
Business managers:				
Grain business	22	37	59	37. 3
Other	201	303	504	39. 9
Professional	36	78	114	31. 6
Semiprofessional	2	12	14	14. 3
Clerical	33	49	82	40. 2
Farmers	43	94	137	31. 4
Manual workers	52	88	140	37. 1

Source: U.S. Department of Agriculture, *Technical Bulletin 1001.*

of Agriculture just once a month and do not indicate intermonth changes in position which would determine profit and loss on the part of the various traders. Hedgers often depress the market or give it a purely technical boost but there is no way of determining if the market is stabilized by speculation and who takes the profit for the stabilization of prices. (See Fig. 36, p. 46.)

THE LARGE SPECULATOR

Ed Wilson is a large speculator, a member of the Chicago Board of Trade, and a man who makes his living assuming risks that other people wish to avoid. Recently he took a position in crude soybean oil for December delivery. Typically he bought the limit allowed by the Commodity Exchange Authority (CEA), 300 contracts, each equal to a 60,000-pound tank car. His average price was 8.2 cents a pound, requiring a margin deposit of $90,000. Three weeks later, he congratulated himself on his analysis of the demand for the high protein oil and decided the price was pretty much in line with his expectations. It was time to get out.

He stepped to the top step of the octagonal pit where soybean oil is traded and waited for a moment to tune into price action. When he found a slight bulge in price he raised his hand, palm out, indicating that he wished to sell. "Sell 25 at 17," he yelled across the pit, indicating that he wished to sell. A man across the pit caught his eye and raised his hand palm in, meaning he wished to place a bid to buy. "Buy 25 at 15," he shouted back, meaning he would buy the 25 contracts at 9.15 cents a pound. Ed

Wilson nodded and the deal was completed for 25 contracts of soybean oil. Mr. Wilson continued to trade throughout the session, keeping his sales below 50 carloads at a time to keep from depressing the market unnecessarily and managed to close out half his position by the close at 1:15 in the afternoon. Two days later he closed out the rest of his holdings at an average price of 9.20 cents a pound for a profit after commissions of $174,000.

Mr. Wilson does not limit his trading to soybean oil. Two years ago, he heard from a friend that supplies of cattle were not keeping up with demand. He went to the Chicago Mercantile Exchange to talk to several traders he knew there and heard enough to whet his appetite. He began digging into Department of Agriculture bulletins listing the number of cattle on feed, last year's spring drop of calves, cattle census on ranches around the country, and so forth. He found that the number of cattle moving into market positions was indeed leveling off. Boosts in social security and a large labor settlement convinced him that personal income was going to rise in the near future. With this research he came to a conclusion that more people were going to be wanting more beef in the next year and that supplies were not going to grow to meet the increased demand. The price would go up. In September through a regular commission house, as he holds no seat on that exchange, he bought 250 carloads of beef on the Chicago Mercantile Exchange. He had guessed right, the price rose, and Mr. Wilson sold back his contracts, seven months later, for a profit of $300,000.

THE SMALL SPECULATOR

Former chairman of the Chicago Mercantile Exchange, Leo Melamed, is more typical of the commodity speculators in the country. He limits himself to smaller positions than does Mr. Wilson and makes a larger number of trades. Mr. Melamed has two signs on the wall where he can brood at them as he plans his trades. The first reads, "I am married to my wife, not my commodity position." To Leo Melamed this means holding no position for more than two weeks. "I'm not looking to capitalize on the entire move of any swing" he explains, "I didn't want the entire top or bottom—just a little slice out of the middle." The exact top or bottom of a price swing cannot be determined by any method, even by a professional speculator standing in the middle of the pit where the contracts are being traded. Mr. Melamed's game is to find an imminent move in price and to play it for what profit is to be had. He limits himself to 100 contracts, a position size he had found "livable" and keeps his money where the action is, which means many trades, as many as 50 in a week, placing his money in position for a profit and removing it immediately if the profit is not to be found.

Mr. Melamed's second sign reads, "Be a lover, not a fighter," which is a philosophy far too often ignored by

FIGURE 36

TABLE 31.—*Aggregate profits and losses of speculators and ratio of profits to losses, by grain and occupational group*

Occupational group	All grains			Wheat			Corn		
	Profits	Losses	Ratio	Profits	Losses	Ratio	Profits	Losses	Ratio
	Dollars	*Dollars*		*Dollars*	*Dollars*		*Dollars*	*Dollars*	
Business managers:									
Grain business	210, 200	743, 600	0. 28	219, 665	587, 135	0. 37	67, 959	169, 668	0. 40
Other	866, 100	5, 466, 600	. 16	469, 786	4, 323, 944	. 11	651, 926	894, 542	. 73
Professional	190, 200	1, 094, 700	. 17	140, 425	836, 440	. 17	78, 694	219, 192	. 36
Semiprofessional	6, 500	61, 300	. 11	4, 711	53, 972	. 09	2, 964	9, 505	. 31
Clerical	44, 100	277, 800	. 16	45, 421	214, 101	. 21	17, 810	74, 849	. 24
Farmers	180, 500	1, 372, 100	. 13	187, 886	1, 162, 210	. 16	63, 232	204, 164	. 31
Manual workers	97, 400	460, 900	. 21	64, 714	382, 299	. 17	66, 188	92, 455	. 72
Retired	241, 300	1, 566, 800	. 15	205, 151	1, 203, 813	. 17	120, 059	351, 317	. 34
Unknown	228, 500	914, 400	. 25	170, 648	647, 706	. 26	115, 161	206, 910	. 56
All speculators	2, 064, 800	11, 958, 200	. 17	1, 508, 407	9, 411, 620	. 16	1, 183, 993	2, 222, 602	. 53

Occupational group	Oats			Rye		
	Profits	Losses	Ratio	Profits	Losses	Ratio
	Dollars	*Dollars*		*Dollars*	*Dollars*	
Business managers:						
Grain business	12, 273	39, 885	0. 31	12, 918	56, 756	0. 23
Other	51, 512	365, 990	. 14	93, 095	362, 868	. 26
Professional	11, 520	65, 115	. 18	58, 534	92, 306	. 63
Semiprofessional	2, 843	4, 068	. 70	383	4, 366	. 09
Clerical	2, 933	15, 075	. 19	3, 669	15, 556	. 24
Farmers	9, 824	72, 611	. 14	14, 370	58, 234	. 25
Manual workers	5, 528	31, 969	. 17	13, 476	34, 470	. 39
Retired	13, 187	108, 195	. 12	67, 131	88, 341	. 76
Unknown	14, 418	69, 224	. 21	29, 466	112, 941	. 26
All speculators	124, 038	772, 132	. 16	293, 042	825, 838	. 35

Source: U.S. Department of Agriculture, *Technical Bulletin 1001.*

speculators. His trades go with the price move, never against them. If at the end of the first day his position is not showing a profit he closes it out. It is possible for a loss to come back but it is much easier to cover it with another trade in another commodity. This policy guarantees that small losses will never grow to be large, for when losses are not given a chance to come back they are not given a chance to grow large.

Mssrs. Wilson and Melamed are both professionals who do quite well in their line of business. Mr. Wilson has averaged over $300,000 a year for the last 10 years on maximum allowed positions. Mr. Melamed specializes in shorter and smaller trades and makes money 10 months a year on the average. On a good month he often brings home $25,000 and on the worst of the bad months he will lose $3,000. Neither has a great advantage over the public speculator in Portland, Oregon, or Denver other than the lower commissions they pay as members of their exchanges. It would be impractical for a public speculator paying full commission of the modest 0.6 percent to make 50 trades in a week but the principles of trading 50 contracts are the same governing the principles of trading 10 or 5. Make more money when you make money than you lose when you lose and you will take money with you when you go.

Ed Wilson bases his beef trades on statistics released once a month by the Department of Agriculture, free of charge to anybody who puts his name on the mailing list, along with data about the economy found in his daily newspaper. Leo Melamed bases his plays on an understanding of fundamental price factors and tight control over his posi-

tions. The playing of commodities requires close watch of price-making factors and past behavior of prices in the market. Any speculator who plays his game properly, as do these men, can make money and have a good time doing it, no matter where he lives or who he uses to execute the mechanical buying and selling for him.

Small traders are not required to file positions reports with the CEA. Their positions are derived by subtracting the large traders' commitments from the total number of contracts open at the end of the month. For this reason, no breakdown is possible of the small traders into hedging and speculative categories. Reporting levels are shown in Figure 37, p. 48.

COMMITMENT OF TRADERS

Each month the Department of Agriculture publishes a bulletin *Commitments of Traders in Commodity Futures*. This bulletin usually comes out before the 15th of the month after the reporting period (February 15th for the month of January, and so on), and lists the total position of six categories of traders. The breakdown is: Large Speculators, long, short, and spreading; Large Hedgers, long and short; and a final category of Small Traders, which includes both hedgers and speculators whose positions are below the reporting level.

Open contracts of large traders show the aggregate positions reported as speculative and hedging, as classified by them in their reports to the Commodity Exchange Authority. A large trader is one who holds a position in any one market and contract month equaling or exceeding the quantities specified as

"Reporting Level." Large traders must report their positions to the CEA.

The *Commitments of Traders* bulletin gives a pretty fair view of the general tenor of a market. How much of the open interest is hedging? How does my position compare to that of the smart money "large traders"? What are the small traders up to? Speculators are much more likely to close their positions if the price moves against them than are hedgers who, after all, are making money on their cash positions when the price moves against their futures position. While the commitment bulletin has not a great deal of predictive value, it provides a timely and honest view of who is using a particular market at a particular time.

Figure 38 opposite gives a breakdown of traders in the corn market on the Chicago Board of Trade on January 31, 1973. The total number of contracts open (open interest) was 490,970. Note that under "Total Open Interest" the number is the same for both long-open contracts and short-open contracts. One long and one short is required to make a contract, someone to deliver, and someone to accept delivery. About four

FIGURE 37

UNITED STATES DEPARTMENT OF AGRICULTURE
Commodity Exchange Authority

GUIDE TO REPORTING LEVELS UNDER THE COMMODITY EXCHANGE ACT, AS OF
JANUARY 20, 1969.

Each trader is required to file reports with the Commodity Exchange Authority when he holds or controls open contracts in any one future of any commodity on any one contract market equal to or exceeding the amounts shown below. A report is to be filed for the first day a trader acquires such a position, for each subsequent day on which he makes a trade, and for the first day his position falls below the reporting level. A trader having a reportable position must report all of his trades and positions, regardless of size, in each future of the commodity on all contract markets. For complete information on reporting requirements, see Parts 15, 18 and 19 of the CEA regulations.

COMMODITY	REPORTING LEVEL	REPORTING FORM NO.
Wheat Corn Oats Rye Soybeans Barley Flaxseed	200,000 bushels	203, 204*
Grain sorghums	11,200,000 pounds (200,000bu.)	
Cotton	5,000 bales	303, 304*
Butter	25 carlots	403
Shell eggs**	25 carlots	503, 504*
Frozen whole eggs**	25 contracts	
Potatoes	25 carlots	603, 604*
Wool** Wool tops**	25 contracts	803
Soybean oil Cottonseed oil	25 contracts	1003
Soybean meal Cottonseed meal	25 contracts	1103
Live cattle**	25 contracts	1203
Cattle products	25 contracts	1303
Live hogs Frozen pork bellies Frozen skinned hams	25 contracts	1403
Hides	25 contracts	1503
Frozen concentrated orange juice	25 contracts	1603

*Series 04 reports are filed weekly by reporting merchandisers, processors, and dealers, showing positions in the cash (spot) commodity when the futures position is reportable.
**A trader with a reportable position in any one future of any one type of contract in this commodity is required to report his trades and positions in all types of contracts in the commodity on all markets. For detailed instructions, see Section 18.00, paragraphs (e) wool and wool tops, (f) shell eggs and frozen eggs, and (g) live cattle.

Source: Reynolds & Co., New York.

FIGURE 38

UNITED STATES DEPARTMENT OF AGRICULTURE
Commodity Exchange Authority
141 West Jackson Blvd., Room A-1
Chicago, Illinois 60604

COMMITMENTS OF TRADERS IN COMMODITY FUTURES

This report gives a breakdown of month-end open interest of large and small
traders in the commodities and markets indicated below.

Open interest of large traders show the aggregate positions reported as speculative (including spreading) and hedging, as classified by them in their reports
to the Commodity Exchange Authority. A large trader is one who holds a position
in any one future of a commodity on any one contract market equaling or exceeding
the quantities specified below as "Reporting Level." Large traders are subject
to the reporting requirements of the CEA.

Open interest of small traders include both speculative and hedging positions.
Small traders are not required to file reports of their futures transactions.
Their positions are derived by subtracting large traders' commitments from total
open interest.

CORN FUTURES
Commitments of traders, Chicago Board of Trade, January 31, 1973

Classification	January 31, 1973		Net change from December 31, 1972	
	Long	Short	Long	Short
CORN				
LARGE TRADERS	(In thousand bushels)			
Speculative				
Long or short only	27,255	9,630	+ 205	+ 2,685
Long and short (spreading)	39,320	38,640	+ 9,215	+ 9,375
Total	66,575	48,270	+ 9,420	+ 12,060
Hedging	304,110	337,455	+ 32,580	+ 41,575
Total reported by large traders	370,685	385,725	+ 42,000	+ 53,635
SMALL TRADERS				
Speculative and hedging	120,285	105,245	+ 13,190	+ 1,555
TOTAL OPEN INTEREST	490,970	490,970	+ 55,190	+ 55,190
Percent held by: Large traders	75.5	78.6	+ 0.1	+ 2.4
Small traders	24.5	21.4	- 0.1	- 2.4

Source: U.S. Department of Agriculture, Commodity Exchange Authority.

fifths of the total open interest of large traders was hedging and short hedging ran higher than long hedging (337,455 to 304,110 thousand bushels). Large speculators made up much of this imbalance by being 27,255 long versus 9,630 short, and the rest was made up of spreaders and small traders who cannot be divided up into hedgers and speculators because they do not report their positions and the statistics are not available.

Speculators long and short (spreading) hold an equal number of contracts on both sides of the market between two contract months with the expectation that the difference between the two contracts will change, so that the trader loses less on one month's contract than he makes on the other. Spreading is explained later in the book. Because the data given is a compilation of all the months that corn is traded (March, May, July, September, and December), it is not possible to tell how the spreaders did (you would have to know which months they were spreading). But for the naked positions of long or short, a guess can be made. During the month of February 1973, the price of corn first declined 10 cents and then advanced 25 cents. For each long speculator (and the speculators had the long side of this market), this market returned from 50 percent to 100 percent profit against their margin. Hedgers lost a similar amount but stood to make the money back on the cash markets when they sold their corn. More fluctuation will occur before the hedgers cover their positions and sell their corn, but whatever they lose or make on the futures markets, they will make on the cash markets.

A healthy well-functioning commodity market requires just three things: (1) a contract which closely fits the needs of the industry so that the country basis will remain constant for as large an area of the country as possible, helping guarantee the efficiency of hedges; (2) sufficient volume to provide liquidity, making the placement of large orders possible without undue price concession; and (3) sufficient speculative interest to balance the lopsided market developed by hedgers who are normally net short. If speculators lose money they hurt themselves and the market at the same time. The greatly increased speculative interest over the sixties is welcomed by all the exchanges and if the new speculators do well everybody will be well served.

4

COMMODITIES AS SEEN BY
THE STOCK TRADER

Similarities between stocks and commodities can be misleading. The public trader does business through brokerage houses, such as E. F. Hutton or Merrill Lynch in both cases, and often the same broker will handle both stocks and commodities. Both brokers will give out tips, brochures, and a dry shoulder when needed. Both brokers will service an established account by phone. Both brokers will take your money. Margin accounts appear to be about the same in function but much lower for commodities; in fact they are entirely different. Both feature nearly instantaneous ticker reporting and any good newspaper will give quotations of daily price movements for both in the same manner. Many of the terms used in one market mean the same thing in the other.

Here are some terms which are used in both stock and commodity trading:

Ask	same
At the market	same
Bear	same
Bid	same
Break	same
Bull	same
Buy on close	same
Buy on opening	same
Cash commodity	no comparison
CEA	SEC
Close, the	same
Closing price	same
Cover (liquidation)	same
Day order	same
Evening up	same
Fundamentals	same
Hedge	same principle

Job lot	odd lot
Leverage	same
Limited order	same
Long	same
Margin (good faith)	in true sense
Market order	same
Net position	same
Offer	ask
On opening	same
Open interest	float
Open order	same
Opening, the	same
Opening price	same
Pit	floor
Point	same
Position	same
Price averaging	same
Privileges	same
Pyramiding	same
Quotations	similar
Range	same
Seasonals	stock cycles
Short	same
Spread	arbitrage
Stop-loss order	same
Straddle	arbitrage
Scalper	specialist
Tape	same
Technical rally	same
Technicals	same
Volume	same

These many similarities in the handling of commodity and stock accounts can lead to the false impression that the two games are played the same way. While the mechanics of trading are much alike, the strategy of play is much different.

Basically a stock trader chooses an issue on any number of criteria with the expectation that the price of the stock will rise within the next year or so. Is the industry healthy? Is the company healthy and moving in the right direc-

51

tion? How are the earnings in the past compared to the earnings of other companies in the industry? Who holds the stock? Is it glamorous? Steady? Growth? If I am correct, where will the price per issue be in a year or two? In five years? How is the stock market doing overall? Will the Dow Jones Industrial Average advance to 1,000 again? (See Fig. 39 below.)

The stock trader is playing price appreciation on one of a dozen issues over a relatively long haul. A 10 percent rise or decline in price can be taken fairly well in stride with the sure expectation that the present recession is beginning to give way to prosperity and higher personal incomes will find their way into the stock market. A bull market will pull nearly any issue along with

FIGURE 39

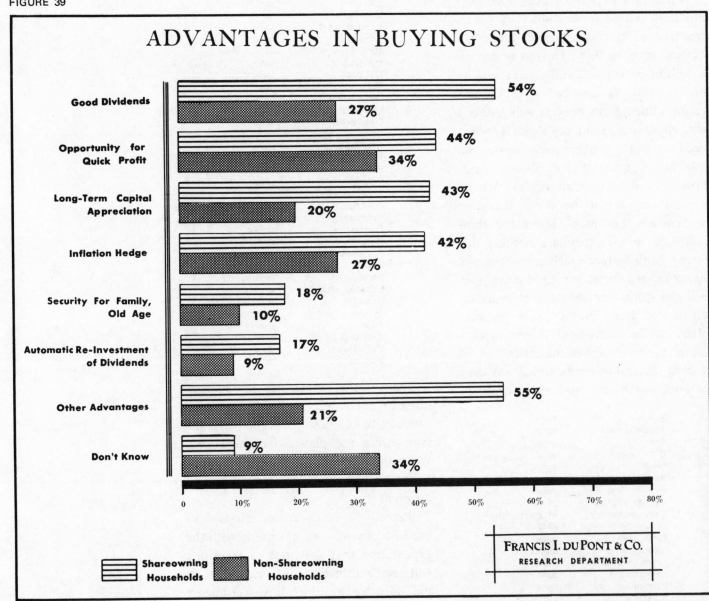

Source: Francis I. DuPont & Co.

it and sooner or later the stock of nearly any healthy company can be expected to hit new levels. Given enough time, a program of buy and hold is nearly guaranteed success.

For any trader with enough capital to deal in round lots, commission is no major consideration and the stock trader has fair mobility in his trading. Stubbornness in the face of hostile price movement can be disastrous, but that same stubbornness is a virtue at the foot of a major price advance. The clever trader can work purely technical adjustments to his advantage in the timing of his purchases and sales and must keep a reasonably interested eye on fundamental aspects of the issues. The major questions during the buildup of a stock portfolio are those of goals and trading mix. Is 10 percent yearly increment good enough? Am I willing to risk more? (See Fig. 40, p. 54, and Fig. 40—*Cont.*, p. 55.)

The commodity trader does not have this question about trading mix. He knows all of his purchases and sales are going to be speculative before he makes any move. His game is not trading mix for he will deal in only two or three commodities at a time, changing his positions often. He may trade wheat futures for several months, then switch to cattle, copper, or coconut oil as prices fluctuate. He makes his money on the small percentage moves on the very large positions he can control with his margin account. He expects to lose money on more than half his trades but if he is a successful trader he keeps these losses extremely small and he is going to be there for the major price moves either up or down. The commodity speculator is playing a game of money

management rather than trading mix. Which commodity he chooses is less important than how he handles his account.

The commodity speculator cannot wait out a setback with the expectation that sooner or later everything rises in price. A contract of July soybeans is going to become soybeans in July and the trader must have made his profit or taken his loss by that time. After the July expiration the contract will have been filled and no longer exist. As commodity margins are so low (about 6 percent for corn and 12 percent for soybeans) a 10 percent price fluctuation can very nearly double the trader's margin account or wipe it out entirely. The seasoned commodity speculator would never sit through a 10 percent move against his position.

Commodity prices have no built-in upward bias equivalent to that in stocks and over the contract life-span prices are as likely to be down as up. Bumper crops in corn, wheat, and cotton can drive prices for these crops down to the government support price, while potatoes skyrocket because of a blight in Idaho and cocoa gyrates madly because of unrest in Nigeria. There are connections between commodities such as the price of hogs and the price of the corn that feeds them, and high-priced corn will eventually raise the price of pork, but these are the exceptions rather than the rule and tie together two or three commodities in a very loose relationship. High-priced corn will do nothing for the price of gold, silver, wool, cotton, plywood, or propane. A rise in the price of palladium does not affect the price of broilers. Each commodity, not the overall market, must be judged. In commodi-

FIGURE 40

Harvard University

(Total general investments: $1,355,704,691)

Name	1972 Number Of Shares	1972 Market Value	1971 Number Of Shares	1971 Market Value
1. Int'l Business Machines	194,299	$76,165,208	191,113	$60,582,821
2. General Reinsurance Corp.	81,162	33,032,934	81,163	19,884,812
3. Eastman Kodak Co.	245,564	32,567,925	244,149	18,952,066
4. Texaco Inc.	837,139	27,207,017	832,587	29,660,911
5. General Motors Corp.	269,257	20,160,617	265,062	20,973,030
6. Standard Oil (N.J.)*	266,956	19,788,113	263,462	19,858,448
7. Ford Motor Co.	293,864	18,770,563	293,578	18,348,625
8. Int'l Tel. & Tel. Corp.	322,607	16,815,889	Not Available	
9. Gulf Oil Corp.	686,797	16,740,676	683,778	21,453,534
10. General Electric Co.	225,253	14,810,384	221,558	13,459,648

* Now called Exxon Corp.

Princeton University

(Grand total, all investments: $542,435,535)

Name	1972 Number Of Shares	1972 Market Value	1971 Number Of Shares	1971 Market Value
1. Int'l Business Machines	71,200	$27,910,400	69,475	$22,023,575
2. Xerox Corp.	180,057	27,188,607	180,000	20,880,000
3. American Home Products	165,668	17,560,808	166,668	12,833,436
4. Texas Oil & Gas (1)	520,954	14,586,712	260,477	11,460,988
5. Louisiana Land & Exploration	322,564	14,515,380	324,564	14,280,816
6. Texaco Inc.	365,243	12,053,019	353,597	12,729,492
7. Coastal States Gas	257,176	11,058,568	257,176	13,373,152
8. Standard Oil (N.J.)*	123,902	9,168,748	123,366	9,252,450
9. Bristol-Myers Co.	140,902	8,876,826	140,902	9,017,728
10. General Reinsurance	18,750	7,631,250	18,750	4,575,000

(1) 2-for-1 split, ex. July 3, 1972.   * Now called Exxon Corp.

Source: *The Exchange* (NYSE), January 1973.

ties there simply is no such thing as an overall market. (See Fig. 41, p. 56.)

On the other side of the coin, the speculator is in the position in commodities of having figured everything right but having the market go to hell. To survive the speculator must manage the risk he assumes in the same manner that an insurance company bears risk. By dividing a determinable risk across a large number of cases, the insurance company can set a program under which it knows it can operate at a profit, even though it does not know what will happen on any particular policy. The insurance company does not know what will happen to any car, only that out of a hundred thousand cars, 12.7 percent will be involved in accidents in any given year. It knows the cost of the average accident and by determining the number of accidents and the cost of the average accident, the company knows how much income it must have to run at a profit and sets its premiums accordingly.

The farmer does not worry about any single grain that he sows but merely about the average germination. If his seed germinates at about 60 percent he knows that he must plant 100 seeds where he wants 60 plants.

The commodity speculator is playing an insurance game, the game of bearing risk. He cannot know whether the price of soybeans is going up or down (although he may try) but he can figure how *far* up or down the price can possibly go and the chance of its going. He knows he is going to lose on at least half his positions, and needs only to see that his average loss is smaller than his average win. There are probably as many different methods of speculation as there are speculators but the trading programs all share two basic functions. The speculator must predict (guess which market to play and which side to take) and manage his position (to ensure the average loss being smaller than the average win).

Commodities trading is what economists term a "zero sum game." Every dollar lost by any trader is made by another trader and the only money that leaves the game is the broker's commission. It is like a poker game with a dime drag out of every pot to pay for the potato chips. While any trader may have a "paper profit" the profit and loss of all traders at all times adds up to zero. This is distinctly different from the stock market where the total value (and profit) goes up in a bull market and down in a bear market. The total value of all commodity futures contracts changes with price movements, but the total value of winnings will change only as the volume of business changes.

While stock traders are bidding for a share of stock which they can place in their safe deposit boxes, the commodity trader is making and closing trading agreements. One share of Acme Dynamic Systems represents ownership of 1/100,000ths of that company. One contract of September cocoa is a written agreement to deliver or accept 30,000 pounds of cocoa in September. The futures contract does not represent ownership of anything, but is rather an agreement to do business at such and such a future date at such and such a set price. One hundred thousand shares of Acme Dynamic Systems are owned by somebody at all times but the number of contracts for delivery of cocoa in

FIGURE 40—*Continued*

University of California
(Total endowment invested: $328,942,000)

| | 1972 | | 1971 | |
Name	Number Of Shares	Market Value	Number Of Shares	Market Value
1. Int'l Business Machines	44,757	$17,544,744	47,515	$15,062,255
2. Caterpillar Tractor	277,664	16,382,176	327,654	15,973,132
3. Eastman Kodak	87,628	11,621,663	83,912	6,513,669
4. General Electric	91,954	6,045,975	90,118	5,474,668
5. Sears Roebuck	50,258	5,553,509	50,425	4,374,368
6. General Motors	61,338	4,592,682	58,505	4,629,208
7. Bankamerica Corp.	91,588	4,041,320	Not Available	
8. Procter & Gamble	39,412	3,675,169	Not Available	
9. American Tel & Tel	85,757	3,569,635	79,890	3,644,981
10. Texaco	97,653	3,173,722	98,058	3,493,316

Yale University
(Total endowment invested: $595,161,754)

| | 1972 | | 1971 | |
Name	Number Of Shares	Market Value	Number Of Shares	Market Value
1. Damon Corp.	226,100	$15,516,114	74,400	$ 3,487,500
2. AMF Corp.	222,500	13,795,000	200,000	7,625,000
3. Florida Nat'l Banks of Fla.	527,000	12,911,500	410,400	8,259,300
4. Mass. Mutual Mtg. & R. I.	385,000	11,790,625	200,500	5,112,750
5. MCA Inc.	361,800	10,311,300	344,700	8,315,888
6. Grace (W.R.) & Co.	402,986	10,225,770	415,986	12,583,576
7. Gillette Co.	200,000	9,750,000	Not Available	
8. Data General	101,000	9,494,000	22,800	1,102,950
9. INA Corp.	203,525	9,311,269	2,325	117,413
10. Eastman Kodak Co.	61,000	8,090,125	Not Available	

Source: *The Exchange* (NYSE), January 1973.

FIGURE 41

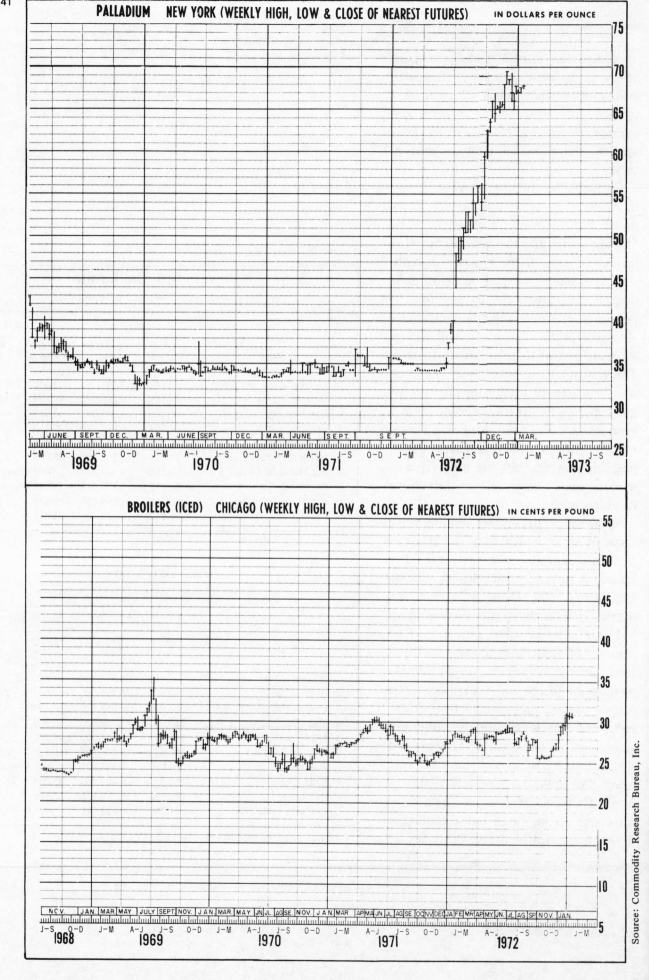

PALLADIUM   NEW YORK (WEEKLY HIGH, LOW & CLOSE OF NEAREST FUTURES)   IN DOLLARS PER OUNCE

BROILERS (ICED)   CHICAGO (WEEKLY HIGH, LOW & CLOSE OF NEAREST FUTURES)   IN CENTS PER POUND

Source: Commodity Research Bureau, Inc.

September changes constantly. Open interest, the number of contracts extant, recently jumped on the cocoa market from 10,000 contracts to 24,000 with no change in the supplies of cocoa and no effect on contract price.

MARGIN

Margin is conceptually different in stock and commodity trading, and the effect of this difference is felt throughout a trader's relationship with his broker. In simple terms, margin in a stock account is used as a downpayment or partial payment for the stock purchased with the remainder made up by a broker loan on which the trader must pay interest. Commodity margin is in the form of a surety bond, assuring the brokerage of the trader's ability and intention to perform as required by the commodity contracts he has entered. Because of the trader not buying anything there is no money owed on the total value of the goods, no broker loan, and no interest payment.

Five thousand bushels of corn (one contract) at $1.20 is worth $6,000, and margin is set at $400. The trader isn't buying the corn, he is merely assuring the broker that he can stand a $400 loss in the value of the contract. The actual $6,000 that the corn is worth is not paid by the brokerage and would never be paid except in the rare event that the trader decided to hold onto the contract past expiration and assume ownership of the 5,000 bushels of corn. In this event the trader must tender a check for the full $6,000 plus handling charges and his $400 surety deposit is returned to him or applied to the purchase.

MAINTENANCE MARGIN

The trader would never be allowed to lose his entire margin deposit of $400 on his contract of corn. To do so would leave the brokerage with an open position for which it held no deposit protection. A deposit of $400 is equivalent to 8 cents per bushel on a contract of 5,000 bushels and the initial deposit will cover a loss of 8 cents. If the trader bought corn at $1.20 the price can drop to $1.12 without incurring loss for the brokerage. If he took the short side of the market at $1.20 the price could rise to $1.28 before completely wiping out the trader's margin account. To protect himself from loss the broker will call for more deposit before the price ever deteriorated to this extent on paper. The trader is generally allowed to lose 25 percent of the original margin deposit. The 75 percent equity he must always maintain is known as "maintenance margin" and serves to protect the brokerage house which is extending credit to the commodity trader. While the trader who bought corn at $1.20 could see the price drop to $1.12 before being completely wiped out he would find himself faced with a margin call for more money at $1.18. He must redeposit enough to bring his equity back up to $400 to protect the house. Should the price continue to deteriorate the trader will be faced with a second margin call at $1.15, and another one each time the price of his contract drops 1 cent or 2 cents.

Soybean margins are set at 22 cents per bushel, which is composed of 7 cents maintenance margin and 15 cents backup. The full margin deposit for soybeans is currently $1,200 which will handle a contract of beans worth $12,500. Soybeans would have to drop 22 cents in order to wipe out a long trader completely, although a margin call could be expected by the time the price dropped 7 cents.

Maintenance margin would work both ways, of course. Each time corn rises 2 cents, a long trader can take $100 out of his account for a return of 25 percent on his money. If soybeans went with the long trader by 6 cents he can take $300 out of his account or use it to finance more contracts in the same or another commodity.

MARGIN FOR SPREAD POSITIONS

Margin rates for spread positions are set much lower than for single "naked" positions. This lower margin allows a trader to handle a much larger position with the same initial cash outlay and provides one of the main attractions of spreads. (A spread is a position long and short in different options of the same commodity.) A trader might have one "leg" in July soybeans and another in August soybeans (see Chapter 9), while the margin for the single naked positions in July would run about $1,000 per contract, the margin for the spread between the two options could run as low as $300 for both legs. An investment of $3,000 would thus control a position of 10 contracts long and 10 contracts short or 3 contracts held naked long or short.

Risk is relatively small in spread positions because as the soybean market moves in price both legs of the spread will move with it. The trader stands to win small percentages of money (but often huge profits or huge losses) as the

legs come closer together or widen (depending on the way in which he spreads the market). In general, the risk is reduced by a spread (although the actual risk may still be very great in some markets) so less protection and margin rates can be set at a lower level. Specific margin requirements for spreading vary according to the commodity, the season, and the current conditions in the market and details of current requirements will have to be verified before any spreads are planned. (See Fig. 42, p. 59, and Fig. 42—Cont., p. 60.)

OTHER MARGIN DIFFERENCES

The initial process of depositing margin is the same for both stocks and commodities, although later on, after the trader is known and his portfolio has grown somewhat, the stock trader can place an order with his broker by telephone and wait four working days to cover the margin on the new shares. In commodities this four-day grace period does not exist. The trader must tender a check on the day of the short sale or purchase and make additional deposits immediately any time his margin account falls below the amount specified for the contracts held open in his account. When a commodity position is offset (closed) the broker must immediately return a check or deposit the money in the client's account.

Contrary to stocks the amount of margin capital required in commodity trading does not normally vary with the value of the commodity. A trader buying 100 shares of Acme Dynamic Systems at $25 a share must come up with $2,500 plus commissions when he opens his account. If he is well enough known

FIGURE 42

SHEARSON, HAMMILL & CO.
INCORPORATED

COMMODITY MARGIN REQUIREMENTS

FIRM POLICY: $1,000.00 deposit is required on all new accounts and to reopen closed accounts. A minimum equity of $500.00 is required by all open accounts with no exceptions. We reserve the right to change requirements without notice. Confirm with Commodity Credit Department

Also of considerable importance is our requirement that no new commodity account is to be opened with a transaction until a deposit of funds has been made either by original receipt or transfer from some other existing account. Stated negatively, no one is permitted to enter a commodity order unless the required cash is on hand in advance. Failure to observe this rule can result in losses which are frequently uncollectable. This, therefore, also serves to remind you that where such losses are sustained, they will be charged on a net basis to the Investment Executive involved.

All sell outs resulting from Margin Calls will be entered here in New York. Branch Offices will not enter this type of order.

No *Hedge Margin* applied to any account unless approved by Commodity Credit Department prior to opening of account.

Day Trading; Account must have excess of $200.00 in account before Day Trading. This applies to all commodities except copper which requires $600.00. $200.00 applies only to a maximum of ten (10) contracts.

EXCHANGE & COMMODITY	TYPE NO.	PRICE RANGE	CUSTOMER CLASSIFICATION	INITIAL MARGIN PER CONTRACT	RESTORATION POINT	SPREAD MARGIN	RESTORATION POINT
Chicago Board of Trade							
CORN	9	All	Speculative	$400.00	25%	$200.00	25%
			Hedge	300.00	$300.00	150.00	25%
OATS	9	All	Speculative	300.00	25%	150.00	25%
			Hedge	200.00	$200.00	100.00	25%
SOYBEANS	9	All	Speculative	750.00	25%	375.00	25%
			Hedge	500.00	$500.00	250.00	25%
SOYBEAN MEAL	9	All	Speculative	500.00	25%	250.00	25%
			Hedge	400.00	$400.00	200.00	25%
SOYBEAN OIL	9	All	Speculative	500.00	25%	250.00	25%
			Hedge	400.00	$400.00	200.00	25%
WHEAT	9	All	Speculative	500.00	25%	250.00	25%
			Hedge	400.00	$400.00	200.00	25%
ICED BROILERS	8	All	Speculative	500.00	25%	250.00	25%
			Hedge	300.00	$300.00	150.00	25%
CHICAGO PLYWOOD	8	All	Speculative	600.00	25%	300.00	25%
			Hedge	300.00	$300.00	200.00	25%
CHICAGO SILVER	8	All	Speculative	600.00	25%	300.00	25%
			Hedge	400.00	$400.00	200.00	25%
Chicago Mercantile BONELESS BEEF	9	All	Speculative	800.00	25%	400.00	25%
			Hedge	600.00	25%	300.00	25%
FRESH EGGS	9	All	Speculative	600.00	25%	300.00	25%
			Hedge	500.00	25%	250.00	25%
SPOT MONTH EGG			Speculative	1500.00	25%	1500.00	25%
			Hedge	750.00	25%	750.00	25%
LIVE BEEF CATTLE	9	All	Speculative	500.00	25%	250.00	25%
			Hedge	400.00	25%	250.00	25%
SPOT MONTH CATTLE			Speculative	600.00	25%	600.00	$400.00
			Hedge	400.00	$400.00	400.00	400.00
LIVE HOGS	9	All	Speculative	400.00	25%	200.00	25%
			Hedge	400.00	25%	200.00	25%
SPOT MONTH HOGS			Speculative	600.00	25%	600.00	25%
			Hedge	600.00	25%	600.00	25%
FROZ. PORK BELLIES	9	All	Speculative	750.00	25%	400.00	25%
			Hedge	750.00	25%	400.00	25%
SPOT MO. BELLIES			Speculative	1000.00	25%	1000.00	25%
			Hedge	1000.00	25%	1000.00	25%
LUMBER 2X4	8	All	Speculative	600.00	25%	300.00	25%
			Hedge	300.00	$300.00	200.00	25%
SPOT MO. LUMBER			Speculative	700.00	25%	450.00	25%
			Hedge	450.00	25%	450.00	25%
IDAHO POTATOES	9	All	Speculative	450.00	25%	225.00	25%
			Hedge	250.00	25%	125.00	$100.00
SPOT MO POTATOE			Speculative	600.00	25%	600.00	25%
			Hedge	500.00	25%	500.00	25%
N. Y. Cocoa Exchange COCOA	8	All	Speculative	750.00	25%	375.00	25%
N. Y. Sugar Exchange Sugar #11	8	All	Speculative	500.00	25%	250.00	25%

Margin levels are set by the exchanges as surety bonds.

FIGURE 42—Continued

EXCHANGE & COMMODITY	TYPE NO.	PRICE RANGE	CUSTOMER CLASSIFICATION	INITIAL MARGIN PER CONTRACT	RESTORATION POINT	SPREAD MARGIN	RESTORATION POINT
Commodity Exch Inc.							
COPPER		Up to 39.99¢	Speculative	$750.00	25%	$500.00	25%
			Hedge	500.00	25%	200.00	25%
DAY TRADE requires	8	40.00¢ to 49.99¢	Speculative	850.00	25%	500.00	25%
$600.00 excess margin			Hedge	600.00	25%	200.00	25%
in account.		50.00¢ and over	Speculative	1000.00	25%	500.00	25%
			Hedge	750.00	25%	200.00	25%
N. Y. SILVER	8	All	Speculative	1200.00	25%	600.00	25%
			Hedge	1000.00	25%	400.00	25%
N. Y. Cotton Exchange							
COTTON #2		Up to 35.00¢	Speculative	1000.00	25%	500.00	25%
	9	35.01¢ to 37.00¢	Speculative	1250.00	25%	625.00	25%
		37.01¢ to 39.00¢	Speculative	1500.00	25%	750.00	25%
		39.01¢ and over	Speculative	2000.00	25%	1000.00	25%
FZN ORANGE JUICE		Up to 50.00¢	Speculative	900.00	25%	450.00	25%
			Hedge	350.00	25%	200.00	25%
		50.05¢ to 60.00¢	Speculative	1200.00	25%	600.00	25%
			Hedge	450.00	25%	200.00	25%
	9	60.05¢ to 70.00¢	Speculative	1500.00	25%	750.00	25%
			Hedge	600.00	25%	200.00	25%
		70.05¢ to 80.00¢	Speculative	1800.00	25%	900.00	25%
			Hedge	750.00	25%	200.00	25%
		80.05¢ and over	Speculative	2000.00	25%	1000.00	25%
			Hedge	900.00	25%	200.00	25%
WOOL (GREASE)	9	Up to 1.500¢	Speculative	600.00	25%	300.00	25%
WOOL TOPS	9	Up to 2.000¢	Speculative	600.00	25%	300.00	25%
N. Y. Mercantile Exch.							
POTATOES MAINE		Up to 3.00¢	Speculative	200.00	25%	200.00	25%
		3.01¢ to 3.50¢	Speculative	250.00	25%	250.00	25%
	9	3.51¢ to 4.00¢	Speculative	300.00	25%	300.00	25%
		4.01¢ to 4.50¢	Speculative	400.00	25%	400.00	25%
*Old and New Cak's		4.51¢ and over	Speculative	500.00	25%	500.00	25%
*Old and New Cak's	*	Margin for all accounts with position in spot month are increased by $125.00 the day prior to first business day of spot month.					
PLATINUM			Speculative	600.00	25%	300.00	25%
			Hedge	600.00	25%	300.00	25%
	8	All					
SPOT MONTH			Speculative	1000.00	25%	1000.00	25%
*Old and New Cak's			Hedge	1000.00	25%	1000.00	25%
U. S. SILVER COIN	8	All	Speculative	1000.00	25%	500.00	25%
			Hedge	750.00	25%	375.00	25%

INTER – COMMODITY SPREADS

COMMODITY	TYPE NO.	PRICE RANGE/REMARKS	INITIAL MARGIN	RESTORATION POINT
1 SOYBEAN MEAL VS. 1 SOYBEAN OIL	9	–	Initial Margin Both sides	25%
5 M SOYBEANS VS. 1 SOYBEAN OIL & 1 SOYBEAN MEAL	9	CRUSH SPREAD	$1000.00	25%
5 M SOYBEANS VS. 1 SOYBEAN OIL CHGO	9	–	1200.00	25%
5 M SOYBEANS VS. 1 SOYBEAN MEAL CHGO	9	–	1200.00	25%
SUGAR – N. Y. #10 VS. #8 and #11	8	–	Initial Margin Both Sides	25%
CHICAGO TWO DIFFERENT GRAINS	9	–	Initial Margin Higher Side	25%
KC WHEAT VS. CHICAGO WHEAT	9	–	Initial Margin Both Sides	25%

OUTSIDE GRAIN MARKET

WHERE TRADED	TYPE NO.	COMMODITY	INITIAL MARGIN	SPREAD MARGIN	RESTORATION POINT
KANSAS CITY	9	WHEAT	10¢	5¢	25%
MINNEAPOLIS	9	WHEAT	10	5	25%
WINNEPEG	8	BARLEY	25	12½	25%
		FLAXSEED	35	17½	25%
		OATS	25	12½	25%
		RAPESEED	35	17½	25%
		RYE	25	12½	25%

Individual brokers may set higher but not lower rates.

by his broker to trade stocks on margin he will need around 65 percent of $2,500 or $1,625. If the same stock is priced at $30 a share he would need $3,000 or $1,950 on a margined account. At $40 he would need $4,000 or $2,600. A contract of pork bellies at 40 cents is worth $14,400 and can be bought and sold with a margin of $750. Were pork bellies to be priced at 45 cents a pound the margin would still be $750. Margin for a contract of wheat is priced at $1,000 whether the wheat is priced at $1.50 or $1.90 a bushel, even though the total value of the contract varies in price by $2,000 at the two times.

While margin does not normally vary according to price levels, it can vary according to the amount of risk that is involved. Brokerages on their own volition will sometimes raise margin requirements above the amount set by the exchanges if they consider the price of a commodity to be extremely volatile and feel in need of extra protection. The exchanges themselves often raise and lower margin requirements which all the brokerages must adhere to. Soybeans have traded with margins set from $500 to $4,000. Corn margins have been set as low as $300 and as high as $1,500. Such fluctuation is common and will not affect a trader's program (although it will affect his leverage).

A final difference between stock and commodity margin accounts is the amount of money which is typically invested. Stocks are often added to over a period of years and the average size of the portfolios handled by the brokerage is considerably larger than the average commodity account. It is not unusual for a brokerage to have many stock accounts containing a hundred thousand dollars' worth of stocks with a correspondingly large margin account. A trader walking into a commodity brokerage and depositing $10,000 may be assured that he has one of the larger accounts on hand. A $2,000 or $3,000 deposit is probably average and the trader starting with $5,000 need feel like nobody's poor cousin. The reason for this, of course, is that an account with $50,000 worth of stocks must have on deposit no less than $35,000 while an account with $50,000 worth of commodities requires no more than $4,000.

COMMISSION HOUSE RULES

Commodity exchanges, like stock exchanges, do business only with members, and the brokerage that does business with the public must either hold a seat on the exchange on which the trade is made, or have arrangements with another brokerage that does hold a seat. (Not all brokerages hold seats on all exchanges; at up to $80,000 and more, seats are expensive and one brokerage will often execute orders through a second at a fee rather than buy its own seat on each exchange.) The contract position which is opened on the commodity exchange is legally binding between "clearing members" of that exchange, rather than between public traders, and the commission house that places a commodity order must honor the contract which was entered.

Because the brokerage must honor all contracts entered by traders who do business through their offices, commodity brokerages are usually more circumspect in their dealings with the public than are stock handling firms. They back up each of their traders with their own funds, in effect, and therefore take precautions that are unnecessary to a stock brokerage. It is for this reason that commodity brokerages may set margin requirements above those set by the exchange or require a minimum initial deposit larger than strictly necessary for trading. The stock brokerage will allow a trader to purchase stock on margin only after the trader is well enough known to justify loaning him money to make up the balance. In commodities *all* trades are made on margin and brokerages make an effort to know *all* of their customers fairly well.

The commission house which accepts commodity business may set other requirements for doing business with the public or have a "trader profile" which they expect customers to fit fairly closely. Some branches of Merrill Lynch will demand an initial opening deposit of as much as $10,000 for a trader new to the field of commodities. They do this not because so large a guarantee is necessary but to assure that traders new to their brokerage and to commodities can truly afford their speculation. Very few brokerages are this strict, but nearly all brokerages will demand various information about new customers. Commission house rules exist for the protection of the house as well as of the public trader entering a risk market, and normally do not impose any real restrictions on the precepts of rational risk bearing. (See Fig. 44, p. 63.)

One major brokerage uses the following formula to determine the amount of *maximum* speculation they will allow a customer, figured as a percentage of the customer's net worth, exclusive of insurance and equity in his home. The per-

centage figure is determined by the formula shown in Figure 43 below.

FIGURE 43

Income	Percent of net worth
Under $10,000	insufficient income
$10,000 to $14,999	*add* 10%
$15,000 to $24,999	*add* 15%
$25,000 to $49,999	*add* 20%
$50,000 and over	*add* 25%
Dependents	
1 dependent	*deduct* 2%
2 dependents	*deduct* 4%
3 dependents	*deduct* 6%
4 dependents	*deduct* 8%
5 or more dependents	*deduct* 10%
Commodity experience	
Under one year	*deduct* 5%
One to five years	zero
Over five years	*add* 5%
Age	
Under 21 years	no minors permitted
21 to 29 years	zero
30 to 59 years	*add* 5%
60 to 64 years	zero
65 and over, retired	*deduct* 10%

Source: Reynolds & Co., New York.

Percentages from the above four categories are added and subtracted to produce a final percentage of total net worth which determines the maximum account size that the brokerage will handle for the prospective customer. Thus, a new customer with an income of $20,000, a wife and three children, one year's previous experience in the commodity markets, 38 years of age, with a total net worth of $40,000 (exclusive of equity in his home and insurance policies), would be allowed to play no more than $4,800 (this particular brokerage rounds up to the nearest thousand, allowing the speculator a maximum of $5,000). This figure is equal to 12 percent of the customer's total net worth and any larger account would be considered more than what should be set

FIGURE 44. EXAMPLE OF LARGE COMMISSION HOUSE NEWSLETTER

EFHutton

Commodity Research Report

COMMODITY OUTLOOK   December 12, 1972

THE FOLLOWING REMARKS ARE DESIGNED TO PROVIDE A LONGER TERM PERSPECTIVE OF

THE SUPPLY/DEMAND SITUATION AND A VIEWPOINT OF THE PRICE PROSPECTS IMPLIED

IN THE BASIC FUNDAMENTAL STATISTICS OF SELECTED COMMODITIES.

METALS - COPPER FUTURES trended higher during the period under review. The
Chilean-Kennecott legal dispute has been a contributing factor. Chile has
made it known that, as a result of Kennecott's legal moves in France and
Holland which have upset Chilean foreign trade, copper shipments to both those
countries were suspended. France imports about 40,000 tons of Chilean copper
a year and has about a two to three month supply. LME stocks as of December 11
were 187,300 metric tons, a decrease of 4,800 tons from the previous week.
Domestically, copper's outlook seems more favorable than a month ago. New
orders booked by fabricators in October rose to 198,127 tons, an increase of
36,628 tons over last September and a 58,575 ton increase over October 1971.
Net consumption by fabricators in October increased 5,017 tons to 182,321
tons while refined copper stocks of fabricators at the end of October decreased
2,326 tons to 470,618 tons. On a world-wide basis, primary production decreased
in October but refined production of copper increased to 425,951 tons as did
stocks, which increased 28,639 tons to 580,708 tons. With favorable forecasts
not only for the U.S. economy but also for the Japanese and West European
economies, the longer term outlook for copper is optimistic. On a short term
basis though, price gains may be limited by increased world production and
high world stocks of copper. SILVER FUTURES made contract highs, penetrating
the 2.00 level, basis March. High bullion prices and a steady flow of silver
from COMEX warehouses have been influential factors. COMEX stocks have declined
over 2.3 million ounces since November 20. Statistics for the first three
quarters of 1972 have been constructive. U.S. new mine production during that
time was 29.3 million ounces, 2% less than the 29.9 million for the first three
quarters of 1971. Consumption for the first nine months of 1972 was 103.9 million
ounces vs. 93.9 million for the corresponding year ago period, an increase of
10.6%. With the U.S. economy expected to improve considerably next year, the
outlook for silver should be for higher prices. PLATINUM prices rose sluggishly
during the period under review. Impala Platinum LTD and General Motors have
agreed to a contract whereby Impala would supply GM with 300,000 ounces of
platinum and 120,000 ounces of palladium a year during the ten year period
1974 to 1983. The only new aspect about the contract, which was originally
disclosed last September 21, was that it would cover ten years. Engelhard
Minerals & Chemicals Corporation and Nissan Motor Company, the Japanese
maker of the Datsun, have signed a letter of intent, serving as a base for a
contract that would supply 400,000 devices for Nissan cars in model years 1975
to 1978. However, the question of whether or not platinum will be used for
auto pollution control still exists. Although it is constructive that Detroit's
auto manufacturers are lining up their sources of platinum in case the EPA
regulations remain the same, there is still the possibility that a substitute
could be found or that the EPA regulations be extended for a year. However,
stiff EPA regulations regarding the petroleum industry and lead-free gasoline,
which would require platinum in the refining process, could provide the needed
momentum for another bull move in platinum.

Source: E. F. Hutton & Co. Inc., New York.

aside for speculation. At no time is the formula allowed to produce a percentage of over 25 percent and if the total figure allowable is above $10,000, the brokerage requires further information to assure that the amount is truly speculative.

COMMISSION

A stock trader pays a commission to his broker when he buys stock for the service provided of purchasing the stock. This commission can vary according to the number of shares bought, the price of the shares, and the trader's standing with the brokerage. The purchase of 10 shares will be charged a commission as much as 6 percent in odd-lot trading although the commission will be much lower for purchases in round lots of 100. Large private traders and industrial traders pay still less. Overall the commission varies with the cost to the brokerage of handling the account. When the stock is sold a second commission is paid, again for the service provided by the brokerage.

Commission is paid only once in commodities at the time that the position is closed. No commission is paid at the opening of a position. Commission is figured by the contract at a set rate and does not vary according to the standing of the trader or the size of the order being executed. The amount varies by commodity but runs in the range of 0.2 percent to 0.6 percent of the total value of the contract. With margin at 10 percent the commission is increased tenfold by the same leverage figure as equity. A percentage of 0.2 becomes 2 percent of the margin deposit, 0.6 percent has the same effect at 6 percent in an unmargined stock account. Because leverage reacts on commission as well as on equity, it is not at all uncommon for a trader to pay a sum in the course of a year equal to or greater than his initial margin deposit. He is literally trading on profits the last half of the year.

When a commodity position is closed the trader receives in the mail a transaction slip which lists the commodity purchased, the price at which the position was opened, price closed, gross profit or loss, total commission, net profit or loss. Combined with the slip received in the mail when the position was first opened, this transaction slip constitutes the trader's official record of his dealings. A monthly statement from the brokerage lists open positions and total equity in the margin account, including any free margin which has been deposited and is not currently being used along with the total value of current open positions. (See Fig. 45 opposite.)

Both stock and commodity commissions have been under recent investigation by the Justice Department for possible restraint of free trade. What was originally set up to avoid price scalping between commission houses may be ruled as an unreasonable exercise of price fixing. The Securities and Exchange Commission is now requiring commission houses using the New York Stock Exchange to barter commission rates with their customers on trades above $300,000. As the effort required of the commodity broker to purchase one contract of a future is no less or greater than the purchase of 10, the policy of charging a set fee 10 times as high for the larger purchase may be struck down. Changes in commission rates can be expected in the not too distant future.

FIGURE 45

SHEARSON, HAMMOL & CO. INCORPORATED FOUNDED IN 1902

PA○ NO.   ○ ACCOUNT WITH   ○ ACCOUNT NUMBER

OFFICES IN PRINCIPAL CITIES FROM COAST TO COAST
MEMBERS OF THE NEW YORK STOCK EXCHANGE

ALL CHECKS, INSTRUCTIONS, ○ SHOULD BE SENT TO THE OFFICE SERVICING YOUR ACCOUNT.

STATEMENT DATE: MO 02 DAY 30 YR 79
ACCOUNT NUMBER: 110 1082 0?

MR BRUCE G GOULD
P O BOX 16
SEATTLE WA 98111

ENTRY DATE MO	DAY YR.	BOUGHT OR RECEIVED	SOLD OR DELIVERED	DESCRIPTION	PRICE	UNREALIZED LOSS	UNREALIZED GAIN	TYPE
				COMMODITY POSITION EQUITY				
				5 BU MAY FLAX WPG	287 1/2		12.50	8
			1	NEW BALANCE JAN 31			231.86	8
				NET EQUITY			244.36CR**	
			1	CAK MCH SB OIL CHI	833		408.00	9
			1	CAK MCH SB OIL CHI	891		360.00	9
			1	CAK MCH SB OIL CHI	901		300.00	9
			1	CAK MCH SB OIL CHI	901		300.00	9
			1	CAK MCH SB OIL CHI	891		420.00	9
			1	CAK MCH SB OIL CHI	909		252.00	9
			1	CAK MCH SB OIL CHI	891		360.00	9
			1	CAK MCH SB OIL CHI	923		168.00	9
			1	CAK MAY SB OIL CHI	873		354.00	9
			1	CAK MAY SB OIL CHI	901		186.00	9
			1	CAK MAY SB OIL CHI	891		245.00	9

THIS IS AN EQUITY STATEMENT

This statement which we refer to as an "EQUITY STATEMENT" is not to be confused with "REGULAR MONTH END STATEMENTS".

The closing balance represents the cash balance as shown on your regular month end statement plus or minus the unrealized gains or losses on your open contract positions as of the above date.

SHEARSON, HAMMOL & CO. INCORPORATED FOUNDED IN 1902

PA○ NO.   ○ ACCOUNT WITH   ○ ACCOUNT NUMBER

OFFICES IN PRINCIPAL CITIES FROM COAST TO COAST
MEMBERS OF THE NEW YORK STOCK EXCHANGE

ALL CHECKS, INSTRUCTIONS, ○ SHOULD BE SENT TO THE OFFICE SERVICING YOUR ACCOUNT.

STATEMENT DATE: MO 01 DAY 30 YR 79
ACCOUNT NUMBER: 110 1082 63

CONTINUED

ENTRY DATE MO	DAY YR.	BOUGHT OR RECEIVED	SOLD OR DELIVERED	DESCRIPTION	PRICE	UNREALIZED LOSS	UNREALIZED GAIN	TYPE
			1	CAK MAY SB OIL CHI	879		318.00	9
			1	CAK MAY SB OIL CHI	942	60.00		9
			1	CAK MAY SB OIL CHI	934	12.00		9
			1	CAK MAY SB OIL CHI	930		12.00	9
			5	M BU JUL WHT K C	135 1/8	143.75		9
				NEW BALANCE JAN 31			8,535.02	9
				NET EQUITY			12,003.27CR**	

THIS IS AN EQUITY STATEMENT

This statement which we refer to as an "EQUITY STATEMENT" is not to be confused with "REGULAR MONTH END STATEMENTS".

The closing balance represents the cash balance as shown on your regular month end statement plus or minus the unrealized gains or losses on your open contract positions as of the above date.

SELLING SHORT

One short and one long is required for each contract traded on futures markets and the speculator must look at both sides before taking any position. Because hedgers are predominately net short, speculators will often be net long, in order to provide a balanced market, but at any time that the market is out of balance, each new trader has an equal chance of making money on either side of the market. Because market price is constantly discounted, it has an exactly equal chance of going up as down and the trader can just as easily take either side. Selling short is not considered unusual in commodities and a short sale is handled in precisely the same manner as a long purchase. An uptick is not required for a short sale as in stock trading and the trader need not borrow contracts to cover his position. Of course, as there are no dividends or splits the short seller in commodities need not pay the same as the stock trader who sells short must.

Margin, commission, technique, and procedures are, of course, exactly the same for short selling in commodities as for a long trade.

CHOOSING A BROKERAGE

Selecting a brokerage firm to handle your commodity account is very similar to choosing one to handle stock transactions. Most big stock brokerages handle commodities and the stock trader can probably stay with the firm he is already using. The largest stock brokerage in the world, Merrill Lynch, Pierce, Fenner & Smith, is also the largest commodity brokerage. E. F. Hutton & Company is also one of the largest firms dealing in the stock and commodity markets. (See Fig. 46, p. 67.)

There are a large number of firms that deal only in commodities. Because the commodity market does not enjoy nearly the volume of public trading seen by the stock exchanges, these firms do not churn nearly as many people through their offices in the course of a year and many commodity brokerages remain unknown to the general public. If you write to the commodity exchange that trades the commodity in which you are interested it will return to you a list of hundreds of smaller firms. Visit several of them before making your choice. You are entering into a business relationship with the brokerage firm and you have every right to look over your prospective partner. He must be able to do half of the job competently and be able to follow your lead on how much advice you wish to hear.

When you first enter a brokerage expect the broker to question you fully about your financial condition and expect some probing into your personality and ability to act responsibly in a risk situation. This brokerage is also entering into a business relationship with you. You may be handed a form asking for information about where you work, income-debt profile, and so on. The brokerage is being honest and straightforward showing itself to be concerned about its patrons as well as its own well-being. Counter, if you wish, with a request to see a financial statement from the brokerage, its health, its research facilities, and its ability to serve you. A businesslike relationship set up at the beginning will pay dividends later.

Whether to choose a brokerage which

FIGURE 46

MERRILL LYNCH OFFICES Throughout the United States and Across the World

Alabama
Birmingham
Huntsville
Mobile
Montgomery

Arizona
Phoenix
Tucson

Arkansas
Little Rock

California
Beverly Hills
Fresno
Hollywood
La Jolla
Long Beach
Los Angeles (2)
Newport Beach
Oakland
Palm Springs
Palo Alto
Pasadena
Riverside
Sacramento
San Diego
San Francisco (2)
San Jose
Santa Ana
Santa Barbara
Sherman Oaks
Westwood

Colorado
Colorado Springs
Denver
Englewood

Connecticut
Hartford
New Haven
New London
Stamford

District of Columbia
Washington (2)

Florida
Bradenton
Clearwater
Cocoa
Coral Gables
Coral Ridge
Delray Beach
Ft. Lauderdale
Gainesville
Jacksonville
Lakeland
Miami (2)
Miami Beach
Orlando
Palm Beach
Pensacola
Pompano Beach
Sarasota
St. Petersburg
Tampa
Vero Beach
Winter Park

Georgia
Athens
Atlanta (3)

Augusta
Columbus
Macon
Savannah

Hawaii
Honolulu

Illinois
Chicago (6)
Evanston

Indiana
Fort Wayne
Indianapolis

Iowa
Davenport
Des Moines

Kentucky
Lexington
Louisville

Louisiana
Baton Rouge
Monroe
New Orleans
Shreveport

Maryland
Baltimore (2)

Massachusetts
Boston (2)
Burlington

Michigan
Birmingham
Detroit (2)
Flint
Grand Rapids
Lansing
Saginaw
Southfield

Minnesota
Minneapolis
St. Paul

Mississippi
Jackson

Missouri
Clayton
Kansas City
St. Louis

Nebraska
Omaha

Nevada
Las Vegas

New Jersey
Morristown
Newark
Paramus
Trenton

New Mexico
Albuquerque
Santa Fe

New York
Albany
Brooklyn
Buffalo

Forest Hills
Garden City
Huntington
Jamestown
Manhasset
New York (12)
Niagara Falls
Poughkeepsie
Rochester
Syracuse
White Plains

North Carolina
Asheville
Charlotte
Greensboro
Raleigh
Wilson
Winston-Salem

Ohio
Akron
Canton
Cincinnati
Cleveland (2)
Columbus
Dayton
Toledo
Youngstown
Zanesville

Oklahoma
Oklahoma City
Tulsa

Oregon
Portland

Pennsylvania
Allentown
Bala Cynwyd
Harrisburg
Jenkintown
Philadelphia
Pittsburgh
West Chester
Wilkes-Barre
Williamsport
York

Rhode Island
Providence

South Carolina
Columbia

Tennessee
Memphis
Nashville

Texas
Amarillo
Austin
Beaumont
Corpus Christi
Dallas (3)
Fort Worth
Houston (3)
San Antonio
Waco
Wichita Falls

Utah
Ogden
Provo
Salt Lake City (2)

Virginia
Norfolk
Richmond

Washington
Seattle (2)
Spokane
Tacoma

Wisconsin
Milwaukee

Puerto Rico
San Juan

Offices of Affiliated Companies

Argentina
Buenos Aires

Belgium
Brussels

Br. Cr. Colony
Hong Kong

Canada
Calgary
Montreal
Toronto
Vancouver

England
London (3)

France
Cannes
Paris

Germany
Duesseldorf
Frankfurt
Hamburg
Munich

Greece
Athens

Italy
Milan
Rome

Japan
Tokyo

Kuwait
Kuwait

Lebanon
Beirut

Netherlands
Amsterdam

Panama
Panama City

Philippines
Manila

Spain
Barcelona
Madrid

Switzerland
Geneva
Lugano
Zurich

Venezuela
Caracas
Maracaibo

Merrill Lynch, Royal Securities Limited

Alberta
Calgary
Edmonton

Br. Columbia
Vancouver
Victoria

England
London

Manitoba
Winnipeg

New Brunswick
Saint John

Newfoundland
St. John's

Nova Scotia
Halifax

Ontario
Hamilton
Ottawa
Toronto

Pr. Edward Island
Charlottetown

Quebec
Montreal
Quebec City

Saskatchewan
Regina

Lionel D. Edie & Co., Inc.

Arizona
Phoenix

California
Los Angeles
San Francisco

Georgia
Atlanta

Illinois
Chicago

Minnesota
Minneapolis

New York
New York

North Carolina
Charlotte

Ohio
Cincinnati

Pennsylvania
Philadelphia
Pittsburgh

Texas
Dallas
Houston

*Hubbard, Westervelt & Mottelay Inc.
New York*

Source: Merrill Lynch, Pierce, Fenner & Smith.

handles only commodities or one which handles both commodities and stocks is a question without an answer. A big firm will have established machinery to deal with complaints, should any come up, and the financial security of a large firm may give you peace of mind. The money in public accounts cannot be mixed with company funds in commodities but should a brokerage firm go under your margin account could be tied up for a while as accounts are unstrung. You will find more printed matter available in large firms and the public relations department will help to make things smoother and more complete. (See Fig. 47, p. 69.)

If you like personal service, however, and the opportunity to develop your own relationship with your broker, a smaller firm will often be less set in its ways. Both large firms and small ones generally have only one wireman who sends orders to the various exchanges and often your order will be executed more rapidly if the volume of business done at that particular office is less. The wire operator is the man whom you will rarely if ever see who types out the actual order. If he has several orders ahead of yours a few minutes delay can result. In a fast-moving game like commodities a few minutes toward the end of a contract life can be significant. If your brokerage handles both stocks and commodities ask if the wireman gives priority to commodity orders over the wire.

Some firms maintain direct phone lines to the floors of the various exchanges in which case you can place an order and know almost immediately if it was fillable as specified and at what price it was filled. It can be very satis-

fying to wait five minutes and know exactly what happened to your order, but really has little to do with the effectiveness or efficiency of the firm. Success in commodities results from carefully planned preset trades and hasty decisions made in the heat of trading can lead to expensive mistakes.

When you first enter a new brokerage either in stocks or commodities, the receptionist will often direct you to the "man of the day" whose turn it is to get all new customers for that day. This is as good a system of matching brokers to customers as any, but don't feel obligated to accept him as your broker. If you are not impressed come again another day or ask to see someone else.

MANAGED ACCOUNTS

Often in stock trading a trader will put his portfolio pretty much in the control of his broker or otherwise try to eliminate the need of personally following the market. Mutual funds work on this principle and it is a good principle for estate building—in the stock market.

Letting another man trade your commodity account is risky business. You won't have any fun and trading commodities is a great deal of fun after you get the feel of it. If your broker suggests that he manage your account either as a "discretionary account" wherein he executes trades at his own discretion and calls you later, or through a Power of Attorney, reject his offer. Such an arrangement can only be set up to make money. Great profits with no effort on your part will not occur in commodity speculation or in any other financial endeavor. Should you wish to allow your broker to do more than execute your

FIGURE 47
EXAMPLE OF SMALL CIRCULATION PRIVATE NEWSLETTER

Dewein Co.

P.O. BOX 1008
DECATUR, IL 62525

Member, Chicago Board of Trade

(217) 122-8581

Letter # 10 -- 72

March, 1972

CORN: The futures market has been strong this past week, with strength coming from new export business and pricing of both old and new contracts, plus the promising outlook for sizable business with Russia and Eastern Europe. Cash corn in some areas is in very good demand and in others very poor. The USDA announced this week that they had achieved their goal on diverted acres of feed grains, although on the low side at 37 million acres. Some people feel that even with this sign-up there will be only a little change from the March intention report of 68.5 million acres for corn. With a good crop year we will need well over 5 billion usage to reduce our carry-over from next September 30th. There has been a great deal of cash corn moved by farmers prior to the April 1st assessment date. No one seems to know if grain will be assessed or not. However, after April 1st we anticipate far less corn being offered from farmers. This, with the good export demand, should correct the wide differential of the cash and futures, and rather quickly.

SOYBEANS: On Tuesday, April 21st we had one of the most hectic trading days in the history of soybeans. Early prices advanced as much as 5¢ per bushel, and with a great deal of public participation. Around 12 o'clock some profit taking came into the pit, followed by an unofficial report that the USDA expected 47 million acres for the 1972 crop. Heavy selling orders then hit the market without any buyers, and July beans fell 11¾¢ in a very short time. The market had just started to recover when the electrical equipment of the Board of Trade broke down and trading was suspended for about 45 minutes. Excepting the breakdown in equipment, this type of market can be expected in a big bull market. However, it cannot help but shake the confidence of the bull. We feel it will be difficult to increase the price of soybean meal without cutting into consumption. It is now costing the consumer about $100.00 per ton and more on 44% protein. If a further good advance is coming in this market, we would expect the present poor cash position in oil to improve, and in the meantime the market would trade in the current area and build a good foundation for the move.

WHEAT: This market is much stronger than most traders expected, especially the new crop futures. During this election year the government will promote export sales as much as possible, and until we get hedging from new crop sales we can only say to follow the market.

QUOTE: "It takes both rain and sunshine to make a rainbow".

Apples of Gold

Source: Victor C. Dewein, Dewein Grain Company.

orders demand to see his "track record" and a few references. If other people with whom he has made such an arrangement are happy they have done business with him and made money perhaps you will, too. If he has no references to give you and waxes vague about his record of trades, he either has not a very long record and is little more knowledgeable than you or his record is bad. "If you are so smart why aren't you rich?" is the question to ask.

In the long run if you are to make money in commodities you are going to have to do it yourself. To anybody who can really afford $2,000 or $5,000 to speculate with the financial rewards are not really so significant as is the feeling of accomplishment that comes of winning in a difficult game. Your goal for the first year ought to be to learn as much as possible without having to add money to your margin account. Look at your first trades with an eye to being able to play again if you lose, and look for a broker who can conservatively guide you, answer your questions, help you hold onto your playing capital, and be as patient and calm as you must be.

Once you are able to play your own game you will probably have little use for your broker other than as an executor of your trades. It is possible to become an expert in two or three commodities and over time you will do so. Then when your broker calls you with advice or a tip, thank him and evaluate his information for yourself. You need not be in the market at all times but ought to take information from all sources such as the Department of Agriculture, *The Wall Street Journal,* the evening news, and your broker, and come to a reasonable decision about the risks and profits of having a position or no position.

If you make it into the 10 percent or so who trade commodities for a consistent profit you will find the game well worth your effort.

5

MECHANICS

The pit, or ring as it is sometimes called, is the natural outgrowth of the time when commodities were traded in the open. Choosing a natural hollow in which to do business allowed more early commodity traders to actively participate while being able to see all the other traders in the market. A short man cannot see any more in a commodity pit than he can at a parade unless he can get up on something a little higher than the man in front of him. A round hollow in the ground solved this problem. Early trading took place without referees; buyers and sellers simply kept finding one another as rapidly as possible while keeping a sharp ear on the trade which was just consummated by other traders. In this way both kept track of the "going price" and had a starting point from which to haggle their trade. They could have as well made their trade in the nearest tavern but trading in the pit assured both of a trade with a price close to what other people were getting and giving.

Modern commodity trading is only slightly more formal and the actual trading still takes place directly between buyer and seller as rapidly as they can find one another and agree upon a price. The hollow is duplicated on the exchange floor by a set of steps rising from the center so that the maximum number of traders can see the entire market. The center of the pit is at floor level with a tier rising around it in an octagonal shape (an eight-sided figure eliminates sharp corners where the view would be congested). A second tier rises above the first and a third above that. On each tier, one month's contracts are traded. One tier is set aside for trading in July contracts, one for September, one for November, one for December, and all the traders of any one option have a pretty good view of all the other traders handling that same option as well as the traders on other tiers. (See Fig. 48, p. 72.)

The trading is done by open auction with each trader calling out the number of contracts he wishes to buy or sell and a price. As nothing can be heard in the din he will back his voice with hand signals. If a seller can find a buyer on the other side of the pit (but not on the same tier) and they come to a price, the deal will be made and the options traded. The pit trader is in effect calling out, "Who will buy 10,000 bushels of corn for delivery in March at $1.40?" He backs up his voice with two fingers thrust into the air (indicating two contracts) palm out. If he finds two fingers up, palm in, across the pit some price haggling may ensue followed by a nod and the sale has been made. Each will

FIGURE 48
NEW YORK COFFEE AND SUGAR EXCHANGE TRADING FLOOR, 1896

Source: New York Coffee and Sugar Exchange.

note the number worn by the other trader, the price, and the number of contracts traded, and use this information to "clear up" at the end of the day. If the trade was made by order from a brokerage then confirmation of the trade will be sent by runner to the teletypes and on to the brokerage. A man on a high bench will note any price change between this trade and the trade previous and send the new price across the teletypes to read out to anyone who owns equipment to pick up the information. No man acts as an auctioneer and each trader must find his opposite and come to a price on his own. A fast-moving market can get pretty aggressive as an overbalance of buyers or sellers compete for the ear and eye of their opposites. (See Fig. 49 below.)

The trader in the pit must find another trader on his own tier. A seller of March contracts cannot trade with a buyer of May contracts, although, of course, he may step onto the next tier and become a seller of May contracts. The two months are not interchangeable. A contract is an agreement to accept or deliver in the future at a set price and in order for the contracts to make sense, both buyer and seller must be trading contracts for the same delivery date. By the same token, a speculator must sell March wheat to close his position. Selling May wheat would simply open a second position, leaving him long in March and short in May.

"Long" and "short" are expressions used in commodities in exactly the same manner they are used in stock handling.

FIGURE 49
TRADING FLOOR—CHICAGO MERCANTILE EXCHANGE

Source: Chicago Mercantile Exchange.

To be long a market means you own something which has not been sold or contracted to be sold. To be short a market is to owe something you do not have at the current time. A magazine subscription makes the reader long magazines and the publisher short. The magazines do not exist and will not until some time in the future, at which time the publisher will fulfill his short obligation by delivering and the subscriber close his long position by taking the magazines to fill his contract. A man who is long March wheat must accept wheat in March according to the contract he has bought or sell his futures position. A man who is short must deliver or sell his obligation to another man who takes the obligation and becomes short.

TRADING UNITS

In order to simplify trading commodities are traded in set units. Grains are traded in contracts of 5,000 bushels and other commodities in quantities set by the trade. One contract of cotton is 100 bales, for a total weight of 50,000 pounds. Hides are traded in 40,000-pound contracts. Soybean oil is traded in a 60,000-pound contract equal to one tank car. Some exchanges also handle trading in job lots similar to odd lots in the stock market with the exception that these job lot contracts cannot be covered by regular contracts. Job lots must be covered by job lots and regular contracts by regular contracts. Job lots are useful to members of the cash trade who can hedge enough for a specific job but are of little value to the speculator and are seldom used. As with stocks trading in job lots is a little more expensive than trading in round lots or full contracts. As commodities are normally held for much shorter periods of time than stocks and leverage return is so much greater, such administrative costs take on much more significance in commodities and discourage job lot trading.

When making an order grains are specified by the number of bushels. All other orders are specified by the number of contracts. An order must specify 5,000 bushels of corn or one contract of frozen pork bellies, 25,000 bushels of soybeans or five contracts of soybean oil. This is strictly a procedural agreement to avoid confusion. An order for "10 March soybeans" can be interpreted as 10 contracts or 10,000 bushels which would equal 2 contracts. An order for 10,000 March corn cannot possibly refer to that number of contracts, the position would be illegal for a speculator even if it could be filled. An order of "10 March soybeans" would be filled by two contracts.

TICKER SYMBOLS

As a matter of policy most brokerages send their orders written out in full or in easily read abbreviations to avoid mistakes and the possibility of a simple typing order error changing the important details of an order. To save time and tape, however, tape readings are usually sent in symbols. Grains are each noted by their first letter, W for wheat, S for soybeans, C for corn, and so on. Months are denoted by the following code:

January	F	July	N
February	G	August	Q
March	H	September	U
April	J	October	V
May	K	November	X
June	M	December	Z

All other commodities are denoted by abbreviations which can be read, with some imagination, as the proper name. July corn would be CN, May soybeans would be SK, February pork bellies would be PBG.

MINIMUM FLUCTUATION

The minimum fluctuation in grains is one-eighth cent per bushel and any new price must vary from the previous high by at least this amount, although, of course, it can be higher or lower by any multiple of eighths. On a contract of 5,000 bushels of a grain one-eighth cent is equal to $6.25. All other contracts fluctuate in points each point being equal to 1/100th of a cent and the minimum number of points is set by commodity. Broilers, cattle, hogs all vary in price by a minimum of two- and one-half points, 2½/100ths of a cent per pound. This is equal to $7 on a 28,000-pound contract of broilers, $10 on a 40,000-pound contract of live steers, and so forth. A list of contract sizes, minimum fluctuations, and commissions is found in Chapter 4.

DAILY TRADING LIMITS

As with stocks, a commodity price which becomes extremely volatile due to major price-making news, will not be allowed to fluctuate too greatly in any single trading session. In the case of a stock, trading will be suspended by the exchange until the public has a chance to digest the news. The same system is used on commodity exchanges with the sole difference that commodity trading ranges from the exchange are preset. Iced broilers, for instance, can trade no

more than 2 cents per pound higher than the close of the previous trading session. Nor can they drop more than 2 cents. In the event of news that would raise or lower prices by such drastic amounts, the pit will remain open for anybody who wishes to trade at a price within the permissible range but no trades will be allowed at prices beyond the published limit. (See Fig. 50, p. 76.)

In the event of really drastic news, trading may not take place for several days. Each day the range will be broadened by the limit amount until the permissible range catches up with the public estimation of fair price. In this event, and only in this rare event, it is possible for a trader to lose his entire margin capital supply and more. It is possible in a case where no trading takes place over a large range of prices for the brokerages to be unable to close a customer's position resulting in a loss of $1,000 or more on an original outlay of $400. This generally will not happen in the stock market.

In the final days of trading, trading limits are often removed to assure that any trader wishing to close his contract can do so. (See Fig. 51, p. 77.)

THE CLEARINGHOUSE

Each exchange has its own clearinghouse which is a distinct legal entity something on the order of check clearinghouses which exist to facilitate the handling of checks issued on accounts of member banks. Nobody would have reason to be a member of a clearinghouse who was not also a seat holder on the exchange serviced, but not all seat holders are clearinghouse members. Those who are not must pay an extra fee

**FIGURE 50
DAILY TRADING
LIMITS CHART**

COMMODITY	Exchange & Trading Hours (N.Y. Time)	Contract Unit	Minimum Fluctuation Per lb., bu., carton, etc.	Minimum Fluctuation Per Contract	Maximum Fluctuation (C) Daily Limit	Maximum Fluctuation (C) Daily Range	CEA Reporting Level
Barley	Winnipeg Grain Ex. 10:30 - 2:15	5,000 bu.	⅛¢	$6.25	10¢	20¢	None
Boneless Beef	Chicago Mercantile Ex. 10:15 - 1:45	36,000 lbs.	.025¢	$9.00	1.50¢	3.00¢	25 Contracts
Boneless Beef, Imported	N.Y. Mercantile Ex. 10:15 - 1:45	30,000 lbs.	.02¢	$6.00	1.50¢	3.00¢	25 Contracts
Broilers (Effective April '72)	Chicago Board of Trade 10:15 - 2:05	28,000 lbs.	.025¢	$7.00	$2.00	$4.00	None
Cattle	Chicago Mercantile Ex. 10:05 - 1:40	40,000 lbs.	.025¢	$10.00	1.00¢	2.00¢	25 Contracts
Cattle, Feeder	Chicago Mercantile Ex. 10:05 - 1:40	42,000 lbs.	.025¢	$10.50	1.00¢	2.00¢	25 Contracts
Choice Steers	Chicago Board of Trade 10:10 - 1:50	40,000 lbs.	.025¢	$10.00	1.50¢	3.00¢	25 Contracts
Cocoa	N.Y. Cocoa Ex. 10:00 - 3:00	30,000 lbs.	.01¢	$3.00	1.00¢	2.00¢	None
Coffee (C)	N.Y. Coffee & Sugar Ex. 10:30 - 2:45	37,500 lbs.	.01¢	$3.75	2.00¢	4.00¢	None
Copper	N.Y. Commodity Ex., Inc 9:45 - 2:10	25,000 lbs.	.05¢	$12.50	2.00¢	4.00¢	None
Corn	Chicago Board of Trade 10:30 - 2:15	5,000 bu.	⅛¢	$6.25	8¢	16¢	200,000 bu.
Cotton (#2)	N.Y. Cotton Ex. 10:30 - 3:00	50,000 lbs.	.01¢	$5.00	2.00¢	2.00¢	50 Contracts
Eggs, Shell (Effective March 72)	Chicago Mercantile Ex. 10:15 - 1:45	(750 cases) 22.500 doz.	.05¢	$11.25	2.00¢	4.00¢	25 Contracts
Fish Meal	Int'l Commerce Ex. (N.Y. Produce) 9:45 - 2:45	100 metric/tons	5¢	$5.00	$5.00	$10.00	None
Flaxseed (Mpls)	Minneapolis Grain Ex. 10:30 - 2:15	1,000 bu.	⅛¢	$1.25	15¢	30¢	200,000 bu.
Flaxseed (Wpg)	Winnipeg Grain Ex. 10:30 - 2:15	1,000 bu.	⅛¢	$1.25	15¢	30¢	None
Hogs	Chicago Mercantile Ex. 10:20 - 1:50	30,000 lbs.	.025¢	$7.50	1.50¢	3.00¢	25 Contracts
Lumber (Effective May '72)	Chicago Mercantile Ex. 10:45 - 2:15	100,000 bd. ft.	10¢ per 1.000 bd. ft	$10.00	$5.00 per 1,000 bd. ft	$10.00	None
Mercury	N.Y. Commodity Ex., Inc 9:50 - 2:30	(760 lbs.) 10 flasks	$1.00	$10.00	$50.00	$100.00	None
Oats (Chgo)	Chicago Board of Trade 10:30 - 2:15	5,000 bu.	⅛¢	$6.25	6¢	12¢	200,000 bu.
Oats (Wpg)	Winnipeg Grain Ex. 10:30 - 2:15	5,000 bu.	⅛¢	$6.25	8¢	16¢	None
Orange Juice (FCOJ)	N.Y. Cotton Ex. 10:15 - 2:45	15,000 lbs.	.05¢	$7.50	3.00¢	3.00¢	25 Contracts
Palladium	N.Y. Mercantile Ex. 10:20 - 12:55	100 ozs.	5¢	$5.00	$4.00	$8.00	None
Platinum	N.Y. Mercantile Ex. 9:45 - 1:30	50 ozs.	10¢	$5.00	$10.00	$10.00	None
Plywood (Chgo)	Chicago Board of Trade 11:00 - 2:00	69,120 sq. ft.	10¢ per 1.000 sq. ft.	$6.91	$7.00	$14.00	None
Plywood (N.Y.)	N.Y. Mercantile Ex. 11:00 - 2:05	70,000 sq. ft.	10¢ per 1.000 sq. ft.	$7.00	$6.00	$12.00	None
Pork Bellies	Chicago Mercantile Ex. 10:30 - 2:00	36,000 lbs.	.025¢	$9.00	1.50¢	3.00¢	25 Contracts
Potatoes, Idaho	Chicago Mercantile Ex. 10:00 - 1:50	(50,000 lbs.) 500 cwt.	1¢	$5.00	35¢	70¢	25 Contracts
Potatoes, Maine	N.Y. Mercantile Ex. 10:00 - 2:00	(50,000 lbs.) 500 cwt.	1¢	$5.00	35¢	70¢	25 Contracts
Propane (L.P. Gas)	N.Y. Cotton Ex. 11:00 - 3:30	100,000 gals.	.01¢	$10.00	.50¢	.50¢	None
Rapeseed	Winnipeg Grain Ex. 10:30 - 2:15	1,000 bu.	⅛¢	$1.25	15¢	30¢	None
Rye (Wpg)	Winnipeg Grain Ex. 10:30 - 2:15	5,000 bu.	⅛¢	$6.25	10¢	20¢	None
Silver (Chgo)	Chicago Board of Trade 10:00 - 2:25	5,000 oz.	.10¢	$5.00	10.00¢	20.00¢	None
Silver (N.Y.)	N.Y. Commodity Ex., Inc 9:30 - 2:15	10,000 oz.	.10¢	$10.00	10.00¢	10.00¢	None
Silver Coins	N.Y. Mercantile Ex. 9:25 - 2:15	$10,000 face value; 10 bags	$1.00 per bag	$10.00	$100.00 per bag	$200.00	None
Sorghum/Milo	Chicago Mercantile Ex. 10:30 - 2:15	200,000 lbs. 3.636.5 bu.	.025¢ per cwt.	$5.00	15¢	30¢	25 Contracts
Soybean Meal	Chicago Board of Trade 10:30 - 2:15	100 tons	5¢	$5.00	$5.00	$5.00	25 Contracts
Soybean Oil	Chicago Board of Trade 10:30 - 2:15	60,000 lbs.	.01¢	$6.00	1.00¢	2.00¢	25 Contracts
Soybeans	Chicago Board of Trade 10:30 - 2:15	5,000 bu.	⅛¢	$6.25	10¢	20¢	200,000 bu.
Sugar, Domestic (#10)	N.Y. Coffee & Sugar Ex. 10:00 - 2:50	112,000 lbs.	.01¢	$11.20	.50¢	1.00¢	None
Sugar, World (#11)	N.Y. Coffee & Sugar Ex. 10:00 - 3:00	112,000 lbs.	.01¢	$11.20	.50¢	1.00¢	None
Tin	N.Y. Commodity Ex., Inc 10:20 - .1:45	11,200 lbs.	.05¢	$5.60	8.00¢	16.00¢	None
Tomato Paste	N.Y. Cotton Ex. 10:45 - 3:15	26,500 lbs.	.02¢	$5.30	2.00¢	2.00¢	None
Wheat (Chgo)	Chicago Board of Trade 10:30 - 2:15	5,000 bu.	⅛¢	$6.25	10¢	20¢	200,000 bu.
Wheat (K.C.)	K.C. Board of Trade 10:30 - 2:15	5,000 bu.	⅛¢	$6.25	10¢	20¢	200,000 bu.
Wheat (Mpls)	Minneapolis Grain Ex. 10:30 - 2:15	5,000 bu.	⅛¢	$6.25	10¢	20¢	200,000 bu.
Wool, Grease	N.Y. Cotton Ex. 10:00 - 2:30	6,000 lbs.	.1¢	$6.00	5.0¢	5.0¢	25 Contracts
Wool Tops	N.Y. Cotton Ex. 10:00 - 2:30	5,000 lbs.	.1¢	$5.00	5.0¢	5.0¢	25 Contracts

Source: Shearson, Hammill & Co.

FIGURE 51
CONTRACT
EXPIRATION
CHART

Commodity	Expiring Contract Daily Trading Limit	First Notice or Delivery Day	Last Trading Day	Final Close N.Y. Time
Barley	Remains 10¢	1st business day of contract month.	Last business day of contract month.	2:15 p.m.
Boneless Beef	Remains 1.50¢	1st business day of contract month.	Business day preceding last 5 business days of contract month.	12:45 p.m.
Boneless Beef, Imported	2.00¢ in Delivery Month; Removed Last Trading Day	After trading ceases.	10th calendar day of contract month. (1)	1:45 p.m.
Broilers	Remains $2.00	Last business day of month preceding contract month.	4th last business day of contract month.	1:00 p.m.
Cattle	Remains 1.00¢	M, T, W or TH, a business day after 6th calendar day of contract month. (1)	20th calendar day of contract month. (1)	12:40 p.m.
Cattle, Feeder	Remains 1.00¢	1st M, T. W or TH of contract month. (1)	20th calendar day of contract month. (1)	12:40 p.m.
Choice Steers	Remains 1.50¢	T or TH of contract month. Notice must be given day preceding delivery.	8th last business day of contract month.	1:00 p.m.
Cocoa	1.00¢; Removed 1st Notice Day	7 business days before 1st business day of contract month.	7th business day prior to last delivery day (usually last business day) of contract month.	12:00 p.m.
Coffee (C)	2.00¢; Removed 1st Notice Day	1st business day before 4th last calendar day of month preceding contract month.	5th calendar day before last business day of contract month. (1)	2:45 p.m.
Copper	2.00¢; Removed 1st Notice Day	2nd last business day of month preceding contract month.	20th calendar day of contract month. (2)	2:10 p.m.
Corn	Remains 8¢	Last business day of month preceding contract month	8th last business day of contract month.	1:00 p.m.
Cotton (#2)	2.00¢; Removed 1st Day of Contract Month	5th last business day of month preceding contract month.	17th last business day of contract month.	12:30 p.m.
Eggs, Shell	Remains 2.00¢	1st business day of contract month.	8th last business day of contract month.	12:45 p.m.
Fish Meal	Remains $5.00	After close of trading on last trading day.	Last business day of month preceding contract month.	2:45 p.m.
Flaxseed (Mpls)	Remains 15¢	Last business day of month preceding contract month.	8th last business day of contract month.	1:00 p.m.
Flaxseed (Wpg)	Remains 15¢	1st business day of contract month.	Last business day of contract month.	2:15 p.m.
Hogs	Remains 1.50¢	M, T, W or TH after 6th calendar day of contract month. (1)	20th calendar day of contract month. (1)	12:50 p.m.
Lumber	Remains $5.00	1st business day after last trading day.	Last business day prior to 16th calendar day of contract month. (2)	1:15 p.m.
Mercury	$50.00; Removed 1st Notice Day	Last business day of month preceding contract month.	Close on 20th calendar day of contract month. (2)	2:30 p.m.
Oats (Chgo)	Remains 6¢	Last business day of month preceding contract month.	8th last business day of contract month.	1:00 p.m.
Oats (Wpg)	Remains 8¢	1st business day of contract month.	Last business day of contract month.	2:15 p.m.
Orange Juice (FCOJ)	3.00¢; Removed 8th Day of Contract Month	1st business day after last trading day. (2)	9th last business day prior to last delivery day (usually last business day) of contract month.	12:00 p.m.
Palladium	$4.00; Removed Last Trading Day	After trading ceases.	14th calendar day of contract month. (1)	Closes early
Platinum	$10.00; Removed Last Trading Day	After trading ceases.	14th calendar day of contract month. (1)	Closes early
Plywood (Chgo)	$7.00; Removed 1st Notice Day	Last business day of month preceding contract month.	8th last business day of contract month.	1:00 p.m.
Plywood (N.Y.)	$6.00; Removed Last Trading Day	1st business day after trading ceases, but no later than 10th calendar day of contract month .	Last business day of month preceding contract month.	Closes early
Pork Bellies	Remains 1.50¢	1st business day of contract month.	Trading day prior to last 5 business days of contract month.	1:00 p.m.
Potatoes, Idaho	35¢; Becomes 50¢ Last Trading Day	1st business day after last trading day.	10th calendar day of contract month. (1)	12:50 p.m.
Potatoes, Maine	50¢; in Delivery Month; Removed Last Trading Day	1st business day after last trading day.	10th calendar day of contract month. (1)	Closes early
Propane (L.P. Gas)	50¢; Removed Last Trading Day	2nd last business day of month preceding contract month.	Last business day prior to 16th calendar day of contract month.	3:30 p.m.
Rapeseed	Remains 15¢	1st business day of contract month.	Last business day of contract month.	2:15 p.m.
Rye (Wpg)	Remains 10¢	1st business day of contract month.	Last business day of contract month.	2:15 p.m.
Silver (Chgo)	Remains 10¢	Last business day of month preceding contract month.	4th last business day of contract month.	1:00 p.m.
Silver (N.Y.)	10¢; Removed 1st Notice Day	2nd last business day of month preceding contract month.	4th last business day of contract month.	2:15 p.m.
Silver Coins	$150 in Delivery Month; Removed Last Trading Day	1st business day after last trading day.	14th calendar day of contract month. (1)	Closes early
Sorghum/Milo	Remains 15¢	1st business day of contract month.	8th last business day of contract month.	1:15 p.m.
Soybean Meal	$5.00; Removed 1st Notice Day	Last business day of month preceding contract month.	8th last business day of contract month.	1:00 p.m.
Soybean Oil	1.00¢; Removed 1st Notice Day	Last business day of month preceding contract month.	8th last business day of contract month.	1:00 p.m.
Soybeans	Remains 10¢	Last business day of month preceding contract month.	8th last business day of contract month.	1:00 p.m.
Sugar, #10	.50¢; Removed Last Trading Day	Same day as last trading day.	14th calendar day before 1st business day of contract month. (1)	2:40 p.m.
Sugar, #11	.50¢; Removed 1st Notice and Last Trading Day	1st business day prior to 15th calendar day of month preceding contract month.	Last business day of month preceding contract month.	2:50 p.m.
Tin	8.00¢; Removed 1st Notice Day	2nd last business day of month preceding contract month.	20th calendar day of contract month. (1)	1:45 p.m.
Tomato Paste	2.00¢; Removed 10th Day of Contract Month	All deliveries are made after trading ceases.	10th business day prior to last business day of contract month.	12:45 p.m.
Wheat (All)	Remains 10¢	Last business day of month preceding contract month.	8th last business day of contract month.	1:00 p.m.
Wool, Grease and Tops	5.0¢; Removed 8th Day of Contract Month	5th last business day of month preceding contract month.	13th last business day of contract month.	12:00 p.m.

(1) Not a holiday, nor a business day preceding a holiday.

(2) At least 3 business days preceding delivery.

(1) Or business day immediately preceding.

(2) Or business day immediately thereafter.

Source: Shearson, Hammill & Co.

Information contained herein has been carefully gathered from reliable sources, but we do not guarantee its completeness or accuracy.

for the services provided by clearinghouse members for them in addition to the normal service fees.

After the close of trading each seat holder on the commodity exchange will tally up the slips made out by the pit traders during the actual trading and submit them to the clearinghouse. These slips contain the pit symbol worn by the trader who took or gave the contracts, price, and number of contracts, and are matched by the clearinghouse to see that an equal number of purchases and sales are accounted for by the day. For every sale there must be a buyer and a seller for every buy listed on the slips of paper. When this balance has been established the clearinghouse accepts the slip and assumes all contract obligations.

Once the slips are accepted at the end of the session, the clearinghouse guarantees performance by each long and each short clearing member. All traders then hold positions with the clearinghouse rather than with other traders. A trade may have been undertaken during the day selling five contracts of cotton on the order of a trader in San Francisco to a trader in Des Moines who placed a buy order with his brokerage. After the clearinghouse has accepted the slips, the trader in San Francisco holds a contract with the clearinghouse to deliver cotton, the trader in Des Moines must accept delivery from the clearinghouse unless he closes his position before the delivery date. Because the clearinghouse holds an equal number of short and long positions it is in no danger of loss due to price changes.

The actual contracts are one step further removed from the speculator by the fact that the clearinghouse will deal only with members of the exchange. The brokerage that took the order from the trader in Des Moines owes the clearinghouse five contracts of cotton rather than the speculator himself. Margin is required of the brokerage and deposited with the clearinghouse to assure performance on the part of the brokerage. This is the main reason that the commission houses are so discreet in their choice of customers and their dealings with them. Should a customer declare bankruptcy or simply drop out of sight, the brokerage that handled his order is still responsible for the contracts it holds for him with the clearinghouse; the brokerage will be required to meet any loss that might occur in the customer's account.

In the event that the brokerage also cannot pay the loss it will be covered by the clearinghouse out of special funds and operating profits. Rules call for backup by solvent clearinghouse members in the event that even more money is required to cover the loss on runaway contracts but this backup has never been called upon. In 125 years of trading no clearing member has left any clearinghouse in a position where it could not cover the commitments of its members out of its own funds, and no trader ever has lost money due to bankruptcy or failure to perform on the part of any other trader or company.

On a modern exchange, the clearinghouse is in fact nothing more than a computer with a single operator backed up by a couple of clerks who match the trading slips as they are given out to them at the end of the trading day. But the existence of the clearinghouse vastly reduces the difficulty of trading commodities because all positions are held by one trader and the clearinghouse rather than between traders. A speculator who bought soybeans in April can sell them back and close his position any time he wants without finding his original contractee. The other party to the trade may have left the market long before or may hold his short position for several months more.

At delivery the clearinghouse matches warehouse receipts tendered by "shorts" to the "longs" that are still in the spot trading option normally giving the first receipt to the oldest standing long. Other systems of ownership dispersal exist but the warehouse receipts are always tendered to the clearinghouse and then handed to the longs who have agreed to accept delivery and stayed around long enough for delivery to become a fact.

PHYSICAL LIMITATIONS OF THE PIT

Direct auction between buyer and seller assures everybody an equal chance at the best possible price, but the physical setup of such a system puts limitations on the efficiency of trading in times when the pit is swamped. The big grain pits measure 30 to 40 feet across and can contain 150 or 200 traders all yelling and waving their arms in the attempt to make quick trades. Sometimes, such as at the opening after price-making news the night before or on the close before a holiday, or at the end of the contract, trading becomes so hectic that communications become snarled. At such times confirmation which is normally immediate can be held up an hour or more or even until after the close of the trading. This is especially true of larger brokerage houses whose wire facilities may not be able to keep up with the large volume in trading. The pit trader

will at all times get the best price he can find for the trades he is given, but this may not be the best price to come across the teletype. Sometimes in the din, a better bid or offer will have been made which simply was not heard or seen by the trader. It is possible for prices to vary from one part of the pit to another in rapid trading although this variation will never exceed a very small fraction. If it did, a scalper fast enough to catch the variation could make a lot of money in a few seconds at no risk.

If the confusion becomes too great, trading will be suspended, just as in stock trading, to allow the traders time to order their decks and prepare for a more rational go at it. But during the flurry that is not suspended even the ticker may not reflect every price hit with complete accuracy. If price is moving rapidly the ticker operator will attempt to report every price hit and will do so to the best of his ability to see or if his assistants in the pit signal him. But at such times even the tape and the quotation board which makes the information available may not show all the activity. Exchange rules reflect this reality and specifically restrict the public trader's recourse in the event of mistakes which cannot be attributed to any person but are rather inherent in the nature of pit trading.

Under exchange rules no trader has recourse if his trade was not made at the best price to come across the ticker so long as it was made in the range of prices coming across reflecting the best price his pit representative could find.

No trader has recourse in the event that a limit order (to be filled at a specified price or better) was not filled even though this price was hit by the market, if such occurred at a time when rapidity of trading made it impossible for his representative to consummate the trade before another buyer or seller stole the deal.

Errors are made, from time to time, and for these arbitration procedures are set out by the exchanges. Should the trader find an error in the handling of his account and not find satisfaction from his broker, he has recourse directly through the exchange on which the trade was made. Should a brokerage or its representative at the exchange simply neglect either to fill an order or close a position the brokerage must pay the trader a sum equal to the amount he lost on the mistake. Mistakes made by brokerages in favor of the trader remain the property of the trader. Further by-laws are obtainable from the various exchanges.

THE COMMODITY
EXCHANGE AUTHORITY

The Commodity Exchange Authority was established by an act of Congress as a branch of the Department of Agriculture to regulate the handling of commodities on the nation's commodity futures exchanges much in the manner that securities are regulated by the Securities and Exchange Commission. Regulated commodities include wheat, corn, oats, grain sorghum, soybeans, soybean meal, soybean oil, cottonseed oil, coconut oil, cotton, wool, frozen orange juice, shell eggs, frozen eggs, potatoes, cattle, frozen boneless beef, live hogs, frozen pork bellies, and frozen hams. Trading in these commodities must take place in accordance to rules set by the CEA. The Commodity Exchange

Authority (1) licenses futures exchanges, (2) licenses brokers and commission houses, (3) audits brokerage houses to see that customers' funds are being properly held, (4) arbitrates complaints between any parties in a commodity transaction, (5) sets limits to positions that may be held by any speculator and watches hedger holding to see that no trader exercises undue control of a market price, and (6) sees to it that all interested parties are given equal access to information that can affect commodity prices. (See Fig. 52, p. 81, and Fig. 52—Cont., p. 82.)

The main purpose of the CEA is to prevent manipulation and provide a market as fair to all participants as can be had through regulation. The CEA attempts to prevent the dissemination of false and misleading crop information which may be released in the hope of disrupting the market. Any fraud or fraudulent practices are prosecuted by the CEA along with violations of CEA regulations by brokerages or individuals handling public funds.

The CEA can be an arbitrator of disputes. Should any trader have a complaint the process of filing charges consists of writing the nearest Commodity Exchange Authority office with a specification of the violations. Specific rules and regulations should be mentioned. Upon investigation a determination will be made by the CEA and if they are found to be valid, or potentially valid, they will be referred to Washington, D.C., where further investigation will occur. Through all the process of bureaucracy a fine or penalty will be imposed on the offending party.

Unregulated commodities are traded without the protection of the CEA.

FIGURE 52

Commodities and designated contract markets with futures trading, 1961-62 to 1970-71

This listing shows the commodities, designated contract markets, the dates their designations became effective, and, for the 10-year period covered in this report, the dates when trading was inaugurated, resumed, or suspended by an exchange. In the commodity tables beginning on page 8, zero (0) is used when there was no trading but trading had not been suspended by a market; leaders (---) are used when a market had suspended trading from 1961-62 to 1970-71.

Commodity	Contract market	Effective date of designation	During 1961-62 to 1970-71	
			Trading began[1]	Trading suspended
Wheat	Chicago Open Board of Trade	Oct. 24, 1922	---	---
	Milwaukee Grain Exchange	Oct. 24, 1922	---	Jan. 17, 1966
	Minneapolis Grain Exchange	May 2, 1923	---	---
	Chicago Board of Trade	May 3, 1923	---	---
	Kansas City Board of Trade	May 5, 1923	---	---
Corn	Chicago Open Board of Trade	Oct. 24, 1922	---	---
	Milwaukee Grain Exchange	Oct. 24, 1922	---	Jan. 17, 1966
	Minneapolis Grain Exchange	May 2, 1923	---	---
	Chicago Board of Trade	May 3, 1923	---	---
	Kansas City Board of Trade	May 5, 1923	---	---
Oats	Chicago Open Board of Trade	Oct. 24, 1922	---	---
	Milwaukee Grain Exchange	Oct. 24, 1922	---	Jan. 17, 1966
	Minneapolis Grain Exchange	May 2, 1923	---	---
	Chicago Board of Trade	May 3, 1923	---	---
Rye	Chicago Open Board of Trade	Oct. 24, 1922	---	July 22, 1970[2]
	Milwaukee Grain Exchange	Oct. 24, 1922	---	Jan. 17, 1966
	Minneapolis Grain Exchange	May 2, 1923	---	---
	Chicago Board of Trade	May 3, 1923	---	July 22, 1970[2]
Barley	Minneapolis Grain Exchange	May 2, 1923	---	---
Flaxseed	Minneapolis Grain Exchange	May 2, 1923	---	---
Grain sorghums	Chicago Board of Trade	May 3, 1923	---	Apr. 10, 1962
	do.		Oct. 17, 1963	June 28, 1966
	Kansas City Board of Trade	May 5, 1923	---	---
	Chicago Mercantile Exchange	Jan. 27, 1971	Mar. 2, 1971	---
Rice	New York Mercantile Exchange	May 5, 1949	---	---
Soybeans	Chicago Board of Trade	Dec. 8, 1940	---	---
	Chicago Open Board of Trade	Dec. 8, 1940	---	---
	Minneapolis Grain Exchange	Sept. 11, 1950	---	---
	Kansas City Board of Trade	Sept. 10, 1956	---	---
	New York Produce Exchange	Aug. 15, 1966	Sept. 7, 1966	---
Soybean meal	Memphis Board of Trade Clearing Assn.	Dec. 8, 1940	---	---
	Chicago Board of Trade	Aug. 22, 1951	---	---
Soybean oil	New York Produce Exchange	Dec. 8, 1940	---	---
	Chicago Board of Trade	June 30, 1950	---	---
Lard	Chicago Board of Trade	Dec. 8, 1940	---	Feb. 26, 1963[3]
Cottonseed oil	Chicago Board of Trade	Dec. 8, 1940	Dec. 9, 1963	---
	New York Produce Exchange	Dec. 8, 1940	---	---
	International Commercial Exch. Inc.	Apr. 9, 1970	Sept. 10, 1970	---
Cottonseed meal	Memphis Board of Trade Clearing Assn.	Dec. 8, 1940	---	---
	New York Produce Exchange	Feb. 11, 1964	July 15, 1964	---
Millfeeds	St. Louis Merchants' Exchange	Apr. 13, 1962[4]	June 1, 1962	Dec. 31, 1962
Cotton	New York Cotton Exchange	Sept. 13, 1936	---	---
	New Orleans Cotton Exchange	Sept. 13, 1936	---	July 9, 1964
	Chicago Board of Trade	Sept. 13, 1936	---	---
Wool	Wool Associates of the New York Cotton Exchange	Oct. 27, 1954	---	---
Wool tops	Wool Associates of the New York Cotton Exchange	June 1, 1938	---	Oct. 21, 1970

Source: U.S. Department of Agriculture, Commodity Exchange Authority.

FIGURE 52—*Continued*

Commodities and designated contract markets with futures trading, 1961-62 to 1970-71--Continued

Commodity	Contract market	Effective date of designation	During 1961-62 to 1970-71	
			Trading began[1]	Trading suspended
Butter	Chicago Mercantile Exchange	Sept. 13, 1936	---	---
	New York Mercantile Exchange	Sept. 13, 1936	---	---
Eggs	Chicago Mercantile Exchange	Sept. 13, 1936	---	---
	New York Mercantile Exchange	Sept. 13, 1936	---	---
Potatoes	Chicago Mercantile Exchange	Sept. 13, 1936	---	---
	New York Mercantile Exchange	Dec. 1, 1941	---	---
Frozen concentrated orange juice	Citrus Associates of the New York Cotton Exchange	July 24, 1968	Oct. 26, 1966	---
Cattle:				
Live beef	Chicago Mercantile Exchange	June 18, 1968	Nov. 30, 1964	---
Choice steers	Chicago Board of Trade	June 18, 1968	Oct. 4, 1966	---
Live feeder	Kansas City Board of Trade	July 2, 1968	June 20, 1966	Oct. 23, 1967
Frozen boneless beef	Chicago Mercantile Exchange	Mar. 13, 1970	Apr. 15, 1970	---
Hides	Commodity Exchange, Inc.	June 18, 1968	---	---
Live hogs	Chicago Mercantile Exchange	June 18, 1968	Feb. 28, 1966	---
Frozen pork bellies	Chicago Mercantile Exchange	June 18, 1968	Sept. 18, 1961	---
	Minneapolis Grain Exchange	Mar. 19, 1971	Apr. 5, 1971	---
Frozen skinned hams	Chicago Mercantile Exchange	July 19, 1968	Feb. 3, 1964	---

[1]/ Leaders indicate that trading began prior to July 1, 1961.
[2]/ Trading suspended except for liquidation.
[3]/ Trading discontinued with the expiration of the 1963 May future.
[4]/ Designated September 13, 1936; vacated August 31, 1957.

Source: U.S. Department of Agriculture, Commodity Exchange Authority.

These include mostly foreign-produced commodities which are not subject to control by our federal government. These include cocoa, sugar, platinum, silver, coffee, and so on, and trading in these commodities is margined from a separate account which consists primarily of internal paper work within the brokerage house which handles the trade for the public speculator.

DAY TRADES

Most exchanges provide for lower commissions on trades which are open and closed on the same day in an attempt to provide a fair chance for the speculator to compete for profits on minor price dislocations such as might occur during the execution of a large order. Day trade commission schedules also apply in the event that a trade is closed and again opened in one day and it is here that the practical importance of day trades exists for the public speculator. The speculator can keep his position closely covered by a stop-loss order and in the event that his stop order is tripped taking him out of the market, and the trader does not wish his position closed, he may economically reestablish himself. He must, however, notify his broker that he wishes the closing and subsequent reopening considered a day trade, as normal accounting procedure may not connect the two resulting in full commission charges being levied on both transactions.

ORDER VARIATIONS

Commodities is a game of control and over the years a number of order variations and restrictions have evolved to allow the public speculator the greatest possible amount of control over his position without the necessity of continual tape reading and order placement. Generally speaking, a broker can execute any order he can understand that can be transmitted into succinct language. The various orders given below are used by traders to exploit the market if and only if it reacts in the manner they wish to exploit. Their whole function is to see that trades are opened and closed when the trader wants them opened and closed, and any of these orders could be replaced by a phone call if the trader wished to keep close enough track of the market tape.

At market (MKT) This is the only order which gives no conditions. It is to be filled immediately upon arrival at the prevailing market price.

At opening (OPG) Order is to be filled as specified at the opening of the market or not at all. If only part can be executed (i.e., 7 contracts of an ordered 10) the remainder will be left unfilled. Such an order would be used to exploit any price aberations expected in the opening trades.

At close (CLO) Similar to the above. Unlike trading in securities, both OPG and CLO orders can contain other restrictions and will simply not be filled if the other conditions cannot be met.

Good through (GT) Order to rest awaiting proper conditions through a stated time limit. If it has not been filled by then it will be canceled. *Good this week (GTW), Good this month (GTM)* are orders which will be canceled if they have not been executed by the end of the week or month. Also, *Good through 2:00* in which case the order will be canceled at 2:00 if it has not been filled; such time orders must conform to the policy of the brokerage, being stated in local time, New York time or Chicago time. *Good till canceled (GTC)* is the most common form.

Fill or kill (FOK) Order must be filled as specified immediately or canceled. If part of the order can be filled, that part will be executed and the remainder canceled.

Stop order (STP) Order rests in the pit trader's deck until other conditions have prevailed, at which time it is executed as a market order to be filled at the best possible price. The most important stop order is the stop-loss order which is designed to take a trader out of the market if price goes against his position, although it is often used to instate positions. Stop orders are not accepted in the orange juice or wool pits.

Limit order Order is to be filled at price specified or better but at no worse price.

Stop-limit order A stop order will not be executed until a certain price level is hit and the stop is "tripped." A limit order gives a minimum (maximum) acceptable price. Stop-limit orders combine the two, to be activated when the price trips the stop, but to be executed at not worse than a stated price.

Market if touched (MIT) Opposite of a stop order, to be filled "at market" once the MIT price has been hit.

Basis orders (BAS) Order is to be filled in one option when the price of a second option hits a significant level; "buy five March bellies when May bellies hit 34.20 cents." In this only the March pork bellies are bought although the May pork bellies are used to trip the stop. Limits and stop orders may be appended to the basis order, specifying the price range for the option to be purchased.

Spread order In instituting a spread position, the trader is primarily interested in the basis difference between the price of the two options, rather than in absolute price levels. A spread order is an order to buy contracts in one month option and sell an equal number in another option, which may be a second month, a second market or a second commodity (March over May wheat; Chicago over Minneapolis wheat; or corn over hogs). In spreads, the basis will be the condition for the sale and when the set spread has occurred both the purchases and sales will be made. In intermarket spreads, it is customary to send the order to the smaller market where the trade is most difficult.

The above orders are all used equally to open or close a position according to signals the trader considers significant. Other conditions can be used to help automatically service an open position.

Enter open stop (EOS) Stop order is being positioned below a buy order or above a sell order. EOS can be set at a stated price or merely at a set range of the opening purchase or sale price. "Buy 2 August cattle, EOS 50 pts." would buy two contracts of cattle at market price and set a stop loss of 50 points below the purchase price.

One cancels other (OCO) (OR) OCO consists of two orders, one entered above the last market price and one entered below the last market price. This is done either to liquidate open positions or initiate new positions when the trader is not exactly sure which way prices will move. Whichever order fills first the other is then automatically canceled—i.e., OCO, one (whichever fills first) cancels the other.

Scale order A scale order can be used to scale in contracts at set intervals. "Buy 5 March wheat at MKT and 5 each 1¢ down total 25 day," would put the trader in at market price and add to his position one contract (5,000 bushels) at a time until five contracts were held only if the market continued to decline. (In grains, "5" is 5,000 bushels, one contract.)

Market if tendered Orders the broker to close a position at market if notice of delivery is received in the delivery month.

As the trader must transmit such orders through his broker, wireman, and pit trader, such variations can be worked out best between the speculator and his individual broker. Usually a form can be found which will economically fill any need the trader may come up with. Such orders, while convenient, can cause problems in some commodity pits if a great many traders use similar trading methods and systems, causing spurts and other dislocations when the price hits a level considered significant by many traders. For this reason some of the pits disallow some of the above orders. At the current time, in *cotton*, only basis, straight limit and market orders are permitted. No EOS is permitted in metals trading except in New York silver and copper. In *orange juice* and *propane*, basis orders and market orders are allowed along with stop-limit orders only when the stop price and limit price are the same. In *wool*, straight limit and market orders are permitted; stop-limit ok if the stop and limit prices are the same. In *metals*, no MIT or other contingency orders are permitted. Straight limit, straight stop, market and stop-limit orders are permitted.

COMMON ORDER ABBREVIATIONS

BAS	basis
CLO	on close
CXL	cancel
DAY	good today only
EOS	enter open stop
FOK	fill or kill
GTC	good till canceled
GTM	good this month
GTW	good this week
GT	good till *(time specified)*
LMT	limit
LVS	leaves
M	thousand (from the roman numeral)
MIT	market if touched
MKT	at market
OB	or better
OPG	at opening
OCO	one cancels the other
PREM	premium
PTS	points
STP	stop

ORDER EXECUTION

Give your broker an order to sell 10,000 bushels of March corn at $1.40 or better, stop loss $1.43, Good Till Canceled. At this time you should have some reason for guessing that the price for March corn is going to drop which is the reason you are selling it and have formed some estimate of how far it might reasonably drop if it does. You should be expecting at least a 3 cent drop equal to a 50 percent return on your margin investment since you are willing to take a 3 cent beating if you are wrong. Your broker will walk out across to the wire room to the operator who will type out "Sell 10m March Corn $1.40 EOS $1.43 GTC." This order will be time stamped to show its time of submission should any dispute arise about its execution. It will then go to the exchange that handles corn futures trading, which would be Chicago. Had you ordered a position in shell eggs your order would have gone to the Chicago Mercantile Exchange as this is where shell eggs are traded. An order for flaxseed would have gone to the Winnipeg Grain Exchange.

This process is the same for stock trading. Had you handed your broker an order to buy 100 shares of Acme he would have handed the order to the wire operator who would have sent it in code to the New York Stock Exchange, American Stock Exchange, or even the Pacific Coast Stock Exchange whichever handles Acme stock. If the stock is traded on two exchanges that must be specified by the wireman and the proper exchange selected for the trade.

The order to sell 10,000 bushels of March corn will be received by another wire operator on the exchange floor where it will be sent by runner to the pit where corn futures are traded. In the case of the Chicago Board of Trade, this will be a separate and distinct pit reserved solely for the trading of corn futures. On smaller exchanges such as the Kansas City Board of Trade, there is only one pit for all the commodities traded in which every order is executed.

The runner will hand the order to the company man who stands physically in the pit and will do the actual selling of the corn as specified. If the pitman can sell 10,000 bushels of March corn for $1.40 or better he will do so immediately. If he cannot he will place the slip of paper containing the order in his hand along with others that have not been filled. This handful of paper is called his "deck" and is arranged so that all slips read in order according to price. By keeping the deck open to the going price he can easily read what orders he holds and fill them. Some of these orders may have been in his deck for a month or more, others for only a few minutes. Some will never leave the deck until the end of trading in that particular commodity because the price will never go high enough or low enough to execute them.

The pit trader will search the pit until he finds another trader indicating he wishes to buy two contracts of March corn—a quick haggle may ensue if either trader thinks he can pick up a fraction on the other and the trade will be made. The man who bought the 10,000 bushels of corn may have been executing an order handed him from the wireman of another brokerage house or he may have been trading for his own account. If he is trading for his own account he may hold the contracts and have an open long position like any other speculator or he may turn around and sell the two contracts to another trader for $1.40⅛. If he does he will have scalped an eighth of a cent on the two contracts for a total of $12.50 in a few seconds.

When the trade is made whether immediately upon receipt from the wire-man or having rested in the pitman's deck for a while, a confirmation will be sent back to the brokerage that originated the order. When the broker receives the confirmation he may or may not immediately call the speculator and confirm the sale according to the agreement made by the trader and his broker beforehand, but he will mail official confirmation of the trade in any event. This confirmation slip contains the price sold at, the numbers of contracts sold or bought if the move was a purchase. This confirmation slip is the only official record of holding that the speculator will receive in the course of holding the position. He will receive no certificate, of course, since none exists. At the same time, the broker will take approximately $800 from the trader's free account to secure the open position. As long as the market price for March corn remains steady nothing further will happen to the trader's account. If the price drops a profit will develop on the open short position and the trader may take funds in excess of the margin requirement out of his margin account. If the price rises the trader will be notified when he has lost his fluctuating margin and asked to bring his margin back up to the specified level.

STOP LOSS

Your original order to your broker was actually two orders, both of which were passed along in code to be executed if possible or enter the pit trader's deck for possible execution later. The first was to sell March corn at $1.40 or better and if the trader could find a buyer at that price he made the sale immediately. If the price was lower than

$1.40 and he could find no takers at the ordered price the order went into his deck. The second order was to buy March corn when and if the price rises to $1.43 or worse and will not be executed unless the first order has been filled. The two will remain attached to another until the first order is filled, at which time the second order, the stop loss, enters the deck as a regular stop order.

The result of such paired orders is to ensure that the trader makes his sale at no worse price than he indicates, in this case $1.40. If he can sell at a higher price he has done better than planned. The second order is designed to take the speculator out of the market should prices rise causing a loss on his original short sale. The speculator has here indicated that he is willing to sit through a rise of less than 3 cents but at 3 cents he is willing to admit his mistake and have his loss stopped. Buying 10,000 bushels at $1.43 will effectively cover his original short position and take him out of the market. If the market shoots past $1.43 before his stop loss can be executed, the trader still wants out at the best price he can get. Thus he has entered one limit order, good until canceled, and one stop-loss order which is not to be executed unless the market acts adversely.

A buy order would have been handled in exactly the same manner. The original purchase might have been "at the market" and fillable at the prevailing price or a limit order to be filled at a given price or less, good until canceled. The stop loss would have entered the deck when the first order was filled or close to it to close the position at the market once the stop point had been hit. "Stop sell at the market if the stop price is traded," would have been the order.

6

THE COMMODITY CONTRACT

A futures contract is simply a legally binding agreement for the delivery and acceptance of a commodity at a certain time and place in the future of a certain grade of commodity. One contract of March wheat traded on the Chicago Board of Trade is a binding contract committing the seller to deliver 5,000 bushels of No. 2 soft red wheat at certain designated warehouses in Chicago at a certain date in March, usually between the 1st and the 20th. February pork bellies is another way of saying 36,000 pounds of bacon of deliverable grade delivered in Chicago in February. (See Fig. 53, p. 89; Fig. 53–*Cont.*, p. 90; and Fig. 53–*Concluded*, p. 91.)

A contract could specify anything. A contract calling for delivery of 3,000 bushels of rye of a certain quality delivered in Walla Walla, Washington, on a certain date could be perfectly acceptable, in fact, the vast majority of the nation's commodities are sold under such "cash forward contracts."

By limiting the delivery points to one city and the delivery months to six or so the volume of business (hence liquidity) is raised and a more efficient market is formed. If all wheat buyers and sellers are willing to choose from the six delivery months offered on the futures markets and are willing to trade a single grade of cash and single delivery position

the market formed serves each of them more efficiently. In a large volume, market orders to buy or sell of nearly any size can be filled with little or no price concession. A farmer may find it difficult to sell 1 million pounds of potatoes for delivery in October in New Jersey without offering a price considerably below the market, but he can fairly easily sell 20 contracts of Maine potatoes (at 50,000 pounds per contract) on the New York Mercantile Exchange for November delivery. (See Fig. 54, p. 92.)

The farmer may have no intention of holding his potatoes until November nor of delivering them to New York and the potatoes sold on the futures exchange may not even be the same grade that he will harvest in the fall, but as the price of potatoes on the futures exchange goes up or down, the price of potatoes at the farmer's local spot market will follow. As the price of potatoes goes up, the price of all potatoes at all delivery positions will follow fairly closely.

COUNTRY BASIS

Commodities are worth less on the farm than they are in the city. This discount reflects the cost of handling and shipping the commodity to the market where it will be sold for cash and is called the country basis. Cash wheat may

FIGURE 53

RAW SUGAR CONTRACT No. 10
(Quota Cane Raw Sugar For U. S. Consumption)

New York............................19....

.... (has)   (sold)
                                                  (have) *this day* (bought) *and agreed to*

(deliver to)
(receive from) ....

50 tons of 2,240 pounds each of Raw Centrifugal Cane Sugar, in bulk, of any grade or grades and qualities as specified in Section 109a at the price of .... cents per pound net cash duty paid or duty free. Such price to be for 96° average polarization outturn, and Standard Quality Range, with additions or deductions for other grades and qualities according to the differentials established or to be established for the delivery month stated below by the Rules of the New York Coffee and Sugar Exchange, Inc., adopted or to be adopted in accordance with the provisions of Section 109a of the By-Laws of said Exchange.

Deliverer shall deliver and Receiver shall receive the Sugar in a vessel berthed at a customary Refiner's Berth in New York or Philadelphia. The port and berth shall be declared by Receiver, who shall discharge the Sugar as customary at said berth at his own expense in accordance with Sugar Trade Rule 10.13. The vessel, which shall be declared by Deliverer, (a) shall be available for discharge at New York and/or Philadelphia and (b) shall be ready and be able to commence discharge during the month of .... Receiver shall not be obliged to discharge the vessel prior to the first regular stevedoring day of said month and the vessel shall arrive in accordance with Section 109a.

So long as Sugar may be processed or consumed only under any quota or allotment plan decreed by any United States Government Department or Agency only Sugar permitted to be so processed or consumed without pentally on the date of delivery under this contract may be delivered in fulfillment thereof. The Receiver guarantees that all Sugar delivered hereunder shall be subjected to such specific processes as shall, following its entry into the continental United States, be required for its classification as Raw Sugar under any plan decreed by any United States Government Department or Agency.

Weight and quality to be determined as provided in Sugar Trade Rules 10.18 and 10.19 and delivery and payment to be made in accordance with Sugar Trade Rule 10.11.

Allowance for delivery to be determined in accordance with Section 109a.

Either party may call for margin as the variations of the market for like deliveries may warrant, which margin shall be kept good.

This contract is made in view of, and in all respects subject to the By-Laws Rules and Regulations of the New York Coffee and Sugar Exchange, Inc.

....
                                                  (Brokers)

(Written across the face is the following)

For and in consideration of One Dollar to .... in hand paid, receipt whereof is hereby acknowledged, ... accept this contract with all its stipulations and conditions.

GRADES DELIVERABLE

    (a) Foreign growth cane Sugars duty paid.
    (b) Duty free cane Sugars.
    (c) Cane Sugars, the product of continental U. S.

So long as Sugar can be processed or consumed only under any quota or allotment plan decreed by any United States Government Department or Agency, only Sugar permitted to be so processed or consumed without penalty on the date of delivery under this contract may be delivered in fulfillment thereof. The Receiver guarantees that all Sugar delivered hereunder shall be subjected to such specific processes as shall, following its entry into the continental United States, be required for its classification as raw Sugar under any plan decreed by any United States Government Department or Agency.

DOCUMENTS DELIVERABLE

    (a) Delivery order on form stipulated in Sugar Trade Rules validated by the Delivery Committee;
    (b) *Pro forma* invoice for 95% of the value of 112,000 pounds of Sugar of 96 degrees polarization and Standard Quality Range for each contract at the Delivery Notice Price;
    (c) Customs consumption entry or other document that may be required by the United States Customs and/or the United States Department of Agriculture to secure release of the Sugar.

SETTLEMENT

Receiver will pay the *pro forma* invoice value between the hours of 10:00 A.M. and 3:00 P.M. within one hour after presentation by Deliverer which shall be not later than 2:00 P.M. on the business day (even though an Exchange holiday, but providing normal afternoon banking facilities are available), that the vessel carrying the Sugar is ready to commence discharging at berth designated in accordance with the By-Laws.

If Receiver's berth is not available and vessel is in all respects ready to discharge, Receiver shall pay the invoice as set forth above.

If Deliverer cannot deliver the above mentioned documents on such day, he shall be responsible for demurrage on the vessel and actual expenses incurred due to his failure to produce the necessary papers for entry, release and discharge of the Sugar.

FIGURE 53—*Continued*

Title shall pass from Deliverer to Receiver at the time documents are presented and payment is made in accordance with the foregoing.

Final settlement shall be made promptly after weights and tests are ascertained.

The Deliverer shall require that payment be made by certified check which shall be, unless otherwise mutually agreed upon, in New York funds.

PRICE MULTIPLES

Quotations are in multiples of 1/100th of 1¢ per pound for each pound of Sugar, equivalent to $11.20 per contract. A fluctuation of 1¢ per pound is equivalent to $1,120 per contract.

TRADING HOURS

10 A.M. to 2:55 P.M.

(When Exchange is open for only a half day—10 A.M. to 11:55 A.M.)

TRADING MONTHS

Trading is conducted in contracts for delivery during 18 months, including the current month.

LAST TRADING DAY

The last trading day for each delivery month in the No. 10 Sugar Contract shall be the fourteenth calendar day before the first full business day of the delivery month, except that if such day is not a full Exchange business day, the last trading day shall be the last full business day prior to such fourteenth calendar day. All contracts outstanding after the close of the Exchange on last trading day shall be completed in accordance with the prescribed delivery procedure of the Exchange.

DELIVERY NOTICES

After the close of business on the last trading day of the coming delivery month, each member holding an open sales contract for that month shall issue a Delivery Notice for the same to the Clearing Association. Delivery Notices shall be presented with clearance sheet on the night of last trading day. Each Notice must be for 112,000 pounds and for Sugar delivered from not more than one country of origin.

All Delivery Notices shall be officially numbered by the Clearing Association, assigned and delivered before 10:00 A.M. of the following Exchange business day to the member(s) holding open purchase contracts in the coming delivery month. Not later than noon of the day the Receiver receives any Notice(s) from the Clearing Association, he shall notify each issuer in writing of the quantity and numbers of such issuer's Delivery Notices so received.

The Clearing Association's assignment of Delivery Notices shall be subject to re-assignment by the Delivery Committee. After receipt from the Clearing Association, Delivery Notices may not be transferred to or exchanged with another member, except as directed by the Delivery Committee or by the Board of Managers as provided in the By-Laws. In the event the Delivery Committee or the Board of Managers subsequently directs a Receiver to exchange one or more specified Notices for a like quantity of specified Notices with another Receiver such exchange shall be effected and the re-assigned Notices treated in all respects as if so assigned initially by the Clearing Association.

Both Deliverers and Receivers shall file with their clearance sheets on the last trading day a signed memorandum addressed to the Exchange stating the number of contracts to be delivered or received by them, which information shall be published by the Executive Director of the Exchange before 10:00 A.M. of the following business day.

Each issuer and stopper of a No. 10 Delivery Notice, shall pay to the Exchange a fee of $1.00 for each Delivery Notice issued and stopped. This fee is not chargeable by the clearing member to his customer.

DELIVERIES

Deliverer shall be responsible for any penalties assessed by any United States Government Department or Agency as well as any penalties assessed for violating the By-Laws and Rules of the New York Coffee and Sugar Exchange, Inc.

Each Receiver shall notify the Delivery Committee, in writing, not later than noon of the first full Exchange business day after the last trading day the number of contracts to be received by him. For the guidance of the Delivery Committee he may, if the information is available, declare the port(s) and Refiner's berth(s) at which he desires to receive the Sugar and the preferred period of arrival in the delivery month.

Each Deliverer shall notify the Delivery Committee, in writing, not later than noon of the first full Exchange business day after the last trading day, (a) the number of contracts to be delivered by him, (b) the country of origin of Sugar being delivered, (c) the approximate arrival date of the vessel carrying the Sugar and the quantity to be loaded or on board such vessel and (d) the name of the carrying vessel and the name of the owners or chartered owners; however, if the vessel's owners or chartered owners have not named the carrying vessel to Deliverer in time to enable the Deliverer to furnish this information to the Delivery Committee on said date, Deliverer shall name the vessel to the Delivery Committee as promptly as possible but not later than 14 calendar days prior to the day vessel is expected to arrive for delivery hereunder, and the Delivery Committee shall promptly notify Receivers of the vessel so named.

On or before 5 P.M. on the second full Exchange business day after the last trading day, the Delivery Committee shall assign the Sugar (or Sugars) to Receivers and shall notify each Receiver of his assignment.

On or before 11 A.M. of the day notification is required under Bulk Sugar Charter—U. S. A. (April, 1962), each Receiver shall declare to the Delivery Committee (in writing) for each contract the port and berth within such port at which the Sugar is to be received, except if such day is not a full Exchange business day, then such declaration shall be made on the preceding full Exchange business day.

FIGURE 53—*Concluded*

On or before 5 P.M. of the day that the Delivery Committee receives the information required from the Receiver, the Delivery Committee shall declare same to the Deliverer. At the request of the Receiver, the Deliverer shall furnish the itinerary of the declared vessel.

If it becomes evident that the carrying vessel declared to the Delivery Committee, due to causes beyond the Deliverer's control, will be unable to arrive in time to fulfill the contracts or is involved in a maritime casualty, the Deliverer may, upon approval of the Delivery Committee, substitute other Sugars which would be good tender under the contract

Delivery under this contract shall be considered timely delivery if the vessel carrying the Sugar reports ready to discharge at its first Exchange Sugar delivery berth not later than 8 A.M. on the last business day of the delivery month. If the vessel reports after the fifth business day prior to the last business day of the month, discharge of sugar to be delivered against Exchange contracts shall be continuous.

A Deliverer and Receiver may mutually agree to deliver and receive at any customary safe berth at any United States port. However, such agreement shall be subject to the approval of the Delivery Committee. Upon approval by the Delivery Committee the delivery so made shall be considered complete and settlement shall be made thereafter between Deliverer and Receiver.

After a carrying vessel has been assigned to a Receiver the Deliverer and Receiver may mutually agree to deliver and receive under conditions other than those stipulated in the By-Laws and Trade Rules. However, such agreement shall be subject to approval by the Delivery Committee. Upon approval by the Delivery Committee, the delivery so made shall be considered complete and settlement shall be made thereafter between Deliverer and Receiver.

ALLOWANCE (FOR DISCHARGING)

Upon receiving a report of the Committee on Sugar Deliveries pursuant to the stipulations contained in the By-Laws and upon any other information which it may deem appropriate, the Board of Managers shall from time to time fix the allowance for discharging Raw Sugar under Contract No. 10 effective upon such date as the Board may determine, and applicable to contracts entered into before such effective date as well as those entered into thereafter. Each such allowance shall be posted on the Bulletin Board of the Exchange and Deliverers shall allow to Receivers such allowance on all Sugar discharged under Contract No. 10 until a new allowance shall become effective.

COMMISSION RATES

(The following rates of Commission including floor brokerage are the lowest that may be charged on each contract, bought or sold, for future delivery under Raw Sugar Contract No. 10.)

Based upon a price of	For customers residing in the United States, its territories, Puerto Rico, Canada; or residing in foreign countries whose Sugar is fully qualified as deliverable in fulfillment of Sugar contracts		For customer residing elsewhere	
	Members	Non-Members	Members	Non-Members
1.99 cents and below......................	$ 5.00	$10.00	$ 7.50	$12.50
2 cents to 3.99 cents incl...................	6.25	12.50	8.75	15.00
4 cents to 5.99 cents incl...................	7.50	15.00	10.00	17.50
6 cents to 7.99 cents incl...................	8.75	17.50	11.25	20.00
8 cents to 9.99 cents incl...................	10.00	20.00	12.50	22.50
10 cents to 11.99 cents incl.................	11.25	22.50	13.75	25.00
12 cents to 13.99 cents incl.................	12.50	25.00	15.00	27.50
14 cents to 15.99 cents incl.................	13.75	27.50	16.25	30.00
16 cents and over..........................	15.00	30.00	17.50	32.50

Upon the delivery or receipt of Sugar under Raw Sugar Contract No. 10, commissions shall be charged and paid as follows:

DELIVERING

1. One commission for the original sale.　　2. One commission for the delivery.

RECEIVING

1. One commission for the original purchase.　　2. One commission for the receipt.

STRADDLES

The lowest commission that may be charged:

60% of the regular rate.

DAY TRADE RATES OF COMMISSION—For each contract bought and sold, both entered into and liquidated upon the same day, for a single account, the commission shall be:

For members—75% of the regular commission exclusive of floor brokerage.

For non-members—50% of the regular commission exclusive of floor brokerage.

The rates of commission to be charged shall in no event be lower than those prescribed above.

For further information, apply to your broker or to the Executive Director's office.

Source: New York Coffee & Sugar Exchange.

FIGURE 54

Chicago Board of Trade

**Agreements of
the Shipper**

The Shipper expressly agrees:

1. that all Stud Lumber tendered in satisfaction of futures contracts shall be graded in accordance with the provisions of Regulation 8020.
2. that all Stud Lumber Shipping Certificates will be registered with the Registrar of the Exchange.
3. to fulfill the duties of the shipper issuing Stud Lumber Shipping Certificates as set forth in Regulation 8022 in the Chapter of the Rules and Regulations of the Board of Trade of the City of Chicago pertaining to Stud Lumber.
4. to abide by the Rules and Regulations of the Exchange applicable to the issuance of Stud Lumber Shipping Certificates, shipping, application of billing, standards and grading of Stud Lumber.
5. that the Exchange may cancel said declaration of regularity, if granted for any breach of said agreements.
6. neither to withdraw as a regular Shipper nor withdraw capacity during the life of the Declaration of Regularity except after sixty (60) days' notice or having obtained the consent of the Exchange.
7. that the signing of this application constitutes a representation that the conditions of regularity are complied with and will be observed during the life of the Declaration of Regularity and, if found to be untrue, the Exchange shall have the right to cancel said Declaration of Regularity immediately.

Company _____

By (title) _____

This application is recommended by the Warehouse, Weighing and Custodian Committee.

Chairman _____

Date _____

Bond in the amount of _____ duly filed (date) _____

Secretary _____

This application is approved and a Declaration of Regularity is granted by the Board of Directors of the Board of Trade of the City of Chicago.

Date _____

Chairman of the Board _____

Secretary _____

Source: Chicago Board of Trade.

be selling for $1.82 in Chicago and $1.74 in Des Moines. The Des Moines figure is not readily available but the Chicago cash price is quoted daily in many newspapers and the cash buyer and seller in Des Moines needs only to know that wheat on his cash market brings 8 cents less than it does in Chicago. The farmer, 20 miles out of Des Moines, needs only to know that wheat on his farm is worth 3 cents less than wheat in Des Moines. By finding the cash Chicago quotation in the newspaper he can subtract 11 cents and have a pretty close estimate of the price he can expect to receive for his crop.

Commodity merchants keep a book of "country basis" charts from which to figure the offering price to make for commodities in each place in the country where they do business and often a purchase agreement will simply specify so many bushels or pounds of goods at "Chicago less 11 cents" from which both the farmer and the merchandiser understand that the farmer will receive that day's closing cash quote from Chicago less the country basis. It is quite possible that neither will know the exact price until the next day. (See Fig. 55, p. 94.)

Country basis is of little direct importance to the commodity speculator who does all of his business on one market but is of great importance to the farmer. Government support programs state a support price for a commodity at a specific locality. Country basis is then subtracted from the support price reflecting the lower value of the goods in different parts of the country. Were this not the case a support price of say $1.25 per bushel for wheat might find no takers in Illinois and buy literally all the wheat produced in Whatcom County,

North Dakota. Through the use of country basis support prices and selling prices are applied evenly across the country. Country basis remains relatively constant in its relationship to a fluctuating futures price. It is not always true but generally if the basis is 10 cents under, 10 cents over, 5 cents under, or 5 cents over the nearby futures price, then it will remain somewhere near that general discount or premium regardless of whether the futures contract is selling at $1 or $1.25. For this reason the farmer or processor can hedge on the Chicago futures market even though he has no intention of delivering or accepting delivery from Chicago as specified in the contract he has entered on the futures market. As the price market varies so will the country basis. Although industry hedgers often make up as much as 80 percent of trading volume on the futures exchanges, fewer than 2 percent of the contracts made for future delivery are filled by actual produce. The rest are closed out (by an opposite order) as the actual goods are sold on the country markets at country prices. Delivery remains a possibility, however, as country basis is equal to the cost of getting goods to the market. Any cash dealer could buy the goods in the country and deliver them in Chicago for a price high enough to cover his costs. This in fact enforces the "country basis."

PREMIUMS AND DISCOUNTS

The number of people who can efficiently use the futures market for hedging is increased (again increasing liquidity) by the specifications in the contract of various grades deliverable at set premiums and set discounts. Corn is traded

FIGURE 55

READING A BASIS CHART
If the basis chart in an area looks like this—what does it mean?

Soybean Basis { Chicago Nov., Mar., Jly. Future
Iowa Track Price }

Oct. 1960 — July 1961

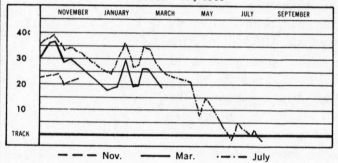

— — — Nov.   ———— Mar.   ·—·— July

For a Farmer it means:

1. Beginning in December, he can look at the November future 11 months ahead, subtract an approximate 20 to 25¢ November basis, and have an estimate of the harvest value of soybeans. He can then:

   a. Decide how many acres to plant

   b. Sell them now — or any time up to harvest — if the futures price looks good to him. If basis holds true, his local price equivalent, figured with the result of the futures transaction, should return about the target price.

   In March, the November future is 276. Basis is 20 to 25¢. He likes the price and sells the future, planning to net 251 to 256 on the beans in November.

   In November, the future is selling at 268. He buys it back 8¢ cheaper than he sold it for, and gains a gross of 8¢. The cash price in his area is 22¢ under the future, or 246, and he sells the grain for 246, adds the 8¢ to make 254. It is in the target price range.

2. All through the growing season a farmer can use basis to check cash price offers—or he can actually sell the crop. Or he might determine that it would pay to carry the crop into the new year.

Supposing he had already sold the November future to lock in an attractive harvest price, but sometime before harvest had a chance to move the hedge to July, eliminating the wide harvest basis and adding about a 13 cent carrying charge. Using the figures of the previous example where he sold the November for 276, aiming for a target price in the 251 to 256 area—he would be looking for about 289 in June (The 276 futures price plus 13 cents carrying charge.) His arithmetic would look like this:

March 15, 1968—Sell November future @ 276 } +6¢
September 25, 1968 { Buy back November contract—270
Sell July at 13¢ over Nov.—283 } +6¢
June 13, 1969—Buy in July future—277
June 13, 1969—Sell cash, same price as July—277

He was aiming at a target price of about 289. Results showed:

Cash price	277
Futures gain	6
Futures gain	6
Gross receipts	289

The example showed this man to be the victim of falling prices if he had not hedged. As it is, he bought the November futures in at lower than the sale price, and the same happened with the July. The gain here, plus his cash price, helped him realize his target price.

He would have achieved the same results had prices gone up, realizing more for his cash sale, but having to subtract losses in the futures market from that. It generally is not good practice to place a hedge, lift it, place it again, lift it, and so on to try to adjust to changing price levels. However, in the event of a genuinely bull market for the cash commodity, a futures position can be readily liquidated.

In short, it is recommended that those who would use the market in their business become thoroughly acquainted with it, then use it as a part of the business when it will help to make or save money.

It's possible to swap a cash speculation for futures speculation by selling cash grain at harvest and buying a futures contract, hoping the price will go up.

Grain has storage charges—live animals do not, otherwise the basis principles and market use are the same for commodities other than grain.

Source: Chicago Board of Trade.

on the Chicago Board of Trade with the contract specifying No. 2 yellow corn. No. 1 yellow may be delivered at a 3 cent premium to the price quoted for the contract grade. The contract similarly makes provision for the delivery of No. 3 yellow at a set discount.

It would be possible to have separate markets for each of the various grades of a commodity, such as corn, but as the value of the different grades remains in a fixed relationship to the value of the contract there is no need. By trading only one grade and allowing delivery of other grades at set premiums and discounts, one market gives a quotation that can be used by all the farmers and processors of that commodity. (See Fig. 56, p. 96.)

If the contract is to serve the largest possible audience it must be set up so that the country basis and the various grade premiums and discounts remain constant and as the industry needs change the contracts will be changed. A farmer who will bring in a crop of No. 1 red wheat cannot hedge his crop by selling contracts of No. 2 red wheat in Chicago unless he is confident that the price differential between the two grades and localities will remain constant. As long as the contract works properly and the relations between the grades hold constant he can hedge in Chicago and remove the risk of a price drop when he harvests his crop.

CONTRACTS CURRENTLY TRADED

Commodities currently traded on futures exchanges can be divided into four main categories. *Grains* include barley, corn, sorghum, flaxseed, oats, rye, wheat, and soybeans, although soybeans are actually an oilseed. Soybean meal and soybean oil each have their own futures contract but might be listed with the beans. Meal and oil are among the few semiprocessed products for which futures markets exist. This category includes the most important commodities in our agricultural industry at the earliest point in their production. Any of these commodities can be used as animal feed and changes in price in these basics will be reflected up the agricultural line.

The second category of commodities traded is *animal products* including live hogs, hams, pork bellies, fish meal, cattle, broilers, eggs, hides, and wool.

Metals include copper, lead, mercury, platinum, palladium, aluminum, tin, silver, and zinc, of which silver and copper are the only ones that receive any public attention to speak of. Zinc, for instance, traded all of three contracts in 1970, nickel 382, and palladium 757. Aluminum traded two contracts. Such exceedingly thin markets are of little value to the hedger who cannot find the buyer or seller he needs and have little attraction to the speculator who must be able to control his position with a phone call. Volume is the Catch-22 of commodities. Those markets which have a lot of volume serve their customers well and get a lot of volume.

A fourth category includes *plant products* such as cocoa, coffee, tomato paste, cotton, orange juice concentrate, Maine potatoes, Idaho potatoes, rubber, sugar, apples, pepper, molasses, cottonseed oil, plywood, and lumber. Some of these markets are quite lively while others do little business.

FIGURE 56

PRICE DIFFERENCE CHART

Lumber prices have long been prominent among the uncertainties associated with the forest products industries. The listing of lumber futures by the Chicago Mercantile Exchange provided the industry with a new management tool with regard to prices paid and received and level of profitability.

While hedging can provide a profit or reduce or eliminate a financial loss due to price changes, careful consideration must be given to the timing of hedges and the grade and species of lumber hedged. Because the futures contract calls for delivery of Hem Fir 2 x 4s, any producer, wholesaler or user of lumber must know his own cost and price situation in relation to the futures contract.

To help you determine more effectively whether you should consider using the futures market, the Chicago Mercantile Exchange has prepared this form.

In using the futures markets you will be concerned primarily with two price differences. 1) You will be concerned with the price difference between the cash and the futures prices and how much that difference changes. This is the futures-cash basis. 2) You will be concerned with the price difference between the cash prices of Hemfir and and the lumber you buy or sell. This we refer to as a cash basis and is important for historical review in order to anticipate price differences more accurately. It is easier to project changes in price differences, than to forecast price movements.

As an example, during 1969, k.d. White Spruce 2 x 4s dropped from $143 MBF in Jan. to $99 MBF in Dec., a $44 price move. At the

same time, *White Fir 2 x 4s dropped from $124 MBF to $80 MBF, also a $44 price move. Therefore, although there was a $44 price move, there was no change in the cash basis, in this case, the difference between the White Spruce and White Fir cash prices.

During the same year, k.d. Douglas Fir dropped $33 MBF while k.d. White Fir cash prices plummeted $44 MBF, a $11 MBF change in the cash basis.

To get a brief idea of a historical comparison, in 1968 the cash basis between White Spruce and White Fir changed $1 from Jan. to Dec. although there were price moves on the rising side of $35. The cash basis change between Douglas Fir and White Fir in 1968 was $4, although Douglas Fir prices moved up $31 MBF.

The record form on the other side provides you with an easy way to keep a running record of futures prices, cash prices and the futures-cash basis and how it relates historically. You have your prices for the past two years. To get the futures prices, ask your commodity futures broker. The less the basis changes between the futures prices and your prices, the more effective a hedge will be. Remember, you hedge to protect yourself against major adverse price moves, especially when the outlook is uncertain and you cannot afford a loss.

With that fundamental data, you can then determine how effective a hedge might be for you.

The original futures contract called for White Fir 2 x 4s, but was changed to Hemfir in 1971 to follow industry interpretations.

Source: Chicago Mercantile Exchange.

NEW CONTRACTS

New markets will come into existence as the needs of industry change, industry leaders become more sophisticated in their marketings, and the advantages of present futures markets become more widely known. In 1970, the New York Cotton Exchange began trading in tomato paste, which will be traded in contracts for delivery in January, March, May, September, and November. In 1968, California which produces 80 percent of the nation's tomato crop saw prices drop from a high of 32 cents per solid pound to 18 cents. Farmers and processors are in no position to absorb this kind of fluctuation and should show quick interest in the chance to hedge the risk onto speculators. A brand new exchange called the West Coast Commodity Exchange opened in 1970 to do business in copper, silver, cocoa, and sugar. Milo (a feed grain), silver coins minted prior to 1965, and a changed plywood contract are new. Contracts for coconut oil, and 2 x 4 lumber, and stock options are also new to be traded. These contracts have nothing in common except that they are in supply that cannot be controlled, have sufficient price fluctuation to attract speculators, and an industry that wants to hedge its bets. (See Fig. 57, p. 98.)

Some of these offerings will fail to attract enough interest to get going. Open interest is self-feeding, high volume makes the market function well, and a well-functioning market attracts heavy use. If the need is great enough they will make it. Some will die out as palladium and steers are presently in the process. Frozen shrimp, short ribs, and lard were all traded at one time in Chicago but now only lard remains as refrigeration has allowed shrimp and the ribs to be kept long enough to vary supply into varying demand. With the ability to hold stocks the need of hedging died out and the markets died. New York and St. Louis had important wheat futures markets at one time but their business declined as changes in the wheat trade and improved communications reduced the special advantages of hedging those markets rather than in Chicago where the great volume lowers the hedging cost. (See Fig. 58, p. 99.)

FIGURE 57

SUMMARY OF INTERCOMMODITY COMPARISONS, YEARS BEGINNING JULY 1961-62 TO 1970-71

Average open interest (based on average number of contracts open at end of month), by commodity, all markets combined

Commodity	1970-71	1969-70	1968-69	1967-68	1966-67	1965-66	1964-65	1963-64	1962-63	1961-62
					Number of contracts					
Wheat	25,050	26,612	42,986	48,168	42,402	32,043	24,258	25,691	29,984	33,994
Corn	66,332	40,364	49,261	46,952	65,142	33,568	31,741	25,334	24,620	38,429
Oats	2,971	5,119	4,268	2,814	5,018	3,223	4,589	5,733	6,762	11,756
Rye	46	581	1,014	1,708	2,013	2,155	1,815	2,921	3,132	6,449
Barley	0	0	0	0	0	0	0	3	2	0
Flaxseed	0	0	0	0	0	1	2	17	101	190
Rice	0	0	0	0	0	0	1	1	0	0
Grain sorghums	199	69	181	184	712	0	0	48	8	11
Soybeans	57,400	38,331	33,386	34,908	42,927	47,843	59,779	51,109	34,005	31,557
Soybean meal	25,326	21,555	15,012	11,390	13,050	12,037	12,445	10,962	9,181	8,602
Soybean oil	30,704	26,923	16,089	10,789	15,135	17,336	17,454	18,424	15,200	9,672
Lard	---	---	---	---	---	---	---	---	39	490
Cottonseed oil	12	0	5	27	224	435	1,357	3,743	4,880	2,667
Cottonseed meal	0	0	0	0	0	0	3	2	4	2
Millfeeds	---	---	---	---	---	---	---	---	34	43
Cotton	5,118	2,290	5,812	5,691	247	205	384	1,233	2,819	4,133
Wool	460	805	1,422	2,217	2,727	4,236	1,958	2,675	3,247	7,548
Wool tops	6	19	17	21	25	34	32	58	141	263
Butter	0	2	1	1	228	30	0	0	0	0
Eggs, shell	5,529	6,982	4,119	1,208	1,152	2,252	1,369	2,509	4,506	5,832
Eggs, frozen	2	5	125	98	132	508	180	968	1,038	1,991
Potatoes	10,686	12,162	16,771	14,702	15,488	13,429	13,244	6,325	7,462	9,870
Frozen concentrated orange juice	4,303	3,317	5,619	3,660	556	---	---	---	---	---
Cattle	13,657	22,210	20,271	18,334	17,936	6,790	1,945	---	---	---
Frozen boneless beef	133	285	---	---	---	---	---	---	---	---
Hides	0	10	116	310	295	331	321	559	296	335
Hogs, live	5,634	3,377	732	731	533	689	---	---	---	---
Frozen pork bellies	17,236	18,445	17,754	15,412	12,086	11,100	6,295	862	73	98
Frozen skinned hams	17	27	15	23	15	20	16	37	---	---
Total	270,821	229,490	234,976	219,348	238,043	188,265	179,188	159,214	147,534	173,932

Source: U.S. Department of Agriculture, Commodity Exchange Authority.

FIGURE 58

ROGER W. GRAY

THE CHARACTERISTIC BIAS IN SOME THIN FUTURES MARKETS

Like a trail through dense undergrowth, a market comes into being only through use, and is improved through increased use. The little used trail, because time and energy are wasted in locating or negotiating it, is more costly to use than the well trodden path. One may pay too much to the guide on a difficult trail to justify the passage; by the same token the payment to the factotum on a thin market may outweigh the advantage of its use. One may, of course learn the trail (or market characteristics) himself; but this too entails a cost.

As the flow of traffic increases, undergrowth is killed, obstacles are moved aside, circumvented, or simply worn away; traffic itself provides an added safety factor; and a trail, in short, becomes more clearly marked and easily traversed. The trail may come to be maintained or artificially improved, as through paving, and traffic over it regulated. Yet should much of its traffic abandon it, a cumulative reversal of the development process is likely to ensue. Maintenance may become slipshod, leading to a further decline in traffic; and in time the trail may be completely abandoned, soon thereafter to disappear.

Most of the literature on the economics of futures markets has pertained to well-developed, thriving markets—especially those for the grains and cotton, the modern turnpikes of our metaphor. These were at one time thin markets, but we lack adequate data for a thorough study of the wheat, corn, or cotton futures markets during their early stages of growth nearly a century ago. Meanwhile other futures markets have been developed, some of them quite recently, and an increasing amount of information has become available about them. Some of these, for examples the soybean and cocoa markets, have recently grown to such proportions that the designation "thin market" is no longer applicable; indeed, these may be the two most thriving markets today. Other markets, after showing promise, have fallen into disuse. The bran and the shorts markets were abandoned by their erstwhile users. The butter market fell a victim of government pricing policies; the government did not eliminate the road, but provided an irresistable alternative which led to its abandonment—a fate which has nearly befallen the cotton futures markets, and has reduced traffic on a number of others. The onion futures market, in contrast, is one which the Congress has closed, without providing any alternative other than the treacherous path which this route superseded.[1]

[1] Public Law 85–839 makes it a misdemeanor to trade in onion futures.

Source: Food Research Institute Studies, Stanford University, Vol. 1, No. 3.

7

HOW THE BIG BOYS DO IT

It is often thought, with good reason, that the big boys have all the advantages in trading commodities. This is true. General Mills, Hershey, Dreyfus, Continental, and Cargill deal in millions of tons of commodities each year. They buy them, use them, store them, export them, and contract sales ahead of their holdings; and they do not handle these commodities in a vacuum. A drop of one penny on a holding of a million bushels of wheat is a loss of $10,000. A drop of a dime can cost a grain merchant $100,000. These companies each hold millions of bushels at any given time, and they stand to be badly hurt by a fluctuating market.

These companies are specialists in what is going on in the cash markets but rarely attempt to predict what will happen even in the near future. Prediction entails risks and the quantities of goods these companies handle simply make such risks untenable. It is the failure of these companies and others to make viable marketing predictions that led to the future markets. All these companies maintain large staffs of commodities experts, but *the whole function of their staffs is to eliminate risk inherent in commodity trading, not to profit from it.* If an exporter can find a buyer in Belgium to take the grain he has bought in Syracuse, New York, at a price that

covers his handling and shipping costs, he knows he has a profit. He is not speculating. If he has not yet bought the grain, or not yet found a buyer, he will use the futures markets to keep from speculating.

Trading cash commodities is fiercely competitive and profits are measured in fractions of a cent over millions of bushels of commodities. Cargill and Continental Grain share about 80 percent of the export trade originating in the United States and the efforts made by one to scoop the other read like a spy novel. Behind a network of midnight meetings and secret contacts is the quiet unrelenting business of squeezing a profit out of a risky business. The backbone of both companies is made up of accountants and actuaries doing business over the telephone. Both Cargill and Continental are privately held, and no publicly held corporation has been able to successfully compete with them. Secrecy is too important for success in the cash commodity business and no public-held corporation can keep the secrets necessary to beat Continental into Romania when a large wheat order is to be made.

Cargill Grain Company headquarters are located in the Wayzeta suburb of Minneapolis in a large mansion built by a millionaire in the twenties who did not survive the great stock market crash. Offices are spread through the three stories of parlors, bedrooms, and closets in a network which might have pleased Franz Kafka. In this comfortable, lazy-looking atmosphere, some of the sharpest and trickiest dealings in the United States take place every day.

The ground floor of the mansion is dominated by what was originally a ball-room, now the seat of the different commodity desks. Around these desks are the people specializing in the buying and selling of commodities throughout the United States. Along one wall is the information complex of lights and figures similar to that in a well-equipped brokerage. The current cash price for each commodity is listed as well as the futures price of the various exchanges for the various trading months. Tickers and telephones manned by several operators line the front of this complex and these people supplement the automated information system through direct links with the exchange floors. A glass wall separates the traders from the board-room wall so that desk operators can check the board at any time but not be disturbed by the noise.

The ballroom itself contains around 50 desks where the bulk of the cash business and much of the hedging operation takes place. It is primarily a business of matching the buying of men in the field with the sales of other men as can be done, and hedging the balance on futures markets. There are three or four desks dealing in corn (the number varies) where men receive phone calls and wires constantly keeping track of how much corn the company owns at any given time and where it is located. They move back and forth constantly from their desks to the board to check prices and refer back across the phone to the man in the field. A basis book allows them to keep track of the proper price in a small town in Kansas in relation to the Chicago price. Normally a buyer in the country will simply bid "12 under" meaning that the corn will be taken at 12 cents less than the price of cash corn at the close in Chicago, although the buyer may call the corn desk at Cargill headquarters and get an exact quotation, in which case his call will send one of the men at the corn desks to the board.

Suppose that on one day, agents in the field buy 1.5 million bushels of corn, stored in elevators around the country. Sellers have contracted to deliver 500,000 bushels in Belgium in three months to be used as chicken feed. Cargill will probably ship grain from its elevators in New Orleans which are much closer to Gulf ports and may have to buy corn in the Midwest in order to fill the order. If the average price paid for the corn in the country was $1.27 a bushel and the corn was sold CIF Belgium for $1.42, Cargill knows it has 15 cents to cover the cost of shipping and handling the grain. If the price rises before the grain is bought and loaded onto barges, this 15 cents will dwindle but is covered by the cash corn hedge, held in elevators around the country. If the price of corn rises, Cargill will lose money on the corn it must buy and ship to Belgium, but it will pick up a windfall profit on the corn already bought and held.

For this day, the corn desk has a net long inventory of 1 million bushels of grain. This position will have to be held overnight if the futures market has already suspended trading for the day, although if the unprotected long position is large, futures hedging may have started in anticipation earlier in the day. If any new sales are to come in from Europe, they will come in early the next morning, due to time differentials, and corn traders will then enter their hedges in the futures market to cover any long or short balances left over from the previous day's trading. In the early morning of the following day, another 500,000 bushels of corn is sold, to be delivered in Rotterdam. The net long position of 500,000 bushels will be protected against price deterioration by a short sale of 100 contracts on the Chicago Board of Trade. These will be added to or lifted as cash dealings dictate over the coming days.

On another day, the corn desk receives a wire from New Delhi, indicating that the Indian government will buy 25 million bushels of corn for early spring delivery, to be paid for in dollars loaned to them by the U.S. Department of Agriculture for that purpose. Cargill salesmen are with Indian officials; can Cargill provide a quotation immediately? The desk men check the quotation board and find corn futures at $1.31 for September delivery, $1.37 for delivery in December, $1.40 for March, and $1.43 for May. Buying 25 million bushels of corn quickly without driving up the price too far is going to be difficult and a plan is quickly laid out. By spreading the buy orders over five corn contracts, the corn men expect to be able to fill the order on the futures market without driving the average price up more than about 2 cents. They should be able to purchase 25 million bushels on the futures market for an average cost of about $1.38. Of this, 5 million bushels

will be bought for May delivery which is too late to fill the sale in India, and when the market calms down after absorbing the large order, May options will be sold and an additional 5 million for March delivery bought.

Shipping schedules are quickly checked. The Suez Canal is closed and if the grain is shipped across the Atlantic, it will have to go around the Cape of Good Hope. An alternative plan would ship grain out of Seattle or Portland. A call is quickly made upstairs to see what shipping is available in both oceans, and if company-owned vessels are tied up for early spring, a cable may go to Greece or Norway seeking tentative offers for cargo space. Cost of shipping by rail is figured from various points in the country to Seattle, Portland, and New Orleans.

The New Orleans figure comes to $1.43 per bushel in elevators along the wharf. Shipping around the Horn will run about 11 cents per bushel, delivered in New Delhi. The Seattle figure is a penny cheaper but the price of corn in position for West Coast delivery could go up 5 cents while Chicago corn prices rose only a penny. The New Orleans route is chosen and a price of $1.58 is arrived at. This price covers $1.38 as the average cost of the corn per bushel, plus 7 cents covering transportation to New Orleans and brief storage, plus 11 cents transportation to New Delhi and 2 cents profit. The cable is returned to salesmen in India. *"Can sell 25,000,000 corn delivery early April stop $1.58 CIF New Delhi stop Cargill."*

If confirmation is received, the futures purchases will be made with extreme care. Phone operators in front of the quotation panel will probably remain in constant contact with Cargill's man on the floor of the Chicago Board of Trade. If the full 25 million bushels can be purchased at the $1.38 estimated average price, Cargill will make 2 cents per bushel on the transaction. This profit is guaranteed once the hedges are placed and amounts to a total of $500,000 on the trade. If the price creeps over $1.38, this guaranteed profit will be endangered, to the tune of $31,250 for every one-eighth cent rise. The final contracts will probably be bought at a higher price. Cargill is mostly interested in the cost of the *average* contract.

Buyers in the field will be immediately notified to pick up their purchases at prices up to 2 cents over current cash prices. For a brief period, Cargill cash buyers will have an edge on the competition, knowing that the price of corn is going to rise, and they will exploit this edge as fully as possible. During the time that it is shy the 25 million bushels it needs to fill the sale, it will keep the futures options and is willing to accept delivery against its short positions if necessary to get the needed grain. Most likely, this will not be necessary and the hedges will be lifted on the futures market as cash corn is bought. Over the spring, Cargill will accumulate the corn and move it to delivery points, slowly lifting its hedges. As it buys 50,000 bushels of the actual commodity, it will sell 10 contracts on the futures market. Ten contracts equals the 50,000 bushels held in warehouses that no longer need to be hedged. As long as the cash price and futures price stay in line, Cargill can pay any price for the cash corn it needs, taking profits from its hedge, if it must pay more for the corn than expected, and losing as much on its hedge as it makes by buying corn cheaper.

If the basis between cash corn and the futures contracts stays in line, Cargill is guaranteed $500,000 profit on the trade. If the basis spreads, it will make more. If the basis narrows, a $500,000 profit can disappear in a blink. The New Orleans route was chosen primarily because the basis between corn for Gulf port delivery holds more firmly with prices on the Chicago Board of Trade. West Coast corn promised a possible larger profit, but was judged too risky, as the hedge is less perfect. So long as basis remains constant—which it does—Cargill has its profit. Cargill does not care what happens to the price of corn it holds after the hedges have been lifted. It could find itself with a stock of 20 million bushels which drop in value, but as the sale is already contracted at a firm price, this grain is naturally hedged. Cargill is both long and short in the cash market and has no need of a futures hedge, once it has bought the corn to cover the sale.

The price of corn futures on the Chicago Board of Trade was driven up by the influx of buying pressure as Cargill placed its hedges. Twenty-five million bushels of corn are going to disappear from American elevators in the spring, and this new source of demand will change the supply and demand balance for cash corn. The futures price is a direct guess of the price of cash corn in the future when cash goes up the price in the corn pit of the Chicago Board of Trade goes up. When the public learns of the new trade, it may drive the option price a little higher, or let it sag a bit according to their opinion of the price effects of a new sale of 25 million bushels. Probably both will happen and the price will fluctuate, *but it will fluc-*

tuate somewhat more than it did before the sale. Had the sale been larger, the price would have been driven yet higher as Cargill placed its long hedges, and the price would fluctuate around this still higher price.

Big commercial producers and exporters have all the advantages in the cash market for many complex reasons. They have the advantage in the futures market for only one reason. They are dispassionate and go about their hedging with a businesslike approach. Cargill does not plan the buying of a grain elevator around the possible profit on a futures transaction. Short-term goals and operating expenses are not allowed to influence the use of their commodity capital. This money is an asset to them, like a ship, an elevator, a computer, or a company airplane. It is not cash; it is not thought of as cash or mixed with company cash. If the remodeling of an executive office were tied directly to the profit of a futures position, commodities traders working for the big exporters would do as poorly as do many public speculators.

The public speculator can be as dispassionate in his den, office, or garage, if he looks at his commodity playing as a game and the money in his margin account as an asset, but not as money. Money can buy a new car or pay the rent; margin can only buy commodities and judge how well the speculator is doing in the game. If margin is mixed up with household money, if a loss on January cocoa means no new car this year, the speculator cannot possibly play the rational game required and he cannot emulate the big commodity companies.

Part two
PRICING

8

CASH COMMODITY PRICING

In the delivery month, futures contracts must "go off" the board at price levels very close to those found in the cash markets for the same commodity in the city where the exchange is located. A contract of July wheat will go off within about 5 cents of the cash price of wheat in Chicago in July. October cotton will trade in its final days on the New York Cotton Exchange at a price very close to that at which raw cotton is selling on the New York wholesale markets. Every trade of a futures option throughout its trading life is made at a price which is simply the best current guess of the cash market price to come in the future.

Dealing with commodities on futures markets requires a good understanding of the various factors which determine prices on the cash market. These factors are called fundamentals, and traders often spend considerable amounts of time pouring over figures of farmers' planting intentions, spring calf drop, layer production, chicks hatched, and so forth, for the various commodities they follow. By far the most important source of fundamental information is the U.S. Department of Agriculture. The USDA keeps close track of farmers' intentions and market conditions in order to aid the farmer and supervise its various regulatory and support programs, and

prints its recommendations and projections in "situation reports" at regular intervals for each commodity. These reports list various figures which determine demand and supply for the commodity, compare figures with years past, and give prognostications for events to come. (See Fig. 59, p. 108.)

Classic demand and supply no longer closely describes pricing in the United States other than in agriculture. Today's farms have grown to become multimillion dollar businesses yet no farmer produces a significant enough proportion of the total production to have any personal control of supply or of the price he will receive for his produce. He must be content with the best price he can get from a market over which he has no control. Buyers of farm produce have similarly grown in size but still very few buyers can set prices effectively against supply and demand. The final price for farm goods is still largely set by how much stock is to be had and how many people want to have it; this is not true of any other significant sector of our economy. (See Fig. 60, p. 109.)

With restrictions, the cash price of a commodity will be as high as suppliers can set it and still account for all their produce and as low as buyers can force the price while still getting all the commodity they need to run their opera-

Feed Market News

GRAIN DIVISION　　**AGRICULTURAL MARKETING SERVICE**
UNITED STATES DEPARTMENT OF AGRICULTURE
Volume 56　　No. 4　　　　Independence, Missouri 64050

WEEKLY SUMMARY AND STATISTICS

January 24, 1973

FEEDSTUFFS MOSTLY HIGHER

Prices for most feed ingredients moved higher on the nations' markets during the week ended January 23. Wheat bulk millfeeds were the exception and prices moved generally lower. Demand for feedstuffs continued at good levels but below the volume of recent weeks. Confusion as to actual values of some ingredients, especially for soybean meal, continuing transportation problems and scarcity of offerings limited trade. Cattle feeds continue to move in good volume along with improving hog feed items and dairy feeds a strong mover. Poultry feeding improved slowly as producers margins teetered between small losses and small gains.

Soybean meal trade is sharply curtailed by confusion as to actual values, dearth of offerings from prime producers, wet beans which prevents manufacture of high protein meal, and dull demand for the 44 percent meal. Most trading is in resale material at mixed prices. Chicago quotes went down $2.50 per ton while other markets held firm or gained as much as $21.00 per ton. Cottonseed meal markets declined under slow demand and pressure from lower priced forward offerings. Declines range $4.50 at Memphis, $5.00 at Kansas City and Lubbock. Solvent linseed meal traded $1.00 higher at Minneapolis.

Meat meal and tankage prices moved sharply higher under strong feed mixer and export demand. Price increases ranged up to $37.50 at Minneapolis. Fish meal shortage continued and the scarcity of synthetic substitutes forced computers to put fish meal back into poultry rations. Prices moved mostly to $400.00 per ton with some scattered material available at lower prices on the West coast. Fishing continued very poor in domestic waters and Peruvian fishing scout boats reported not enough catch to resume operations.

Gluten feed sold steadily with good demand taking the moderate production. Gluten meal continued in tight supply, up $8.00 for the week and with a $6.00 advance announced for Wednesday. Brewers' dried grain prices moved up mostly $1.00 per ton. Distillers' dried grains advanced as much as $12.00 at Chicago as strong competition for the light offerings forced prices up.

Wheat bulk millfeeds came under pressure as some resale material was offered in a period of slack mixer demand and a steady milling schedule. Price declines ranged $6.00 at Kansas City to $10.00 at Buffalo. Rice bran traded up $1.50 at Louisiana mills but $4.00-5.00 lower at Arkansas and Texas mills. Yellow hominy feed came under pressure Chicago-east when lower corn markets in the East provided competition. West coast markets firmed after earlier weakness and prices closed steady to up $1.00 per ton.

Dehydrated alfalfa meal moved to market only an occasional car at a time. Price advances ranged up to $18.00 per ton at Buffalo. Traders reported some feeders importing material from Canada. Alfalfa center prices advanced $10.00 and some traders speculated prices could go $10.00-20.00 per ton higher. Some feed mixers became sellers as reduced formulation freed some contracted supplies. Sun-cured production was interrupted by thawing fields and prices held firmly or advanced $2.00 or more. Feeding cane blackstrap molasses met with strong buyer resistance to recent price advances. Some feedlots turned to corn and milo, reporting molasses now priced above feed grains. Kansas City buyers found material easier to buy, though still tight, and the average price moved 50¢ lower. Corn hydrol sold nominally steady.

Yellow corn traded mixed, up $2.50 at Kansas City, up 40¢ at Chicago and 70¢ per ton lower at Omaha. Barley traded generally 85¢ lower. Oats prices moved down $3.20 at Minneapolis and $5.70 lower at Chicago. Grain Sorghum sold up about $1.00 at Kansas City and Fort Worth.

Index Numbers With Comparisons			
Index (1967 = 100)	This week	Last week	Last year
Feedstuff Index	222.8	217.2	108.2
Feed Grain Index	126.1	125.0	97.6
Hog-Corn Ratio (Omaha)	21.7	20.8	20.5
Steer-Corn Ratio (Omaha)	27.4	25.8	29.2

Source: U.S. Department of Agriculture, Agricultural Marketing Service.

FIGURE 60
EXAMPLES OF CASH GRAIN PRICES AT VARIOUS POINTS IN THE UNITED STATES

CASH GRAIN PRICES
Cents per bushel except grain sorghum per cwt.

GRAINS	MARKETS	GRADE	1972 NOMINAL LOAN VALUE 1/ AT MATURITY	1-18-73 LESS STORAGE	Jan. 18, 1973	Jan. 11, 1973	Jan. 20, 1972	Dec. AVERAGE 2/ 1972
WHEAT	Kansas City	No. 1 Hard Winter (Ord. Prot.)	150	146	266	271	158-160	262
		No. 1 Hard Winter (13% Prot.)	154½	150½	267	271	165	265
	Houston	No. 1 Hard Winter (Ord. Prot.)	158	154	284	288-289	172-173	278
	Omaha	No. 1 Hard Winter (Ord. Prot.)	150	146	254-256	259-261	154-156	251
	Chicago	No. 2 Yellow Hard Winter	146	142	264	267	170	257
		No. 2 Soft Red Winter	146	142	266	269	170	260
	Toledo 6/	No. 2 Soft Red Winter	145	141	268	269	162	264
		No. 2 Soft White	145	141	268	269	160	264
	St. Louis	No. 2 Hard Winter	146	142	250	256	155-158	254
		No. 2 Soft Red Winter	146	142	264	269	155-158	259
	Minneapolis	No. 1 Dark No. Spring (Ord. Prot.)	163	158	239-240	240-241	157-159	232
		No. 1 Dark No. Spring (13% Prot.)	167½	162½	243	244	163	241
		No. 1 Dark No. Spring (15% Prot.)	173½	168½	242	244	176-177	242
		No. 1 H. Amber Durum	168	163	249-260	254-260	170-175	239
	Portland	No. 1 Soft White	148	143	278-280	283-284	156	278
		No. 1 Hard Winter (Ord. Prot.)	148	143	277-279	282	160-161	275
	Baltimore	No. 2 Soft Red Winter (garlicky)	155	151	244-245	246-248	157	240
RYE	Minneapolis	No. 2	113	109	111-115	111-115	101-105	115
CORN	Kansas City	No. 2 White	126	118	197-200	190-193	124-127	200
		No. 2 Yellow	126	118	170	160-164	123-130	164
	Omaha	No. 2 Yellow	120	112	148-150	148-158	120-128	149
	Chicago	No. 2 Yellow	125	117	158	158	123	157
		No. 3 Yellow	123	115	149-153	152-156	118-122	154
	Toledo 6/	No. 2 Yellow	125	117	132	140	114	160
	St. Louis	No. 2 Yellow	127	119	158	162	116-118	155
	Minneapolis	No. 2 Yellow	115	107	141-145	140-144	111-113	139
OATS	Kansas City	No. 2 White	75	72	100	105	76-87	102
	Chicago	No. 2 Extra Heavy White	72	69	96	98	80-81	101
	Toledo 6/	No. 2 Heavy White	75	72	100	101	82	109
	Minneapolis	No. 2 Extra Heavy White	69	65	92	89	68	91
BARLEY	Kansas City	No. 3	107	103	141-144	141-144	110-122	139
	Minneapolis	No. 3 or better Malting (Choice)	109	104	160	160	118-122	145
		No. 3 or better	109	104	126-146	126-142	100-114	127
	Portland	No. 2 Western 45 lbs.	117	111	184	184	119-120	166
	Stockton	No. 2 Western 46 lbs.	126	122	181-184	181-182	149-151	178
	Los Angeles	No. 2 Western 46 lbs.	129	125	188-191	190-192	157-160	188
GRAIN SORGHUM	Kansas City	No. 2 Yellow	208	194	308-313	303-305	205-207	288
	Texas 5/	No. 2 Yellow	—	-	305-310	295-300	210-215	298
	Los Angeles	No. 2 Yellow (NTFE) 3/	270	256	394-396	388-390	278-280	386
SOYBEANS	Chicago	No. 1 Yellow	247	240	454	432	313	413
	Toledo 6/	No. 1 Yellow	246	239	441	405	306	404
	Minneapolis	No. 1 Yellow	237	230	432	408	304	391
	Illinois Pts.	No. 1 Yellow 4/	237	230	453-460	426-429	306-310	407
FLAXSEED	Minneapolis	No. 1	281	276	395	385	270	341

1/ Nominal loan values indicated by adjusting loan rates of tributary counties for Uniform Grain Storage Agreement charges and approximate transportation costs.
2/ Average of daily prices.
3/ Non-transit from the East.
4/ Prices paid by Central Illinois processors. Truck prices starting November 2, 1972.
5/ Texas High Plains, F.O.B. elevator.
6/ All Toledo prices are truck delivered to elevator beginning January 4, 1973.

Source: U.S. Department of Agriculture, Agricultural Marketing Service.

tions. In the course of the year, price will adjust to assure that all of the commodity finds a home somewhere. Restrictions of pure demand and supply pricing are regulated by the Department of Agriculture, largely in the form of price floors designed to protect the farmer against too low a price for his production. These floors are administered in a number of ways, through planting restrictions on supply, loan levels, and outright purchase.

SUPPLY DETERMINANTS

Total supply breaks down into three sections, which, added together, will give the total amount of the commodity to be disposed of over the year. This figure can be compared to years past, and when compared to projected demand, provides a basis for estimating cash prices in the near future. The three sources of supply are: (1) carryover from previous years; (2) farmer's planting intentions, the total crop to be available; and (3) government offerings. Government offerings are set in price by a formula based on support prices, rather than on the market price, and significantly alter supply only if the market price rises sufficiently to make the government offerings attractive to buyers looking for merchandise. For commodities grown in the United States, situation reports neatly sum all of the above information in a manner readily understood by the student of fundamentals. (See Fig. 61 below.)

Changes in projected supply occur throughout the year and will, of course, affect the futures price which attempts to forecast the cash price in an altered supply and demand market. "Farmers' planting intentions" will later be released as "total estimated acreage" nor-

FIGURE 61

OATS

World Production of Oats   In Thousands of Metric Tons[3]

Crop Year	United States	Canada	Argentina	Australia	Turkey	U.S.S.R.	W. Germany	Spain	Netherlands	Denmark	France	Sweden	Un. King.	Poland	World Total
1959	1,050	418	68	59	28	750	140	39	22	39	194	55	153	172	3,710
1960	1,153	456	58	95	35	750	150	30	27	47	188	81	144	190	3,955
1961	1,010	284	49	69	30	600	132	34	30	47	179	93	128	203	3,410
1962	1,012	494	34	86	31	385	161	35	32	42	178	75	122	189	3,375
1963	966	453	64	85	33	255	160	32	29	46	198	81	101	195	3,180
1964	852	357	55	88	29	270	159	26	29	57	159	100	93	154	2,890
1965–6	927	415	33	73	31	317	141	24	25	54	173	92	85	173	2,995
1966–7	801	375	37	134	31	517	161	29	25	60	178	80	77	184	3,147
1967–8	789	304	48	50	33	661	187	34	25	62	192	96	96	194	3,255
1968–9[3]	13,633	5,591	490	1,710	450	9,700	2,893	522	318	863	2,528	1,523	1,225	2,891	50,800
1969–0	13,787	5,728	425	1,678	468	10,700	2,976	533	336	765	2,309	1,129	1,319	3,063	51,761
1970–1[1]	13,190	5,673	360	1,613	415	11,400	2,484	409	201	631	2,070	1,685	1,233	3,209	50,868
1971–2[2]	12,712	5,817	450	1,296	450	11,400	3,037	577	201	704	2,500	1,781	1,369	3,205	52,465
1972–3															

1 Preliminary.   2 Estimated.   3 Data prior to 1968–9 are in MILLIONS OF BUSHELS.
Source: Foreign Agricultural Service, U.S.D.A.

Source: Commodity Research Bureau, Inc.

mally with some adjustment as farmers changed their minds. Right after harvest, this figure will be encompassed in "stocks in all positions," and give a yet more accurate picture of total supply for the coming year. These adjustments are again spelled out in the USDA situation reports for each commodity. Other factors which will affect supply are found in the daily news. These include weather, disease, and the world situation as it affects individual commodities. (See Fig. 62, p. 112.)

Ideal weather conditions exist for each agricultural commodity and any trader quickly learns what to look for in the evening national weather report. Soybeans flower in summer and if temperatures are too high or humidity too low through the Midwest, fewer blooms will develop and the crop size will be lowered. Ample rainfall will persuade the farmers to wait while the plants pick up the added moisture—making the harvest later and determining whether the September soybean contracts will reflect new crop or old crop prices. Winter wheat is planted and sprouts in the fall, lays dormant under the snow, to be harvested in the spring and early summer. The best yields are produced when soil moisture level is 15-18 percent throughout germination, and this figure may drop to no less than 9 percent after germination without damaging the crop. After full structural growth, temperatures in the 80-100° F. range help to firm the kernels and mature the crop. Relative humidity below 50 percent will raise the quality of the crop by lowering the risk of rot in storage.

Such parameters, of course, exist for weather conditions of each agricultural commodity and the trader must learn

the conditions that will lead to bonus crops and low prices, and those which will damage the crop but raise the price per unit. As a practical matter, no trader need hang on the news each day to see that supplies of the commodity he trades are not damaged. Droughts take time to do their damage and wet corn will not alter government offerings until the following year when the Commodity Credit Corporation (CCC) finds itself holding stockpiles of corn which are in danger of rotting, long after the news is known. Commodity letters received by the trader and his broker will keep the trader well appraised of weather conditions and spell out their significance for the futures market.

World conditions will affect supply in the event of poor competing crops in other countries. Fall 1972 wheat prices were at extremely high levels both on cash and futures markets due to poor Russian crops and the sale of 400 million bushels to the Russians to be delivered over the coming year. Other world crop conditions will affect supply of competing products such as sunflower oil, olive oil, and various fish oils that directly compete with the high-protein soybean oil produced in the United States. Again, it takes little time for the student of the fats and oils situation to get a good feel of world fats conditions and newsletters will keep him appraised of expected changes in current price structures.

INTERCOMMODITY RELATIONSHIPS

Any commodity which comes from an animal will be affected by changes in the feed complex that feeds the animal before it is slaughtered. High-priced corn will eventually result in high-priced hogs

FIGURE 62
EXAMPLE OF STOCKS IN ALL POSITIONS

stocks of grains

In All Positions

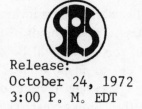

Release:
October 24, 1972
3:00 P. M. EDT

FEED GRAIN STOCKS UP -- WHEAT SLIGHTLY LOWER

Total stocks of the four feed grains (corn, oats, barley, and sorghum) on October 1, 1972 amounted to 61.6 million tons, 23 percent more than the 50.2 million tons a year earlier, according to the Crop Reporting Board. Large increases were noted in corn and sorghum grain while oats and barley were down moderately.

Stocks of all wheat were slightly below a year earlier and durum stocks were down 10 percent. Rye stocks were 4 percent lower and flaxseed 45 percent under a year ago.

All wheat in storage on October 1 totaled 1,879 million bushels, slightly below the 1,881 million of a year earlier but 5 percent above October 1, 1970. Farm holdings of 739 million were down 11 percent from the record high stocks of a year earlier, more than offsetting a 9-percent increase in off-farm stocks. Disappearance from all storage positions during July-September is indicated at 545 million bushels, compared with 489 million a year earlier. The Commodity Credit Corporation owned 295 million bushels of the total wheat stocks and had loans outstanding on an additional 329 million.

Durum wheat stocks in all positions on October 1 totaled 116.2 million bushels, nearly 10 percent less than a year earlier but 10 percent more than 2 years ago. Farm holdings of 91.5 million were 10 percent less than October 1, 1971 and off-farm stocks of 24.7 million were down 9 percent. Disappearance during July-September 1972 is indicated at 27.4 million, compared with 13.1 million a year earlier and 22.2 million 2 years ago.

Rye stocks in all storage positions on October 1 totaled 63.0 million bushels, 4 percent less than a year earlier but 28 percent above October 1, 1970. Off-farm stocks, at 40.3 million bushels, were 11 percent greater than a year earlier but farm stocks were down 22 percent. Indicated disappearance during July-September was 13.8 million bushels, compared with 13.4 million a year earlier. The Commodity Credit Corporation owned 33.3 million bushels of the total rye stocks and had loans outstanding on 11.8 million.

UNITED STATES DEPARTMENT OF AGRICULTURE
STATISTICAL REPORTING SERVICE   CROP REPORTING BOARD
GrLg 11-1 (10-72)   WASHINGTON, D.C. 20250

Source: U.S. Department of Agriculture, Crop Reporting Board.

and a lowering in the number of pigs farrowed. Fewer hogs brought to market will result in a lowered supply of pork bellies which are traded on their own futures market. Commodities can be related to other commodities in three different ways and examples of all three are traded on futures markets.

Some commodities are part of larger markets so that increased supplies of a competing product is essentially the same as an increase in the supply of the commodity. Soybean oil is in direct competition to other digestible high-protein fats and increases in olive production in the Mediterranean will tend to lower the price of soybean oil as though more beans had been grown. Soybean meal is used as animal feed, along with corn, rye, oats, milo, and so on, and as any one of these feeds increases in supply, it will affect the market for the other feeds. The overall feed market is viewed by the USDA in the *Feed Situation* report.

Some commodities are direct by-products of other commodities, such as pork bellies and hogs from which they are cut. The supply of hogs will be determined by the demand for pork, hams, and so forth, and the cost of feed. Pork bellies which eventually become bacon come two from each hog and the supply of hogs will directly determine the supply of pork bellies. The trader studying the supply of pork bellies, looks immediately to the hogs' situation, then to the feeds which will feed them. Hides are traded on the New York Commodity Exchange and the trader wishing to take a position in hides must look to the upcoming slaughter of cattle. (See Fig. 63 opposite.)

A third category of interrelated com-

FIGURE 63

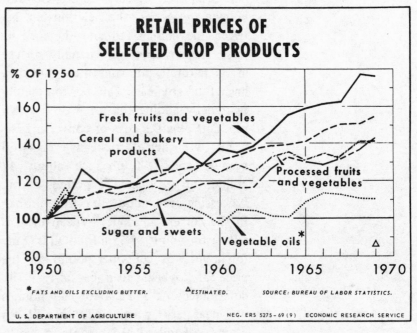

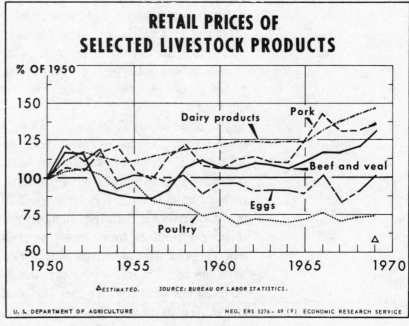

Source: U.S. Department of Agriculture, Economic Research Service.

modities might consist of those semi-processed goods which are directly dependent on other commodities. Rather than being by-products as the previous category, these may account for the entire demand for the unprocessed original crop. The hog-corn ratio is the best known, reflecting the relationship between the animal fed and the feed he eats. The soybean has virtually no use in its natural state and the value of a bushel of soybeans can be completely figured by adding the price of the two products plus the cost of converting the beans. A bushel of soybeans weighs 60 pounds and will produce about 47 pounds of meal and 11 pounds of oil. Processing costs about 30 cents a bushel. In the current market, soybean meal is selling for about $125 a ton. Oil is going for about 9.50 cents per pound and the price of soybeans can be fairly easily determined. At $125 a ton, 47 pounds of meal are worth $2.93¾. Eleven pounds of oil at 9.50 cents is worth $1.04½. Added together, the gross revenue to the soybean crusher from a bushel of beans is $3.98¼; he must have 30 cents per bushel to cover the cost of his operation and can pay no more than $3.68¼ for his beans. (See Fig. 64 opposite.)

The price of soybeans can go up only if the price of oil or meal goes up enough to allow the crusher to pay more. It cannot drop substantially below $3.68 without holding out a very large windfall profit to crushers, causing them to run their operations 24 hours a day or open new facilities. The speculator who would trade soybeans must look to supplies of beans along with the demand for meal and oil. To figure supplies of oil he must look to competing products in digestible oils. Meal must be compared with other supplies of feed stock.

DEMAND DETERMINANTS

Factors of demand for each commodity are bunched together in the situation reports under the classification "disappearance." "Disappearance" refers to all the individual sales made on cash markets, regardless of the disposition of the commodity. It may be eaten, processed, dumped, given away under a government program, or exported. "Disappearance" is easily compared to total supply and to disappearance in previous years to judge the demand and supply conditions to come. Will there be a great excess in the near future? Is the nation using up its supplies too quickly? This information is used to form the base price found in the newspapers as the current quote for the commodity. Changes in disappearance will change with new sources of demand. (See Fig. 65, p. 116.)

While supply changes with farmers' opinions before planting and weather after the crop is in the ground, new demand factors change daily with all kinds of conditions. While the trader will find most supply information in USDA bulletins, demand changes make national news and are felt immediately in the cash and futures markets. Longshoremen's strikes, railway walkouts, and large grain exports resulting from Henry Kissinger's secret travels will all affect the market by altering demand or the ability of suppliers to get their goods to market.

Particularly in livestock, demand can act as a function of disposable income. As individual incomes go up, the market will demand more high-priced beef in

FIGURE 64

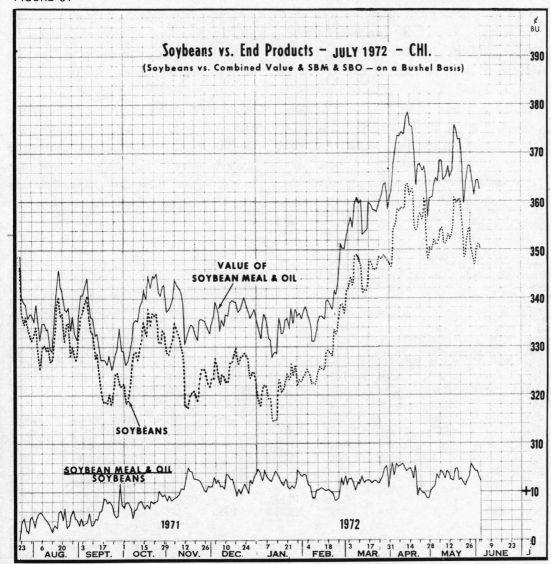

Soybeans vs. End Products – JULY 1972 – CHI.
(Soybeans vs. Combined Value & SBM & SBO – on a Bushel Basis)

VALUE OF
SOYBEAN MEAL & OIL

SOYBEANS

SOYBEAN MEAL & OIL
SOYBEANS

1971   1972

Source: Commodity Research Bureau, Inc.

place of relatively cheaper pork, chicken, and fish. The result of lowered disposable income will tend to be increased demand for pork in place of beef. But unlike shipping strikes and world summits, recessions and booms take time to develop and make themselves felt in overall demand for agricultural products, and the trader in livestock must make his judgment of the overall economy a year in advance.

Demand and supply pricing is extremely complex, made up of minutiae from all parts of the economy all over the world and a trader can easily snow himself down in tables and logarithms before he realizes that of all the complexity, only a few fundamentals are changing at any given time. The trader need not know all the factors that go to make up price, but only those that are unusual or likely to change. To compare this year's crop size and disappearance with last year's, he need really only know the significant unusual factors as understood and explained in newsletters describing the general makeup of a market. The trader really needs only to know the factors which set the tone for the current market. Is the price higher than usual? Why? His job is made easier by a series of price floors and ceilings and other restrictions placed on the free market by USDA policy.

GOVERNMENT PROGRAMS

Tampering with a supply and demand market has proven to be extremely difficult and government programs are in flux just about as rapidly as other conditions which make up the total agricultural complex. When the Department of Agriculture attempted to limit surplus production by restricting the acreage planted, farmers gave more care to the acres they did plant, bringing supply back up to old levels. Changes

FIGURE 65

Supply and Distribution of American Cotton in the United States   In Thousands of Running Bales

Crop Year	At Mills	Public Ware-houses	Farms & in Transit	Total Carry-over	Govern-ment Stock	"Free" Stock	Pro-duction[1]	Season Supply	Consump-tion	De-stroyed[3]	Net Ex-ports	Total Season Distri-bution
1959	1,069	7,553	220	8,843	7,094	1,749	14,830	23,673	8,918	50	7,182	16,150
1960	1,390	5,919	215	7,523	5,055	2,468	14,532	22,055	8,186	50	6,632	14,868
1961	1,886	4,754	490	7,187	1,503	5,684	14,495	21,682	8,844	134	4,915	13,893
1962	1,504	6,095	190	7,789	4,707	3,082	15,051	22,840	8,316	50	3,351	11,717
1963	1,196	9,647	280	11,123	8,230	2,893	15,404	26,527	8,509	50	5,662	14,221
1964–5	1,120	10,916	270	12,306	10,437	1,869	15,249	27,555	9,081	191	4,060	13,332
1965–6	1,472	12,521	230	14,223	11,689	2,534	14,975	29,198	9,405	50	2,942	12,397
1966–7	1,339	15,274	188	16,801	12,356	4,445	9,851	26,652	9,398	110	4,669	14,177
1967–8	1,757	10,318	400	12,475	5,829	6,646	7,280	19,755	8,886	261	4,206	13,353
1968–9	1,825	4,277	300	6,402	207	6,195	11,035	17,437	8,167	50	2,731	10,948
1969–0	1,623	4,466	400	6,489	2,911	3,578	10,013	16,502	7,950	50	2,769	10,769
1970–1	1,411	3,962	360	5,733	3,035	2,698	10,331	16,064	8,037	50	3,740	11,827
1971–2[2]	1,630	2,207	400	4,237	314	3,923	10,562	14,799	8,070	50	2,900	11,020
1972–3[4]				3,779								

[1] Includes city crop.   [2] Preliminary.   [3] Includes adjustment items, if any.   [4] Estimate.   *Source: New York Cotton Exchange*

Source: Commodity Research Bureau, Inc.

in government policy can be expected literally with every session of Congress and new legislation will continue to have profound influence on the commodity markets. The intended effect of government policy is to prevent large surpluses while keeping farmer income at some percentage of parity with a previous base period. If surpluses grow, or farmer income either jumps or drops radically, changes in programs and their administration can be expected.

Changes in government programs are usually the result of pressure on Congress when someone is either making too much or too little money and Congress feels compelled to react.

In the past, the majority of changes have been a matter of tinkering with the current system, with a total revamping of the system about every 10 years. The framework of the present system is given below, although changes in loan rates, parity, and surplus disposal can be expected from time to time.

Parity is the theoretical formula, attempting to keep current farm prices "on par" with nonagricultural prices as they were in some base period. Nonagricultural prices used in determining parity include a sample of all the costs incurred by the farmer in running his farm or maintaining his household, such as labor, real estate prices, taxes, machinery, and clothing. If in the base period, 1910-19, a farmer could buy a suit of clothes with his return from 30 bushels of wheat, and if he can still do so, farm prices are said to be at full parity. In fact, farm efficiency has increased more rapidly than efficiency in other parts of the economy, and as farmer production has increased, parity has been allowed to slip somewhat.

Parity is now maintained at 75-90 percent for basic crops (wheat, corn, cotton, rice, tobacco, and peanuts) and 60-90 percent for nonbasic crops (wool, mohair, milk, butterfat, honey, and tung nuts). As farmer income falls or grows relative to nonagricultural prices, adjustments in parity formula can be expected from the Department of Agriculture. As parity is enforced through the various programs by which the USDA supports farm prices, changes will be felt in these programs as the effect of parity slippage.

Government price support programs break into two categories: (1) direct purchase of the farmer's crop or subsidy making up the difference between the market price and the pegged parity price (loan rate, direct purchases, incentive payment plans, subsidized exports), and (2) payments to farmers for reducing production (the New Deal, AAA, the Soil Bank and Land Diversion Payments). Payments to farmers for reducing production are of little immediate practical importance to the speculator (although they are, of course, to the farmer). The speculator will find their effect in "Farmer's Planning Intentions" and the total size of the crop. The speculator deals in terms of the total actual crop planted or harvested and need not be overly concerned with the number of acres diverted into other crops or left fallow. Outright purchase and loan rates, however, simply change the ownership of grain which is produced and harvested, and this grain finds its way off the cash markets and back on again, affecting prices. (See Fig. 66, p. 118.)

The loan program is the most effective government policy for supporting farm prices and has the most profound effect on the cash and futures markets. Before planting has begun, the Department of Agriculture will announce its "loan rate" for each commodity under the program. Farmers know this to be the minimum price they will have to accept for their produce and can plan their crops accordingly. The 1972 loan rate for wheat is set at $1.25 a bushel. At harvest, the farmer can "borrow" this amount from the Commodity Credit Corporation (an administrative wing of the Department of Agriculture) if the cash market price is near $1.25 or below this amount. In order to qualify for the loan, he must have his crop in elevators which have been inspected and approved by the CCC. The money he receives from the CCC is secured by the stored grain, and the farmer can use it to pay the machinery rental costs, labor, and so forth, that he has run up over harvest and any other bank loans he may have outstanding, which are normally due soon after harvest.

The farmer has until January 31, following harvest to place most grains under loan (May 31 for corn, April 30 for cotton) and any time he does so he has secured an effective bottom price for his crop. Two months after the cutoff date for making loans (which would be March 31 for most grains) the CCC owns the wheat and the farmer keeps the loaned money. He has no further obligation to the CCC. At any time before March 31, the farmer may repay the loan and take possession of the grain to sell on the cash market. If he takes repossession, he must pay storage costs for the time the grain was in elevators, unless he stored it in approved elevators on his own farm. The loan rate thus forms an effective floor to the price of commodities. If the cash price does not rise above the loan rate, by enough to cover storage and red tape costs to the farmer, the farmer will simply default on his loan and let the CCC have the wheat effectively keeping the grain off the market.

The loan can be pegged at $1.25 (it can vary each year depending on the rate set for that year) and the farmer may receive less than this amount reflecting country basis. This loan value often sets an effective floor on how low the cash and futures market will decline since a farmer who qualifies for the loan program will simply sell his crops to the government at the loan rate whenever the free market is paying less. However, not all farmers qualify for government loans since they did not comply with acreage or other program restrictions. When this nonloan supply is sold on the open market it can (and often has) forced both futures and cash prices below the equivalent Chicago govern-

FIGURE 66

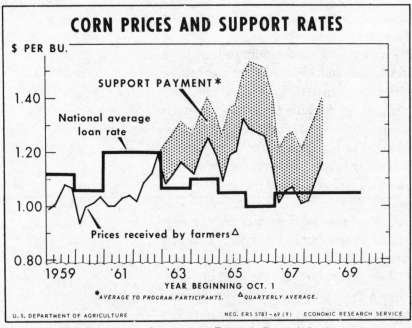

Source: U.S. Department of Agriculture, Economic Research Service.

ment loan rate. Thus the floor is not perfect and the market price can drop below the loan floor by small amounts, but it will not drop far. Especially immediately after harvest, there simply may not be enough storage elevators to go around, which will force some grain onto the market at any price it can obtain, for the CCC will not loan money on grain that is not properly stored in inspected elevators. Also the cash market price must drop below the loan rate to entice some farmers to go through the red tape and charges connected with the loan. Some misjudgment of market price can occur after the final day for taking the CCC loan, which means some unprotected grain may make it to market even at rates below the loan rate. Finally, some hedging activity will take place on the futures markets regardless of price level; if this hedging is net short in the normal pattern, it can force futures prices below the loan rate on near months immediately after harvest. (See Fig. 67 opposite.)

Outright government purchases are similar in effect and execution to the loan program. The farmer may contract to sell certain quantities of his produce to the CCC at a pegged price, which is usually the same as the loan rate and deliver or not deliver according to whether he can get a better price somewhere else. Under the purchase program, the farmer does not receive his money until he relinquishes the grain and gives up all right to take it back, and storage becomes the responsibility of the CCC.

Occasionally the Department of Agriculture will announce direct purchases on the cash market of commodities whose prices have fallen too low. Such purchases help to buoy up the market

and are announced several weeks in advance. These are looked at simply as new demand purchases taking place in a low-priced market. This type of support is usually limited to sporadic entries into such markets as the butter, milk, cottonseed, and cheese. The produce purchased is then given away in such programs as the School Lunch Program.

Other price support programs are designed to help the movement of U.S. surpluses overseas. The Department of Agriculture makes direct subsidies to exporters when domestic prices rise above world prices, which is most of the time. Rather than let huge surpluses build up, overwhelming the cash markets and storage facilities, the Department of Agriculture will pay the difference between the domestic and world prices, allowing exporters to do business in the world markets. Under Public Law 480,

FIGURE 67

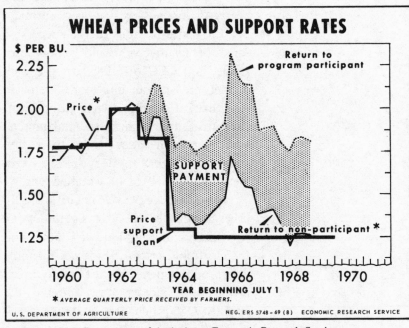

Source: U.S. Department of Agriculture, Economic Research Service.

the CCC can give its stocks of commodities to needy nations, use them for barter at less than their total worth, or sell them on long-term loans. When the goods exported come directly from CCC stocks, no effect is felt on the cash or futures markets, as these stocks were not competing with "free" stocks and had no price effect. Public Law 480 does allow the CCC, however, to make loans in dollars to foreign nations, with the stipulation that the money be spent on specific commodities, which are then purchased on cash markets in this country. Such purchase arrangements have in the past accounted for over half our exports of edible oils.

GOVERNMENT DISPOSAL

While government purchase and loan programs form a rough but effective floor under commodity prices, government disposal forms a much simpler and more effective ceiling to how high prices can climb. CCC held stocks are not nearly as large now as they were throughout the sixties, owing to the success of some of its diversion and export programs, but CCC offerings on the cash market are still an important factor in cash market pricing when price levels rise sufficiently to make them attractive. Whenever cash prices rise to within grasp of support resale prices, government offerings must be watched closely.

The Department of Agriculture publishes a monthly CCC sales list indicating what stocks of commodities it holds and their offering prices. The price formula is figured independently of cash demand and supply factors, to eliminate the absurdity of purchasing grains at a support price while dumping the same

grains on a market that cannot sustain the supply at reasonable price levels. The CCC sells wheat at no less than 115 percent of the current support price plus reasonable carrying charges. If wheat is supported at a net loan rate of $1.25, the total cost of the grain to the CCC, including interest, storage, handling, and so on (the gross loan rate) is $1.47. The resale offering in Chicago will be 115 percent of this gross loan rate of $1.47 plus transportation to Chicago of, say, 10.5 cents per bushel, or $1.80. The CCC is supporting wheat at $1.25 at harvest and can offer it later in the winter at $1.80. If the market price rises above this amount, the CCC will sell the grain at market, but it will not sell it for less than $1.80, · and no trader need figure CCC held stocks into supply unless the market price rises close to this amount. (See Fig. 68 opposite.)

An exception to the resale formula exists only in the case that the stocks of grains are endangered. Any time the CCC fears that the commodity is likely to spoil, due to too much moisture in the kernels, or for whatever reason, it may sell the endangered goods at the best market price it can fetch. Such sales can be important in corn holdings which do not store well when the corn is full of moisture. Drying processes are available but expensive, and wet corn held by the CCC often makes it to market at prices below the formula.

Soybeans are offered by the CCC at the support price plus 1½ cents per month storage for each month after August of each year. As the cash market price for soybeans is normally well above the loan rate, very few farmers default on their loans and CCC stockpiles of soybeans are not a significant market

FIGURE 68

Feist   (202) 44-73134
McDavid (202) 44-74026

NEWS

U. S. DEPARTMENT OF AGRICULTURE

CCC ISSUES MONTHLY SALES LIST FOR OCTOBER 1972:

WASHINGTON, September 29 -- The U. S. Department of Agriculture announced today the minimum prices at which Commodity Credit Corporation (CCC) commodity holdings are available for sale beginning at 2:30 p.m., (EDT) September 29, 1972. These prices, subject to amendment, will continue until superseded by the November Monthly Sales List.

Listed for unrestricted use sale are wheat, rye, corn, barley, oats, grain sorghum, flaxseed, rice, linseed oil, butter, nonfat dry milk, cotton and tung oil. Listed for export are linseed oil, nonfat dry milk, butter and wheat. Peanuts are offered for restricted use. The list of commodities offered for sale in October is unchanged from a month earlier except for the deletion of rye and oats for export. With the 1972 crop marketing year beginning October 1, formula pricing for corn and grain sorghum is based on 1972 loan rates.

CCC will sell warehouse stocks of grains (except rice) and oilseeds (except peanuts) for deferred delivery up to 120 days from the date of sale. Prices of such sales will be in accordance with the CCC Monthly Sales List in effect at the time of sale with interest beginning for the account of the buyer the day after the date of sale. Such sales made on an in store delivery basis will require storage to begin for the account of the buyer 10 days after the date of sale. Such sales made on an FOB delivery basis will require storage for the account of the buyer beginning on the day after the date of sale. Storage charges will be in accordance with Uniform Grain Storage Agreement rates. Interest to date of payment will be at 6½ percent. No cash advance will be required from responsible buyers, but buyers will be required to furnish CCC an irrevocable letter of credit covering the purchase price plus estimated storage and interest to the end of the delivery period.

In this Sales List; "market price" and "transit value" apply to prices and values as determined by CCC. "Unrestricted use" applies to sales, which permit either domestic or export use and "export" applies to sales, which require export. "Announcement GR-212" means the third revision, Nov. 30, 1970, as amended. "Designated terminals" are listed in grain price support regulations. "Export market price" means a price as determined by CCC and generally reflects the price at which commodities are being sold for export.

A listing of USDA offices involved in CCC sales operations is shown at the end of the list. Information on elevator stocks of feed grains, rye, and wheat is available at the Kansas City ASCS Commodity Office and the Chicago, Minneapolis and Portland Branch Offices. Information on CCC binsite stocks can be obtained from Agricultural Stabilization and Conservation Service State Offices. Binsite stocks of corn are not offered for sale because they are being held for application against requirements of the Emergency Livestock Feed Program.

Source: U.S. Department of Agriculture, Commodity Credit Corporation.

factor, either as a floor or market ceiling.

Corn is currently offered by the CCC at 105 percent of the loan rate plus carrying charges for the time of storage and the transportation costs. At times over half the corn delivered in Chicago is CCC owned, and resale prices can be very significant in corn markets. Most other grains are offered at 115 percent of the loan rate plus costs. Because government stockpiles are normally very large, offering prices set a very effective ceiling to the cash and futures prices. The price can rise to the offering rate but cannot effectively puncture it until government stocks are depleted.

WHERE TO FIND CASH PRICES

The trader does not have to study the various government policies, demand determinants, and supplies to find the cash price of a commodity. He simply looks in his newspaper. Cash prices for most commodities are easily found in one of three sources: *The Wall Street Journal*, the *New York Journal of Commerce*, and the *Winnipeg Quotation Service* (for commodities on the Winnipeg Exchange). Every day *The Wall Street Journal* publishes cash market prices for most major commodities with a few major exceptions such as world sugar, orange juice, and some wheat prices. Those prices which are not available in *The Wall Street Journal* are available in the *New York Journal of Commerce*. This daily newspaper devotes nearly half a page to cash commodity prices and three or four pages to discussion of commodity statistics and news items. Winnipeg cash prices are generally available only through a private grain reporting service operated by a former president of the Winnipeg

Commodity Exchange, Mr. Stanley N. Jones. His report costs about $4 per month airmailed to the United States and can be secured by writing to Mr. Jones, c/o the Winnipeg Commodity Exchange, Winnipeg, Manitoba, Canada. (See Fig. 69 opposite and Fig. 70, p. 124.)

Since most commodity traders follow only a few commodities at a time, subscriptions to any one of these newspapers will keep them informed. A subscription to all of them will ensure that the trader has available all the cash prices for any future he wishes to trade. The majority of other cash price-making data are contained in government releases, and subscription to these will bring the trader all the information that is available to anyone in the country.

GOVERNMENT REPORTS

Government reports contain just about all the information that is to be had about the commodity markets and most other sources of information are derivative from them. They are free and released to all people at the same time, which effectively eliminates insiders from the commodity markets. These are had by placing your name on the automated mailing lists for the bulletins you wish to receive.

The Situation Reports are released by the Department of Agriculture monthly during the most important part of the season for the commodity covered, bimonthly or quarterly thereafter. These contain reviews of major price-making factors and give opinions as to probable price movement in the future, domestic use, exports, and so forth. They also contain statistics of past use and supply, and

FIGURE 69
GRAIN EXCHANGE PRICES

THURSDAY,		WINNIPEG FUTURES JUNE,			22/72.

MONTH	OATS	BARLEY	RYE	FLAX	RAPESEED THUNDER BAY	RAPESEED VANCOUVER
Jul	$69\frac{1}{8}$	$109\frac{3}{4}$	$101\frac{1}{4}$B	$278\frac{1}{4}$	Jul $239\frac{3}{8}$B	Jun $252\frac{3}{8}$B
Oct	$70\frac{1}{4}$a	110B	$99\frac{7}{8}$B	$279\frac{1}{4}$	Oct $241\frac{3}{4}$a	Sep $256\frac{1}{4}$B
Nov	–	–	–	$277\frac{1}{2}$B	Nov $242\frac{1}{2}$B	Nov $255\frac{3}{4}$&1
Dec	$70\frac{1}{8}$nnt	$109\frac{7}{8}$B	$99\frac{5}{8}$a	$274\frac{1}{4}$a	Dec $234\frac{1}{2}$B	Jan $254\frac{1}{2}$
May	–	111nnt	$100\frac{1}{2}$nnt	$282\frac{3}{4}$nnt	May $236\frac{1}{4}$Bnt	Mch 250B

OATS	SPOT	TOUGH	BARLEY	SPOT	TOUGH	RYE	SPOT
2cw	$\frac{1}{2}$–Jul	$2\frac{1}{2}$–	1 & 2cw6r	$\frac{5}{8}$–Jul	$3\frac{5}{8}$–	2cw	$\frac{5}{8}$–Jul
x3cw	3–	5–	1cw2r	$\frac{5}{8}$–	$3\frac{5}{8}$–	3cw	$5\frac{5}{8}$–
3cw	$3\frac{1}{4}$–	$5\frac{1}{4}$–	2cw2r	$2\frac{5}{8}$–	$5\frac{5}{8}$–	tf2cw	$3\frac{5}{8}$–
x1fd	$3\frac{1}{4}$–	$5\frac{1}{4}$–	3cw6r	$2\frac{5}{8}$–	$5\frac{5}{8}$–	tf3cw	$10\frac{5}{8}$–
1fd	$4\frac{1}{4}$–	$6\frac{1}{4}$–	3cw2r	$3\frac{3}{8}$–	$6\frac{1}{4}$–	4cw	30–
2fd	$7\frac{1}{4}$–	$9\frac{1}{4}$–	1fd	$3\frac{3}{4}$–	$6\frac{1}{4}$–	Ergoty	39–
3fd	$10\frac{1}{4}$–	$12\frac{1}{4}$–	2fd	$5\frac{1}{2}$–	8–	Track	$\frac{1}{2}$–
4xgr	$15\frac{1}{4}$–		3fd	$8\frac{1}{2}$–	11–		
Mxd. Fd.	21¢		3xgr	$14\frac{1}{2}$–			

						VOLUME AND OPEN INTEREST

FLAX	SPOT		RAPESEED T. BAY	CASH CLOSE		JUNE 21, 1972.
1cw	$\frac{7}{8}$–Jul		1 Can. $\frac{5}{8}$–Jul	Rye		Flax
2cw	$5\frac{7}{8}$–		2 Can.$15\frac{7}{8}$–	1&2cw $101\frac{1}{8}$		Jul 174–2800
3cw	30–			3cw $95\frac{5}{8}$		Oct 559–4294
Track	$\frac{5}{8}$–		INSPECTIONS	Tf2cw $98\frac{1}{8}$		Nov 97–387
SCREENINGS			Wht 933	Tf3cw $90\frac{5}{8}$		Dec 40–585
REFUSE – TON			Oats 42	4cw $71\frac{1}{4}$		May 0–0
MINNEAPOLIS WHEAT			Bly 414	Ergoty $62\frac{1}{2}$		
			Rye 2	Track $100\frac{1}{4}$		Rye
Jul 152			Flax 34			Jul 147–1679
Sep 154			Rapes'd 35	Flax		Oct 94–2020
Dec 157			June 19th.	1cw $277\frac{3}{8}$		Dec 25–308
			DELIVERIES	2cw $272\frac{3}{8}$		May 0–0
KANSAS CITY WHT.			Oats –	3cw $248\frac{1}{4}$		
Jul $140\frac{1}{4}$			Bly –	Track $277\frac{5}{8}$		Rapeseed Van
Sep $141\frac{7}{8}$			Rye –			Jun 17–188
Dec 145			Flax –	Rapeseed T.B.		Sep 983–5263
Mch $146\frac{1}{4}$			Rapes'd 74M Vanc	1 Can $238\frac{7}{8}$		Nov 392–1756
			June 22nd.	2 Can $223\frac{5}{8}$		Jan 48–825
						Mch 0–75

CHICAGO WHt	Oats	Soyoil	SOYBEANS	CORN		Rapeseed T.B.
Jul $141\frac{3}{8}$	$69\frac{1}{8}$a	1035/33	$342\frac{1}{4}$&$\frac{1}{2}$	$120\frac{1}{4}$		Jul 250–1539
Aug –	–	1035/36	$342\frac{5}{8}$&$\frac{1}{2}$	–		Oct 128–1472
Sep $142\frac{1}{2}$	$67\frac{1}{2}$	1036	$330\frac{1}{4}$	$122\frac{5}{8}$		Nov 448–448
Nov –	–	–	$317\frac{3}{8}$&$\frac{1}{2}$	–		Dec 0–26
Dec $146\frac{5}{8}$	$70\frac{3}{8}$	–	(Jan$321\frac{3}{8}$&$\frac{5}{8}$,	$121\frac{7}{8}$		May 0–0
Mch $148\frac{7}{8}$	–	–	$325\frac{1}{4}$	$126\frac{1}{2}$		

Source: Stanley N. Jones, Winnipeg Commodity Exchange.

so on. The *Situation Reports* currently published are: *The Demand and Price Situation; The Wheat Situation; The Feed Situation; The Fats and Oils Situation; The Wool Situation; The Cotton Situation; The Poultry and Egg Situation; The Vegetable Situation; The Farm Income Situation;* and *The Livestock and Meat Situation.* (See Fig. 71 opposite.)

Other government reports include the *Weekly Grain Market News* which lists weekly price changes, CCC sales, stocks, and exports. Comparisons are given with previous years, along with crop estimates loans entries, domestic consumption, and export figures.

The Foreign Agriculture Bulletin covers world production, trade and price prospects, emphasizing foreign output and the world market condition. This bulletin is especially important for trading in coffee, cocoa, and sugar where the bulk or all of the product comes from overseas. Information is gathered by U.S. embassies and can vary significantly from the "official" crop reports and estimates given out by foreign governments. As foreign governments have an interest in the prices brought by major export crops, their estimates can be low, especially in peak years and the *Foreign Agriculture Bulletin* is a good check against

FIGURE 70

Stanley N. Jones, 745 Grain Exchange, Winnipeg, Canada — Phone 942-7918

EXPORT — IN STORE T-BAY

WHEAT	ST. GD.	TOUGH	REJ'D 'HTD	REJ'D ADMIX
1°	171	167	165	168
2°	169	165	163	166
3°	164	160	158	161
4°	161	157	155	158
5				
6				
FD				

LAKEHEAD & EASTERN
2CW Red Spring Wht.
14% 4- 1 CW Red Spng
13% 4- "
12% 4- "
3CW same as 2CW 12%

1 CW Red Spring	
15%	-
14½%	171
14%	169
13½%	-
13%	163
12½%	-
12%	157

CANADIAN WHEAT BOARD PRICES

IN STORE PACIFIC			C.I.F. ATL.	ST.L.	PORT CARTIER BAIE COMEAU
1°	178¼		189⅝	189	190
2°	177¼		187⅝	187	188
3°	172¼		182⅝	182	183
4°	170¼		179⅝	179	180

1 CW Red Spring			C.I.F. ATL.	ST.L.	BAIE COMEAU
15%	-		-	-	-
14½%	178¼		189⅝	189	190
14%	177¼		187⅝	187	188
13½%	173¼		-	-	-
13%	-		181⅝	181	182
12½%	-		-	-	-
12%	-		175⅝	175	176

INSTORE CHURCHILL
1CW RedSpring 13½% 175

Bank of Canada Noon rate
U.S. Funds $0.97 25/32.

DOMESTIC

		1CW RedSpring	
1nor	195½	15%	199½
2nor	193½	14½%	197½
3nor	188½	14%	195½
4nor	185½	13½%	193½
5	148½	13%	189½
6	146½	12½%	187½
Fd	141½	12%	183½
1MxGr	127		

	S.W.SP.	MXD WHT	ARW/GAR		ARW/GAR	S.W.SP.
1	171	143⅞	161	1	170¼	178¼
2	169	142⅞	160	2	169¼	177¼
3	164	141⅞	159	3	168¼	172¼
4	161	141⅞	148	4	167¼	170¼

	ARW/GAR.	S.W.SP.
1		185½
2		184½
3		183½
4		182½

DURUM EXPORT IN STORE T-BAY

	IN STORE T-BAY	IN STORE PACIFIC	C.I.F. ATL.	C.I.F. ST.L	C.I.F. COMEAU CARTIER
1	167⅝	176⅛	186¼	185⅝	186⅝
2	166⅝	175⅛	185¼	184⅝	185⅝
3	157⅝	166⅛	176¼	175⅝	176⅝
Ex4	163⅝		182¼	181⅝	182⅝
4	153⅝		172¼	171⅝	172⅝
5					

OATS SPOT		BARLEY SPOT	
2 cw	69¼	1&2CW6R	118½
x3CW	66½	1&2CW2R	118½
3CW	66¼	3CW6R	116½
X1FD	66¼	3CW2R	116½
1FD	65¼	1FD	106¼
2FD	62¼	2FD	104¾
3FD	59¼	3FD	101¾

DURUM	
1	195½
2	194½
3	185½
x4	191½
4	181½

TUESDAY, JUNE 13/72.

Source: Stanley N. Jones, Winnipeg Commodity Exchange.

FIGURE 71

LIVESTOCK AND MEAT SITUATION

CONTENTS

• • •

Approved by
The Outlook and Situation Board
and Summary released
March 17, 1972

Principal contributors:
Donald Seaborg
John T. Larsen
George R. Rockwell

Economic and Statistical Analysis Division

Economic Research Service

U.S. Department of Agriculture
Washington, D.C. 20250

• • •

The *Livestock and Meat Situation* is published in February, March, May, August, October, and November.

SUMMARY

Larger beef supplies in 1972 and further gains during the next several years are indicated by recent cattle inventory figures. The Nation's cattle herd rose nearly 3½ million head during 1971 to 117.9 million at the beginning of this year for the sharpest increase since 1962. Beef cattle accounted for all of the gain. Beef cow numbers totaled 38.7 million, up 1.2 million, or 3 percent. This increase was about in line with those of the past several years and indicates that the 1972 calf crop will be up. Also, there are enough feeder cattle to permit increased placements on feed this year.

Fed cattle marketings rose less than 2 percent in 1971. This was a much smaller gain than in other recent years. Marketings in the first half of 1972 will be up moderately from a year ago. On January 1, there were 9 percent more cattle on feed, and cattle feeders planned to ship 7 percent more cattle this winter than last. However, winter marketings probably were up less than that. Spring marketings will be moderately larger than a year ago and larger than in the winter.

First half placements on feed will largely govern the pace of fed cattle marketings in the second half. With a larger feeder cattle supply, lower feed costs, and relatively high fed cattle prices, increased first half placements seem likely. January-February placements in 6 major feeding States were up 7 percent.

Choice steer prices at Omaha rose steadily during the fall and early winter, from $32 per 100 pounds in mid-October to about $36.50 in late January. Prices then weakened somewhat and by early March were $35.40, still about $4 above a year earlier. Although some further decline is likely, prices will stay above the April-June 1971 average when Choice steers at Omaha were $32.60. Strong consumer demand is continuing to bolster the cattle market.

The voluntary restraint level for 1972 of meat subject to the Meat Import Law is 1,240 million pounds (product weight), nearly a tenth above 1971 actual imports. This will put limited downward pressure on cattle prices. These imports consist mainly of frozen boneless beef, so cow prices will be affected more than fed cattle prices.

Hog slaughter rates will continue sharply lower than a year ago through midyear, but will be down less this spring than the 13 percent drop in January and February. Last December 1 there were 7 percent fewer market hogs on farms in weight groups that typically supply the bulk of spring slaughter supplies. Farmers

biased figures. (See Fig. 72, p. 127.)

The Commitments of Traders in Commodity Futures is released by the Commodity Exchange Authority and gives information about the futures markets of commodities which are regulated by the Department of Agriculture. These reports come out on the 11th of the month unless this is a Saturday, Sunday or holiday, covering the previous month, and give the total commitments of traders in three categories: hedgers, speculators, and small traders. Positions for each category of trader are broken into long, short, and spreading. This report is useful for giving a feeling for the general tone of the market. (See Fig. 73, p. 128.)

Monthly Commodity Futures Statistics is published by the Commodity Exchange Authority and contains statistics about futures trading for each regulated commodity and each futures market if there is more than one. Statistics gathered cover volume of trading, month-end open interest, and month-end closing price.

Special commodity reports by the CEA cover *Futures Trading in Maine Potatoes, Futures Trading in Fresh Shell Eggs, Futures Trading in Frozen Concentrated Orange Juice,* and *Trading in Live Beef Cattle Futures.* (See Fig. 74, p. 129.)

EXCHANGE INFORMATION SHEETS

Most commodity exchanges publish yearbooks containing information about futures contracts traded on their various pits. Monthly historical highs and lows (see Chapter 13) are found in these yearbooks along with a great deal of source material about the futures contracts themselves. These are had by writing the exchanges at addresses given in the back of this book.

In addition to annual yearbooks, many exchanges produce daily or weekly newspapers containing information pertinent to the commodities traded at that exchange. The Kansas City Board of Trade has a daily newspaper covering grain conditions. The New York Cocoa Exchange has a daily paper giving complete coverage of exports from major centers; cocoa loading or afloat to the United States along with lists of daily, monthly, and annual arrivals, licensed warehouse stocks of cocoa and major news items affecting cocoa trade. Other exchanges have information distribution of varying degrees of regularity. These are uniformly useful to the trader who can find out what is available and costs from the exchange in question. (See Fig. 75, p. 130.)

It is fairly easy for a trader to snow himself under in fundamental information. Most of the sources of information are repetitious, however, and subscribing to the pertinent *Situation Report, The Wall Street Journal* and the exchange sheet where the commodity is traded will generally give the trader all the information about fundamentals he would care to know. Daily reading is much more important in developing a feel for the market than are all the correlations and paper work that a man can do with the information he is given. Keeping abreast of the market is mostly a matter of reading one or two regular sources and subscription to the proper sources above will give the trader all he need know to trade the commodity futures markets. (See Fig. 76, p. 131.)

FIGURE 72
SAMPLE OF MONTHLY FOREIGN AGRICULTURAL BULLETIN

WORLD AGRICULTURAL PRODUCTION AND TRADE

Statistical Report

DECEMBER 1972

CONTENTS

WORLD SUMMARIES

UNITED STATES DEPARTMENT OF AGRICULTURE
FOREIGN AGRICULTURAL SERVICE

FIGURE 73

UNITED STATES DEPARTMENT OF AGRICULTURE
Commodity Exchange Authority
141 West Jackson Blvd., Room A-1
Chicago, Illinois 60604

COMMITMENTS OF TRADERS IN COMMODITY FUTURES

This report gives a breakdown of month-end open interest of large and small traders in the commodities and markets indicated below.

Open interest of large traders show the aggregate positions reported as speculative (including spreading) and hedging, as classified by them in their reports to the Commodity Exchange Authority. A large trader is one who holds a position in any one future of a commodity on any one contract market equaling or exceeding the quantities specified below as "Reporting Level." Large traders are subject to the reporting requirements of the CEA.

Open interest of small traders include both speculative and hedging positions. Small traders are not required to file reports of their futures transactions. Their positions are derived by subtracting large traders' commitments from total open interest.

Market and Commodity	Reporting Level
Chicago Board of Trade:	
Wheat	200 thousand bushels
Corn	200 thousand bushels
Oats	200 thousand bushels
Soybeans	200 thousand bushels
Soybean Oil	25 contracts (1.5 million pounds)
Soybean Meal	25 contracts (25 hundred tons)
Kansas City Board of Trade:	
Wheat	200 thousand bushels
Minneapolis Grain Exchange:	
Wheat	200 thousand bushels
Chicago Mercantile Exchange:	
Shell Eggs	25 carlots (562,500 dozen)
Frozen Pork Bellies	25 contracts (900 thousand pounds)
Live Beef Cattle	25 contracts (1 million pounds)
Live Hogs	25 contracts (750 thousand pounds)

This report is scheduled for release on the 11th of each month or the next business day if the 11th is a Saturday, Sunday, or holiday.

Source: U.S. Department of Agriculture, Commodity Exchange Authority.

FIGURE 74

**UNITED STATES
DEPARTMENT
OF AGRICULTURE**

COMMODITY
EXCHANGE
AUTHORITY

Monthly
Commodity Futures Statistics

ON FUTURES TRADING IN COMMODITIES REGULATED
UNDER THE COMMODITY EXCHANGE ACT

September 1972

Vol. 6, No. 3   Released October 16, 1972

Source: U.S. Department of Agriculture, Commodity Exchange Authority.

FIGURE 75
EXAMPLE OF
MONTHLY
STATISTICAL
REPORTS ISSUED

COMMODITY CALENDAR - JUNE 1972

SCHEDULED SPECIFIC REPORTS AND APPROXIMATE RELEASE DATES

GRAINS

June 5 Report: Weekly grain export inspections. (every Monday)

9 Report: Indicated yield of Winter Wheat as of June 1 and indicated production of Winter Wheat.

15 Report: Grain loan entries through May 31.

30 Report: World Estimate of 1971-72 Corn acreage & production.

CANADIAN GRAINS

7 Report: Telegraphic Crop Report - Canada.

16 Report: Progress of Seeding; Winter killing & Spring condition of Winter Wheat, Fall Rye, Tame Hay & Pasture; Rates of Seeding.

21 Report: Telegraphic Crop Report - Prairie Provinces.

30 Last day of trading for June Rapeseed.

SOYBEANS, SOYBEAN MEAL AND SOYBEAN OIL

5 Report: Weekly Soybean export inspections. (every Monday)

15 Report: Grain loan entries through May 31.

23 Report: Soybean Products production for May.

30 Report: Soybean Products consumption for May.

CITRUS

9 Report: Indicated 1971-72 production of Citrus crops.

16 Report: Cold storage stocks of Frozen Orange Juice Concentrate as of June 1.

COTTON AND COTTONSEED OIL

16 Report: N.Y. Cotton Exch. Service Report of domestic cotton consumption for Apr. 30 - May 27.

19 Report: Cotton Stocks as of May 27 and Consumption & Spindle Activity for Apr. 30 - May 27.

23 Report: Cottonseed products production for May.

30 Report: Cottonseed Products consumption for May.

EGGS AND POULTRY

7 Report: Egg Products production for April.

7 Report: Commercial Broiler Production and Broiler Chicks placed. (every Wed.)

16 Report: Cold storage stocks of Shell, Frozen Eggs & Iced Broilers as of June 1.

16 Report: Hatchery Production Pullet Chicks for Broiler Hatchery Supply Flocks & Poultry and Egg Production for May.

21 Last day of trading for June Shell Eggs.

27 Last day of trading for June Iced Broilers.

LIVESTOCK MEATS AND PORK BELLIES

13 Report: Cattle & Calves on feed as of June 1.

14 Report: Conditions of Western Range and Livestock as of June 1.

16 Report: Cold storage stocks of Pork Bellies, Meats & Products as of June 1.

20 Last day of trading for June Live Hogs & Live Cattle.

23 Report: Dec.-May Pig Crop 1972, June-Nov. 1972 farrowing intentions & June 1 inventory.

29 Report: Commercial livestock slaughter & Meat production during May.

METALS

20 Report: Copper Institute data indicating U.S. and Foreign production, stocks and deliveries of Copper during May.

27 Last day of trading for June Silver. (N.Y. & Chicago)

POTATOES

9 Report: Yield & Production of Early Spring, Late Spring and Early Summer Potatoes.

16 Report: Cold storage stocks of Frozen French Fries as of June 1.

SUGAR

9 Report: Yield, Production & Value 1970 & 1971 Sugar Beets and Sugar Cane Crops.

19 Last day of trading for July Sugar #10.

30 Last day of trading for July Sugar #11.

30 Report: World Sugar estimate for 1971-72 production.

PARITY AND FARM PRICES

30 Report: Parity & farm prices as of June 15.

SPECIAL USDA SITUATION REPORTS

1 The Cotton Situation.

2 The Agricultural Outlook Digest.

26 The Tobacco Situation.

29 The Poultry & Egg Situation.

30 The Fats and Oils Situation.

30 The World Agricultural Production & Trade Statistical Report.

Source: Commodity Research Bureau, Inc.

FIGURE 76

 Daily Information Bulletin

Thursday, May 17, 1973 - #94

CHICAGO MERCANTILE EXCHANGE STATISTICAL DEPARTMENT

444 WEST JACKSON BLVD. • CHICAGO, ILL. 60606 • (312) 648 1000

DAILY PRICE RANGE, VOLUME & OPEN INTEREST -- May 16,

	OPEN	HIGH	LOW	CLOSE	SETT. PRICE	VOL.	OPEN INTEREST	VOL.	OPEN INTEREST	SETT. PRICE
LIVE BEEF CATTLE										
Jne	45.75	46.10	45.52	46.10@.05	46.07	3114	8940 – 303	1938	5239	36.60
Aug	45.55	45.90	45.35	45.90@.85	45.87	2886	6788 – 125	1363	5066	35.47
Oct	45.22	#45.50	45.02	45.45@.47	45.45	1422	4956 + 70	701	3956	34.45
Dec	45.30	#45.65	45.20	45.55@.52	45.52	1179	3954 – 13	702	3179	34.52
Feb	45.50	45.70	45.40	45.57	45.57	123	1262 – 3	171	1028	34.72
Apr74	45.27	#45.60	45.20	45.35	45.35	137	641 – 13	22	566	34.52
								4897	20034	
				Total Beef Cattle:		8861	26541 – 387			
FEEDER CATTLE										
May	53.80	54.60	53.80	54.30	54.30	19	42 – 13	11	90	38.50
Aug	52.85	53.00	52.85	53.00	53.00	8	252 – 1	1	49	38.15
Sep	52.65	52.85	52.50	52.85	52.85	7	224 unch	---	27	38.00
Oct	52.45	52.50	52.25	52.50	52.50	26	367 – 8	2	104	37.45
Nov	---	---	---	52.05N	52.05	---	41 unch	4	24	37.75
								18	294	
				Total Feeder Cattle:		60	926 – 22			
SHELL EGGS										
May	46.30	46.90	45.70	46.75	46.75	44	102 – 33	125	635	28.25
Jne	48.60	48.60	46.95	48.15@8.00	48.10	408	918 + 7	88	438	28.05
Jly	53.30	53.30	51.35	52.50	52.50	86	358 + 4	24	293	32.45
Aug	54.00	54.00	53.00	53.50	53.50	10	134 – 2	2	33	35.25
Sep	59.40	59.40	58.10	58.90@.60	58.75	1276	2606 + 243	748	1819	39.80
Oct	55.50	55.50	54.50	55.00	55.00	10	206 – 1	6	58	38.75
Nov	---	---	---	56.50A	56.50	---	199 – 1+	3	34	41.75
Dec	59.90	59.90	58.05	59.10@58.90	59.00	207	739 + 49	77	457	42.05
								1073	3767	
				Total Shell Eggs:		2041	5262 + 266			
FROZEN EGGS										
Oct	---	---	---	36.50N	36.50	---	3 unch	---	--	---
				Total Frozen Eggs:		---	3 unch	---	--	---
IDAHO RUSSET POTATOES										
May	---	---	---	---	---	---	70 – 1	---	--	---
				Total Idaho Potatoes:		---	70 – 1	---	--	---
LIVE HOGS										
Jne	38.50	39.15	38.50	39.02@38.92	38.97	746	2010 + 43	913	2260	28.17
Jly	38.85	39.37	38.50	39.25@.30	39.27	1777	3387 + 75	1632	3624	28.42
Aug	38.40	38.70	38.22	38.60@.57	38.60	593	1182 + 14	633	1761	27.90
Oct	37.10	37.30	36.75	36.90	36.90	439	1270 + 2	295	1349	26.82
Dec	37.00	37.22	36.50	36.90	36.90	544	1840 + 28	1762	4505	26.87
Feb74	37.50	37.60	37.10	37.42@.45	37.45	85	508 – 17	283	1491	26.42
Apr	35.70	35.70	35.15	35.70	35.70	61	460 – 19	42	163	25.07
Jne	35.70	#35.75B	*35.65A	35.75B	35.75	1	2 + 1	---	--	---
Jly	---	---	---	35.70N	35.70	---	1 unch	5560	15153	
				Total Live Hogs:		4246	10660 + 127			
FROZEN PORK BELLIES										
May	56.00	56.90	55.90	56.80@.70	56.75	206	671 – 129	284	1301	39.72
Jly	56.20	56.87	55.95	56.60@.65	56.62	2561	4482 + 118	736	9359	39.97
Aug	55.75	56.32	55.05	55.90@56.05	55.97	1844	3739 + 34	321	5152	38.57
Feb	55.10	55.50	54.75	55.00@.05	55.02	601	1173 + 131	271	3276	41.82
Mar	55.00	55.20	54.55	54.80A	54.80	29	127 + 8	8	436	41.35
May74	---	#54.50B	---	54.50B	54.50	---	3 unch	---	126	41.50
				Total Pork Bellies:		5241	10195 + 162	1620	19650	
LUMBER										
May	---	---	---	---	---	5+	40 – 8	---	11	---
Jly	135.0	137.0	133.4	133.4@.5	133.5	440	952 + 14	35	827	117.9
Sep	125.0	125.5	*120.5A	120.5A	120.5	136	531 + 2	7	379	113.3
Nov	120.3	120.5	*118.0	119.0	119.0	49	251 – 3	6	272	109.0
Jan	114.9	115.0	*113.0	113.0	113.0	12	85 + 7	---	52	108.4
				Total Lumber:		642	1865 – 49	48	1541	
GRAIN SORGHUM-(Milo)										
May	3.10	3.10	3.08A	3.08A	3.08	2	2 + 1	---	2	2.055
Jly	---	---	---	3.14N	3.14	---	20 unch	---	44	2.102
Sep	---	---	---	2.92N	2.92	---	11 – 1+	---	--	---
Dec	---	---	---	2.78N	2.78	---	12 unch	---	46	---
				Total Sorghum:		2	45 unch			
				Total May 16:		21,093	55567 + 96	13216	60485	

WEDNESDAY'S DELIVERIES-Shell Eggs - 1, Lumber - 8, and Idaho Potatoes - 1.
*Contract #high, *low. ++Vol adj.*

CHICAGO PORK BELLY STORAGE MOVEMENT-In 11 CME approved warehouses.

	Tuesday In	Out	On Hand	YEAR	Hses	On Hand	Net Mvmt
May 15	56,000	NONE	11,094,000	AGO:	11	34,978,000	87,000 In

ESTIMATED DAILY LIVESTOCK SLAUGHTER-Under federal Inspection.

	Wednesday	Wk Ago	Yr Ago		Wednesday	Wk Ago	Yr Ago
Hogs	249,000	311,000	278,000	Cattle	118,000	120,000	123,000
Total Week	780,000	926,000	909,000		352,000	352,000	364,000

CASH GRAIN SORGHUM-(#2 yellow, per cwt)

	Wednesday	Prev Day	Year Ago
Kansas City	3.05@3.10	3.00@3.05	2.07
Ft. Worth	3.48@3.56	3.48@3.63	2.46@2.54

4 STATE (EGG-TYPE) HATCHERY OPERATIONS-Wk Ending May 12

	This Week	Last Week	Year Ago	% Year Ago
Settings	3,173,000	3,705,000	2,699,000	+ 18
Hatchings	2,704,000	2,755,000	2,621,000	+ 3

U. S. CHICK PLACEMENTS-Based on the preliminary chick placements, the number of fryers available for marketing during the week ending July 4 is estimated at 62,200,000. This compares to 63,100,000 head the prev week and to 64,300,000 head the same week a year ago.

DPSC EGG PRICES
EXPORTS-No purchases May 16.

CAMPS-	May 16	May 15
East (Mdms)	45.90	44.00@44.62
S.Calif. (Mdms)	44.89	44.29

HOUSING STARTS-The Census Bureau reported that privately owned housing starts in April were at an annual rate of 2,103,000 units on a seasonally adjusted basis. This compares with the adjusted rate of 2,248,000 units in March and 2,204,000 units in April, 1972.

9

FUTURES CONTRACT PRICING

Cash price forms an effective floor and ceiling to the futures contract price and the two will be very near the same in the expiration month of the contract. Most traders give the fact little thought unless they are trading into the final days of the contract but the concept of cash floor and ceiling provides a good example of how the futures market discounts any available information so that no speculative advantage can accrue to any speculator or hedger, long or short. When a fact becomes known (such as the fact that cash price and futures price are not coming into line) it involves no risk, and where there is no risk, the futures market will grant no profit. (See Fig. 77 opposite.)

Since the futures price of a commodity is merely a guess of what the cash price of that commodity will be in a certain number of months, it follows that when the month guessed at arrives, the futures price will be approximately equal to the cash price. Where the guess was proven wrong, it was altered. In September, the futures market may guess that the cash price of soybeans will be $3.28 in March and futures contracts for the delivery of soybeans in March will sell for that price. In March, a cash price of $3.28 will mean that the September guess was correct. Should the cash price be other than $3.28, the guess was

wrong and will have been altered as the facts became clearer and the guesses more accurate. Reasonably enough, it becomes easier to forecast prices, the closer the time of prediction. The simple fact that it is easier to predict the future three weeks in advance than three months is the first reason that cash and futures contract prices come together toward the close of the contract term.

FLOOR

The second reason cash and futures prices coincide is more ironclad and forms the floor for the futures contract price. People in the cash commodity business, be they in silver, copper, hogs, lumber, rapeseed, grain sorghum, propane, oats, rye, or barley, are also close watchers of the futures market prices. On April 1st a dealer wanting to buy wheat had only one option—he had to buy it in the cash market regardless of price. Buying the May future at that time would have done him no good for he would have had to wait a month before he could possibly have received delivery of the wheat. But as May approaches, a second option becomes feasible. The dealer can buy cash wheat as usual or he can buy the May futures option as a source of wheat. Contracts normally expire between the 1st and

20th of the delivery month and if the trader buys the May futures, the longest he would have to wait for delivery would be three weeks and he might get it the next day. This new alternative, the fact that the user of the cash commodity can buy the future and take delivery acts as a floor on the price of the commodity futures. This possibility of using the futures market as a means of procurement also explains why care is taken to see that the contracts are so written that they can actually be used by the industry.

Assume that the price of May wheat futures fell to $1.40 a bushel while cash wheat was bringing $1.60. If the miller can wait the three weeks necessary before being sure of delivery, he will most certainly buy the May future at a savings of 20 cents over the price of the cash commodity. He would simply hold his long futures position into delivery and take possession of the actual grain at the bargain price as shorts were forced to deliver. A 20 cent profit to the dealer is huge since he typically makes only 1 cent or 2 cents per bushel in his handling and processing operation. The shorts who deliver either held wheat which they could have sold much more profitably on the cash market or must buy

cash wheat in order to fulfill their contract obligations. Either way, they stand to lose the 20 cents per bushel that the dealer is making.

Dealers who are not able to secure sufficient cash commodities on the cash market may do their buying on the futures market. This buying in the futures may or may not have an impact on the cash market depending upon the then prevailing activity in both cash and futures markets.

Futures option prices will never fall far enough below the cash price to make it profitable for the merchant or processor to buy futures contracts and wait the time required to take delivery.

Dealers taking their guaranteed profits in such a dislocated market would drive the futures price up, and when the time came to accept delivery, the dealer who bought at the futures price would probably find that the two had come into line. He then covers his futures position and buys from his cash dealer in the normal fashion. He has still made his 20 cent guaranteed profit on his long position in the rising futures market. The dealer's ability to buy futures and take a profit if the price is too low reaches back farther in time than the first of the month. Any time the futures price is too

FIGURE 77

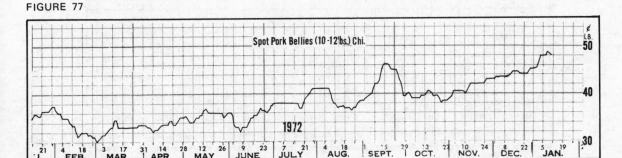

Source: Commodity Research Bureau, Inc.

low a guess of the cash price in the expiration month, dealers will move in and establish long positions, driving the option price up and guaranteeing that the futures price will be the best possible guess of all the people in the industry of what the cash price is going to be.

CEILING

Cash price also sets a ceiling on how high futures prices can climb. A futures contract rarely rises above the commodity cash price plus the cost of storing it, handling it, and insuring it until the delivery month. If it did, people would do just that. Buy cash goods, store, handle, and insure them and redeliver them against short futures positions. (See Fig. 78 below.)

Carrying costs for wheat run about 1.5 cents a month. Should the current

FIGURE 78

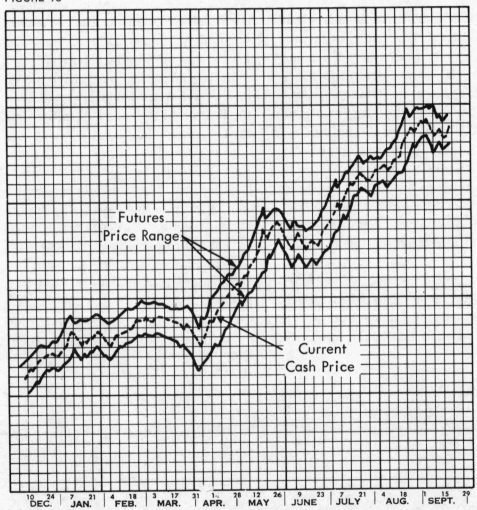

Futures prices are the best possible guess of cash prices to come in the future and cannot deviate far from concensus opinion. A futures price which is too high guarantees a profit to short traders who can buy cash and deliver to fill their high-priced contracts. Too low a price will prompt longs to buy futures, take delivery and redeliver on the cash market.

cash price for wheat be $1.40 a bushel and the futures option price for delivery four months hence be $1.50, any dealer could simply buy cash goods and sell futures contracts. He would then store the commodity for four months at a known cost of 1.5 cents per month or 6 cents altogether and deliver against his short futures position for a guaranteed profit of 4 cents a bushel. He could not lose.

Assume that a warehouseman in September is faced with a cash market of $3.19 a bushel for soybeans he is holding, which price he would normally be happy with. He notices a little too much glint in his dealer's eye and before selling checks the soybean futures in the newspaper. Here he finds a price of $3.38 for January soybeans. He can store, insure, and handle his soybeans for about 2.5 cents a month and is very happy to do so as it keeps his elevator occupied and an empty elevator brings no revenues. January is four months off and continued storage of the beans will cost him about 10 cents a bushel. He adds together the $3.19 he could get now for his beans and the 10 cents a bushel cost of storage for a total of $3.29. He can deliver the soybeans in January for $3.38, a guaranteed profit of 9 cents per bushel. Not only will he withhold his soybeans from the cash market, he will buy every soybean he can get his hands on at any price from the current quote of $3.19 up to the break-even price of $3.28. He sells an equal amount of beans in January futures contracts and sits back for his guaranteed profit.

Should the futures price of $3.38 prove wrong as a guess of the cash price in January, the warehouseman may have to accept less for his beans. He will make an equivalent profit, however, on his short position on a falling futures market. If the futures market does not fall enough—he will simply deliver the beans to fill his contracts rather than covering them with contract purchases.

A futures option price which is either too high or too low will grant somebody a guaranteed profit, and taking his profit, the trader will beat the option price back into line. The futures markets do not grant guaranteed profits for long, and this process of taking profits will always assure that the option price is the best possible guess of the coming cash price for the commodity. It is by finding option prices that are too high or too low that the speculator makes his profit on the commodity marts. For this reason, speculators keep a sharp eye on the supply and demand factors that determine cash price.

Like most price factors in commodities, the floor and ceiling provided for the futures contract by the cash market price is not absolute and the expiring contract can vary a small amount from the cash price. Users of the cash commodity have grade requirements which are not necessarily the same as those specified in the futures contract and this fact will allow the two possible sources of goods to vary to some extent. Grade requirements are not absolute, however, and if the two prices vary by too much, a user of one grade will quickly find that he can make do with the bargain grade offered. Insufficient volume is a great cause of price disparity. As hedgers close their position and speculators leave the market, price dislocations can occur strictly caused by the technical function of traders leaving the market. Such price differences between cash and expiring contracts are kept small enough not to tempt traders to exploit them. If the profit offered is large enough to make trading worth someone's while, he will make the trade and take the profit, forcing the two prices back into line. Normal disparity is thus kept to a couple of cents in the delivery month.

INTERMONTH BASIS

The rule that basis (price difference) can never exceed carrying costs applies as well to intermonth relationships as to the relationship between an option and the cash price. Each unprocessed commodity that has ever been alive (excludes metals, butane, and so on) has a seasonal curve starting with prices fairly low during and immediately after harvest when the market is glutted with the cash goods. Each month that the goods are held adds a slight increment to the price at which they will be sold. If no changes in supply and demand occur, soybeans worth $3 in October will be worth $3.05 in December, for the simple reason that it costs a nickel to store them for the two months. Were the price to be the same at both times, no dealer would have reason to go to the expense of holding the commodity for the two months.

While other market conditions (new customers, demand changes, and so forth) will enter into the price to be found for a commodity in later months pushing the price up or down, they will tend to push all the futures options up or down together, preserving intact the monthly basis between commodity contracts. This is especially true of the later options which are less affected by short-term conditions in the cash market.

The assumption behind intermonth basis is that a higher price for later months following harvest is necessary to avoid a complete market glut as all farmers and warehousemen dump their produce immediately after harvest. The market must pay them to hold the goods for a while before selling them. In fact, overselling immediately after harvest does occur, and quickly sets up a premium for the later months as cash prices are depressed and later month's bids remain buoyant. The premium for far months is enforced by traders in a manner similar to that by which futures prices are kept in line with cash prices. When a dislocation occurs, someone is offered a guaranteed profit.

Intermonth basis is clearest in those commodities such as oats, soybeans, and corn, that are harvested at one time with supplies rationed out over the year. (Wheat is harvested twice a year, in the spring and late summer but may be added to the list.) Soybeans provide a good example of the normal monthly basis. (See Fig. 79 opposite.)

The soybean year begins in October with harvest, and the first new crop contracts are usually for delivery in November, followed at two-month intervals by January, March, May, July, and August which is the "clean-up month." September (and sometimes August) can be either a "new crop" month or finish off the last of the old crop, depending on when the new crop comes in, and is therefore a very volatile option in soybeans, jumping up in price if the new crop appears to be late (meaning that September will see the scarce remains of the old crop) or dropping in price if the new crop abundance hits the market in September.

FIGURE 79

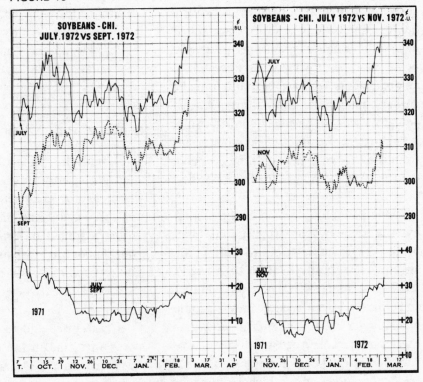

Source: Commodity Research Bureau, Inc.

Disregarding September contracts, the price of soybeans is usually set with the November contract when the size of the soybean crop is first known. Prices for the ensuing months will tend to rise on an even scale, representing the cost of storing the soybeans throughout the year. *The Wall Street Journal* (September 12, 1972) lists the following prices for soybean futures at Chicago (Fig. 80).

September is an old crop month this year and soybeans are selling at a 10 cent premium over the price expected to come in November, representing the scarcity of beans on the current market and the glut to come when the new crop comes in. November sets the new crop price at 334¾ bid and 335 asked. January's price is set approximately 4 cents higher at $339\frac{5}{8} - \frac{3}{4}$ per bushel. March

FIGURE 80
SOYBEANS

	Open	High	Low	Close	Change
September	345¾	346¼	344¾	345¼	$-\frac{1}{2}$ to $\frac{5}{8}$
November	336½	336½	334¼	334¾–335	$-2\frac{1}{2}$–$2\frac{1}{4}$
January 73	342	342	339⅜	339⅝–¾	$-2\frac{3}{4}$–$2\frac{5}{8}$
March	346	346⅛	344	344¼	$-2\frac{7}{8}$
May	349¼	349¼	347½	347⅞	$-2\frac{1}{8}$
July	351¼	351¼	349¼	349½–350	$-2\frac{1}{2}$–2
August	347¼	347½	346	346½	$-1\frac{1}{2}$

is set 5 cents higher yet, allowing storage costs for the four months from November to March. May and July are set at somewhat smaller premiums over the nearer months showing some uncertainty among traders who are hesitant to make guesses so far in the future. August actually sells at a discount to July, reflecting the possibility that some beans from the following new crop might make it to market by August 1973, depressing prices.

If the new crop does enter the market by August next year, August prices will be lower yet in relation to July (they are now set at July $3.49½ to August's $3.46½, a basis difference of 3 cents) and this basis difference may become much larger. If the new crop does not enter the market, August will rise above July in a normal basis relationship. Traders don't know now which is going to happen 11 months from now and are splitting the difference. Rather than bidding the August contract to 2.5 cents more than July (a normal relationship) or 20 cents less (as will be the case if the new crop comes in by August 1973), they have bid the price to 3 cents lower.

In January, the Department of Agriculture will release a "stocks in all positions" report on soybeans, probably making some adjustment in the reported size of the crop over the current estimates. When this happens the price of all soybean options may rise or fall according to whether the crop is found to be larger or smaller, but intermonth basis will remain about the same.

If the basis between months is not sufficient to cover the cost of storing the beans (or wheat or corn, and so on) farmers will sell their beans right away, depressing current prices and leaving later prices untouched. This action will act to restore the normal basis. Speculators can also act to keep basis in line by exploiting any imbalance in prices that may occur by taking a spread position.

SPREADS AND STRADDLES

Should the price difference between contract months be greater than carrying costs, or not great enough, the speculator can exploit the dislocation by instituting a spread or straddle position and waiting for the two months' options to come back into line. "Spread" and "straddle" are two words for the same maneuver.

If cash price and futures price do not come into line in the delivery month, a dealer can make a guaranteed profit by buying futures and forcing delivery at bargain prices (if the option is priced lower than cash prices), or by selling short on the futures exchange and delivering cheap cash grain to fill his high-priced options (if the futures price is too high). The speculator in grain futures can do the same thing with futures options alone if the monthly basis between option months gets out of line. In so doing he helps force the options back into line in the same manner that dealers taking their guaranteed profits will force cash and option prices back into line.

Assume that the basis between the soybean option for January delivery and March delivery on the Chicago Board of Trade is 8 cents. Cash price is going to be determined by conditions in the cash markets for soybeans with little consideration given to the futures markets. If no reason exists for the overlarge premium between January and March, the cash prices for the two months will follow the normal basis pattern, trading in March 5 cents higher than in January and the futures price guess will be proven wrong. In this case it will be adjusted to fit the reality found in the cash markets. If good reason exists to believe that soybeans are going to go up in value by March, farmers and warehousemen will withhold beans from the cash market in January and hold them until March to pick up the 3 cent bonus. Withholding beans from the cash market in January will tend to raise January's price, while the excess beans to be dumped in March will tend to lower this price, bringing

the two back into the normal 5 cent premium basis.

If everybody does their job properly—i.e., makes as much money as is offered—the market will settle in the normal basis pattern. (See Fig. 81 below.)

The speculator can exploit an intermonth basis which is too great by buying contracts for delivery in January and selling short for delivery in March. In so doing, he applies downward pressure on the March contract price while strengthening the January price. He thus speeds the futures market prices back to normalcy.

If the basis between the two months is to return to 5 cents from the bloated

FIGURE 81

Source: Commodity Research Bureau, Inc.

8 cents, either the March price must fall relative to the January price or the January price must rise relative to the March price. Both prices can go up or down according to changes in supply and demand for soybeans, but March must go up less or fall more than January. In no other way will the two contracts come into line. The trader in a spread position between the two months may lose a good deal on one leg of his spread if the entire market moves, but he will make more on the other. A trader in a spread position can lose money only if the basis becomes greater and make money only as the two come closer together. He is not affected by the overall market movement. As risk is relatively small, margin required of a trader in a spread or straddle position is less. With less risk, less security bond is required by the brokerage.

Should the market basis not come into line but remain at 8 cents, someone is guaranteed a profit. Any dealer who was long January soybeans and short March could simply take delivery in January to fill his long position, hold the beans for two months at a cost of 5 cents and redeliver in March for a guaranteed profit of 3 cents a bushel. This is a return of 100 percent in two months against the low margins required for spread positions. Consequently this does not happen. The market does not allow guaranteed profits. (See Fig. 82 below.)

Spreads between commodities are common. Wheat is normally harvested in July and August and the cash market suffers pressure from overburdensome supplies during this period of the year. After July and August the wheat market usually goes up in a normal basis pattern. Corn is not harvested until October and does not feel pressure until then. From

FIGURE 82

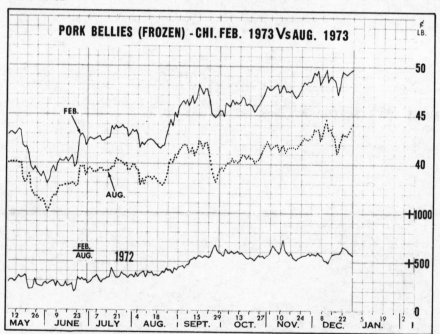

Source: Commodity Research Bureau, Inc.

August until October, corn is usually declining in price while wheat is advancing. Many traders then place a spread, buying wheat and selling corn. This is a common spread widely used whose success will depend upon wheat prices advancing more than corn prices during this period. The contracts for wheat are already bid up, of course, reflecting their normal rise, as are corn contracts at a low level. The trader is merely playing with the seasonal pattern, figuring a weak market is more likely to drop (in corn) than is a strong market (wheat). Conversely, if either option rises, wheat will likely be the one or go farther. (See Fig. 83 below.)

Intercommodity spreads are common between wheat and corn, hogs and pork bellies, oats and corn, since oats are harvested about the same time as wheat and usually advance in price earlier in the year than corn. The two compete directly as a feed source. Intercommodity spreads are also common in the soybean complex, meal and oil versus the beans from which they are processed. Such spreads are also possible in Idaho and Maine potatoes which are harvested at different times of the year. (See Fig. 84 below.)

FIGURE 83

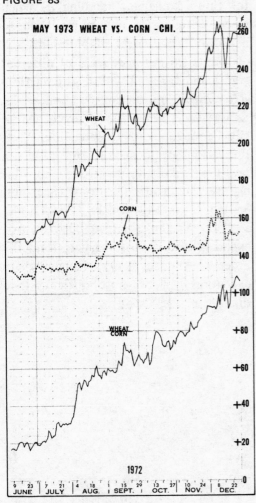

Source: Commodity Research Bureau, Inc.

FIGURE 84

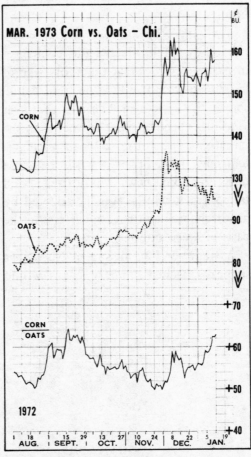

Source: Commodity Research Bureau, Inc.

Spreads in two trading months of the same commodity are also common. Soybeans are harvested in September and October. During the summer months, it may become obvious that there is a great shortage of soybeans for "near-term demand." The incoming crop cannot alleviate the early summer shortage but promises to be of excellent size, dampening later prices substantially but leaving near option prices buoyant.

The trader takes a "bull market spread" in soybeans, buying all the August and September contracts he wishes with the idea that prices will not drop far in a tight market. He balances the purchase with an equal sale of November soybean futures. He has gone long old crop beans and short new crop beans.

Tight old crop contracts will generally not fall by much, which a glutted market in November prevents the short side of his spread from climbing on him. A bull spread is so named because the near "leg" is expected to rise further than the far "leg." The entire soybean price system may move up or down in response to international news, but both near and far contracts will be equally affected by major changes and have no effect on the basis between options.

A trader wishing to spread November soybeans against January beans would probably take a "bear market spread," with both legs in the same crop year. Such a spread placed a month or two before harvest can exploit a widening of the basis between the two options if the near month falls more than the far. This often happens when the market glut comes to pass, depressing spot prices beyond the normal basis pattern. If insufficient elevator storage space is available, cash prices can be depressed severely.

Spreads are also occasionally placed between markets trading in the same commodity. The most common form of intermarket spread is in wheat among the three exchanges handling it. When wheat prices move, they normally do so nationwide and a set of premiums and discounts exists for delivery of different grades and types of wheat. The relationship between options on the Minneapolis, Kansas City, and Chicago exchanges is close enough to invite spreading. When the various options move out of line, a profit is held out to the trader who helps restore the proper positions. (See Figs. 85 and 86, p. 143; and Fig. 87, p. 144.)

When placing a spread between two exchanges, it is customary to send the order to the smaller exchange, where execution can be more difficult. (See Fig. 88, p. 145.)

FIGURE 85

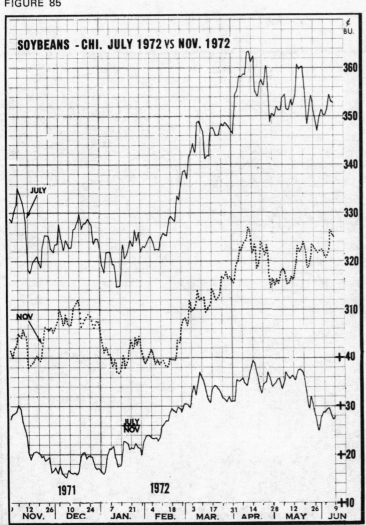

SOYBEANS - CHI. JULY 1972 vs NOV. 1972

Source: Commodity Research Bureau, Inc.

FIGURE 86

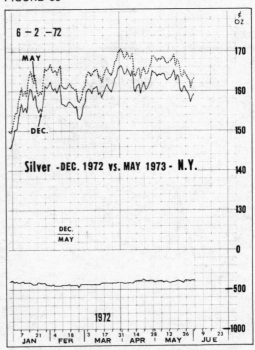

Silver -DEC. 1972 vs. MAY 1973 - N.Y.

Source: Commodity Research Bureau, Inc.

FIGURE 87

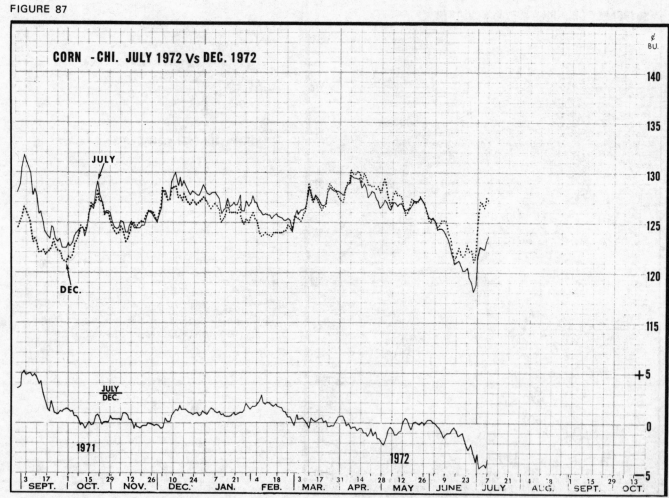

CORN - CHI. JULY 1972 Vs DEC. 1972

Source: Commodity Research Bureau, Inc.

144   Dow Jones-Irwin guide to commodities trading

FIGURE 88

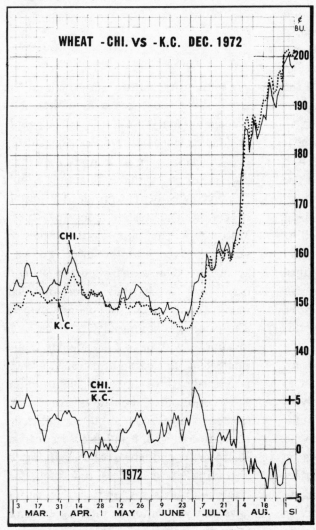

Source: Commodity Research Bureau, Inc.

INVERSIONS

Should intermonth basis grow too large, traders will take their guaranteed profits and force the two contracts back into a normal basis arrangement. Too small a basis, however, has no limit and the near month can actually rise to sell for more than the later month when the near month is competitive with cash

goods. This is known as an *inversion* of the normal intermonth relationship.

Should a shortage of wheat develop in Chicago (or Kansas City, Minneapolis, or Winnipeg where wheat is also traded), it is possible for the cash price of wheat to be bid very high on the cash market as processors and millers compete for the limited supplies. Wheat from outlying areas will be brought in to alleviate the shortage as soon as the price is bid high enough to cover transportation costs. The higher the price at Chicago, the more a supplier can afford to pay for shipping the further from Chicago he can be, and still afford to get into the cash market. If this occurs in March, say, the March contracts will offer buyers an alternative source of their needed wheat and it is possible for the price of March wheat futures to be bid higher than the May contracts. The result is an "inversion" in the normal March-May wheat prices. The market, in effect, is telling the warehouseman that it will not only *not* pay him for storing his wheat until May, it will actually pay him less for holding it. The market wants wheat *now*. There is no theoretical limit to this inversion until the price gets so high the millers simply can't afford to mill flour, but outside shipping will react as fast as possible to keep the shortage short lived.

Inversions occur, reflecting a mistake in the figuring of the people who supply wheat to the cash markets in Chicago. January cash and futures prices become higher than March prices because traders *know* there is a shortage in January and expect the shortage to be gone by the time March rolls around. The price of a futures contract is just an estimate of what the cash price will be and if traders expect the shortage to be gone in March, they expect the cash price will drop and the March contracts will sell at this lower guess.

Inversions needn't confuse trading; they simply reflect what traders know to be the case in the current market and what they expect to happen in the future. Avoiding inversions is as simple as staying out of delivery months, which most speculators do as a matter of prin-

ciple. It is not their game. (See Fig. 89 opposite.)

OPEN INTEREST

Commodity futures contracts differ from things sold in cash markets and especially from stocks, in that the supply of March wheat futures or the futures of any month or commodity is in as great a supply as there are people willing to make agreements to trade. The supply of common shares of stock in General Motors, or the supply of bushels of wheat is fixed and the price will vary according to how many people want to hang onto what they have and how many people want to become owners. The price of a commodity or stock fixed in supply will be set by demand, and interest in that commodity or stock will necessarily show up as a higher price. But commodity contracts come into existence any time a buyer and seller come to agreement and bind a contract. Reasonably enough, at the beginning of a trading cycle only a few such contracts will exist as only a few people have as yet entered into agreements. Over the course of the trading period, more people usually enter the market, both as sellers and as buyers. The number of agreements extant is called the *open interest*, which is just a name for the number of contracts which are "open" at any given time. (See Fig. 90, p. 148.)

When a trader holds a short position in any commodity, he is offset by some other person who holds a long position and an "open" position exists. At any time, the holder of, say, five open short contracts of March wheat can buy five long contracts. He is now completely balanced, holding essentially contracts with himself to deliver and accept wheat in March. In effect his position has been "closed" and he drops out of the market. The number of open contracts and the volume of "open interest" will drop by five contracts when he closes out.

A buyer can enter a long position in the market by making an agreement with a trader taking the opposite position, in which case, the open interest increases by one contract, or whatever number of contracts the two people agree upon, or he can simply buy a long position from another long trader, taking his former position and leaving the open interest unchanged. The original holder of, say, five contracts sells five contracts and leaves the market. The buyer of his contracts then assumes his position on the long side of the market.

When a sell order reaches the trading

FIGURE 89

┌How a 'straddle' can lower the risks─────

Speculating in commodities may be the most dangerous game in town. But market veterans say there is at least one device that can lessen the risk—and sometimes yield a tax saving, too—and that is the "straddle" or "spread."

The most common type of straddle involves taking long and short positions in the same commodity by simultaneously buying and selling contracts with different delivery dates—for instance, buying March cocoa and selling December cocoa. Because futures contracts of the same commodity often move in tandem, the risk of being wiped out by a sudden erratic price swing is reduced.

Ordinarily, a speculator buys a straddle because he thinks that some temporary factor will affect one futures contract more than another. He may decide, for example, that fears of a pending dock strike will drive up the price of a contract with a near delivery date, without influencing the more distant month. So he buys March cocoa, sells July cocoa, and if the March contract does take a jump, he closes out both positions at a nice profit.

But a straddle can also be used, and often is, to defer a short-term gain until the next tax year or to convert a short gain into a long-term gain.

The technique. Take a speculator sitting with a $20,000 short-term gain, made in commodities or in the stock market. This time he buys a straddle in a commodity where he thinks most futures

contracts will move together—silver being a favorite tax-straddle vehicle. As soon as the price has fluctuated enough to produce a $20,000 loss in one leg of the straddle (and conversely a $20,000 gain in the other), he takes the loss and immediately straddles again by taking a similar position in another delivery month. He has now offset his original short-term gain and, assuming both sides of the straddle continue to move together, is locked into a new $20,000 gain. (Of course, he hopes that the movement won't be precisely uniform, so that he can wind up with an even bigger gain.)

If the trader's new gain is in his long position, and the price stays up, he simply waits six months and closes out both sides of the straddle—turning a short gain into a long-term gain. On the other hand, if his gain is in his short position, he waits until the start of the next tax year and then closes out the straddle. His short gain has been deferred to a new tax year in which his tax liability may be less.

Plainly, this whole approach takes careful planning. Eugene Krieger, a tax manager at Price Waterhouse & Co. in New York, says that "it's crucial to work with a knowledgeable tax man and a broker who specializes in straddles." A Wall Street commodities man agrees. "If you're unlucky or careless," he warns, "you can wind up by converting your initial gain into a hefty loss."

Source: *Business Week*, December 23, 1972.

area (the pit), it is matched at auction with whatever buy orders exist. The seller cannot know and has no reason to care whether he is buying the position formerly held by another person or whether his sell order was matched to a new buy order and gave rise to a brand new contract. Sell orders and buy orders are matched constantly and the number of open contracts changes just as constantly. A trader can thus enter a long position into the market without driving the price up, creating an altogether new agreement and changing open interest, or he can buy the position of another trader, changing only volume for the day. Price will be changed not by the amount of business done but by the mix. If a great many more people want to sell at the going price than want to buy, the price will be driven down. If there are more buy orders on the trading floor, the price will rise until some of the buying traders lose interest or other traders are enticed into entering the short side. (See Fig. 91 opposite.)

Open interest begins to taper off as the delivery month nears and speculators who neither wish delivery nor to deliver get out and as industry hedgers lift their hedges. At the delivery date any open contracts stand to be filled by actuals as shorts must deliver and longs accept. Industry users of the futures market could stand for delivery or make delivery, but rarely do, choosing rather to lift their hedges as actuals come into their warehouses or are shipped, and no longer need to be hedged. Finally, usually by the 20th of the delivery month, the contract simply dies out. Open interest tapers down to nothing, to be revived the next year. (See Fig. 92, p. 150.)

FIGURE 90
OPEN INTEREST

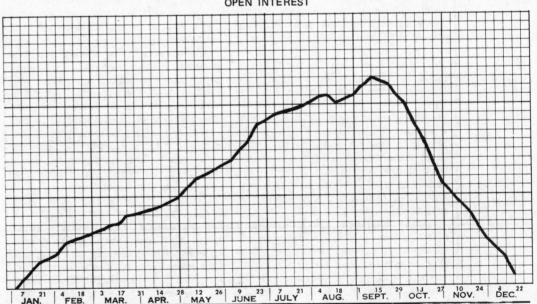

Start of Trading
Contract Expiration

As the season progresses, more and more people usually enter into agreement. Open interest then peaks and tapers back down to nothing as stocks of cash goods are used up and contracts held as hedges are closed.

FIGURE 91

Table 4. Open contracts in commodity futures, all contract markets combined

Commodity	Unit	Open contracts at end of month				
		Aug. 1970	July 1970	Net change	Aug. 1969	July 1969
Wheat	1,000 bu.	150,074	145,548	+ 4,526	166,567	165,899
Corn	do.	357,901	164,223	+193,678	235,905	243,708
Oats	do.	17,900	11,653	+ 6,247	29,437	22,750
Rye	do.	427	692	- 265	3,929	3,683
Soybeans	do.	248,068	289,829	- 41,761	161,334	156,168
Grain sorghums	Million lb.	29.7	14.8	+ 14.9	31.4	9.8
Cotton	1,000 bales	125.1	105.8	+ 19.3	209.9	228.7
Wool	6,000 lb.	391	444	- 53	1,095	1,004
Wool tops	5,000 lb.	12	18	- 6	12	15
Butter	Carlots	0	0	0	11	11
Eggs - shell	do.	10,288	6,540	+ 3,748	8,764	7,667
" - frozen	36,000 lb.	6	6	0	8	8
Potatoes	Carlots	9,948	6,558	+ 3,390	10,799	8,249
Soybean oil	60,000 lb.	26,171	28,312	- 2,141	15,789	16,261
Soybean meal	1,000 tons	2,413.9	2,337.2	+ 76.7	1,248.8	1,301.1
Cattle, live beef	40,000 lb.	11,782	13,562	- 1,780	31,082	29,104
Steers, choice	27,600 lb.	32	80	- 48	1,011	1,145
Boneless beef, frozen	36,000 lb.	317	306	+ 11	---	---
Hogs, live	30,000 lb.1/	2,440	2,352	+ 88	2,227	1,652
Pork bellies, frozen	36,000 lb.2/	8,772	10,921	- 2,149	13,493	14,168
Skinned hams, frozen	36,000 lb.	44	9	+ 35	0	0
Hides	40,000 lb.	0	0	0	32	32
Orange juice, frozen concentrated	15,000 lb.	2,905	2,526	+ 379	4,217	4,378

Source: U.S. Department of Agriculture, Commodity Exchange Authority.

FIGURE 92

Volume and Open Interest

The Commodity Exchange Authority reported grain futures trading on the Chicago Board of Trade as of the close of business Monday, Jan. 15, 1973 (in thousands of bushels):

	March	May	July	Sept.	Dec.	Total
Wheat	5,130	4,265	4,495	1,190	680	15,760
Corn	31,255	15,245	17,065	3,035	4,490	71,090
Oats	190	450	250	....	....	890

Soybeans: January, 9,115; March, 39,025; May, 21,040; July, 17,440; August, 3,560; September, 1,785; November, 8,835; January '74, 545; Total 101,345.

Soybean oil trading totaled 2,386 tank cars of 60,000 pounds each. Soybean meal trading totaled 2,866 contracts of 100 tons each.

Open Interest (in thousands of bushels):

	Wheat	Corn	Oats	Soybeans	r-Meal	s-Oil
January	....	....	....	15,910	1,120	638
March	33,750	163,225	4,590	113,465	5,370	13,276
May	25,760	123,750	2,710	86,280	4,416	8,937
July	27,450	98,770	1,800	69,800	3,583	6,108
August	....	....	....	24,050	1,991	2,106
September	13,085	22,440	....	8,545	703	1,541
October	....	....	....	....	1,640	1,001
November	....	....	....	45,565	....	....
December	1,950	66,445	....	....	1,472	1,608
January '74	....	....	....	2,060	....	1
Total	101,995	474,630	9,100	365,675	20,295	35,216

r-In hundreds of tons. s-In tank cars of 60,000 pounds.

Open contracts for Jan. 15 and changes from Friday: **Frozen Pork Bellies** (36,000 pounds each), Feb. 7,620, March 5,185, May 3,470, July 4,575, Aug. 1,381. Total 22,231, down 75. **Hogs** (30,000 pounds each), Feb. 5,948, April 4,583, June 1,174, July 1,549, Aug. 406, Oct. 908, Dec. 553. Total 15,121, down 185. **Cattle** (40,000 pounds each), Feb. 9,120, April 9,318, June 7,043, Aug. 2,618, Oct. 1,574, Dec. 661. Total 30,334, up 751. **Fresh Eggs** (750 cases each), Jan. 1,266, Feb. 1,820, March 807, April 568, May 1,528, June 73, July 21, Aug. 15, Sept. 112. Total 6,210, down 9. **Maine Potatoes** (50,000 pounds each), March 3,378, April 2,257, May 9,598, Nov. 612. Total 15,845, up 71. **World Sugar No. 1 1**(112,000 pounds each), March 8,788, May 6,681, July 3,859, Sept. 1,213, Oct. 1,720, March 635, May 87. Total 22,983, up 256. **Cocoa** (30,000 pounds each), March 5,522, May 4,489, July 2,618, Sept. 1,819, Dec. 2,868, March 257, May 1,260. Total 18,853, down 54. **Copper** (25,000 pounds each), Jan. 91, March 7,376, May 5,568, July 5,606, Sept. 1,859 Oct. 532, Dec. 1,145, Jan. 202. Total 21,379, up 193. **Silver** (10,000 troy ounces each), Jan. 839, Feb. 38, March 10,283, May 10,292, July 10,688, Sept. 10,624, Dec. 7,994, Jan. 5,233, March 4,210, May 785. Total 60,986, down 1,909. **Cotton** (500-pound bales), March 347,900, May 323,100, July 174,400, Oct. 50,700, Dec. 247,000, March 32,100, May 4,000. Total 1,179,200, down 15,200. **Orange Juice** (15,000 pounds each), Jan. 1,521, March 1,855, May 970, July 323, Sept. 232, Nov. 49, Jan. 52, March 5. Total 5,007, down 32.

As reproduced daily in *The Wall Street Journal.*

CASH PRICE EFFECTS OF FUTURES TRADING

It has been said throughout this book that futures contracts expire at the cash price in the delivery month and have no effect on the cash market which determines the expiration price. As a matter of shorthand, this practice is excusable but it is not strictly true. Futures contracts *will* expire at the going cash rate without altering that rate—*in the delivery*

month. Farmers are businessmen and like any businessmen, they will use all the data available in deciding whether to sell their produce or to hold it for a higher price. Farmers do look to the futures markets for help in deciding whether to sell or hold, and to this extent, futures option prices will have a feedback effect onto the cash market. Futures prices will help determine cash prices for each month over the course of the sales year. To the extent that the futures markets present an ordered, fair price over the year—normal intermonth basis, smooth transition from contract to contract—they will help to provide a smooth cash market over the year, without the erratic jogs that can plague an illiquid cash market without the "crystal ball" provided by a futures market quotation.

In 1958, Congress passed a law prohibiting futures trading in onions at the request of onion farmers and wholesalers. Industry spokesmen feared and attempted to prove that futures trading in onions tended to wildly accelerate price swings which were ruining the cash market. Figures taken from the cash onion market before, during, and after the time that the futures market was functioning tend to underline the fact that speculation quiets price gyrations rather than accelerating them as claimed by the cash traders.

Onions are a particularly good example of a futures market in action because both crop size and demand are as variable as with any other commodity with the improvement (for study) that onions cannot be carried over from year to year. All onions grown must be consumed, for old onions cannot compete with new onions on the cash market. If the stored onions are consumed too quickly during the winter or if the early Rio Grande crop is late in being harvested, onion prices can skyrocket in the last weeks before the onslaught of new onions. Alternately, if stocks of onions are underestimated and too many onions crowd the market prior to the new crop or if the new crop comes early, onions can drop to very low price levels on the cash market.

The seasonal price of onions typically rises from September to March with a fairly wild flip at the end of the season if an estimated six-week national supply of onions must be made to last eight weeks or consumed in four. The following chart shows the seasonal movement in cash onion prices in Michigan. Michigan onions were those used in futures trading with other onions at discount or premium to them and thus reacted most closely to the futures prices. (See Fig. 93, p. 152.)

In the years without futures trading price variations were much greater than in the years with futures trading and when late season price adjustments became necessary it was executed with extreme price gyrations. The country simply ran out of onions. In years with futures trading, not only were the price movements less violent, they started much earlier and about as often tapered down as up. The market had been fully discounted and had about as much chance of being overpriced as underpriced. Higher prices started earlier in the presence of futures trading, making a 12-week supply of onions last 14 when necessary or setting the price so that 14 weeks' worth of onions disappeared in 12. Without futures trading the case seems to have been one of trying to

make a four-week supply last six weeks.

The process of feedback between the futures and cash market for onions is what led to the confusion and the blame placed on the futures exchange. An onion farmer had a choice of selling his onions at the going price or holding them because the futures quotation convinced him that prices were going up. The wholesaler wishing to buy onions found that farmers were refusing the offer he was making. When he found out why farmers were withholding he had a source on which to vent his anger. Higher prices on the futures exchanges did have the direct effect of immediately hurting the buyer of onions. They also had the effect of lowering prices to come, but this fact did not stand out. Had the futures markets gyrated as charged, the farmers would quickly have lost confidence in their predictive value, and their feedback onto cash market pricing would have lost its strength.

It is probably unfair to attribute the evidence heard in Congress against onion futures trading to industry insiders who wished to scalp the cash crop, or warehousemen trying to preserve windfall profits at the expense of the farmer, but it is also unfair to characterize the speculator as the grand manipulator for his role in leveling price swings. Leveling swings hurts a little in the immediate market, but it helps later when the overselling has to be balanced. Unfortunately, it is the small immediate pain that causes the wincing, and not the later soothing that is felt. The potato market has been under investigation by Congress as a possible candidate for shutdown. Hopefully, the same ignorance that killed the onions futures market will not kill the futures market for potatoes.

FIGURE 93

Monthly High and Low Prices of Onions to Michigan Growers, and Monthly National Average Prices to Growers, September–March

(Dollars per 50-pound sack at 1947–49 price level)

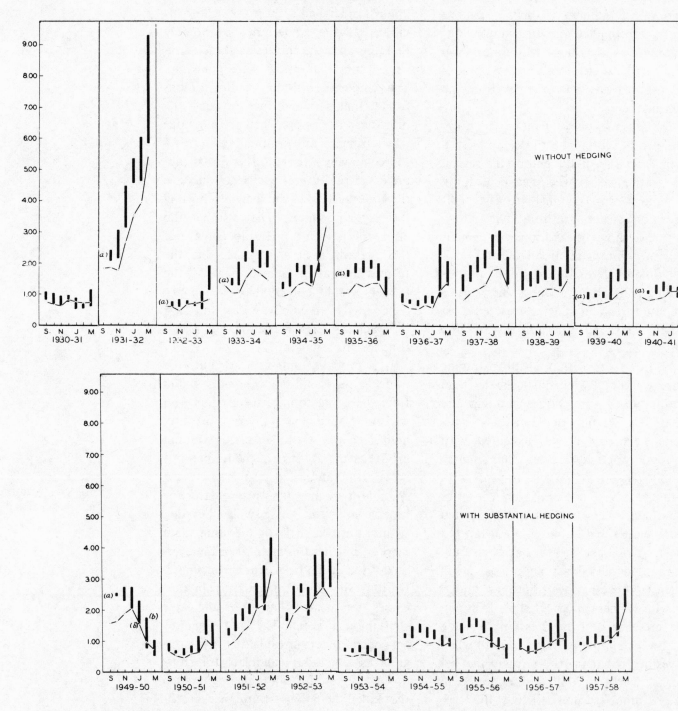

* Michigan price range shown by vertical bars.
^a Quotations lacking or insufficient to establish price range for the month.
^b Missing high or low Michigan price quotation estimated on the basis of Chicago spot quotations.

Source: Holbrook Working, "Price Effects of Futures Trading."

INTERPRETING FUTURES QUOTATIONS

Figure 94 opposite and Figure 95 on page 154 are from *The Wall Street Journal* for November 21, 1972 and quote cash and futures price activity for the day before. Hard red wheat on the cash markets of Kansas City is selling for $2.23¾ a bushel, down nearly 2 cents over the weekend but up roughly 70 cents over a year ago, reflecting high wheat prices caused by the recent large wheat sales to Russia. The nearest futures option for Kansas City wheat is for delivery in December and is in its final days of trading. Kansas City December wheat closed at $2.21 bid and $2.21¼ asked. Notice that the option and cash prices are very close.

As the futures price is always the best possible guess of cash price to come in the future, the closeness of cash and December option prices is to be expected. If the December futures price were much higher than the current cash quote, any trader could buy cash, sell futures, store the cash grain for two weeks or so, and deliver for a guaranteed profit. Similarly, a futures quote much below cash prices would encourage any dealer who could wait the two weeks for delivery to forsake the cash market and buy the December future at the bargain prices. The financial link between the cash and futures markets is dealt with in detail in the next chapter.

Cash wheat prices on the Kansas City markets are off 2⅛ cents per bushel for the day. The December option price is off 2⅜–2⅛ cents for the day due to the split close. The similarity in price movement is expectable. The other options follow: were they not to stay in line

with cash prices on the current market, basis between months would become skewed, making the later delivery months prices other than the best possible guess of prices to come, and offering someone a profit for bringing them back into line. (See Chapter 6 for inter-month basis.) When cash dropped 2⅛ cents, December dropped with it, March dropped 1¾ cents; May 2⅛ cents; July 2⅛ cents; and September 1¼ cents.

FIGURE 94

Cash Prices

Monday, November 20, 1972
(Quotations as of 4 p.m. Eastern time)

FOODS

	Mon.	Fri.	Yr. Ago
Flour, hard winter NY cwt	n$8.10	$8.10	$6.85
Coffee, Santos 4s NY lb	n.57½	.57½	.44
Cocoa, Accra NY lb	n.37¾	.38	.23⅞
Sugar, Refined NY lb	.1295	.1295	.1270
Sugar, Raw NY lb	.0902	.0902	.0865
Butter, Fresh A-92 sc NY lb	.71 .70¾-.71	.68¾
Eggs, Lge white, Chgo., doz	n.42½	.42½	.33
Broilers, Dressed "A" NY lb	x.28½	.28½	.25½
Pork Bellies, 10-12 lbs., Chgo., lb	.42	.42	.24
Hogs, Omaha avg cwt	27.55	27.05	18.45
Steers, Omaha choice avg cwt	32.40	33.10	33.50
Pepper, black NY lb	a.46½	.46½	.45

GRAINS AND FEEDS

Wheat, No. 2 ord hard KC bu	2.23¾	2.25⅞	1.54
Corn, No. 2 yel Chicago bu	1.32¾	1.34½	1.04
Oats, No. 1 wh. hvy, Chgo., bu	n.88½	.88	.75¼
Rye, No. 2 Minneapolis bu	1.19	1.19	.91
Barley, top qlty., Mpls., bu	1.35	1.35	1.20
Soybeans, No. 1 yel Chicago bu	n3.67	3.75¾	2.93½
Flaxseed, Minneapolis bu	n3.14	3.14	2.60
Bran, Buffalo ton	n72.00	72.00	46.00
Linseed Meal, Minneapolis ton	109.00	107.00	64.00
Cottonseed Meal, Memphis ton	118.00	110.00	68.00
Soybean Meal, Decatur, Ill. ton	121.00	120.00	71.50

FATS AND OILS

Cottonseed Oil, crd Miss Vly lb	.10¼	.10⅜	.13½
Corn Oil, crude Chicago lb	n.16¼	.16¼	.19¼
Soybean Oil, crd Decatur, Ill. lb	a.0961	.0966	.1247
Peanut Oil, crd Southeast lb	n.18¼	.18⅛	.16½
Coconut Oil, crd Pac Cst lb	a.09⅛	.09⅛	.11¾
Lard, Chicago lb	.1050	.1050	.1025
Tallow, bleachable, NY lb	b.07½	.07½	.06⅞
Linseed Oil, raw NY lb	a.1151	.1151	.1021

TEXTILES AND FIBERS

Cotton, 1 1-16 in. mid Memphis lb	.3100	.3100	.3005
Print Cloth, 64x60 39½ in. NY yd	.21	.21	.17½
Print Cloth, 78x78 43-in. NY yd	.37	.37	.26½
Sheetings, 56x60 40-in. NY yd	.27	.27	.22¾
Burlap, 10 oz. 40 in. NY yd	n.1855	.1855	.1950
Wool, fine staple terr. Bstn, lb	1.47	1.47	.59
Rayon, Satin Acetate NY yd	.26	.26	.25

METALS

Steel Scrap, 1 hvy melt Chg. ton	38.00	38.00	31.00
Copper, per lb	r.50½-¾	.50½-¾	.52⅞
Copper Scrap, No. 2 wire NY lb	n.37½	.37½	.34½
Lead, NY lb	.14½-.15	.14½-.15	.14¼
Zinc, per lb	18	.18	.17
Tin, NY lb	1.7¼	1.77¾	1.76½
Aluminum, ingot, NY lb	.25	.25	.29
Quicksilver, NY 76 lb flask	n260.00	260.00	258.00
Silver, (H&H) NY oz.	1.789	1.795	1.333

MISCELLANEOUS

Rubber, smoked sheets NY lb	n.20½	.20⅝	.17½
Hides, light native cows Chgo lb	n.48	.47	.18
Gasoline, 92 oct. mid-Cont. gal	.13¼	.13¼	.13¼
Fuel Oil, No. 2 mid-Cont. gal	.09¾	.09¾	.09¾

a-Asked. b-Bid. n-Nominal. x-Less than truckloads.

Source: *The Wall Street Journal.*

FIGURE 95

Futures Prices

Monday, November 20, 1972

CHICAGO—WHEAT

	Open	High	Low	Close	Change	Season's High	Season's Low
Dec	229¾	230½	226¾	227-227½	−2⅜to1⅞	233	145¼
Mar 73	231⅛	232⅝	229⅛	229¾-230	−1⅜to1⅛	236¼	147⅞
May	225½	227½	224½	225	−1⅛	233	146⅞
July	207¼	209¾	206½	207	−⅛	215½	178⅛
Sept	209½	211¼	209¼	209½	−⅛	217¼	181½

CORN

	Open	High	Low	Close	Change	Season's High	Season's Low
Dec	138½	138½	136⅛	136¼-⅛	−2½to2⅝	147¾	120⅞
Mar 73	142¼	142¼	140⅛	140⅛-⅜	−2⅜to2⅛	153	125
May	144⅞	144⅞	143	143⅛-¼	−2⅛to2	155½	128
July	146½	146½	144⅝	144⅝-¾	−2to1⅞	157½	130¾
Sept	143¼	143¼	142¼	142¼	−1½	146¼	141
Dec	139	139	137⅝	137¾	−1¾	143½	134

OATS

	Open	High	Low	Close	Change	Season's High	Season's Low
Dec	89⅞	89⅞	89	89	−⅞	90	68
Mar 73	88¾	88¾	88¼	88¼-⅜	−1⅛to1	89⅝	78
May	88¼	88¼	87⅝	87⅞	−¾	88⅞	79¼
July	83½	83½	83	83	+¼	84⅝	79¾

SOYBEANS

	Open	High	Low	Close	Change	Season's High	Season's Low
Nov	381½	381¾	367¾	372-367¾a	−5¾to10	386¾	295¾
Jan 73	375½	375½	366½	369-368½	−3¾to4¼	377½	300
Mar	374½	374½	368⅜	370-370½	−2¼to1¾	375½	319½
May	376	376	370	371¾-372	−1⅞to1⅝	376	328⅛
July	376¾	376¾	371¼	373¼-½	−1⅜to1⅛	376¾	331¾
Aug	373¾	374	369	371-371⅛	−1¼to1⅛	374	342
Sept	354½	354¾	350½	352	−2¼	357	332¾
Nov	339	339	335	336-336¼	−2¾to2⅛	342½	323

SOYBEAN OIL

	Open	High	Low	Close	Change	Season's High	Season's Low
Nov	9.63	9.63	9.54	9.59-.56	− .07to.10	11.85	9.09
Dec	9.68	9.68	9.56	9.65-.67	− .02to unch	11.80	9.17
Jan 73	9.77	9.77	9.65	9.75	− .01	11.78	9.25
Mar	9.94	9.94	9.82	9.92-.93	− .02to.01	11.75	9.37
May	10.03	10.04	9.93	10.02-.03	− .02to.01	10.87	9.47
July	10.14	10.14	10.00	10.09-.11	− .04to.02	10.76	9.56
Aug	10.14	10.14	10.02	10.11	− .02	10.65	9.56
Sept	10.10	10.10	10.05	10.10	....	10.60	9.55
Dec	9.75	9.75	9.75	9.75	− .15	10.26	9.55

SOYBEAN MEAL

	Open	High	Low	Close	Change	Season's High	Season's Low
Nov	121.75	121.75	120.10	120.5-121.5	+2.0to3.0	134.75	78.00
Dec	122.00	122.00	120.10	121.00-.25	+ .35to.60	127.95	78.00
Jan73	118.00	118.30	117.25	117.80-.95	+ .90to1.05	124.00	79.25
Mar	116.00	116.30	115.40	115.75-116.	+ .90to1.15	120.50	87.50
May	115.10	115.10	114.50	115.-114.90	+1.25to1.15	119.25	92.50
July	115.00	115.20	114.60	115.20	+1.40	118.75	102.75
Aug	114.75	114.90	114.55	114.90b	+1.15	118.00	104.25
Aug	14.75	114.90	114.55	114.90b	+1.15	118.00	104.25
Sept	111.50	111.50	111.50	111.50b	+ .70	114.00	110.80
Dec	103.00	103.00	102.60	102.50b	− .25	104.50	93.00

ICED BROILERS

	Open	High	Low	Close	Change	Season's High	Season's Low
Nov	26.75	26.75	26.75	26.75	− .15	27.15	25.30
Jan 73	27.90	27.90	27.85	27.90	− .10	28.00	26.75
Mar	28.60	28.60	28.60	28.60	....	28.60	26.95

PLYWOOD

	Open	High	Low	Close	Change	Season's High	Season's Low
Nov	164.00	167.00	161.00	167.-165.5	+5.8to4.3	199.50	95.10
Jan73	142.00	145.50	136.00	145.-144.5	+5.9to5.4	173.60	97.40
Mar	134.00	138.00	131.00	137.5-138.	+6.3to6.8	156.00	98.80
May	130.00	135.10	129.00	135.10b	+7.00	148.90	100.00
July	127.00	132.00	126.50	132.00b	+7.00	141.00	114.50
Sept	126.50	130.00	126.00	130.00b	+7.00	137.00	115.00

CHICAGO—SILVER

	Open	High	Low	Close	Change	Season's High	Season's Low
Dec	178.60	179.70	177.90	179.50	+1.00	196.40	137.80
Feb73	180.90	182.00	180.20	181.90-.60	+1.3to1.0	198.60	140.10
Apr	182.80	183.90	182.00	183.70	+1.10	200.50	152.70
June	184.80	185.90	184.20	185.80	+1.30	202.50	161.80
Aug	187.40	187.90	186.40	187.90	+1.50	204.20	163.30
Oct	189.20	189.80	189.20	189.80	+1.40	205.50	176.50
Dec	190.80	191.70	190.40	191.70	+1.60	207.00	178.50
Feb74	193.00	194.00	192.40	193.60b	+1.80	201.60	191.80

KANSAS CITY—WHEAT

	Open	High	Low	Close	Change	Season's High	Season's Low
Dec	223½	223½	221	221-221¼	−2⅜to2⅛	233	144⅛
Mar 73	223¼	223¼	220⅞	221	−1¾	233½	145⅜
May	217	217¼	215	215⅛	−2⅛	225	146¼
July	198½	199¼	197¾	197⅞	−2⅛	202¼	183½
Sept	200½	201¼	200	200	−1¼	201¼	192½

MINNEAPOLIS—WHEAT

	Open	High	Low	Close	Change	Season's High	Season's Low
Dec	210¾	210¾	207½	208-207½	−2to2½	231	156¾
Mar 73	212¼	212¼	208	209-208	−2¾to3¾	234¾	186
May	213¾	214¼	210¼	210½	−2¾	235½	194¼

WINNIPEG—RAPESEED (VANCOUVER)

	Open	High	Low	Close	Change	Season's High	Season's Low
Nov	292½	292½	288½	289b	−¼	297⅛	242½
Jan 73	287½	289⅛	284⅝	286¼-½	−1to¾	293½	240½
Mar	282¼	284⅝	280	281¼b	−1	290⅝	242
June	278¼	278⅜	275½	276½	−½	284¼	259

RYE

	Open	High	Low	Close	Change	Season's High	Season's Low
Dec	127½	127½	127	127⅛b	−⅛	127⅝	97
May 73	134	134⅛	133	133¾	+⅛	135	102⅛
July	134	134	132½	132⅝b	−⅞	134	124

OATS

	Open	High	Low	Close	Change	Season's High	Season's Low
Dec	94¼	96¼	94¼	95⅝	+1⅝	96¼	70½
May 73	95⅜	96⅞	95⅜	95¾	+⅜	96⅞	71½
July	95⅝	95⅝	95⅝	95⅝	+⅞	95⅝	81⅝

BARLEY

	Open	High	Low	Close	Change	Season's High	Season's Low
Dec	126¾	127	126¾	127	+¼	130½	109⅝
May 73	129⅞	130⅛	129⅞	130	+½	132½	117
July	131⅛	131⅛	131⅛	131⅛b	+⅛	132¼	126

FLAXSEED

	Open	High	Low	Close	Change	Season's High	Season's Low
Nov	367	373¾	367	373¾	+10	374	266
Dec	336	336¼	334	335½a	+¼	342¼	266⅞
May 73	341¾	342	340⅛	341⅛a	+⅛	347½	284¾
July	340	340½	338½	339½a	+¼	346	315¾

CATTLE (CHICAGO MERCANTILE EXCHANGE)

	Open	High	Low	Close	Change	Season's High	Season's Low
Dec	34.50	34.50	34.25	34.40-.37	− .25to.28	37.45	31.00
Feb 73	36.75	36.97	36.67	36.82-.85	− .13to.10	38.45	32.00
Apr	37.12	37.42	37.05	37.30	+ .05	38.20	32.35
June	37.25	37.50	37.10	37.42-.40	+ .10to.98	238.40	34.17
Aug	35.35	36.55	36.25	36.40	− .10	38.05	33.95
Oct	35.70	35.75	35.70	35.75	− .05	36.85	35.70

Sales estimated at: 5,568 contracts.

FRESH EGGS

	Open	High	Low	Close	Change	Season's High	Season's Low
Dec	36.60	36.60	35.85	36.20-.10	− .80to.90	45.80	35.50
Jan 73	37.70	37.70	36.85	37.25-.20	− .70to.75	44.60	36.50
Feb	38.00	38.20	37.65	37.90-38.05	− .55to.40	43.40	37.15
Mar	38.00	38.30	37.90	37.95-38.	− .25to.20	42.00	37.30
Apr	38.30	38.30	37.75	37.75	− .50	40.75	36.55
May	34.50	35.00	34.50	34.55	− .65	37.00	33.80

Sales estimated at: 2,267 contracts.

POTATOES (IDAHO RUSSET)

	Open	High	Low	Close	Change	Season's High	Season's Low
May 73	7.40	7.40	7.30	7.30	− .10	8.23	5.95

Sales: 4 contracts.

FROZEN PORK BELLIES

	Open	High	Low	Close	Change	Season's High	Season's Low
Feb 73	47.55	47.57	47.15	47.20-.15	− .42to.47	48.40	31.90
Mar	46.00	46.05	45.67	45.72-.70	− .28to.30	47.42	31.85
May	45.20	45.25	44.80	44.87-.80	− .28to.35	46.60	32.75
July	43.95	44.17	43.77	43.95-.87	− .05to.13	44.55	36.80
Aug	41.75	42.05	41.52	41.72-.77	− .03to+.02	42.55	34.30

Sales estimated at: 4,929 contracts.

HOGS

	Open	High	Low	Close	Change	Season's High	Season's Low
Dec	29.97	30.00	29.82	29.95-.97	+ .05to.07	30.10	22.65
Feb 73	29.30	29.32	29.12	29.20	− .12	30.25	22.97
Apr	26.30	26.40	26.20	26.32	− .03	28.20	23.65
June	26.95	27.05	26.95	27.05	− .05	28.60	24.80
July	26.97	27.00	26.97	27.00	− .05	28.40	24.80
Aug	25.00	25.05	25.00	25.05	....	26.50	23.50
Oct	23.60	23.60	23.45	23.55	+ .05	24.65	22.37

Sales estimated at: 1,078 contracts.

LUMBER

	Open	High	Low	Close	Change	Season's High	Season's Low
Jan73	139.00	141.00	137.20	140.80-.90	+1.2to1.3	165.00	104.50
Mar	135.50	140.00	134.50	138.6-140.	+3.5to3.9	155.00	106.50
May	132.50	135.50	132.00	135.50	+3.50	147.90	124.50

Sales estimated at: 264 contracts.

NEW YORK—SILVER

	Open	High	Low	Close	Change	Season's High	Season's Low
Dec	178.30	179.10	178.00	178.90	+ .30	195.20	137.50
Jan73	179.30	180.00	179.10	180.00	+ .30	196.00	138.60
Mar	181.20	182.50	181.20	182.10	+ .30	198.40	140.10
May	183.70	184.50	183.30	184.10	+ .30	200.20	149.40
July	185.50	186.40	185.30	186.10	+ .30	202.30	158.20
Sept	187.70	188.10	187.20	188.10	+ .60	204.00	163.90
Dec	190.40	191.20	190.10	191.00	+ .40	206.50	176.50
Jan74	192.00	192.10	191.10	192.10	+ .40	207.40	179.00
Mar	193.60	194.00	193.50	194.00	+ .40	202.80	193.50

Sales: 2,795 contracts.

COPPER

	Open	High	Low	Close	Change	Season's High	Season's Low
Dec	46.05	46.30	46.05	46.10	− .15	54.90	46.05
Jan 73	46.50	46.60	46.50	46.50	− .15	54.90	46.45
Mar	47.20	47.45	47.20	47.30	− .10	55.20	47.10
May	47.90	48.00	47.90	47.95	− .05	55.05	47.80
July	48.50	48.65	48.50	48.60	....	54.40	48.35
Sept	49.15	49.20	49.10	49.20	....	54.80	49.00
Oct	49.50	49.55	49.40	49.55	+ .05	54.20	49.30
Dec	50.05	50.15	50.05	50.15	+ .05	51.95	49.90

Sales: 1,638 contracts.

SUGAR (WORLD CONTRACT)

	Open	High	Low	Close	Change	Season's High	Season's Low
Mar 73	7.40	7.42	7.32	7.36-.37	− .15to.14	8.90	4.84
May	7.30	7.35	7.26	7.27-.30	− .12to.09	8.80	5.49
July	7.22	7.23	7.17	7.18b	− .10	8.70	5.51
Sept	7.05	7.05	7.03	7.03b	− .11	8.10	5.44
Oct	6.92	6.98	6.90	6.91	− .11	8.01	5.37
Mar 74	6.65	6.70	6.65	6.69n	− .10	7.44	6.60

Sales: 1,065 contracts. Spot: 7.15n.

COCOA

	Open	High	Low	Close	Change	Season's High	Season's Low
Dec	32.45	32.69	32.35	32.45	− .30	33.85	21.88
Mar 73	32.60	32.69	32.40	32.48	− .26	33.80	22.34
May	32.30	32.45	32.25	32.25	− .25	33.94	22.75
July	32.42	32.49	32.30	32.31	− .24	34.60	27.25
Sept	32.55	32.60	32.44	32.44	− .23	34.25	28.24
Dec	32.74	32.79	32.58	32.58	− .25	34.50	30.20

Sales: 1,234 contracts.

WOOL FUTURES

	Open	High	Low	Close	Change	Season's High	Season's Low
July73	135.0	135.0	135.0	135.0	+0.3	158.0	108.5

Spot: 149.5n.

ORANGE JUICE (FROZEN CONCENTRATED)

	Open	High	Low	Close	Change	Season's High	Season's Low
Jan 73	43.70	44.50	43.50	44.50	+ .80	56.25	40.15
Mar	44.60	45.50	44.45	45.35	+ .60	55.75	41.00
May	45.50	46.25	45.50	46.15b	+ .50	50.25	41.50
July	46.15	46.70	46.15	46.65b	+ .40	51.00	41.90
Sept	46.20	46.20	46.20	47.15b	+ .45	49.85	42.40
Jan 74	44.00	44.25	44.00	44.00b	+ .40	45.00	41.00

Sales estimated at: 400 contracts.

COTTON

	Open	High	Low	Close	Change	Season's High	Season's Low
Dec	32.90	33.10	32.55	33.10	+1.10	33.40	26.34
Mar 73	32.50	32.95	32.26	32.83-.90	+ .93to1.0	33.45	27.03
May	32.40	33.00	32.35	32.85	+ .85	33.60	27.59
July	32.45	33.05	32.40	32.90	+1.02	33.30	27.85
Oct	31.35	32.03	31.35	31.96	+ .71	33.05	27.77
Dec	30.98	31.03	30.90	31.00	+ .40	32.15	27.70
Mar 74	31.35	31.50	31.30	31.30b	+ .42	32.36	28.30

Sales estimated at: 2,150 contracts.

SILVER COIN FUTURES (IN DOLLARS)

	Open	High	Low	Close	Change	Season's High	Season's Low
Jan 73	1340	1340	1334	1334	−10	1432	1149
Apr	1355	1355	1355	1355	−10	1450	1179
July	1385	1385	1378	1378	−8	1465	1235
Oct	1400	1400	1395	1395	−5	1483	1250
Jan 74	1418	1420	1415	1418	−2	1500	1312
Apr	1445	1445	1434	1435	−5	1488	1434

Sales: 58 contracts.

PLATINUM

	Open	High	Low	Close	Change	Season's High	Season's Low
Jan73	136.70	138.50	136.70	138.10	+ .90	163.70	98.00
Apr	139.00	140.70	138.60	140.30	+1.20	165.00	98.00
July	140.70	142.80	140.70	142.20	+1.20	165.00	101.00
Oct	142.70	143.80	142.70	144.20b	+1.20	165.20	105.20
Jan74	145.00	146.90	145.00	146.50a	+1.30	164.50	137.50

Sales: 326 contracts.

POTATOES (MAINE CONTRACT)

	Open	High	Low	Close	Change	Season's High	Season's Low
Mar 73	4.92	4.92	4.88	4.90	....	4.92	3.05
Apr	5.10	5.10	5.09	5.10	+ .02	5.10	3.28
May	5.70	5.70	5.65	5.65	− .01	5.71	3.70

Sales: 545 contracts.

a-Asked. b-Bid. n-Nominal.

Source: *The Wall Street Journal.*

September is a new crop contract for the wheat traded in Kansas City and is not as tightly linked with the other options which all reflect prices for the same year's crop.

The Wall Street Journal quotes prices for wheat at Kansas City, Chicago, and Minneapolis and the three must be kept separate. Chicago wheat cannot be delivered against Kansas City contracts nor against Minneapolis contracts. The three markets are distinct and price disparity between them is to be expected. However, when wheat prices move, *all* wheat prices follow and Chicago and Minneapolis wheat options also closed down for the day.

Corn is traded on the Chicago Board of Trade and the corn trader finds the following closes for the day:

Cash	$1.32¾
December	1.36¼–⅜
March 1973	1.40⅛–⅞
May	1.43⅛–¼
July	1.44⅝–¾
September	1.42¼
December	1.37¾

These quotations are the best going guess of cash prices to come in the future in each of the contract months. At the current time, traders foresee a cash chart for corn reflecting the normal inter-month basis, climbing at an even rate through the winter and spring, then tapering back down into harvest. Corn is generally lowest in price around October and November, following harvest with a market peak in the late spring. As news enters the market, corn prices will jog up and down, but the normal cash seasonal pattern will remain the same as all options jog together and March can be expected to remain priced about 4 cents over December, May about 4 cents over March, tapering down toward the September and December deliveries. As December represents a new crop, the relationship between December and previous month prices is expected to be less closely related by intermonth basis.

Usually bid *or* offer are quoted when there is no trade at the close; the split price represents a range in which prices traded during the closing period. When no split quotation is given, the bidding price offered by buyers and the asking price of sellers was the same and a trade was made. *Nominal* refers to a price which is a pretty good representation of the prices current in the market at the close. No trade necessarily took place at this price although it is the best single quotation for the closing activity.

10

SOMETHING TO START WITH

WHEAT

Wheat futures are among the oldest commodities traded on futures exchanges and one of the most important. It is one of the three major crops of the United States, along with corn and soybeans. Wheat futures are traded on the Chicago Board of Trade, the Kansas City Board of Trade, and the Minneapolis Grain Exchange, with the Board of Trade (at Chicago) taking by far the lion's share of the business. (See Fig. '96 opposite.)

In the United States, the winter wheat harvest starts in the South in late May and ends along the Canadian border in late July. A second crop, spring wheat, is harvested in the late summer. The crop season for wheat runs from July 1 through June 30 of the year following so that May is generally an old crop contract with July seeing the first of the newly harvested crop and lower prices. March, May, July, September, and December are the five contract months traded. The trading unit is 5,000 bushels as with all grains. Margin runs from $500 per contract to a high of $2,500 when prices are considered volatile. Wheat contract prices may move in a range no greater than 10 cents above or below the closing quote of the previous trading session. Any trader who holds a position

in excess of 200,000 bushels must report his position to the Commodity Exchange Authority and no trader may hold a position of more than 3 million bushels. (See Fig. 97 opposite.)

The *Statistical Yearbook* of the Chicago Board of Trade and the Commodity Research Bureau's *Commodity Yearbook* both give full layout on the supply and demand of and for wheat throughout the world, along with vital statistics for other commodities. The Department of Agriculture issues its *Crop Production Report* regularly during harvest including a Prospective Planting Report and other crop reports which keep the trader up-to-date with statistics. The Department of Agriculture also periodically issues the *Wheat Situation* report which is probably the most useful publication available to the trader (Fig. 98, p. 158). This is available free to anyone who puts his name on the automated mailing list. The *Grain Market News* also from the Department of Agriculture is published weekly and gives the trader a good feel for the current supply and demand in cash markets.

Four times a year, the Department of Agriculture issues *Quarterly Stocks of Grains in All Positions* which outlines the stocks of wheat throughout the United States by size, location, and ownership along with other grains. This

FIGURE 96

DEC. 1, 1972

WHEAT CHICAGO BOARD OF TRADE MONTHLY HIGH, LOW & CLOSE OF NEAREST FUTURES CONTRACT IN CENTS PER BUSHEL

PREPARED BY
COMMODITY RESEARCH BUREAU, INC.
140 BROADWAY NEW YORK, N. Y. 10005

Source: Commodity Research Bureau, Inc.

FIGURE 97
WHERE WHEAT IS GROWN IN
THE UNITED STATES

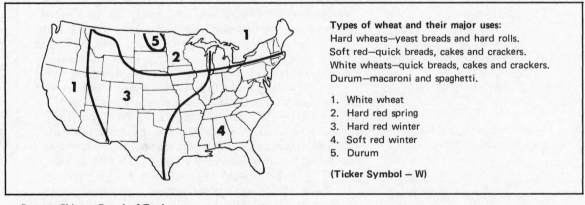

Types of wheat and their major uses:
Hard wheats—yeast breads and hard rolls.
Soft red—quick breads, cakes and crackers.
White wheats—quick breads, cakes and crackers.
Durum—macaroni and spaghetti.

1. White wheat
2. Hard red spring
3. Hard red winter
4. Soft red winter
5. Durum

(Ticker Symbol — W)

Source: Chicago Board of Trade.

FIGURE 98
SAMPLE OF PAGE 1 FROM A *WHEAT SITUATION* REPORT

WHEAT SITUATION

CONTENTS

• • •

Approved by
The Outlook and Situation Board
and Summary released
May 15, 1972

Principal contributors:
James J. Naive
Frank R. Gomme

Economic and Statistical Analysis Division

Economic Research Service

U.S. Department of Agriculture
Washington, D.C. 20250

• • •

The next issue of the *Wheat Situation* will be published in August 1972.

SUMMARY

Domestic use of wheat this marketing year is rising to the highest level in over 2 decades, thanks to heavy use for feed. However, exports are running sharply lower and total wheat disappearance is expected to fall about 5% from last season's 1,526 million bushels. Since the 1971 harvest boosted supplies sharply, around 200 million bushels will be added to stocks, pushing them to the highest level since 1963. Carryovers of Hard Red Spring (HRS), Hard Red Winter (HRW), and Durum wheats will be heaviest.

Farm prices for the season will average moderately above the loan rate and close to the $1.33 per bushel of last season, despite the much larger wheat supply and smaller disappearance. Prices were still strong early in the season when a large part of the crop was marketed. Farmers have used the loan program judiciously this year and privately held supplies have been maintained in good balance with demand.

World wheat production rose 10% to a record 318 million metric tons in 1971. Generally favorable weather was the main reason for output being up for all major producers except the USSR and Mainland China. The larger wheat harvest has dropped world import demand about 5% from last season's 53.8 million metric tons. Europe will buy less, accounting for most of the reduction. World wheat prices have dropped 10 to 20 cents a bushel as a result of larger supplies, lower import demand, and lower feed grain prices.

Farms that are enrolled in the 1972 wheat program account for 94% of the eligible national domestic allotment of 19.5 million acres, about the same as last year. Set-aside acreage was up a half totaling 20.3 million, including 15.3 million required and 5.0 million voluntary additional. Total harvested acreage is estimated at about 47.0 million acres, down 3% from last year. Harvested spring wheat acreage may be down nearly a third but winter wheat acreage was increased.

Winter wheat production as of May 1 was indicated at 1,149 million bushels, down 1% from last year. Assuming spring wheat yields are on trend, total wheat production may be around 1,500 million bushels, down 9% from this season's record. However, a crop this size would indicate some price pressures, and unless exports recover sharply from this season's low level, there could be an increase in carryout at the end of the 1972/73 marketing year. Prospects point to larger soft wheat crops, sharply reduced HRS and durum harvests, and little change in HRW.

Source: U.S. Department of Agriculture, *Wheat Situation.*

is one of the most important reports issued by the government and often will set the stage for a rapid price advance or decline. This report is issued as of the 1st of January, April, July, and October and is available about the 20th-25th of the month.

All of these reports rely almost exclusively on statistical data viewed from different perspectives, although the *Situation Reports* also include conclusions and forecasts in paragraph form. The tables can be difficult to consume unless the trader is looking for specific information and each of these reports is usually used as reference material after the trader has decided what he is looking for. Figure 99, page 160, is a typical table from the *Wheat Situation* report.

Wheat makes a seasonal low normally during the month of June or July, dipping during harvest and rallying over the ensuing months. It is said that a wealthy trader once left his son all he needed to make a fortune: "Buy wheat July 1st and sell wheat December 1st." While this does not work every year, it is in conformity with the general price trend.

A wheat future is characterized by wide swings in normal range of an active market. A rise of 6 cents followed by a drop of 8 cents and another rise of 5 cents can occur as a regular pattern. Because of this wide-swinging pattern, wheat is one of the more difficult of the commodity markets, making harder the manipulation of a position through the use of stops and requiring substantial backup for the trader who wishes to ride out the storm.

Additional statistical data pertaining to the preceding section on "Wheat" is shown in Figures 100, 101 and 102 on pages 161, 162, and 163.

FIGURE 99

Table 1.--Wheat: Supply, distribution and prices, total and by class
July-June average 1964-68 and annual 1969-72 1/

Item and Year	Average 1964-68	1969/70	1970/71 preliminary	1971/72 projected	1972/73 projected
	- - - - Million bushels - - - -				
Beginning carryover	644	819	885	730	927
Production	1,402	1,460	1,370	1,640	1,500
Imports 2/	1	3	1	1	1
Total supply	2,047	2,282	2,256	2,371	2,428
Food 3/	513	520	519	520	
Seed	68	57	63	64	
Feed (residual) 4/	111	214	206	285	
On farms where grown	(43)	(61)	(62)	(73)	
Domestic disappearance	692	791	788	869	
Exports 2/	728	606	738	575	
Total disappearance	1,420	1,397	1,526	1,444	
Ending carryover	627	885	730	927	
Privately owned--"Free"	(194)	(152)	(169)		
	- - - - Dollars per bushel - - - -				
Price Support					
National average loan rate	1.26	1.25	1.25	1.25	
Average certificate payment	.50	.65	.75	.54	
Season Average Price Received					
By non-participants	1.39	1.24	1.33	1.31	
By program participants	1.89	1.89	2.08	1.86	

	Hard winter	Red winter	Hard spring 5/	Durum	White
	- - - - Million bushels - - - -				
Average 1964-68					
Beginning carryover	411	13	161	43	16
Production	700	225	205	73	199
Total supply	1,111	238	367	116	215
Domestic disappearance	303	146	138	39	66
Exports 2/	422	73	76	34	123
Total disappearance	725	219	214	73	189
1969/70					
Beginning carryover	524	33	163	41	58
Production	790	194	189	106	181
Total supply	1,314	227	355	147	239
Domestic disappearance	353	176	137	35	90
Exports 2/	336	28	89	34	119
Total disappearance	689	204	226	69	209
1970/71 Preliminary					
Beginning carryover	625	23	129	78	30
Production	760	183	198	50	179
Total supply	1,385	206	328	128	209
Domestic disappearance	385	165	124	35	79
Exports 2/	450	26	113	39	110
Total disappearance	835	191	237	74	189
1971/72 Projected					
Beginning carryover	550	15	91	54	20
Production	759	221	367	88	205
Total supply	1,309	236	459	142	225
Domestic disappearance	426	180	142	36	85
Exports 2/	308	37	90	40	100
Total disappearance	734	217	232	76	185
Carryover, June 30, 1972	575	19	227	66	40

1/ Data by class, except production, are approximations. Projected disappearance figures should be regarded as midpoint of estimated ranges. 2/ Imports and exports include flour and other products in terms of wheat. 3/ Used for food in the United States, U.S. territories, and by the military at home and abroad. 4/ Assumed to roughly approximate total amount used for feed, including mixed and processed feed, also includes negligible quantities used in distilled spirits and beer. 5/ Total supply of Hard spring includes imports.

Source: U.S. Department of Agriculture, *Wheat Situation*, May 1972.

FIGURE 100

Wheat: Comparison of 1971 and 1972 Program Provisions

Item	1971 Set-aside Program	1972 Set-aside Program
National domestic wheat allotment	19.7 million acres	19.7 million acres
Loan	$1.25 per bushel	$1.25 per bushel
Domestic certificate	Difference between the $1.30 received by farmers in the first 5 months (July-Nov. 1971) of the marketing year and 100 percent of wheat parity on July 1, 1971.	Difference between average price received by farmers in the first 5 months (July-Nov. 1972) of the marketing year and 100 percent of wheat parity on July 1, 1972.
Total support or guarantee to program participants for certificated production	100 percent of parity ($2.93)	100 percent of parity
Production eligible for domestic certificates	Production on 100 percent of farm domestic wheat allotment.	Same as for 1971
Production eligible for loan	Total production on participating farms	Same as for 1971
Certificated production on participating farms-estimated	535 million bushels	Same as for 1971
Preliminary payments	75 percent of estimated value of certificates soon after July 1, 1971. Final payments made after December 1. If preliminary payment is larger than value of certificates finally determined, no refund will be required	Same as for 1971
Payment limitations	Maximum value of 1971 wheat certificates to any person $55,000	Same as for 1971
Limitation on acreage planted to wheat	Participant who sets aside cropland equal to the required percentage of his domestic wheat allotment and maintains his conserving base may plant all the remaining cropland on the farm to wheat or any other crop he wishes-without loss of certificates (planting of quota crops limited by other programs).	Same as for 1971 except for the voluntary set-aside requirement which limits planting of spring wheat.
Required set-aside	75 percent of farm domestic wheat allotment	83 percent of farm domestic wheat allotment
Compensation for required set-aside	Value of wheat certificates and loan eligibility	Same as for 1971
Voluntary set-aside for payment	None	Up to 75 percent of a farm's domestic allotment. Spring wheat producer's planted acreage plus voluntary set-aside cannot exceed his total planted acreage in 1971.
Payment for voluntary set-aside	None	94 cents per bushel times farm yield times acre voluntarily set-aside.
Planting requirement to prevent loss of allotment	Producer who fails to plant 90 percent of his domestic allotment to wheat in 1971 will have his 1972 allotment reduced by the underplanting--up to 20 percent. Acreage planted to corn or sorghum is considered planted to wheat. Acreage not planted due to natural disaster or conditions beyond producers control will be considered planted and producer who makes a set-aside but elects to receive no payment will not suffer an allotment loss.	With the inclusion of barley and soybeans, same as for 1971
Substitution	Any producer who sets aside cropland equal to the required percentages of his base and allotment and maintains his conserving base can plant his entire acreage to wheat, corn or sorghum without loss of payments, certificates, base acreage or allotment. A producer with only a base or only an allotment can participate in one program and plant all wheat or all feed grains without loss of benefits, base or allotment.	With the inclusion of barley and soybeans, same as for 1971
Conserving base	Acreage diverted must be in addition to the conserving base, i.e., average acreage of conserving crops in 1959 and 1960.	Same as for 1971
Farm program yield (used to calculate benefits)	Projected from 1967-69 average	Projected from 1968-70 average

Source: U.S. Department of Agriculture.

FIGURE 101

World Production of Wheat In Thousands of Metric Tons[3]

Crop Year	Argentina	Australia	Canada	China	France	W. Germany	India	Italy	Pakistan	Spain	Turkey	Un. Kingdom	U.S.S.R.	United States	World Total[1]
1959	215	198	445	(880)	425	166	350	311	144	175	215	104	1,900	1,118	8,175
1960	150	274	518	N.A.	405	182	377	250	145	130	260	112	1,700	1,355	8,185
1961	190	246	283	N.A.	352	148	404	305	141	126	225	196	1,900	1,232	7,880
1962	190	307	566	N.A.	509	168	442	349	149	177	250	146	2,000	1,092	8,760
1963	328	328	723	N.A.	377	178	398	299	155	179	290	112	1,470	1,147	8,315
1964	415	369	600		508	191	362	315	154	146	257	139	2,100	1,283	9,327
1965–6	228	260	649	808	542	160	452	359	170	173	273	153	1,700	1,316	9,075
1966–7	234	462	827	764	415	167	394	346	146	177	301	128	2,939	1,312	10,276
1967–8	269	277	593	845	513	214	419	353	161	206	331	143	2,352	1,522	10,185
1968–9	211	544	650	772	551	228	608	355	238	201	309	131	2,815	1,576	11,318
1969–0[3]	7,020	10,835	18,623	22,300	14,459	6,000	18,652	9,536	6,600	4,691	8,300	3,364	62,300	39,740	287,412
1970–1[2]	4,250	7,890	9,023	24,500	12,922	5,662	20,093	9,630	7,399	4,060	8,000	4,174	80,000	37,291	287,913
1971–2[1]	5,200	8,453	14,253	23,500	15,100	7,142	23,247	10,070	6,588	5,387	10,500	4,824	75,000	44,620	313,640
1972–3															

[1] Estimated. [2] Preliminary. [3] Data prior to 1969–70 are in MILLIONS OF BUSHELS.
Source: Foreign Agricultural Service, U.S.D.A.

Seeded Acreage, Yield and Production of All Wheat in the United States

Year	Seeded Acreage—1,000,000 Acres					Yield Per Harvested Acre—In Bushels					Production—1,000,000 Bushels				
	Winter	Spring	Not Durum	Durum	All	Winter	Spring	Not Durum	Durum	All	Winter	Spring	Not Durum	Durum	All
1959	43.6	13.1	11.9	1.2	56.7	23.2	16.5	16.3	17.7	21.6	917.8	200.0	179.8	20.2	1,117.7
1960	42.7	12.2	10.5	1.7	54.9	27.8	20.5	20.5	20.8	26.1	1,111.4	243.3	208.9	34.4	1,354.7
1961	43.5	12.2	10.4	1.8	55.7	26.4	14.6	14.8	13.1	23.9	1,074.8	157.6	136.2	21.3	1,232.4
1962	38.9	10.4	7.9	2.4	49.3	24.4	27.0	·26.2	29.7	25.0	822.9	269.1	198.8	70.3	1,092.0
1963	42.3	11.1	9.0	2.1	53.4	26.3	21.8	20.8	25.7	25.2	914.1	232.7	181.3	51.4	1,146.8
1964	43.6	12.0	9.5	2.5	55.7	26.8	22.5	21.1	27.6	25.8	1,021.0	262.4	194.2	68.1	1,283.4
1965	45.1	12.2	9.9	2.4	57.4	27.1	24.9	23.6	30.4	26.5	1,017.1	298.5	228.7	69.9	1,315.6
1966	43.0	11.4	8.9	2.5	54.4	27.4	22.6	21.6	25.9	26.3	1,062.5	249.2	186.6	62.6	1,311.7
1967	54.1	13.7	10.9	2.8	67.8	26.6	23.6	23.5	24.1	25.9	1,206.8	315.6	249.1	66.4	1,522.4
1968	49.3	13.2	9.5	3.7	62.5	29.1	26.6	26.1	27.9	28.5	1,235.1	341.2	241.7	99.5	1,576.3
1969	43.1	11.2	7.8	3.4	54.3	31.2	28.8	27.5	31.9	30.7	1,147.2	313.0	206.9	106.1	1,460.2
1970	38.4	11.1	9.0	2.1	49.5	33.3	24.0	23.7	25.0	31.0	1,110.3	259.9	209.4	50.5	1,370.2
1971[1]	38.7	15.9	13.1	2.8	54.6	35.2	30.9	30.7	31.9	33.8	1,163.4	476.1	388.3	87.8	1,639.5
1972[2]	42.2	14.8	12.1	2.7	57.1						1,291.4				
1973															

[1] Preliminary. [2] Estimate. Source: Crop Reporting Board, U.S.D.A.

Salient Statistics of Wheat in the United States

Crop Year	Acreage Harvested 1,000 Acres			Avg.—All Yield Per Acre In Bushels	Farm Disposition (Million Bushels)				Farm Value 1,000 Dollars	Foreign Trade[5] Million Bushels		Per Capita[1] Consumption In Pounds	
	Winter	Spring	All		Used for Seed	Fed to Livestock	Home Use	Sold		Domestic Exports[2]	Imports[3]	Flour	Cereal
1959	39,562	12,154	51,716	21.6	43.3	28.0	1.1	1,045	1,969,546	485.2	7.4	120	2.8
1960	40,027	11,852	51,879	26.1	42.2	24.9	1.0	1,287	2,361,212	631.1	8.1	118	2.8
1961	40,754	10,817	51,571	23.9	37.6	22.4	—	1,172	2,254,675	684.7	5.5	118	2.8
1962	33,734	9,954	43,688	25.0	36.7	16.1	—	1,039	2,225,738	603.7	5.1	115	2.9
1963	34,807	10,699	45,506	25.2	40.5	15.2	—	1,091	2,125,315	815.7	3.6	113	2.9
1964	38,075	11,687	49,762	25.8	41.2	31.4	—	1,211	1,756,969	684.9	.8	114	2.9
1965	37,586	11,974	49,560	26.5	39.6	41.7	—	1,234	1,774,537	832.3	.5	113	2.9
1966	38,816	11,051	49,867	26.3	46.8	26.1	—	1,239	2,140,655	712.8	1.3	111	2.9
1967	45,406	13,365	58,771	25.9	46.3	42.9	—	1,433	2,110,197	735.6	.5	112	2.9
1968–9	42,428	12,834	55,262	28.5	39.7	60.8	—	1,476	1,950,462	519.1	.5	112	2.9
1969–0	36,723	10,854	47,577	30.7	34.2	61.1	—	1,365	1,815,732	581.9	2.6	110	2.9
1970–1[4]	33,300	10,841	44,141	31.0	34.7	62.3	—	1,281	1,826,060			110	2.9
1971–2[4]	33,049	15,404	48,453	33.8					2,167,711			111	2.9

Source: Commodity Research Bureau, Inc.

FIGURE 102

U.S. Wheat Foreign Trade and Domestic Disappearance   In Millions of Bushels

Crop Year	Imports (Grain Only) July-Sept.	Oct.-Dec.	Jan.-Mar.	Apr.-June	Total	Exports (Grain Only) July-Sept.	Oct.-Dec.	Jan.-Mar.	Apr.-June	Total	Domestic Disappearance July-Sept.	Oct.-Dec.	Jan.-Mar.	Apr.-June	Total
1959	.8	1.9	2.2	3.0	7.8	88.8	73.6	116.8	138.7	418.0	197.0	183.6	199.0	113.0	692.6
1960	.7	2.0	3.1	1.9	7.8	120.7	129.4	162.9	148.1	561.2	203.0	149.9	201.4	149.1	703.4
1961	.7	1.1	1.9	1.6	5.4	141.9	177.8	133.4	155.1	608.1	185.7	157.9	208.7	166.8	719.0
1962	.5	.8	2.3	1.5	5.1	124.0	107.4	121.4	181.8	534.7	220.2	146.9	193.0	129.0	689.1
1963	.5	.5	1.6	1.0	3.6	151.3	186.9	215.6	200.5	754.3	247.7	142.9	194.5	104.8	690.0
1964–5	.3	.1	.4	.3	1.1	159.3	181.1	113.4	182.9	636.7	191.9	149.7	179.3	122.7	643.6
1965–6	.2	.1	.3	.3	.9	187.4	166.4	212.8	217.4	784.0	221.6	179.8	190.3	139.5	731.2
1966–7	1.0	.2	.2	.3	1.7	211.1	184.4	135.2	136.0	666.7	179.5	180.5	198.8	120.5	679.3
1967–8	.1	.2	.3	.3	.9	188.5	181.5	184.6	143.0	697.6	188.6	151.6	169.1	138.5	647.8
1968–9	.2	.2	.3	.4	1.1	120.5	142.6	66.2	141.7	471.0	293.1	174.9	158.2	127.7	753.9
1969–0	.3	1.0	.8	1.1	3.2	108.4	127.2	148.4	145.9	529.9	279.8	192.7	169.7	149.0	791.2
1970–7[1]	.2	.2	.3	.4	1.1	154.2	191.7	167.1	161.6	674.6	293.2	168.5	171.3	154.2	787.2
1971–2[1]	.2	.2				149.5	116.3				324.9	200.3			
1972–3															

[1] Preliminary.   Source: Crop Reporting Board, U.S.D.A.

Wheat Government Loan Program Data in the United States

Year Beginning July	Total Support Rate	Loan Rates (Cents Per Bushel) National Avg.[1]	Average Extra Payment	No. 1 Dk. No. Spring Minneapolis	No. 1 Hard Red Winter Kansas City	No. 1 Soft White Portland	Under Price Support (Loans)	Delivered to CCC[5]	Owned by CCC[2]	Stocks—End of Marketing Year (June 30) Under Loan Current Crop	Earlier Crops	Total	"Free" Wheat[3]	Total Stocks[4]
1960	178	178	—	215	207	199	405.8	260.5	1,243	42.0	45.4	1,330	43	1,411
1961	179	179	—	216	208	199	262.4	119.9	1,097	18.0	40.0	1,155	130	1,322
1962	200	200	—	235	227	218	280.7	245.0	1,083	41.9	25.7	1,150	16	1,195
1963	200	182	18	216	206	200	161.6	85.2	829	16.6	36.0	882	10	901
1964	173	130	43	163	153	147	197.9	86.9	607.7	47.8	26.9	682	135	817
1965–6	169	125	44	158	143	144	170.1	11.3	262.1	32.2	43.1	340	195	535
1966–7	184	125	59	156	143	146	132.7	12.3	123.6	32.6	37.1	201	224	425
1967–8	173	125	48	155	143	144	281.0	63.8	102.3	165.7	55.2	323	216	539
1968–9	180	125	55	156	144	144	445.0	108.0	162.7	278.8	174.2	616	203	819
1969–0	190	125	65	157	145	145	406.9	55.1	301.2	179.7	251.6	733	152	885
1970–1[6]	200	125	75	159	147	146	254.2	4.9	362.6	76.2	127.6	561	169	730
1971–2[6]	179	125	54	162	149	147	385							

[1] The national average loan rate at the farm as a percentage of the parity priced wheat at the beginning of the marketing year.
[2] Includes open market purchases, and accordingly may include some new crop wheat.   [3] Less by the amount of new wheat in the stocks owned by CCC.   [4] Carryover of old-crop wheat only.   [5] Includes purchase agreement wheat delivered to CCC.
[6] Preliminary.   Source: Agricultural Marketing Service, U.S.D.A.

Volume of Trading in Wheat Futures at All "Contract" Markets in the U.S.   In Millions of Bushels

Year	July	Aug.	Sept.	Oct.	Nov.	Dec.	Jan.	Feb.	Mar.	Apr.	May	June	Total
1959–60	366.4	268.8	230.4	183.3	195.4	181.2	145.7	175.2	234.8	197.7	237.5	160.7	2,577.1
1960–61	282.6	278.9	151.4	165.0	261.7	178.2	225.7	197.8	207.4	134.4	141.8	264.0	2,489.0
1961–62	445.0	540.6	292.8	309.0	217.9	208.9	308.6	255.8	267.7	349.7	475.9	468.8	4,140.8
1962–63	507.1	664.0	690.2	516.3	394.2	317.6	346.4	294.0	329.5	365.6	436.7	289.7	5,151.5
1963–64	532.9	320.2	654.7	581.0	403.4	364.6	278.6	333.3	583.5	476.1	413.4	413.2	5,354.9
1964–65	602.1	387.9	290.4	201.9	206.2	222.8	177.1	131.6	156.7	148.8	122.9	177.4	2,825.9
1965–6	366.1	590.2	494.5	429.5	677.1	668.0	389.4	300.5	336.4	305.6	470.1	972.6	6,000.1
1966–7	806.9	684.1	926.6	719.0	653.3	637.8	648.1	698.3	1,531	1,201	953.7	967.7	10,425.4
1967–8	1,088	1,303	864.9	608.2	832.6	500.0	420.6	417.0	464.2	471.4	447.2	447.3	6,930.2
1968–9	813.3	859.5	742.3	724.0	623.4	271.0	200.0	299.1	221.2	238.9	256.1	302.9	3,714
1969–0	571.9	471.1	365.8	282.6	233.2	293.3	230.2	247.6	230.7	338.2	267.1	424.1	4,235
1970–1	458.3	534.0	491.1	377.4	343.0	338.7	273.3	244.2					
1971–2	421.1	371.0	328.9	330.4	322.3								
1972–3													

Source: Commodity Exchange Authority

Note: All data on this page is from the Commodity Research Bureau, Inc.

CORN

The feed corn crop is the most valuable farm product produced in this country. The United States grows more corn than all the rest of the world combined. With a crop in excess of 5 billion bushels, corn far exceeds the crops of wheat at 1.5 billion bushels and soybeans at 1.1 billion bushels.

Corn futures are traded on the Chicago Board of Trade, the Chicago Open Board of Trade, and the Kansas City Board of Trade with 99 percent of all corn futures traded in Chicago. (See Fig. 103 below.)

The size of the contract is 5,000 bushels and the months in which it can be traded are March, May, July, September, and December. The trading units are one-eighth cents per bushel with each minimum price fluctuation equaling $6.25 per contract. The trading range from the low to the high is a maximum of 20 cents with the market allowed to fluctuate within a limit from 10 cents higher to 8 cents lower than the previous day's closing price.

The most important publication relating to corn is the *Feed Situation* report issued by the U.S. Department of Agriculture (Fig. 104 opposite). This cites the past history of the corn market and forecasts prices for the upcoming months based on current and projected supply

FIGURE 103

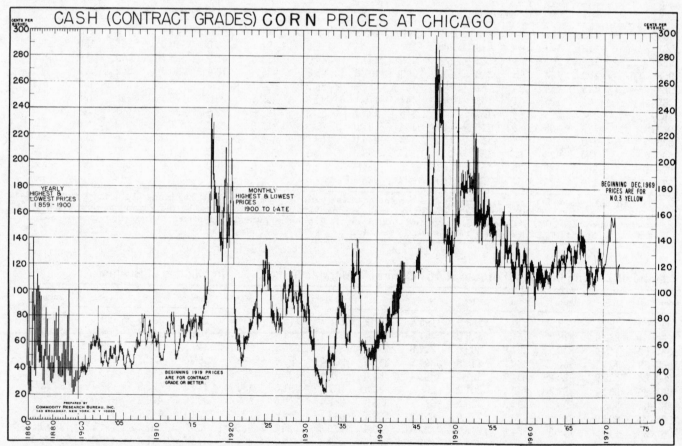

Source: Commodity Research Bureau, Inc.

FIGURE 104. EXAMPLE OF *FEED SITUATION* REPORT

THE FEED SITUATION

CONTENTS

● ● ●

Approved by
The Outlook and Situation Board
August 23, 1972

The summary and a feed grain supply-use
table was released on the above date.

Principal contributor
Jack S. Ross

Economic and Statistical Analysis Division
Economic Research Service

U.S. Department of Agriculture
Washington, D.C. 20250

● ● ●

The *Feed Situation* is published in February, April, May,
August, and November.

SUMMARY

The 1972/73 feed grain supply will total 233 million tons on the basis of August indications, a little below last year's big supply. Production, forecast at 183 million tons, is some 23 million below last year's record output. The smaller crop will be harvested from the least acreage of this century as farmers participated heavily in the voluntary set-aside under the 1972 Feed Grain Program.

Domestic consumption of feed grains in 1972/73 probably will make a further modest gain after the sizable increase occurring this season. Prospects for 1-2% more grain consuming animal units and continued favorable livestock-feed price ratios will likely maintain heavy feeding rates per animal unit.

The 1972/73 feed grain export picture looks bright. Boosted by substantial sales to the USSR, U.S. feed grain exports in 1972/73 will probably exceed the estimated 26 million tons for 1971/72, a volume that is second largest of record.

With expanding use in 1972/73, a sizable reduction in the carryover is likely. For the season now ending, the carryover is estimated at 50 million tons, 17 million more than last year.

Farm prices at harvesttime will be stronger than the low levels in 1971. For example, corn prices this November will be higher than last year's low 97 cents a bushel, perhaps a few cents above the $1.05 loan rate. However, as the year progresses, prices may rise less than seasonally because of moderating effects of relatively large stocks under loan and owned by CCC.

This year's corn crop, forecast at 4.9 billion bushels on August 1, plus an estimated carryover of more than a billion bushels this October 1, gives a 1972/73 supply of 6.1 billion bushels, a little below last year. Production at this level would be short of projected requirements, resulting in a sizable dip in the carryout at the close of 1972/73. Domestic use probably will make a modest gain from this season's 4.3 billion bushels. Exports could be considerably larger than the 750 million estimated for this year.

Sorghum production, forecast at 803 million bushels, would be 10% below last year's record crop. Adding an estimated 160-million-bushel carryover this October 1, however, gives a supply only slightly below the 986 million bushels in 1971/72. With more cattle on feed and prospects for less wheat feeding, livestock producers and demand statistics. This is published five times a year in February, April, August, May, and November. *The Grain Market News* which is a source of information for wheat trading is also valuable for the corn market. Likewise the *Crop Production Reports* issued on the 10th of each month are significant in that they set the existing supply of corn for the current crop year. As in the case of the corn blight in 1970, a production report which first indicated a damaged crop set the tone of the market for the next two years. This report is watched very closely by the trade when following corn statistics. For those traders who desire to position themselves on the side of the large and professional traders, the *Commitment of Traders* report allows them to size up their own positions with those of the professional large traders.

In addition to corn, oats and barley constitute a portion of the feed grain supplies. When prices of corn are high enough, wheat also becomes a substitute for feed corn with wheat a more nutritious but also more expensive feed for animals. When the trader studies the supply of corn in the United States he must also study the supply of barley and oats to enable him to assess the total feed grain situation without depending too heavily upon the supply of corn only.

Most corn is fed to hogs and livestock such as feeder cattle and a significant amount goes to the feed of chickens and broilers throughout the United States. Available from the Department of Agriculture and the Commodity News Service at most brokerage offices is the hog/corn ratio. This ratio is the number of bushels of corn equivalent in price to a hundred pounds of live hogs. If the price of hogs is relatively high as compared to corn prices then farmers will feed more corn to their hogs rather than sell the corn on the open market. The price of corn, therefore, has a definite effect upon the supply of pork and indirectly thereby, beef prices in the United States. The hog feed, and cattle feed, and broiler feed ratios are closely watched by farmers who must decide whether hog prices are high enough to justify heavy feeding or whether the return does not make the effort worthwhile. (See Fig. 105 opposite.)

Most of the corn which is grown by farmers throughout the United States never leaves the farm. It is grown primarily for the feeding of animals raised on the farm and after harvest is chopped up and stored away in silos. Some dry processed corn is used for breakfast food, cornmeal, or grits and some corn is used for brewing and industrial purposes. The wet processing of corn involves turning corn into corn syrup, corn sugar, and corn oil.

One of the most significant factors in analyzing the corn market is government price support and loan programs. By agreeing to loan farmers a certain price for their corn, provided they divert a portion of their acreage, the government places an artificial floor below which the cash and the futures market normally will not dip. Since the farmer is able to default on his loans with no penalty and turn his corn over, the government consequently ends up with large supplies of corn. These are owned by the Commodity Credit Corporation which can sell them on the open market when prices reach a certain level. This acts as a ceiling on which the market normally will not advance above. Thus govern-

FIGURE 105

Table 1.--Statistical summary of prices, indexes and price ratios, recent years and months

Item	Unit	Season average 1969-70	1970/71	1971 July	1972 April	1972 May	1972 June	1972 July
FEED GRAIN AND HAY PRICES								
Corn, No. 3 Yellow, Chicago	Dol. per bu.	1.25	1.44	1.49	1.26	1.29	1.27	*1.29
Price received by farmers	do.	1.15	1.33	1.36	1.13	1.15	1.13	1.14
Oats, No. 1 White, Chicago	do.	.624	.729	.712	**	.775	**	**
No. 2 White, Minneapolis	do.	.632	.709	.663	.697	.726	.728	.698
Price received by farmers	do.	.586	.626	.626	.635	.638	.666	.655
Barley, No. 3, Minneapolis	do.	1.08	1.21	1.17	1.16	1.18	1.21	1.17
Price received by farmers	do.	.872	.959	1.07	.990	1.04	1.09	1.04
Grain sorghum, No. 2 Yellow, Kansas City	Dol. per cwt.	2.10	2.42	2.54	2.10	2.09	2.09	2.15
Price received by farmers	do.	1.91	2.05	2.37	1.87	1.88	1.90	1.98
All hay, baled, price received by farmers	Dol. per ton	24.70	26.10	24.10	28.00	31.10	30.90	28.50
Alfalfa hay, baled, price received by farmers	do.	23.90	24.70	24.60	29.20	32.60	32.60	30.50
PROCESSED FEED PRICES, BULK								
Soybean meal, 44% solvent, Decatur	Dol. per ton	78.40	78.50	84.25	94.50	95.30	95.00	101.40
49-50% solvent, Decatur	do.	86.60	84.30	90.00	101.75	103.30	104.90	111.60
Cottonseed meal, 41% expeller, Memphis	do.	72.50	73.40	74.60	73.60	72.25	70.30	81.40
Linseed meal, 34% solvent, Minneapolis	do.	67.90	62.60	64.50	73.25	74.50	75.00	80.50
Peanut meal, 50%, S.E. mills	do.	80.40	77.70	75.75	**	96.00	97.50	102.00
Tankage digester, 60%, Chicago	do.	109.50	99.60	97.20	120.00	120.00	120.60	124.25
Meat meal, 50%, Chicago	do.	107.00	95.60	92.20	122.50	116.00	118.10	122.80
Fish meal, 65%, Imported, East Coast	do.	191.70	173.20	152.75	171.50	181.80	180.00	182.25
Gluten feed, 21%, Chicago	do.	47.80	49.50	45.00	48.75	46.40	43.50	45.10
Brewers' dried grains, 24%, Milwaukee	do.	48.90	51.50	45.50	51.25	51.70	49.40	46.00
Distillers' dried grains, 28%, Cincinnati	do.	57.90	64.40	64.00	60.10	62.25	64.25	64.00
Wheat bran, Minneapolis	do.	41.80	43.80	37.60	40.50	36.40	36.40	36.75
Buffalo	do.	44.50	50.00	40.50	50.90	45.50	42.00	47.50
Wheat middlings, Minneapolis	do.	42.30	43.90	38.25	40.00	35.90	36.40	37.50
Buffalo	do.	48.50	51.60	44.40	51.00	45.80	44.00	48.75
Hominy feed, Chicago	do.	43.20	45.70	45.50	41.25	34.30	33.75	37.50
Molasses blackstrap, New York	do.	27.40	27.67	29.10	29.10	29.10	29.10	29.20
Beet pulp (molasses), Los Angeles	do.	50.40	54.90	55.40	55.60	56.20	58.60	58.60
Alfalfa meal, 17%, dehydrated, Kansas City	do.	45.30	48.10	45.75	49.40	49.70	45.80	47.10
Tallow, inedible prime, Chicago	Cents per lb.	7.5	7.6	7.2	6.5	6.5	6.4	6.6
Urea, 42%, N., Ft. Worth (bagged)	Dol. per ton	71.00	70.00	**	69.50	69.50	67.00	67.00
PRICES PAID BY FARMERS								
Soybean meal, 44%	Dol. per cwt.	5.52	5.69	5.76	6.14	6.27	6.32	6.53
Cottonseed meal, 41%	do.	5.26	5.54	5.54	5.65	5.69	5.71	5.74
Wheat bran	do.	3.64	4.01	4.02	4.02	4.01	3.96	3.94
Wheat middlings	do.	3.72	4.09	4.08	4.05	4.02	3.98	3.96
Broiler grower feed	Dol. per ton	93.00	99.00	99.00	96.00	96.00	96.00	96.00
Laying feed	do.	83.00	88.00	89.00	85.00	85.00	86.00	87.00
Dairy feed, 16%	do.	73.00	79.00	79.00	78.00	78.00	78.00	78.00
Beef cattle feed, 30% and over	Dol. per cwt.	4.80	4.99	5.00	5.04	5.05	5.05	**5.07**
Hog feed, over 29%	do.	6.65	6.77	6.82	7.18	7.23	7.29	7.43
Alfalfa hay, baled	Dol. per ton	34.10	36.00	36.50	40.70	40.20	39.10	38.00
PRICE INDEXES (1967=100)								
Feed grains, prices received by farmers	Pct.	97	110	113	97	98	98	99
Eleven high-protein feeds, at principal markets	do.	105	105	109	120	122	122	130
Five oilseed meals	do.	103	103	109	120	122	122	130
Tankage, meat meal, and fish meal	do.	128	116	111	129	130	132	139
Gluten feed, brewers' dried grains and distillers' dried grains	do.	103	107	101	105	106	104	106
Feed, prices paid by farmers	do.	100	107	108	105	105	105	106
LIVESTOCK AND POULTRY/FEED PRICE RATIOS 1/	Average (July)							
Hog-corn, Omaha 2/	1967-71=18.1	20.2	12.7	13.9	18.2	19.7	21.5	22.8
Hog-corn, U.S.	1967-71=18.4	20.8	12.8	14.0	19.9	21.7	22.5	24.1
Beef steer-corn, Omaha 3/	1967-71=23.1	23.6	22.2	22.6	27.4	27.8	30.5	30.4
Milk-feed, U.S.	1967-71=1.61	1.76	1.69	1.61	1.74	1.70	1.68	1.71
Egg-feed, U.S.	1967-71=7.9	9.9	7.4	6.4	6.4	6.4	6.4	7.0
Broiler-feed, U.S.	1967-71=3.3	3.0	2.8	3.2	2.7	2.8	3.0	3.3
Turkey-feed, U.S.	1967-71=4.6	5.2	4.5	4.5	4.7	4.5	4.5	4.4

1/ Units of corn or other concentrates ration equal in value to 100 pounds of hog or beef steer, one pound of chicken, milk, or one dozen eggs. 2/ Based on packer and shipper purchases of hogs and No. 2 Yellow corn. 3/ Based on price of beef steers all grades sold out first hands for slaughter, and No. 2 Yellow corn. *No. 2 yellow. **Not reported.

Prices compiled from Chicago Board of Trade, Minneapolis Daily Market Record, Kansas City Grain Market Review, National Provisioner, Feedstuffs, and reports of the Agricultural Marketing Service.

Source: U.S. Department of Agriculture, *Feed Situation*, August 1972.

ment action becomes a very significant factor in the corn markets of the United States.

Corn is harvested during the months of September and October and makes a harvest low normally during these months. The astute trader is reluctant to take a long position prior to harvest for fear of a price decline as corn supplies are being harvested. The corn futures market is very large and often has an open interest three times that of the wheat or soybean markets. Normally price swings in corn are far more moderate than in wheat and therefore easier to trade.

Additional statistical data pertaining to the preceding section on "Corn" is shown in Figures 106 and 107 on pages 169 and 170.

FIGURE 106

World Production of Corn or Maize   In Millions of Metric Tons[4]

Crop Year	United States[2]	Argentina	Brazil	Mexico	Rep. of So. Afr.	France	China	India	Italy	Bulgaria	Hungary	Yugoslavia	Roumania	Indonesia	U.S.S.R.	World Total
1959	3,825	175	335	219	150	1963-	1955-9	160	153	48	140	263	224	82	175	7,265
1960	3,907	190	335	205	190	67	Avg.	158	150	46	138	243	218	97	300	7,565
1961	3,598	210	373	219	220	Avg.	(435)	168	155	45	107	179	215	91	500	7,465
1962	3,606	180	400	215	240	(3.6		180	128	61	128	208	194	126	385	7,470
1963	4,019	211	370	253	168	M.T.)	1960-	179	136	68	140	212	237	105	335	8,060
1964	3,484	202	465	295	177		64	179	156	81	138	274	263	161	360	7,835
1965-6	4,084	277	394	295	199		Avg.	182	131	49	140	233	231	90	252	8,133
1966-7	4,117	335	488	323	389		(425)	197	138	84	154	314	316	197	268	8,944
1967-8	4,760	258	490	335	209			247	152	81	139	284	270	117	315	9,444
1968-9[4]	111.1	6.9	11.5	8.6	5.0	5.4		5.7	4.0	1.7	3.8	6.8	7.1	3.0	7.6	229.8
1969-0	116.4	9.4	14.2	6.5	6.1	5.7	24.5	5.7	4.5	2.4	4.8	7.8	7.7	2.3	10.1	258.3
1970-1[1]	104.4	9.9	13.5	9.2	8.6	7.4	25.0	7.4	4.7	2.4	4.1	6.9	6.4	2.9	7.5	252.1
1971-2[3]	141.0			9.5		8.5		6.5	4.5	3.0	5.0	7.2	9.0	2.1	9.5	293.5

1 Preliminary.   2 Grain only.   3 Estimated.   4 Data prior to 1968-9 are in MILLIONS OF BUSHELS.
Source: Foreign Agricultural Service, U.S.D.A.

Domestic Disappearance and Foreign Trade of Corn in the United States   In Millions of Bushels

Crop Year	Exports—Grain Only					Imports—Grain Only					Domestic Disappearance				
	Oct.-Dec.	Jan.-Mar.	Apr.-June	July-Sept.	Total	Oct.-Dec.	Jan.-Mar.	Apr.-June	July-Sept.	Total	Oct.-Dec.[2]	Jan.-Mar.	Apr.-June	July-Sept.	Total
1959	61.9	45.1	53.1	49.4	209.4	.3	.3	.3	.2	1.2	900.1	985.0	788.7	683.7	3,358
1960	73.0	68.3	70.0	64.9	276.1	.3	.3	.5	.2	1.2	925.5	954.4	779.3	743.3	3,403
1961	90.4	117.7	118.1	89.1	415.3	.3	.3	.6	.2	1.4	1,032.6	984.9	788.8	741.5	3,548
1962	102.2	81.3	124.0	90.0	397.3	.2	.3	.1	.3	1.0	946.7	1,081.2	794.0	675.3	3,497
1963	143.7	114.2	105.6	114.0	477.5	.2	.2	.3	.2	1.0	896.2	952.3	796.7	726.1	3,371
1964	145.8	115.5	145.5	143.2	550.0	.2	.3	.2	.3	1.0	1,000.4	954.4	766.5	603.5	3,325
1965	197	171	177	142	687	.2	.3	.2	.2	.9	994	1,007	903	801	3,705
1966-7	140	126	107	114	487	.2	.3	.2	.2	.8	1,141	837	865	805	3,648
1967-8	183	158	129	163	633	.2	.1	.3	.2	.9	1,143	895	899	852	3,789
1968-9	158	71	134	173	536	.2	.3	.3	.2	1	1,165	1,121	839	782	3,907
1969-0	186	139	133	154	612	.5				1	1,193	1,187	935	771	4,086
1970-1[1]	156	120	93	147	516					4	1,208	1,092	872	751	3,923
1971-2[1]	160										1,402				
1972-3															

1 Preliminary.   2 Includes all corn fed in silage and forage or hogged off, part of which is consumed after January 1.
Source: Economic Research Service, U.S.D.A.

Distribution of Corn in the United States   In Millions of Bushels

Year Begin. October	Breakfast Foods[1]	Food & Industrial Products[7]	Cornmeal, etc.[2]	Wet-Process Products[3]	Alcohol & Products	Seed	Live-Stock Feed[4]	Exports (Incl. Grain Equiv. of Pdt's.)	Total Utilization	Domestic Disappearance
1959	16	278	95	154.0	31.0	12.4	3,043	230	3,563	3,333
1960	16	284	96	154.8	32.8	11.1	3,092	292	3,679	3,387
1961	17	304	102	168.7	36.4	10.9	3,212	435	3,962	3,527
1962	18	311	105	179.4	28.2	11.6	3,157	416	3,895	3,479
1963	19	352	112	195.0	25.8	11.2	3,009	500	3,848	3,348
1964	19	358	110	201.0	28.0	11.0	2,957	570	3,875	3,305
1965-6	20	365	111	204.0	30.0	13.0	3,347	687	4,392	3,705
1966-7	21	376	117	205.0	33	14.0	3,284	487	4,135	3,648
1967-8	21	385	117	213	34	12	3,412	633	4,422	3,789
1968-9	22	390	114	221	33	12	3,521	536	4,443	3,907
1969-0	22	395	116	226	31	13	3,692	612	4,698	4,086
1970-1[5]	22	402	120	230	30	14	3,526	516	4,439	3,923
1971-2[6]							3,902	600	4,904	4,304
1972-3										

1 Estimated quantities used during the calendar year following the corn harvest.   2 Estimated quantities used in producing cornmeal, flour, hominy, and grits during the calendar year following the corn harvest.   3 Starch, sirup, sugar, etc.   4 Feed, and waste (residual, mostly feed).   5 Preliminary.   6 Forecast.   7 Total quantities processed and breakdown between domestic use and exports.   *Source: Economic Research Service, U.S.D.A.*

Note: Data on this page is originally from Commodity Research Bureau, Inc.

FIGURE 107

U.S. Exports[2] of Corn (Including Seed), By Country of Destination   in Thousands of Bushels

Yr. Begin. October	Austria	Belg. & Luxem.	Canada	France	W. Germany	Greece	Israel	Italy	Japan	Mexico	Netherlands	Norway	Spain	United Kingdom	Total All Exports
1959	7,210	12,356	23,229	254	17,776	2,343	4,681	411	7,372	859	34,147	1,886	N.A.	71,483	210,195
1960	6,751	18,432	37,076	200	17,406	3,445	5,672	4,209	21,428	1,564	46,658	2,253	9,323	75,726	275,475
1961	10,467	23,257	59,850	25	22,108	3,494	6,069	20,408	39,025	664	59,092	3,627	11,130	101,405	413,938
1962	2,277	20,922	68,764	460	17,465	5,995	6,723	39,589	33,305	15,981	54,506	3,175	30,023	61,938	396,392
1963	4,207	24,848	70,598	1,165	35,961	7,052	7,801	35,193	62,690	967	64,123	3,658	25,416	68,174	476,019
1964–5	10	32,015	78,204	3,853	34,367	8,909	6,745	79,279	90,168	709	74,300	3,836	38,275	63,395	549,397
1965–6	5,000	37,134	65,643	3,755	51,277	12,174	6,242	94,283	94,280	421	87,135	3,413	59,661	84,250	669,420
1966–7	8	22,503	41,095	1,160	32,816	6,126	5,634	21,820	61,351	484	90,327	1,603	30,519	64,020	465,544
1967–8	7	22,123	48,504	11,399	53,623	7,560	6,068	78,595	102,358	950	119,869	2,291	32,750	65,336	613,059
1968–9	11	19,924	71,843	2,628	31,084	11,231	4,294	62,978	121,231	513	72,719	11	11,633	55,572	519,968
1969–0	9	24,931	61,731	601	36,390	13,432	4,525	36,037	180,323	24,205	78,297	1,630	21,432	53,501	601,408
1970–1[1]	1,991	24,341	27,082	2,099	45,522	8,980	4,490	47,379	116,178	1,221	89,537	47	504	46,284	500,957
1971–2															

[1] Preliminary.   [2] Exports of grain only.   Does not include corn exported under the food for relief or charity program.
Source: Foreign Agriculture Service, U.S.D.A.

Average Price Received by Farmers for Corn in the U.S., as of 15th of Month   In Cents Per Bushel

Year	Oct.	Nov.	Dec.	Jan.	Feb.	Mar.	Apr.	May	June	July	Aug.	Sept.	Average[1]
1959	99.1	98.8	97.8	99.9	101	102	106	108	109	109	107	106	105
1960	99.2	90.2	91.9	97.0	101	101	96.8	102	103	105	104	104	100
1961	102	99.2	99.4	99.3	99.6	100	102	104	104	105	103	104	110
1962	103	98.7	104	107	109	110	110	111	116	119	119	121	112
1963	111	105	109	112	111	113	115	117	116	112	112	117	111
1964–5	113	107	116	118	120	121	123	126	125	122	118	118	117
1965–6	110	104	113	119	120	117	119	121	120	127	134	135	116
1966–7	129	126	129	128	126	128	126	125	126	121	111	112	124
1967–8	104	97.5	103	104	106	106	106	109	107	104	98.6	101	103
1968–9	96.2	104	105	108	109	109	112	119	118	118	118	115	108
1969–0	112	107	109	112	114	113	115	118	121	124	127	138	115
1970–1	134	129	136	142	143	143	141	138	143	136	119	111	133
1971–2	100	97.4	108	109	109								
1972–3													

[1] Weighted average by sales.   *Source: Statistical Reporting Service, U.S.D.A.*

Note: Data originally from Commodity Research Bureau, Inc.

SOYBEANS

The soybean market has only come into play in recent times. Prior to World War II, Manchuria was the source of the world supply of soybeans with only a handful of soybeans grown in the United States. Now soybeans are the number one dollar export of the United States and involve a crop in excess of 1 billion bushels, nearly as large as the wheat crop in this country. (See Fig. 108 opposite.)

Soybean futures are traded on the Chicago Board of Trade as are soybean meal futures and soybean oil futures. The options are traded in January, March, May, July, August, September, and November. The contract size is 5,000 bushels and price is quoted in one eighths with a minimum fluctuation equaling the sum of $6.25 per contract. Soybean futures are allowed to fluctuate

10 cents above and below the close of the previous day giving the market a 20 cent daily range. Since the margin required to trade soybean futures can be as low as 10 cents per bushel, the return on invested capital can be quite substantial in a short period of time. This is one of the reasons that soybean futures have attracted such a wide following among the speculative public.

Soybeans are harvested during a short period of time from September to November. Often the crop will almost equal the demand for the year with carryover for the next year being quite small.

Because of this, prices normally rise evenly after harvest to ration out the supply which is available. (See Fig. 109, p. 172.)

The situation report which covers soybeans and soybean by-products is the *Fats and Oils Situation* report which is published five times annually. This report sets forth the current and past supply and demand situation for soybeans and soybean by-products and makes a price forecast for the upcoming season. These situation reports reflect what the U.S. Department of Agriculture actually thinks will happen to the

FIGURE 108

Source: Commodity Research Bureau, Inc.

price of a commodity during the up-coming season and therefore offer un-usually valuable information to the commodity trader. (See Fig. 110 opposite.)

Soybeans are crushed into soybean meal and soybean oil which are then consumed as the major by-products of the soybean itself. Soybean oil is the major vegetable oil in the United States today and is used heavily in all vegetable oils found on the grocery shelves. Except for Mazola which labels its product as corn oil, most vegetable oils (Wesson, and so on) are soybean oil.

Soybean meal is a feed used much like feed corn but with a much higher protein value. Each month the U.S. Department of Agriculture issues a report on the previous month's crush of soybeans and how many tons of meal and oil were produced. This "crush report" is significant since it gives the demand for the current product as the crushers usually only crush the amount of beans they feel they can sell, and if prices are low for both the by-products of soybean oil and soybean meal, then the crusher will simply shut down his plant and wait for

prices to advance before crushing any further soybeans.

A 60-pound bushel of soybeans when crushed yields 11 pounds of soybean oil and 48 pounds of soybean meal with 1 pound of waste lost in the process. To determine whether it is worthwhile for the crusher to crush soybeans at the current price the trader will multiply the current price of soybean oil times 11, multiply the price of meal per pound by 48 to reach a price at which the bushel of soybeans will bring on the products market. If soybeans are selling for $3.16 a bushel, soybean oil at 11.06 cents per pound, and soybean meal at $71 per ton, the gross crushing margin would be 30 cents per bushel, which is normal.

Often speculators will play the spread between the price of oil and meal and the price of beans buying futures contracts of whichever is the cheapest relative to the other and figuring that eventually the processor will come into the market and thereby bring the prices back into line, at which time the speculator will liquidate his holdings for a profit. If the speculator feels that prices will continue to deteriorate and the spread will widen between the price of beans and meal and oil, he will play a "reverse crush spread" in which he buys soybean oil and soybean meal and sells soybeans in the futures market figuring that the products will rise in value faster than the actual cash price of beans.

Soybeans have become one of the most active of all commodities traded on futures exchanges due to their wide price swings which offer substantial profit potentials for the commodity speculator. Undoubtedly in the future they will continue to retain their glam-

FIGURE 109
WHERE SOYBEANS ARE GROWN
IN THE UNITED STATES

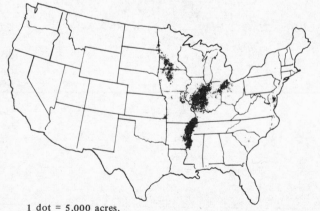

1 dot = 5,000 acres.
Source: U.S. Department of Commerce, Bureau of Census.

FIGURE 110

Table 4.--Soybeans, soybean meal and soybean oil: U.S. exports by country of destination, and total value, 1967-71

Continent and country of destination	Soybeans 1/ Year beginning September					Soybean meal Year beginning October					Soybean oil Year beginning October				
	1967	1968	1969	1970	1971 2/	1967	1968	1969	1970	1971 2/	1967	1968	1969	1970	1971 2/
	1,000 bu.	1,000 bu.	1,000 bu.	1,000 bu.	1,000 bu.	1,000 tons	1,000 tons	1,000 tons	1,000 tons	1,000 tons	Mil. lb.	Mil. lb.	Mil. lb.	Mil. lb.	Mil. lb.
North America															
Canada	21,736	37,856	69,952	42,162	31,279	227.8	262.9	270.9	242.1	204.5	25	29	51	50	43
Dominican Republic	---	---	37	324	223	4/	4/	.4	.9	3.5	50	28	25	24	20
Haiti	---	---	---	---	---	---	---	.2	1.2	---	17	19	19	26	27
Mexico	308	824	5,004	2,192	658	2.7	.9	2.8	116.3	64.3	11	4	18	1	5/
Panama	---	---	---	37	1,804	1.1	1.4	1.0	3.5	10.6	11	5/	17	23	11
Other	3/	---	358	109	3/	21.6	20.9	27.1	60.3	65.7	14	19	21	23	21
Total	22,044	38,680	75,351	44,824	33,964	253.2	286.0	302.4	424.3	348.6	128	99	151	147	122
South America															
Argentina	1	4	3/	2	2	.2	4/	---	---	---	---	2	---	5/	---
Brazil	6	---	---	2	---	.1	---	---	---	---	21	9	10	-6	2
Chile	---	---	---	---	---	---	---	3.3	10.1	1.9	33	31	28	-8	2
Colombia	---	---	---	837	---	---	---	---	---	---	9	9	17	17	15
Ecuador	---	---	---	---	---	---	---	---	---	---	5	9	12	23	28
Peru	---	---	202	---	404	4/	---	4/	---	---	5	9	59	111	74
Venezuela	1,336	1,650	2,070	3,042	1,599	.1	.1	4/	2.9	32.3	2	3	5/	5/	5/
Other	---	---	---	---	---	4/	.2	.2	.3	.6	1	5/	3	5	3
Total	1,343	1,654	2,272	3,883	2,005	.4	.3	3.5	13.3	34.8	77	71	139	219	124
Western Europe															
Austria	---	---	---	2	---	7.0	1.3	5.2	1.5	---	---	---	---	5/	---
Belgium-Luxembourg	8,698	10,237	16,115	13,222	5,658	240.7	166.9	219.0	308.8	328.4	5/	5/	6	5/	1
Denmark	15,516	11,797	18,408	21,442	16,156	66.0	18.3	32.5	85.6	95.5	---	5/	5/	5/	---
Finland	---	---	---	---	184	---	---	---	---	---	---	5/	5/	---	---
France	551	284	4,988	13,223	12,807	495.4	471.8	622.8	712.1	610.3	5/	5/	2	---	5/
Germany, West	31,966	30,515	41,778	52,980	51,988	508.2	636.5	855.9	987.4	705.0	5/	5/	2	5/	5/
Greece	---	---	---	2	---	2.1	.3	---	20.2	---	---	---	---	12	---
Ireland	---	---	---	---	---	31.0	43.2	60.4	36.5	72.4	---	---	---	---	---
Italy	14,788	16,428	25,413	25,978	22,960	190.5	231.9	309.5	330.8	295.6	5/	5/	5/	5/	5/
Netherlands	36,835	42,660	57,397	57,932	64,096	546.9	515.8	659.0	675.4	480.8	5/	5/	1	1	1
Norway	4,959	4,247	5,434	7,462	7,284	---	4/	4/	2.2	---	5/	5/	5/	5/	5/
Spain	29,498	31,172	36,349	38,691	43,991	15.0	96.1	34.1	10.7	4.5	1	---	---	---	---
Sweden	1	3	8	309	245	.5	.3	1.1	.1	4/	5/	5/	5/	5/	5/
Switzerland	431	380	495	188	40	9.4	64.3	111.8	76.1	32.5	---	---	---	2	5/
United Kingdom	3,919	4,840	7,510	5,990	5,432	82.0	38.5	42.9	100.1	58.3	5/	1	12	10	1
Other	3/	352	1,047	1,600	1,261	28.0	33.4	18.5	9.2	39.4	4	2	5	1	5/
Total	147,163	150,915	214,942	239,021	232,102	2,222.7	2,318.6	2,972.7	3,336.5	2,794.9	5	3	25	26	3
Eastern Europe															
Bulgaria	---	---	17	---	---	41.4	32.7	40.3	32.8	---	---	---	---	---	---
Czechoslovakia	149	240	470	115	---	11.6	2.2	36.2	99.4	72.3	---	---	---	---	---
Hungary	---	---	499	1,187	---	50.4	28.6	170.6	156.0	94.1	---	---	---	---	---
Poland	1,256	1,381	4,928	3,063	2,423	80.6	103.0	109.9	112.3	65.8	16	4	10	7	---
U.S.S.R. (Europe and Asia)	---	---	---	---	---	---	---	---	---	---	---	---	---	---	---
Yugoslavia	---	---	---	1,127	1	113.7	143.3	173.8	186.8	116.2	---	---	1	271	199
Other	---	195	---	567	3/	5.7	11.0	5.7	---	6/99.9	5/	1	---	---	---
Total	1,405	1,816	5,914	6,059	2,424	303.3	320.9	536.5	587.4	448.3	16	4	12	278	199
Africa															
Algeria	---	---	---	---	---	---	---	---	---	---	---	3	1	---	---
Egypt	---	---	---	---	---	.5	1.8	3.6	6.0	---	---	---	29	2	1
Morocco	---	---	---	---	---	---	---	---	---	---	55	28	53	90	122
Tunisia	---	---	---	---	---	---	---	---	---	---	97	57	95	76	135
Other	---	---	---	307	2	4/	4/	---	6.5	7.5	12	19	35	43	25
Total	---	---	---	307	2	.5	1.8	3.6	12.5	7.5	164	107	213	211	283
Asia and Oceania															
Australia	4	4	211	181	---	27.1	25.4	34.3	33.0	17.6	8	2	8	8	4
Bangladesh	---	---	---	---	---	---	---	---	---	---	---	---	---	---	135
Hong Kong	73	57	96	38	---	3.1	1.7	2.0	.4	---	12	4	12	2	5/
India	4	---	---	---	---	2.4	.6	4/	.5	.4	196	328	249	284	144
Iran	11	---	---	---	---	2.5	1.8	1.1	1.1	1.1	7	48	159	134	113
Israel	9,515	6,541	8,279	12,793	12,236	4/	4/	4/	---	.1	49	34	38	41	44
Japan	73,739	69,883	101,382	102,791	106,714	15.3	19.9	83.9	22.0	24.5	---	0	11	5/	1
Korea, South	639	632	1,338	2,519	1,066	4/	3.9	20.1	26.1	13.7	3	2	3	4	2
Pakistan	---	---	---	2	---	---	---	---	---	---	224	114	355	276	142
Philippines	---	---	---	---	2	47.7	43.8	49.1	53.8	58.0	3	5/	5/	5/	1
South Viet Nam	---	---	---	---	---	---	.2	.4	21.3	16.3	37	41	6	29	33
Taiwan	10,632	16,590	21,226	19,582	23,853	---	---	1.1	---	---	5	---	9	16	4
Turkey	---	---	---	---	---	---	---	1.1	---	---	3	5/	6	31	16
Other	5	2	1,591	1,801	1,798	20.3	13.4	24.7	27.0	39.6	24	10	22	31	17
Total	94,622	93,709	134,124	139,707	145,669	119.4	116.7	216.7	185.2	171.3	571	585	879	900	657
Total	266,577	286,776	432,602	433,801	416,165	2,899.5	3,044.3	4,035.4	4,559.3	3,805.3	963	870	1,420	1,742	1,388
Value of Exports															
Total (Mil. dol.)	749	772	1,149	1,337	1,315	243	251	337	405	358	106	89	176	250	191
Per unit	$2.81	$2.69	$2.66	$3.08	$3.16	$83.81	$82.45	$83.52	$88.83	$94.06	11.0¢	10.2¢	12.4¢	14.4¢	13.8¢

1/ Census export data to Canada overstated since Canada contains major transit ports and ultimate destination was unknown at time of shipment. Transshipment through Canadian ports are mainly destined for Western Europe and Asian countries. Census data to these countries are understated by the amount of transshipment via Canada. 2/ Preliminary. 3/ Less than 500 bushels. 4/ Less than 50 tons. 5/ Less than 500,000 pounds. 6/ Includes 43 million pounds to East Germany and 57 million pounds to Rumania.

Source: U.S. Department of Agriculture, *Fats and Oils Situation* Report.

our as the great speculative medium of the nation's commodity markets.

Additional statistical data pertaining to the preceding section on "Soybeans" is shown in Figures 111, 112, 113, and 114 on pages 174, 175, 176, and 177.

FIGURE 111

Year beginning September	Soybean oil Yield Pounds	Soybean oil Price 1/ Cents	Soybean oil Value Dollars	Soybean meal Yield Pounds	Soybean meal Price 1/ Cents	Soybean meal Value Dollars	Total value Dollars	Soybean price No. 1 yellow, Illinois Received by farmers Dollars	Soybean price No. 1 yellow, Illinois points Dollars	Spread between value of products and soybean price No. 1 yellow Received by farmers Dollars	Spread No. 1 yellow, Illinois points Dollars
1947	9.5	23.4	2.22	47.5	4.15	1.97	4.19	3.33	3.69	.86	.50
1950	9.7	17.9	1.74	46.8	3.16	1.48	3.22	2.47	2.95	.75	.27
1951	10.0	11.6	1.16	46.7	4.07	1.90	3.06	2.73	2.96	.33	.10
1952	10.8	12.0	1.30	47.3	3.52	1.66	2.96	2.72	2.83	.24	.13
1953	11.0	13.4	1.47	47.4	3.90	1.85	3.32	2.72	3.24	.60	.08
1954	10.9	12.2	1.33	45.9	3.06	1.40	2.73	2.46	2.60	.27	.13
1955	11.1	12.5	1.39	46.2	2.68	1.24	2.63	2.22	2.51	.41	.12
1956	10.9	12.7	1.38	47.5	2.36	1.12	2.50	2.18	2.33	.32	.17
1957	10.8	11.0	1.19	46.8	2.64	1.24	2.43	2.07	2.20	.36	.23
1958	10.6	9.6	1.02	47.3	2.82	1.33	2.35	2.00	2.12	.35	.23
1959	11.0	8.3	91	46.5	2.77	1.29	2.20	1.96	2 07	24	.13
1960	11.0	11.2	1.23	47.0	3.00	1.41	2.64	2.13	2.53	.51	.11
1961	10.9	9.7	1.06	47.2	3.11	1.47	2.53	2.28	2.41	.25	.12
1962	10.7	8.8	.94	46.9	3.57	1.67	2.61	2.34	2.50	.27	.11
1963	10.9	8.4	.92	48.0	3.58	1.72	2.64	2.51	2.59	.13	.05
1964	10.9	11.2	1.22	47.7	3.48	1.66	2.88	2.62	2.81	.26	.07
1965	10.7	11.8	1.26	47.5	4.02	1.91	3.17	2.54	2.91	.63	.26
1966	10.7	10.4	1.11	47.7	3.98	1.90	3.01	2.75	2.86	.26	.15
1967	10.6	8.6	.91	47.7	3.82	1.82	2.73	2.49	2.61	.24	.12
1968	10.6	8.2	.87	47.4	3.76	1.78	2.66	2.43	2.54	.23	.12
1969 2/	10.7	11.0	1.17	47.5	3.96	1.84	3.01	2.44	2.53	.57	.48

1/ Simple average price per pound using the following quotations: Soybean oil, crude, tank cars, f.o.b. Decatur; soybean meal, bulk, Decatur, quoted as 41% prior to July 1950, 44% beginning July 1950.
2/ Preliminary.

Source: *Soybean Digest.*

FIGURE 112

Table 1.--U.S. Fats and Oils Situation at a Glance

Item	Unit	Marketing year total or average 1970-71	Marketing year total or average 1971-72 preliminary	1971 September	1971 October	1972 July	1972 August	1972 September	1972 October
SOYBEANS (Year beg. Sept.)									
U.S. average price received by farmers	$ bu.	2.85	3.01	2.95	2.96	3.34	3.36	3.26	3.13
U.S. support price	$ bu.	2.25	2.25	2.25	2.25	2.25	2.25	2.25	2.25
Price, No. 1 yellow, Illinois points	$ bu.	3.00	3.24	3.01	3.01	3.48	3.45	3.45	3.30
Price, No. 2 yellow, f.o.b., Gulf	$ bu.	3.19	3.45	3.21	3.21	3.69	3.69	3.62	3.52
Price, No. 2 yellow, f.o.b., Baltimore	$ bu.	3.21	3.46	3.25	3.20	3.68	3.71	3.59	3.53
Receipts at mills	Mil. bu.	769.0	716.3	45.6	145.2	34.7	28.6	26.4	141.9
Crushings	Mil. bu.	760.1	720.5	54.5	59.5	58.2	57.9	52.2	67.1
Oil yield per bushel crushed	Lb.	10.83	10.98	10.97	10.84	11.15	11.15	11.13	10.66
Meal yield per bushel crushed	Lb.	47.37	47.43	47.88	47.23	47.56	47.68	47.55	46.77
Stocks at mills, end of month	Mil. bu.	42.3	38.1	33.5	119.1	67.4	38.1	12.3	87.1
Exports	Mil. bu.	433.8	416.2	29.2	29.4	26.3	24.2	15.0	N.A.
SOYBEAN OIL (Year beg. Oct.)									
Production	Mil. lb.	8,264.7	7,891.5	597.5	645.2	648.6	645.7	581.0	715.3
Domestic disappearance	Mil. lb.	6,253.2	6,452.2	504.3	543.7	508.5	592.9	555.7	N.A.
Exports	Mil. lb.	1,742.3	1,388.4	136.8	143.0	110.6	63.5	83.9	N.A.
Stocks, end of month	Mil. lb.	772.6	782.2	772.6	725.9	854.1	841.6	782.2	9.6
Price, crude, Decatur	¢ lb.	12.8	11.3	12.8	13.2	10.3	10.1	9.8	9.6
SOYBEAN MEAL (Year beg. Oct.)									
Production	Thou. ton	18,035.2	17,024.2	1,303.8	1,405.9	1,383.7	1,381.1	1,240.6	1,568.8
Domestic disappearance	Thou. ton	13,405.6	13,110.2	882.0	1,182.9	1,003.8	1,191.4	922.9	N.A.
Exports	Thou. ton	4,559.3	3,805.3	487.9	156.9	324.1	204.8	341.9	N.A.
Stocks at mills, end of month	Thou. ton	145.8	191.7	145.8	205.2	243.2	221.6	191.7	180.8
Price, 44% protein, bulk, Decatur	$ ton	78.50	90.20	73.25	74.75	101.40	101.00	107.75	109.00
Price, 49-50% protein, bulk, Decatur	$ ton	84.30	98.20	80.00	80.75	111.60	111.00	117.90	118.60
COTTONSEED (Year beg. Aug.)									
U.S. average price received by farmers	$ ton	56.40	56.80	58.40	55.80	---	45.00	44.10	47.40
U.S. support price, basis grade	$ ton	37.00	1/	1/	1/	1/	1/	1/	1/
Receipts at mills	Thou. ton	3,865.9	3,977.2	192.8	1,167.5	19.3	145.6	396.1	1,784.5
Crushings	Thou. ton	3,728.5	3,959.9	108.9	349.4	169.3	195.7	174.9	427.7
Stocks at mills, end of month	Thou. ton	217.8	235.0	205.8	1,023.9	235.0	215.3	462.4	1,819.3
COTTONSEED OIL (Year beg. Aug.)									
Production	Mil. lb.	1,210.9	1,274.5	34.3	111.8	54.4	61.2	53.4	133.3
Domestic disappearance	Mil. lb.	898.6	815.3	57.1	72.5	56.5	68.7	58.6	N.A.
Exports	Mil. lb.	357.4	421.2	26.2	3.1	33.5	58.3	13.0	N.A.
Stocks, end of month	Mil. lb.	167.2	203.9	93.8	130.0	203.9	137.9	119.6	N.A.
Price, crude, Valley	¢ lb.	14.7	13.2	15.6	14.3	11.3	11.1	10.56	10.00
COMMERCIAL LARD (Year beg. Oct.)									
Production	Mil. lb.	2,018.0	1,645.6	156.0	148.0	107.0	126.0	113.0	N.A.
Domestic disappearance	Mil. lb.	1,619.0	1,459.4	140.7	117.6	113.2	132.2	106.9	N.A.
Exports	Mil. lb.	329.4	170.8	19.6	12.2	12.7	5.4	14.5	N.A.
Shipments to U.S. Territories	Mil. lb.	52.7	49.0	.5	12.6	.3	.3	.1	N.A.
Stocks, end of month	Mil. lb.	76.9	43.8	76.9	82.7	64.1	52.3	43.8	N.A.
Price, loose, tanks, Chicago	¢ lb.	11.1	10.4	11.1	10.8	10.0	10.0	10.3	10.5
CREAMERY BUTTER (Year beg. Oct.)									
Production	Mil. lb.	1,148.2	1,128.6	69.4	79.9	89.4	76.3	65.4	N.A.
Domestic disappearance	Mil. lb.	1,072.5	1,051.7	90.2	101.1	72.0	89.2	84.5	N.A.
Stocks, end of month, total	Mil. lb.	222.0	178.2	222.0	188.9	211.4	198.2	178.2	148.3
Stocks, end of month, CCC	Mil. lb.	195.3	160.4	195.3	154.7	183.3	174.1	160.4	131.0
Price, 92-score, Chicago	¢ lb.	68.9	68.2	68.1	68.0	67.8	69.5	70.2	69.4
FLAXSEED (Year beg. July)									
U.S. average price received by farmers	$ bu.	2.40	2.41	2.31	2.25	2.49	2.55	2.69	2.76
U.S. support price, farm basis	$ bu.	2.50	2.50	2.50	2.50	2.50	2.50	2.50	2.50
Price, No. 1, Minneapolis	$ bu.	2.66	2.70	2.61	2.58	2.79	2.85	3.00	3.12
Receipts at mills	Thou. bu.	19,596	20,328	2,873	1,065	1,974	1,170	1,958	1,928
Crushings	Thou. bu.	18,946	20,980	1,707	1,771	1,660	2,016	2,036	1,768
Exports	Thou. bu.	3,331	1,904	---	---	1,040	919	1,691	N.A.
Stocks at mills, end of month	Thou. bu.	3,396	2,688	5,033	4,327	3,003	2,157	2,079	2,239
LINSEED OIL (Year beg. July)									
Production	Mil. lb.	381.8	426.0	35.4	36.5	33.2	40.4	41.1	34.0
Domestic disappearance	Mil. lb.	253.8	286.7	26.5	2.7	17.4	20.1	16.4	N.A.
Exports	Mil. lb.	52.5	65.9	6.1	10.0	28.4	30.8	18.8	N.A.
Stocks, end of month	Mil. lb.	203.8	276.6	179.9	203.7	263.8	253.3	259.1	N.A.
Price, raw, Minneapolis	¢ lb.	9.7	8.9	8.8	8.8	9.5	9.5	9.5	9.5
INEDIBLE TALLOW & GREASE (Year beg. Oct.)									
Production	Mil. lb.	5,251.7	5,099.4	469.6	410.9	391.1	414.3	437.7	N.A.
Domestic disappearance	Mil. lb.	2,627.7	2,730.5	236.9	208.7	201.0	241.8	237.4	N.A.
Exports	Mil. lb.	2,589.9	2,446.7	247.6	210.8	206.6	192.9	186.5	N.A.
Stocks, end of month	Mil. lb.	409.7	332.4	409.7	401.2	339.1	318.5	332.4	N.A.
Price, bleachable fancy, Chicago	¢ lb.	8.1	6.8	7.6	7.4	7.1	7.4	7.5	7.8
COCONUT OIL (Calendar year's 1970 and 1971)									
Production	Mil. lb.	247.1	N.A.	N.A.	N.A.	N.A.	N.A.	N.A.	N.A.
Imports	Mil. lb.	594.7	627.7	79.3	67.8	53.1	47.0	31.7	N.A.
Domestic disappearance	Mil. lb.	788.9	N.A.	N.A.	N.A.	N.A.	N.A.	N.A.	N.A.
Stocks, end of month	Mil. lb.	100.8	103.9	108.2	115.8	157.8	121.5	111.1	N.A.
Price, crude, Pacific Coast	¢ lb.	16.3	13.6	14.1	13.2	9.4	9.3	9.2	9.4
PALM OIL (Calendar year's 1970 and 1971)									
Imports	Mil. lb.	140.9	216.9	15.4	25.9	84.6	30.8	25.4	N.A.
Domestic disappearance	Mil. lb.	127.5	213.2	24.8	9.1	53.7	39.0	27.7	N.A.
Stocks, end of month	Mil. lb.	42.9	39.9	36.0	51.7	115.8	99.8	93.3	N.A.
Price, Congo, tanks, New York	¢ lb.	13.2	13.3	14.0	14.0	9.9	9.8	9.8	9.8
PEANUTS (Year beg. Aug.)									
U.S. average price received by farmers	¢ lb.	12.8	13.6	13.5	13.8	---	13.0	14.8	14.5
U.S. support price - Farmers' stock basis	¢ lb.	12.75	13.42	13.42	13.42	13.42	14.25	14.25	14.25
Millings, all types, Farmers' stock basis	Mil. lb.	2,615.9	2,650.3	209.3	326.1	45.6	78.1	209.6	N.A.
Production of shelled edibles	Mil. lb.	1,373.1	1,385.6	135.4	176.6	15.0	41.8	132.8	N.A.
Total edible uses - shelled basis	Mil. lb.	1,065.3	1,087.1	99.5	97.7	79.0	102.4	100.7	N.A.
Crushings - shelled basis	Mil. lb.	600.9	612.3	23.1	48.8	37.4	41.4	28.2	N.A.
Commercial stocks, end of month - FS	Mil. lb.	453.2	391.8	1,765.9	2,127.5	391.8	484.5	1,614.0	N.A.
CCC stocks, end of month - FS	Mil. lb.	---	---	618.0	744.5	---	80.2	578.1	N.A.
PEANUT OIL (Year beg. Aug.)									
Production	Mil. lb.	253.5	260.0	9.4	21.1	16.6	17.3	12.0	15.8
Domestic disappearance	Mil. lb.	193.1	194.7	14.5	18.7	13.9	13.8	17.1	N.A.
Exports	Mil. lb.	43.9	74.9	4.3	.3	.1	4.9	7.6	N.A.
Stocks, end of month	Mil. lb.	41.8	32.1	23.7	25.8	32.1	30.7	18.0	N.A.
Price, crude, Southeast mills	¢ lb.	17.1	17.0	17.2	16.4	17.8	16.4	15.8	16.1

1/ No support announced. N.A.--Not available.

Source: U.S. Department of Agriculture, *Fats and Oils Situation* Report.

FIGURE 113

Average Cash Price of No. 1 Yellow Soybeans at Chicago   In Cents per Bushel

Year	Oct.	Nov.	Dec.	Jan.	Feb.	Mar.	Apr.	May	June	July	Aug.	Sept.	Average
1959	214	223	216	218	215	216	219	219	215	216	219	215	217
1960	212	211	223	249	276	294	323	310	273	266	262	242	260
1961	239	245	248	248	247	251	256	254	253	254	255	245	249
1962	245	250	253	264	269	265	261	264	266	265	263	267	259
1963	278	279	278	278	270	269	262	256	252	252	258	270	267
1964–5	273	281	291	296	303	301	304	286	297	289	275	268	288
1965–6	249	254	266	284	291	286	298	308	338	359	373	319	298
1966–7	296	299	300	296	291	291	288	287	290	283	281	269	293
1967–8	260	261	264	269	273	271	271	274	271	271	272	261	269
1968–9	246	253	259	263	264	264	269	272	269	270	261	249	263
1969–0	238	242	247	255	259	258	264	270	271	289	279	281	263
1970–1	290	300	293	303	306	304	291	303	321	338	329	312	308
1971–2	312	300	308	309	318								
1972–3													

Source: Consumer & Marketing Service, U.S.D.A.

Soybeans Crushed (Factory Consumption) in the U.S.   In Millions[2] of Bushels—One Bushel = 60 Pounds

Year	Oct.	Nov.	Dec.	Jan.	Feb.	Mar.	Apr.	May	June	July	Aug.	Sept.	Total
1959	35,340	36,053	34,070	34,150	30,917	34,810	33,237	33,197	31,327	31,337	32,067	26,872	393,417
1960	35,637	37,057	38,107	38,997	34,553	34,797	32,963	34,297	31,853	30,970	30,033	22,953	402,217
1961	36,493	38,503	38,733	40,967	36,303	38,847	36,477	38,600	34,303	34,800	34,374	30,440	438,840
1962	39,937	42,840	42,753	42,810	38,807	41,890	35,957	41,057	39,030	38,220	39,010	32,186	474,497
1963	40,517	39,417	39,203	35,987	34,563	33,793	35,307	36,327	35,037	37,293	37,190	36,283	440,917
1964[2]	44.3	43.6	43.2	43.0	37.8	40.9	38.2	40.9	37.1	36.6	37.1	30.4	473.1
1965–6	44.1	48.2	48.9	50.2	45.1	49.4	43.9	50.1	44.7	42.0	40.4	35.3	542.4
1966–7	45.2	49.6	48.9	50.1	44.0	46.4	46.8	49.2	48.8	47.5	45.4	42.2	563.9
1967–8	50.4	51.6	50.6	51.2	48.6	48.3	44.6	48.8	47.5	47.6	44.9	38.2	572.4
1968–9	54.7	55.6	52.2	49.9	45.0	54.6	50.4	54.5	50.6	52.1	48.2	47.5	615.3
1969–0	61.8	62.0	63.1	62.9	58.8	62.9	62.5	67.4	63.7	62.7	62.0	53.3	743.1
1970–1	66.8	65.9	68.6	67.7	60.1	63.6	63.8	63.8	61.1	62.4	63.7	54.5	761.5
1971–2[1]	59.5	59.8	68.6	64.5									
1972–3													

[1] Preliminary.   [2] Prior to Oct. 1964 data are in THOUSANDS OF BUSHELS.   Source: Bureau of the Census

Volume of Trading in Soybean Futures at the Chicago Board of Trade[1]   In Millions of Bushels

Year	Jan.	Feb.	Mar.	Apr.	May	June	July	Aug.	Sept.	Oct.	Nov.	Dec.	Total
1959	231.9	181.7	208.2	210.0	166.0	226.6	438.3	312.7	332.1	621.0	737.0	686.0	4,351.5
1960	546.6	485.0	416.5	316.6	334.8	316.0	396.2	498.5	416.5	597.0	726.1	788.1	5,837.9
1961	1,694	1,342	1,721	1,599	1,452	1,215	662.3	527.3	495.4	572.9	429.9	337.3	12,048.1
1962	431.5	260.6	245.5	241.3	296.5	300.0	318.5	501.3	566.1	798.1	461.1	310.8	4,731.3
1963	1,095	913.5	745.9	643.2	788.8	1,144	1,454	953.7	1,426	2,137	1,694	1,236	14,231.0
1964	1,331	793.9	848.3	597.1	504.9	563.7	534.9	1,191	1,515	1,594	1,575	1,893	13,129.4
1965	2,002	1,825	1,900	1,766	1,682	1,821	1,754	1,018	1,090	890.4	961.0	1,118	17,827.4
1966	1,791	1,456	1,313	1,300	1,410	1,927	1,291	1,300	1,020	1,067	1,096	790.2	15,761.2
1967	793.1	429.7	478.6	312.6	310.6	462.4	409.1	428.4	449.0	635.6	493.9	322.2	5,525.2
1968	432.1	275.3	283.6	311.0	302.5	408.1	465.6	447.8	400.4	676.0	435.4	280.5	4,718.3
1969	355.5	306.9	320.6	360.1	329.2	286.1	341.0	261.9	482.2	983.0	604.6	373.5	5,004.6
1970	485.9	412.8	394.1	497.7	389.1	1,132	1,485	874.5	722.9	1,470	1,185	1,107	10,156
1971	1,266	837.0	903.2	934.9	1,039	1,440	1,548	1,384	1,384	1,925	1,678	1,226	15,565
1972	1,441	1,371											

[1] Trading on this market represents approximately 98% to 99% of all trading in Soybeans.
Source: Commodity Exchange Authority

Note: Data on this page was taken originally from Commodity Research Bureau, Inc.

FIGURE 114

Highest and Lowest Prices of May Soybeans Futures on the Chicago Board of Trade In Cents per Bushel

Year of Delivery		Year Prior to Delivery							Delivery Year					
		June	July	Aug.	Sept.	Oct.	Nov.	Dec.	Jan.	Feb.	Mar.	April	May	Range
1961	High	—	226½	229⅝	227½	230	231⅜	238⅝	270	314	310½	334½	331	314
	Low	—	220½	224⅜	222	222	220½	222⅛	237½	259	282	297	301½	220½
1962	High	264¼	265¼	257½	252¾	253½	252	249½	250⅛	248½	249¼	252½	251⅛	265¼
	Low	255½	256¼	252⅛	247⅞	247¾	246⅛	246⅜	246½	242⅞	243½	247	247¾	242⅞
1963	High	246	243¾	246¼	250¼	258	253¾	253	281¼	272½	267½	262⅞	264¾	281¼
	Low	241¾	239½	238⅝	241¾	245	246½	249¼	251	260¼	253½	254	256	238⅝
1964	High	272	289	269¾	290½	300	302¾	296½	288⅝	273	270	260¾	256⅛	302¾
	Low	259¾	261¾	259	261¾	277¼	269	269¾	266½	263⅝	258¼	254	245½	245½
1965	High	257¼	254¾	267¾	288	291	299	302⅝	314½	317¼	309¾	307¾	290	317¼
	Low	294¾	246¾	251¼	261¼	273⅛	276¼	280½	280¼	294½	288¾	286½	278½	246¾
1966	High	259¾	266	260	261¼	258⅜	263⅝	274⅜	294	298⅜	289¾	307¼	308¾	308¾
	Low	253⅝	252¼	253½	254⅝	255	257¼	263⅜	270½	282½	281½	285¼	297⅛	252¼
1967	High	323¼	342¼	343¼	342	311¾	304	300	291⅝	289¾	292½	288⅜	284½	343¼
	Low	291⅝	310	320¾	305⅞	299	295⅛	290¼	286	283⅝	285	280⅜	279¾	279¾
1968	High	294	281¼	279¾	278	275½	276⅝	277	279¼	279	278¼	273¼	273½	294
	Low	281½	277⅛	275⅛	270⅝	270⅜	272½	273⅛	274	276	272⅝	269	270⅛	269
1969	High	271¼	268¼	264⅝	264¼	264¼	268⅜	267	268⅝	268⅛	266½	266¾	268	271¼
	Low	264⅛	260⅜	260	257⅝	258	262¼	263	264⅞	265¾	262⅜	261¾	265	257⅝
1970	High	249⅛	252⅝	250⅜	252⅞	260⅞	263¼	258	260⅝	263½	262½	266⅞	270	270
	Low	244⅜	245⅞	246¾	246⅝	250¼	253¼	252¼	254¾	257⅞	258½	259½	262¾	244⅜
1971	High	308	314½	314	305¾	322½	318¾	308¾	317	314	309¼	299⅜	299¾	322½
	Low	298⅛	295½	289¾	288½	298⅜	304½	298¼	301⅜	306	297¾	286½	290½	286½
1972	High	332½	351¼	343	338¾	340	334¾	329⅞	325½	336½				
	Low	309½	328	322	315	317⅛	312¼	318¾	310	316¾				
1973	High													
	Low													

Source: Chicago Board of Trade

Note: Data originally from Commodity Research Bureau, Inc.

SOYBEAN MEAL

Soybeans and soybean meal are fairly new arrivals in American agriculture. Only in the past 20 years has a market grown for high protein oils which are largely used in this country as vegetable oil, in margarine, and as a protein supplement to processed foods. The establishment of commercial beef-feeding operations after World War II similarly increased demand for high-protein processed feeds, including soybean meal. (See Fig. 115, p. 178.)

There are currently about 150 soybean crushing plants in the United States, mostly in the Midwest where the soybeans are grown. When the bean is crushed, oil is extracted, refined, and sold as a separate product. The remaining flakes are treated with chemical solvent, then desolventized, toasted, and ground to produce the high-protein animal feed. The meal which results is up to 50 percent protein, too rich a feed to be used straight. It is normally cut down to 44 percent protein or less before being fed to animals. As soybean meal competes directly with other animal feed, the *Feed Situation* report of the Department of Agriculture is important. Soybean meal must be looked at as a part of a complex of feeds and will vary in price along with competing products.

Other important sources of information to the soybean meal trader are found in the Chicago Board of Trade *Statistical Annual* and, of course, the *Commodity Yearbook.* A reasonable eye must be kept on the overall feed needs of farmers, found in the *Livestock and Meat Situation* report of the USDA. The *Weekly Grain Market News* (USDA) keeps track of grain movements and inventories, including soybeans and meal, along with support price data.

Of all soybean meal produced, 99 percent is fed to animals or exported for animal feed. Most goes to the feeding of steers for beef production, some goes to hogs with an increasing amount going to the poultry industry. Soybean meal prices have risen above $350 a ton and fallen as low as $30, although recent prices have been on the higher end of the scale. Over the decade of the sixties the entire soybean complex has shifted upward dramatically in price as new uses are found for the produce, and any averaging of soybean, meal or oil prices must discount the lower prices prevalent in the early sixties to avoid an artificially

FIGURE 115

DEC. 1, 1972

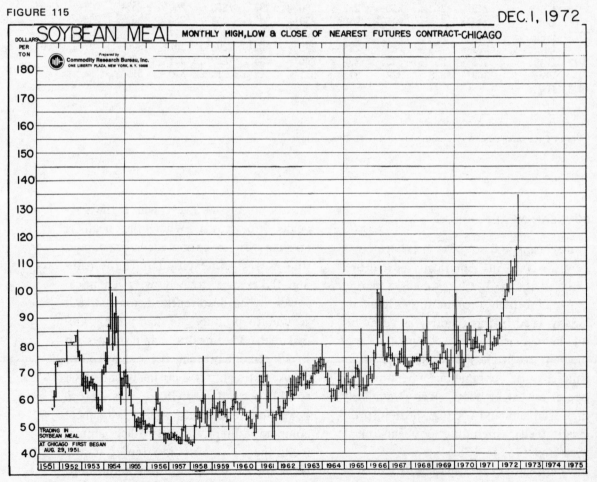

Source: Commodity Research Bureau, Inc.

low result. A $5 movement in the price of a ton of meal is equal to a return of 100 percent on margin capital.

The delivery months for futures are January, March, May, July, August, September, October, and December. There is only one deliverable grade on the futures contract with no provision for other grades at discount or premium to it. The contract grade is 44 percent protein, contract size is 100 tons. Commission runs $33 per contract. Daily trading limit is set at $5 per ton above or below the close of the previous session and no trades will be allowed beyond this limit with the exception of the delivery months when limits are removed after the first notice day. The largest position a trader may hold is 480 contracts or 48,000 tons of soybean meal, which should satisfy most people. Trading hours are 9:30 A.M. to 1:15 P.M., Chicago time.

Additional statistical data pertaining to the preceding section on "Soybean Meal" is shown in Figures 116 and 117 on pages 180 and 181.

FIGURE 116

Table 9.--High-protein feed: Quantity available for feeding and high-protein
feed-consuming animal units, 1960-72

Year beginning October	Quantity available for feeding (in terms of 44% protein soybean meal equivalent)				High-protein consuming animal units			Total per animal unit
	Oilseed meal	Animal protein	Grain protein	Total	Livestock	Poultry	Total	
	-- 1,000 tons --				Million	Million	Million	Pounds
1960	11,259	3,281	947	15,487	70.0	51.8	121.8	254
1961	11,687	3,421	1,052	16,160	71.0	51.3	122.3	264
1962	11,976	3,543	1,069	16,588	73.0	52.0	125.0	265
1963	11,656	3,753	1,136	16,545	72.4	53.4	125.8	263
1964	11,804	3,557	1,181	16,542	69.9	55.9	125.8	263
1965	12,689	3,577	1,238	17,504	68.6	59.7	128.3	273
1966	12,561	3,950	1,250	17,761	71.0	62.0	133.0	267
1967	12,240	4,290	1,283	17,813	71.5	60.3	131.8	270
1968	13,520	3,868	1,298	18,686	72.2	62.5	134.7	277
1969	15,310	3,444	1,321	20,075	72.2	66.1	138.3	290
1970	15,227	3,533	1,319	20,079	74.6	66.6	141.2	284
1971 1/	15,106	3,569	1,360	20,035	74.3	68.7	143.0	280
1972 2/	16,185	3,275	1,400	20,860	75.5	69.0	144.5	288

1/ Preliminary. 2/ Forecast based on November indications.

Table 10.--Soybean meal: Supply, disposition, meal equivalent of exports of soybeans, and price, 1960-72

Year beginning October	Supply				Disposition				Soybeans (Meal equivalent) of exports) 2/	Price per ton, Bulk, Decatur	
	Production	Imports	Stocks, Oct. 1 1/	Total	Exports	Shipments to U.S. Territories	Domestic disappearance			44% protein	49 or 50% protein
							Total	Per high protein animal unit			
	-- 1,000 tons --							Pounds	1,000 tons	-- Dollars --	
1960	9,452	---	83	9,535	590	---	8,867	146	3,090	60.60	66.50
1961	10,342	---	78	10,420	1,064	---	9,262	151	3,639	63.60	69.40
1962	11,127	---	94	11,221	1,476	---	9,586	153	4,282	71.30	77.10
1963	10,609	---	159	10,769	1,478	---	9,168	146	4,539	71.00	78.70
1964	11,286	---	122	11,408	2,036	23	9,243	147	4,890	70.20	79.20
1965	12,901	---	106	13,007	2,604	52	10,219	159	5,968	81.50	89.60
1966	13,483	---	132	13,615	2,657	49	10,772	162	6,327	78.80	86.30
1967	13,660	---	138	13,798	2,899	60	10,693	162	6,415	76.90	84.30
1968	14,581	---	145	14,726	3,044	56	11,469	170	6,797	74.10	82.50
1969	17,596	---	157	17,753	4,035	67	13,514	195	10,669	78.40	86.60
1970	18,035	---	137	18,172	4,559	61	13,406	190	10,286	78.50	84.30
1971 3/	17,024	---	146	17,170	3,805	63	13,110	183	9,545	90.20	98.20
1972 4/	18,130	---	192	18,322	4,300	65	13,765	190	12,125	110	

1/ Stocks at processors' plants. 2/ Calculated at 47.5 pounds of meal per bushel. 3/ Preliminary. 4/ Forecast except October 1 stocks.

Table 11.--Oilseed cake and meal: Supply, disposition, and price, year beginning October, 1971-72

Item	Supply				Disposition				Price per ton 2/
	Stocks, October 1 1/	Production	Imports	Total	Domestic disappearance	Exports	Shipments to U.S. Territories	Total	
	-- 1,000 tons --								Dollars
1971-72 3/									
Soybean	146	17,024	---	17,170	13,110	3,805	63	16,980	90.20
Cottonseed	82	1,843	---	1,925	1,858	6	26	1,891	76.30
Linseed	5	405	3	413	263	144	---	407	72.50
Peanut	5	172	---	177	175	---	---	175	85.50
Copra	---	100	---	100	100	---	---	100	---
Total	238	19,544	3	19,785	15,506	3,955	89	19,553	
1972-73 4/									
Soybean	192	18,130	---	18,322	13,765	4,300	65	18,130	110
Cottonseed	34	2,520	---	2,554	2,375	75	25	2,475	90
Linseed	6	400	---	406	285	115	---	400	90
Peanut	2	200	---	202	200	---	---	200	110
Copra	---	100	---	100	100	---	---	100	---
Total	234	21,350	---	21,584	16,725	4,490	90	21,305	

1/ Stocks at processing mills. 2/ Soybean meal, 44 percent protein, bulk, Decatur. Cottonseed meal, 41 percent protein, bulk, Memphis. Linseed meal, 34 percent protein, bulk, Minneapolis. Copra meal, bulk, San Francisco. Peanut meal, 50 percent protein, Southeast milling points. 3/ Preliminary. 4/ Based on November 1971 indications.

Source: U.S. Department of Agriculture, *Fats and Oils Situation*, November 1972.

FIGURE 117

Supply and Distribution of Soybean Meal in the United States   In Thousands of Short Tons

| Year Begin. Oct. | Supply | | | Distribution | | | | Price (44%) $ Per Ton Decatur—Bulk |
	Stocks Oct. 1	Production	Total	(Domestic) Feed[2]	Exports	Shipments to U.S. Territories	Total	
1964	122	11,286	11,408	9,243	2,036	23	11,302	70.20
1965–6	106	12,901	13,007	10,219	2,604	52	12,875	81.50
1966–7	132	13,483	13,615	10,772	2,657	49	13,478	78.80
1967–8	138	13,660	13,798	10,693	2,899	60	13,652	76.90
1968–9	145	14,581	14,726	11,469	3,044	56	14,569	74.10
1969–0	157	17,596	17,753	13,514	4,035	67	17,616	78.40
1970–1[1]	137	18,035	18,172	13,406	4,559	61	18,126	78.50
1971–2[3]	146	17,150	17,300	13,200	3,900	60	17,160	78.10

[1] Preliminary.   [2] Includes small quantities used for industrial purposes, estimated at 30,000 tons annually.   [3] Estimate.
Source: Economic Research Service, U.S.D.A.

U.S. Exports of Soybean Cake & Meal by Country of Destination   In Thousands of Tons

Year Begin. Oct. 1	Belgium Luxembourg	Bulgaria	Canada	Denmark	France	W. Germany	Hungary	Ireland	Italy	Netherlands	Philippines	Poland	United Kingdom	Yugoslavia	Grand Total
1964–5	177.0	—	249.4	110.9	358.4	300.7	—	18.1	143.2	245.2	7.1	—	34.4	108.9	2,036
1965–6	163.9	19.5	234.0	147.8	464.9	513.0	12.4	14.0	155.0	325.5	3.1	64.1	105.4	78.5	2,602
1966–7	221.4	27.8	238.4	109.4	431.5	458.1	30.3	22.7	192.0	417.9	30.4	51.2	86.1	159.3	2,657
1967–8	240.7	41.4	227.8	66.0	495.4	508.2	50.4	31.0	190.5	546.9	47.7	80.6	82.0	113.7	2,900
1968–9	166.9	32.7	262.9	18.3	471.8	636.5	28.6	43.2	231.9	515.8	43.8	103.0	38.5	143.3	3,044
1969–0	219.0	40.3	270.9	32.5	622.8	855.9	170.6	60.4	309.5	659.0	49.1	109.9	42.9	173.8	4,035
1970–1[1]	308.8	32.8	242.1	85.6	712.1	994.4	156.0	36.5	330.8	675.4	53.8	112.3	100.1	186.8	4,559

[1] Preliminary.   *Source: The Bureau of the Census, U.S.D. of Commerce*

Average Price of Soybean Meal (44% Protein) at Chicago   In Dollars per Ton (Bagged)

Year	Jan.	Feb.	Mar.	Apr.	May	June	July	Aug.	Sept.	Oct.	Nov.	Dec.	Average
1960	64.50	60.65	59.35	60.40	57.40	55.90	54.75	54.30	57.80	52.75	48.00	55.15	56.75
1961	59.00	65.25	68.20	77.00	75.00	67.85	68.85	71.10	63.60	59.50	63.30	64.10	66.90
1962	63.50	61.40	64.90	66.30	68.20	71.00	72.50	74.00	80.90	73.30	74.50	74.70	70.40
1963	75.80	76.50	74.70	72.00	71.50	74.20	76.50	79.50	79.40	77.60	79.20	81.70	76.55
1964	81.50	78.80	77.60	74.00	69.80	70.70	69.80	68.10	73.90	73.40	70.30	72.10	73.35
1965	72.10	74.20	72.70	73.60	72.80	79.70	78.90	74.40	81.30	75.20	80.20	75.70	75.85
1966	83.20	81.50	75.90	80.00	84.80	96.90	101.50	102.30	92.70	86.60	83.40	89.10	88.15
1967	86.10	73.70	81.10	78.90	78.10	82.50	82.60	83.00	83.60	76.30	76.30	77.80	80.85
1968	79.50	78.90	79.30	79.00	79.60	83.90	87.20	88.90	89.60	82.50	78.10	76.10	81.90
1969	74.20	74.40	77.00	77.80	80.60	82.00	81.90	81.30	77.30	79.90	74.60	87.90	79.10
1970	92.50	90.25	76.80	79.60	76.20	79.90	88.10	89.20	86.00	82.40	83.20	87.40	84.35
1971	85.60	82.60	82.40	80.25	84.25	87.50	90.25	84.75	79.25	80.75	79.80	86.60	83.65
1972													

Source: Consumer Marketing Service, U.S.D.A.

Note: Data originally from Commodity Research Bureau, Inc.

SOYBEAN OIL

Soybean oil, when first processed, has a very objectionable taste, and it took researchers several years to develop a method of removing this taste to produce a bland oil which can be left unflavored or flavored artificially to produce an eatable product. Since this development, soybean oil has become so important to the food industry that it has changed the United States from a net importer of edible oils (we used to import a lot of olive oil) to a net exporter. We now export much of our product to underdeveloped countries on special programs, such as Public Law 480, or at retail prices to western Europe (including Italy, which must irritate local chauvinists) and elsewhere. Today when an American housewife buys Wesson Oil or other oils or margarine, the chances are about 80 percent that she is buying soybean oil. Soybean oil is also used to a lesser degree in the production of paints and plastics. (See Fig. 118 below.)

The futures price of oil can fluctuate from a low of 6 cents a pound on up to 15 or 20 cents a pound and like most commodities can be volatile at its extremes. One-half cent movement (50 points) equals a 100 percent return on margin. Many people are attracted to the market as one of the more manageable and volume is growing yearly. Spreads between soybeans, oil and meal, are one of the popular forms of speculation. Contracts are traded for delivery in January, March, May, July, August, September, October, and December. Each contract is equal to 60,000 pounds (one tank car) of oil.

Commission for a contract of soybean oil is $33. The daily trading range is 100

FIGURE 118

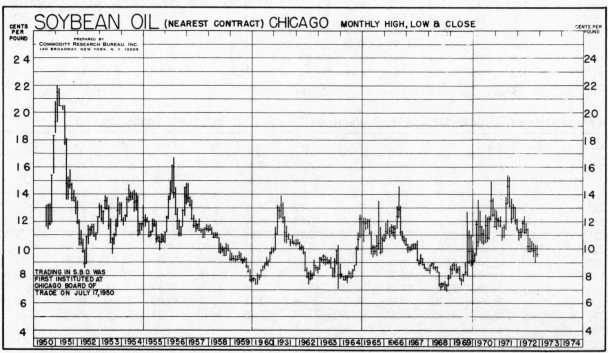

Source: Commodity Research Bureau, Inc.

points (1 cent) above or below the previous closing quotation. The maximum number of contracts that can be held by a speculator is 320, which is equal to 19,200,000 pounds. Holding a contract into delivery is not recommended in any commodity, but a tank car of soybean oil can be carried at $1.80 per day plus interest and insurance.

A great number of good stories exist about the soybean complex. It was soybean oil that Tony de Angeles pumped back and forth between a dozen tanks to assure the Department of Agriculture that they were all full. I personally made $13,000 in a single day on a long position of 48 contracts in soybean oil, which is a lot of money for a man who doesn't normally hold such large positions.

Trading begins at 9:30 A.M. and closes at 1:15 P.M., Chicago time.

Additional statistical data pertaining to the preceding section on "Soybean Oil" is shown in Figures 119, 120, 121 and 122 on pages 184-87.

FIGURE 119

Table 5.--Soybean oil: Supply, disposition, oil equivalent of exports, and price, 1949-72

Year beginning October	Supply: Production	Stocks October 1	Total	Exports	Shipments to U.S. Territories	Domestic disappearance: Total	Per capita	Soybeans (oil equivalent of exports) 1/	Price per pound (tank cars): Crude, Decatur	Refined, N.Y.
	-- Million pounds --			-- Million pounds --			Pounds	Million pounds	-- Cents --	
1949	1,937	113	2,050	291	---	1,646	10.9	128	12.3	---
1950	2,454	113	2,567	490	---	1,906	12.4	272	17.8	21.5
1951	2,444	171	2,615	271	---	2,150	13.7	167	11.3	14.1
1952	2,536	194	2,730	93	---	2,462	15.5	320	12.1	14.8
1953	2,350	174	2,525	71	---	2,326	14.4	436	13.5	16.2
1954	2,711	127	2,838	50	---	2,609	15.9	666	11.9	14.8
1955	3,143	179	3,322	556	---	2,539	15.2	741	12.5	15.5
1956	3,431	227	3,658	807	---	2,565	15.0	937	12.7	15.4
1957	3,800	286	4,085	804	---	3,051	17.6	939	10.8	13.7
1958	4,251	2/281	4,532	930	---	3,304	18.8	1,209	9.5	11.8
1959	4,338	298	4,636	953	---	3,376	18.8	1,552	8.3	10.4
1960	4,420	308	4,728	3/721	---	3,329	18.2	1,431	11.3	13.6
1961	4,790	677	5,467	3/1,308	---	3,540	19.0	1,685	9.5	11.7
1962	5,091	618	5,709	3/1,165	---	3,624	19.2	1,984	8.9	11.1
1963	4,822	920	5,742	3/1,106	17	4,058	21.2	2,103	8.5	10.7
1964	5,146	578	5,724	3/1,340	25	4,069	21.0	2,265	11.3	13.4
1965	5,800	297	6,097	923	28	4,687	23.9	2,764	11.8	13.6
1966	6,076	462	6,538	1,077	30	4,837	24.4	2,930	10.1	12.4
1967	6,032	596	6,628	963	29	5,096	25.4	2,972	8.4	10.5
1968	6,531	540	7,071	870	29	5,756	28.4	3,148	8.4	10.4
1969	7,904	415	8,319	1,420	29	6,328	30.9	4,941	11.2	13.1
1970 4/	8,265	543	8,808	1,742	40	6,253	30.3	4,764	12.8	14.6
1971 5/	7,592	773	8,665	1,388	42	6,452	30.9	4,421	11.3	12.7
1972 5/	8,260	782	9,042	1,500	50	5,450	31	5,600	6/9.6	6/11.1

1/ Calculated at 11.0 pounds of oil per bushel. 2/ Adjusted to new Census basis which includes hydrogenated oils and stearin. 3/ Includes estimates of foreign donations of fats and oils, not reported by Census, 1960-64. 4/ Preliminary. 5/ Forecast except October 1 stocks. 6/ October average.

Table 6.--Soybean oil: Utilization, by products, 1949-71

Year beginning October	Food: Shortening	Margarine	Cooking and salad oils 1/	Other edible	Total	Non-Food: Paint and varnish	Resins and plastics	Other drying oil products	Linoleum and oilcloth	Other inedible 2/	Foots and loss	Total	Total domestic disappearance
	-- Million pounds --					-- Million pounds --							
1949	776	265	288	---	1,329	112	---	---	30	97	78	317	1,646
1950	795	459	344	---	1,599	91	62	11	7	50	87	308	1,906
1951	800	583	404	---	1,786	109	68	11	19	60	97	364	2,150
1952	879	735	462	---	2,077	155	61	9	12	42	106	386	2,462
1953	905	661	437	---	2,002	138	56	7	7	32	84	324	2,326
1954	979	741	545	---	2,264	138	71	11	7	15	107	344	2,609
1955	803	725	668	---	2,196	115	72	9	2	39	107	337	2,539
1956	764	836	627	---	2,227	117	54	9	3	31	132	325	2,565
1957	993	1,041	692	---	2,726	103	66	9	1	28	133	343	3,051
1958	1,136	1,082	665	77	2,960	102	74	6	---	37	147	375	3,304
1959	1,183	1,114	680	23	3,000	101		4	---	48		376	3,376
1960	1,097	1,073	793	26	2,989	96	64	4	1	36	139	340	3,329
1961	1,353	1,036	771	20	3,180	88	74	4	---	43	151	359	3,540
1962	1,222	1,069	933	15	3,239	90	78	6	---	48	163	385	3,624
1963	1,391	1,126	1,146	21	3,684	97	84	6	---	42	146	374	4,058
1964	1,404	1,107	1,100	32	3,643	94	105	5	---	57	165	426	4,069
1965	1,739	1,241	1,200	38	4,218	100	104	6	---	53	206	469	4,687
1966	1,591	1,273	1,353	58	4,375	86	97	5	---	61	201	462	4,837
1967	1,816	1,234	1,494	44	4,588	87	97	7	---	59	259	508	5,096
1968	1,978	1,290	1,957	36	5,271	94	94	7	---	61	236	485	5,756
1969	2,255	1,415	2,150	37	5,857	94	79	7	---	48	243	471	6,328
1970	2,077	1,381	2,288	34	5,780	82	65	6	---	92	267	472	6,253
1971 3/	1,992	1,412	2,591	29	6,024	81	55	4	---	40	249	429	6,452

1/ Adjusted for exports of refined and further processed salad oil. Prior to January 1965 no adjustment made for exports of undeodorized hydrogenated oil. 2/ Includes soap, fatty acids and other miscellaneous. 3/ Preliminary.

Source: U.S. Department of Agriculture, *Fats and Oils Situation*, November 1972.

FIGURE 120

Table 7.--Cottonseed and soybean oil: U.S. exports for dollars and under
P.L. 480, by country of destination, and total value, 1968-71 1/

Country of destination	1968 Public Law 480	1968 Commercial 2/	1968 Total	1969 Public Law 480	1969 Commercial 2/	1969 Total	1970 Public Law 480	1970 Commercial 2/	1970 Total	1971 Public Law 480	1971 Commercial 2/	1971 Total
						-- Million pounds --						
North America												
Canada	3/	45	45	---	79	79	---	77	77	---	60	60
Dominican Republic	12	16	28	16	17	33	23	1	24	20	5	25
Haiti	1	18	19	1	18	19	3	23	26	1	26	27
Mexico	---	4	4	3/	52	52	---	8	8	---	3/	3/
Other	1	19	20	5	34	39	3	46	49	4	31	35
Total	14	102	116	22	200	222	29	155	184	25	122	147
South America												
Argentina	---	2	2	---	---	---	3/	3/	3/	---	3/	3/
Brazil	9	---	9	10	3/	10	6	---	6	---	2	2
Chile	20	11	31	2	36	38	4	54	58	2	---	2
Colombia	8	---	8	115	2	17	10	7	17	8	7	15
Ecuador	2	7	9	4	8	12	5	18	23	11	17	28
Peru	4	5	9	6	53	59	4	107	111	1	73	74
Venezuela	1	72	73	---	44	44	---	63	63	---	44	44
Other	1	1	2	2	1	3	3	1	4	3	---	3
Total	45	97	142	39	144	183	32	250	282	25	143	168
Western Europe												
Spain	---	---	---	---	3/	3/	---	3/	3/	---	3/	3/
Sweden	---	7	7	---	13	13	---	23	23	---	32	32
Germany, West	---	15	15	3/	38	38	---	57	57	---	40	40
Netherlands	---	11	11	3/	35	35	---	22	22	---	23	23
Greece	---	---	---	---	---	---	---	12	12	---	---	---
Italy	---	3/	3/	---	3/	3/	---	3/	2/	]---	3/	3/
Belgium-Luxembourg	---	3/	3/	3/	6	6	---	1	1	---	2	2
United Kingdom	1	---	1	3/	83	83	---	46	46	---	44	44
Other	1	---	1	1	9	10	---	9	9	---	6	6
Total	2	34	36	1	184	185	---	170	170	---	146	146
Eastern Europe												
Poland	4	---	4	6	27	33	---	39	39	---	5	5
Yugoslavia	3/	---	3/	1	2	3	---	271	271	---	199	199
Other	---	---	---	1	---	1	---	---	---	---	1	1
Total	4	---	4	8	29	37	---	310	310	---	205	205
Africa												
Algeria	3	---	3	1	---	1	---	---	---	---	---	---
Egypt	---	17	17	---	100	100	2	78	80	1	185	186
Guinea	6	---	6	3/	3/	3/	10	---	10	2	---	2
Morocco	28	---	28	20	45	65	58	37	95	95	32	127
Tunisia	54	3	57	72	23	95	74	2	76	119	16	135
Other	13	---	13	15	21	36	17	21	38	8	14	22
Total	104	20	124	108	189	297	161	138	299	225	247	472
Asia and Oceania												
Australia	---	2	2	1	7	8	1	11	12	---	5	5
Bangladesh	---	---	---	---	---	---	---	---	---	4/136	---	136
Burma	---	---	---	---	---	---	---	---	---	---	---	---
Hong Kong	1	3	4	1	11	12	---	2	2	---	3/	3/
India	328	---	328	188	62	250	284	---	284	5/144	---	144
Iran	30	---	30	64	134	198	6	130	136	3/	139	139
Israel	34	---	34	38	---	38	41	---	41	41	3	44
Japan	---	2	2	3/	17	17	---	1	1	---	16	16
Pakistan	130	1	131	284	89	373	214	64	278	97	45	142
South Viet Nam	41	---	41	4	3	7	29	---	29	34	---	34
Taiwan	---	---	---	---	9	9	---	18	18	---	4	4
Turkey	3/	---	3/	6	---	6	---	31	31	6	10	16
Other	9	5	14	15	16	31	16	20	36	9	13	22
Total	573	13	586	601	348	949	591	277	868	467	235	702
Grand total	743	266	1,009	779	1,093	1,872	813	1,300	2,114	741	1,099	1,840
Value of Exports												
Total (Mil. dol.)			101			216			309			256
Per pound (Cent)			10.0			11.6			14.6			13.9

1/ Census data. Breakdown between P.L. 480 and commercial provided by the Fats and Oils Division, FAS. 2/ Includes Barter,
CCC credits. 3/ Less than 500,000 pounds. 4/ Includes relief shipments to Bangladesh beginning May 1, 1972, handled by UNROD
and other relief agencies. 5/ Includes relief shipments for East Pakistan refugees financed under Title II.

Source: U.S. Department of Agriculture, *Fats and Oils Situation*, November 1972.

FIGURE 121

U.S. Production of Refined Soybean Oil   In Millions of Pounds

Year	Oct.	Nov.	Dec.	Jan.	Feb.	Mar.	Apr.	May	June	July	Aug.	Sept.	Total
1965–6	353.2	423.2	445.2	468.6	416.5	476.4	418.0	450.9	430.2	359.7	425.8	402.1	5,070
1966–7	411.5	427.0	465.3	460.4	410.4	446.0	387.4	424.8	450.3	377.0	432.7	398.2	5,091
1967–8	428.2	414.8	442.6	429.1	457.7	431.9	424.2	447.1	425.2	392.6	427.1	444.4	5,165
1968–9	446.7	439.5	462.4	460.1	448.3	506.4	479.1	466.3	498.7	452.4	459.4	489.3	5,609
1969–0	513.0	526.2	560.8	533.0	509.2	566.4	545.9	505.6	531.9	488.1	516.5	491.9	6,289
1970–1[1]	534.5	514.5	538.8	543.5	511.1	557.9	495.0	506.7	526.7	482.9	532.8	568.6	6,313
1971–2[1]	534.5	504.2	534.1	525.5									

[1] Preliminary.   *Source: Bureau of the Census*

U.S. Exports of Soybean Oil (Crude & Refined)   In Millions of Pounds

Year	Jan.	Feb.	Mar.	Apr.	May	June	July	Aug.	Sept.	Oct.	Nov.	Dec.	Total
1961	75.3	43.9	14.0	61.5	22.1	84.4	62.5	73.5	32.2	55.5	42.0	35.6	602.4
1962	38.9	66.2	55.2	152.1	94.4	165.5	170.4	137.5	110.8	54.1	75.1	93.4	1,213.6
1963	49.4	36.2	153.4	179.4	95.5	77.7	82.2	87.0	142.7	99.6	42.1	57.3	1,102.6
1964	70.2	74.7	69.2	127.3	62.7	99.5	127.1	132.1	124.8	110.2	117.8	157.6	1,273.2
1965	68.4	72.7	146.6	91.7	85.1	78.2	61.0	99.3	89.9	28.5	36.6	168.7	1,026.7
1966	44.6	42.1	45.6	33.2	47.2	64.6	55.1	97.1	78.5	30.4	48.6	97.8	684.8
1967	24.3	45.7	120.2	41.0	66.5	131.0	107.4	43.1	118.0	79.1	114.3	40.1	912.3
1968	30.3	68.4	80.9	41.4	48.0	119.2	46.2	29.7	124.2	67.2	56.4	111.5	823.4
1969	58.9	19.1	18.6	77.1	43.2	120.3	69.6	20.2	90.9	45.3	100.8	97.2	761
1970	62.7	46.2	151.7	73.8	81.1	197.8	136.0	126.7	165.2	103.9	52.7	174.6	1,372
1971	112.0	109.3	156.0	168.0	191.8	140.9	189.0	78.1	122.2	143.0	43.5	153.8	1,612
1972	157.8												

Source: Dept. of Commerce

Average Prices of Crude Domestic Soybean Oil (in Tank Cars) F.O.B. Decatur   In Cents per Pound

Year	Oct.	Nov.	Dec.	Jan.	Feb.	Mar.	Apr.	May	June	July	Aug.	Sept.	Average
1960–61	9.4	10.2	10.0	10.9	12.2	13.0	13.3	12.7	11.6	10.9	10.9	10.5	11.3
1961–62	10.7	10.4	10.5	10.5	10.2	10.1	9.9	9.3	8.4	8.0	8.2	8.1	9.5
1962–63	8.7	8.6	8.6	8.9	9.2	9.3	9.1	9.2	9.1	9.0	8.3	8.5	8.9
1963–64	9.2	9.1	8.3	8.1	8.0	8.1	7.9	8.4	8.2	8.5	8.8	9.7	8.5
1964–65	10.9	12.2	12.0	11.6	12.1	12.2	12.1	10.4	10.2	10.0	10.5	11.4	11.4
1965–6	11.5	11.2	11.2	11.9	12.0	11.3	11.6	11.3	11.2	12.3	12.3	12.3	11.8
1966–7	10.9	10.8	10.6	10.3	10.3	10.3	10.3	10.3	9.8	9.1	9.6	9.3	10.1
1967–8	8.8	8.6	8.6	8.7	9.5	9.1	8.8	8.7	7.8	7.4	7.5	7.5	8.4
1968–9	7.3	7.9	8.1	8.6	9.1	8.8	8.4	8.4	7.8	8.2	8.9	9.7	8.4
1969–0	10.6	10.9	9.6	9.6	11.5	12.2	12.2	11.3	11.1	11.5	11.6	12.1	11.2
1970–1	14.0	13.9	12.4	12.3	12.1	12.2	11.2	11.4	12.8	14.5	14.5	12.8	12.8
1971–2	13.2												

Source: Bureau of Labor Statistics

Note: Data originally from Commodity Research Bureau, Inc.

FIGURE 122

Supply & Distribution of Soybean Oil in the U.S.   In Millions of Pounds

Year Begin. Oct.	Production	Stocks Oct. 1	Exports & Shipments	Total	Food Short-ening	Mar-garine	Cooking & Salad Oils	Other Edible	Total Food	Non-Food Paint & Varnish	Resins & Plastics	Other Drying Oil Pdt's	Other Inedible[3]	Foots & Loss	Total Non-Food
1959–0	4,338	298	953	3,376	1,183	1,114	680	23	3,000	101	74	4	48	147	375
1960–1	4,420	308	721	3,329	1,097	1,073	793	26	2,989	96	64	4	36	139	340
1961–2	4,790	677	1,308	3,540	1,353	1,036	771	20	3,180	88	74	4	43	151	359
1962–3	5,091	618	1,165	3,624	1,222	1,069	933	15	3,239	90	78	6	48	163	385
1963–4	4,822	920	1,106	4,058	1,391	1,126	1,146	21	3,684	97	84	6	42	146	374
1964–5	5,146	578	1,357	4,069	1,404	1,107	1,100	32	3,643	94	105	5	57	165	426
1965–6	5,800	297	948	4,687	1,739	1,241	1,200	38	4,218	100	104	6	53	206	469
1966–7	6,076	462	1,105	4,837	1,691	1,273	1,353	58	4,375	96	97	7	61	201	462
1967–8	6,032	596	993	5,096	1,816	1,234	1,494	44	4,588	86	97	7	59	259	508
1968–9	6,531	540	899	5,756	1,978	1,290	1,967	36	5,271	87	94	7	61	236	485
1969–0	7,904	415	1,448	6,328	2,255	1,415	2,150	37	5,857	94	79	7	48	243	471
1970–1[1]	8,265	543	1,782	6,253	2,077	1,381	2,302	34	5,794	82	65	6	52	267	472
1971–2[2]	7,825	773	1,250	6,450											
1972–3															

[1] Preliminary.   [2] Forecast.   [3] Includes soap, fatty acids and other miscellaneous.
Source: Economic Research Service, U.S.D.A.

Note: Data originally from Commodity Research Bureau, Inc.

COTTON

Cotton futures are traded on the New York Cotton Exchange from 10:30 A.M. to 3:00 P.M., New York time.

Contract size is 50,000 pounds with each 1 cent price advance or decline in cotton futures returning a $500 profit or loss to the commodity dealer.

The margin for trading cotton futures varies with the prices at which cotton is selling. When cotton is priced from 1 cent to 35 cents per pound, the margin per contract is $1,000. When cotton is selling from 35 cents to 37 cents per pound, the margin for trading the future is $1,250 per contract. From 37 cents to 39 cents the margin is upped to $1,500 per contract. When cotton is priced from 39 cents to 41 cents the margin required to trade the future is $1,800. Above 41 cents the margin for cotton is $2,300 per contract.

After there has been a net paper loss in the position held by the trader of 25 percent, the trader must bring his margin up to the balance initially required. The margin for a spread position is $500 when prices are below 35 cents per pound and $600 when cotton is priced above 35 cents per pound.

The commission for trading a contract of cotton is $45 per contract. The day trade commission is $22.50 with a spread position of both long one cotton future and short another cotton future costing a commission for both positions of $54. (See Fig. 123, p. 188.)

The United States and the Soviet Union compete for the world cotton production record with 40 percent of the world crop grown in these two countries. China is the third largest producer of cotton in the world followed by Brazil and Egypt.

The Soviet Union and the United States almost equally consume cotton with each using approximately 80 percent of their own production. China consumes more cotton than it produces as does India which is also a substantial cotton-producing country.

Most of the cotton produced in the United States is harvested by October. Texas is by far the largest cotton-producing state in the Union having produced 3,247,000 bales in 1970. Mississippi is second, followed by California, and then by Arkansas.

The U.S. government plays a major role in the cotton markets as it does in the feed and bread grain markets. By a system of price supports and government loans there is no longer a free laissez-faire cotton market. With the CCC holding a large portion of the free stock supply, whenever prices do rise there is always the threat that the government will unload its surpluses onto the open market and depress prices. (See Fig. 124 opposite.)

At one time in American history, the cotton markets were among the most active in existence. The big rollers such as "Bet a Million Gates" and "Jessie Livermore" often played the cotton

FIGURE 123

Source: Commodity Research Bureau, Inc.

FIGURE 124
Cotton Situation at a Glance

Item	Unit	1971			1972[1]		
		July	Aug.	Sept.	July	Aug.	Sept.
GENERAL ECONOMY							
BLS wholesale price indices							
All commodities	1967=100	114.6	114.9	114.5	119.7	119.9	120.2
Cotton broadwoven goods	do.	112.1	112.2	111.6	123.3	123.1	124.4
Indices of industrial production[2]							
Overall including utilities	do.	106.1	105.6	106.2	113.7	114.3	
Textiles, apparel and leather products	do.	100.2	100.1	102.5	104.4	105.9	107.2
Personal income payments[2]	Bil. dol.	857.7	866.1	869.9	932.9	939.8	
Retail apparel sales[2]	Mil. dol.	1,729	1,749	1,683	1,800		
COTTON							
Broadwoven goods industry							
Average gross hourly earnings	Dollars	2.53	2.53	2.56	2.71		
Ratio of stocks to unfilled orders[3]	Percent	30	33	33	23	22	
Consumption of all kinds by mills							
Total (4-week period except as noted)	1,000 bales	515	637	[4]771	493	587	[4]716
Cumulative since August 1	do.	8,068	637	1,408	8,010	587	1,303
Daily rate							
Seasonally adjusted[5]	do.	31.4	31.2	30.9	30.0	28.7	28.7
Unadjusted	do.	25.8	31.8	30.9	24.7	29.3	28.6
Spindles in place on cotton system[6]	Thousands	19,231	19,233	19,198	19,104	19,093	19,084
Consuming 100 percent cotton	do.	11,459	11,425	11,422	10,826	10,656	10,505
Consuming blends	do.	5,058	5,068	5,061	5,283	5,386	5,463
Mill margin data, expanded series[7]							
Average gray goods price	Cents	N.A.	76.51	76.62	89.90	90.00	89.85
Average cotton price	do.	N.A.	30.87	31.30	37.78	36.19	31.21
Margin	do.	N.A.	45.64	45.32	52.12	53.81	58.64
Prices of American upland							
Received by farmers (mid-month)	do.	23.73	27.00	27.00	30.99	30.98	24.35
Parity (effective following month)	do.	51.74	51.99	52.12	55.16	55.16	55.67
Farm as percentage of parity	Percent	44	52	52	56	56	44
Stocks							
Mill, end of month	1,000 bales	1,641	1,512	1,263	1,540	1,235	1,006
Public storage and compresses	do.	2,211	1,712	1,498	1,614	1,478	2,028
Trade							
Raw cotton							
Exports							
Total	do.	213	162	310	110	59	
Cumulative since August 1	do.	3,738	162	473	3,229	59	
Imports							
Total	Bales	1,141	2,503	4,986	5,462	4,010	
Cumulative since August 1	do.	36,665	2,503	7,489	72,205	4,010	
Textile manufactures (equivalent raw cotton)							
Exports							
Total	1,000 bales	34.9	44.0	51.0	45.7	53.3	
Cumulative since August 1	do.	413.6	44.0	95.0	560.7	53.3	
Imports							
Total	do.	86.7	90.0	119.4	98.5	122.8	
Cumulative since August 1	do.	945.6	90.0	209.4	1,207.5	122.8	
MAN MADE FIBERS							
Consumption, daily rate by mills[8]							
Non-cellulosics	1,000 pounds	3,664	3,678	3,551	4,608	4,452	4,527
Rayon and acetate	do.	2,044	1,954	1,972	2,073	1,919	1,865
Prices							
Non-cellulosic staple, 1.5 denier							
Acrylic	Dollars	.56	.56	.56	.56	.56	.56
Polyester	do.	.61	.61	.61	.61	.61	.61
Rayon viscose							
Staple							
Modified, 1.5 and 3.0 denier	do.	.38	.38	.38	.38	.38	.38
Regular, 1.5 denier	do.	.28	.28	.28	.31	.32	.32
Yarn, 150 denier	do.	.98	.98	.98	1.03	1.03	.95

[1] Preliminary. [2] Seasonally adjusted. [3] Not seasonally adjusted. [4] 5-week period. [5] Combined upland and extra-long staple. [6] End of month. [7] Net weight. [8] On cotton-system spinning spindles, seasonally adjusted. N.A. Not available.

Source: U.S. Department of Agriculture, *Cotton Situation*, October 1, 1972.

markets during the 1920s to 1940s when the action in cotton exceeded the action on all other commodity markets combined nearly exceeding the value of the New York Stock Exchange. With the heavy role of the government, however, and price supports, this situation changed and the cotton market is no longer as active.

In most commodities the demand picture is not very difficult to compute though forecasting it is usually time-consuming. In the cotton market, however, demand is very much complicated by the trading program requiring an accurate estimate of cloth inventories, the quantity and quality of raw cotton inventories held by mills, the competition from other new fibers which have changed over the years, and the need for cotton in foreign countries. Thus by having to estimate these various independent factors, the trader may have a difficulty in sizing up the cotton demand situation. (See Fig. 125 opposite.)

The most important economic report for the trader to study is the *Cotton Situation* report issued by the U.S. Department of Agriculture. This report sizes up the cotton market as the government sees it and makes forecasts for price advances or declines throughout the season.

Once these reports and estimates have been made, then the trader will wish to follow closely the *Cotton Production Reports,* issued periodically throughout the crop years, to see if the production is in fact falling into line with the estimates of the government. Besides these two crop reports, the trader will wish to follow the cotton ginnings reports which indicate the usage of cotton throughout the year. There is also a monthly report issued by the U.S. Census Bureau which gives the consumption of cotton throughout the United States as well as the current stocks at mills and in storage. There are further reports on the quality of cotton available and monthly reports which show the production of cotton goods which enable the trader to estimate usage as the season rolls along. Finally, there are the export figures which the trader will follow as a reduction of supply in the United States. (See Fig. 126, p. 192.)

Cotton is harvested in the United States primarily in the southern states and Texas and California. As the harvest comes along there is considerable pressure put upon the cash markets to absorb the great influx of supply. This pressure causes prices to dip normally during the harvest months of October and November and to rally thereafter when the pressure from harvest has lifted. Thus the trader finds that the seasonal price variations in cotton are very significant and he wants to be aware of them prior to their occurring. By timing his sales to a period in advance of harvest and his purchases to a period either during or after harvest, the trader can often maximize his profits in the market.

Additional statistical data pertaining to the preceding section on "Cotton" is shown in Figures 127 and 128 on pages 193 and 194.

FIGURE 125

Table 12.—Cotton: Supply distribution, by type in 480-pound net weight bales, U.S. 1957 to date

Year beginning August 1	Carry over August 1	Ginnings Current crop less ginning[1]	Ginnings New crop[2]	Imports	City crop	Total	Mill consumption[3]	Exports	Total
		Supply					Distribution		

1,000 480-pound net weight bales[4]

All kinds

Year	Carry over	Current crop less ginning	New crop	Imports	City crop	Total	Mill consump.	Exports	Total
1957	11,442.5	10,716.2	213.7	141.2	58.4	22,572.0	8,076.3	5,959.3	14,035.6
1958	8,789.6	11,280.6	150.7	136.5	51.3	20,408.7	8,793.5	2,894.7	11,688.2
1959	8,931.0	14,376.2	139.5	130.7	50.1	23,627.5	9,025.9	7,394.3	16,420.2
1960	7,566.5	14,097.9	227.0	[5]127.2	62.9	22,081.5	8,271.8	6,857.3	15,129.1
1961	7,212.9	14,055.6	286.7	[5]152.4	63.8	21,771.4	8,928.0	5,056.0	13,984.0
1962	7,808.6	14,540.7	244.8	136.6	67.8	22,798.5	8,399.8	3,429.3	11,829.1
1963	11,190.2	15,048.7	152.1	[6]134.8	102.0	26,627.8	8,610.3	5,776.5	14,386.8
1964	12,380.9	14,992.2	180.2	118.2	70.0	27,741.5	9,169.0	4,194.9	13,363.9
1965	14,287.6	14,771.2	9.9	118.4	87.6	29,274.7	9,500.7	3,035.5	12,536.2
1966	16,869.3	9,545.6	256.7	104.6	50.0	26,826.2	9,479.1	4,831.8	14,310.9
1967	12,525.6	7,186.7	6.1	149.1	30.0	19,897.5	8,987.1	4,361.3	13,348.4
1968	6,452.2	10,919.9	8.0	67.6	40.0	17,487.7	8,249.0	2,824.7	11,073.7
1969	6,526.2	9,982.2	6.0	51.9	40.2	16,606.5	8,031.9	2,876.3	10,908.2
1970	5,790.3	10,186.1	125.4	36.7	40.3	16,178.8	8,123.4	3,897.4	12,020.8
1971	4,286.3	10,347.6	41.1	72.2	40.9	14,788.1	8,174.4	3,362.8	11,537.2
1972[10]	3,391.3	[11]13,670.1	---	50.0	50.0	17,161.4	8,200.0	3,517.0	11,717.0

Upland (other than extra-long staple)

Year	Carry over	Current crop less ginning	New crop	Imports	City crop	Total	Mill consump.	Exports	Total
1957	11,388.4	10,634.6	213.7	96.6	58.4	22,391.7	7,974.5	5,949.1	13,923.6
1958	8,665.3	11,197.2	150.7	51.0	51.3	20,115.5	8,682.4	2,869.7	11,552.1
1959	8,775.4	14,305.9	139.5	47.5	50.1	23,318.4	8,886.2	7,392.7	16,278.9
1960	7,409.8	14,030.8	227.0	41.5	62.9	21,772.0	8,121.2	6,849.5	14,970.7
1961	7,072.7	13,993.3	286.7	68.2	63.8	21,484.7	8,754.1	5,049.0	13,803.1
1962	7,717.0	14,428.4	244.8	54.5	67.8	22,512.5	8,235.5	3,426.6	11,662.1
1963	10,987.9	14,884.9	152.1	[6]54.4	102.0	26,181.3	8,467.3	5,773.9	14,241.2
1964	12,124.6	14,872.7	180.2	35.5	70.0	27,283.0	9,013.0	4,173.2	13,186.2
1965	14,021.2	14,683.4	9.9	30.8	87.6	28,832.9	9,356.2	3,029.7	12,385.9
1966	16,574.8	9,473.9	256.7	28.9	50.0	26,384.3	9,343.1	4,818.6	14,161.7
1967	12,270.4	7,117.2	6.1	57.6	30.0	19,481.3	8,857.4	4,345.0	13,202.4
1968	6,258.8	10,841.0	8.0	37.9	40.0	17,185.7	8,121.6	2,816.0	10,937.6
1969	6,369.6	9,904.8	6.0	30.1	40.2	16,350.7	7,919.4	2,861.1	10,780.5
1970	5,682.2	10,128.8	125.4	11.1	40.3	15,987.8	8,025.3	3,885.7	11,911.0
1971	4,223.6	10,249.5	41.1	42.0	40.9	14,597.1	8,078.7	3,355.9	11,434.6
1972[10]	3,316.0	[11]13,574.7	---	25.0	50.0	16,965.7	8,100.0	3,500.0	11,600.0

Extra-long staple (other than upland)[7]

Year	Carry over	Current crop less ginning	New crop	Imports	City crop	Total	Mill consump.	Exports	Total
1957	54.1	81.6	---	44.6	---	180.3	101.8	10.2	112.0
1958	124.3	83.4	---	85.5	---	293.2	111.1	25.0	136.1
1959	155.6	70.3	---	83.2	---	309.1	139.7	1.6	141.3
1960	156.7	67.1	---	85.7	---	309.5	150.6	7.8	158.4
1961	140.2	62.3	---	84.2	---	286.7	173.9	7.0	180.9
1962	[8]91.6	112.3	---	82.1	---	286.0	164.3	2.7	167.0
1963	[8]202.3	163.8	---	[6]80.4	---	446.5	143.0	2.6	145.6
1964	[8]256.3	119.5	---	82.7	---	458.5	156.0	21.7	177.7
1965	[8]266.4	87.8	---	87.6	---	441.8	144.5	5.8	150.3
1966	[8]294.5	71.7	---	75.7	---	441.9	136.0	13.2	149.2
1967	[8]255.2	69.5	---	[9]91.5	---	416.2	129.7	16.3	146.0
1968	193.4	78.9	---	29.7	---	302.0	127.4	8.7	136.1
1969	156.6	77.4	---	21.8	---	255.8	112.5	15.2	127.7
1970	108.1	57.3	---	25.6	---	191.0	98.1	11.7	109.8
1971	62.7	98.1	---	30.2	---	191.0	95.7	6.9	102.6
1972[10]	75.3	[11]95.4	---	25.0	---	195.7	100.0	17.0	117.0

Source: U.S. Department of Agriculture, *Cotton Situation.*

FIGURE 126
SAMPLE OF *COTTON SITUATION* REPORT

COTTON SITUATION

OUTLOOK AND RECENT DEVELOPMENTS

1973 UPLAND COTTON LOAN RATE

The U.S. Department of Agriculture announced on October 17 that there would be no change in the loan rate for the 1973 crop of upland cotton. The announcement, stated, in part:

"The national average loan rate for Middling 1-inch upland cotton (miconaire 3.5 through 4.9) net weight, at average location is 19.5 cents per pound, the same as for 1972. After determining 90 percent of the average world price of Middling 1-inch cotton for the 2-year period ending July 31, 1972, an adjustment was made to take into account the unusually high world prices which prevailed during much of this period. The adjustment is in accordance with provisions of the Agricultural Act of 1970 which specifically provides for it whenever needed in order to keep U.S. cotton competitive and to retain an adequate share of the world market.

Loans available to program cooperators for different individual qualities will be based on the Middling 1-inch rate. A schedule of premiums and discounts for these various qualities and the base loan rate for Middling 1-inch cotton at each warehouse location will be issued at a later date. As in 1972, loans will be available to cooperators for a term of 10 months from the first day of the month in which the loan is made. Loan amounts will be reduced for any unpaid storage charges in excess of 60 days, as provided by law."

Other major provisions of the 1973 Upland Cotton Program, such as the national base acreage allotment, the acreage set-aside requirement, and the preliminary set-aside payment rate will be announced by November 15.

DEMAND AND SUPPLY HIGHLIGHTS

The domestic cotton outlook for 1972/73 is dominated by increased supplies stemming from sharply larger production. Output is expected to be up 31%, boosting supplies nearly 2½ million bales above 1971/72's 14-3/4 million (480 pounds net weight) despite smaller beginning stocks. Disappearance may increase only slightly above last season's 11½ million

bales. Thus, stocks next summer may total about 2 million bales above last August's 3.4 million (table 12 and figure 1).

To assess more accurately the actual quantity of U.S. cotton moving off the farm into domestic and foreign markets, supply and distribution data have been converted from running bales to 480-pound net weight bales. A comparison of the 2 sets of data, as shown in tables 12 and 13, reveals a substantial difference in 1971/72. With the switch to net weight trading last year, average bale weights increased to 491.6 pounds, about 2% above the average of recent years. Thus, the use of data expressed in running bales tends to understate the actual pounds involved.

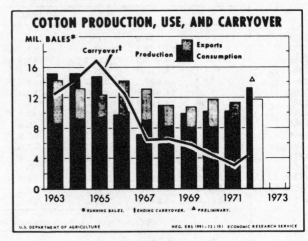

Figure 1

DOMESTIC OUTLOOK AND DEVELOPMENTS

**Large 1972 Crop Replenishing Supplies;
Acreage and Yields Up Sharply**

The 1972 cotton crop was estimated at 13.7 million 480-pound net weight bales as of October 1, slightly above earlier indications, and about 3.2 million above the 1971 crop. The increase reflects 15% more acres and 14% higher yields. Larger acreage mirrors last season's relatively high cotton prices, while higher yields reflect favorable growing conditions across much of the Cotton Belt.

Larger production in the Delta and Southwest is mainly responsible for this season's larger U.S. output.

Source: U.S. Department of Agriculture, *Cotton Situation,* November 1972.

FIGURE 127

COTTON: ACREAGE, YIELD, AND PRODUCTION

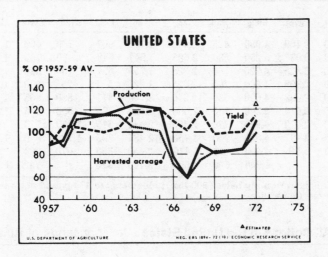

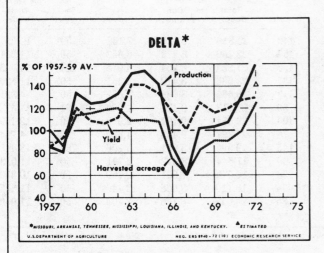

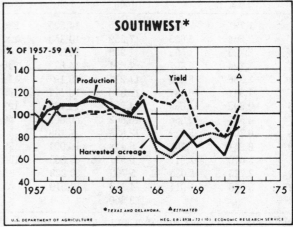

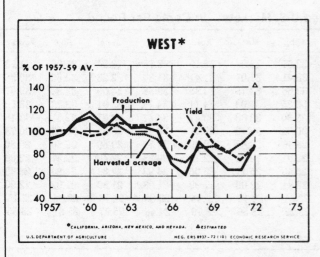

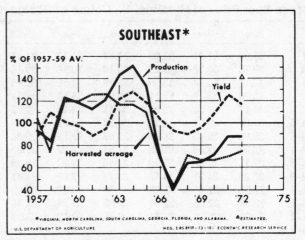

YEAR BEGINNING AUGUST 1

Source: U.S. Department of Agriculture, *Cotton Situation.*

FIGURE 128
World Production of Cotton   In Thousands of Bales[3]

Year Begin. Aug. 1	Argen-tina	Brazil	China	Egypt	India	Iran	Mex-ico	Pakis-tan	Peru	Sudan	Syria	Tur-key	United States	U.S.S.R.	World Total
1962–3	615	2,250	4,300	2,109	4,950	425	2,400	1,702	667	750	690	1,130	14,920	6,850	48,223
1963–4	460	2,325	4,700	2,037	5,250	530	2,085	1,944	648	470	705	1,185	15,340	8,100	50,469
1964–5	635	2,075	5,500	2,325	4,920	560	2,385	1,754	627	700	810	1,500	15,245	8,300	52,141
1965–6	480	2,500	5,800	2,398	4,600	700	2,615	1,925	544	755	830	1,500	14,920	8,930	53,390
1966–7	400	2,050	6,500	2,098	4,600	530	2,240	2,149	471	890	655	1,760	9,860	9,480	48,921
1967–8	340	2,750	7,000	2,014	5,300	545	2,000	2,400	390	900	585	1,825	7,215	9,370	47,746
1968–9	520	3,320	6,800	2,013	4,900	770	2,450	2,440	515	1,050	710	2,005	11,030	9,200	53,661
1969–0	645	3,100	7,000	2,497	4,850	760	1,750	2,485	393	1,135	690	1,845	9,950	8,850	51,893
1970–1[1]	400	2,300	7,000	2,346	4,400	710	1,440	2,450	355	1,070	690	1,845	10,269	10,800	51,529
1971–2[2]	500	3,000			4,900	600	1,600	2,700	420		745	2,200	10,500	10,800	54,300

[1] Preliminary.   [2] Estimate.   [3] U.S. is in running bales (500 lbs.); all others are 478 pound net weight bales.
Source: International Cotton Advisory Committee

Supply and Distribution of All Cottons in the United States   In Thousands of Running Bales

Year Begin. Aug. 1	Carryover—August 1			Produc-tion[2]	City Crop[4]	Imports	Total Supply	Con-sumption	Exports	De-stroyed[4]	Total Distri-bution
	Free	Gov't.	Total								
1959	1,791	7,094	8,885	14,505	286	140	23,816	9,025	7,182	50	16,257
1960	2,504	5,055	7,559	14,353	120	157	22,189	8,279	6,632	50	14,961
1961	5,725	1,503	7,228	14,384	64	158	21,834	8,954	4,915	134	14,003
1962	3,124	4,707	7,831	14,822	246	137	23,036	8,419	3,351	50	11,820
1963	2,986	8,230	11,216	15,197	173	113	26,699	8,609	5,662	50	14,321
1964–5	1,941	10,437	12,378	15,177	69	89	27,713	9,171	4,060	191	13,422
1965–6	2,602	11,689	14,291	14,763	193	104	29,351	9,497	2,942	50	12,489
1966–7	4,506	12,356	16,862	9,809	50	76	26,797	9,485	4,669	110	14,264
1967–8	6,704	5,829	12,533	7,188	30	145	19,896	8,981	4,206	261	13,448
1968–9	6,241	207	6,448	10,991	39	66	17,544	8,242	2,731	50	11,023
1969–0	3,610	2,911	6,521	9,863	136	50	16,570	7,991	2,769	50	10,810
1970–1	2,725	3,035	5,760	10,229	85	36	16,110	8,068	3,740	50	11,858
1971–2[1]	3,938	314	4,252	10,519	43	36	14,850	8,100	2,900	50	11,050
1972–3[3]			3,800								

[1] Preliminary.   [2] Includes in-season ginnings.   [3] Estimated.   [4] And adjustments, if any.   *Source: New York Cotton Exchange*

Average Spot Price of Middling, 1″, Cotton at Designated U.S. Markets   In Cents Per Pound

Year	Aug.	Sept.	Oct.	Nov.	Dec.	Jan.	Feb.	Mar.	Apr.	May	June	July	Average
1959	31.95	31.77	31.66	31.61	31.78	31.91	32.01	32.04	32.10	32.18	32.24	31.96	31.93
1960	30.75	30.52	30.22	30.19	30.16	30.14	30.41	31.07	31.41	31.80	32.22	32.65	30.96
1961	33.11	33.38	33.59	33.59	33.56	33.60	33.66	33.75	33.85	33.88	34.09	33.98	33.67
1962	33.36	33.02	33.01	32.98	33.13	33.42	33.75	34.04	34.11	34.13	33.91	33.43	33.52
1963	33.17	33.09	33.08	33.11	33.15	33.22	33.30	33.38	33.41	33.37	33.27	32.57	33.18
1964–5	31.20	30.67	30.58	30.58	30.57	30.56	30.63	30.72	30.77	30.84	30.91	30.69	30.73
1965–6	29.98	29.72	29.68	29.62	29.53	29.51	29.46	29.46	29.49	29.57	29.60	29.60	29.60
1966–7	22.04	21.86	21.83	21.84	21.92	21.97	22.01	22.08	22.17	22.23	22.40	22.57	22.08
1967–8	22.77	23.22	23.40	24.98	27.02	26.19	25.40	25.21	25.06	24.93	24.83	24.94	24.83
1968–9	25.05	24.97	24.29	23.27	22.67	22.47	22.21	22.09	21.99	21.93	21.89	21.92	22.90
1969–0	21.59	21.43	21.68	21.94	22.02	22.00	22.11	22.19	22.44	22.60	22.78	22.96	22.15
1970–1	22.99	22.98	23.00	22.82	22.58	22.81	23.22	23.56	23.79	24.46	25.07	25.31	23.55
1971–2	26.78	27.27	27.71	28.05	30.12	32.88							
1972–3													

Source: Department of Agriculture

Note: Data originally from Commodity Research Bureau, Inc.

FROZEN ORANGE JUICE

Orange juice futures (frozen concentrate orange juice) are traded on the New York Cotton Exchange from 10:15 A.M. to 2:45 P.M., New York time.

The contract consists of 15,000 pounds with each 1 cent price advance or decline resulting in a $150 profit or loss for the futures trader. (See Fig. 129 below.)

The margin for trading orange juice futures varies from $900 to $2,000. When the future is priced below 50 cents per pound the margin is $900. When the future is priced from 50 cents to 60 cents the margin is $1,200. When the future is priced from 60 cents to 70 cents the margin is $1,500. When the future is priced from 70 cents to 80 cents the margin is $1,800. When the future is priced above 80 cents the margin is $2,000.

The hedge margin varies from $350 to $900 with divisions at each range the same as for the speculative position. When the paper position results in a 25 percent paper loss the margin must be restored to full value.

FIGURE 129

Source: Commodity Research Bureau, Inc.

The margin for a spread position varies from $200 for a hedge spread and $450 for a speculative spread up to $900 for a speculative spread.

The commission for trading a contract of frozen concentrated orange juice is $45 per contract. The day trade commission is $22.50 with a spread position of long one option of orange juice and short another option costing a commission for both positions of $54.

The United States is by far the largest world producer of oranges. From a total 1970 supply of 708 million boxes, the United States produced 243 million boxes or nearly 38 percent. Japan is the second largest producer of oranges, producing 86 million boxes, followed by Spain with 65, Brazil with 56, Italy with 51, and Argentina with 34.

In the United States about 90 percent of the total production is grown in the states of Florida and California with Florida producing most of the oranges. California uses most of its land for other crops and with a lack of rainfall sufficient to produce the moist juicy orange demanded by today's housewife.

This is naturally to the advantage of the commodity trader who has only one state or at the most two states to watch for freezes and crop production estimates. The trader who trades in wheat, corn, soybeans, silver, and so forth, must follow supply statistics from across the country, while the orange juice trader has a very limited area in which to be concerned about the crops. (See Fig. 130 opposite.)

The orange juice market is often very thin which makes trading often quite hazardous. When the news of a freeze or crop abundance is released, the price of the future may move in one direction

for several days without the opportunity for the trader to liquidate his position. At one time during a freeze, the future ran up the "limit" for 7 consecutive days with no opportunity for the trader who was short to cover his position.

For traders in orange juice futures there is the *Fruit Situation* report which compares with the *Wheat Situation,* the *Feed Grain Situation,* the *Hogs and Pigs Situation,* the *Livestock Situation,* and so on.

This is released four times a year in February, July, September, and November and sums up the feelings of the U.S. Department of Agriculture with respect to the orange juice crop for the upcoming year. Annually the *Summary of Fruit,* officially entitled the *Summary of the Citrus Fruit Industry,* is issued outlining the salient factors in the citrus fruit market for the previous year.

Also significant to the orange juice trader is the *Crop Production Report* issued six times a year, the *Monthly Cold Storage Reports* which indicates the frozen orange juice stocks on the first of each month, and numerous other smaller and private publications which outline the Florida citrus crop situation. Especially helpful here are some private crop reports which are sold by private firms who are in the business of estimating crop production for the industry and the trader who specializes in orange juice futures. Prices and other data may also be received from the Florida Department of Agriculture which naturally takes a deep interest in the state of its citrus crops due to the significance to the Florida economy of the citrus crops.

See also Figures 131, 132 and 133 on pages 198-200.

FIGURE 130

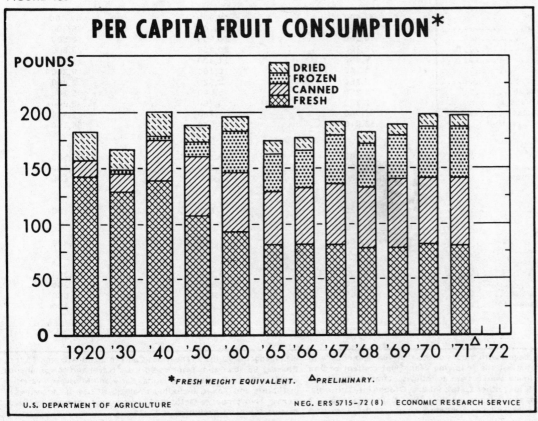

PER CAPITA FRUIT CONSUMPTION*

POUNDS

DRIED
FROZEN
CANNED
FRESH

200

150

100

50

0

1920 '30 '40 '50 '60 '65 '66 '67 '68 '69 '70 '71△ '72

*FRESH WEIGHT EQUIVALENT. △PRELIMINARY.

U.S. DEPARTMENT OF AGRICULTURE   NEG. ERS 5715-72(8)   ECONOMIC RESEARCH SERVICE

Source: U.S. Department of Agriculture, *Fruit Situation*, February 1972.

FIGURE 131

Table 22—Citrus fruits: Production, 1969/70, 1970/71, and indicated 1971/72[1]

Crop and State	1969/70	1970/71	1971/72
	1,000 boxes[2]	*1,000 boxes[2]*	*1,000 boxes[2]*
Oranges:			
Early, Midseason and Navel varieties:[3]			
California	21,200	17,900	22,000
Florida	72,900	82,100	69,500
Texas	2,800	4,000	3,800
Arizona	990	760	800
Total	97,890	104,760	96,100
Valencias:			
California	17,800	19,600	21,000
Florida	64,800	60,200	68,000
Texas	1,400	2,200	2,000
Arizona	3,640	2,800	3,700
Total	87,640	84,800	94,700
All Oranges:			
California	39,000	37,500	43,000
Florida	137,700	142,300	137,500
Texas	4,200	6,200	5,800
Arizona	4,630	3,560	4,500
Total oranges	185,530	189,560	190,800
Grapefruit:			
Florida, all	37,400	42,900	47,400
Seedless	27,900	31,100	36,300
Pink	10,200	10,900	12,500
White	17,700	20,200	23,800
Other	9,500	11,800	11,100
Texas	8,100	10,100	9,200
Arizona	3,160	2,520	2,400
California, all	5,250	5,040	5,100
Desert Valleys	2,950	3,260	3,200
Other areas	2,300	1,780	1,900
Total grapefruit	53,910	60,560	64,100
Lemons:			
California[4]	12,700	13,500	13,500
Arizona	2,820	3,150	3,300
Total lemons	15,520	16,650	16,800
Limes:			
Florida	725	880	1,100
Tangelos:			
Florida	2,500	2,700	3,800
Tangerines:			
Florida	3,000	3,700	3,300
Arizona	350	390	300
California	760	1,140	600
Total tangerines	4,110	5,230	4,200
Temples:			
Florida	5,200	5,000	5,400

[1] The crop year begins with bloom of the first year and ends with completion of harvest the following year. [2] Net content of box varies. Approximate averages are as follows: Oranges-California and Arizona, 75 lbs.; other States, 90 lbs.; Grapefruit-California, Dersert Valleys, and Arizona, 64 lbs.; other California areas, 67 lbs.; Florida, 85 lbs. and Texas, 80 lbs.; lemons-76 lbs.; Limes-80 lbs.; Tangelos-90 lbs.; Tangerines-California and Arizona, 75 lbs.; Florida, 95 lbs.; and Temples-90 lbs. [3] Navel and Miscellaneous varieties in California and Arizona. Early and Midseason varieties in Florida and Texas, including small quantities of tangerines in Texas. [4] November 1-October 31 crop year through 1970/71. August 1-July 31 beginning 1971/72.

Source: U.S. Department of Agriculture, *Fruit Situation*, February 1972.

FIGURE 132

Table 9.—Fruits, per capita consumption: Fresh-weight equivalent, 1950-71[1]

Year	Citrus						Apples						Other fruit						All fruit[4]
	Fresh[2]	Canned[2]	Canned juice[2]	Chilled[3]	Frozen	Total	Fresh[4]	Canned	Canned juice	Frozen	Dried	Total	Fresh	Canned	Canned juice	Frozen	Dried	Total	
	Pounds	Pounds	Pounds	Pounds	Pounds	Pounds	Pounds	Pounds	Pounds	Pounds	Pounds	Pounds	Pounds	Pounds	Pounds	Pounds	Pounds	Pounds	Pounds
1950	41.7	1.5	19.8	...	10.8	73.8	22.7	3.5	.9	.5	1.2	28.8	44.4	20.6	5.9	2.4	13.3	86.6	189.2
1951	45.8	1.7	20.8	...	15.2	83.5	25.7	3.4	.8	.4	1.2	31.5	46.5	17.9	6.5	2.2	12.7	85.8	200.8
1952	45.1	1.5	17.0	...	21.5	85.1	21.6	4.0	.8	.5	1.0	27.9	47.7	19.6	7.4	2.7	12.5	89.9	202.9
1953	44.1	1.8	16.0	...	24.4	86.3	20.9	3.5	.8	.4	.9	26.5	44.4	20.0	7.3	2.6	12.5	86.8	199.6
1954	42.0	1.9	15.8	...	27.1	86.8	20.0	3.6	1.1	.5	.9	26.1	43.1	20.0	6.6	2.6	12.4	84.8	197.7
1955	41.8	2.2	14.9	1.7	30.9	91.5	19.6	4.0	.8	.7	.9	26.0	38.0	20.7	7.5	3.2	12.0	81.8	199.3
1956	39.1	2.0	14.3	2.4	30.3	88.1	18.9	4.4	1.0	.9	.8	26.0	40.9	19.4	8.4	3.3	12.0	84.0	198.1
1957	37.1	1.5	14.1	3.6	33.0	89.3	19.3	4.4	1.0	.6	.7	26.0	40.3	20.0	8.9	3.2	11.9	84.3	199.6
1958	31.0	2.1	14.3	3.8	25.8	77.0	22.5	4.7	1.2	.7	.7	29.8	40.5	19.8	9.8	3.1	10.8	84.0	190.8
1959	34.0	1.6	10.9	3.8	32.6	82.9	21.1	4.5	1.5	.7	.8	28.6	40.6	19.5	8.5	2.9	10.3	81.8	193.3
1960	33.7	2.0	11.6	4.4	34.2	85.9	18.3	4.8	1.4	.7	.8	26.0	41.4	19.3	9.0	3.1	10.8	83.6	195.5
1961	30.8	1.8	10.7	3.7	32.1	79.1	16.4	5.0	1.5	.6	.8	24.3	41.4	19.4	8.0	3.2	10.4	82.4	185.8
1962	29.5	1.9	10.5	4.5	37.2	83.6	17.4	4.8	1.6	.5	.8	25.1	36.5	18.8	8.0	3.5	10.6	77.4	186.1
1963	22.1	1.3	10.7	3.5	25.1	62.7	16.7	5.1	1.9	.7	.9	25.3	35.7	19.0	9.6	3.5	10.2	78.0	166.0
1964	26.2	1.7	8.7	3.5	23.5	63.6	17.8	5.1	2.3	.7	.7	26.6	34.7	18.6	8.3	3.3	10.1	75.0	165.2
1965	29.1	1.8	8.1	4.4	29.6	73.0	16.3	5.4	2.4	.8	.7	25.6	35.7	18.8	7.6	3.3	10.4	75.8	174.4
1966	29.1	2.0	9.5	7.1	28.0	75.7	16.0	4.5	1.8	.7	.9	23.9	36.3	18.7	8.5	3.2	10.6	77.3	176.9
1967	31.6	2.2	11.1	9.3	40.0	94.2	16.2	5.1	2.1	.9	1.0	25.3	33.1	18.0	7.0	3.3	10.4	71.8	191.3
1968	26.3	2.1	10.5	8.9	34.3	82.1	15.7	4.9	2.6	.8	.9	24.9	36.3	17.9	8.0	3.4	9.9	75.5	182.5
1969	28.3	1.7	14.6	8.7	34.5	87.8	15.1	5.0	3.7	.9	1.1	25.8	35.6	20.1	7.7	3.3	9.6	76.3	189.9
1970	28.6	1.8	13.4	9.8	41.4	95.0	18.5	5.2	4.1	.8	1.2	29.8	34.3	18.9	7.1	2.9	9.4	72.6	197.4
1971[5]	29.3	2.0	15.1	9.8	41.2	97.4	16.2	5.0	4.9	.9	.8	27.8	34.6	17.8	6.9	3.2	9.2	71.7	196.9

[1] Excludes quantities consumed as baby food. Unless otherwise noted, data represent a calendar year (adjustments to a calendar year, when necessary, were made by combining proportional parts of each pack year involved). Civilian consumption only. Beginning 1960, includes Alaska and Hawaii. [2] Crop and pack year beginning October or November prior to year indicated. [3] Includes juice beginning 1955 and fruit beginning 1956. [4] Includes apples grown in commercial areas. [5] Preliminary.

Note: See September 1970 (TFS-176) *Fruit Situation* for data prior to 1950.

Source: U.S. Department of Agriculture, *Fruit Situation*, February 1972.

FIGURE 133

World Production of Oranges (Including Tangarines)   In Millions of Boxes

Season	Al-geria	Argen-tina	Bra-zil	Aus-tralia	Greece	Israel	Italy	Japan	Mex-ico	Mor-occo	Spain	Tur-key	South Africa	United States	World Total
1959	11.8	19.3	24.0	1960-	6.1	15.5	26.2	30.8	20.8	12.5	49.3	5.6	11.4	129.6	391.8
1960	6.7	22.6	25.0	64	6.7	12.6	27.2	35.2	21.5	14.1	48.2	7.5	8.5	121.5	389.6
1961	8.0	21.5	25.0	Avg.	7.2	12.1	29.2	35.0	14.0	14.2	52.1	7.6	12.7	142.1	413.5
1962	13.2	21.8	26.0	(6.3)	7.2	17.3	26.1	34.1	24.8	13.9	48.0	7.8	11.3	106.9	394.5
1963	11.0	22.5	24.0		7.0	19.4	33.6	38.8	25.2	19.2	58.3	10.7	16.0	96.3	420.3
1964	12.4	22.5	25.7		10.1	21.3	37.3	48.4	27.1	16.1	54.9	9.0	16.3	125.2	465.7
1965	12.0	16.4	40.4	6.6	10.0	20.8	37.0	52.0	27.2	18.8	58.9	10.5	16.7	177.9	523.0
1966–7	12.0	23.8	49.2	7.3	12.8	25.1	43.1	65.6	27.7	21.3	73.9	11.6	15.8	241.5	650.1
1967–8	13.0	25.7	49.8	8.7	6.6	29.9	45.3	61.7	27.8	24.4	65.4	14.0	16.4	165.7	573.7
1968–9	14.8	32.7	51.1	7.7	11.2	26.6	52.8	89.2	28.3	22.7	54.5	16.8	14.7	237.0	681.1
1969–0[1]	13.9	34.4	63.1	10.1	14.6	28.6	53.4	76.3	29.5	25.8	67.2	14.9	15.9	241.2	708.7
1970–1[2]	14.0	38.3	65.1	8.0	12.5	32.6	51.6	95.8	32.1	23.7	63.6	15.7	16.7	249.7	740.6
1971–2															

[1] Preliminary.   [2] Estimate.   *Source: Foreign Agricultural Service, U.S.D.A.*

Salient Statistics of Oranges in the United States

Season	Ari-zona	Cali-fornia	Production[2] Florida	Texas	Total	Farm Price $ Per Box	Farm Value Million $	Foreign Trade[3] Domestic Exports	Imports	Quan-tities Pro-cessed	Frozen Concen-trates	Florida Crop Processed Chilled Pdt's Sections Juice & Salads	Other Pro-cessed	Total Pro-cessed
1959–0	1.5	30.8	91.5	2.7	126.8	2.40	210.4	5.8	.2	68.7	Not Available			
1960–1	1.2	25.0	86.7	3.5	116.6	3.41	282.4	5.1	.4	67.6	Not Available			
1961–2	1.4	20.7	113.4	2.3	137.9	2.33	253.8	5.0	.2	89.4	Not Available			
1962–3	1.6	28.8	74.5	.1	104.7	2.16	229.2	4.4	.8	61.1	47.2	5.6 .5	9.2	62.5
1963–4	2.2	32.0	58.3	.2	92.5	5.01	274.9	5.1	1.7	43.0	34.2	4.9 .6	5.7	45.5
1964–5	2.4	31.6	86.2	.9	120.7	2.99	246.8	5.7	1.1	67.8	54.5	7.3 .5	7.3	69.6
1965–6	2.6	36.9	100.4	1.3	140.6	2.26	216.6	6.9	.7	80.5	61.8	12.3 .8	8.0	82.9
1966–7	3.9	36.8	139.5	2.7	182.9	1.85	337.5	8.2	1.1	134.1	96.8	16.5 .8	10.2	124.3
1967–8	3.1	19.2	100.5	1.8	124.6	3.08	384.1	7.3	2.0	92.1	62.0	16.0 .8	6.8	85.5
1968–9	5.4	44.3	129.7	4.5	183.9	2.60	479.4	7.0	1.8	137.7	92.1	17.8 .8	9.4	120.1
1969–0	4.6	39.0	137.7	4.2	185.5	2.43	450.8	6.6	2.0	140.9	100.7	18.6 .8	8.2	128.4
1970–1[1]	3.6	38.6	142.3	6.2	190.7	2.09	387.6			146.5	103.5	19.8 .7	8.8	132.8
1971–2[1]	4.7	43.0	136.0	6.0	189.7	2.33	442.0							
1972–3														

[1] Preliminary.   [2] Fruit ripened on trees, but destroyed prior to picking is not included.   [3] Year beginning Nov. 1.
Source: Economic Research Service, U.S.D.A.

Note: Original data is from Commodity Research Bureau, Inc.

FROZEN PORK BELLIES

Frozen pork bellies are the glamour item of the commodity markets. When anyone mentions commodities, he normally goes on to talk about pork bellies. A pork belly is uncured bacon which comes from the underside of a hog, each hog having two. Pork bellies have only been traded since 1961 and acceptance of this new contract has been phenomenal, providing the exception to the rule that speculative interest follows hedging volume. (See Fig. 134 below.)

Trading months are February, March, May, July, and August. The size of the contract is 36,000 pounds which is equal to a car lot commonly used by the trade.

Each 1 cent movement in price returns $360 for each contract held by a speculator. The deliverable grade is 12-14 pound bellies with the minimum fluctuation for the futures contract price being 2½ points, or hundredths of a cent. The maximum daily trading range is 3 cents per pound with the maximum daily fluctuation set at 150 points or 1.5 cents above or below the close of the previous session.

The supply of pork bellies is directly determined by the slaughter of pigs. Statistics on hog farrowing and slaughter are closely followed by the pork belly trader. As in the case of corn, the pork belly trader closely follows the hog feed ratio to determine whether feed is cheap

FIGURE 134

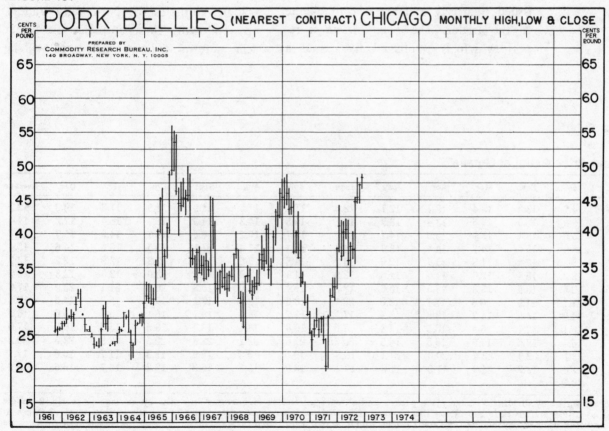

Source: Commodity Research Bureau, Inc.

relative to the price of hogs and, therefore, the farmer will continue to feed his hogs as long as possible. A low hog-corn ratio indicates that the price of corn as compared to the price of hogs is relatively high and, therefore, the farmer will be encouraged to slaughter his hogs early rather than to continue feeding them at high feed prices. (See Fig. 135 below.)

Cold storage reports are also closely watched by the pork belly trader as an indication of the current supply and the buildup in supply at the cold storage warehouses approved for storage by the Department of Agriculture. (See Fig. 136 on p. 203.)

The major sources of information for the pork belly trader are the *Livestock and Meat Situation* reports which are issued quarterly and are free of charge to the trader. The *Feed Situation* report which is published five times a year is also important. *Hogs and Pigs* reports are issued quarterly in December, March, June, and September. This report shows the sows farrowing, pigs per litter, and the total pig crop by six-month periods. The hogs available and slaughtered are useful for the trader in estimating the number of hogs which will come to the market during the upcoming months. The monthly cold storage report cited above is probably the monthly report most significant to the commodity trader in pork bellies as these storage figures are followed extremely closely, often having a violent effect on the market with a limit advance or decline occurring the day after the release of this report.

The Chicago Mercantile Exchange publishes a *Yearbook* which gives the salient statistics for pork belly traders. By following these statistics the trader can determine how much pork will be

FIGURE 135

Hog-Corn Price Ratio[1] at Omaha[2]

Year	Jan.	Feb.	Mar.	Apr.	May	June	July	Aug.	Sept.	Oct.	Nov.	Dec.	Average
1959	14.2	13.2	13.4	12.7	12.7	12.6	11.4	11.5	11.9	11.9	11.6	10.8	12.3
1960	10.9	12.0	13.5	13.4	13.3	14.1	14.8	14.3	14.3	16.7	18.4	17.2	14.4
1961	15.8	16.1	15.9	15.9	14.7	15.0	15.7	16.2	16.6	15.7	14.9	15.7	15.7
1962	16.0	15.5	14.7	14.4	13.6	14.9	16.4	17.0	17.1	15.5	15.6	14.6	15.4
1963	13.3	12.8	11.9	11.7	12.6	13.7	14.5	13.5	11.9	13.3	12.9	12.2	12.7
1964	12.2	12.4	12.0	11.6	11.8	12.9	14.3	13.9	13.5	13.0	12.5	12.8	12.7
1965	12.5	13.5	13.3	13.5	15.6	18.5	19.4	21.0	19.3	20.0	21.1	23.0	17.6
1966	21.7	21.9	20.6	17.7	18.6	20.1	18.6	18.6	17.1	15.9	15.0	14.5	18.4
1967	14.8	14.9	14.2	13.8	16.8	17.1	17.7	18.0	16.7	16.1	16.0	15.6	16.0
1968	16.1	17.1	16.4	16.5	15.8	17.6	19.0	18.4	18.4	16.5	15.3	16.6	17.0
1969	16.4	17.5	17.8	16.5	18.5	20.2	21.6	22.1	22.8	22.5	22.8	23.6	20.2
1970	23.1	22.9	22.4	20.0	19.3	18.3	19.6	15.8	14.9	13.3	11.7	10.6	17.7
1971	11.0	13.2	11.9	11.3	11.8	12.2	13.9	15.1	16.3	17.2	16.7	16.6	13.9
1972	19.7												

[1] Ratio computed by dividing average price packer and shipper purchases of barrows and gilts by average price No. 2 yellow corn both at Chicago. This ratio represents the number of bushels of corn required to buy 100 pounds of live hogs. [2] Prices at Omaha are being used to replace the CHICAGO prices which were discontinued in May, 1970. *Source: Department of Agriculture*

Note: Data originally from *Commodity Research Bureau Yearbook, 1972.*

available and base his positions on his estimates. (See Fig. 137, p. 204, and Fig. 138, p. 205.)

The primary source for demand for pork bellies is the weekly sliced bacon production figures issued by the USDA. About 65 percent of the pork bellies sliced into bacon are inspected and reported by the Department of Agriculture. By following these statistics the trader can estimate what the general demand will be, since it is assumed that all the bellies sliced into bacon are consumed. As demand begins to grow the trader can closely follow the increases on the weekly statistics.

Pork bellies, as do the other agricultural commodities, show a seasonal price pattern whereby prices advance and decline throughout the year in a cyclical pattern. Normally, pork belly prices are low in the fall and winter and then advance into the spring with the normal contract highs reached in July and August. However, the pork belly future

seems to follow this more in the breach than in the concurrence and the trader who hopes to buy on seasonal lows in the month of December will as often be wrong as he will be right.

A great many traders use the pork belly market for "day trading" going in on the opening in the morning and closing out the position at the end of the day. In general, day trading is not a successful technique and in pork bellies it can often prove disastrous. All too often the trader will take a position for a $50 profit in the morning, be locked into a $100 loss by nightfall and hold on until he had earned or received a $200 or $300 loss. It is simply not worth it to take such a substantial beating for a mere $50 profit, and day trading in pork bellies should be undertaken very carefully.

Another trading technique often found in pork bellies is the taking of spreads whereby a trader buys one option and sells another hoping that the spread

FIGURE 136

Federally Inspected Hog Slaughter in the United States In Thousands of Head

Year	Jan.	Feb.	Mar.	Apr.	May	June	July	Aug.	Sept.	Oct.	Nov.	Dec.	Total
1959	5,885	5,686	5,733	5,652	4,970	4,902	5,184	4,977	5,767	6,646	6,337	6,968	68,708
1960	6,516	5,841	6,116	5,571	5,483	5,086	4,304	5,203	5,165	5,407	5,707	5,753	66,153
1961	5,744	5,078	6,110	5,048	5,597	5,093	4,320	5,114	5,240	6,223	6,327	5,738	65,632
1962	6,098	5,312	6,225	5,672	5,800	5,041	4,699	5,214	4,737	6,643	6,376	5,954	67,770
1963	6,333	5,665	6,559	6,343	5,910	4,880	4,995	5,174	5,868	6,775	6,380	6,695	71.577
1964	6,956	5,898	6,420	6,481	5,476	5,038	4,928	4,841	5,630	6,804	6,546	6,648	71,667
1965	6,047	5,301	6,534	5,802	4,719	4,717	4,429	4,750	5,475	5,421	5,503	5,010	63,708
1966	4,719	4,650	5,806	5,303	4,913	4,673	4,228	5,088	5,888	6,047	6,200	6,215	63,729
1967	6,292	5,661	6,728	5,867	5,310	5,178	4,743	5,808	6,114	6,684	6,431	6,100	70,915
1968	6,496	5,697	6,238	6,483	6,407	5,125	5,454	5,942	6,348	7,410	6,571	6,619	74,789
1969	6,814	6,245	6,809	6,852	6,045	5,591	5,739	5,708	6,611	7,100	5,825	6,344	75,682
1970	6,170	5,507	6,415	6,678	5,877	5,685	5,774	6,045	7,034	7,662	7,350	7,990	78,187
1971	7,489	6,379	8,266	7,794	6,932	6,983	6,220	6,922	7,379	7,190	7,569	7,547	86,670
1972	6,395												

Source: Statistical Reporting Service, U.S.D.A.

Note: Original data is from Commodity Research Bureau, Inc.

FIGURE 137

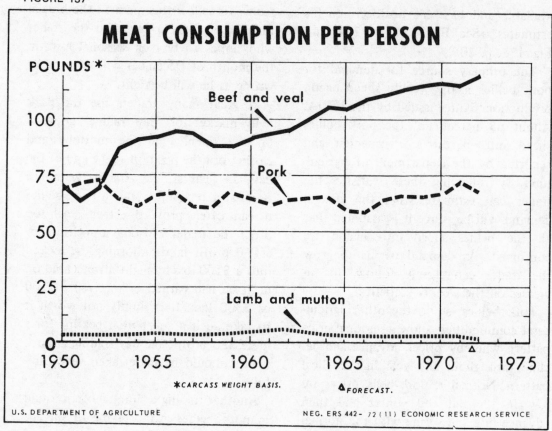

MEAT CONSUMPTION PER PERSON

POUNDS*

Beef and veal

Pork

Lamb and mutton

100

75

50

25

1950   1955   1960   1965   1970   1975

*CARCASS WEIGHT BASIS.   △ FORECAST.

U.S. DEPARTMENT OF AGRICULTURE

NEG. ERS 442– 72 (11) ECONOMIC RESEARCH SERVICE

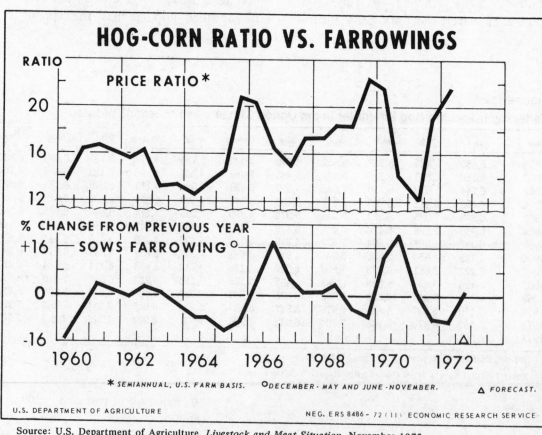

HOG-CORN RATIO VS. FARROWINGS

RATIO

PRICE RATIO*

20

16

12

% CHANGE FROM PREVIOUS YEAR

SOWS FARROWING °

+16

0

-16

1960   1962   1964   1966   1968   1970   1972

* SEMIANNUAL, U.S. FARM BASIS.   ° DECEMBER - MAY AND JUNE - NOVEMBER.   △ FORECAST.

U.S. DEPARTMENT OF AGRICULTURE

NEG. ERS 8486– 72 (11) ECONOMIC RESEARCH SERVICE

Source: U.S. Department of Agriculture, *Livestock and Meat Situation*, November 1972.

between the two options will widen with time and return a profit. Trading spreads is probably one of the more popular techniques for trading the belly market but as pork belly futures, more than any other commodity, tend to move independently of each other, basis spreads can be dangerous. One cannot be sure that intermonth basis will remain true in the pork belly market as it does in corn, wheat, oats, and other grains and oilseeds.

Additional statistical data pertaining to the preceding chapter on "Frozen Pork Bellies" is shown in Figures 139, 140, 141 and 142 on pages 206-8.

FIGURE 138

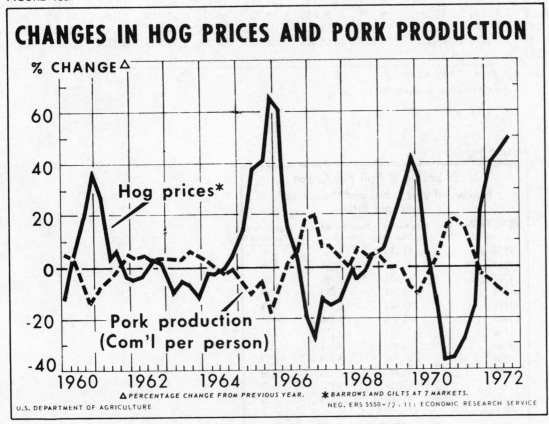

Source: U.S. Department of Agriculture, *Livestock and Meat Situation*, November 1972.

FIGURE 139

U.S. Frozen Pork Belly Storage Stocks (In Thousand Pounds, as of First of the Month)

Year	Jan.	Feb.	Mar.	Apr.	May	June	July	Aug.	Sept.	Oct.	Nov.	Dec.
1959	45,873	54,762	86,255	113,741	127,397	121,215	97,340	65,720	38,768	22,455	25,540	42,393
1960	73,023	92,488	108,393	115,771	131,992	130,720	113,278	75,580	44,691	18,813	15,828	20,732
1961	33,510	43,038	58,880	74,812	78,095	79,984	64,811	33,787	11,710	5,553	7,153	22,825
1962	39,352	44,445	60,956	84,599	99,428	109,525	91,355	61,623	34,493	12,482	15,863	35,107
1963	57,822	64,240	73,277	103,411	119,888	112,447	94,813	65,919	36,842	22,142	23,146	38,455
1964	60,800	84,180	113,713	139,494	156,572	154,758	133,160	86,272	46,487	22,238	33,649	54,195
1965	74,589	84,859	97,900	113,770	120,908	103,142	73,520	40,867	21,607	8,768	8,958	16,164
1966	25,318	29,472	36,053	48,768	62,688	65,838	47,659	27,019	12,495	7,034	9,310	19,847
1967	44,921	50,191	67,803	91,284	108,506	100,453	88,993	60,577	33,275	20,796	32,098	48,756
1968	68,882	66,810	77,182	92,099	115,682	129,377	102,949	59,462	27,393	15,809	20,437	33,774
1969	49,076	46,699	56,173	76,035	96,249	96,670	84,284	46,755	21,719	12,167	19,565	26,074
1970	38,697	37,017	47,094	61,068	74,004	82,061	67,250	39,300	20,393	9,823	21,043	42,054
1971	76,437	82,823	84,534	113,457	133,428	148,379	138,938	106,996	71,525	51,474	53,857	68,926
1972[1]	86,325	84,372										

[1] Preliminary. *Source: U.S. Dept. of Agriculture*

Note: Original data is from the Commodity Research Bureau, Inc.

FIGURE 140

U. S. Spring & Fall Pig Crops — Number of pigs saved and the number saved per litter			
SPRING CROP—	Pigs Saved (In Thou.)	Sows Farrowing (In Thou.)	Pigs Saved Per Litter
1960	47,288	6,782	6.96
1961	50,366	7,018	7.18
1962	49,535	6,996	7.08
1963	50,749	7,099	7.15
1964	47,682	6,596	7.23
1965	42,525	5,890	7.22
1966	45,422	6,201	7.32
1967	48,205	6,570	7.34
1968	49,146	6,669	7.37
1969	46,788	6,360	7.36
1970	52,551	7,171	7.33
*1971	51,905	7,231	7.18
FALL CROP—			
1960	40,998	5,839	7.02
1961	42,347	5,918	7.16
1962	44,073	6,098	7.23
1963	43,307	5,987	7.23
1964	39,862	5,525	7.21
1965	36,415	5,006	7.27
1966	42,141	5,811	7.25
1967	43,540	5,899	7.38
1968	45,071	6,129	7.35
1969	42,019	5,727	7.34
*1970	49,768	6,905	7.21
**1971	45,735	6,265	7.30
*Preliminary	**Indications		

Source: Commodity Research Bureau, Inc.

FIGURE 141

PORK BELLIES

Weekly Federally Inspected Hog Slaughter / Weekly Sliced Bacon Production Prepared under Federal Inspection

Week Ending	(In Thousand Head)					(In Thousand Pounds)				
	1972	1971	1970	1969	1968	1972	1971	1970	1969	1968
Jan. 1	1,381	1,382	1,183	1,239	1,208	25,300	24,186	17,930	22,647	23,352
8	1,492	1,841	1,334	1,532	1,541	28,100	32,380	27,846	28,873	28,572
15	1,672	1,947	1,616	1,631	1,440	30,100	33,632	29,462	28,688	27,191
22	1,524	1,933	1,513	1,503	1,483	30,900	33,831	27,488	27,915	25,902
29	1,363	1,709	1,391	1,514	1,334	26,600	32,524	25,310	25,592	23,850
Feb. 5	1,435	1,528	1,393	1,538	1,443	24,900	29,680	24,847	25,063	22,673
12	1,396	1,647	1,365	1,552	1,389	21,100	28,779	23,125	25,479	22,177
19	1,542	1,540	1,374	1,571	1,250	27,100	26,374	22,427	25,076	21,925
26	1,516	1,664	1,375	1,588	1,393	24,800	26,120	22,745	25,170	23,124
Mar. 4	1,638	1,723	1,482	1,624	1,448	.....	27,718	24,406	25,910	23,992
11	1,778	1,823	1,497	1,654	1,485	.....	28,800	24,217	24,888	24,549
18	1,654	1,762	1,459	1,559	1,499	.....	28,700	25,604	23,432	24,547
25	1,759	1,891	1,441	1,630	1,521	.....	27,600	23,756	25,170	22,934
Apr. 1	....	1,802	1,447	1,503	1,524	.....	29,300	24,316	22,698	23,814
8	....	1,729	1,562	1,552	1,382	.....	27,900	25,923	24,236	21,746
15	....	1,759	1,555	1,577	1,511	.....	28,100	24,438	24,795	23,386
22	....	1,850	1,401	1,582	1,510	.....	29,400	26,568	25,872	23,402
29	....	1,760	1,574	1,582	1,460	.....	28,900	25,225	25,213	22,860
May 6	....	1,765	1,460	1,524	1,471	.....	30,600	25,729	26,185	24,904
13	....	1,757	1,431	1,399	1,460	.....	30,800	25,941	27,603	25,378
20	....	1,687	1,393	1,409	1,413	.....	28,800	24,700	25,459	24,887
27	....	1,662	1,263	1,099	1,197	.....	29,900	25,546	23,335	23,631
June 3	....	1,457	1,326	1,358	1,405	.....	26,900	27,513	25,235	27,184
10	....	1,630	1,353	1,351	1,277	.....	33,100	27,813	26,194	28,668
17	....	1,623	1,262	1,287	1,217	.....	30,100	28,183	25,094	28,233
24	....	1,445	1,254	1,337	1,213	.....	30,000	29,949	27,535	28,195
July 1	....	1,442	1,151	1,025	957	.....	32,400	25,479	24,534	24,215
8	....	1,229	1,236	1,326	1,279	.....	27,800	28,574	28,110	28,705
15	....	1,500	1,277	1,330	1,211	.....	32,200	26,794	26,804	28,702
22	....	1,410	1,270	1,284	1,226	.....	32,300	24,255	29,229	26,680
29	....	1,490	1,343	1,296	1,292	.....	32,300	28,570	30,274	28,172
Aug. 5	....	1,464	1,272	1,365	1,286	.....	31,800	28,903	27,385	29,115
12	....	1,601	1,447	1,329	1,362	.....	33,800	29,717	27,303	29,633
19	....	1,555	1,479	1,365	1,357	.....	33,000	28,218	26,967	28,569
26	....	1,635	1,540	1,384	1,425	.....	33,300	31,135	26,273	30,256
Sept. 2	....	1,671	1,549	1,279	1,320	.....	32,300	31,228	24,219	26,077
9	....	1,476	1,406	1,549	1,540	.....	29,000	26,538	26,314	29,213
16	....	1,767	1,731	1,586	1,626	.....	34,600	31,617	27,956	28,002
23	....	1,752	1,664	1,590	1,545	.....	33,900	34,288	27,768	26,687
30	....	1,737	1,683	1,545	1,628	.....	31,000	31,617	24,985	27,087
Oct. 7	....	1,624	1,642	1,507	1,590	.....	29,500	29,358	25,558	26,725
14	....	1,713	1,739	1,555	1,641	.....	29,000	29,770	24,983	26,338
21	....	1,736	1,763	1,570	1,604	.....	29,600	30,572	25,824	25,769
28	....	1,637	1,815	1,548	1,628	.....	27,400	30,502	26,799	26,411
Nov. 4	....	1,823	1,854	1,536	1,667	.....	28,900	31,643	26,434	27,235
11	....	1,805	1,784	1,529	1,555	.....	28,400	29,379	25,206	26,775
18	....	1,801	1,828	1,453	1,618	.....	30,200	30,071	25,439	27,687
25	....	1,336	1,526	1,297	1,357	.....	30,000	24,644	21,406	23,041
Dec. 2	....	1,862	1,923	1,529	1,700	.....	30,800	26,933	25,009	26,465
9	....	1,837	1,866	1,479	1,665	.....	30,400	30,631	26,545	25,838
16	....	1,726	1,905	1,448	1,522	.....	30,800	29,735	25,041	25,620
23	....	1,437	1,315	1,035	1,144	.....	22,700	21,987	17,766	19,281

Source: U.S. Department of Agriculture

Note: Original data from Chicago Mercantile Exchange.

FIGURE 142

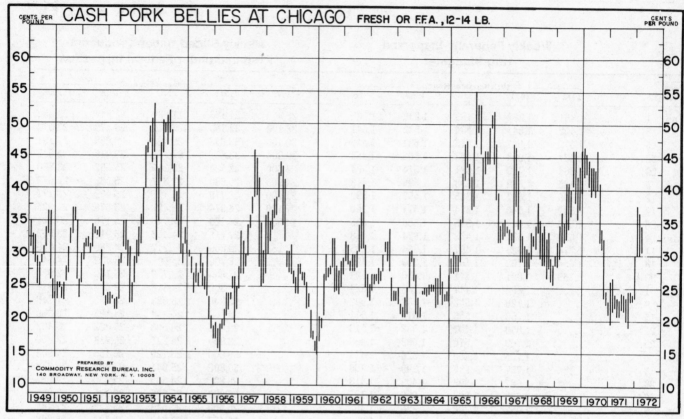

Source: Commodity Research Bureau, Inc.

LIVE CATTLE

The cattle market has followed pork bellies as one of the more active commodity futures traded on the Chicago Mercantile Exchange. Initiated in 1964, this commodity future has steadily grown in volume until it is now one of the 10 most active commodities traded in the United States.

The demand for red meats has always been high in the United States, second only to Argentina in worldwide per capita consumption. Despite rising prices during the inflation period of the early 1970s, the demand for beef has remained steady. Since there is a limited supply of cattle, the rationing device to restrict usage has been high prices.

There are a large number of producers of cattle throughout the United States and few large buyers. Until the early 1960s, it had been a buyer's market with the sellers at the mercy of the few buyers who were in the market. The futures market left an alternative for the producer but usually prices on the futures market were so low as not to offer an attractive hedging situation.

As a result of a favorable ruling by the tax courts, many investors now raise cattle as strictly a tax write-off procedure. Feed for cattle is deductible from ordinary income in the year it is purchased. The profits from sales of cattle are capital gains. Thus, an investor would be wise to purchase feed for his cattle during the years when he has a large income to reduce the same and sell the cattle for a capital gain in later years. Like oil investing, this offers a method for converting ordinary income into capital gains and reducing the maximum taxes from 75 percent to 35 percent, which for individuals with high income can be a substantial saving. (See Fig. 143 below.)

Live cattle are traded in contracts of 40,000 pounds. Prices are quoted in dollars per hundredweight (dollars per cwt.) and the minimum fluctuation is 2½ points, equal to $10. Contracts are traded for February, April, June, August, October, and December deliveries. Daily fluctuation is limited to 100 points above or below the previous close. The largest position that can be legally held is 300 contracts long or short in any delivery month or combination of delivery months. Trading hours are from 9:05 A.M. to 12:40 P.M., Chicago time. (See Fig. 144, p. 210.)

FIGURE 143

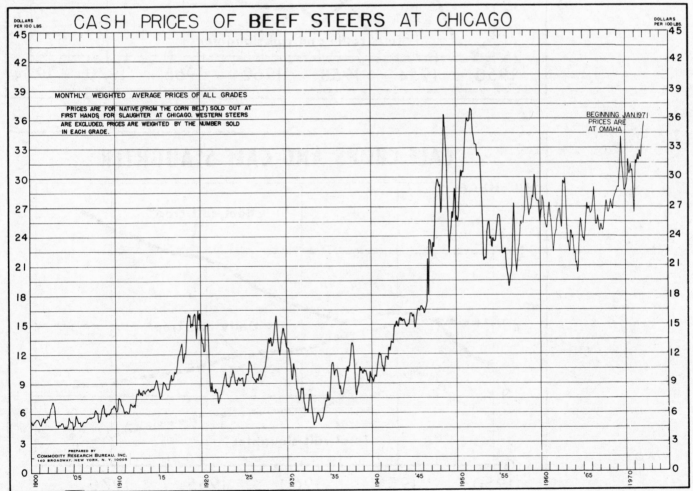

Source: Commodity Research Bureau, Inc.

FIGURE 144

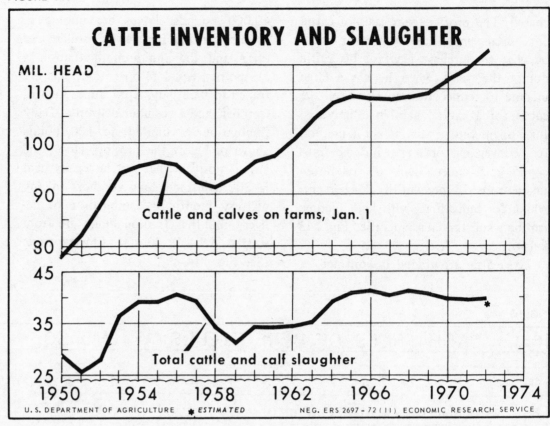

CATTLE INVENTORY AND SLAUGHTER

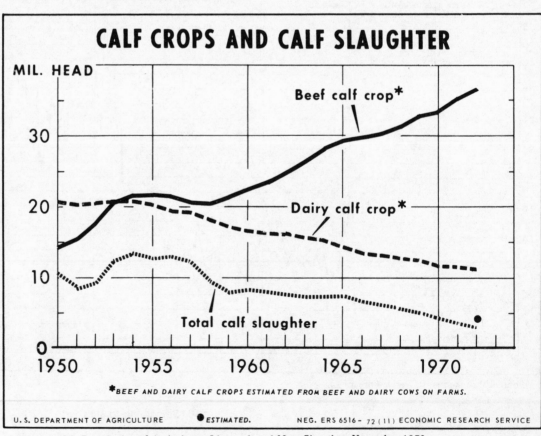

CALF CROPS AND CALF SLAUGHTER

Source: U.S. Department of Agriculture, *Livestock and Meat Situation*, November 1972.

The trader who wishes to follow cattle statistics will subscribe to the *Cattle and Calves Report*, the *Livestock and Poultry Inventory Report*, *Meat Animals Annual Summary*, *Shipments of Stocker and Feeder Cattle*, *Cattle on Pastures*, *Livestock Slaughter*, *Western Range Reports*, and the various livestock reports mentioned for the trader on pork bellies.

By following these reports he can learn the size of the cattle available in the United States, the cattle currently on feed and the cattle projected to be on feed in the future, the conditions of pastures throughout the United States, the average weight of the animals being slaughtered, the stocks of beef at cold storage plants, the supplies of competitive meats such as pork, lamb, and poultry, and the current cash prices for cattle at the major markets.

Cattle prices do not have an annual rise and dip as do the agricultural products and the pork market. Rather, cattle prices run in cycles often lasting several years. Prices will be relatively high for two or three years and then decline for two or three years. This is why marginal producers hold onto their farms and ranches during the lean years because they know that eventually prices will rise again and they can pay off their notes.

During periods of prosperity everyone decides to get into the cattle market and cattle are raised in abundance. This increase in supplies depresses the market and cattle prices go into a slump for several years. During the slump many individuals leave the market and begin to raise hogs or chickens and thereby reduce the supply of cattle for the market. This forces prices up again in response to a relatively steady demand and the cycle has repeated itself.

A great deal of money has been spent by large companies and economists in an attempt to forecast periods of high and low prices accurately but so far no foolproof system seems to have been developed. For the trader he need only know that after two or three years he should look for a reversal in the trend of prices and trade his futures positions accordingly.

Additional statistical data pertaining to the preceding section on "Live Cattle" is shown in Figures 145, 146 and 147 on pages 212-14.

FIGURE 145

Table 2.—Average retail price of meat per pound, United States, by months, 1966 to date

Year	Jan.	Feb.	Mar.	Apr.	May	June	July	Aug.	Sept.	Oct.	Nov.	Dec.	Av.
	Cents	Cents	Cents	Cents	Cents	Cents	Cents	Cents	Cents	Cents	Cents	Cents	Cents
Beef, Choice grade													
1966 ...	81.0	83.1	84.1	84.6	83.8	81.7	81.5	81.7	82.2	81.3	80.3	83.6	82.4
1967 ...	80.4	80.9	80.8	80.4	79.6	81.9	83.3	84.0	85.5	85.3	84.4	85.3	82.6
1968 ...	84.3	85.1	85.6	85.6	85.8	85.8	87.1	87.0	88.4	87.7	88.1	88.5	86.6
1969 ...	89.5	89.6	90.9	93.3	97.8	101.9	102.4	101.1	99.1	95.2	96.5	96.9	96.2
1970 ...	97.5	97.3	99.4	99.9	99.4	98.5	100.7	100.4	98.7	97.9	97.6	96.5	98.6
1971 ...	97.2	101.3	102.2	104.0	104.8	105.7	104.7	105.7	105.9	105.1	106.3	108.5	104.3
1972 ...	111.5	115.8	115.8	112.0	111.4	113.5	117.3	115.8	112.9				
Veal, retail cuts													
1966 ...	85.1	89.2	89.4	90.3	88.5	90.7	91.1	90.6	91.3	91.3	90.5	91.4	90.0
1967 ...	92.0	90.1	91.4	92.8	93.3	93.7	93.9	96.1	96.3	96.7	97.4	97.2	94.2
1968 ...	99.8	99.2	100.0	102.0	100.0	102.5	101.7	101.4	101.9	101.1	101.9	100.9	101.0
1969 ...	102.5	103.7	104.6	107.5	108.6	112.5	114.0	115.0	115.2	114.6	116.3	110.8
1970 ...	117.2	119.3	120.8	123.3	123.9	124.9	125.7	126.6	127.0	127.4	127.6	127.9	124.3
1971 ...	128.9	129.5	130.8	133.2	134.2	135.4	139.3	140.2	140.6	141.4	141.9	142.4	136.5
1972 ...	144.3	148.6	149.7	151.0	151.8	154.3	156.5	157.4	157.7				
Pork													
1966 ...	80.0	80.2	77.5	72.6	71.1	73.5	74.1	75.8	74.4	71.8	69.4	68.1	74.0
1967 ...	67.5	66.2	64.5	63.2	66.0	70.0	71.0	70.2	69.3	66.6	66.6	64.9	67.2
1968 ...	65.4	66.7	67.1	66.3	66.7	67.8	69.4	69.0	68.8	67.8	67.1	67.0	67.4
1969 ...	67.9	68.6	69.0	69.1	71.6	75.0	76.9	78.3	78.9	78.7	78.1	79.7	74.3
1970 ...	82.1	81.8	81.4	79.9	80.0	80.0	80.6	79.7	76.7	74.6	70.8	68.4	78.0
1971 ...	68.4	69.4	69.9	68.7	68.2	69.6	71.4	71.6	71.0	71.3	71.4	72.9	70.3
1972 ...	76.3	81.3	79.4	78.2	79.4	82.0	85.6	86.0	86.6				

Table 4.—U.S. meat imports and exports and percentage comparisons (carcass weight), 1971 and 1972

Months	Beef and veal			Lamb and mutton[1]			Pork			Total meat		
	1971	1972	Change	1971	1972	Change	1971	1972	Change	1971	1972	Change
	Mil. lb.	Mil. lb.	Pct.	Mil. lb.	Mil. lb.	Pct.	Mil. lb.	Mil. lb.	Pct.	Mil. lb.	Mil. lb.	Pct.
IMPORTS												
January	128	143	+12	9	3	-68	35	63	+81	172	209	+21
February	100	130	+30	6	5	-18	38	45	+18	144	179	+25
March	137	120	-12	10	6	-40	47	50	+7	194	176	-9
April	134	144	+8	9	27	+220	38	44	+13	181	215	+19
May	119	152	+28	12	27	+125	40	36	-10	171	215	+26
June	165	157	-5	13	14	+4	41	31	-24	219	202	-8
July	150	162	+8	9	16	+79	42	41	-3	201	219	+9
August	175	230	+31	3	23	+696	38	37	-2	216	290	+34
September	237	230	-3	20	15	-23	41	31	-24	298	276	-7
October	121			6			18			145		
November	97			3			32			132		
December	193			3			49			245		
Total	1,756			103			459			2,318		
EXPORTS												
January	3.45	4.03	+17	0.17	0.22	+30	4.55	3.28	-28	8.17	7.53	-8
February	4.22	3.89	-8	.17	.11	-34	3.68	3.53	-4	8.07	7.53	-7
March	5.61	4.93	-12	.24	.16	-36	3.36	4.29	+28	9.22	9.38	+2
April	5.27	5.45	+3	.17	.10	-47	3.78	10.43	+176	9.22	15.98	+73
May	4.43	5.70	+29	.18	.23	+22	4.88	19.40	+298	9.49	25.33	+167
June	4.63	5.04	+9	.13	.12	-13	4.65	13.73	+196	9.41	18.89	+101
July	3.63	4.78	+32	.11	.19	+81	3.46	6.48	+87	7.20	11.45	+59
August	3.54	4.48	+27	.21	.21	+3	7.12	5.39	-24	10.86	10.08	-7
September	4.10	13.99	+241	.18	.52	+183	7.52	20.18	+168	11.80	34.69	+194
October	3.25			.13			6.62			10.00		
November	5.82			.21			12.41			18.44		
December	4.92			.20			10.35			15.47		
Total	52.87			2.10			72.38			127.35		

[1] Includes goat meat.

Source: U.S. Department of Agriculture, *Livestock and Meat Situation*, February 1973.

FIGURE 146
Selected price statistics for meat animals and meat

Item	1971 September	1971 October	1972 August	1972 September	1972 October
	Dollars per 100 pounds				
CATTLE AND CALVES					
Beef steers, slaughter, Omaha					
Prime	33.72	33.18	36.32	35.51	35.52
Choice	32.62	32.34	35.66	34.85	34.85
Good	30.94	31.11	34.22	33.48	33.79
Standard	27.36	27.96	31.42	32.21	32.30
Utility	25.27	26.27	30.00	29.65	30.86
All grades	32.21	32.11	35.18	34.69	34.68
Choice 900-1100 pounds, California	32.60	32.47	34.80	34.38	35.62
Choice 900-1100 pounds, Colorado	32.63	32.05	35.06	34.66	34.75
Cows, Omaha					
Commercial	21.45	21.96	25.76	26.19	25.91
Utility	21.84	22.30	26.18	26.57	26.19
Cutter	20.66	20.46	24.95	25.18	24.68
Canner	18.94	19.55	23.63	23.87	23.18
Vealers, Choice, S. St. Paul	48.46	48.10	57.24	58.78	60.50
Stocker and feeder steers, Kansas City[1]	31.72	34.07	38.20	41.29	40.87
Price received by farmers					
Beef cattle	29.20	29.30	33.50	33.20	34.20
Cows	20.90	20.80	25.30	25.00	25.10
Steers and heifers	31.20	31.40	35.60	35.30	36.40
Calves	36.30	36.90	45.00	45.70	47.10
Beef steer-corn price ratio[2]	28.0	28.2	29.0	27.1	27.1
HOGS					
Barrows and gilts, U.S. No. 1 and 2, Omaha					
180-200 pounds	---	---	---	---	---
200-220 pounds	19.19	20.19	29.11	29.50	28.66
220-240 pounds	19.19	20.11	29.07	29.47	28.57
Barrows and gilts, 7 markets[3]	18.91	19.80	28.86	29.10	28.09
Sows, 7 markets[3]	16.08	16.95	25.22	25.92	25.05
Price received by farmers	17.90	19.50	28.00	28.00	27.50
Hog-corn price ratio[4]					
Omaha, barrows and gilts	16.3	17.2	23.5	22.6	21.8
Price received by farmers, all hogs	16.1	19.5	24.3	23.0	23.1
SHEEP AND LAMBS					
Sheep					
Slaughter ewes, Good, San Angelo	8.20	7.62	9.80	10.12	9.38
Price received by farmers	6.39	6.05	7.47	7.47	7.41
Lamb					
Slaughter, Choice, San Angelo	25.70	26.06	31.52	29.44	28.50
Feeder, Choice, San Angelo	24.95	25.19	29.70	29.56	29.38
Price received by farmers	25.90	25.40	29.90	28.90	28.10
ALL MEAT ANIMALS					
Index number price received by farmers					
(1967=100)	120	123	151	150	152
	Dollars per 100 pounds				
MEAT					
Wholesale, Chicago, Carlot					
Steer beef carcass, Choice, 600-700 pounds	52.75	51.60	54.56	53.36	52.95
Heifer beef, Choice, 500-600 pounds	51.58	50.74	53.33	52.04	51.49
Cow beef, Canner and Cutter	46.74	45.57	52.73	53.38	51.15
Lamb carcass, Choice and Prime, 45-55 pounds	59.47	59.84	65.35	62.48	60.75
Fresh pork loins, 8-14 pounds	45.99	48.69	61.68	62.19	64.38
	Cents per pound				
Retail, United States average					
Beef, Choice grade	105.9	105.1	115.8	112.9	
Pork, retail cuts and sausage	71.0	71.3	86.0	86.6	
Lamb, Choice grade	112.9	111.2	120.7	120.1	
Index number all meats (BLS)					
Wholesale (1967=100)	115.5	115.7	131.4	129.7	
Retail (1967=100)	118.8	118.3	132.5	132.3	
Beef and veal	127.7	127.1	140.2	138.3	
Pork	106.4	105.8	125.4	127.1	

[1] Average all weights and grades. [2] Bushels of No. 2 Yellow Corn equivalent in value to 100 pounds of slaughter steers sold out of first hands, Omaha, all grades. [3] St. Louis N.S.Y., Kansas City, Omaha, Sioux City, S. St. Joseph, S. St. Paul, and Indianapolis. [4] Number bushels of corn equivalent in value to 100 pounds of live hogs.

Source: U.S. Department of Agriculture, *Livestock and Meat Situation,* February 1973.

FIGURE 147

World Cattle and Buffalo Numbers   In Millions of Heads

Year	Argentina	Australia	Brazil	Canada	China	Colombia	France	W. Germany	India[1]	Mexico	Rep. of South Africa	USSR	United Kingdom	United States	World Total[2]
1959	41.2	16.3	71.4	10.1	65.0	14.8	18.4	12.1	206.5	20.0	11.3	70.8	11.0	93.3	983.2
1960	43.4	16.5	72.8	10.5	65.4	15.1	18.7	12.5	N.A.	21.0		74.2	11.5	96.2	1,007
1961	43.2	17.3	74.0	10.9		15.4	19.4	12.9	226.8	21.1		75.8	11.7	97.7	1,041
1962	43.3	18.0	76.2	10.9		15.6	20.3	13.3		22.5		82.1	11.6	100.4	1,060
1963	40.1	18.5	79.1	11.2		15.6	20.3	13.4		25.4		87.0	11.6	104.5	1,057
1964	40.5	19.1	79.9	11.6		15.6	20.1	13.0		21.6		85.4	11.4	107.9	1,070
1965	45.0	18.8	84.1	11.9		16.5	20.2	13.1		23.0	12.4	87.2	11.7	109.0	1,100
1966		17.9	90.6	11.6		17.1	20.6	13.7		23.3	12.2	93.4	12.0	108.9	1,129
1967	51.2	18.3	90.1	11.7		17.9	21.2	14.0		23.3	11.9	97.1	12.2	108.6	1,166
1968	51.5	19.2	90.0	11.8		18.8	21.7	14.0		23.6	12.1	97.2	12.0	109.2	1,191
1969	51.2	20.6	92.8	11.5		19.6	22.1	14.1		24.9	11.8	95.7	12.1	109.9	1,191
1970[3]	49.4	22.2	95.3	11.8		20.4	21.7	14.3		25.1	11.7	95.2	12.3	112.3	1,198
1971[2]	49.6	22.6	97.1	12.2		21.2	21.6	14.0		25.4	12.6	99.1	12.5	114.6	1,212
1972															

[1] Data includes buffaloes.   [2] Estimate.   [3] Preliminary.   Source: Foreign Agricultural Service, U.S.D.A.

Cattle Supply and Distribution in the United States   In Thousands of Heads

Year	Cattle & Calves on Farms Jan. 1	Calves Born	Total Supply	Livestock Slaughter—Cattle and Calves				Total Slaughter	Deaths on Farms	Total Slaughter and Deaths
				Commercial						
				Federally Inspected	Other[2]	All Commercial	Farm			
1959	93,322	38,938	132,260	22,333	8,280	30,613	1,181	31,794	3,876	35,670
1960	96,236	39,355	135,591	24,654	8,795	33,449	1,195	34,637	4,100	38,735
1961	97,700	40,180	137,880	24,973	8,363	33,336	1,218	34,550	4,018	38,571
1962	100,369	41,441	141,810	25,319	8,258	33,577	1,194	34,762	4,125	38,885
1963	104,488	42,268	146,756	26,197	7,867	34,064	1,213	35,277	4,040	39,317
1964	107,903	43,809	151,712	29,953	8,119	38,072	1,242	39,314	4,232	43,546
1965	109,000	43,928	154,828	31,690	8,077	39,767	1,196	40,963	4,248	45,211
1966	108,862	43,526	152,388	31,751	8,623	40,374	661[3]	41,035	4,038	45,073
1967	108,645	43,765	152,410	31,782	8,006	39,788	617	40,405	4,038	44,443
1968	109,152	44,239	153,391	33,468	7,001	40,469	558	41,027	3,986	45,013
1969	109,885	45,196	155,081	34,173	5,927	40,100	486	40,586	4,150	44,734
1970	112,303	45,908	158,211	33,817	5,280	39,097	463	39,560	4,318	43,878
1971[1]	114,470	46,974	161,444	34,225	5,042	39,267				
1972[1]	117,916									
1973										

[1] Preliminary.   [2] Wholesale and retail.   [3] Data beginning 1966 not comparable with previous year due to change in definition.
Source: Economic Research Service, U.S.D.A.

Number of Cattle & Calves on U.S. Farms & Ranches on Jan. 1, by Classes   In Thousands of Heads

Year	Total Cattle & Calves	Cows & Heifers That Have Calved			Heifers 500 lbs. & Over				Steers 500 lbs. & Over	Bulls 500 lbs. & Over	Heifers, Steers & Bulls Under 500 lbs.
		Beef Cows	Milk Cows	Total	For Beef Cow Replacement	For Milk Cow Replacement	Other Heifers	Total			
1965	109,000	33,400	15,380	48,780	5,700	4,780	5,980	16,460	14,050	2,180	27,530
1966	108,862	33,500	14,490	47,990	5,760	4,450	5,990	16,200	14,770	2,150	27,752
1967	108,645	33,740	13,770	47,510	5,810	4,220	6,090	16,120	14,750	2,140	28,125
1968	109,152	34,460	13,250	47,710	5,940	4,120	6,010	16,070	14,700	2,170	28,502
1969	109,885	35,250	12,835	48,085	6,020	4,040	5,900	15,960	14,850	2,190	28,800
1970	112,303	36,404	12,578	48,982	6,253	3,974	6,065	16,292	15,080	2,245	29,704
1971	114,470	37,533	12,414	49,947	6,475	3,941	6,046	16,462	15,375	2,305	30,381
1972[1]	117,916	38,725	12,279	51,004	6,840	3,942	6,331	17,113	15,711	2,365	31,723
1973											

[1] Preliminary.   Source: Crop Reporting Board, U.S.D.A.

Note: Original data from Commodity Research Bureau, Inc.

ICED BROILERS

At one time, broilers (chickens) were raised on small farms and consumed locally. Per capita consumption at the end of World War II was just 5 pounds a year. By 1969, consumption of broilers had risen to 35 pounds per person countrywide. Spurred on by Colonel Sanders and the fast-food chicken take-out industry, the demand for broilers (and "iced" broilers which could be shipped) was born. Production has radically changed to meet the demand; today more than 90 percent of broilers are produced by large corporations on integrated farms where production and processing is one continuous system. The integrated farmer usually buys his chicks from an independent producer, then feeds, processes, and markets himself. As the production cycle from egg to marketed chicken is as little as 10 weeks, a hard view at the marketing of chicks can be valuable to the speculator who would estimate coming supplies of broilers. (See Fig. 148 below.)

The relatively short 10-week cycle

FIGURE 148

Source: Commodity Research Bureau, Inc.

between egg and packaged fryer lends the iced broiler market its characteristic cyclic pattern but pretty much eliminates larger, sweeping price changes. At low prices, production can be cut back almost immediately or raised within 10 weeks of a high-priced market. The vast majority of iced broilers are produced in the Old South. (See Fig. 149 below.)

Information about the broiler market, consumption, production, and so on can be found in the Chicago Board of Trade *Yearbook*. *The Poultry and Egg Situation* is helpful along with the *Feed Situation* which will aid in estimating costs incurred by producers.

The trader has the option of trading virtually every month of the calendar in broilers, usually scheduled as much as 10 months from inception to delivery. Deliverable grade is USDA Grade A

broiler fryers, wrapped and iced, ready to cook. The size of the contract is 28,000 pounds, traded on the Chicago Board of Trade. Three hundred contracts is the maximum allowed position.

Prices are quoted in dollars and cents per hundredweight (cwt.) with a minimum fluctuation of 2.5 cents per hundred pounds. Daily trading limits are set at $2 per hundredweight above or below the previous close, except after the first delivery day until the expiration of the contract, during which time no limits are enforced. The pit is open from 9:15 A.M. to 1:15 P.M., Central time.

Additional statistical data pertaining to the preceding section on "Iced Broilers" is shown in Figs. 150 and 151, p. 217; Figs. 152 and 153, p. 218; and Fig. 154, p. 219.

FIGURE 149
TEN STATES ACCOUNT FOR MAJORITY OF U.S. BROILER PRODUCTION

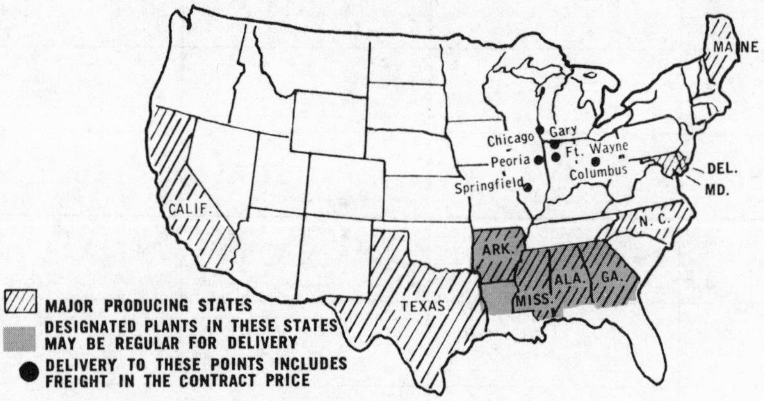

Source: Chicago Board of Trade.

FIGURE 150

Average Wholesale Broiler Prices Delivered at Chicago[1] In Cents Per Pound

Year	Jan.	Feb.	Mar.	Apr.	May	June	July	Aug.	Sept.	Oct.	Nov.	Dec.	Avg.	9-City Weighted Avg.[2]	Frying Chicken Urban Areas[3]
1966	28.1	28.5	29.6	27.7	29.2	29.0	29.1	28.0	26.7	24.2	24.5	22.5	27.3	27.64	41.3
1967	24.8	27.0	25.8	25.4	25.0	25.2	27.1	24.8	24.6	23.5	22.6	22.7	24.9	25.15	38.1
1968	25.2	27.7	27.6	27.0	27.2	27.8	28.7	27.9	27.3	24.6	25.2	25.3	26.8	27.15	39.8
1969	26.8	27.9	28.5	28.1	29.3	29.9	32.4	30.6	29.3	28.0	27.0	26.1	28.7	29.06	42.2
1970	28.2	27.2	27.7	26.4	26.5	26.1	25.9	25.4	26.0	24.6	25.5	24.8	26.2	26.41	40.8
1971	26.1	27.1	26.7	26.4	28.2	29.1	30.0	27.6	27.0	25.4	24.4	24.1	26.8	27.16	41.0
1972	26.7														

[1] Trucklots (U.S. & plant, Grade A). [2] Grade A ice packed, ready-to-cook. [3] In retail stores, whole or cut-up ready to cook.
Source: Bureau of Labor Statistics

Note: Data taken originally from the Commodity Research Bureau, Inc.

FIGURE 151

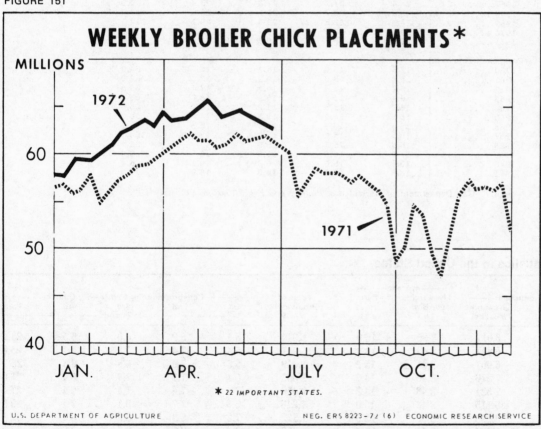

Source: U.S. Department of Agriculture, *Poultry and Egg Situation*, February 1973.

FIGURE 152

Table 10.— Per Capita Consumption of broilers, turkey and red meat by quarters, 1960-71

Item and year	First quarter	Second quarter	Third quarter	Fourth quarter	Total[1]
	Pounds	Pounds	Pounds	Pounds	Pounds
Broilers					
1960	5.1	6.2	6.6	5.5	23.4
1961	5.4	7.4	7.3	5.7	25.8
1962	5.6	7.0	6.8	6.3	25.7
1963	6.1	7.1	7.4	6.4	27.0
1964	6.4	7.4	7.4	6.4	27.6
1965	6.6	7.7	8.1	7.1	29.5
1966	7.2	8.3	8.8	8.0	32.3
1967	7.6	8.7	8.7	7.8	32.8
1968	7.7	8.4	8.9	8.1	33.1
1969	8.0	9.1	9.3	8.8	35.2
1970	8.8	9.9	9.8	8.8	37.3
1971	8.8	9.4	9.8	9.2	37.2
Turkey:					
1960	.6	.8	1.3	3.4	6.1
1961	.6	1.0	1.7	4.1	7.4
1962	.7	.9	1.5	3.9	7.0
1963	.5	.9	1.5	3.9	6.8
1964	.7	.9	1.8	4.0	7.4
1965	.7	.9	1.8	4.1	7.5
1966	.7	1.0	2.0	4.1	7.8
1967	.8	1.1	2.2	4.5	8.6
1968	.9	1.1	1.9	4.0	7.9
1969	1.0	1.2	2.0	4.1	8.3
1970	.9	1.0	2.1	4.2	8.2
1971	1.0	1.2	2.1	4.2	8.5
Beef and veal:					
1960	22.3	22.3	24.1	22.5	91.2
1961	22.3	23.7	24.0	23.4	93.4
1962	23.4	23.4	24.3	23.3	94.4
1963	23.8	24.6	25.7	25.3	99.4
1964	25.1	26.7	26.7	26.6	105.1
1965	25.9	25.2	26.7	26.9	104.7
1966	26.6	26.7	28.1	27.4	108.8
1967	27.4	27.7	27.8	27.4	110.3
1968	28.0	27.7	29.2	28.4	113.3
1969	28.1	27.5	29.4	29.1	114.1
1970	29.1	28.6	29.7	29.2	116.6
1971	28.4	28.7	30.0	28.6	115.7
Pork, excluding lard:					
1960	17.5	15.6	15.1	16.7	64.9
1961	15.8	15.0	14.2	17.0	62.0
1962	16.2	15.4	14.5	17.4	63.5
1963	16.4	15.8	15.2	18.0	65.4
1964	16.7	15.5	15.2	18.0	65.4
1965	15.8	14.5	13.8	14.6	58.7
1966	13.8	13.9	13.9	16.5	58.1
1967	16.5	15.0	15.4	17.2	64.1
1968	16.6	15.8	15.9	17.9	66.2
1969	17.0	16.0	15.5	16.5	65.0
1970	15.4	15.6	16.3	19.1	66.4
1971	18.3	17.8	18.0	18.9	73.0

Source: U.S. Department of Agriculture, *Poultry and Egg Situation,* February 1973.

FIGURE 153

Broiler Salient Statistics in the United States

Year	Production — Number Millions	Production — Liveweight Mil. Lbs.	Average Liveweight Per Bird Lb.	Farm Price ¢ Lb.	Value of Production Mil. $	Consumption Per Capita 1st (In Pounds)	2nd	3rd	4th	Total
1960	1,795	6,017	3.35	16.9	1,014	5.1	6.2	6.6	5.5	23.4
1961	1,991	6,832	3.43	13.9	947	5.4	7.4	7.3	5.7	25.8
1962	2,023	6,907	3.41	15.2	1,049	5.6	7.0	6.8	6.3	25.7
1963	2,102	7,276	3.46	14.6	1,063	6.1	7.1	7.4	6.4	27.0
1964	2,161	7,521	3.48	14.2	1,070	6.4	7.4	7.4	6.4	27.6
1965	2,334	8,115	3.48	15.0	1,218	6.6	7.7	8.1	7.1	29.5
1966	2,572	8,993	3.50	15.3	1,372	7.2	8.3	8.8	8.0	32.3
1967	2,593	9,187	3.55	13.3	1,223	7.6	8.7	8.7	7.8	32.8
1968	2,621	9,332	3.50	14.2	1,326	7.7	8.4	8.9	8.1	33.1
1969	2,788	10,046	3.60	15.2	1,531	8.0	9.1	9.3	8.8	35.2
1970[1]	2,984	10,808	3.64	13.5	1,462	8.8	9.9	9.8	8.8	37.3
1971[1]	3,100	11,000	3.68	13.8	1,518	8.9	9.5	10.0	9.0	37.4
1972										

[1] Preliminary.   Source: *Economic Research Service, U.S.D.A.*

Note: Original data from Commodity Research Bureau, Inc.

FIGURE 154

Table 8.— Broilers: Eggs set and broilers placed weekly in important commercial broiler producing States, 1970 to date

		Eggs set			Percent of previous year		Chicks placed			Percent of previous year	
		1970	1971[1]	1972	1971	1972	1970	1971[1]	1972	1971	1972
		Thou.	Thou.	Thou.	Pct.	Pct.	Thou.	Thou.	Thou.	Pct.	Pct.
January	2 ...	74,211	70,018	73,305	94	105	56,218	56,311	58,059	101	103
	9 ...	76,344	72,013	72,468	94	101	57,580	56,833	57,466	99	101
	16 ...	75,800	69,341	73,838	91	106	57,609	55,666	58,614	97	105
	23 ...	76,924	70,370	76,065	91	108	58,002	56,312	59,746	97	106
	30 ...	77,178	71,675	77,328	93	108	59,118	57,597	59,302	97	103
February	6 ...	77,701	71,689	77,628	92	108	59,157	54,686	60,065	92	110
	13 ...	78,997	72,745	78,210	92	108	60,200	56,052	61,432	93	110
	20 ...	79,317	73,091	78,211	92	107	60,304	57,221	62,224	95	109
	27 ...	80,819	74,826	78,375	93	105	61,036	57,653	62,724	94	109
March	6 ...	81,317	74,588	79,089	92	106	61,648	58,462	63,376	95	108
	13 ...	81,197	75,886	79,101	93	104	62,342	58,799	63,538	94	108
	20 ...	81,742	76,366	79,146	93	104	63,279	59,824	63,133	95	106
	27 ...	82,165	77,364	79,705	94	103	64,173	60,313	64,245	94	107
April	3 ...	82,051	76,825	80,359	94	105	63,871	60,732	64,287	95	106
	10 ...	81,386	77,066	80,682	95	105	64,353	61,467	64,263	96	105
	17 ...	81,196	76,166	78,958	94	104	64,529	62,077	64,424	96	104
	24 ...	81,839	76,210	78,589	93	103	64,609	61,496	64,902	95	106
May	1 ...	80,821	76,848	79,681	95	104	63,944	61,498	65,808	96	107
	8 ...	81,307	76,565	78,822	94	103	63,926	60,637	64,517	95	106
	15 ...	81,486	76,865	79,180	94	103	63,974	60,965	63,987	95	105
	27 ...	81,860	77,917	79,508	95	102	63,364	61,943	64,702	98	104
	29 ...	80,933	77,184	78,981	95	102	63,354	61,461	64,346	97	105
June	5 ...	80,327	77,093	78,652	96	102	63,505	61,722	63,746	97	103
	12 ...	77,993	76,784	78,947	98	103	63,545	61,975	63,412	98	102
	19 ...	72,147	71,249		99		62,960	61,422		98	
	26 ...	74,656	72,899		98		62,513	61,122		98	
July	3 ...	75,924	74,588		98		60,648	60,266		99	
	10 ...	75,042	73,831		98		55,308	55,374		100	
	17 ...	73,462	74,285		101		56,427	56,699		100	
	24 ...	73,453	74,168		101		58,244	58,490		100	
	31 ...	72,803	73,110		100		57,165	58,020		101	
August	7 ...	71,493	73,122		102		56,060	58,131		104	
	14 ...	68,875	72,327		105		56,624	57,686		102	
	21 ...	66,989	71,109		101		55,806	57,027		102	
	28 ...	64,453	69,616		108		54,813	57,564		105	
September	4 ...	58,440	62,407		107		52,384	56,914		109	
	11 ...	62,442	63,482		102		51,719	56,169		109	
	18 ...	66,733	69,881		105		49,593	54,437		110	
	25 ...	64,958	67,563		104		44,938	48,472		108	
October	2 ...	58,324	62,244		107		47,775	49,556		104	
	9 ...	59,660	60,355		101		51,991	54,581		105	
	16 ...	66,434	65,394		98		50,773	53,410		105	
	23 ...	68,970	69,791		101		45,432	49,131		108	
	30 ...	70,488	71,250		101		46,929	47,160		100	
November	6 ...	69,997	70,400		101		51,905	51,929		100	
	13 ...	71,641	72,230		101		54,284	55,509		102	
	20 ...	71,099	72,490		102		55,820	57,036		102	
	27 ...	71,365	72,645		102		55,230	56,477		102	
December	5 ...	66,202	69,795		105		55,582	56,603		102	
	12 ...	71,432	71,275		100		55,966	56,179		100	
	19 ...	71,791	71,712		100		55,688	56,598		102	
	26 ...	70,152	72,578		103		52,176	52,344		100	
52 weeks total		3,851,947	3,755,468		97		2,998,338	2,976,008		99	

[1] Data revised to reflect latest weekly revisions.

Source: U.S. Department of Agriculture, *Poultry and Egg Situation*, February 1973.

FRESH SHELL EGGS

The fresh shell egg futures markets, traded on the Chicago Mercantile Exchange, is one of the more dynamic markets. Many traders follow egg and chicken statistics almost exclusively and restrict their trading to this one commodity. Egg prices are as cyclical as frozen broilers and for the same reasons. When egg prices start to swing, they are known to advance and decline in rapid sequence so that it is possible for a trader to net many thousands of dollars on both the long and short side of the market as he plays the swings. (See Fig. 155 opposite.)

Like the cattle market, but with a shorter duration, the egg producer in the United States operates on a limited budget and hopes to make enough during the fat years to carry him through the lean years. When prices are high every egg producer makes money (unfortunately prices are only rarely high in the egg markets) but when prices are low most producers lose money. In an effort to make a bundle during the periods of high prices, the egg producer increases his flocks as fast as he can during the peak price periods. This increase in flock size forces prices downward in response to the increased available supply. When prices fall the producer then culls his flock as best he can or goes out of business, since at low-price periods it often costs more for the farmer to raise an egg than he gets from the distributor. An egg which he may sell for 30 cents a dozen may have cost him 35 cents a dozen to produce. During these low-price periods the farmer cuts back his flock to almost nothing to survive. With flocks cut back, price begins to rise in response to a limited supply and the cycle starts all over again. (See Fig. 156, p. 222.)

Thus in the egg market when prices are high they almost always remain high for several weeks until more egg-laying chickens can be added to the producing flocks and then prices nosedive until the increased egg layers are again cut back. (See Fig. 157, p. 222.)

The egg production cycle becomes one of the most dependable and most volatile in the industry and one which attracts many commodity speculators to trading in the egg futures market.

The U.S. Department of Agriculture provides four times a year the *Poultry and Egg Situation* report which summarizes the outlook for egg prices for the upcoming months. The trader who wishes to understand egg statistics in depth will undoubtedly have his name added to this report. *Dairy and Poultry News* is available also from the U.S. Department of Agriculture out of its Chicago office and is available free to anyone who wishes his name added to the mailing list. In addition other important reports are the *Production Report*, the *Cold Storage Report*, and the *Chicago Mercantile Exchange Yearbook* which provides sufficient data on supply and demand for the egg trader to gain a grasp on past year's fundamentals.

The use of stop-loss orders when trading the egg futures market is most essential. A small loss of 1 cent per dozen can run into 10-12 cents within a matter of days or a few weeks and the trader who hopes to hold onto his position in the desire to see prices rebound to previous levels will usually be most disappointed. It is much easier to take a sharp but quick loss at a point and

FIGURE 155

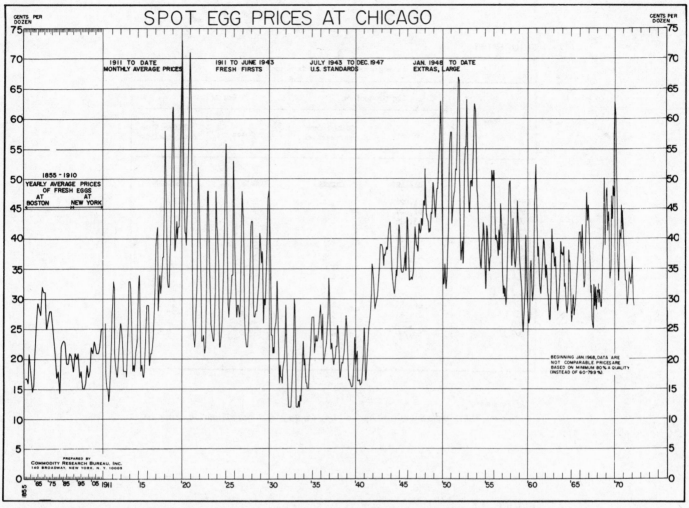

SPOT EGG PRICES AT CHICAGO

CENTS PER DOZEN

1911 TO DATE
MONTHLY AVERAGE PRICES

1911 TO JUNE 1943
FRESH FIRSTS

JULY 1943 TO DEC. 1947
U.S. STANDARDS

JAN. 1948 TO DATE
EXTRAS, LARGE

1855 - 1910
YEARLY AVERAGE PRICES
OF FRESH EGGS
AT BOSTON   AT NEW YORK

BEGINNING JAN 1968, DATA ARE
NOT COMPARABLE. PRICES ARE
BASED ON MINIMUM 80% A QUALITY
(INSTEAD OF 60-79.9 %)

PREPARED BY
COMMODITY RESEARCH BUREAU, INC.
140 BROADWAY, NEW YORK, N.Y. 10005

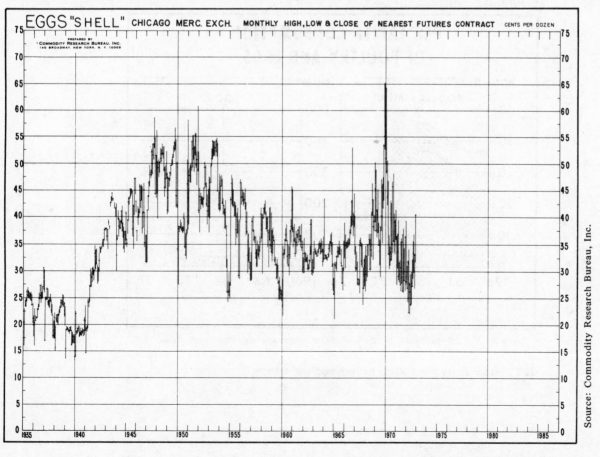

EGGS "SHELL" CHICAGO MERC. EXCH.   MONTHLY HIGH, LOW & CLOSE OF NEAREST FUTURES CONTRACT   CENTS PER DOZEN

PREPARED BY
COMMODITY RESEARCH BUREAU, INC.
140 BROADWAY, NEW YORK, N.Y. 10005

Source: Commodity Research Bureau, Inc.

FIGURE 156

Year	Egg production		Egg prices	
	Volume	Change from year earlier	Per dozen	Change from year earlier
	Million	Percent	Cents	Percent
1957	61,026	-1.1	35.9	-8.7
1958	61,607	0	38.5	7.2
1959	63,335	1.8	31.4	-18.4
1960	61,602	-3.7	36.1	15.0
1961	62,423	.4	35.6	-1.4
1962	63,569	.8	33.8	-5.1
1963	63,500	-1.1	34.5	2.1
1964	65,215	1.7	33.8	-2.0
1965	65,692	.7	33.7	.3
1966	66,484	1.2	39.1	16.0
1967	70,031	5.3	31.2	-20.2
1968	69,326	-1.0	34.0	9.0
1969 1/	68,700	-0.9	37.0	8.8

Caption: Changes in egg production and farm prices, 1957-69

1/ Forecast.

Source: U.S. Department of Agriculture, *Poultry and Egg Situation*, June 1972.

FIGURE 157

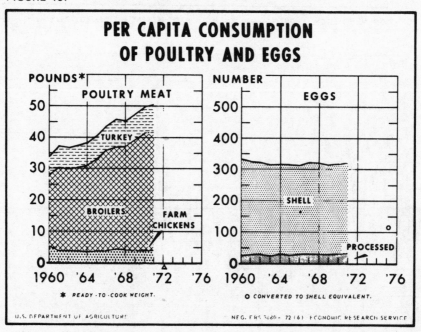

Source: U.S. Department of Agriculture, *Poultry and Egg Situation*, June 1972.

then reenter the market at a later more favorable date than to hold onto a poor position in the hope (usually misguided hope) that you will recover your loss at a later date. Some commodities offer this opportunity but egg futures are not one of them.

Egg prices are quoted in cents per dozen with the minimum fluctuation set at 5 points (5/100ths of a cent), which is worth $11.25 on a contract size of 22,500 dozen. Contracts are traded in all months, though some are more actively traded than others.

Additional statistical data pertaining to the preceding section on "Fresh Shell Eggs" is shown in Figure 158 below and Figures 159-61 on pages 224-26.

FIGURE 158

Eggs: Production, rate of lay, and average number of layers, 1957-69 1/						
	Egg production		Rate of lay 2/		Layers	
Year	Total	Percentage of 1957-59	Eggs per layer	Percentage of 1957-59	Average number	Percentage of 1957-59
	Million dozen	Percent	Number	Percent	Thousands	Percent
Average: 1957-59	5,475	100.0	203	100.0	305,612	100.0
1957	5,442	99.4	199	98.0	306,676	100.3
1958	5,442	99.4	202	99.5	304,441	99.6
1959	5,542	101.2	207	102.0	305,720	100.0
1960	5,339	97.5	209	103.0	295,284	96.6
1961	5,358	97.9	210	103.4	296,648	97.1
1962	5,403	98.7	212	104.4	299,834	98.1
1963	5,345	97.6	213	104.9	298,476	97.7
1964	5,435	99.3	217	106.9	301,136	98.5
1965	5,474	100.0	218	107.4	301,687	98.7
1966	5,540	101.2	218	107.4	305,142	99.8
1967	5,836	106.6	221	108.9	316,962	103.7
1968	5,777	105.5	220	108.4	315,220	103.1
1969 3/	5,725	104.6	219	107.9	314,000	102.7

1/ 1957-59 excludes Alaska and Hawaii. 2/ Eggs produced during the year divided by the average number of layers on hand during the year. 3/ Estimated.

Data published currently in Poultry and Egg Situation (ERS).

Source: U.S. Department of Agriculture, *Poultry and Egg Situation*, June 1972.

FIGURE 159

Table 4.—Per capita consumption of eggs by quarters, 1960-71

Year	Shell					Processed egg[1]	Total eggs
	First quarter	Second quarter	Third quarter	Fourth quarter	Total		
	Number	Number	Number	Number	Number	Number	Number
1960	79.9	74.6	73.4	77.8	306	29	335
1961	75.9	72.2	72.7	77.3	298	30	328
1962	76.5	72.1	71.4	76.4	296	31	327
1963	73.9	70.7	70.9	74.6	290	28	318
1964	74.1	69.4	70.4	73.6	288	30	318
1965	72.0	70.5	70.2	72.9	286	28	314
1966	71.3	69.0	69.7	74.0	284	30	314
1967	72.4	70.1	71.6	75.1	289	35	324
1968	74.8	71.1	70.4	72.9	289	32	321
1969	72.6	70.8	70.7	72.4	287	31	318
1970	71.7	69.9	70.4	73.5	286	33	319
1971	72.2	70.9	69.5	72.4	285	37	322

[1] Shell egg equivalent.

Table 3.—Eggs: Supply and utilization, 1960-71

Year	Supply						Utilization							
	Pro-duction	Im-ports	Beginning stocks[1]			Total supply	Ending stocks	Exports and shipments			Domestic disappearance			
			Com-mercial	USDA	Total			Com-mercial	USDA	Total	Eggs used for hatch-ing	Mili-tary[2]	Civilian	
													Total	Per capita
	Mil. doz.	Mil. doz.	Mil. doz.	Mil. doz.	Mil. doz.	Mil. doz.	Mil. doz.	Mil. doz.	Mil. doz.	Mil. doz.	Mil. doz.	Mil. doz.	Mil. doz.	No.
1960 . . .	5,339	3	65	---	65	5,407	51	42	2	44	282	63	4,967	334
1961 . . .	5,358	3	51	---	51	5,412	48	40	2	42	302	64	4,956	328
1962 . . .	5,403	2	48	---	48	5,453	50	32	---	32	303	70	4,998	327
1963 . . .	5,345	1	50	---	50	5,396	44	42	1	43	304	67	4,938	318
1964 . . .	5,435	2	44	---	44	5,481	46	30	2	32	312	76	5,015	318
1965 . . .	5,474	1	46	---	46	5,521	41	39	---	39	333	94	5,014	314
1966 . . .	5,540	15	41	---	41	5,596	28	41	---	41	365	102	5,060	314
1967 . . .	5,836	4	28	---	28	5,868	71	55	---	55	361	110	5,271	324
1968 . . .	5,773	6	71	---	71	5,850	56	46	---	46	364	108	5,276	321
1969 . . .	5,757	9	56	---	56	5,822	34	41	---	41	395	83	5,269	318
1970 . . .	5,853	28	34	---	34	5,915	39	46	---	46	400	66	5,364	319
1971[3] . .	5,978	10	39	---	39	6,027	58	51	---	51	391	52	5,475	322

[1] Storage stocks include shell eggs and the approximate shell-egg equivalent of frozen eggs. [2] Includes USDA donations to military and military feedings of civilians in occupied territories. [3] Preliminary.

Table 1.— Eggs: Production, disposition and value, 1960-71[1]

Year	Average Number layers on hand during the year	Eggs						
		Produced		Consumed on farms where produced	Sold	Price per dozen	Value of-	
		Per layer on hand during	Total				Sales	Sales and consump-tion
	Millions	Number	Millions	Millions	Millions	Cents	Million dollars	Million dollars
1960	295	209	61,602	3,782	57,680	36.1	1,731	1,841
1961	297	210	62,423	3,364	59,509	35.6	1,750	1,848
1962	300	212	63,569	3,026	60,543	33.8	1,703	1,787
1963	298	213	63,500	2,729	60,770	34.5	1,747	1,824
1964	301	217	65,215	2,439	62,776	33.8	1,770	1,836
1965	302	218	65,692	2,056	63,636	33.7	1,788	1,844
1966	305	218	66,484	1,612	64,872	39.1	2,114	2,165
1967	317	221	70,031	1,558	68,473	31.2	1,781	1,820
1968	315	220	69,270	1,393	67,877	34.0	1,921	1,959
1969	314	220	69,086	1,172	67,914	40.0	2,261	2,300
1970[2]	321	218	70,023	1,062	68,961	39.1	2,246	2,280
1971[2][3]	322	223	71,644	998	70,646	31.4	1,849	1,875

[1] Data cover both farm and commercial operations. [2] Estimates for 1970-71 were made on the basis of a marketing year, December 1 through November 30. [3] Preliminary.

FIGURE 160

U. S. MONTHLY EGG PRODUCTION
(In Thousand Cases)

Year	Jan.	Feb.	Mar.	Apr.	May	June	July	Aug.	Sept.	Oct.	Nov.	Dec.	Total
1959	15,217	14,389	16,733	16,325	16,189	14,539	14,056	13,533	12,992	13,647	13,586	14,725	175,931
1960	15,089	14,317	15,544	15,347	15,747	14,400	13,942	13,336	12,656	13,097	13,150	14,103	170,728
1961	14,414	13,647	15,889	15,461	15,556	14,386	14,139	13,689	13,178	13,889	13,931	14,775	172,958
1962	14,831	13,847	16,081	15,764	15,981	14,747	14,489	14,006	13,511	14,178	14,019	14,669	176,122
1963	14,503	13,433	15,814	15,722	15,939	14,769	14,617	14,217	13,633	14,264	14,194	14,794	175,900
1964	14,964	14,572	16,153	15,819	16,131	15,100	14,914	14,511	14,075	14,703	14,425	15,250	180,617
1965	15,586	14,261	16,033	15,725	16,217	15,300	15,217	14,794	14,244	14,819	14,525	15,203	181,925
1966	15,255	13,936	15,939	15,725	16,131	15,225	15,181	14,978	14,714	15,511	15,372	16,169	184,128
°1967	16,411	15,011	16,972	16,628	17,000	16,122	16,272	16,050	15,539	16,197	15,822	16,506	194,530
1968	16,619	15,656	17,067	16,642	16,872	15,914	16,072	15,653	15,050	15,744	15,322	15,806	192,417
1969	15,861	14,683	16,686	16,356	16,939	16,050	16,150	15,914	15,336	15,978	15,608	16,344	191,905
1970	16,369	14,856	16,833	16,478	16,928	16,039	16,317	16,178	15,675	16,389	16,103	16,928	195,093
1971	17,067	15,456	17,228	16,728	17,200	16,419	16,597	16,406	15,883	16,642	16,458	17,133	199,217
1972	17,300	. . . . .	. . . . .	. . . . .	. . . . .	. . . . .	. . . . .	. . . . .	. . . . .	. . . . .	. . . . .	. . . . .	

° Effective with 1967, production reflects U.S., rather than 48 states. As reported thereto.

World Production[2] of Eggs   In Billions of Eggs

Year	Argentina	Australia	Bel. & Lux.	Brazil	Canada	Denmark	France	W. Germany	Italy	Japan	Netherlands	Poland	U.S.S.R.	United Kingdom[3]	United States
1960	3.5	2.4	2.8	6.2	5.4	2.4	8.5	7.9	6.4	9.6	5.8	5.6	27.5	11.3	61.5
1961	3.7	2.5	3.1	6.5	5.2	2.2	9.0	8.4	6.6	12.9	6.0	6.1	29.3	13.6	62.1
1962	2.9	2.5	3.0	6.9	5.2	1.9	9.2	8.9	6.8	14.6	6.1	6.1	30.1	13.6	63.1
1963	2.5	2.5	2.9	7.3	5.0	1.8	9.4	10.0	7.5	15.3	5.3	5.8	28.5	14.4	63.5
1964	2.4	2.5	3.2	7.8	5.3	1.7	9.7	11.2	9.9	17.9	5.1	6.0	26.7	14.6	62.2
1965	2.7	2.7	2.9	8.1	5.2	1.5	9.2	11.9	10.0	19.4	4.3	6.3	29.1	15.2	65.7
1966	3.1	2.7	2.9	8.5	5.0	1.5	9.7	12.9	10.6	19.6	4.2	6.3	31.7	14.6	66.5
1967	2.5	2.3	3.0	8.8	5.3	1.5	10.3	13.8	10.5	23.3	3.7	6.3	33.9	14.4	70.0
1968	2.9	2.3	3.4	9.5	5.4	1.5	10.8	14.1	9.8	24.7	4.0	6.3	35.7	14.9	69.3
1969	2.9	2.4	4.0	9.7	5.7	1.5	11.2	14.7	10.3	27.9	4.4	6.7	37.2	14.8	69.1
1970[1]	3.0	2.5	4.5	9.6	5.9	1.5	11.2	15.4	10.6	30.0	5.5	6.9	40.4	14.8	70.3

[1] Preliminary.   [2] Relates to farm production in Canada and the United States, but information for many countries is not explicit on this point.   [3] Farm production, years ending May.   *Source: Foreign Agricultural Service, U.S.D.A.*

Note: Original data is from Chicago Mercantile Exchange.

FIGURE 161

Eggs: Civilian Per Capita Disappearance in the United States Number of Eggs

Year	Jan.	Feb.	Mar.	Apr.	May	June	Shell July	Aug.	Sept.	Oct.	Nov.	Dec.	Total[1]	Processed[2]	Total
1959	29.0	25.5	29.0	26.4	26.2	24.4	25.6	25.6	25.1	26.7	26.6	28.4	319	33	352
1960	27.5	24.7	27.7	26.6	24.9	23.1	24.9	24.4	24.0	25.3	25.6	26.9	306	29	335
1961	26.2	23.3	26.3	25.3	24.4	22.5	24.4	24.3	23.9	25.3	25.2	26.7	298	30	328
1962	26.3	23.5	26.5	25.3	24.4	22.4	23.6	24.0	23.6	24.9	25.0	26.4	296	31	327
1963	25.5	22.5	25.8	24.2	23.9	22.5	23.6	23.8	23.3	24.5	24.5	25.5	290	28	318
1964	25.2	23.4	25.4	23.5	23.7	22.1	23.3	23.9	23.1	24.3	23.9	25.3	287	30	318
1965	25.3	22.1	24.5	24.1	24.1	22.1	23.6	23.6	22.9	24.4	23.7	24.7	285	28	314
1966	24.5	22.0	24.6	23.4	23.6	21.8	23.3	23.4	22.8	24.6	24.2	25.1	283	30	314
1967	25.0	22.1	25.2	23.8	23.9	22.2	24.0	24.0	23.4	24.6	24.5	25.8	289	35	324
1968	25.7	23.5	25.4	24.2	24.2	22.5	23.7	23.5	23.0	24.1	23.7	24.8	288	32	321
1969	24.8	22.2	25.6	23.9	24.4	22.5	23.6	23.9	23.2	23.9	23.7	24.8	287	31	318
1970[3]	24.9	21.9	24.9	23.7	24.0	22.1	23.7	23.9	22.9	24.1	24.0	25.4	286	33	319
1971[3]	25.4	22.3	24.7	23.9	24.6	22.8	24.1	24.2	22.9	24.3	23.8	25.2	288	35	323
1972															

[1] Monthly totals do not necessarily add to yearly figures due to rounding. [2] Liquid, frozen, & dried egg (egg solids) converted to shell egg equivalent. [3] Preliminary. *Source: Economic Research Service, U.S.D.A.*

Egg-Feed Ratio[1] in the United States

Year	Jan.	Feb.	Mar.	Apr.	May	June	July	Aug.	Sept.	Oct.	Nov.	Dec.	Average
1959	10.9	10.5	10.0	8.2	7.3	7.4	8.9	9.1	9.9	9.6	9.6	9.5	9.2
1960	9.1	8.9	9.8	10.7	9.7	9.3	9.6	10.4	11.7	13.4	14.3	13.8	10.9
1961	12.0	11.8	10.9	10.0	9.5	9.1	10.1	10.3	10.5	11.1	10.8	10.5	10.6
1962	10.6	10.8	9.9	9.3	8.5	8.3	8.6	9.6	10.6	10.7	10.8	10.6	9.9
1963[2]	8.6	8.8	8.6	7.7	7.0	7.0	7.3	7.7	8.5	8.4	8.6	8.4	8.0
1964	8.9	8.2	8.1	7.5	7.1	7.3	7.6	8.3	8.4	8.3	8.2	7.9	8.2
1965	7.4	7.4	7.4	7.9	7.1	7.2	7.5	8.1	8.7	8.9	9.1	9.9	7.6
1966	8.9	9.8	9.9	9.2	7.9	7.8	8.1	9.0	9.6	9.3	9.5	9.3	9.5
1967	8.6	7.5	7.9	6.9	6.7	6.3	7.0	7.0	7.5	6.8	7.2	7.7	7.9
1968	7.9	7.5	7.6	7.2	6.8	7.6	8.2	8.7	10.9	9.6	9.9	10.7	7.4
1969	10.9	9.9	10.1	9.3	7.6	7.8	9.4	8.9	10.0	10.1	12.3	13.5	9.9
1970	13.0	11.4	10.2	8.5	7.3	7.3	8.7	7.9	9.0	7.6	8.5	8.8	10.9
1971	8.2	7.4	7.2	7.2	6.7	6.5	6.3	7.0	7.1	6.8	7.2	8.2	7.6
1972	7.1												

[1] Pounds of laying feed equivalent in value to one dozen eggs. [2] NEW SERIES. Comparable earlier data not available.
Source: Department of Agriculture

Salient Egg Statistics in the United States

Year	Hens & Pullets On Farms Jan. 1 (Millions)	Hens & Pullets Avg.[9] Number During Year (Millions)	Rate of Lay Per Layer On Farms Jan. 1[2] (Number)	Rate of Lay Per Layer During Year[3] (Number)	Farm Prod. (Billions)	Used for Farm Hatching (Billions)	Consumed[4] on Farms (Billions)	Sold	Gross Income[5] Billion $	Total Egg Prod.[6]	Imports[7] (Million Dozen)	Exports[8] & Shipments (Million Dozen)	Used for Hatching (Million Dozen)	Consumption Total	Consumption Per Capita Eggs
1960	351.8	295.3	175	209	61.5	—	3.8	57.8	1.85	5,339	3	44	282	4,963	334
1961	347.9	296.6	170	210	62.4	—	3.4	59.1	1.85	5,358	3	42	302	4,953	328
1962	358.8	299.8	171	212	63.6	—	3.03	60.54	1.79	5,403	2	32	303	4,993	326
1963	357.3	298.5	170	213	63.5	—	2.73	60.77	1.82	5,345	1	43	304	4,933	317
1964	363.6	301.1	176	217	62.2	—	2.44	62.78	1.84	5,435	2	32	312	5,017	318
1965	312.9[10]	301.7	182	218	65.7	—	2.06	64.64	1.84	5,474	1	39	333	5,014	314
1966	309.9[10]	305.1	179	218	66.5	—	1.61	64.87	2.17	5,540	15	43	365	5,058	313
1967	324.8[10]	317.0	183	221	70.0	—	1.56	68.47	1.82	5,836	4	55	361	5,271	324
1968	329.3[10]	315.0	183	220	69.3	—	1.39	67.88	1.96	5,773	6	46	364	5,276	321
1969	316.2[10]	314.1	192	220	69.1	—	1.17	67.91	2.30	5,757	9	41	395	5,269	318
1970[1]	326.6[10]	321.3		218	70.0	—	1.06	69.25	2.20	5,833	28	46	411	5,359	320
1971[1]	335.1[10]	321.8		223	71.6					5,967					323
1972[1]	328.3														

[1] Preliminary. [2] Number of eggs produced during the year divided by number of hens & pullets on hand Jan. 1. [3] Number of eggs produced during the year divided by the average number of hens & pullets of laying age on hand during the year. [4] Consumed in households of farm producers. [5] Value of sales plus value of eggs consumed in households of producers. [6] Farm production, plus nonfarm output estimated at 10% of farm through 1954; thereafter, 1 percentage point less each year. [7] Shell-egg equivalent of eggs and egg products. [8] Shell eggs & shell equivalent of frozen & dried egg products. [9] Average number of layers on farms during the year. [10] Of laying age. *Source: Agricultural Marketing Service, U.S.D.A.*

11

THE RANDOM NATURE OF MARKET PRICE

It is useful at some point to talk about the nature of price itself, divorced from the fundamental and technical factors that make it up. Economists speak of price changes in terms of negative and positive serial correlation—whether or not one price in a series is correlated to other prices in the series. If prices are related in the series, technical study of past market prices can give valid forecasts of prices to come. If they are not related, no technical study of the market has any value whatsoever. In order to study the commodity markets and the nature of supply and demand pricing, economists posit a theoretical Ideal Market and measure actual markets against it. This is called the random walk market, and it serves about the same function in economic studies that a 1,000 batting average serves for baseball fans, or a 300 game for bowlers. With an ideal game in mind, something exists by which to measure the real.

DISCOUNTING

Any trader who stays with the commodity markets for a while will undoubtedly have the experience of seeing a bullish change in fundamental supply and demand cause prices to drop. Consider the trader who subscribed to *The Eastern European Review* for other reasons than commodity trading, and ran across an article stating that the Soviet Union had decided to put emphasis on self-sufficiency on feed grains this year and was planting rye and corn in fields normally given to sunflowers. Russia was to export no edible fats for the year. The trader checked Russian exports of edible fats in the past, and found them to be a significant factor in international trade, especially in the Asian and African markets. Safflower oil is in direct competition to the high-priced, high-quality soybean oil exported from the United States.

The trader bought soybean oil and waited for the world to start buying tons of the stuff as competing products ran out. Sure enough, in December alone, 30 million additional pounds of soybean oil were sold for export, the news coming across the wire Friday afternoon after the close of trading in soybean oil futures. Monday morning the price fell in active trading and never rallied up to its Friday close. Soybean oil traders had been expecting sales of at least 50 million pounds and were discouraged by such a small sale announcement. The price had already been bid up to reflect traders' expectations and when the expectations were not fulfilled, prices dropped.

Demand for orange juice doesn't

change much with price changes, and the critical factor in orange juice concentrate prices is supply. The market will normally discount all available information and *established odds,* when finding equilibrium price for future delivery. If all the oranges in the current crop make it to market, traders may figure orange concentrate to be worth 50 cents a pound, but the market doesn't trade at this price. A major freeze hits about every other year, and the average freeze over the last 10 years has raised orange concentrate prices about 10 cents a pound. With a 50-50 chance of a freeze which will raise orange concentrate prices by 10 cents, the market simply plays the odds and raises its 50 cent estimate by 5 cents. If there is no freeze, prices will drop 5 cents. If a freeze does occur, the price will rise by 5 cents. Orange concentrate has one of the most volatile and "dangerous" markets on any of the commodity exchanges, because of the extreme and unpredictable effects of weather, but to the extent that unforeseeable weather conditions can be figured into the going price, they will be. In the case of light and scattered freeze damage, the trader might watch the price of orange concentrate *go down* on news of a partially damaged crop.

PRICE EFFECTS OF TAKING PROFITS: DISCOUNTING CONTINUED

In an undiscounted orange concentrate market, contracts might sell for 50 cents a pound. Any trader who recognized the possibility of a freeze could take a long position and if the freeze did not occur, price ought to stay about where it was, leaving him in a zero-loss, zero-profit position. If a freeze did occur, he would make 10 cents for nearly a 300 percent return on his margin. He stands to win a little or lose a little in the event of no freeze as the market fluctuates, with the added kicker on the long side of a large win if the freeze did occur. Such a market would heavily favor the speculator on the long side; placing his order, such a speculator would help firm the price for orange concentrate futures. Other speculators doing the same, would help push the price up yet more, until finally the price rests at the point at which speculators are no longer offered the lopsided odds. This would be a price which simply no longer tempted speculators into taking long positions. At this level, the price has an exactly equal chance of dropping or rising and the market is fully discounted.

Should the price rise above the point at which it has a 50-50 chance of advancing or falling the same amount, some speculators will find that they are risking 7 cents in the event there is no freeze (if the price were at 57 cents) and standing to gain only 3 cents if there is (if the average freeze brings the price to 60 cents). With an equal chance of a freeze or no freeze, speculators who are risking 7 cents against 3 cents will prudently leave the market, weakening price until it drops back to the point that no further speculators wish to leave the market.

Any time any trader can find an advantage on one side of the market or the other, either because price is more likely to move in one direction than the other, or because it is likely to move *farther,* in one direction than the other, he is offered a premium for instituting a position. In so doing, he firms up a too low estimate or weakens one that is too high, speeding the market price closer to a better guess of the price that is going to occur on the cash market at contract expiration. As price adjusts up or down into speculator demand taking advantage of the too-low or too-high price, the premium will shrink until it no longer exists and tempts no further speculators into exploiting it. It is by the process of offering profits, either at the opening of a position or at its closing, that the market discounts itself. Any time the price does not include all known factors and known odds of change in fundamental factors, a profit is held out, which will be exploited until it disappears. A buy or sell order has the same market effect whether it is used to close an open short position or open a long position and it makes no difference whether the speculator takes a profit offered at the opening or the closing of his position.

The net effect of market discounting is that price in an efficient, discounted market has at all times an exactly equal chance of going the same distance in either direction. Variations exist, of course. If the market has a 25 percent chance of going up (such as a history of freeze one year in four) this fact will be reflected in the price. The resting price in all events will be the price at which no speculative advantage is held out to any trader.

Holbrook Working, in his academic study of the profits accruing to different players in commodity futures markets, concluded that speculators exist essentially on the crumbs of the market as speculative advantage is exploited by a field of eager market watchers before it has time to hold out a substantial meal to anyone. This is an adequate metaphor for a fully discounted market as long as it is remembered that *nobody* is getting the meal. If the market is working efficiently, crumbs are all that are allowed to exist. The metaphor ought not to be taken too literally, however. Even in the most efficient market, the leverage given traders by low margins can return 100 to 1,000 percent in a matter of weeks.

THIN MARKETS

The best discounted markets are those that see the greatest volume of trading. The more traders doing business on a market and seeking advantage by different methods, the less likely is the market to hold out any sizable speculative advantage to any of them. Such markets will hand out profits, in a random manner. Thin markets can be expected to react to news in a more jerky manner and show a generally more volatile price pattern.

Thin markets often hold out greater advantages to the speculator because of reduced competition for profits, but they also hold out greater risk. Lack of trading volume can make execution of plays at planned levels difficult or impossible, and once a poorly discounted market takes off, its price moves tend to be greater than on better discounted markets. The markets for frozen orange concentrate and frozen pork bellies both enjoy speculator interest out of proportion to hedging primarily because of the greater profits they make possible. The trader must balance against these potentially greater profits, the risk of greater losses if he is wrong and the potential danger of not being able to control his position if liquidity falls so low that his order cannot be executed.

Extremely thin markets, such as those for most metals, pepper, molasses, propane, rubber, and hides, ought to be avoided altogether. Volume is so thin on these markets that the speculator has virtually no control over his position in times of price movement.

RANDOM WALK MARKET

No such thing as a random walk market exists but by studying this "perfect game" an understanding of the real markets can be had. Where the real-world markets deviate from the ideal, a speculative advantage can be found. Where real-world price movement is not random, the chart trader can make money by reading past price behavior. Theory has been largely avoided throughout this book for the simple reason that the vast majority of it has absolutely no pragmatic value to the speculator. Random walk is an exception and will be given in some brief detail in the hope of providing some basis by which the trader can determine exactly what his forecasting system attempts to measure.

Some very efficient commodity markets, such as those for wheat, corn, soybeans, and cotton have been shown to closely approximate the ideal over comparatively long periods of time. Price movement is random and the market is considered fully discounted, free of trends. In shorter terms, inefficiency creeps in—price dips to accept large seasonal hedging sales, new information is not immediately and fully understood, traders do not all receive the same information at the same time and come to the same conclusions. Because of these shorter term inefficiencies, trends exist and it is these trends that allow a trader to develop better than 50-50 odds in his playing. Technical chart rules attempt to mechanically exploit these inefficiencies and it is for this reason that theoretical economists have given study to the rules of chart traders. The effect of chart rules is a direct measure of nonrandomness. (See Fig. 162 opposite.)

FIGURE 162

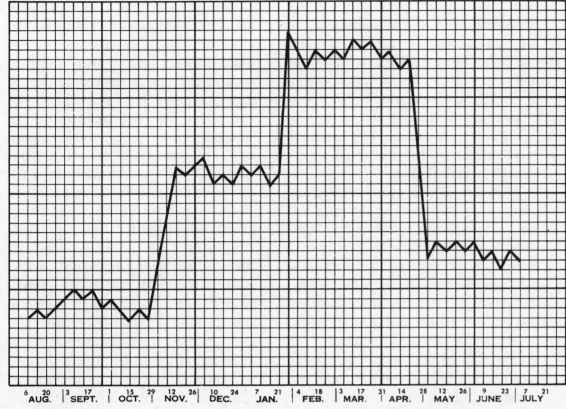

6 20	3 17	1 15 29	12 26	10 24	7 21	4 18	3 17	31 14	28 12 26	9 23	7 21
AUG.	SEPT.	OCT.	NOV.	DEC.	JAN.	FEB.	MAR.	APR.	MAY	JUNE	JULY

In a random walk market, price change will occur without pattern in the manner of a coin flip. Jogs in the chart occur when new, unpredictable information reaches the market and leave price at a new level of random fluctuation.

THE MODEL

In a random walk market, the price will fluctuate daily in a narrow range for as long as no new information or expectation of new information applies to the judgment of traders. This random price movement could be accurately duplicated by the simple flip of a coin and is insignificant to any trader who must pay full commission because movements are too small to cover the cost of exploiting them. These small random fluctuations are called "noise" and any series of upticks would give the trader no more information about his next position than would a series of heads to the bettor on a coin flip. In large efficient markets, such noise has been found to account for 75 percent of all new prices coming across the ticker. About 75 percent of all new prices are in the direction opposite the one preceding them, with the result that the price ends in almost exactly the same level that it started for any length of time during which the market is fully discounted. The market may in fact move in one direction or the other, rewarding long or short traders, but no such movement would give information about future movement or help a trader in instituting a position.

According to the model, all information pertaining to price that can be applied has been, and no trader who has the money to open a new position has the desire. No trader with the desire has the money. Such fluctuation as occurs is caused by traders closing their positions to go on vacation or opening new positions simply because they have the money, and come in a completely unpredictable, erratic fashion.

When new information is released and becomes generally known, the price will jump or drop to a new level and begin the meaningless fluctuation that characterizes a market at rest. In the theoretically perfect market, all traders receive the information at the same time and are equally talented in interpretation. Thus the price moves quickly and smoothly to its new level. There ought to be very little disagreement about the direction dictated by the new information and only a slight bit more about the amount of movement justified. Some traders will consider the new information to justify a 4 cent upward adjustment, some might think 5 cents closer to reality, but agreement ought to be quickly reached and a new consensus price established. If the new information was expected and the market already discounted in anticipation, the price may rise or drop with the news according to whether the anticipated news was as good or not as good as expected.

A possible refinement to the model exists if traders are not considered to be equally able to acquire and interpret news, but fall into two classes according to the rapidity of their response. In such a case, the "insiders" must not only come to a conclusion about the import of the news but also predict the reaction of their less able fellows. In such a case, the price might be expected to jog upward or downward at the release of news which affected market price, and then jog a second time as the second class of traders adjusted their position. At the second jog, the price could rise if the "insiders" underestimated the enthusiasm of the "outsiders" or it could fall if "insiders" bid the price too high in the first place and many of them took their profits when they had the opportunity to sell their positions to the newcomers.

As news is by definition "new," its effect on a market is random. It can be as likely bearish or bullish. The Department of Agriculture takes great precautions to avoid leaks of information and to see that all traders have equal access to Department releases. This is done to see that all traders have a fair chance at profits in the commodity markets and serves to bring the real markets closer to the theoretically perfect market.

The random walk market is random in the short term as price reacts up and down to essentially nonfundamental purchases and sales, characterized by small sales just sufficient to set a new price. It is also random in the medium term as incoming news is random and the new price level is quickly fitted to the new information. Only in the long run is any bias expected as commodity prices in general inflate in value along with other prices in the economy. Long-term bias spreads across a period longer than the life-span of any contract and will not thus affect the random nature of the market. If corn prices are to rise, the contract for corn delivery will start at a higher price in a perfect market.

THE THEORY AND THE REALITY

The model fits the short- and long-term reality of actual markets fairly well, sometimes extremely well. In the medium term of several weeks or months, however, statisticians have found distinct trends. Some markets such as those for cocoa, sugar, eggs, wool, cattle, broilers, potatoes, and flaxseed show distinct trends, sometimes very large in size and generally explosive once they start. This indicates to the market student that these markets are not fully discounting information, either because the information is not generally and equally distributed or because lack of volume inhibits the orderly execution of positions.

Were the actual markets perfect, there would be no possibility of improving profit from technical study of past price performance. The next price would bear absolutely no relation to the last price or any number of past prices. The trader would do as well to buy and sell at random as according to any schedule. Because the markets are not perfect, trends exist and the speculator takes some of his profit by identifying these trends in time to go along with them. If he is right in his analysis, his order will help push a trending price to its final goal, and probably a little past, to being back again. This trading has the effect of eliminating the trend by simply ending it—the price more rapidly reaches its destination and the market more fully approximates the random walk. The more trading done on a market, and the more bidding into price changes, the more the market will approach the theoretically perfect market.

IMPLICATIONS OF RANDOM WALK

If market price did not walk randomly, there would be no need of futures markets and the unique process of discounting they provide. If agricultural prices could be controlled, or even accurately forecast by any single system, large farmers and processors would do so and be able to adequately control their yearly budgeting with cash forward contracts and other commercial devices that are commonly used in all markets in this country. Because commodity markets *do* walk randomly, no computer has yet been programmed that can take over the function of an open auction by a large number of traders.

Random walk theory allows prediction techniques to be viewed as exceptions to a rule rather than as distinct entities that exist without relation to anything else. Viewing technical study as the measurement of flaws in the perfect market gives the trader some method of measuring the worth of his prediction methods, and some measure of the confidence he ought to put in them. Such an approach is rather negative but perhaps it is better to be a flaw in a theory than to be in no theory at all. Especially if money is being bet on it.

The theory of random walk allows improvement on random buying and selling only if one of the following conditions are met. Under these conditions, the market is still considered to walk randomly, although with flaws which hold out a speculative advantage to one side of the market or the other. Such a view seems to most accurately describe actual markets.

1. The entire demand and supply bal-

ance which makes up the current market can be biased. This can happen due to conditions in the cash market such as the glut immediately at harvest, or because of marketing peculiarities such as the seasonal lifting of hedges or repeating unknowable factors. This would be a flaw in market discounting and would be found in a study of seasonal behavior for the commodity and each of its contracts. This is one of the most promising predictive avenues.

2. A time lag can exist in the discounting of information. Experienced traders are normally quite humble about their own opinions and a trader who has learned of bullish news will often buy a few contracts and wait for market price to confirm his opinion before buying more. Rather than jogging neatly to the next resting area, market price may trend toward it. Several technical devices attempt to define and exploit such trends and exploit them while profit possibilities still exist. Obviously, the first trader to find the trend will make the most money.

3. Market price may react randomly at a price set by supply and demand which is fully discounted but which is near a nonrandom price factor such as the government loan rate which provides a floor under a price, or the price at which the CCC is offering large stockpiles of the commodity. In such a case the price has an equal chance of going up or down but can go *further* in one direction than the other.

4. Fundamental price factors may be found which have not been fully discounted because of their obscurity. The trader has found an "angle" all his own which he can exploit until it becomes common knowledge. This is the case of the reader of *Eastern European Review* and the Russian sunflower seed oil, and is extremely risky. Fundamental prediction of price movement supposes that a trader can outjudge his competition.

5. Some market characteristics can be the result of self-fulfilling prophecy. A collection of stop-loss orders at a point gauged significant by chart traders may actually cause the price to spurt when it hits the clustered stop orders.

6. The trader can manage his positions so that he wins more on his correct guesses than he loses when he is wrong. Of the six, this possibility presents the most theoretically sound procedure and the only one which is not subject to discounting. To win more than he loses on a 50-50 chance, the trader must either:

a) win more on winning positions than he loses on losing positions
b) win on more contracts when he wins than he loses on when he loses
c) choose his risks through some combination of the previous five conditions.

The next four chapters will explore each of these six possibilities as an aid toward the development of a trading program which can coexist with the random walk.

SOURCES FOR FURTHER STUDY

The majority of theoretical work on random walk and serial correlation relating to futures markets has been published by the Stanford Food Institute and can be had by ordering the appropriate reprint through a bookstore. Orders should be made to Stanford University

Press, Stanford, California and cost $1 apiece.

Much of this data is too theoretically inclined to be of pragmatic use to the trader of commodities and the various authors universally warn against direct application of their conclusions, although their methods and conclusions may aid a trader in forming his own. Some background in economics and statistics is required, but the authors take care to place their contributions in context with the body of work that exists and an inexperienced reader can interpret their papers with some patience.

As a practical matter, study of academic research is of little value, and the following are offered only for the rare trader who is interested in the academics behind his trading practices. Only the most pertinent articles are listed here. Under the name of any of the people below, the researcher will find many more articles from which to choose. The list is, of course, not intended to be exhaustive.

Sidney Alexander (M.I.T.), *Trends or Random Walk I and II* (two volumes)

Paul Cootner, *Comments on the Variation of Certain Speculative Prices; Preface: Origins and Justification of the Random Walk Theory; Refinement and Empirical Testing of the Random Walk Theory; The Random Walk Hypothesis Reexamined; Speculation and the Stability of Futures Markets.*

Roger Gray, *Seasonal Pattern of Wheat Futures Under Loan. The Search for a Risk Premium*

Hendrick Houthaker (Harvard), *Systematic and Random Elements in Short-Term Price Movements; Can Speculators Forecast Prices?*

Arnold Larson (University of Hawaii), *Price Prediction on the Eggs Futures Market; Measurement of a Random Process in Futures Prices*

Charles Rockwell (Yale), *Backwardation, Forecasting and Returns to Speculators*

Seymour Schmidt (Cornell), *A Test of Serial Independence in Soybean Futures; A New Look at Random Walk*

Holbrook Working (Stanford), *New Concepts Concerning Futures Markets and Prices* (Many articles resulting from a long career as an academic student of the futures markets)

Part three
A TRADING PROGRAM

12

THE ART OF
PRICE FORECASTING

Market forecasting systems are divided into fundamental and technical studies. Fundamental forecasting relies on study of the demand and supply elements—the "fundamentals"—that make up market price in the attempt to find changing aspects which have not yet been found and discounted by the market at large. Technical study attempts to find trends in the marketplace itself, rather than in the basic demand and supply for the commodity. Although some traders claim to rely solely on one or the other of the two major types of systems, the best forecast probably includes elements of both, closely checked against the seasonal pattern of what usually happens, with close management of the position.

FUNDAMENTAL FORECASTING

Two basic types of information are found in the study of fundamental price factors. The trader can determine the possible *range* in which the commodity must trade, largely through the study of natural and government-imposed floors and ceilings to price. The trader can also attempt to find elements of supply and demand which are likely to *change* in the future. In so doing, he is attempting to scoop his competitors by being among the first to discount news which will not

be announced until some future date.

How far can price go without running into major flak from competing products or government policy? What factors have determined the present price and how stable are they? What will be the effect of the most likely possible change? If the trader can answer any of these questions he has a good fundamental basis for "guesstimating" prices in the near future. The number of factors which determine the price of any commodity are nearly infinite but often less than a half-dozen are in any degree transient enough to be important. Factors which *never* change, never change prices and can be ignored. The number of certified grain storage elevators in the Chicago area will have a direct price effect in the delivery month, but it does not fluctuate from year to year. (See Chapter 10 for data significant to fundamental price forecasting.)

PRICE RANGES

Floors and ceilings to the cash price of a commodity have already been discussed and must be known for each commodity the speculator may wish to trade. With corn priced at $1 a bushel and CCC wheat offered at $1.47, a set of price parameters exists for wheat. Near-month wheat selling at $1.40 has an exactly equal chance of going up or down in price, but it is going to begin running into heavy flak at $1.47 as large CCC held stockpiles enter the market. If the wheat price exercises its option to fall, it can fall all the way to about $1.15 before it enters a large new demand curve as cattlemen and hog farmers start making purchases to feed their animals. In the absence of other information, wheat is a better sale than purchase in such a situation. The trader has no idea in which direction the price is going to change, but he knows it can climb no more than about 7 cents. It can drop 25 cents if the extreme thing happens. In commodities, extreme things happen all the time.

The first rule of fundamental forecasting is *choose your risks* so that potential profit is several times potential loss. *Never sell a price that is near its natural or government-imposed floor. Never buy a price that is near its ceiling.*

As a general rule, the trader will not enter a position unless the potential profit is at least three times the *known* loss. In the above case, 7 cents is far too much money to lose with a short position in a climbing market, and the trader would limit this loss through the placement of a stop loss at a price above his sale price, to take him out of the market if the price goes against him.

FORECASTING THE NEWS

In attempting to find fundamental factors which are on the verge of changing, the trader is essentially trying to scoop his competition by predicting news before it becomes news. He is attempting to find an *angle* that will produce a position prior to the jog in price which will occur when the news

occurs and becomes known. Like the trader who bought soybean oil to fill the world market when the Russians ran out of sunflower oil to sell, or the trader who discovered the freezes in the Florida orange belt, the fundamentalist who attempts to forecast the news runs into the risk that other fundamentalists are doing the same thing, and that the market has already discounted their scoop, long before the news occurs—if it occurs at all.

TECHNICAL FORECASTING

Technical forecasting, in commodities as in stocks, relies on the study of the marketplace itself, rather than the factors that weigh on the commodity that is being traded on the market. The underlying assumption is that fundamental factors are essentially unpredictable and that they are of less significance than the interaction of traders themselves. It makes no difference whether price drops due to an altered supply and demand curve, the seasonal lifting of long hedges, or if some trader closed his position to use the money for other purposes. The price will drop in any event and it is the drop which is significant to the trader. The best measure of price, according to technical traders, can be found by the study of charts showing past price behavior. If the price has shown difficulty passing a certain level, nobody wants to buy or sell past that level. *Why* doesn't matter.

If price moved in neat jogs as predicted by the random walk model, technical trading would consist of a mere set of mechanical rules. Buy any price above the resting area represented by random minor fluctuation with the sure knowledge that price is speeding to a new level, and hold the position until the price drops, reversing its trend. Sell any price that is hit below the resting area and hold the short position until the price stops sinking. Such rules would serve to speed the price to its new level, making the unpredictable jogs extremely abrupt and short-lived. The context would be one of getting on the price movement as early as possible through the use of resting stop orders, without setting the stop order so close that it is tripped by insignificant fluctuation in the resting market. Traders who set their stops too far from the resting area would find their orders unfillable or filled at a price far away from their stop as no trading took place during the rapid spurt to the new level. (See Fig. 163 below.)

It is easily established that random walk is not a perfect description of the reality found on commodity markets, and the prediction has to be somewhat more complicated than a mechanical buy and sell rule. The existence of trends in the real markets requires some technical method of determining when a trend is about to begin and when it is about to end. Most technical tools attempt to define these two functions.

"A price at rest tends to stay at rest. A price in motion tends to stay in motion" are the essential tenets of the

FIGURE 163
RANDOM WALK WITH BUY–SELL SIGNALS

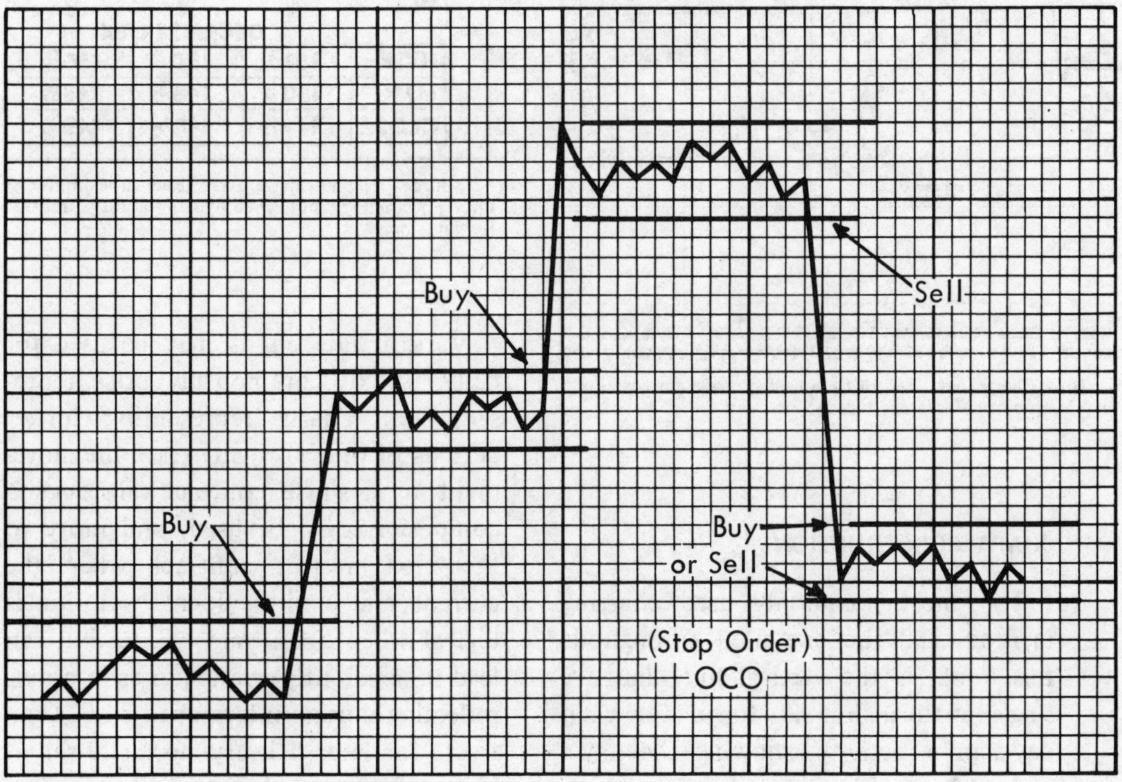

Were random walk an accurate description of real markets, buying any rise and selling any dip beyond a level of significance would yield effortless profits.

chart trader. A price at rest exhibits an establishable floor or ceiling for itself which is merely the graphic presentation of demand and supply conditions too complex to be understood. When the price breaks through its resting channel, a buy or sell signal is received. A price that is trending establishes a similar floor or ceiling for its trend. When the floor or ceiling is ruptured, the trend can be expected to end. (See Fig. 164 below.)

A second horizontal line crosses the first, indicating the close for the day. Vertical line charts have the advantage over other charts of being commonly used, so that charts from different sources may be compared. They are also easily maintained on a daily basis. Normally price is shown on the vertical axis of the chart, and the dates of trading on the horizontal. (See Fig. 165 below.)

FIGURE 164
CHART FORMATIONS

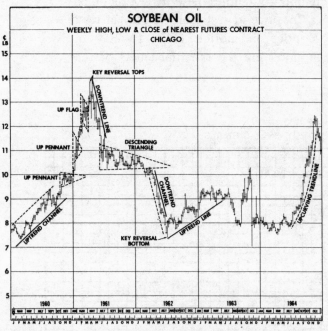

Source: "How Charts Are Used in Commodity Price Forecasting," published by Commodity Research Bureau, Inc.

FIGURE 165
VERTICAL LINE CHART

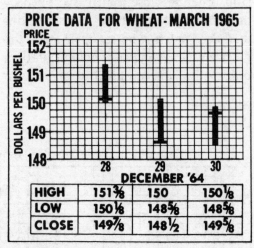

Source: "How Charts Are Used in Commodity Price Forecasting," published by Commodity Research Bureau, Inc.

CHART CONSTRUCTION

The most commonly used charting method, and the one used throughout this book, is the vertical line chart. A single vertical line is drawn for each day's price activity, showing the day's high and low prices connected by a line.

Vertical line charts may be used for daily, weekly, or monthly price representation. Charts representing longer periods of time normally trace the movement of a single contract (although a composite could be used) and move to the next nearest contract when the current one expires. Such a solution is logical when a contract expires but can lead to apparently erratic jumps in prices, reflecting normal intermonth basis. Contracts for later delivery normally sell at higher prices and this job will be picked up by the continuation method, showing an apparently very active trading session which did not in fact exist. Such jumps can be especially large when the next nearest contract is for delivery of the new crop year, which sells at prices not directly related to the old contract prices. (See Fig. 166 below.)

FIGURE 166
CONTINUATION CHART

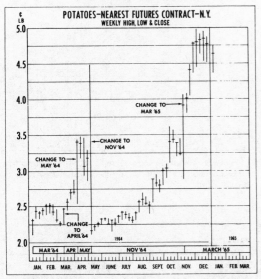

Source: "How Charts Are Used in Commodity Price Forecasting," published by Commodity Research Bureau, Inc.

The above chart shows the apparently large price jumps which occur as the old contract expired and the new contract was picked up. The change to November 1964, is a new crop year which sells at a much lower price than did the expiring old crop contract. At crossover, old contract potatoes sold as high as 4.5 cents per pound in the final days, while the new contract started out at just above 2 cents. The apparent large jump in prices must be ignored by the chart trader.

READING CHART FORMATIONS

Charts exhibit certain basic patterns which repeat themselves. Most of these patterns are consistent with a basic understanding of market discounting and if a pattern can be shown to occur before a major price move with any consistency, it can be used for prediction. Chart traders maintain that such consistency does occur and have formulated a number of patterns which are used in chart trading.

CHANNELS

A market which is trending presents profit for any trader who goes with the trend before it comes to its end at the next resting area. Trend lines are commonly drawn to show the channel in which such trending prices have traded. A line is drawn under uptrending prices connecting the lowest prices in the trend. Prices may fluctuate within the channel for weeks without significance to the chart trader so long as they continue higher. Once the line under the uptrend has been broken, prices are considered to be weakening, unable to maintain their climb. For downward trending prices, a line is drawn connecting the high points in the market channel. When the line above a downtrending channel is broken, the price is considered to be firming, no longer able to continue its drop. Sidewise trending prices commonly have a line drawn above and below the highest and lowest prices delineating the sidewise channel and similar significance is given to a breakthrough of either trendline. Here, a second dotted line has been drawn above the uptrend and below the downtrend to emphasize the channel. (See Fig. 168.)

SUPPORT AND RESISTANCE LEVELS

Pressure levels are denoted by chartists by a number of commonly described formations. A pressure level is defined as a level which the price has a hard time penetrating. It may enter this area several times but fail to penetrate it and move onward. The simplest such formation is the *double top* or *double bottom*. In the cocoa chart for 1964, price climbed to 28.80 cents before running out of steam and descending. When it climbed to the 28.80 cent level a second time and failed to penetrate it, the sign was given that long pressure was simply not sufficient to support higher prices. Price could

only trend sidewise or drop and a short sale was indicated. (See Fig. 167 below.)

FIGURE 167
DOUBLE TOP FORMATION

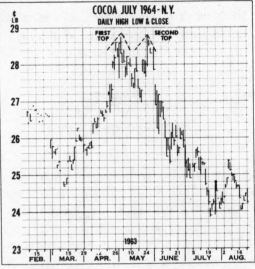

Source: "How Charts Are Used in Commodity Price Forecasting," published by Commodity Research Bureau, Inc.

FIGURE 168
TRENDLINES AND CHANNELS

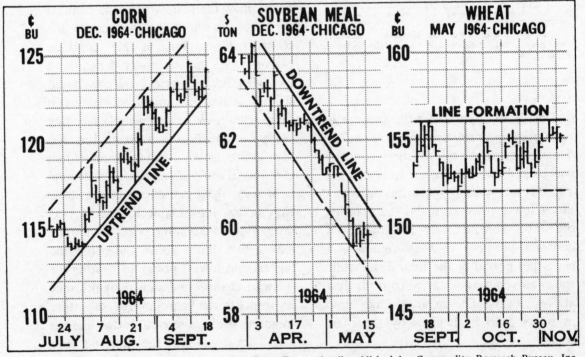

Source: "How Charts Are Used in Commodity Price Forecasting," published by Commodity Research Bureau, Inc.

The price of 28.80 cents in 1964 cocoa was found to be a resistance area preventing further price advances. The same formation can be found at the bottom of price drops, indicating a long position is in order. Double bottoms form at price levels termed *support areas.*

A common variation on price action in a support or resistance level is the *head and shoulders formation.* A head and shoulders formation is found when price ends a trend with a mild reaction before making a second attempt at furtherance of the trend. This second attempt also fails as does a third, giving the final formation of a left shoulder, head, and right shoulder. The significant chart signal in a head and shoulders formation is formed by a line, called the "neckline" joining three lowest points of the formation. When the neckline is broken, a major trend reversal is foreseen, commonly believed to be at least as long as the distance from the lowest point in the formation to the top of the head. (See Fig. 169 below.)

An inverse head and shoulders can be formed at the bottom of a downtrend

and is read in the same manner. Heads and shoulders, like double tops and bottoms, are simply the graphic representation of a price at the end of its trending. When the key sign is read, the trader is given notice that the current trend is over and can act accordingly.

RESTING AREAS

A market at rest is indicated by a number of chart formations. Major among these are *pennants* and *triangles.* (See Fig. 170 below.) When a price slows to a stop, it will often go through a period of discounting represented on a chart by an ever narrowing range of fluctuation as the day's trading ranges narrow and opinion concensus is more tightly formed. The pictorial result is a triangle with a wider range of prices slowly narrowing off toward the tip of the formation. As with a trendline, a line is drawn connecting the highest prices in the formation. A second line connects the lowest prices. When either of these lines is broken, new information is read to have entered the market, upsetting the discounting which was taking place

FIGURE 169
HEAD AND SHOULDERS FORMATION

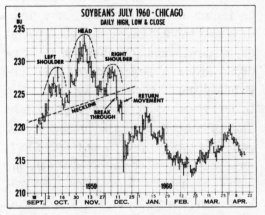

Source: "How Charts Are Used in Commodity Price Forecasting," published by Commodity Research Bureau, Inc.

FIGURE 170
TRIANGLES AND PENNANTS FORMATION

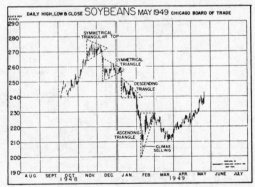

Source: "How Charts Are Used in Commodity Price Forecasting," published by Commodity Research Bureau, Inc.

and setting the price for a change. A breakout of the upper line, of course, indicates a new uptrend.

OTHER CHART FORMATIONS

The list of possible chart formations is nearly endless, seemingly limited only by the imagination of the people who use them. Spires, diamonds, bells, cornucopias, wedges, and so forth, are all found by different traders and all indicate information in a manner similar to the ones explained here. Some technical information is taken from chart performances which are not actually formations, but single events, often transpiring in a single trading session. *Gaps, islands,* and *reversals* are figures considered important by chart traders which often occur in a single day. (See Fig. 171 below.)

A session which trades above both the previous trading range and the one to follow is called an *island.* It takes its name from the fact that on a chart, such a day's trading is isolated from other trading, with a gap below it. A *gap* is formed any time no trading takes place at a price level and these can be significant as an indication of market frenzy. In the case of an *island,* the price jumped so fast as to leave ground uncovered. The resultant price was unsustained by trading to follow and can often indicate a major reversal. *Reversals* are often characterized by active trading and a wide range for the day's prices, indicated by a comparatively long vertical bar. Such lines at the end of a long trend are read as indication of a possible reversal of the trend. If they are confirmed by trading in the days to follow, a position is indicated for the coming trend. *Gaps* are normally considered to fall into one of three categories: (1) The common gap, which occurs when no trading takes place at a certain price between two days. These are normally filled in by subsequent trading. (2) The breakaway or runaway gap, which is formed as prices move rapidly out of resting or trending area; and (3) The exhaustion gap, which produces an island and marks the reversal of a trend.

Often more than one formation can be found in a chart at the same time, such as a triangle inside a larger uptrend or a downtrend channel which may occur inside a larger, longer lived uptrend channel. Generally speaking, the trader gives weight to the formation that suits his purposes according to the period of time he prefers to trade. Short-term trading will be more strongly affected by smaller formations than will long-term trading. For the trader who wishes to hold an open position for several months or the life of the con-

FIGURE 171
GAP FORMATION

Source: "How Charts Are Used in Commodity Price Forecasting," published by Commodity Research Bureau, Inc.

tract, smaller formations which occur along the way can be disregarded so long as they don't indicate a major change in the long-term direction of price.

Different commodities have different chart characteristics and the technical trader can narrow the field of formations according to the commodity he is watching. Heads and shoulders are common and considered important in cotton trading, while the most common figurations in wheat are usually trendlines and triangles. Often a technical trader who believes he has found a significant formation in a particular contract will check the charts of other options for the same commodity and look for confirmation of his findings. The interrelationship between option months of a com-

modity often carries over to the formations which appear in each of their charts, particularly between options for months close to each other on the calendar.

In the reading of any chart formation, it is important that the underlying explanation of what is happening is held in mind. Random walk, trending, discounting and the floors and ceilings for each commodity all help in the interpretation of charts and help prevent some of the more spurious reasoning that can come from technical study. Finding chart formations in time to profit from their predictions is easier, if the trader knows what to look for. (See Fig. 172, p. 248.)

FIGURE 172. FOUR CHARTS WITH FORMATIONS

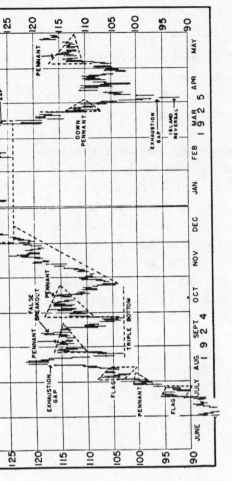

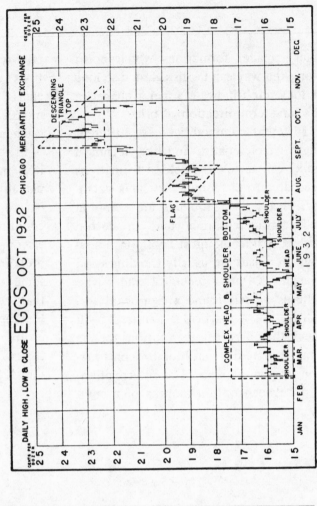

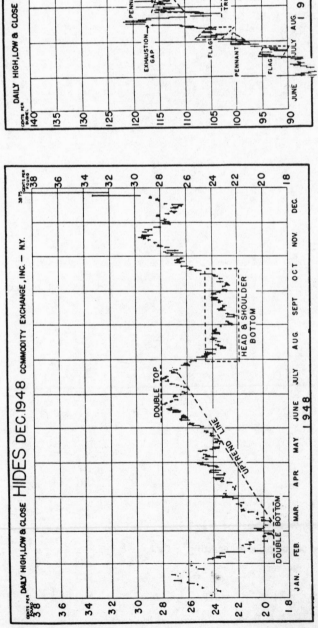

Source: "How Charts Are Used in Commodity Price Forecasting," published by Commodity Research Bureau, Inc.

MOVING AVERAGES

Technical devices universally attempt to measure impending change. What is done graphically through the study of graph formations can also be undertaken mathematically through the computation of moving averages. The trader can take any number of days for his average and plot a second line along with the vertical bar chart, chart of closing prices, or chart of daily midranges. The result will be a line representing each day's activity joined by a second line indicating a weighted average. When the average crosses daily activity, price movement is found to have substantially changed its general trend.

A moving average is made by adding together the daily closing or midrange prices for a number of days and dividing by the number of days used, to produce an average for the set. Each day, the average is refigured by dropping the first day in the series and adding a new day on the end. The new average is then plotted along with the daily information. As technical traders are interested in trends, sidewise, uptrending or downtrending, a moving average clearly shows when a trend has changed.

The number of days used in the average is arbitrary. Longer averages will require more substantial price changes to affect the moving average and will help filter out meaningless short-lived price changes. They will also, of course, take longer to alert the trader to new trends in the market and limit his trading to longer range movements. Variations of moving average sometimes overlay a 3-day average and a 10-day to clarify trends which run counter to the longer term price movement. When the shorter average pierces the longer, a change in market trend has been found. (See Fig. 173 below.)

FIGURE 173
MOVING AVERAGES

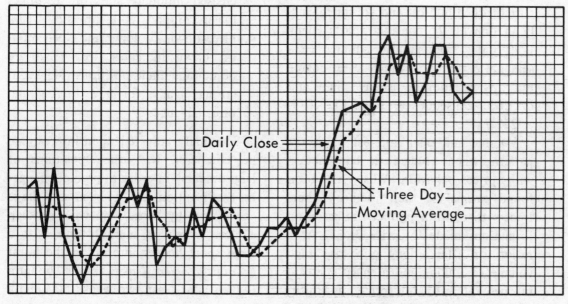

VOLUME AND OPEN INTEREST
AS PREDICTIVE DEVICES

Volume and open interest refer to the trading activity for the day, and the number of open contracts which exist. These two figures are reported daily along with market prices in most newspapers and reporting services and used by technical traders primarily as a backup to confirm predictions and interpretations of market price behavior. Used alone, they are usually considered of little predictive value. (See Fig. 174 opposite.)

Open interest normally builds over the life of a contract before tapering off at expiration and exhibits a seasonal pattern which must be consulted before raw data can be interpreted. It is not enough to know the total open interest on a given date; the trader must also know the seasonal pattern and what is normal for that date. He is interested in whether open interest is unusually high rather than in its absolute net value. Any good chart service will provide the seasonal open interest pattern along with current open interest and volume, usually in one of the contract charts giving price data. Volume also adheres to a seasonal pattern to a much lesser degree but this variation is usually slight and of little consequence. (See Fig. 175, p. 252.)

Volume and open interest exhibit a pattern when studied in conjunction with price behavior. What has been found normal is then used by chart traders to confirm predictions based on formations made by price alone. At a major top after a long price rise, high volume of trading and a sharp decrease in open interest is interpreted as confir-

mation of the end of the trend. Positions are being closed in a hurry. At a major bottom, found through chart analysis, a sharp decrease in open interest is considered confirmation of the chart signal. Conversely, a large increase in open interest under heavy trading is considered confirmation of a new move about to get under way. When a chart formation breakout has been found, the trader expects a new trend and will look at volume and open interest for confirmation.

Traders have formed four rules regarding volume and open interest:

1. Price is up—Volume and open interest up indicates longs are in control raising price by intensive bidding for contracts. Price is strong.
2. Price is up—Volume and open interest down indicates that the primary source of buying pressure is shorts' covering their positions with purchases. Price is weak.
3. Price down—Volume and open interest up means shorts are in control of the market coming into it in increased numbers and forcing prices lower. Market is technically weak.
4. Price down—Volume and open interest down indicates tired longs are liquidating their positions. Market is strong, ready for new buying and price advance.

Seasonally adjusted open interest can be compared with the "positions of large traders" in order to predict changes in the positions of hedgers and large speculators by those who wish to keep a close watch on market tone. With a large short hedger interest in the latest *Commitment of Large Traders* bulletin (which is at least two weeks old) and a

FIGURE 174

Month-End Open Interest of All Wheat Futures Contracts at the Chicago Board of Trade
In Millions of Bushels

Year	Jan.	Feb.	Mar.	April	May	June	July	Aug.	Sept.	Oct.	Nov.	Dec.	Chicago[2]	Minneapolis[3]	Kansas City[4]
1959	90.9	87.5	85.8	72.5	62.4	78.7	112.2	116.4	114.5	101.8	88.1	65.2	76.8	5.4	11.4
1960	62.4	50.5	49.6	55.7	43.7	61.9	108.6	114.6	101.1	82.8	72.7	67.7	79.2	6.4	13.0
1961	63.1	71.2	60.2	54.6	61.5	91.5	147.1	182.1	165.3	154.6	147.7	139.5	139.9	7.1	22.5
1962	123.5	118.1	122.1	125.9	115.3	137.1	164.7	154.8	151.8	152.0	142.5	128.5	120.0	5.5	23.9
1963	112.3	92.7	81.0	87.5	78.6	93.4	123.9	130.1	113.5	124.2	121.4	110.9	101.8	5.1	21.1
1964	92.5	88.1	72.5	73.0	67.4	103.7	171.6	172.2	143.0	127.2	110.4	92.8	97.6	4.2	19.1
1965	79.2	74.4	59.4	48.6	38.7	53.1	92.1	135.0	138.9	133.3	150.6	150.3	123.1	7.6	28.9
1966	144.6	118.5	94.5	88.9	88.1	142.3	176.6	176.7	167.5	165.7	174.0	170.9	164.9	9.2	37.2
1967	138.7	150.7	171.3	155.5	161.6	169.5	222.1	243.8	240.2	232.2	213.8	210.4	179.2	9.4	50.4
1968	173.9	143.0	121.9	103.1	110.7	135.1	189.5	202.9	218.7	227.4	215.7	208.9	167.2	9.8	36.4
1969	182.9	144.0	119.6	104.6	97.3	95.1	118.0	121.6	122.1	114.5	101.6	99.0	96.4	6.7	28.6
1970	91.7	93.5	81.2	76.9	66.5	69.5	93.1	90.4	96.8	98.0	88.6	85.5			
1971[5]	86.0	74.6	32.1	61.3	58.7	73.1	80.6	81.1	81.6	79.6	83.9	66.3			
1972[5]	61.7	66.2													

1 Fiscal year beginning July. 2 Chicago Board of Trade. 3 Minneapolis Grain Exchange. 4 Kansas City Board of Trade. 5 Preliminary. *Source: Commodity Exchange Authority, U.S.D.A.*

Volume of Trading in All Potato Futures[1], on N.Y. Mercantile Exchange   In Carlots (50,000 Pounds Per Car)

Year	Jan.	Feb.	Mar.	Apr.	May	June	July	Aug.	Sept.	Oct.	Nov.	Dec.	Total
1959	7,339	8,209	16,365	24,122	17,954	3,765	3,087	4,375	9,737	17,236	24,093	24,180	160,462
1960	28,666	34,080	69,144	49,410	19,236	1,378	2,123	6,430	10,071	9,158	11,470	14,549	255,715
1961	17,300	29,477	41,481	21,428	13,934	11,490	8,754	9,905	12,388	11,970	14,559	16,703	209,389
1962	17,640	27,677	42,149	41,177	26,443	5,324	7,610	7,893	6,925	12,619	9,007	7,423	211,887
1963	21,527	23,304	32,010	13,192	8,505	2,041	3,882	3,237	2,633	3,951	3,494	2,461	120,237
1964	14,189	23,351	35,909	61,388	20,065	4,120	7,641	16,123	33,584	56,622	51,360	68,674	393,026
1965	75,138	74,957	89,077	81,200	30,965	17,180	15,901	24,141	33,526	39,037	19,522	30,013	530,657
1966	37,433	18,539	84,975	77,978	24,733	7,172	27,215	56,049	62,069	72,982	62,211	58,982	590,338
1967	70,860	74,294	86,399	71,099	42,682	17,618	16,596	19,191	41,488	53,115	24,667	28,817	546,826
1968	29,732	40,956	34,931	81,588	34,850	5,542	10,611	30,279	52,500	41,665	45,986	46,208	454,848
1969	39,084	50,988	67,796	65,984	23,296	4,013	7,270	9,201	13,340	33,821	19,288	31,494	365,575
1970	45,995	36,815	58,995	52,471	30,764	5,303	8,493	15,739	18,703	24,418	12,560	16,437	326,693
1971	19,332	17,065	30,106	28,662	12,761	1,418	3,571	5,355	7,060	10,046	7,567	8,426	151,369
1972	22,435	25,945											

1 Maine grown. *Source: Commodity Exchange Authority, U.S.D.A.*

Note: Original data from Commodity Research Bureau, Inc.

decrease in open interest resulting in higher prices, the trader is left with the hypothesis that hedgers are lifting their hedges, leaving the market to speculators. For confirmation of chart formations, seasonal adjustment can be forgotten on a day-to-day basis as the trader is interested in major changes on a single day. Seasonal adjustment cannot be ignored in the look at market tone.

CHART SERVICES

A number of chart services are available to the chart trader, of which the Commodity Research Bureau is by far the most prestigious. The Commodity Research Bureau prepares 150 different charts a week covering daily fluctuation, volume and open interest, cash price, London futures, commodity indices,

FIGURE 175

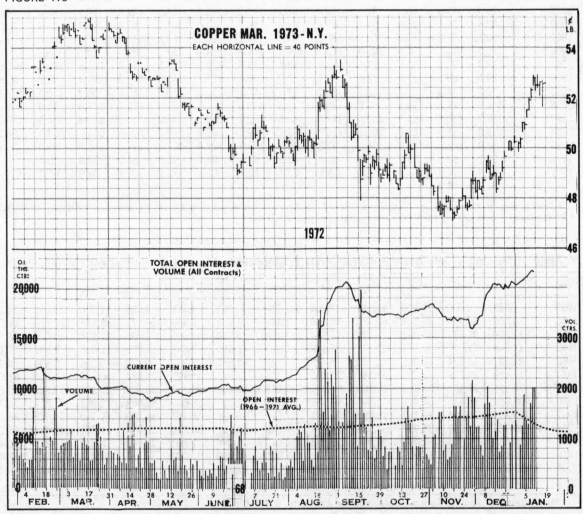

Source: Commodity Research Bureau, Inc.

weekly basis charts, long-term trends, along with interpretation of the market by technical traders on their staff. Charts are contained in a single booklet airmailed on Fridays. Rates for the CRB reports run $65 for three months, to $200 for the year (subject to change). Inquire at Commodity Research Bureau, Inc., One Liberty Plaza, New York, New York 10006.

Other services are available ranging across all variations of forecasting skills and at a variety of prices. For the most current listings and an appraisal, see your broker.

LIMITS OF TECHNICAL FORECASTING

Even the staunchest random walk theorists recognize the existence of trends in the actual commodity markets but considerable dispute is aroused between random walkers and market technicians on the subject of their readability. Both agree that trends can be found *post hoc* but the free walker presents a convincing case against their predictability. Anybody can look back at a string of heads on a coin flip, free walkers declare, and agree that a string has occurred that would have rewarded the man who bet on heads. The question is left open whether any technical system can predict when the string of heads is going to begin or end.

Debaters on both sides can find academic backup for their opinions. Arnold Larson (see Chapter 11) found a distinct pattern in price movement which runs counter to random walk. Prices, he found, will move 81 percent on the first day of their trend, followed by a reversal against the trend of 8 percent over

several days before the trend continues with a 27 percent move in the original direction over the next weeks, bringing the price to its new resting area. (81% − 8% + 27% = 100%.) He did not try the impossible—determining what the news meant, or even what the news was—but of the moves that occurred, up or down, 81 percent happened on the first day, followed by a reaction equal to 8 percent of the total move before the final 27 percent brought the price home. If a trend can be analyzed mathematically, some basis exists for chart formations. Sidney Alexander (again see Chapter 11) is another academician who has found meaningful nonrandom elements in commodity prices. He found, reasonably enough, that a price which had fallen or risen 5 percent would go further. The fewer prices which made it to 10 percent would go still further. It would be absurd to expect anything else, that the price would rise 10 percent and stop on a dime, and Mr. Alexander's findings are nothing more than would be dictated by common sense. They also indicate that a rule of buying prices which have risen 5 percent will return a positive profit. His results confirm the profitability of such "filters" for values ranging from 5 percent to 30 percent. Filters below 5 percent generated too many trades which returned for a loss. Filters above 30 percent generated too few trades to give meaningful results. Reasonable as Mr. Alexander's findings are, they would not be predicted in a coin flip chart and cannot exist in a random walk market.

The best way of looking at technical trading is as a "guesstimating" input to be added along with other information and guesses to form a final composite conclusion. If any one market device returned profits effortlessly, it would be used, returning profit until it was discounted away by the speculators it was rewarding. Both technicians and random walkers might agree on one thing—that is, how difficult it is to predict the future and make money on the commodity markets.

13

SEASONALS AND ODDS

Should you buy wheat in August? What are the chances of making money on a short sale in cocoa in March? Through the study of seasonals and odds, the trader can tell if an offered risk is a long shot or the house favorite.

Any unprocessed commodity that has ever been alive has a seasonal price pattern that can be calculated and graphed. Every plant has a time of harvest when the market is well supplied with the produce, and a time when the produce is scarce. Every animal eats feed that is expensive at one time of the year and cheap at another. Most animals have a natural mating season, a time of farrowing, and an optimum marketing time; to hold them longer costs space and feed and raises their marketing price. Any trader wishing to trade commodities must know when his commodity is cheap and when it is dear—he must know its seasonal price pattern.

Rarely buy a commodity after it has passed its seasonal highs. Rarely sell a commodity after it has passed its seasonal lows. The price of a commodity in a glutted market may well go up, but it is not going up far. Any commodity at its time of scarcity may drop in value on the cash markets, but it is not going to drop far, and it is large price moves that bring profit to the futures trader. Processed commodities may or may not reflect the seasonal pattern of the raw materials from which they are made. Soybean oil and meal have seasonal graphs which are derived from the cash seasonal of soybeans. There is current debate on whether plywood and lumber futures will reflect a seasonal price pattern. More trees are cut in the good weather months, but milling is carried on throughout the year at a fairly even rate. Commodities which have never been alive (or at least not recently) such as the metals and propane generally seem to exhibit no discernible seasonal pattern. Trading in nonseasonal commodities is rendered more difficult by the lack of crop information, leaving the trader to rely upon world market conditions, new discoveries, and so forth, which are difficult by nature to quantify and predict.

As commodities are traded on both cash and futures markets, all commodities that have a futures market will have two sets of seasonals. The cash seasonal gives the pattern of highs and lows for the commodity over the year, telling the trader exactly when his commodity is scarce on the cash markets, when it is abundant, and the rate of price change between these two times. All traders, whether they chart seasonal patterns or not, must have a fair idea of cash seasonal patterns in their heads to avoid selling a commodity at a time when it has almost no chance of going down in price. Each commodity that is traded on futures markets also has a set of seasonal patterns, one for each option. Cotton is traded *March, May, July, October,* and *December,* and each of these contracts' months exhibits seasonal characteristics of its own, reflecting storage costs from the time of harvest to the time of contract expiration, new crop months and other factors which distinguish one contract month from others for the same commodity.

To trade a commodity future, the trader must know where he stands in the commodity's seasonal year; he must know the cash seasonal pattern. To open the actual position on the market, he must choose a single option to purchase or sell. For this he needs a second seasonal, for the particular trading month he chooses. As price characteristics of the different delivery months are different, he must inspect the pattern individually for the option month he wishes to trade.

CHARTING CASH SEASONAL PRICES

Cash seasonals can be calculated quite easily by averaging the official monthly cash price data found in the *Commodity Yearbook* (New York: Commodity Research Bureau, Inc., annual) or in the USDA situation report for the particular commodity. Constructing a cash seasonal graph consists of simply averaging the monthly data for a number of years and plotting the results on graph paper. The cash prices listed for January from several years are added together and divided by the number of years in the sample to produce an average cash price for January for the commodity. This point is plotted on the graph. All February figures are added together and divided by the number of Februaries to produce an average figure for the month, which is then plotted next to January on the graph. Doing so for all 12 months will produce a chart of the cash seasonal pattern, indicating visually the average highs and lows for the commodity over a year.

Premade charts are readily available showing visually the cash behavior for various lengths of time, daily for the past year, weekly for the past 10 years, or monthly for the whole century, and these can be of use to the trader interested in how his commodity is shaping up against its normal position on the market. Charts can be made by applying to graph paper the seasonal pattern of the nearby futures contract which is similar in shape and information to a cash chart for a single year. Nearest future graphs are made by charting the price behavior of a contract until it expires and then immediately resuming with the next nearest contract until it expires, and so on. These charts can be useful in focusing on the current market and its place in history but must not be confused with a chart of *average* cash price seasonal patterns. The three different charts contain different information. A cash seasonal chart pictures the *average* seasonal pattern, rather than the pattern of individual years, months, weeks, or days in a string, as do the other two kinds of graphs. (See Figs. 176, 177, 178, 179 and 180, pp. 257-59.)

Basing the averages from which you make your cash seasonal graph on a large number of years (20 or so), helps

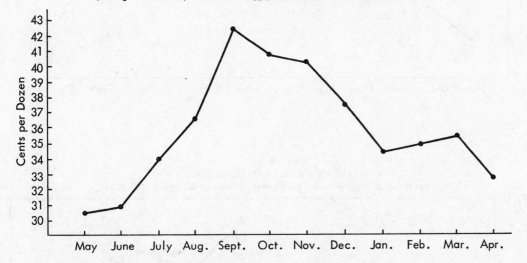

FIGURE 176
EGG CASH SEASONAL
(average wholesale price of shell eggs, extra large at Chicago, 1955-1967)

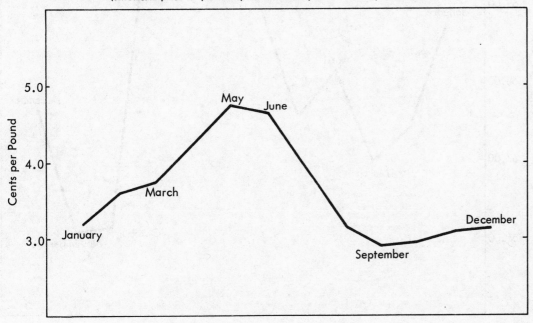

FIGURE 177
POTATO CASH SEASONAL
(wholesale price of potatoes, white eastern, at New York, 1961-1967)

FIGURE 178
CORN CASH SEASONAL
(monthly average price of No. 3 yellow corn at Chicago, January 1956–December 1967)

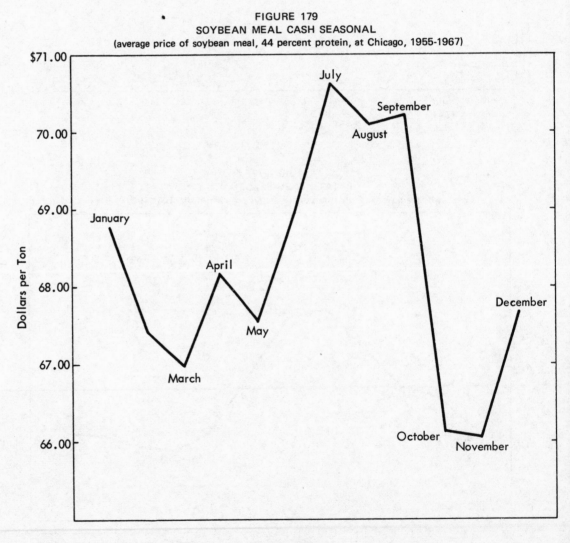

FIGURE 179
SOYBEAN MEAL CASH SEASONAL
(average price of soybean meal, 44 percent protein, at Chicago, 1955-1967)

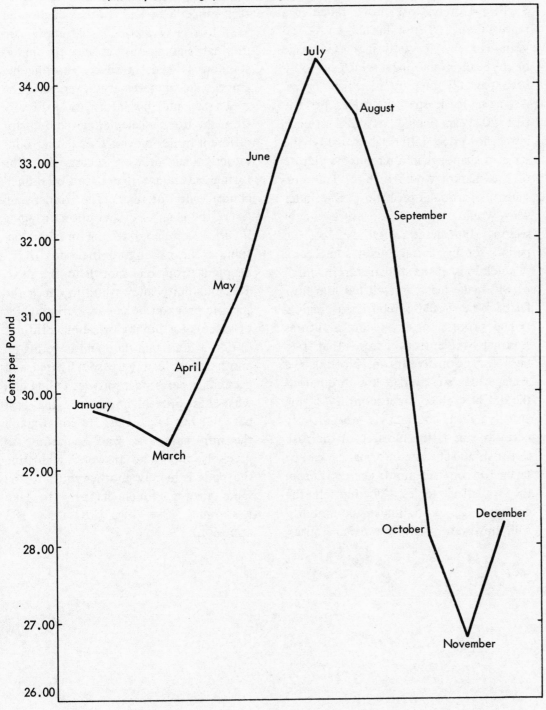

FIGURE 180
PORK BELLIES CASH SEASONAL
(monthly cash average price of Chicago pork bellies, 1949 through 1968)

correct for any distortion that might be introduced by an extremely aberrant year. Chartists will often go back in years as far as they have data which comes from a market similar to the modern conditions in today's market. Soybeans for instance, now traded in a range about $7 per bushel above 10 years ago, due to vastly increased usage of soybean oil and meal which has only been partially met by increased crops. Averaging cash soybean prices for the past 20 years would produce a chart lower in price (although roughly the same in shape) than a reasonable picture of the market would dictate. This presents no particular problem to the trader who would generate an average cash seasonal, but dictates that he choose the period for his average with some care. A quick look at the statistics from which he will make his chart will tell him how far back he should extend his averaging.

The process for producing a futures seasonal is identical, except that two lines are normally drawn, plotting the average high and average low throughout the life of each contract month. Plotting visually each contract is not strictly necessary, as is the plotting of the cash seasonal, and specific information can be taken for contract months directly from the statistical tables. Plotting all the contracts for a particular commodity will, however, produce a visual impression of what is going on and might well be undertaken for at least one commodity. When done, the trader will have one seasonal graph for cash and four or five futures graphs, one for each option.

Charting the information found in cash price lists and futures highs and lows lists gives a good visual impression of what is going on, but once the understanding is had, however, charting becomes an unnecessary exercise. The trader can pull his information directly from the lists by calculating the odds for different price moves. Calculating odds rather than drawing charts has the further advantage that it can be refined almost without end. The trader can figure the chances of an option dropping in price compared to the previous option, or he can figure the odds of its dropping from one month to the next. This flexibility allows him to check the specific program he is considering. Odds of success for buying or selling a futures option at a certain date and covering on another date can be easily figured and presents a percentage answer, telling him what has proven normal in the past between the two dates. He could graph the information as well and come to precisely the same answer. Calculating the odds is merely another route to the same answer, which happens to take less time. (See Figs. 181 and 182 opposite.)

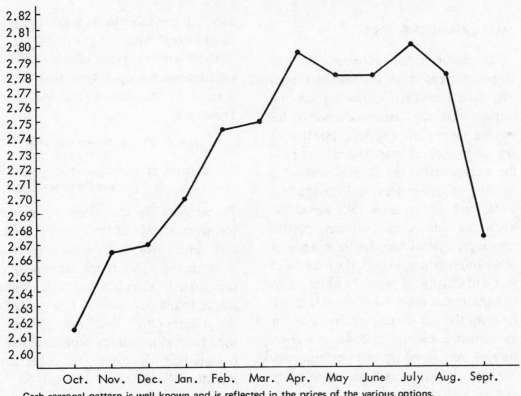

FIGURE 181
SOYBEANS CASH SEASONAL
(No. 1 yellow, average monthly cash price at Chicago 1960-1970)

Cash seasonal pattern is well known and is reflected in the prices of the various options.

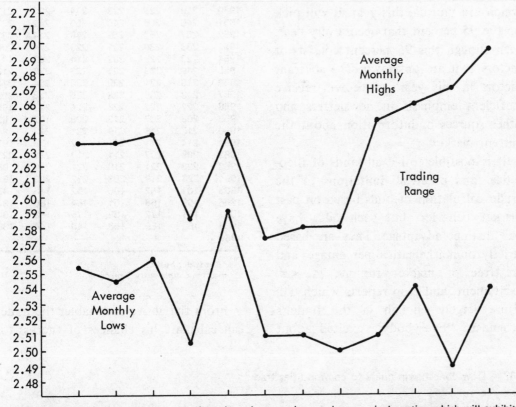

FIGURE 182
SEPTEMBER SOYBEAN CONTRACT AVERAGE HIGHS AND LOWS
(Chicago Board of Trade, 1961-62 to 1970-71)

The trader, of course, does not trade cash soybeans and must choose a single option which will exhibit a seasonal pattern of highs and lows all its own. The wide divergence between highs and lows in August and September reflects the fact that the September contract can be a new crop or old crop contract.

CALCULATING THE ODDS

The trader makes approximately 5 to 10 percent profit on his margin capital with each 1 cent rise or fall in grains, no matter what the historic chance of his making money on a specific position at any given time of year. The market pays the same whether the chances are for his winning or against him, and the prudent trader will simply never take a position when the odds based on past performance are against him. In the absence of other information, *expect the usual,* and you will *usually* be right. In order to do this the trader must know what is usual. He does this by calculating the odds for a contract going up or down at a given time of year based on past performance. The current market is made up of many factors both normal and unique to this particular year, as were the markets of each of the years in the past, and while a crude calculation of odds will leave out the 5 percent of market conditions which are unusual this year, it will pick up the 95 percent that occur every year, even though this 95 percent consists of factors that are unknown. The aberrant factors in this year's price will receive sufficient emphasis in newsletters and other sources of information about the current market.

It is possible to list all kinds of theoretical and practical limitations to the crude calculation of odds based on past market behavior, but such odds have one distinct advantage. They are based strictly on mathematical percentages and are free of market rumors, guesses, excitement, and crop reports which will figure largely enough in the trader's prognosis. "Everybody's excited about cocoa, the market looks good, the price should rise." What are the odds?

There are two types of odds and two subdivisions for each type that are important to the commodity speculator. These are:

CASH ODDS	General Cash Odds
	Specific Cash Odds
FUTURE ODDS	General Future Odds
	Specific Future Odds

To calculate the cash odds, the speculator needs a table of the monthly average cash prices for the commodity he is interested in. This is the same information used to calculate the cash seasonal graph, found in *Situation* reports and in the *Commodity Yearbook*. Wheat is used here, although the procedure would be identical, of course, for other commodities. (See Fig. 183 below.)

FIGURE 183
MONTHLY AVERAGE CASH PRICE OF WHEAT AT CHICAGO CASH MARKETS*

Year	Jan.	Feb.	March	April	May	June
1950	219	225	233	234	232	217
1951	246	255	245	250	242	237
1952	257	253	253	248	244	233
1953	233	230	231	226	221	205
1954	222	228	232	214	203	197
1955	240	233	227	223	225	212
1956	213	221	229	238	224	213
1957	243	235	228	225	218	209
1958	222	222	228	224	227	195
1959	203	207	213	208	192	192
1960	215	213	219	221	212	194
1961	214	211	211	192	188	193
1962	208	207	211	217	221	221
1963	222	221	219	221	219	198
1964	223	219	203	212	203	155
1965	161	162	160	152	148	147
1966	169	168	161	164	166	182
1967	171	172	182	175	169	164
1968	155	159	158	148	144	136
1969	—	—	—	—	—	—

*Cents per bushel.
Source: *Commodity Yearbook*.

From the above cash table, the trader can calculate his chances of success for any wheat position he is contemplating. From his broker, his newsletter, his own study of fundamentals, or technical behavior, or a combination of all of these sources, the trader might decide in April that the price of wheat is going to rise over the course of the summer. He is considering opening a long position in wheat sometime in April and wishes to know what the chances are historically of wheat going up in price between the time he buys, around April 1st, and the end of June, at which time he wants to close his position. Once he has his position in mind, he has a formalized question that can be answered mathematically with odds from the chart of cash prices.

Question: In the last 19 years how many times has Chicago cash wheat averaged a higher price during the month of June than it did during the month of April?

Answer: From the above table by comparing the April average cash price of wheat to the June average cash price of wheat we find that the answer is 3 years out of the total of 19 years.

General odds: 16 percent chance for an advance in cash prices. 84 percent chance for decline in cash prices.

Conclusion: General odds favor a decline in monthly average cash wheat prices in Chicago during April through June period.

CALCULATING SPECIFIC CASH ODDS

The price of wheat has historically dropped over the course of the summer. This answer is given from the figuring of the crude odds for cash wheat and is confirmed by a glance at the cash seasonal chart for wheat. Explanations are fairly easy to supply, once the conclusion is known; in this case, scarcity of wheat stored over the winter is being eased by new crop harvestings. On nearly any commodity at any time, explanations are easily found for conclusions that are already made. The trader can refine his question, by limiting his sample of years to those in the past which exhibited behavior similar to this year's. He knows the behavior of the early part of the current year (to April in this case, the current date) and he can simply eliminate from his figuring, those years which were markedly different from this year's known behavior. He is looking for years similar to the one he is trading, from which to calculate the specific odds of success for the position he is thinking about assuming. In essence, he is merely redrawing a new cash seasonal chart based solely on years similar to the known part of the current year.

Question: This year we know that cash wheat prices in Chicago averaged a higher price during the month of March than they did during the month of February. How many years out of the last 19 years in our table has a similar price pattern occurred?

Answer: From the above table we find the answer to be 9 years out of the total of 19 years. [1950, 1953, 1954, 1956, 1958, 1959, 1960, 1962, 1967]

Question: In these specific nine years then which demonstrated a market pattern similar to the market pattern being demonstrated this year, how many times has Chicago cash wheat averaged a higher price during the month of June than it did during the month of April? [Merely repeat same question used in calculation of general odds except now use only 9 years rather than total of 19 used for general odds.]

Answer: From the above table by comparing the April average cash price of wheat to the June average cash price of wheat in these specific nine years we find the answer to be one year out of the total of nine years.

Specific odds: 11 percent chance for advance in cash prices. 89 percent chance for decline in cash prices.

Conclusion: Specific odds favor a decline in the monthly average cash price of Chicago wheat during the April through June period.

This calculation simply tells the trader what has happened in years past that were similar to the year he is trading. The *why* of past year's price performance is known and can be found if the trader cares to research past issues of situation reports, newsletters and *The Wall Street Journal.* The *why* of the current year is not known. The trader can only *expect the normal.* While wheat prices dropped in 89 percent of years past which were similar to this year up to the present, wheat prices could rise over this particular summer. The calculation of specific odds merely tells the trader that rising prices over the coming year would be a statistical abnormality. Boardroom rumors, market letters, and technical information might suggest a long position in wheat over the summer, and they might be correct, but it is statistically a long shot. Long shots and "house bets" all pay the same, so there is simply no reason to play the long shots.

The successful commodity speculator will not take a futures position unless the general and specific cash odds are greater than 50 percent in his favor.

CALCULATING FUTURES CONTRACT ODDS

The trader knows that the cash wheat market traditionally drops in price over the summer and is warned by this normality against taking any long positions in wheat. The price might well rise, but chances are, any large new orders for wheat will wait until a little later in the summer when supplies are greater. If the price rises, it isn't going to rise far.

The trader, however, trades futures not cash wheat, and contract months later in the summer are already depressed in price, reflecting the normal late summer low prices for wheat. These contract prices have sold at lower prices throughout their trading lives in reflection of this normal cash seasonal pattern and the trader cannot make money by selling September's wheat option and necessarily watching it go down. It is already down and has been throughout its existence. The trader has no use for a prediction that the September future is selling for less than the July future. He *knows* this to be the case. He is interested in the odds of the September future dropping farther yet, or of having to adjust upward in price between now and expiration in September. To answer this question, he recalculates his odds for the September contract. His calculation is made in the same manner as that for cash odds, but now he is using different tables of information referring to the September contract rather than to the cash market.

The chances for a contract going up in price during a particular segment of the trading year are calculated from a "Monthly Highs Historical Table." The chances of a contract dropping in price between one date and another are figured from a "Monthly Lows Historical Table." Because contract prices often cover a considerable spread of prices and the use of stop order allows the trader to use the particular part of the spread he wishes to use (high for selling, low for buying) an average monthly price table has no meaning. The chance of an option entering new high-price territory must be figured from the highs chart; new low-ground odds must be figured independently from the historical lows chart. Both of these charts are found in Exchange *Annuals.* Each commodity exchange puts out a yearbook which gives the monthly historical highs and lows tables for each trading month for each commodity, along with a good deal of other information. These are had by writing the exchange on which the commodity is traded.

The tables used here are for the September wheat contract from the Chicago Board of Trade *Yearbook.* (See Figs. 184 and 185 opposite.) The trader wishes to know the chances of the September contract going up in price between April 1st and the end of June. Had he wanted to know the chances for the November contract, he would use the historical table for highs and lows of the November option. Had he wished to know the odds for July cotton going up in price between April 1st and June 30th, he would have looked up the historical tables for July cotton in the New York Cotton Exchange *Yearbook.*

FIGURE 184
SEPTEMBER WHEAT FUTURE: MONTHLY HIGHS
HISTORICAL TABLE*

Year	Jan.	Feb.	March	April	May	June
1950	193.4	196.0	209.6	218.0	223.4	222.4
1951	252.4	257.6	250.2	254.3	251.6	243.4
1952	251.7	249.0	248.7	245.5	239.3	237.0
1953	240.0	236.1	236.2	230.3	224.5	208.4
1954	209.4	218.0	223.5	222.0	203.4	199.1
1955	218.1	216.3	206.7	199.0	205.1	205.0
1956	202.3	205.7	212.3	219.2	214.7	212.7
1957	233.7	228.3	227.5	219.0	213.2	218.5
1958	192.5	199.0	201.2	194.7	191.1	189.0
1959	186.0	190.6	191.1	193.1	191.0	191.4
1960	187.4	189.2	187.4	187.4	188.6	188.2
1961	197.7	203.2	199.0	192.3	193.0	197.3
1962	214.6	213.6	213.4	216.7	219.3	218.6
1963	195.2	196.0	194.6	192.0	190.1	192.0
1964	181.1	173.0	165.1	160.5	157.2	153.5
1965	148.3	149.3	148.0	145.7	143.7	143.7
1966	166.0	163.2	159.5	162.2	171.6	197.4
1967	175.7	180.2	189.4	184.4	185.1	173.4
1968	156.2	155.1	161.4	155.0	144.3	141.2
1969	—	—	—	—	—	—

*Cents per bushel.
Source: *Chicago Board of Trade Annual Yearbook.*

FIGURE 185
SEPTEMBER WHEAT FUTURE: MONTHLY LOWS
HISTORICAL TABLE*

Year	Jan.	Feb.	March	April	May	June
1950	189.7	186.2	194.0	203.0	214.1	209.7
1951	235.2	240.1	237.4	246.0	237.7	233.7
1952	246.2	245.2	243.6	235.1	235.4	229.1
1953	230.6	224.4	227.4	221.4	208.0	189.0
1954	200.1	205.2	213.2	201.4	192.5	191.5
1955	211.7	200.2	197.2	193.2	194.7	197.6
1956	195.6	197.1	197.0	207.5	202.5	203.5
1957	226.0	222.7	217.3	211.2	205.0	204.4
1958	186.7	188.4	190.7	188.2	185.4	185.2
1959	182.7	184.7	186.0	185.4	186.6	186.2
1960	185.2	186.2	185.4	185.6	186.6	184.7
1961	188.7	200.1	189.4	189.3	188.6	189.4
1962	209.1	209.7	211.0	212.7	214.6	214.0
1963	190.0	192.0	189.4	187.7	182.4	186.0
1964	170.5	162.6	156.5	151.2	149.4	142.2
1965	144.1	146.6	143.5	141.4	140.0	140.2
1966	157.6	157.3	154.5	156.1	158.6	170.0
1967	163.4	163.6	175.2	165.4	166.4	154.7
1968	152.4	152.6	152.6	140.3	140.0	130.3
1969	—	—	—	—	—	—

*Cents per bushel.
Source: *Chicago Board of Trade Annual Yearbook.*

The above two tables contain the highest and lowest prices reached by the September wheat future during the years and months listed. Thus, the trader can determine how high or how low the September future went in any particular month or period. He can also determine the crude odds of an advance or decline in the price of the September option between April 1st and June 30th.

CALCULATING GENERAL FUTURES ODDS

Using the "Monthly Highs and Lows Historical Tables," the trader merely chooses the period he wishes to trade and calculated the odds as he did for the general cash odds calculation. If he wishes to buy wheat on April 1st and sell it at the end of June, he wants to know whether the September wheat future usually goes higher in the month of June than it does during the month of April.

Question: In the last 19 years how many times has the September wheat future gone higher during the month of June than it did during the month of April?

Answer: From the above tables by comparing the June high of the September wheat future to the April high of the September wheat future over the past 19 years we find the answer to be 6 years out of the total of 19 years.

General odds: 32 percent chance for advance in September future prices. 68 percent chance for decline in September future prices.

Conclusion: General odds favor a decline in the September wheat future during the April through June period.

The above questions are answered from the information contained in the "Monthly Highs Historical Table," for the trader is calculating the chances of the price reaching recent new highs over

the three-month stretch. Had he been interested in the chances of a price drop, he would have asked the same questions of the "Monthly Lows Historical Table."

CALCULATING SPECIFIC FUTURES ODDS

From the general odds, the trader knows that past performance favors a drop in the price of the September wheat contract between April 1st and June 30th. He can refine his calculations any way he wishes. The most obvious refinement would be to eliminate those years which were different than the current year in the months which are already known in the current year. He could as well eliminate those years when wheat sold above $2 a bushel, or focus in on years when September contracts rose in price from January to March. Through all his refinements, he is simply redrawing his graph, basing it on only those years which are similar in some way to the current year.

Question: This year we know that the September wheat future did not go as high during the month of March as it did during the month of February. In how many years out of the past 19 has a similar market pattern occurred?

Answer: From an examination of the above tables we find the answer to be 11 years of the past 19. [1951, 1952, 1955, 1957, 1960, 1961, 1962, 1963, 1964, 1965, 1966]

Question: In those 11 years then which demonstrated a similar market pattern to the pattern being demonstrated this year, how many times did the September wheat future go higher during the month of June than it did during the month of April?

Answer: From the above tables by comparing the June high of the September wheat future to the April high of the September wheat future in only those 11 years we find the answer to be 5 years out of 11 years.

Specific odds: 45 percent chance for advance in September future prices. 55 percent chance for decline in September future prices.

Conclusion: Specific odds do not favor an advance in the September wheat future from April through June.

A WORD ABOUT PLAYING THE ODDS

Speculators make their money on futures markets by selling prices which are a little too high and buying prices which are a little too low. It makes no difference if the dislocated price was caused by excess hedging or by a cumulative incorrect guess on the part of all traders. Any system of pointing out incorrect prices for exploitation is simply trying to mechanically determine these incorrect prices so that the speculator can profit from them. Figuring the odds to determine how many times the futures market has been too low and had to adjust upward, is a method of prediction based on the idea that cumulative mistakes made in the past with a history of being repeated will be repeated in the future. It should not happen, but it appears to.

If the market is correctly discounted, figuring the odds will not return a profit because the market will not make mistakes in judgment over and over. No technical system of prediction will return profit theoretically. But the market is not perfect and patterns of mistakes do appear to occur. All of the factors that encourage hedgers to hedge and speculators to speculate add together to make the market. These things cannot be understood, but they do seem to be fairly constant from one year to the next. If they are, and if they tend to have the same effect on futures market prices, some basis is found for prediction by the figuring of odds. Traders who find an 80 percent possibility of the price of a contract going up from April 1st to June 30th have the opportunity to profit from it, and by so doing, help to correct it by buying the current price and selling it later at a higher price.

Speculators finding dislocations in market price and exploiting them help to make the markets function more smoothly by eliminating historical mistakes—but the fact that speculators *do* smooth out market price makes it impossible for a simple odds sheet to be printed up and handed out. So many speculators working the same odds would quickly render the exercise profitless. The market would be relieved of one flaw, but this is not the only goal of the speculator. If he also wishes to profit from his trading he will have to find and use his own odds.

WORKSHEET

POSITION CONTEMPLATED: I wish to buy the _____ future for the commodity called _____. I want to buy during the month of _____ and sell during the month of _____.

EVALUATION OF POSITION: The odds for success of the contemplated position are as follows:

a) General Cash Odds are _____% chance of success.
b) Specific Cash Odds are _____% chance of success.
c) General Future Odds are _____% chance of success.
d) Specific Future Odds are _____% chance of success.

CONCLUSION: The odds indicate that the contemplated position [should] [should not] be taken.

CHAPTER 13 APPENDIX
(Figs. 186-94, pp. 268-80)

FIGURE 186
WHEAT
Monthly Range of Futures Prices
(dollars per bushel)

March Delivery

	APRIL		MAY		JUNE		JULY		AUGUST		SEPTEMBER		OCTOBER		NOVEMBER		DECEMBER		JANUARY		FEBRUARY		MARCH	
	High	Low	High	Low	High	Low	High	Low	High	Low	High	Low	High	Low	High	Low	High	Low	High	Low	High	Low	High	Low
1970–71	1.53⅛	1.46⅛	1.52⅞	1.42¾	1.54¾	1.42½	1.57¼	1.47	1.70	1.49	1.76½	1.65	1.78¼	1.69⅝	1.80¼	1.69	1.74	1.64⅝	......	......	......	......	......	......
1969–70	1.45	1.38½	1.45⅝	1.39½	1.42½	1.37¾	1.40⅞	1.29¼	1.37½	1.30⅛	1.39¼	1.35½	1.41¾	1.37¼	1.43⅞	1.38⅛	1.48	1.41¼	1.47⅝	1.42⅝	1.54¼	1.42⅞	1.53⅜	1.45¾
1968–69	1.64¼	1.50¾	1.55	1.50⅛	1.51¾	1.41½	1.43½	1.36½	1.36⅞	1.27⅜	1.31¼	1.23¾	1.35½	1.25⅝	1.39⅛	1.31⅞	1.35⅝	1.29½	1.36¾	1.32	1.35	1.27¾	1.32⅛	1.25⅞
1967–68	1.93½	1.75⅛	1.83¾	1.76¼	1.87¼	1.66⅛	1.69	1.60¾	1.67⅝	1.54¾	1.63	1.55	1.61⅜	1.56⅝	1.58½	1.49	1.52¾	1.47¼	1.49½	1.45⅞	1.49⅞	1.45⅜	1.53¼	1.44⅞
1966–67	1.69⅝	1.64½	1.79⅞	1.66	2.05½	1.78¼	2.04¾	1.91¾	2.04⅝	1.95	2.07¼	1.79⅛	1.84⅜	1.72½	1.86⅝	1.73⅞	1.86¾	1.75¼	1.77⅛	1.60¾	1.77⅞	1.60½	1.86¼	1.73¼
1965–66	......	......	1.51	1.47⅜	1.51⅜	1.47	1.55¾	1.49	1.62½	1.54½	1.66	1.60¼	1.66¾	1.60½	1.69¼	1.62	1.73	1.64¼	1.70½	1.66	1.69⅞	1.61¼	1.63	1.56¼
1964–65	1.63⅛	1.59⅝	1.64½	1.57½	1.62¼	1.50¾	1.54½	1.49¼	1.52⅝	1.51½	1.55⅝	1.50⅝	1.55⅜	1.51½	1.56½	1.54⅛	1.54¾	1.48½	1.52⅜	1.45⅞	1.51⅜	1.48¼	1.51½	1.46⅛
1963–64	1.96⅛	1.92½	1.95	1.82½	1.98	1.91	1.97¼	1.84½	1.89⅞	1.85⅛	2.09¾	1.87¼	2.18¼	2.05	2.19	2.07¼	2.20¼	2.14¾	2.24	2.17¼	2.23¾	2.10¼	2.11	1.94
1962–63	2.22⅞	2.20⅝	2.25⅞	2.21⅜	2.25½	2.21½	2.25¾	2.21⅞	2.23⅛	2.16	2.20¾	2.03⅜	2.16½	2.05⅜	2.12⅝	2.07⅝	2.11¾	2.08⅞	2.12⅞	2.05½	2.11¾	2.04¾	2.09	2.01½
1961–62	2.03¼	1.99¾	2.03¾	1.99¼	2.08⅜	2.00½	2.09⅞	2.04	2.12½	2.08⅛	2.12	2.08	2.10¾	2.06½	2.10¼	2.07½	2.10⅜	2.06¼	2.07¼	2.01¼	2.04¼	1.99¼	2.06¾	1.99⅝

May Delivery

	JUNE		JULY		AUGUST		SEPTEMBER		OCTOBER		NOVEMBER		DECEMBER		JANUARY		FEBRUARY		MARCH		APRIL		MAY	
	High	Low	High	Low	High	Low	High	Low	High	Low	High	Low	High	Low	High	Low	High	Low	High	Low	High	Low	High	Low
1970–71	1.53½	1.41¼	1.56	1.46¾	1.67⅞	1.47⅝	1.74¾	1.62½	1.75⅞	1.67⅛	1.78¾	1.68⅛	1.72⅞	1.63¼	......	......	......	......	......	......	......	......	......	......
1969–70	1.46¼	1.38¾	1.41¾	1.30¼	1.37¾	1.31⅛	1.39½	1.35¾	1.42¾	1.37¾	1.44	1.39¼	1.47	1.41½	1.45¼	1.40⅛	1.49¾	1.40⅜	1.48¼	1.42⅞	1.53	1.44½	1.51¾	1.45¼
1968–69	1.53½	1.43¾	1.46	1.39¼	1.39⅜	1.29⅞	1.33⅞	1.27	1.39½	1.29⅜	1.42¼	1.35⅜	1.37⅞	1.32⅜	1.39¼	1.34¾	1.37¼	1.31¼	1.34⅛	1.25⅛	1.33⅛	1.25¾	1.35	1.28½
1967–68	1.87½	1.68	1.70⅝	1.62	1.69⅝	1.57⅜	1.65½	1.57⅝	1.63¾	1.59⅜	1.61½	1.52½	1.56¼	1.50½	1.53½	1.49⅜	1.52⅞	1.49¼	1.56	1.46¾	1.48	1.33⅛	1.38⅛	1.32⅜
1966–67	2.02	1.76¾	2.02	1.88	2.03½	1.92	2.07	1.80½	1.86½	1.74¼	1.89⅜	1.74½	1.89¼	1.77⅜	1.79⅝	1.63⅞	1.80½	1.63⅜	1.87	1.72¼	1.82¼	1.60½	1.66¾	1.60
1965–66	1.51⅜	1.47	1.54¾	1.49	1.60	1.53½	1.63¼	1.57⅝	1.65½	1.58¼	1.68	1.60	1.73	1.62¾	1.72¼	1.66⅝	1.70⅞	1.62½	1.64¾	1.56½	1.64¼	1.56½	1.66¼	1.58¼
1964–65	1.63¼	1.51½	1.55	1.50	1.53¾	1.52⅜	1.56	1.51½	1.55¾	1.52¼	1.57⅛	1.54⅜	1.55½	1.48¾	1.53	1.47	1.53	1.49⅜	1.52½	1.48	1.51¾	1.43½	1.48	1.42¾
1963–64	1.92	1.83	1.92¼	1.77¾	1.85	1.80¼	2.07	1.84	2.14½	2.02⅛	2.15⅛	2.04	2.15⅜	2.10½	2.19⅜	2.12¾	2.18	2.06	2.06¾	1.89¼	2.09½	1.97⅞	2.10¼	1.94¼
1962–63	2.24	2.13¾	2.24	2.18¾	2.21⅜	2.14¼	2.18¼	2.02⅜	2.15¼	2.04⅞	2.11¼	2.06⅞	2.10	2.07⅜	2.12⅞	2.05	2.12⅛	2.04	2.08⅝	2.00¼	2.11⅛	2.06	2.28⅝	2.00⅝
1961–62	2.09¾	2.00½	2.11	2.06	2.14½	2.09⅜	2.13⅞	2.10½	2.12⅞	2.08¾	2.12⅜	2.09¾	2.12½	2.09⅛	2.10¼	2.04¼	2.08⅛	2.02⅞	2.07⅞	2.03⅞	2.13⅜	2.07⅜	2.17	2.12⅝

July Delivery

	AUGUST		SEPTEMBER		OCTOBER		NOVEMBER		DECEMBER		JANUARY		FEBRUARY		MARCH		APRIL		MAY		JUNE		JULY	
	High	Low	High	Low	High	Low	High	Low	High	Low	High	Low	High	Low	High	Low	High	Low	High	Low	High	Low	High	Low
1970–71	1.64½	1.42	1.64	1.54	1.63½	1.55¾	1.68½	1.58	1.63	1.55¼	......	......	......	......	......	......	......	......	......	......	......	......	......	......
1969–70	1.37	1.28	1.35½	1.32½	1.38¼	1.33½	1.39¾	1.34⅝	1.41⅜	1.36¼	1.39⅛	1.35¼	1.41¼	1.35	1.38⅝	1.36⅛	1.44⅜	1.36⅜	1.42½	1.34	1.43⅞	1.33¼	1.44	1.36⅛
1968–69	1.40⅜	1.30	1.33¾	1.27⅛	1.39⅛	1.30⅞	1.42⅛	1.35	1.37⅝	1.32¼	1.36⅛	1.32½	1.35⅛	1.30	1.32½	1.25¼	1.33	1.26	1.34⅞	1.27¾	1.31⅝	1.24½	1.29	1.24½
1967–68	1.67	1.56½	1.63¼	1.56⅛	1.61¾	1.58½	1.60½	1.53⅛	1.55⅞	1.50½	1.53½	1.49¼	1.52¼	1.49⅞	1.58	1.49⅜	1.51	1.37	1.40½	1.36½	1.37⅜	1.26⅛	2.29⅜	1.24½
1966–67	1.91	1.75½	1.95	1.69	1.74½	1.64¾	1.84⅜	1.66¾	1.85	1.70½	1.73½	1.61⅛	1.77½	1.61¼	1.86	1.72¼	1.80⅞	1.62¼	1.70⅜	1.63	1.75¼	1.50½	1.53	1.46⅝
1965–66	1.49¼	1.44⅝	1.50¾	1.46⅛	1.51	1.46⅜	1.55½	1.50⅛	1.63¼	1.53¼	1.64¼	1.56	1.61⅜	1.55¼	1.57⅝	1.52⅝	1.60½	1.54	1.69⅛	1.56⅜	1.95	1.67	1.90⅞	1.78
1964–65	1.50	1.43	1.51	1.47⅜	1.51½	1.48	1.55	1.50	1.52¼	1.43¼	1.46⅛	1.42	1.47¼	1.44¼	1.45⅞	1.41½	1.43⅞	1.39⅝	1.41⅞	1.37⅞	1.45	1.38	1.46	1.39¼
1963–64	1.58½	1.54	1.71½	1.57⅜	1.79	1.64⅝	1.77	1.62⅝	1.79½	1.69¾	1.79½	1.69¾	1.71¼	1.61½	1.63⅜	1.54½	1.58¾	1.49½	1.53⅜	1.46¾	1.49½	1.37½	1.43	1.37
1962–63	......	......	1.92⅝	1.88½	1.97	1.89⅝	1.92⅜	1.89⅞	1.91⅜	1.87¼	1.93	1.87⅝	1.93¾	1.90	1.94¾	1.87⅝	1.90¾	1.86⅜	1.88¾	1.80	1.90	1.84⅝	1.86½	1.78⅛
1961–62	2.15	2.09	2.15¼	2.12¼	2.14⅛	2.10¾	2.13⅜	2.11½	2.13¼	2.11	2.12	2.06½	2.10⅞	2.06¼	2.10¼	2.07¾	2.14⅞	2.09⅞	2.17⅛	2.12¼	2.16	2.11	2.13⅜	2.10⅝

September Delivery

	OCTOBER		NOVEMBER		DECEMBER		JANUARY		FEBRUARY		MARCH		APRIL		MAY		JUNE		JULY		AUGUST		SEPTEMBER	
	High	Low	High	Low	High	Low	High	Low	High	Low	High	Low	High	Low	High	Low	High	Low	High	Low	High	Low	High	Low
1970–71	1.65	1.59¾	1.70½	1.60½	1.64⅝	1.57	......	......	......	......	......	......	......	......	......	......	......	......	......	......	......	......	......	......
1969–70	1.40⅝	1.34⅝	1.41½	1.37⅜	1.43⅛	1.38½	1.41⅛	1.37⅛	1.42⅞	1.37⅛	1.40½	1.38⅛	1.46¼	1.38¾	1.44⅝	1.35⅝	1.45½	1.35¼	1.49	1.38¼	1.61¾	1.43¾	1.69½	1.54⅞
1968–69	1.43¼	1.30⅛	1.44¾	1.37	1.40½	1.35	1.38¾	1.34¾	1.37⅞	1.32¾	1.35½	1.28	1.35⅝	1.28¾	1.37⅜	1.30¼	1.34	1.27⅜	1.31¾	1.19½	1.28⅝	1.20¾	1.32¾	1.27⅝
1967–68	1.65½	1.61⅝	1.63⅝	1.56⅛	1.59⅛	1.53¾	1.56¼	1.52½	1.55⅛	1.52¾	1.61½	1.52¾	1.55	1.40⅜	1.44⅜	1.40	1.41¼	1.30⅜	1.32½	1.24¼	1.24⅝	1.15¼	1.20	1.14¼
1966–67	1.75¼	1.67¼	1.86½	1.68⅞	1.87½	1.73	1.75⅞	1.63½	1.80¼	1.63¾	1.89½	1.75¼	1.84½	1.65½	1.75⅛	1.66½	1.79	1.54¾	1.57¼	1.49⅜	1.56	1.42⅜	1.50½	1.43⅞
1965–66	1.53	1.49⅜	1.57⅛	1.51¾	1.64¾	1.54¾	1.66	1.57¾	1.63¼	1.57⅜	1.59⅝	1.54⅝	1.62½	1.56⅛	1.71¾	1.58¾	1.97½	1.70	1.94¾	1.82	1.93⅝	1.84	1.93	1.81
1964–65	1.53⅝	1.50¼	1.57	1.52	1.54½	1.45¼	1.48⅜	1.44⅛	1.49⅜	1.46¾	1.48	1.43⅝	1.45⅞	1.41½	1.44¼	1.40	1.47¾	1.40½	1.48½	1.43	1.56½	1.48¼	1.60	1.54
1963–64	1.81	1.52	1.78½	1.63	1.80½	1.71	1.81⅛	1.70⅝	1.73	1.62¾	1.65⅛	1.56⅝	1.60⅝	1.51¼	1.56	1.48⅝	1.52	1.40¾	1.45	1.39½	1.43¾	1.38½	1.51⅞	1.41¼
1962–63	1.99¾	1.92½	1.95¼	1.92⅞	1.94¼	1.90⅛	1.95¼	1.90	1.96	1.92	1.94¾	1.89½	1.92	1.87⅞	1.90⅛	1.85½	1.92	1.86	1.88⅝	1.76	1.81¼	1.76⅛	1.95	1.77¼
1961–62	2.17⅛	2.13½	2.16⅝	2.14¾	2.16	2.13¾	2.14¾	2.09⅛	2.14	2.09⅞	2.13⅛	2.11	2.16⅞	2.12⅞	2.19⅜	2.14¾	2.18¾	2.14	2.16⅝	2.12⅛	2.12¾	2.04½	2.09½	2.00⅝

December Delivery

	JANUARY		FEBRUARY		MARCH		APRIL		MAY		JUNE		JULY		AUGUST		SEPTEMBER		OCTOBER		NOVEMBER		DECEMBER	
	High	Low	High	Low	High	Low	High	Low	High	Low	High	Low	High	Low	High	Low	High	Low	High	Low	High	Low	High	Low
1970	1.45⅜	1.41¼	1.47½	1.41¼	1.45	1.43⅛	1.50⅜	1.43¼	1.49¼	1.40⅞	1.50¾	1.40⅝	1.54⅜	1.43½	1.66⅛	1.49	1.73¼	1.61⅛	1.77	1.67⅛	1.79⅝	1.66⅜	1.73	1.63¼
1969	1.43⅞	1.39⅞	1.42⅞	1.37⅞	1.40¾	1.33¾	1.41⅛	1.34¼	1.42¼	1.35¾	1.39⅜	1.33⅜	1.37	1.25¼	1.34	1.26⅛	1.36⅛	1.32½	1.38¼	1.33⅞	1.42⅛	1.34⅞	1.48¼	1.40⅛
1968	1.61⅜	1.57¾	1.60	1.57⅞	1.67	1.58¼	1.60½	1.46¼	1.50½	1.45¾	1.46⅝	1.36¾	1.38¾	1.30½	1.31	1.21½	1.25⅝	1.17¾	1.29⅞	1.19¾	1.33⅝	1.27½	1.34¼	1.25
1967	1.81	1.68½	1.85	1.68¾	1.94¾	1.80¼	1.89⅞	1.71⅜	1.79½	1.72	1.84¼	1.61½	1.64	1.56	1.62⅝	1.49⅛	1.57½	1.49⅞	1.56	1.50¾	1.52⅜	1.42¾	1.47¼	1.43½
1966	1.70	1.62¼	1.68⅛	1.62⅛	1.64⅜	1.59½	1.67⅜	1.61	1.77	1.63⅝	2.02½	1.75¼	2.00½	1.88	2.00¼	1.90½	2.00½	1.72½	1.77¾	1.66⅛	1.80	1.68	1.79¾	1.73½
1965	1.52⅜	1.48¼	1.53¾	1.51⅛	1.52½	1.48½	1.50⅝	1.46⅛	1.48¼	1.44¾	1.50½	1.44½	1.53⅝	1.47⅞	1.61⅝	1.53	1.66	1.60	1.66	1.59¾	1.66½	1.61¼	1.72	1.63¼
1964	1.85	1.75⅞	1.77⅝	1.67½	1.70⅛	1.61½	1.65¾	1.55¾	1.60½	1.53⅝	1.56⅞	1.46¾	1.50¾	1.44¼	1.48¾	1.44	1.51⅛	1.46½	1.51¼	1.47¼	1.53	1.48¾	1.50	1.46¾
1963	1.99½	1.94¾	2.00¼	1.97½	1.99	1.93½	1.95⅞	1.91¾	1.94½	1.86	1.97	1.91¼	1.94½	1.82	1.86⅞	1.82¼	2.07	1.83⅞	2.17	2.04	2.18½	2.05½	2.19½	2.12⅝
1962	2.20¾	2.13⅞	2.19	2.15⅛	2.18¼	2.15¾	2.20⅞	2.18⅛	2.24⅛	2.19⅝	2.23⅝	2.19⅛	2.22⅜	2.18½	2.19	2.11⅜	2.15⅞	1.98½	2.12¼	2.00¼	2.09¾	2.03	2.10½	2.05¾
1961	2.03¾	1.94½	2.09½	2.00⅜	2.05	1.95½	1.98⅛	1.95½	1.98¾	1.94⅝	2.03½	1.95⅝	2.04¾	1.98⅝	2.07½	2.02⅞	2.07¾	2.02⅞	2.05½	2.01½	2.06	2.02	2.06⅝	2.03½

Source: Chicago Board of Trade, *Statistical Annual 1970.*

FIGURE 187
CORN
Monthly Range of Futures Prices
(dollars per bushel)

March Delivery

Trading Year	Delivery Year	APRIL High	Low	MAY High	Low	JUNE High	Low	JULY High	Low	AUGUST High	Low	SEPTEMBER High	Low	OCTOBER High	Low	NOVEMBER High	Low	DECEMBER High	Low	JANUARY High	Low	FEBRUARY High	Low	MARCH High	Low
1970-71	1972													1.57¾	1.55½	1.64¼	1.57	1.62½	1.54½						
	1971	1.28½	1.21⅜	1.27¼	1.24⅜	1.43¼	1.25⅜	1.40	1.29½	1.63¼	1.30½	1.65	1.52¼	1.61	1.48¼	1.58½	1.48¾	1.56¾	1.51¾						
1969-70	1971																			1.24	1.21⅜	1.22¾	1.20¼	1.22⅛	1.20⅜
	1970	1.27⅞	1.17	1.32⅜	1.25¼	1.31	1.26	1.33¼	1.20¼	1.22¾	1.19	1.22¾	1.20⅜	1.27	1.20½	1.24⅞	1.21¾	1.20¾	1.16½	1.22½	1.20¼	1.23¼	1.20¼	1.24½	1.20½
1968-69		1.31½	1.23¾	1.26½	1.23¾	1.24½	1.18¼	1.19½	1.10	1.11⅜	1.08¼	1.08⅞	1.06	1.19¼	1.06½	1.22⅜	1.14½	1.20⅝	1.16½	1.21¾	1.17¾	1.19¾	1.17¼	1.15½	1.12½
1967-68		1.48¼	1.37¾	1.42	1.35¼	1.47	1.33¼	1.35¼	1.24¾	1.25¾	1.21¾	1.22¾	1.20⅜	1.20¾	1.17½	1.20	1.16¼	1.21¾	1.17¾	1.20½	1.17¾	1.19¼	1.17¼	1.20¾	1.17¾
1966-67		1.25⅜	1.23¼	1.27¼	1.23¾	1.45¼	1.26¼	1.54	1.39¼	1.58¾	1.47	1.55¼	1.40⅜	1.43⅜	1.37¾	1.48½	1.42½	1.49¾	1.41¾	1.44½	1.38¼	1.41¼	1.34½	1.41½	1.37⅛
1965-66		1.26½	1.24	1.25½	1.20¼	1.26¾	1.21½	1.25¼	1.21¼	1.23¼	1.20¾	1.23½	1.20¼	1.20¼	1.18	1.22½	1.18¼	1.27¼	1.22½	1.31	1.24⅞	1.29¾	1.26¾	1.31¼	1.27¼
1964-65		1.23¼	1.21½	1.22⅜	1.20¼	1.23¼	1.19⅜	1.21¼	1.17	1.26¼	1.18⅜	1.28	1.23¾	1.27¾	1.22¾	1.27½	1.23¼	1.27¼	1.25¼	1.28	1.25½	1.29¼	1.26¾	1.31¼	1.27¼
1963-64		1.18¼	1.15½	1.19¾	1.15⅜	1.21¼	1.18½	1.29	1.15½	1.17	1.14¾	1.28	1.18½	1.27	1.19½	1.24	1.19¾	1.13½	1.09¾	1.17½	1.12¼	1.19	1.13½	1.19¼	1.15
1962-63		1.22⅜	1.20½	1.23¾	1.16	1.19¾	1.14½	1.16⅜	1.10¼	1.12¾	1.08¾	1.12½	1.10½	1.19¼	1.07½	1.11½	1.08	1.13½	1.09¾	1.10¾	1.05½	1.07¼	1.03¼	1.11¾	1.05¾
1961-62		1.24¼	1.18¼	1.28	1.22¼	1.27¾	1.22⅛	1.28	1.21¼	1.21¾	1.18	1.19¾	1.13½	1.17¾	1.12¼	1.14¾	1.12½	1.12¾	1.09⅜	1.10¾	1.05½	1.07⅜	1.03⅜	1.11⅛	1.05¾

May Delivery

Trading Year	JUNE High	Low	JULY High	Low	AUGUST High	Low	SEPTEMBER High	Low	OCTOBER High	Low	NOVEMBER High	Low	DECEMBER High	Low	JANUARY High	Low	FEBRUARY High	Low	MARCH High	Low	APRIL High	Low	MAY High	Low
1970-71	1.44⅜	1.28½	1.42¾	1.32½	1.66¼	1.33½	1.67½	1.55¼	1.64½	1.51⅜	1.62	1.51½	1.59¼	1.54½										
1969-70	1.35¼	1.29	1.36½	1.23¾	1.25¼	1.22¼	1.25⅜	1.23½	1.30¼	1.24	1.28¼	1.24⅜	1.26¾	1.23⅜	1.25⅛	1.22½	1.24½	1.21½	1.23¾	1.22¼	1.28⅜	1.23	1.30¼	1.27¼
1968-69	1.27½	1.21¼	1.22½	1.13	1.14⅜	1.11½	1.12¾	1.09½	1.22¼	1.09½	1.26	1.17⅜	1.23½	1.19½	1.23¼	1.19¾	1.20¾	1.17	1.19½	1.15¼	1.26½	1.16¼	1.16½	1.12½
1967-68	1.49¼	1.36	1.38	1.27¼	1.28½	1.24¾	1.25¼	1.21½	1.24½	1.20¾	1.25½	1.21¼	1.25½	1.21¼	1.24⅜	1.21½	1.23¼	1.21½	1.23½	1.20¾	1.20¾	1.13½	1.33½	1.28¼
1966-67	1.47	1.29¼	1.56	1.41	1.61¼	1.49¾	1.58¾	1.42½	1.47	1.39½	1.51½	1.45⅜	1.52½	1.43¾	1.47	1.41	1.44⅜	1.37¼	1.44⅞	1.39¾	1.43½	1.27¾	1.33½	1.28¼
1965-66	1.29¼	1.24	1.27¼	1.24	1.25¾	1.23⅜	1.25⅜	1.23	1.23½	1.20¼	1.25	1.21½	1.30	1.24¾	1.29¾	1.27¼	1.30½	1.27¾	1.33½	1.30¼	1.34½	1.31½	1.35¼	1.32½
1964-65	1.25½	1.22¼	1.23¾	1.19¼	1.24⅜	1.21	1.30⅜	1.26½	1.30	1.25½	1.29⅜	1.26	1.29½	1.27¼	1.30¼	1.27¾	1.31¼	1.29¼	1.33¼	1.30¼	1.34⅛	1.31½	1.25½	1.23¼
1963-64	1.23½	1.20⅜	1.31	1.17¾	1.19	1.16⅜	1.30	1.17¾	1.29½	1.21½	1.27¼	1.22	1.24½	1.22	1.24	1.21	1.22¾	1.19¾	1.19¼	1.14¾	1.18¾	1.15¼	1.21¼	1.17¾
1962-63	1.21½	1.16½	1.18¾	1.13	1.15½	1.11½	1.15¼	1.12¾	1.21½	1.10	1.14¼	1.10¾	1.16	1.12½	1.18¼	1.14¼	1.19¼	1.14¼	1.19½	1.16½	1.18¾	1.15¼	1.21¼	1.17¾
1961-62	1.29¾	1.25⅜	1.31	1.24¾	1.25	1.21½	1.23¾	1.17½	1.21½	1.16½	1.21½	1.15¼	1.18⅜	1.15¼	1.16	1.12¼	1.14¼	1.09¾	1.14⅜	1.08⅜	1.16	1.10½	1.15	1.10¾

July Delivery

Trading Year	AUGUST High	Low	SEPTEMBER High	Low	OCTOBER High	Low	NOVEMBER High	Low	DECEMBER High	Low	JANUARY High	Low	FEBRUARY High	Low	MARCH High	Low	APRIL High	Low	MAY High	Low	JUNE High	Low	JULY High	Low
1970-71	1.66⅛	1.35¼	1.68	1.56	1.66	1.53½	1.64	1.53¼	1.61⅜	1.55¼	1.27	1.24	1.25⅛	1.22½	1.24½	1.23¼	1.30½	1.24	1.30½	1.28	1.40¼	1.29	1.41	1.33½
1969-70	1.28	1.24½	1.28	1.26½	1.32¼	1.26¾	1.30⅜	1.26¾	1.28¾	1.25¼	1.24¾	1.22½	1.23½	1.20	1.22¼	1.17¼	1.28¼	1.18¼	1.31½	1.25	1.30½	1.25¾	1.30½	1.25¾
1968-69	1.17	1.14¼	1.15¾	1.12½	1.24¾	1.12¼	1.27½	1.19¾	1.25½	1.22	1.24¾	1.22½	1.27¾	1.24¾	1.26⅜	1.25	1.27¼	1.24⅜	1.18¾	1.15¼	1.16	1.10½	1.21¼	1.09¼
1967-68	1.30⅜	1.27¼	1.28½	1.23¾	1.26¼	1.23¾	1.25¼	1.22½	1.28	1.24	1.27¾	1.24¾	1.26⅜	1.25	1.47½	1.43¼	1.47⅜	1.31¾	1.36½	1.31¾	1.41½	1.29¾	1.33	1.25¾
1966-67	1.63½	1.50¾	1.61¼	1.44½	1.48¼	1.41	1.53¼	1.47¾	1.54	1.45	1.48¼	1.42½	1.46¾	1.39¾	1.29¾	1.25¾	1.28¼	1.26	1.36¼	1.26¼	1.43½	1.31¾	1.43½	1.31¼
1965-66	1.27¾	1.24¼	1.27½	1.24¾	1.27¼	1.24¼	1.26½	1.22¾	1.31½	1.26	1.33¾	1.28⅜	1.33½	1.26½	1.29¾	1.25¾	1.28¾	1.26	1.34½	1.31½	1.32⅜	1.26¾	1.43½	1.31¼
1964-65	1.29¾	1.23¾	1.31	1.27½	1.31¼	1.27¼	1.31⅜	1.27⅝	1.31	1.28½	1.31¼	1.28½	1.33	1.30½	1.34	1.31½	1.35¼	1.32¾	1.34½	1.31½	1.32⅜	1.26¾	1.34¾	1.18⅜
1963-64	1.21¼	1.17¼	1.31½	1.19¼	1.30¼	1.23¾	1.29¼	1.24	1.26	1.24	1.25½	1.22⅜	1.24¾	1.21¾	1.25¼	1.22½	1.26	1.23	1.24½	1.22	1.28¾	1.23¾	13.1⅛	1.26
1962-63	1.18⅜	1.13⅜	1.17½	1.13⅜	1.23½	1.11⅜	1.16¼	1.13½	1.18	1.14¼	1.19¼	1.15¾	1.20⅜	1.16⅜	1.20¼	1.18¼	1.19½	1.17	1.23¾	1.18⅜	1.28¾	1.23¾	1.12½	1.08
1961-62	1.27¼	1.24¼	1.26½	1.21	1.25	1.19¾	1.21⅜	1.18	1.18⅜	1.15⅜	1.17½	1.12⅜	1.15¼	1.11½	1.18½	1.12½	1.19¼	1.13⅜	1.17⅜	1.12½	1.15¼	1.09¼	1.12⅜	1.08

September Delivery

Trading Year	OCTOBER High	Low	NOVEMBER High	Low	DECEMBER High	Low	JANUARY High	Low	FEBRUARY High	Low	MARCH High	Low	APRIL High	Low	MAY High	Low	JUNE High	Low	JULY High	Low	AUGUST High	Low	SEPTEMBER High	Low
1970-71	1.65	1.51½	1.62¼	1.53¼	1.60⅜	1.54¼	1.24¼	1.21⅜	1.22½	1.20⅛	1.23¼	1.20⅜	1.29½	1.22⅛	1.29½	1.26¼	1.40¼	1.27¾	1.37⅛	1.29¼	1.60¼	1.30½	1.60¼	1.45
1969-70	1.29¼	1.24¼	1.26¼	1.23½	1.26	1.23⅜	1.24¼	1.21¾	1.22½	1.19½	1.21¼	1.18	1.27⅛	1.18¼	1.32½	1.24½	1.29	1.24⅛	1.28½	1.18½	1.24⅜	1.20¾	1.24½	1.21
1968-69	1.24½	1.13	1.25½	1.20	1.23½	1.20¾	1.23	1.20¼	1.22½	1.19⅜	1.21¼	1.18	1.26½	1.18¼	1.20⅜	1.17¾	1.14	1.06	1.07½	1.04¼	1.07½	1.04	1.21	1.04
1967-68	1.27¼	1.23	1.25½	1.20	1.28¼	1.24½	1.28⅜	1.26¼	1.28¼	1.27	1.44¼	1.37	1.47½	1.42¼	1.48½	1.33¼	1.44	1.30½	1.32½	1.23¾	1.23¼	1.18½	1.21	1.17
1966-67	1.46	1.36	1.47	1.41½	1.48½	1.38½	1.27½	1.22	1.30	1.24½	1.25¾	1.22¾	1.48½	1.33¼	1.25¼	1.22½	1.38¼	1.26	1.45¼	1.34¼	1.52¾	1.40	1.46¼	1.37
1965-66	1.21¾	1.20	1.21⅛	1.20¼	1.28⅜	1.24½	1.28½	1.24¼	1.29¼	1.27½	1.29½	1.27¾	1.30¼	1.28½	1.29¼	1.24¼	1.29½	1.25¾	1.27½	1.23⅜	1.24½	1.20¼	1.26½	1.21
1964-65	1.27¾	1.24¾	1.28⅜	1.25¼	1.28⅜	1.24½	1.28⅛	1.24¼	1.29¼	1.27¼	1.29½	1.27½	1.24⅛	1.21½	1.23½	1.20⅜	1.22½	1.19¼	1.25	1.18	1.28½	1.22⅛		
1963-64	1.27	1.20⅜	1.27½	1.22½	1.24¼	1.23	1.24½	1.21½	1.18½	1.15	1.18¼	1.16¼	1.18	1.16¼	1.21	1.17¼	1.24½	1.20½	1.27¼	1.20½	1.26	1.20⅜	1.36	1.23¾
1962-63	1.21¼	1.10½	1.14¼	1.11¼	1.16¼	1.13	1.17¾	1.13¼	1.18¼	1.15	1.19¼	1.15½	1.20⅜	1.16⅜	1.19⅜	1.14½	1.16⅜	1.11¼	1.13¾	1.07⅜	1.08⅜	1.03½	1.09½	1.06
1961-62	1.25½	1.21⅜	1.21⅜	1.19	1.20¼	1.17½	1.19⅜	1.14	1.17¼	1.14	1.19¼	1.15½	1.20⅜	1.16⅜	1.19⅜	1.14½	1.16⅜	1.11¼	1.13¾	1.07⅜	1.08¼	1.03½	1.09½	1.06

December Delivery

Trading Year	Delivery Year	JANUARY High	Low	FEBRUARY High	Low	MARCH High	Low	APRIL High	Low	MAY High	Low	JUNE High	Low	JULY High	Low	AUGUST High	Low	SEPTEMBER High	Low	OCTOBER High	Low	NOVEMBER High	Low	DECEMBER High	Low
1970	1971																			1.53¼	1.50	1.61	1.52⅜	1.58	1.50¼
	1970	1.20	1.17¼	1.19	1.16½	1.18⅜	1.16½	1.24	1.17¼	1.23⅜	1.20⅛	1.37¼	1.21½	1.35¼	1.25¼	1.58½	1.26	1.59¼	1.47¼	1.55½	1.43½	1.52¾	1.42¼	1.51¼	1.45¾
1969		1.19½	1.15⅜	1.16¼	1.14½	1.16⅜	1.12¾	1.23¼	1.13¾	1.28½	1.21	1.26¼	1.21⅜	1.27¼	1.15½	1.17¼	1.14¼	1.17¼	1.15¼	1.14½	1.01¾	1.19	1.10	1.17¼	1.12½
1968		1.27¼	1.24¼	1.29½	1.27¼	1.29	1.26¼	1.27¾	1.19¾	1.21¼	1.18¼	1.20	1.14¼	1.05½	1.03⅜	1.03¼	1.01¼	1.03½	1.01½	1.15½	1.12½	1.15½	1.11½	1.18	1.13½
1967		1.35¼	1.31¼	1.37½	1.30¾	1.42¼	1.35¼	1.44½	1.33½	1.37⅜	1.31	1.43¼	1.28¾	1.30¼	1.20¾	1.21⅜	1.17¼	1.53¾	1.42¼	1.49¾	1.35⅜	1.42⅜	1.36½	1.46	1.39½
1966		1.25	1.20¼	1.22½	1.18½	1.21½	1.19⅜	1.22½	1.20½	1.21½	1.17½	1.22⅜	1.17¼	1.21¾	1.17¾	1.19½	1.16¼	1.19¼	1.16½	1.16¼	1.13¼	1.18½	1.13¾	1.24¾	1.18½
1965		1.21¼	1.17¼	1.21⅜	1.17½	1.23½	1.18½	1.20¼	1.18½	1.19¼	1.17¼	1.19⅛	1.16¼	1.17¼	1.13¼	1.22½	1.14½	1.24¾	1.20½	1.23¼	1.19¼	1.24¼	1.20⅜	1.19⅛	1.14⅜
1964		1.20¾	1.16	1.21¾	1.17¾	1.23½	1.18⅜	1.15½	1.12¾	1.16½	1.13	1.18¼	1.15⅜	1.25	1.12½	1.14	1.11½	1.24½	1.12¾	1.23½	1.15½	1.19¾	1.15	1.19⅛	1.14⅜
1963		1.14¾	1.10¼	1.15½	1.12½	1.15½	1.12¾	1.15½	1.12¼	1.16½	1.13	1.16⅜	1.11¼	1.13	1.07⅜	1.09	1.05½	1.09	1.06¾	1.15¼	1.05	1.08½	1.05	1.12½	1.07¼
1962		1.21¼	1.12½	1.17¾	1.14½	1.19½	1.15¾	1.19¼	1.16½	1.19¼	1.12¼	1.16½	1.11½	1.24½	1.17	1.17½	1.13½	1.14	1.09⅛	1.12¾	1.07¼	1.11½	1.08¼	1.09½	1.05¼
1961		1.24	1.13½	1.26¼	1.17⅜	1.20¼	1.12	1.20⅜	1.15	1.23¼	1.18½	1.23⅜	1.17½	1.24⅜	1.17	1.17½	1.13½	1.14	1.09⅛	1.12¾	1.07¼	1.11½	1.08¼	1.09½	1.05¼

Source: Chicago Board of Trade, *Statistical Annual 1970.*

FIGURE 188
SOYBEANS
Monthly Range of Futures Prices
(dollars per bushel)

January Delivery

Trading Year	Delivery Year	FEBRUARY		MARCH		APRIL		MAY		JUNE		JULY		AUGUST		SEPTEMBER		OCTOBER		NOVEMBER		DECEMBER		JANUARY	
		High	Low	High	Low	High	Low	High	Low	High	Low	High	Low	High	Low	High	Low	High	Low	High	Low	High	Low	High	Low
1970-71	1972	...	...	...	...	...	...	...	...	...	...	...	...	...	...	...	...	2.82	2.80	2.92¾	2.80¾	2.90⅝	2.81¼	...	...
	1971	2.57⅝	2.51⅝	2.59	2.56	2.68⅛	2.57⅛	2.66⅜	2.60⅛	3.01¼	2.62⅛	3.07	2.87	3.03½	2.81	2.97¼	2.80	3.15	2.90⅛	3.11¼	2.97	3.00¾	2.89½	...	...
1969-70		2.49½	2.42½	2.43¾	2.36⅞	2.40½	2.38¼	2.42¼	2.37⅞	2.41¼	2.37⅞	2.44⅜	2.38	2.42⅜	2.39¼	2.45¼	2.39½	3.53⅜	2.41⅜	2.53	2.43¾	2.48⅛	2.42⅞	2.52⅝	2.46
1968-69		2.75⅞	2.74	2.77⅛	2.70⅝	2.71⅛	2.65½	2.67	2.65⅝	2.65⅞	2.58¾	2.61¾	2.55½	2.59⅝	2.54¾	2.58½	2.51⅜	2.57¼	2.51¾	2.61¾	2.55⅜	2.60⅝	2.56⅛	2.61¾	2.58⅛
1967-68		2.83⅛	2.79⅛	2.86½	2.81¾	2.83⅞	2.79¾	2.87⅜	2.79¼	2.95⅛	2.76⅛	2.76⅛	2.71½	2.73⅞	2.69¼	2.72⅝	2.65⅜	2.70¼	2.64⅜	2.69	2.64⅞	2.68	2.65	2.70⅝	2.65
1966-67		2.75⅛	2.68⅞	2.74⅛	2.70⅛	2.90⅝	2.75	2.87⅝	2.80¾	3.19	2.85⅝	3.37¾	3.05	3.37	3.15½	3.34½	2.98¼	3.03¾	2.92	3.00¾	2.91⅝	3.03¼	2.95¾	2.98	2.86
1965-66		2.60¾	2.54	2.60⅞	2.57	2.62¾	2.58	2.58½	2.46	2.54½	2.47½	2.60⅝	2.46⅝	3.54¼	2.48¼	2.58⅛	2.48½	2.52¾	2.48	2.59	2.51⅛	2.68½	2.58¾	2.89¼	2.65
1964-65		2.62⅞	2.56¼	2.59½	2.47¾	2.51⅜	2.43⅞	2.48	2.42⅛	2.70⅞	2.43⅞	2.49	2.41½	2.62⅛	2.44½	2.83¼	2.56	2.85½	2.68⅛	2.94⅜	2.72	2.98½	2.77	3.01	2.75¾
1963-64		2.54¾	2.50	2.55½	2.45¼	2.54½	2.47	2.58⅜	2.51¼	2.67¼	2.54½	2.83¾	2.57½	2.65	2.54¾	2.84	2.55⅞	2.95	2.71¾	2.95	2.65½	2.90	2.63¼	2.81	2.69⅝
1962-63		2.44½	2.41	2.43⅞	1.42¼	2.45	2.41⅞	2.43	2.39	2.40¼	2.37	2.38¾	2.34¼	2.39¾	2.32⅞	2.44⅛	2.36½	2.53	2.40	2.48¾	2.41⅝	2.47⅞	2.44⅜	2.62¾	2.46⅜
1961-62		2.53¼	2.29¼	2.49	2.35½	2.67½	2.44¾	2.65	2.53¼	2.57¼	2.48¼	2.58¾	2.49¾	2.50¾	2.45⅝	2.46⅛	2.41	2.48¼	2.39⅞	2.46½	2.41⅞	2.45	2.42⅞	2.45⅜	2.41⅝

March Delivery

	APRIL		MAY		JUNE		JULY		AUGUST		SEPTEMBER		OCTOBER		NOVEMBER		DECEMBER		JANUARY		FEBRUARY		MARCH	
	High	Low	High	Low	High	Low	High	Low	High	Low	High	Low	High	Low	High	Low	High	Low	High	Low	High	Low	High	Low
1970-71	2.71⅜	2.61	2.70	2.64	3.05⅛	2.65⅞	3.11	2.92	3.06⅛	2.86	3.02	2.84¾	3.19	2.94⅞	3.15¾	3.00½	3.04½	2.94	...	...	...	...	...	...
1969-70	2.44¼	2.41⅞	2.46	2.41¾	2.45½	2.41⅝	2.49⅛	2.42½	2.47	2.43¾	2.49⅞	2.43⅝	2.58	2.46¾	2.58¾	2.49⅛	2.54	2.48⅜	2.56⅛	2.51¼	2.58½	2.53⅝	2.57¾	2.53⅞
1968-69	2.74½	2.69⅛	2.70½	2.69⅛	2.69⅜	2.62⅛	2.65½	2.58⅜	2.62⅜	2.57⅝	2.61⅞	2.54⅞	2.61¾	2.55⅝	2.66⅛	2.59½	2.64⅜	2.60½	2.65¼	2.62¼	2.64⅞	2.61⅛	2.61¾	2.58¼
1967-68	2.87	2.82⅞	2.90⅝	2.82⅝	2.98¼	2.79⅛	2.79¼	2.74⅝	2.76⅞	2.72¼	2.75⅝	2.68¾	2.73½	2.67⅞	2.72⅞	2.69½	2.72⅞	2.69¼	2.75¾	2.70	2.75¾	2.71⅝	2.73¾	2.69½
1966-67	2.99¾	2.78½	2.91	2.84½	3.21¾	2.89	3.40½	3.08¼	3.41¼	3.18½	3.40⅝	3.03	3.08¾	2.95⅝	3.01¼	2.92	3.00	2.91¾	2.93⅞	2.86⅝	2.92⅞	2.84⅝	2.93¼	2.84½
1965-66	2.65⅞	2.61¼	2.61⅞	2.49¼	2.57½	2.50¾	2.64	2.50	2.58	2.51⅛	2.61⅞	2.52	2.56¼	2.52	2.61½	2.54⅞	2.71⅝	2.61⅛	2.92¼	2.68	2.96¼	2.79¼	2.85¾	2.78½
1964-65	2.54	2.46¾	2.51	2.45⅛	2.52¼	2.44⅛	2.65¼	2.44½	2.65¾	2.47½	2.86½	2.59⅛	2.89	2.71¼	2.97½	2.75¼	3.01¼	2.79½	3.11¾	2.78½	3.13½	2.90¾	3.05½	2.88
1963-64	2.57¼	2.50	2.61½	2.54	2.69¾	2.57⅜	2.89	2.59¾	2.67⅝	2.57⅝	2.87½	2.59¼	2.98	2.74¼	2.98¾	2.68	2.93	2.66½	2.85⅛	2.63¾	2.70¾	2.62⅛	2.71⅜	2.56½
1962-63	2.48	2.45	2.46¼	2.42⅜	2.43⅝	2.40	2.41¾	2.37¼	2.42⅞	2.36	2.47½	2.39⅝	2.56½	2.43	2.51⅝	2.44½	2.50½	2.47	2.78¾	2.48⅞	2.69	2.58¼	2.65¼	2.52
1961-62	2.71¼	2.48¼	2.68¼	2.56¾	2.61	2.52¼	2.62¾	2.53½	2.54½	2.49¼	2.49¾	2.44¾	2.50⅞	2.43⅝	2.49½	2.44½	2.47⅜	2.45	2.47⅞	2.43½	2.45⅛	2.38¾	2.46⅛	2.39¼

May Delivery

	JUNE		JULY		AUGUST		SEPTEMBER		OCTOBER		NOVEMBER		DECEMBER		JANUARY		FEBRUARY		MARCH		APRIL		MAY	
	High	Low	High	Low	High	Low	High	Low	High	Low	High	Low	High	Low	High	Low	High	Low	High	Low	High	Low	High	Low
1970-71	3.08⅛	2.69⅛	3.14½	2.95½	3.14	2.89¼	3.05¼	2.88½	3.22½	2.98⅜	3.18¼	3.04½	3.08¾	2.98¼	...	...	...	...	...	...	...	...	...	...
1969-70	2.49⅛	2.44⅜	2.52⅝	2.45⅞	2.50⅜	2.46¾	2.52⅞	2.46⅛	2.60⅞	2.50¼	2.63¼	2.53¼	2.58	2.52¼	2.60⅜	2.54¾p	2.63½	2.57⅞	2.62½	2.58½	2.66⅞	2.59½	2.70	2.62¾
1968-69	2.71¼	2.64⅛	2.68¼	2.60⅜	2.64⅝	2.60	2.64¼	2.57⅝	2.65¼	2.58	2.68⅜	2.62¼	2.67	2.63	2.68⅝	2.64⅞	2.68⅛	2.65¾	2.66½	2.62⅜	2.66¾	2.61¼	2.68	2.65
1967-68	2.94	2.81⅜	2.81¼	2.77⅛	2.79¾	2.75⅛	2.78	2.70⅝	2.75½	2.70⅜	2.76⅝	2.72½	2.77	2.73⅛	2.79¼	2.74	2.79	2.76	2.78¼	2.72⅝	2.73¼	2.69	2.73½	2.70⅛
1966-67	3.23¼	2.91⅝	3.42¼	3.10	3.43¼	3.20¾	3.42	3.05⅞	3.11¾	2.99	3.04¼	2.95⅛	3.00	2.90¼	2.91⅝	2.86	2.89¾	2.83⅜	2.92½	2.85	2.88⅜	2.80⅜	2.84½	2.79¾
1965-66	2.59¾	2.53⅝	2.66	2.52¼	2.60	2.53½	2.63⅝	2.54⅝	2.58⅜	2.55	2.63⅜	2.57¼	2.74⅜	2.63⅛	2.94¼	2.70½	2.98⅜	2.82½	2.89¾	2.81½	3.07¼	2.85¼	3.08¾	2.97⅞
1964-65	2.57¼	2.49¾	2.54¾	2.46¾	2.67¾	2.51¼	2.88	2.61¼	2.91	2.73⅛	2.99	2.67½	3.02⅝	2.80⅝	3.14½	2.80¼	3.17¼	2.94½	3.09¾	2.88¾	3.07¾	2.86½	2.90	2.78½
1963-64	2.72	2.59⅞	2.89	2.61¾	2.69¾	2.59	2.90½	2.61¾	3.00	2.77¼	3.02¾	2.72½	2.93½	2.69¾	2.88⅝	2.66½	2.73	2.63⅜	2.70	2.58¼	2.60¾	2.54	2.56⅛	2.45½
1962-63	2.46	2.41¾	2.43¾	2.39½	2.45¼	2.38⅝	2.50¼	2.41¾	2.58	2.45⅛	2.53¾	2.46½	2.53	2.49¼	2.81¼	2.51	2.72½	2.60¼	2.67½	2.53½	2.62⅞	2.54	2.64¾	2.56
1961-62	2.64¼	2.55½	2.65¼	2.56¼	2.57½	2.52⅛	2.52¾	2.47⅞	2.53½	2.46⅞	2.52	2.46⅛	2.49½	2.46⅜	2.50⅛	2.46½	2.48½	2.47⅞	2.49¼	2.43½	2.52½	2.47	2.51⅛	2.47¾

July Delivery

	AUGUST		SEPTEMBER		OCTOBER		NOVEMBER		DECEMBER		JANUARY		FEBRUARY		MARCH		APRIL		MAY		JUNE		JULY	
	High	Low	High	Low	High	Low	High	Low	High	Low	High	Low	High	Low	High	Low	High	Low	High	Low	High	Low	High	Low
1970-71	3.13	2.91½	3.07	2.89	3.22½	2.99½	3.19¼	3.06⅛	3.11½	3.01	...	...	...	...	...	...	...	...	...	...	...	...	...	...
1969-70	2.52⅜	2.47¾	2.54¼	2.48	2.62⅛	2.52	2.65⅜	2.54¾	2.60⅛	2.54½	2.63½	2.56⅞	2.66¾	2.59⅞	2.66¼	2.62¼	2.71⅜	2.64⅛	2.72½	2.66½	2.99⅜	2.70¾	2.98	2.84½
1968-69	2.64⅞	2.60	2.64¾	2.58¼	2.66⅛	2.58⅝	2.69¼	2.63	2.67¼	2.63½	2.68⅞	2.65¼	2.69½	2.67	2.69	2.65⅞	2.70⅞	2.65⅝	2.71¾	2.66⅝	2.67½	2.63¼	2.70	2.64⅝
1967-68	2.81	2.76½	2.78⅞	2.71½	2.76⅝	2.71⅜	2.78⅞	2.73⅞	2.79⅛	2.75⅝	2.80½	2.76⅛	2.80⅛	2.78¼	2.81⅝	2.78⅝	2.76¼	2.72⅛	2.74¼	2.70½	2.72¼	2.63⅛	2.70¼	2.64⅞
1966-67	3.44½	3.21¾	3.44	3.07⅞	3.13	3.00¼	3.05	2.96¾	3.00⅛	2.89⅝	2.90¾	2.85¼	2.88	2.82	2.92	2.85¼	2.87⅞	2.81⅜	2.89½	2.81	2.95½	2.81¾	2.86½	2.79¼
1965-66	2.62½	2.54¾	2.64½	2.55⅝	2.59¾	2.56	2.64⅛	2.58	2.75	2.63¾	2.95	2.71½	2.99	2.83⅜	2.91½	2.82¾	3.11⅛	2.86⅞	3.17¼	3.01¾	3.77¼	3.12¾	3.72	3.41½
1964-65	2.68¾	2.53	2.88¼	2.61⅝	2.90	2.73	2.98¼	2.76¾	3.01¼	2.78½	3.14½	2.78¼	3.17½	2.96	3.10¾	2.90½	3.08¾	2.88½	2.91¾	2.72¼	3.00¾	2.80¼	2.98¼	2.73⅛
1963-64	2.70¾	2.60½	2.91½	2.62⅞	3.01¾	2.78½	3.04½	2.71½	3.00	2.70¼	2.90⅞	2.68⅛	2.74	2.64¾	2.69¼	2.55½	2.58¼	2.50	2.53	2.46¼	2.51¾	2.47⅜	2.55⅝	2.46⅝
1962-63	2.42⅜	2.16¼	2.50¾	2.42¼	2.57¾	2.45⅝	2.54⅜	2.46⅝	2.54⅛	2.50⅛	2.83	2.52	2.74½	2.61	2.68⅜	2.54⅝	2.61⅛	2.55	2.66	2.57½	2.67	2.58¼	2.81	2.57
1961-62	2.59¼	2.54⅜	2.55¼	2.50	2.55¾	2.49⅝	2.53¼	2.46⅛	2.49⅝	2.46⅞	2.50⅜	2.47⅛	2.49⅛	2.14⅞	2.49¾	2.46⅜	2.51⅜	2.47	2.49½	2.46¼	2.50⅝	2.44¼	2.57	2.47⅞

August Delivery

	SEPTEMBER		OCTOBER		NOVEMBER		DECEMBER		JANUARY		FEBRUARY		MARCH		APRIL		MAY		JUNE		JULY		AUGUST	
	High	Low	High	Low	High	Low	High	Low	High	Low	High	Low	High	Low	High	Low	High	Low	High	Low	High	Low	High	Low
1970-71	3.03½	2.86½	3.16½	2.96	3.15¾	3.03¼	3.08¾	2.99	...	...	...	...	...	...	...	...	...	...	...	...	...	...	...	...
1969-70	2.51⅝	2.45⅝	2.58½	2.49¾	2.61¾	2.53½	2.57⅜	2.53½	2.60⅝	2.53½	2.64¾	2.57⅜	2.65⅝	2.61⅜	2.69½	2.62½	2.70	2.64⅝	2.98½	2.68⅛	2.97⅝	2.80½	2.94	2.73¾
1968-69	2.63½	2.55	2.62¾	2.54	2.64½	2.59⅝	2.62¼	2.58⅞	2.65	2.60¼	2.65⅝	2.63½	2.65¼	2.61	2.67⅜	2.62⅛	2.68¾	2.62½	2.65¼	2.61⅜	2.65¼	2.60¼	2.74	2.63½
1967-68	2.77	2.69⅝	2.74⅞	2.70⅛	2.78¾	2.72⅜	2.78¼	2.75¼	2.79½	2.75⅜	2.78⅞	2.77⅜	2.81	2.75½	2.76⅜	2.72⅛	2.73⅜	2.69½	2.71¼	2.63⅝	2.67¾	2.64⅝	2.70½	2.65
1966-67	3.40	3.04½	3.09½	2.96	3.01¼	2.93½	2.97	2.86¾	2.87¼	2.82¼	2.85⅝	2.79⅜	2.89¾	2.83⅜	2.86½	2.80⅜	2.88½	2.80⅜	2.95⅜	2.78⅞	2.80¾	2.74¾	2.80	2.72¼
1965-66	2.61¾	2.52¾	2.57	2.53⅝	2.60¼	2.54¾	2.70¾	2.59⅞	2.90¾	2.68¼	2.95¼	2.80	2.88¼	2.80	3.08½	2.83⅝	3.13¾	2.98⅝	3.68¼	3.11	3.65¾	3.30½	3.98	3.34
1964-65	2.83	2.59¾	2.84	2.67½	2.91⅝	2.70¼	2.95¼	2.72¾	3.07	2.73¼	3.10½	2.90	3.04¾	2.84¼	3.02¼	2.83¾	2.86½	2.68½	2.90⅞	2.74	2.87¼	2.71	2.83½	2.69⅛
1963-64	...	...	2.99¼	2.75	2.99	2.67	2.92½	2.67½	2.85¾	2.63¾	2.70¼	2.61	2.65¾	2.51¼	2.54	2.47	2.50¼	2.44	2.50¾	2.44⅜	2.49⅝	2.44½	2.60	2.48¾
1962-63	2.48⅜	2.42½	2.51	2.42⅛	2.51½	2.42¾	2.52¼	2.47⅝	2.81¼	2.49⅝	2.73½	2.59½	2.66⅞	2.53⅛	2.62⅛	2.52¾	2.65¾	2.57⅝	2.65½	2.58⅝	2.81	2.57½	2.65½	2.55¼
1961-62	2.55¼	2.50⅞	2.56⅝	2.51	2.53¼	2.45½	2.48⅝	2.45½	2.48¾	2.46½	2.49	2.44⅞	2.49¼	2.46½	2.50¼	2.45⅞	2.46¾	2.43⅞	2.46¾	2.40⅞	2.48¾	2.44⅛	2.56½	2.38½

Source: Chicago Board of Trade, *Statistical Annual 1970.*

FIGURE 188—*Continued*
SOYBEANS
Monthly Range of Futures Prices
(dollars per bushel)

September Delivery

	OCTOBER		NOVEMBER		DECEMBER		JANUARY		FEBRUARY		MARCH		APRIL		MAY		JUNE		JULY		AUGUST		SEPTEMBER	
	High	Low	High	Low	High	Low	High	Low	High	Low	High	Low	High	Low	High	Low	High	Low	High	Low	High	Low	High	Low
1970–71	2.91	2.80¾	2.97	2.86½	2.94	2.85¾	......	......	......	......	......	......	......	......	......	......	......	......	......	......	......	......	......	......
1969–70	2.49¼	2.42¾	2.51	2.46⅛	2.50½	2.45¼	2.55⅝	2.46⅞	2.56½	2.51½	2.56¾	2.53⅞	2.65¾	2.55¾	2.74¾	2.59	2.96	2.61⅝	2.99¾	2.81¼	2.92⅞	2.75	2.86	2.71½
1968–69	2.50½	2.40½	2.49	2.45⅛	2.49	2.44⅝	2.51¼	2.46⅝	2.50½	2.47½	2.49¼	2.42½	2.47	2.44	2.49⅛	2.44⅝	2.46⅝	2.44⅛	2.47⅞	2.44¼	2.48⅞	2.43½	2.49⅛	2.43½
1967–68	2.71	2.66¼	2.75⅝	2.69¾	2.74½	2.72¼	2.74⅞	2.71⅝	2.75	2.73⅛	2.76	2.68¾	2.69⅝	2.64⅝	2.65⅞	2.64⅛	2.65	2.57¼	2.60⅝	2.55½	2.63⅞	2.54⅝	2.69	2.57½
1966–67	3.01	2.86¼	2.92	2.86	2.91¼	2.83	2.84½	2.79⅛	2.82	2.77⅛	2.85⅛	2.80⅛	2.82½	2.78	2.85¾	2.77	2.93	2.74½	2.74⅝	2.69¼	2.80	2.68	2.79¼	2.71¾
1965–66	2.49¾	2.46⅞	2.53⅝	2.47¼	2.64⅝	2.53	2.76½	2.66	2.79¼	2.70½	2.75⅛	2.71	2.94	2.74¾	2.92⅝	2.82⅞	3.¾½	2.91⅝	3.46	3.11½	3.62¾	3.23¼	3.43½	3.03
1964–65	2.60	2.50¼	2.63½	2.51½	2.66¼	2.54½	2.70½	2.54¾	2.68	2.59¼	2.67¾	2.59	2.67½	2.60¼	2.61¼	2.47⅛	2.59¼	2.49¾	2.61¾	2.48⅝	2.56¼	2.47¼	2.72¼	2.49
1963–64	2.73½	2.62½	2.68¾	2.47	2.69½	2.55½	2.63⅝	2.54⅛	2.61¼	2.54⅝	2.58¼	2.45¾	2.49½	2.41¾	2.45⅞	2.39⅞	2.47½	2.41⅛	2.45⅞	2.38¾	2.58	2.43¼	2.79¾	2.52⅛
1962–63	2.41	2.32¾	2.38⅞	2.33⅛	2.43¼	2.30¾	2.58¾	2.42	2.55½	2.49½	2.55⅛	2.43	2.53⅝	2.45¾	2.57⅝	2.49¾	2.64¼	2.53½	2.80	2.54½	2.63½	2.53	2.69½	2.53¾
1961–62	2.48⅝	2.43⅞	2.45¼	2.33¾	2.39⅛	2.35½	2.42	2.38⅝	2.41⅞	2.37¾	2.41⅞	2.39⅝	2.43⅝	2.40¼	2.41⅝	2.35½	2.37⅛	2.33¼	2.35½	2.30½	2.35⅞	2.28⅝	2.44	2.32½

November Delivery

Trading Year	Delivery Year	DECEMBER		JANUARY		FEBRUARY		MARCH		APRIL		MAY		JUNE		JULY		AUGUST		SEPTEMBER		OCTOBER		NOVEMBER	
		High	Low	High	Low	High	Low	High	Low	High	Low	High	Low	High	Low	High	Low	High	Low	High	Low	High	Low	High	Low
1970–71	1972	......	......	......	......	......	......	......	......	......	......	......	......	......	......	......	......	......	......	......	......	......	......	......	......
	1971	2.86⅞	2.75¾	......	......	......	......	......	......	......	......	......	......	......	......	......	......	......	......	......	......	......	......	......	......
1969–70	1971	......	......	......	......	......	......	......	......	......	......	......	......	......	......	......	......	......	......	......	......	2.79¾	2.75½	2.88¼	2.76¼
	1970	2.86⅞	2.75¾	2.50¾	2.42⅞	2.52¾	2.47	2.54	2.51¼	2.77¾	2.52¾	2.62	2.55¾	2.95⅞	2.57¾	3.02	2.81¾	2.97½	2.76	2.92	2.75	3.10¼	2.84¾	3.06¾	3.00⅞
1968–69		2.43¼	2.39¼	2.45¾	2.40¼	2.42¼	2.38½	2.39¾	2.33¼	2.36½	2.34¼	2.38⅜	2.33⅝	2.36¼	2.33⅝	2.39½	2.33⅛	2.37¾	2.34¼	2.40½	2.34⅝	2.48	2.36⅛	2.48	2.41⅝
1967–68		2.72⅜	2.69¼	2.72	2.68½	2.72½	2.70⅜	2.73¼	2.66⅝	2.67¼	2.61¾	2.63¼	2.61¾	2.62⅜	2.55⅛	2.58	2.52⅞	2.55½	2.51¾	2.55⅛	2.47¼	2.53¼	2.47¾	2.58	2.51¼
1966–67		2.88¼	2.80¼	2.81⅞	2.76½	2.79½	2.74½	2.83⅛	2.78	2.80½	2.76	2.83¾	2.75½	2.91⅜	2.72¼	2.72½	2.67⅞	2.70	2.65½	2.69¾	2.62⅝	2.67⅛	2.61¼	2.65½	2.62¼
1965–66		2.59¾	2.49⅝	2.69½	2.58	2.72	2.65¼	2.71	2.66⅜	2.86⅝	2.71½	2.83¾	2.77	3.15¼	2.81¾	3.34½	3.01	3.32¾	3.11½	3.28¼	2.93¼	3.00	2.87¾	3.07	2.88½
1964–65		2.58½	2.48	2.58	2.49¾	2.57¼	2.50½	2.57½	2.53⅛	2.59⅛	2.54⅜	2.54⅞	2.42¼	2.50½	2.43¾	2.57	2.43⅛	2.50¾	2.44⅛	2.54⅞	2.44¾	2.49⅛	2.44½	2.55⅛	2.52⅞
1963–64		2.64½	2.52	2.59⅞	2.52	2.59¾	2.52⅝	2.56¼	2.44½	2.48	2.40¼	2.44½	2.38½	2.47	2.40	2.45	2.37⅝	2.58¼	2.41¾	2.79½	2.52	2.82½	2.64¼	2.82¼	2.68½
1962–63		2.41½	2.35½	2.52½	2.40⅛	2.51⅞	2.47¼	2.52⅜	2.42¼	2.51	2.43¾	2.55	2.48⅛	2.61	2.51	2.82⅝	2.53¾	2.61¼	2.51	2.80	2.52¼	2.90	2.67¼	2.91½	2.66½
1961–62		2.37¾	2.33¼	2.41	2.36⅜	2.41	2.37	2.40⅛	2.38¼	2.41¼	2.37⅞	2.39⅛	2.35	2.36½	2.33⅛	2.35	2.30⅝	2.36¼	2.29¼	2.40½	2.33¼	2.50	2.36⅝	2.48	2.39⅝
1960–61		2.18¾	2.12¾	2.31½	2.15¾	2.49⅞	2.26¼	2.45½	2.31½	2.63½	2.40½	2.60½	2.49	2.52¼	2.43¾	2.53¾	2.54¼	2.46¾	2.41⅝	2.42⅛	2.36⅜	2.44⅛	2.35⅛	2.44¼	2.39¼

Source: Chicago Board of Trade, *Statistical Annual 1970.*

FIGURE 189
SOYBEAN MEAL
Monthly Range of Futures Prices
(dollars per ton)

January Delivery

Trading Year	Delivery Year	FEB High	FEB Low	MAR High	MAR Low	APR High	APR Low	MAY High	MAY Low	JUN High	JUN Low	JUL High	JUL Low	AUG High	AUG Low	SEP High	SEP Low	OCT High	OCT Low	NOV High	NOV Low	DEC High	DEC Low	JAN High	JAN Low
1970-71	1972																								
	1971																			75.25	75.00	76.50	75.00		
1969-70		77.70	69.00	70.10	68.80	70.50	68.55	69.90	68.80	82.70	69.30	83.45	75.40	83.50	74.90	80.20	76.50	81.00	76.70	83.10	78.10	84.10	78.65		
1968-69		69.20	68.00	68.25	66.75	68.45	67.20	69.40	67.80	68.85	68.20	69.80	66.85	68.75	67.00	68.95	67.35	72.90	68.00	69.85	66.30	83.25	68.15	98.50	76.40
1967-68		74.15	73.80	74.45	73.30	73.35	72.90	73.35	72.95	74.90	73.30	75.05	73.35	75.15	73.30	74.85	72.70	75.00	72.95	74.95	71.50	72.80	70.35	71.65	69.40
1966-67		65.20	63.55	65.50	64.35	68.75	65.00	69.30	67.10	79.00	69.40	82.70	73.50	82.40	75.80	80.20	74.50	77.75	73.40	75.85	73.10	79.70	75.50	78.95	74.25
1965-66		62.00	59.75	62.10	60.75	62.60	61.75	61.90	60.60	63.70	60.90	64.60	60.90	62.90	59.60	65.00	59.55	62.25	59.55	62.90	61.10	66.45	62.45	75.75	64.75
1964-65		68.00	67.25	62.15	63.15	64.25	61.40	61.70	59.35	62.70	60.65	62.40	58.95	65.80	60.35	69.25	63.15	68.85	63.50	66.15	62.75	66.90	62.00	66.10	62.00
1963-64				62.40	59.65	62.35	59.25	63.45	61.25	66.75	63.10	71.50	64.75	69.60	65.80	74.70	67.50	76.10	71.40	75.40	71.10	78.80	71.45	74.60	71.90
1962-63										59.15	56.50	60.90	55.90	60.35	55.85	62.75	59.00	66.70	59.80	66.20	61.50	68.10	63.85	69.60	64.50
1961-62										57.30	54.30	57.25	55.10	55.60	51.80	52.35	49.50	54.75	48.25	55.25	52.50	57.45	54.10	57.35	52.50

March Delivery

Trading Year	APR High	APR Low	MAY High	MAY Low	JUN High	JUN Low	JUL High	JUL Low	AUG High	AUG Low	SEP High	SEP Low	OCT High	OCT Low	NOV High	NOV Low	DEC High	DEC Low	JAN High	JAN Low	FEB High	FEB Low	MAR High	MAR Low
1970-71	70.75	69.30	70.75	69.60	83.00	70.20	83.20	75.70	83.45	75.35	79.85	76.90	80.95	77.40	81.65	78.10	81.70	78.65						
1969-70	69.40	68.30	70.20	68.55	69.95	69.30	71.25	68.55	70.00	68.20	70.00	68.40	72.90	69.00	70.40	67.35	76.75	68.25	81.50	72.90	86.50	77.20	81.00	69.50
1968-69	73.90	73.50	74.05	73.40	75.30	73.75	75.10	73.80	74.95	73.95	73.00	70.40	75.70	73.75	75.80	72.65	73.85	71.75	73.10	71.00	72.80	70.20	72.50	70.70
1967-68	72.15	70.40	72.80	70.35	74.80	71.00	72.40	70.90	73.00	70.40	72.40	70.60	73.00	70.55	74.75	72.25	74.65	72.85	75.60	73.20	75.05	73.10	74.45	73.45
1966-67	68.90	65.25	69.45	67.25	78.95	69.60	82.70	73.00	82.50	76.00	81.00	74.75	77.95	73.70	75.60	73.20	76.90	74.90	76.45	73.70	76.80	73.50	75.00	72.00
1965-66	63.20	62.15	62.50	61.50	64.50	61.90	65.05	61.45	63.60	60.45	64.50	60.65	61.95	59.85	62.35	60.75	65.50	62.25	70.85	64.40	71.85	67.25	69.00	65.75
1964-65	64.25	61.85	62.15	59.95	63.00	61.10	62.65	59.50	66.60	60.95	66.60	60.95	64.00	60.15	69.10	64.00	67.15	63.70	67.92	64.00	69.80	65.50	67.20	63.00
1963-64	61.70	61.15	64.10	61.45	67.00	63.25	72.50	65.15	69.35	66.05	74.60	67.55	77.25	71.85	75.85	72.20	80.00	72.45	76.45	71.60	72.95	67.70	69.45	65.50
1962-63					61.15	56.60	60.60	56.20	62.00	59.55	66.00	60.10	64.60	61.20	66.55	63.40	72.00	64.90	69.45	66.90	69.75	64.05
1961-62					56.90	53.20	53.90	51.55	54.75	50.20	55.00	52.75	54.60	53.25	55.75	53.20	55.45	52.30	59.55	54.95

May Delivery

Trading Year	JUN High	JUN Low	JUL High	JUL Low	AUG High	AUG Low	SEP High	SEP Low	OCT High	OCT Low	NOV High	NOV Low	DEC High	DEC Low	JAN High	JAN Low	FEB High	FEB Low	MAR High	MAR Low	APR High	APR Low	MAY High	MAY Low
1970-71	84.00	70.90	84.00	76.50	84.00	76.00	80.10	77.40	80.85	78.25	81.70	78.95	81.45	78.75										
1969-70	71.20	70.40	72.35	70.00	71.10	69.30	71.20	69.45	73.25	70.00	71.50	68.60	74.80	69.40	75.65	72.05	77.50	72.80	75.25	70.30	77.70	70.20	74.50	71.35
1968-69	75.70	74.20	75.25	74.20	75.60	74.25	75.55	74.10	76.40	74.60	76.60	73.80	74.85	72.90	74.55	72.40	74.20	72.05	73.75	72.05	76.20	72.65	77.95	74.20
1967-68	76.00	71.45	72.70	71.50	73.25	70.85	72.70	71.05	73.60	71.05	75.25	72.65	75.20	73.70	76.10	74.20	75.60	74.25	75.40	74.20	75.15	73.55	74.95	73.40
1966-67	78.75	69.50	82.70	73.25	82.65	76.00	81.75	75.40	78.00	74.10	76.00	73.80	76.35	74.55	75.20	73.20	76.30	74.90	76.45	73.70	72.40	68.30	69.95	68.10
1965-66	64.00	63.85	65.60	62.25	64.40	61.15	64.70	61.35	62.55	60.75	63.05	61.10	65.70	63.15	69.70	65.05	70.25	66.65	69.20	66.25	77.85	67.00	78.20	74.50
1964-65			60.50	59.85	67.10	61.40	66.60	60.95	66.60	60.95	64.40	61.15	68.60	65.90	72.00	65.90	71.75	67.20	69.65	64.25	67.65	64.30	66.75	63.85
1963-64	67.20	63.90	72.75	65.80	69.20	66.30	74.75	67.40	77.10	72.25	76.40	72.75	80.35	73.05	78.10	72.00	73.40	69.60	71.20	65.15	67.60	62.45	63.75	58.85
1962-63			59.00	57.25	60.90	56.55	62.60	60.00	66.70	60.20	63.85	61.25	66.10	63.20	72.45	64.40	69.95	67.00	68.95	63.50	66.75	63.75	66.10	63.60
1961-62					55.15	52.90	55.20	51.40	55.50	53.45	54.40	53.40	55.40	53.85	55.85	53.30	57.65	55.10	59.80	56.45	61.75	57.45

July Delivery

Trading Year	AUG High	AUG Low	SEP High	SEP Low	OCT High	OCT Low	NOV High	NOV Low	DEC High	DEC Low	JAN High	JAN Low	FEB High	FEB Low	MAR High	MAR Low	APR High	APR Low	MAY High	MAY Low	JUN High	JUN Low	JUL High	JUL Low
1970-71	84.50	76.75	80.25	77.80	81.75	78.15	82.25	79.50	82.05	79.60														
1969-70	72.20	70.60	71.95	70.40	74.15	71.00	72.80	69.70	75.10	71.00	75.40	72.50	75.40	72.70	74.00	71.60	77.30	71.40	74.75	71.90	84.00	73.10	84.75	78.60
1968-69	76.00	74.70	75.75	74.70	77.20	75.35	77.30	74.80	75.75	73.90	75.70	73.60	75.35	73.70	75.20	73.35	76.25	74.65	76.20	74.75	79.90	76.65	77.60	76.00
1967-68	73.50	71.55	73.00	71.55	74.30	71.50	75.70	73.65	75.80	74.30	76.95	75.20	76.35	75.35	76.40	75.20	76.25	74.65	76.20	74.75	81.60	75.65	84.25	79.50
1966-67	82.85	77.60	82.10	76.85	78.20	74.65	76.75	74.35	76.55	74.90	75.10	73.50	74.85	72.95	74.75	72.35	72.70	69.60	74.55	69.65	77.35	72.85	78.40	74.75
1965-66	64.75	61.85	64.75	61.80	63.15	61.50	63.75	61.85	66.10	63.80	69.70	65.65	70.50	67.05	69.45	66.70	76.30	67.50	79.85	73.75	100.00	79.15	98.85	88.00
1964-65	67.25	64.00	70.40	64.40	69.75	64.90	69.10	64.90	69.30	66.80	73.50	66.85	73.00	69.00	70.90	66.15	69.70	66.40	68.35	65.10	74.05	67.70	72.35	67.85
1963-64	68.85	66.60	74.50	67.30	75.75	72.50	76.45	73.10	80.50	73.10	78.50	72.00	73.45	70.35	71.70	65.75	67.35	62.65	63.05	60.15	63.75	60.50	63.35	60.25
1962-63	60.90	60.40	62.05	60.60	66.00	60.30	63.60	61.10	65.95	63.15	72.50	64.45	70.05	67.20	68.85	63.75	67.25	63.90	66.85	64.95	68.35	65.95	72.30	65.60
1961-62			55.00	54.00	55.75	52.60	55.75	54.00	54.90	53.50	55.40	54.40	55.90	53.95	57.05	55.40	58.30	56.25	62.75	56.90	65.30	61.10	67.55	62.15

Source: Chicago Board of Trade, *Statistical Annual 1970.*

FIGURE 189—*Continued*
SOYBEAN MEAL
Monthly Range of Futures Prices
(dollars per ton)

August Delivery

	SEPTEMBER		OCTOBER		NOVEMBER		DECEMBER		JANUARY		FEBRUARY		MARCH		APRIL		MAY		JUNE		JULY		AUGUST	
	High	Low	High	Low	High	Low	High	Low	High	Low	High	Low	High	Low	High	Low	High	Low	High	Low	High	Low	High	Low
1970–71	80.20	77.60	81.25	78.10	82.20	79.40	82.00	79.50																
1969–70	71.90	70.60	74.15	71.00	73.05	70.40	75.05	71.25	75.10	72.50	74.90	72.30	73.50	71.65	76.25	71.45	74.50	72.00	84.15	73.20	86.85	78.75	87.60	81.50
1968–69	75.55	74.60	76.75	75.20	76.80	75.05	75.75	73.90	75.50	73.55	75.25	73.75	74.95	73.40	77.30	74.30	80.25	76.25	79.85	77.60	78.35	74.30	78.10	73.25
1967–68	71.95	71.60	74.10	71.55	76.00	73.50	75.75	74.30	76.75	75.30	76.30	75.45	76.40	75.40	76.45	74.85	76.65	75.30	79.85	76.05	76.00	72.15	76.30	72.95
1966–67	81.00	76.00	78.00	74.50	76.50	74.30	76.45	74.90	69.70	65.80	70.35	67.25	69.65	67.05	76.35	67.50	79.65	73.25	96.00	79.00	95.00	82.05	108.50	84.00
1965–66	64.55	62.10	63.35	62.00	63.90	62.20	66.40	64.10																
1964–65			69.15	64.70	68.90	64.75	68.70	66.60	72.25	66.65	72.05	68.70	70.75	66.00	69.45	66.70	68.40	65.50	73.95	67.60	72.35	67.15	70.50	62.30
1963–64	74.40	67.40	77.00	73.50	75.75	72.90	80.15	73.25	77.75	71.60	72.50	69.80	71.10	65.65	66.90	62.65	63.00	60.20	63.80	60.90	63.35	59.20	63.30	59.60
1962–63	61.10	61.10	64.75	60.30	63.00	60.90	65.35	62.45	72.50	63.95	70.00	66.95	68.60	63.75	67.35	64.00	66.90	65.15	68.80	66.05	72.75	66.10	74.00	68.80
1961–62									55.30	54.50	55.90	54.30	57.00	55.50	57.75	56.20	62.00	56.85	64.00	60.05	66.05	60.60	68.50	61.05

September Delivery

	OCTOBER		NOVEMBER		DECEMBER		JANUARY		FEBRUARY		MARCH		APRIL		MAY		JUNE		JULY		AUGUST		SEPTEMBER	
	High	Low	High	Low	High	Low	High	Low	High	Low	High	Low	High	Low	High	Low	High	Low	High	Low	High	Low	High	Low
1970–71	78.00	76.30	79.50	76.30	79.50	77.50																		
1969–70	71.15	69.50	70.75	69.20	73.50	69.65	73.50	70.40	73.75	71.25	72.50	70.75	73.90	70.40	72.80	70.90	83.90	71.70	85.00	77.80	87.05	79.20	86.80	78.75
1968–69	74.40	72.75	74.10	71.75	72.70	71.40	72.80	71.55	72.95	71.65	72.65	71.10	74.00	72.30	76.80	73.50	76.05	73.95	74.50	72.00	74.95	71.30	74.00	69.10
1967–68	72.55	71.10	75.00	72.25	74.55	73.10	75.50	73.50	73.75	72.00	73.30	71.85	73.35	71.80	72.35	70.00	73.10	69.95	76.25	71.70	73.65	71.00	83.00	75.70
1966–67	74.00	72.35	74.00	72.50	75.00	73.50	73.75	72.00	73.30	71.85	73.35	71.80	72.35	70.00	72.75	69.95	76.50	70.30	79.50	74.80	83.50	76.75	83.00	75.70
1965–66			62.90	62.50	65.40	63.50	68.15	64.80	68.65	66.25	68.07	65.90	67.75	66.85	72.55	66.85	76.50	70.30	91.10	80.50	98.10	82.40	85.50	63.00
1964–65	64.00	61.80	63.75	59.80	64.00	61.90	65.50	63.10	64.60	63.25	64.70	62.50	65.60	63.60	64.50	62.70	68.50	64.00	67.80	64.40	65.90	60.85	71.00	63.15
1963–64	71.30	68.50	70.30	66.10	74.40	68.50	70.70	67.25	68.80	66.40	65.55	63.85	65.70	61.50	65.30	61.50	64.75	63.25	67.85	64.75	73.40	68.00	73.05	69.60
1962–63			60.10	58.85	63.00	59.70	66.30	62.10	65.55	63.85	65.70	61.50	65.30	61.50	64.75	63.25	67.85	64.75	72.70	65.60	72.00	56.50	68.25	62.25
1961–62									54.00	54.00	55.60	54.55	58.25	54.10	59.75	56.75	62.00	56.50	62.40	56.40				

October Delivery

	NOVEMBER		DECEMBER		JANUARY		FEBRUARY		MARCH		APRIL		MAY		JUNE		JULY		AUGUST		SEPTEMBER		OCTOBER	
	High	Low	High	Low	High	Low	High	Low	High	Low	High	Low	High	Low	High	Low	High	Low	High	Low	High	Low	High	Low
1970–71	76.50	73.90	77.80	75.70																				
1969–70	69.00	67.90	70.30	68.00	72.30	68.75	72.10	70.05	71.35	69.60	71.25	69.50	70.40	69.50	83.35	69.60	84.00	76.90	85.45	76.05	83.85	77.75	81.60	74.90
1968–69	72.00	69.90	70.30	69.25	70.70	69.50	69.80	68.75	69.00	67.40	69.90	68.25	72.00	69.50	71.35	69.95	71.20	68.50	70.00	68.10	70.40	67.90	77.90	70.10
1967–68					74.00	73.00	74.30	73.65	74.55	73.45	73.40	72.85	73.35	72.85	75.10	73.30	76.60	73.50	77.90	74.70	78.30	74.10	79.40	74.25
1966–67	73.00	71.25	73.50	72.00	72.60	71.70	72.15	71.40	73.15	71.65	66.05	64.40	69.75	65.10	71.70	68.00	77.90	74.70	78.30	74.10	79.40	74.25	80.15	75.15
1965–66					65.60	63.50	66.05	64.20	66.05	64.40	66.05	64.40	69.75	65.10	71.70	68.00	83.00	71.00	85.40	75.50	86.00	77.50	85.25	75.20
1964–65	61.75	58.50	61.50	59.80	61.60	60.00	62.25	59.50	62.75	59.50	62.95	61.60	61.75	60.60	64.60	61.25	65.70	61.55	64.00	59.95	69.40	60.25	67.80	61.75
1963–64	68.20	64.50	71.00	66.00	68.50	66.10	67.45	65.65	67.05	62.80	64.00	60.65	61.05	58.75	62.50	60.30	62.10	58.50	65.50	59.70	69.25	62.80	70.00	64.65
1962–63					63.50	60.45	62.25	61.20	62.25	59.30	62.35	58.75	63.40	61.00	66.70	63.05	71.50	64.75	71.00	66.25	73.00	68.30	74.00	69.05
1961–62									54.20	53.30	53.75	53.00	57.05	53.40	58.50	56.05	60.70	55.50	60.75	55.50	63.85	59.25	66.60	61.20

December Delivery

Trading Year	Delivery Year	JANUARY		FEBRUARY		MARCH		APRIL		MAY		JUNE		JULY		AUGUST		SEPTEMBER		OCTOBER		NOVEMBER		DECEMBER	
		High	Low	High	Low	High	Low	High	Low	High	Low	High	Low	High	Low	High	Low	High	Low	High	Low	High	Low	High	Low
1970	{1971}																					75.70	73.50	75.80	74.90
	{1970}	70.05	67.75	70.80	69.00	70.30	68.75	70.35	68.55	69.70	68.70	82.60	69.00	83.00	75.55	84.40	74.90	81.00	77.05	81.50	76.60	83.15	78.00	85.50	78.20
1969		70.00	69.15	69.25	68.00	68.20	66.55	68.45	67.10	69.45	67.80	68.80	68.15	69.65	66.60	68.40	66.50	68.75	67.05	74.40	68.35	71.20	66.50	90.50	69.20
1968		73.75	73.00	74.30	73.60	74.45	73.35	73.30	72.85	73.20	72.75	74.85	73.10	72.15	69.95	72.80	69.60	72.65	70.15	73.25	70.10	75.25	71.25	72.90	70.05
1967		72.50	71.50	72.20	71.40	73.05	71.65	71.95	69.95	72.55	69.85	74.55	70.70	72.15	69.95	82.75	73.50	82.00	75.60	81.00	74.50	78.15	73.80	82.50	75.50
1966		64.30	63.55	65.40	63.15	65.90	64.30	68.70	64.90	69.30	67.05	79.25	69.30	82.75	73.50	82.00	75.60	81.00	74.50	78.15	73.80	76.75	73.30	82.50	75.50
1965		61.65	60.00	62.10	59.00	62.20	60.50	62.45	61.30	61.60	60.35	62.55	60.00	63.50	60.65	62.15	58.70	65.00	59.10	64.25	59.40	64.90	62.75	68.45	63.55
1964		68.65	66.25	67.65	65.95	64.25	63.10	64.25	61.20	61.45	59.05	62.55	58.70	64.45	60.85	62.65	59.45	65.00	59.10	65.15	62.50	65.15	62.50	67.25	63.40
1963				62.60	61.30	62.40	59.40	62.35	59.00	63.45	61.00	66.45	63.05	71.45	64.60	69.60	65.40	74.00	67.50	75.80	70.95	75.15	70.60	80.00	70.30
1962								53.95	53.00	57.35	53.60	58.50	56.30	60.60	55.40	59.90	55.35	62.00	58.40	67.90	59.90	68.20	62.80	72.50	65.00
1961								58.00	52.55	56.90	54.70	56.60	53.50	55.00	50.90	51.50	48.45	54.25	47.20	54.25	47.20	55.60	52.00	60.50	54.25

Source: Chicago Board of Trade, *Statistical Annual 1970*.

FIGURE 190
SOYBEAN OIL
Monthly Range of Futures Prices
(dollars per 100 lbs.)

January Delivery

Trading Year	Delivery Year	FEBRUARY		MARCH		APRIL		MAY		JUNE		JULY		AUGUST		SEPTEMBER		OCTOBER		NOVEMBER		DECEMBER		JANUARY	
		High	Low	High	Low	High	Low	High	Low	High	Low	High	Low	High	Low	High	Low	High	Low	High	Low	High	Low	High	Low
1970-71	1972																				11.10	10.78	10.70	9.70		
	1971	8.85	8.24	9.00	8.65	9.87	8.91	9.83	9.07	10.20	9.38	10.65	9.53	10.46	9.65	11.07	9.67	13.29	10.79	13.20	12.04	12.54	11.55		
1969-70		7.59	7.20	7.58	7.28	7.36	7.11	7.39	7.09	7.21	7.00	7.35	7.19	7.56	7.23	8.15	7.28	9.20	7.75	10.55	8.20	9.34	8.52	9.70	8.95
1968-69				9.04	8.62	8.67	8.29	8.36	8.22	8.21	7.50	7.70	7.23	7.34	7.09	7.51	7.00	7.48	7.00	8.13	7.34	8.57	7.75	8.87	8.10
1967-68		9.80	9.63	10.04	9.70	10.06	9.83	10.24	9.95	10.40	9.32	9.38	9.05	9.51	8.95	9.35	8.94	9.07	8.56	8.73	8.43	8.67	8.42	8.49	8.23
1966-67		10.80	10.24	10.67	10.23	11.04	10.59	11.00	10.50	11.30	10.45	12.48	11.08	13.00	11.60	12.44	10.86	11.17	10.66	10.85	10.37	10.68	10.17	10.33	9.74
1965-66		9.70	9.30	9.70	9.25	9.85	9.41	9.53	8.62	8.85	8.38	9.02	8.43	9.21	8.64	9.57	9.00	9.76	9.07	10.51	9.55	10.78	10.28	11.94	10.68
1964-65						8.55	8.11	8.75	8.40	8.70	8.27	8.82	8.39	8.98	8.67	10.12	8.92	10.79	9.85	12.20	10.63	12.11	10.85	12.02	10.54
1963-64				9.58	9.25	9.58	9.21	9.51	9.18	9.50	9.18	9.70	8.81	8.97	8.32	9.55	8.23	10.10	9.08	10.42	7.05	9.12	7.90	8.24	7.92
1962-63										9.00	8.52	8.70	7.92	8.75	8.04	8.60	8.12	9.25	8.28	8.90	8.48	8.77	8.22	9.27	8.45
1961-62								11.07	10.90	11.11	10.27	11.22	10.34	11.07	10.59	10.88	10.59	11.05	10.44	10.62	10.38	10.81	10.33	10.73	10.35

March Delivery

Trading Year	APRIL		MAY		JUNE		JULY		AUGUST		SEPTEMBER		OCTOBER		NOVEMBER		DECEMBER		JANUARY		FEBRUARY		MARCH	
	High	Low	High	Low	High	Low	High	Low	High	Low	High	Low	High	Low	High	Low	High	Low	High	Low	High	Low	High	Low
1970-71	9.75	8.86	9.71	9.01	10.20	9.29	10.64	9.54	10.37	9.65	10.80	9.67	12.85	10.56	12.82	11.73	12.18	11.28						
1969-70	7.40	7.15	7.43	7.14	7.26	7.08	7.41	7.23	7.59	7.28	8.12	7.32	8.80	7.75	10.05	8.20	9.06	8.36	9.58	8.64	12.07	9.45	13.56	11.10
1968-69	8.70	8.30	8.44	8.30	8.31	7.58	7.78	7.32	7.43	7.14	7.58	7.11	7.56	7.07	8.17	7.44	8.47	7.78	8.70	8.18	8.95	8.37	8.88	8.33
1967-68	10.03	9.83	10.25	9.98	10.40	9.35	9.44	9.11	9.55	9.03	9.48	9.05	9.21	8.70	8.88	8.55	8.80	8.57	8.84	8.50	8.95	8.73	9.04	8.49
1966-67	11.00	10.59	10.95	10.50	11.18	10.43	12.37	11.02	12.90	11.55	12.43	10.90	11.18	10.72	10.81	10.35	10.61	10.15	10.31	9.89	10.18	9.84	10.33	9.94
1965-66	9.81	9.40	9.52	8.66	8.88	8.41	9.03	8.43	9.13	8.65	9.52	8.93	9.59	9.03	10.25	9.47	10.60	10.07	11.65	10.58	12.05	11.05	11.30	10.78
1964-65	8.65	8.21	8.85	8.48	8.79	8.40	8.93	8.50	9.07	8.77	10.11	9.02	10.65	9.82	12.00	10.49	11.89	10.68	12.30	10.45	12.25	11.35	12.20	11.60
1963-64	9.60	9.31	9.60	9.28	9.63	9.30	9.80	8.93	9.07	8.48	9.70	8.42	10.20	9.22	10.62	7.30	9.55	8.10	8.49	7.85	8.03	7.66	7.97	7.67
1962-63					8.83	8.00	8.89	8.19	8.70	8.27	9.39	8.45	9.03	8.63	8.95	8.40	9.42	8.58	9.44	9.03	9.30	8.92		
1961-62					10.95	10.50	11.03	10.44	11.21	10.63	11.00	10.71	11.13	10.54	10.73	10.50	10.97	10.51	10.90	10.32	10.52	9.90	10.25	9.92

May Delivery

Trading Year	JUNE		JULY		AUGUST		SEPTEMBER		OCTOBER		NOVEMBER		DECEMBER		JANUARY		FEBRUARY		MARCH		APRIL		MAY	
	High	Low	High	Low	High	Low	High	Low	High	Low	High	Low	High	Low	High	Low	High	Low	High	Low	High	Low	High	Low
1970-71	10.25	9.18	10.61	9.52	10.29	9.62	10.63	9.66	12.59	10.42	12.60	11.63	11.92	11.11										
1969-70	7.33	7.15	7.45	7.28	7.60	7.30	8.11	7.32	8.68	7.76	9.80	8.20	8.90	8.27	9.46	8.55	10.80	9.25	11.25	9.72	12.80	10.55	11.74	10.37
1968-69	8.33	7.66	7.86	7.38	7.50	7.20	7.63	7.20	7.65	7.15	8.23	7.53	8.47	7.85	8.54	8.12	8.75	8.24	8.66	8.21	8.72	8.30		
1967-68	10.40	9.43	9.52	9.18	9.59	9.13	9.58	9.16	9.33	8.85	9.02	8.67	8.95	8.68	8.96	8.68	9.05	8.85	9.10	8.52	8.70	8.35	8.71	8.27
1966-67	11.15	10.43	12.35	10.97	12.70	11.55	12.41	10.91	11.16	10.71	10.82	10.36	10.60	10.15	10.32	9.95	10.21	9.84	10.41	9.99	10.40	9.96	10.24	9.96
1965-66	8.85	8.43	9.03	8.45	9.05	8.65	9.17	8.86	10.09	9.06	10.58	9.83	10.15	9.40	10.51	10.01	11.47	10.48	11.88	10.93	11.60	10.74	11.65	10.85
1964-65	9.02	8.72	9.19	8.63	9.42	8.88	9.52	8.95	10.15	9.40	11.79	10.61	11.47	10.48	12.35	10.40	12.25	11.35	12.09	11.51	12.17	11.09	11.26	10.14
1963-64	9.72	9.40	9.89	9.03	9.19	8.63	9.83	8.61	10.29	9.35	10.73	7.45	9.75	8.27	8.71	8.05	8.27	7.92	8.13	7.71	8.03	7.51	8.21	7.86
1962-63			8.93	8.68	8.95	8.29	8.80	8.38	9.49	8.59	9.12	8.73	9.05	8.81	9.55	8.68	9.49	9.05	9.55	9.10	9.45	8.78	9.42	9.14
1961-62					11.20	10.67	11.03	10.68	11.20	10.62	10.79	10.54	11.03	10.55	10.97	10.52	10.70	10.13	10.37	10.03	10.21	9.55	9.83	8.90

July Delivery

Trading Year	AUGUST		SEPTEMBER		OCTOBER		NOVEMBER		DECEMBER		JANUARY		FEBRUARY		MARCH		APRIL		MAY		JUNE		JULY	
	High	Low	High	Low	High	Low	High	Low	High	Low	High	Low	High	Low	High	Low	High	Low	High	Low	High	Low	High	Low
1970-71	10.24	9.59	10.42	9.64	12.28	10.22	12.38	11.47	11.78	11.00														
1969-70	7.64	7.35	8.07	7.36	8.60	7.65	9.70	8.16	8.77	8.20	9.30	8.46	10.29	9.15	10.50	9.42	11.96	10.02	11.47	10.24	11.35	10.25	12.50	10.38
1968-69	7.56	7.27	7.68	7.26	7.70	7.22	8.24	7.60	8.45	7.87	8.49	8.07	8.66	8.18	8.57	8.15	8.57	8.09	8.70	8.26	7.75	7.32	7.94	7.62
1967-68	9.50	9.16	9.61	9.19	9.37	8.99	9.13	8.81	9.09	8.84	9.09	8.82	9.12	8.97	9.17	8.63	8.72	8.41	8.70	8.26	8.26	7.30	7.54	7.00
1966-67	12.70	11.60	12.36	10.93	11.16	10.74	10.80	10.38	10.59	10.15	10.32	9.95	10.21	9.85	10.42	9.98	10.47	10.06	10.37	10.08	10.55	9.12	9.18	8.78
1965-66			9.30	8.82	9.46	8.95	10.02	9.35	10.46	9.91	11.36	10.47	11.79	10.82	11.48	10.70	11.76	11.05	11.69	10.95	11.70	10.68	13.10	11.49
1964-65	9.15	9.14	10.05	9.12	10.47	9.78	11.75	10.29	11.70	10.55	12.35	10.31	12.20	11.30	11.99	11.31	11.98	10.92	11.06	9.60	10.33	9.36	10.15	9.62
1963-64	9.30	8.77	9.90	8.74	10.40	9.40	10.83	7.95	9.85	8.41	8.88	8.18	8.45	8.13	8.33	7.89	8.20	7.72	8.40	8.05	8.27	7.83	8.51	7.86
1962-63	8.40	8.37	8.85	8.58	9.43	8.72	9.15	8.80	9.15	8.60	9.65	8.76	9.57	9.12	9.61	9.17	9.49	8.87	9.41	8.91	9.21	8.93	9.44	8.60
1961-62			10.97	10.85	11.20	10.70	10.88	10.62	11.07	10.61	11.02	10.68	10.82	10.29	10.50	10.17	10.37	9.75	10.03	8.39	8.64	7.91	8.12	7.40

Source: Chicago Board of Trade, *Statistical Annual 1970.*

FIGURE 190—Continued
SOYBEAN OIL
Monthly Range of Futures Prices
(dollars per 100 lbs.)

August Delivery

	SEPTEMBER		OCTOBER		NOVEMBER		DECEMBER		JANUARY		FEBRUARY		MARCH		APRIL		MAY		JUNE		JULY		AUGUST	
	High	Low	High	Low	High	Low	High	Low	High	Low	High	Low	High	Low	High	Low	High	Low	High	Low	High	Low	High	Low
1970-71	10.31	9.74	11.96	10.11	12.17	11.35	11.51	10.90																
1969-70	7.92	7.38	8.52	7.68	9.65	8.10	8.62	8.10	9.13	8.43	10.09	9.01	10.14	9.25	11.63	9.83	11.19	10.01	11.15	10.20	12.16	10.16	12.31	11.01
1968-69	7.58	7.20	7.62	7.17	8.15	7.54	8.37	7.80	8.37	8.05	8.64	8.15	8.55	8.13	8.47	8.04	8.41	7.60	7.75	7.33	8.10	7.53*	8.96	8.07
1967-68	9.24	9.20	9.38	9.02	9.08	8.86	9.09	8.90	9.10	8.88	9.15	9.00	9.17	8.69	8.74	8.43	8.64	8.26	8.25	7.35	7.55	7.11	7.44	7.16
1966-67	11.60	10.75	11.10	10.74	10.75	10.38	10.58	10.13	10.27	9.95	10.12	9.85	10.36	9.96	10.44	10.08	10.41	10.12	10.60	9.23	9.27	8.79	9.62	8.87
1965-66	9.20	9.00	9.28	8.91	9.84	9.20	10.12	9.76	11.17	10.24	11.69	10.74	11.34	10.63	11.70	10.97	11.65	10.93	11.78	10.73	12.92	11.52	14.58	12.33
1964-65					11.60	11.20	11.58	10.50	12.25	10.20	12.06	11.19	11.73	11.00	11.62	10.76	10.80	9.45	10.05	9.24	9.90	9.43	11.00	9.50
1963-64					10.77	7.85	9.70	8.55	8.88	8.10	8.53	8.22	8.34	7.96	8.28	7.78	8.47	8.10	8.36	7.88	8.53	7.95	8.78	8.41
1962-63			9.40	8.95	9.11	8.80	9.14	8.65	9.63	8.77	9.57	9.14	9.60	9.16	9.48	8.92	9.41	8.93	9.18	8.96	9.36	8.60	8.62	7.94
1961-62									11.02	10.71	10.87	10.38	10.48	10.24	10.40	9.81	10.06	8.47	8.73	8.04	8.29	7.50	8.37	7.95

September Delivery

	OCTOBER		NOVEMBER		DECEMBER		JANUARY		FEBRUARY		MARCH		APRIL		MAY		JUNE		JULY		AUGUST		SEPTEMBER	
	High	Low	High	Low	High	Low	High	Low	High	Low	High	Low	High	Low	High	Low	High	Low	High	Low	High	Low	High	Low
1970-71	11.47	9.92	11.87	11.10	11.25	10.48																		
1969-70	8.26	7.56	9.10	7.97	8.34	7.92	8.99	8.20	9.83	8.85	9.95	9.13	11.22	9.60	10.77	9.80	11.02	10.10	11.55	9.93	11.53	10.46	12.35	10.65
1968-69	7.36	7.05	8.02	7.34	7.94	7.59	8.13	7.52	8.35	7.80	8.32	7.92	8.09	7.74	8.13	7.30	7.82	7.41	8.49	7.75	7.52	7.09	7.56	7.23
1967-68	9.22	9.00	9.10	8.85	9.07	8.92	9.12	8.88	9.14	9.01	9.13	8.69	8.74	8.42	8.51	8.25	8.24	7.36	7.54	7.18	9.59	8.96	9.30	9.04
1966-67	10.93	10.63	10.59	10.20	10.45	10.06	10.04	9.92	10.04	9.79	10.27	9.92	10.36	10.07	10.48	10.11	10.57	9.31	9.32	8.90	14.10	12.22	13.13	9.04
1965-66	9.12	8.75	9.73	9.01	10.12	9.66	10.97	10.17	11.37	10.60	11.08	10.59	11.50	10.91	11.50	10.86	11.77	10.76	12.90	11.52	10.34	9.18	13.50	9.95
1964-65	10.05	9.63	10.78	9.86	10.85	9.70	11.05	9.50	10.93	10.31	10.74	10.14	10.70	10.15	10.26	9.00	9.51	8.78	9.59	9.07				
1963-64			10.44	7.91	8.55	8.50	8.83	8.32	8.50	8.25	8.38	7.97	8.30	7.80	8.53	8.14	8.40	7.96	8.58	8.02	8.79	8.48	9.88	8.75
1962-63			9.06	8.96	9.10	8.65	9.43	8.73	9.49	9.07	9.60	9.12	9.49	8.96	9.40	8.96	9.26	9.01	9.45	8.64	8.70	7.98	8.75	7.85
1961-62					10.80	10.77	10.90	10.68	10.84	10.35	10.55	10.19	10.35	9.76	10.04	8.52	8.79	8.14	8.43	7.60	8.50	7.72	8.21	7.77

October Delivery

	NOVEMBER		DECEMBER		JANUARY		FEBRUARY		MARCH		APRIL		MAY		JUNE		JULY		AUGUST		SEPTEMBER		OCTOBER	
	High	Low	High	Low	High	Low	High	Low	High	Low	High	Low	High	Low	High	Low	High	Low	High	Low	High	Low	High	Low
1970-71	11.54	10.82	10.95	10.05																				
1969-70	8.55	7.90	8.15	7.80	8.54	8.00	9.33	8.50	9.40	8.90	10.68	9.32	10.44	9.47	10.70	9.78	10.98	9.73	11.00	10.13	12.43	10.22	14.90	12.11
1968-69	7.84	7.18	7.69	7.38	7.88	7.33	7.85	7.32	7.86	7.43	7.52	7.27	7.59	7.13	7.28	6.98	7.40	7.17	7.82	7.33	9.27	7.58	11.30	8.85
1967-68					9.00	8.86	9.07	8.93	9.02	8.57	8.60	8.28	8.38	8.16	8.15	7.38	7.57	7.13	7.30	7.05	7.56	7.23	7.18	6.91
1966-67	10.43	10.18	10.34	9.98	10.12	9.85	9.92	9.73	10.14	9.82	10.17	9.95	10.30	10.02	10.47	9.28	9.30	8.95	9.56	9.00	9.26	8.81	8.89	8.51
1965-66	9.50	8.99	9.95	9.45	10.77	10.57	11.03	10.45	10.84	10.41	11.25	10.75	11.25	10.62	11.50	10.60	12.68	11.24	13.43	11.87	12.74	10.95	11.25	10.56
1964-65	10.45	9.75	10.17	9.35	10.12	8.98	10.02	9.51	10.02	9.52	10.16	9.65	9.80	8.75	9.05	8.49	9.30	8.68	9.67	8.87	10.70	9.38	11.60	10.17
1963-64	10.50	8.30	9.55	8.55	8.88	8.40	8.65	8.42	8.55	8.10	8.40	7.92	8.63	8.26	8.54	8.11	8.66	8.15	8.86	8.54	10.20	8.82	11.20	9.93
1962-63					9.28	8.71	9.44	9.06	9.57	9.10	9.46	9.04	9.36	9.01	9.31	9.05	9.52	8.63	8.72	8.06	9.26	7.93	9.85	8.88
1961-62									10.33	10.13	10.27	9.76	9.98	8.62	8.83	8.25	8.49	7.64	8.54	7.77	8.27	7.87	8.70	7.98

December Delivery

Trading Year	Delivery Year	JANUARY		FEBRUARY		MARCH		APRIL		MAY		JUNE		JULY		AUGUST		SEPTEMBER		OCTOBER		NOVEMBER		DECEMBER	
		High	Low	High	Low	High	Low	High	Low	High	Low	High	Low	High	Low	High	Low	High	Low	High	Low	High	Low	High	Low
1970	1971																					11.16	10.76	10.78	9.80
1970	1970	8.42	7.87	8.95	8.20	9.10	8.75	10.15	9.07	10.03	9.20	10.37	9.48	10.79	9.50	10.55	9.70	11.42	9.72	13.95	11.15	13.70	12.38	12.93	11.79
1969		7.82	7.25	7.60	7.20	7.59	7.28	7.36	7.10	7.40	7.05	7.19	6.97	7.31	7.13	7.55	7.21	8.29	7.27	9.79	7.93	11.04	8.71	9.88	8.85
1968		9.03	8.86	9.07	8.95	9.03	8.60	8.65	8.26	8.34	8.18	8.18	7.45	7.66	7.18	7.30	7.07	7.46	6.96	7.43	6.95	8.09	7.28	8.73	7.75
1967		10.09	9.82	9.89	9.65	10.04	9.74	10.06	9.85	10.24	9.95	10.40	9.29	9.34	9.04	9.53	8.95	9.31	8.88	9.00	8.48	8.64	8.40	8.64	8.40
1966		10.85	9.90	10.73	10.29	11.10	10.31	11.10	10.65	11.07	10.56	11.37	10.45	12.49	11.16	13.10	11.65	12.49	10.84	11.17	10.64	10.90	10.41	10.77	10.48
1965		9.90	9.22	9.75	9.30	9.78	9.30	9.92	9.45	9.58	8.62	8.88	8.39	9.04	8.42	9.29	8.64	9.72	9.05	10.06	9.18	10.88	9.65	12.38	11.53
1964		8.80	8.55	8.82	8.57	8.70	8.26	8.50	8.05	8.72	8.37	8.64	8.23	8.75	8.32	8.92	8.60	10.16	8.87	10.96	9.90	12.46	10.77	12.38	11.53
1963				9.42	9.40	9.60	9.18	9.51	9.13	9.45	9.11	9.44	9.14	9.61	8.74	8.87	8.21	9.47	8.14	10.01	9.02	10.30	7.05	8.80	7.80
1962								10.25	9.79	10.01	8.71	8.95	8.43	8.61	7.81	8.69	7.94	8.50	8.03	9.23	8.18	8.84	8.42	8.73	8.40
1961				11.35	10.32	11.17	10.50	12.00	10.81	11.89	10.20	11.10	10.20	11.20	10.24	11.02	10.47	10.78	10.48	11.00	10.37	10.58	10.27	10.74	10.23

Source: Chicago Board of Trade, *Statistical Annual 1970.*

FIGURE 191
RYE
Monthly Range of Futures Prices
(dollars per bushel)
(Chicago Board of Trade Stopped Trading Rye Futures in December 1970)

March Delivery

	APRIL		MAY		JUNE		JULY		AUGUST		SEPTEMBER		OCTOBER		NOVEMBER		DECEMBER		JANUARY		FEBRUARY		MARCH	
	High	Low	High	Low	High	Low	High	Low	High	Low	High	Low	High	Low	High	Low	High	Low	High	Low	High	Low	High	Low
1970–71																								
1969–70	1.27	1.23¼	1.28	1.20⅞	1.25¼	1.19¾	1.24½	1.15¾	1.18	1.15	1.19¾	1.15	1.19½	1.16¾	1.19	1.12	1.15¼	1.12⅛	1.19	1.11½	1.19	1.16¼	1.19	1.13½
1968–69	1.30	1.23¾	1.26¾	1.23¼	1.24¼	1.21	1.22½	1.16	1.17	1.10¾	1.18¼	1.14¼	1.21½	1.14½	1.21½	1.14	1.22½	1.16	1.24½	1.20½	1.23¼	1.15	1.17¼	1.13¾
1967–68	1.40½	1.31½	1.36½	1.31¾	1.38	1.28¼	1.38¾	1.29¾	1.36¼	1.24	1.28¾	1.25⅛	1.26⅜	1.22¼	1.24¼	1.17	1.19¼	1.17	1.21⅛	1.16⅜	1.24⅜	1.20¼	1.23¾	1.17
1966–67	1.39	1.30¼	1.35	1.28¼	1.45	1.30⅝	1.49	1.37	1.47	1.36	1.44½	1.28	1.32	1.26	1.33¾	1.27½	1.31⅜	1.26	1.26⅞	1.20½	1.23¾	1.17½	1.26¼	1.18½
1965–66			1.25¼	1.23	1.23¾	1.21	1.26⅝	1.20⅞	1.30	1.25¼	1.29½	1.24⅜	1.30½	1.25⅞	1.28⅜	1.21⅝	1.28⅞	1.22⅛	1.41	1.26⅞	1.35¼	1.26	1.29	1.20¾
1964–65	1.39⅝	1.31¾	1.36¼	1.28½	1.34½	1.30⅛	1.34¼	1.28⅜	1.34	1.28½	1.39¼	1.31	1.33¾	1.24¼	1.28¼	1.24¾	1.26½	1.23	1.25¾	1.19	1.23¼	1.18¾	1.23⅞	1.19
1963–64	1.32	1.30⅞	1.32¼	1.27½	1.37¼	1.31½	1.39¼	1.30½	1.38½	1.31	1.69	1.36⅜	1.62	1.48¾	1.62¼	1.42	1.55¼	1.44½	1.57	1.48¼	1.50	1.33¾	1.35⅝	1.27½
1962–63	1.37⅛	1.34½	1.36½	1.27⅝	1.32¾	1.26¾	1.31¼	1.23¼	1.24¾	1.19¼	1.25	1.19¾	1.32⅛	1.17⅝	1.36⅛	1.21¾	1.33½	1.24⅜	1.42½	1.31⅝	1.36¾	1.30⅝	1.34⅞	1.27
1961–62			1.32	1.26a	1.40	1.27	1.44¾	1.35¼	1.42½	1.33¾	1.40¼	1.32	1.44⅝	1.35	1.42¾	1.36⅛	1.41¼	1.37	1.38¼	1.33½	1.37¼	1.31	1.35¾	1.26

May Delivery

	JUNE		JULY		AUGUST		SEPTEMBER		OCTOBER		NOVEMBER		DECEMBER		JANUARY		FEBRUARY		MARCH		APRIL		MAY	
	High	Low	High	Low	High	Low	High	Low	High	Low	High	Low	High	Low	High	Low	High	Low	High	Low	High	Low	High	Low
1970–71																								
1969–70	1.28¾	1.23	1.27	1.17	1.20	1.15½	1.20¾	1.17	1.20½	1.18½	1.22	1.16	1.18¼	1.15	1.16½	1.11⅜	1.16⅞	1.14	1.14½	1.09	1.15¾	1.06½	1.12	1.03¼
1968–69	1.24½	1.22	1.24	1.17¾	1.18⅝	1.12¼	1.19¾	1.15½	1.22¼	1.15⅝	1.22¾	1.14¼	1.23½	1.17¾	1.25½	1.20¼	1.22½	1.16½	1.19¼	1.13⅜	1.25⅛	1.15	1.26	1.19¼
1967–68	1.36½	1.30¾	1.40½	1.31½	1.38½	1.26⅜	1.31½	1.27½	1.29¼	1.25⅛	1.27	1.20½	1.22¾	1.19¾	1.23⅞	1.19⅜	1.25¼	1.22½	1.26	1.18½	1.19¼	1.11¼	1.15⅝	1.10½
1966–67	1.45¾	1.31¾	1.50	1.37½	1.49½	1.38½	1.47½	1.32	1.35⅜	1.29¼	1.38	1.30¼	1.35¾	1.30¼	1.31	1.24½	1.27¾	1.21½	1.29⅛	1.22½	1.26¾	1.16¾	1.23⅜	1.16¼
1965–66			1.27¾	1.23½	1.30¼	1.26½	1.30¼	1.25⅞	1.32½	1.27¾	1.30½	1.23¾	1.31⅝	1.24¾	1.43½	1.29⅛	1.38	1.28¼	1.31	1.23¼	1.29¾	1.18¾	1.22¼	1.16
1964–65	1.34½	1.30¾	1.34¾	1.28¾	1.34	1.28⅜	1.39½	1.32¾	1.35¾	1.26¼	1.30¼	1.26¼	1.28⅜	1.24¾	1.27¾	1.20¼	1.26	1.21¾	1.24½	1.19½	1.19⅝	1.16	1.20¼	1.14½
1963–64	1.36	1.32¼	1.36¼	1.29¼	1.38	1.29⅜	1.68	1.35½	1.61½	1.48¾	1.60⅞	1.44½	1.56½	1.46¼	1.58½	1.50½	1.52	1.37½	1.39¼	1.28½	1.36	1.27	1.30⅛	1.20¾
1962–63	1.32	1.27½	1.30¼	1.24	1.25	1.19⅝	1.25	1.20	1.32¼	1.17⅞	1.26¼	1.21⅛	1.30	1.24⅛	1.39⅛	1.28¼	1.35¼	1.29⅛	1.34	1.26	1.32¾	1.27	1.29¼	1.23¼
1961–62	1.40¾	1.32¼	1.45¼	1.36	1.42¼	1.34	1.40½	1.32	1.45	1.35¼	1.40½	1.35½	1.38	1.33½	1.35⅝	1.29½	1.35½	1.30⅞	1.34½	1.26½	1.32	1.27	1.28	1.24⅛

July Delivery

	AUGUST		SEPTEMBER		OCTOBER		NOVEMBER		DECEMBER		JANUARY		FEBRUARY		MARCH		APRIL		MAY		JUNE		JULY	
	High	Low	High	Low	High	Low	High	Low	High	Low	High	Low	High	Low	High	Low	High	Low	High	Low	High	Low	High	Low
1970–71																								
1969–70			1.19	1.16¼	1.21½	1.17½	1.20	1.15½	1.17¼	1.15¼	1.15½	1.11¾	1.14½	1.11⅜	1.11	1.06	1.11	1.08¼	1.09⅝	1.06¼	1.09¼	1.00	1.04¼	1.00
1968–69	1.18⅞	1.14¼	1.20	1.16	1.23¾	1.16⅝	1.23½	1.16	1.24	1.18	1.25½	1.20½	1.21¾	1.17½	1.19½	1.14	1.25⅜	1.15¾	1.25	1.17½	1.20	1.14	1.17¼	1.11¼
1967–68	1.29	1.26½	1.31	1.28¾	1.30	1.26⅝	1.27½	1.22¾	1.25	1.21⅞	1.25¼	1.21⅜	1.26¼	1.23⅜	1.27¾	1.20½	1.22¼	1.14¾	1.17½	1.13½	1.14¾	1.10	1.19½	1.08¼
1966–67	1.44	1.35¼	1.46¾	1.31	1.35½	1.30¼	1.40	1.31½	1.38¼	1.32½	1.32¾	1.26¼	1.30¾	1.24	1.32¼	1.26¼	1.30½	1.20⅝	1.26¼	1.20¼	1.28	1.17¼	1.25⅜	1.17½
1965–66	1.28	1.25	1.28½	1.24¼	1.30	1.27⅜	1.29⅞	1.24⅜	1.32½	1.25⅝	1.44½	1.30½	1.38½	1.29¼	1.32½	1.25¼	1.32½	1.21½	1.24¼	1.19	1.34½	1.19¼	1.36¼	1.24¼
1964–65	1.31	1.25½	1.34½	1.29⅞	1.33¼	1.26½	1.29¾	1.27½	1.29¼	1.25½	1.27⅛	1.22	1.26¾	1.23¾	1.25¾	1.21¼	1.21¼	1.17½	1.20¼	1.15¾	1.17¼	1.12	1.14½	1.10
1963–64	1.33⅜	1.27⅜	1.55½	1.30¾	1.51¼	1.38⅞	1.52	1.41	1.50½	1.43¼	1.51½	1.44¼	1.45	1.35	1.37¼	1.28¾	1.35¼	1.26¾	1.30½	1.22	1.27¼	1.21¼	1.26⅜	1.21½
1962–63			1.18¾	1.17¼	1.27¾	1.13¾	1.22¼	1.18	1.26½	1.21	1.33½	1.24¼	1.31¼	1.26¼	1.29½	1.25½	1.30¾	1.27	1.28⅜	1.24	1.29¾	1.26⅛	1.31	1.23
1961–62	1.38	1.32¼	1.36¾	1.30	1.37	1.31¼	1.34	1.29	1.31¾	1.25¾	1.29¼	1.25	1.30¼	1.26½	1.29¼	1.25	1.31¾	1.26¼	1.30⅜	1.24	1.39½	1.28½	1.32¼	1.18

September Delivery

	OCTOBER		NOVEMBER		DECEMBER		JANUARY		FEBRUARY		MARCH		APRIL		MAY		JUNE		JULY		AUGUST		SEPTEMBER	
	High	Low	High	Low	High	Low	High	Low	High	Low	High	Low	High	Low	High	Low	High	Low	High	Low	High	Low	High	Low
1970–71																								
1969–70			1.20½	1.20¼	1.17½	1.15¾	1.16¼	1.13	1.15¼	1.13	1.12¾	1.09	1.13	1.09¼	1.11⅞	1.10	1.12¼	1.05	1.06⅞	1.03½	1.13½	1.03½	1.04	1.00
1968–69	1.23¾	1.18	1.23	1.18¼	1.24⅜	1.18¼	1.25¾	1.20½	1.22¼	1.17¾	1.20¼	1.14¾	1.22½	1.15¾	1.23	1.16⅛	1.20½	1.15¾	1.20¼	1.09¼	1.11¾	1.08	1.11	1.06¾
1967–68			1.25½	1.24¼	1.26	1.23½	1.27	1.23	1.27⅛	1.24½	1.28¾	1.22¾	1.23½	1.16¾	1.19¾	1.16¼	1.17¼	1.12¼	1.15½	1.10½	1.12¼	1.06½	1.15⅜	1.09
1966–67	1.36	1.31	1.40½	1.32½	1.39⅝	1.35½	1.35½	1.29	1.33¼	1.27	1.35¼	1.29¼	1.33¼	1.23½	1.28¾	1.23¼	1.31	1.20½	1.29½	1.21½	1.27½	1.15⅛	1.19½	1.15⅛
1965–66	1.30	1.27½	1.30½	1.25⅜	1.33⅜	1.27½	1.43½	1.31½	1:38¼	1.31	1.33½	1.27	1.34½	1.23½	1.28	1.21¾	1.39½	1.23	1.40½	1.27¾	1.35½	1.24¼	1.31	1.22½
1964–65					1.28¾	1.27½	1.28	1.24	1.27½	1.25¼	1.26½	1.23⅛	1.23⅛	1.19	1.20¾	1.18⅜	1.19¾	1.15¾	1.19	1.13¾	1.22½	1.17¾	1.20¾	1.17
1963–64					1.48¾	1.40	1.49	1.41½	1.43¼	1.34	1.37¼	1.29	1.35	1.26½	1.30¼	1.23⅛	1.28¾	1.24	1.27½	1.22¾	1.29½	1.24¾	1.36¼	1.28⅛
1962–63					1.26	1.24¼	1.31¾	1.23½	1.31¼	1.26¼	1.30¼	1.26	1.30⅝	1.27¼	1.28¾	1.24¼	1.31	1.26¾	1.34	1.25	1.31¾	1.24¾	1.50½	1.28¾
1961–62					1.32¼	1.24¾	1.29⅜	1.25⅛	1.30½	1.27	1.29¾	1.26⅛	1.33¼	1.27¼	1.32¼	1.25¾	1.32⅞	1.25¼	1.29¼	1.19⅜	1.23¼	1.17¾	1.21¼	1.15½

December Delivery

	JANUARY		FEBRUARY		MARCH		APRIL		MAY		JUNE		JULY		AUGUST		SEPTEMBER		OCTOBER		NOVEMBER		DECEMBER	
	High	Low	High	Low	High	Low	High	Low	High	Low	High	Low	High	Low	High	Low	High	Low	High	Low	High	Low	High	Low
1970					1.11½	1.11	1.14½	1.11¼	1.14½	1.11½	1.15½	1.09	1.11½	1.07	1.18	1.06	1.16	1.09	1.18	1.16	1.19	1.16	1.19	1.15
1969	1.27	1.22½	1.24½	1.20⅝	1.22½	1.17¾	1.24½	1.20	1.26	1.18½	1.23½	1.18⅛	1.23½	1.12½	1.15¾	1.12½	1.16¼	1.12¼	1.15½	1.12	1.15¼	1.08	1.14½	1.08
1968	1.30⅝	1.26¾	1.30⅞	1.28½	1.32½	1.26¼	1.27½	1.20⅞	1.23¾	1.20	1.21	1.16⅛	1.18½	1.13¼	1.14¼	1.07¾	1.15	1.11¾	1.19¼	1.12⅛	1.19½	1.13	1.21¾	1.15½
1967	1.38⅛	1.32½	1.37	1.31	1.38⅞	1.33¼	1.37⅜	1.27½	1.32⅞	1.27¾	1.35	1.24¼	1.35	1.26¼	1.32½	1.20⅛	1.24½	1.20¼	1.21¾	1.18	1.20¾	1.12⅛	1.16	1.11¾
1966	1.45½	1.35½	1.41¼	1.33¾	1.36⅜	1.31	1.37⅛	1.27½	1.32½	1.24¾	1.41¾	1.27	1.45½	1.33½	1.41¼	1.30¾	1.38¾	1.22	1.26	1.19¾	1.26¾	1.21¾	1.27¼	1.21¾
1965	1.30	1.26¼	1.29⅝	1.27¾	1.29⅛	1.26	1.25½	1.21⅝	1.23½	1.20¾	1.22⅝	1.19	1.23¼	1.17¾	1.27	1.22	1.25½	1.21¼	1.25½	1.21¾	1.24½	1.17⅜	1.25¾	1.17¾
1964	1.48¼	1.45¾	1.46¼	1.36⅞	1.40	1.32½	1.37¾	1.30	1.33⅜	1.26	1.32½	1.27½	1.31½	1.25⅝	1.31¾	1.26¾	1.37	1.27½	1.30	1.21¼	1.24¾	1.21½	1.23¼	1.19¼
1963			1.30¾	1.29¼	1.30¾	1.27¾	1.32¾	1.28½	1.30½	1.26	1.34	1.29½	1.36½	1.27⅝	1.35⅝	1.28	1.64½	1.33¾	1.60¼	1.45¾	1.60	1.39	1.50	1.40¾
1962	1.31¾	1.27¼	1.33	1.29	1.32¼	1.29	1.35¾	1.30¼	1.35	1.26⅞	1.32¼	1.25¾	1.29½	1.21	1.23	1.17¾	1.22½	1.17½	1.30¾	1.16⅜	1.23⅜	1.20½	1.36	1.21⅝
1961			1.33	1.32¾	1.38½	1.22½	1.28	1.21¼	1.31	1.22½	1.35	1.22½	1.41¼	1.31	1.38	1.29¾	1.38	1.28¼	1.44	1.32	1.43½	1.35¼	1.43¼	1.36¾

Source: Chicago Board of Trade, *Statistical Annual 1970.*

FIGURE 192
OATS
Monthly Range of Futures Prices
(dollars per bushel)

March Delivery

	APRIL		MAY		JUNE		JULY		AUGUST		SEPTEMBER		OCTOBER		NOVEMBER		DECEMBER		JANUARY		FEBRUARY		MARCH	
	High	Low	High	Low	High	Low	High	Low	High	Low	High	Low	High	Low	High	Low	High	Low	High	Low	High	Low	High	Low
1970–71	......	......	......	......	.70¾	.65½	.71	.67⅝	.86¾	.69⅛	.85	.78	.82	.75	.83	.77	.83¾	.76⅜	......	......	......	......	......	......
1969–70	.72¼	.69⅛	.72	.67⅛	.69⅜	.65¼	.69	.64¼	.68½	.64½	.69½	.66⅛	.69	.64½	.65½	.61⅝	.64⅝	.61½	.65½	.60⅝	.61⅜	.58	.61	.58
1968–69	.76	.73¾	.73¾	.70⅜	.72	.67	.68	.63⅜	.64	.60½	.65	.61¾	.68¼	.63	.71	.67½	.72⅝	.67⅞	.75	.71⅜	.75⅞	.69¾	.69½	.64¾
1967–68	......	......	......	......	.78½	.74¼	.73⅞	.71½	.74⅝	.70½	.72⅛	.70¼	.72⅜	.70⅜	.72	.70¼	.74	.71⅛	.76⅝	.73¾	.80	.75⅝	.84⅜	.79½
1966–67	......	......	.72¾	.72	.81½	.71⅜	.81⅞	.76	.86⅛	.77⅛	.83⅜	.74¾	.81¼	.76⅛	.80½	.78	.79¼	.75½	.77¾	.74⅜	.74⅞	.68½	.75	.70
1965–66	.75⅝	.71½	.75⅛	.70⅞	.73⅜	.71½	.72¾	.70¾	.72⅝	.68½	.70⅛	.67⅜	.69¼	.67½	.70⅞	.69	.72¼	.70	.73⅞	.71⅛	.73¼	.70¾	.73⅜	.71½
1964–65	.72⅝	.69⅛	.70¼	.68⅝	.69¾	.66¼	.67⅞	.65⅞	.69⅞	.66¾	.71½	.68¾	.70⅜	.67½	.71	.68¾	.72⅞	.69½	.73½	.71¼	.72⅛	.66½	.71⅞	.66⅝
1963–64	.72⅞	.71⅜	.72	.69⅞	.73⅛	.70¾	.75½	.68½	.70	.67¾	.75½	.69⅝	.75	.71⅜	.74¾	.69½	.72¼	.70	.73	.68⅛	.68½	.63⅞	.65¾	.63¾
1962–63	.78¾	.75	.77	.72¼	.73½	.71⅛	.72⅝	.67¼	.68⅜	.66¼	.69¼	.64⅜	.70	.63¼	.69⅞	.64¾	.74¼	.68⅝	.74¾	.70¾	.74¾	.70½	.75⅜	.71
1961–62	......	......	.77⅜	.74⅛	.77⅝	.72¼	.80	.75⅜	.79¼	.75¼	.79⅞	.72½	.74¼	.69¾	.72¼	.69¾	.73¼	.70¼	.73¾	.66⅝	.68⅝	.61⅜	.68⅜	.64⅛

May Delivery

	JUNE		JULY		AUGUST		SEPTEMBER		OCTOBER		NOVEMBER		DECEMBER		JANUARY		FEBRUARY		MARCH		APRIL		MAY	
	High	Low	High	Low	High	Low	High	Low	High	Low	High	Low	High	Low	High	Low	High	Low	High	Low	High	Low	High	Low
1970–71	.72¼	.65⅞	.70¾	.68	.86	.69⅛	.83	75⅜	.79¾	.74¾	.80¾	.75⅜	.80¼	.75½	......	......	......	......	......	......	......	......	......	......
1969–70	.71	.65⅜	.68¼	.64½	.69	.64½	.70¼	.67	.70¾	.66⅝	.68¼	.65⅛	.66⅝	.65	.67⅝	.63	.63½	.60⅞	.63⅜	.60⅜	.65¾	.63	.69½	.65
1968–69	.70½	.67¼	.67⅞	.63⅜	.64	.60½	.64⅜	.61⅝	.68	.62⅞	.69⅞	.65	.69⅝	.65⅝	.73⅞	.69⅜	.73½	.67¾	.67⅞	.65	.67⅞	.64	.69	.65⅜
1967–68	.75¾	.74⅝	.73½	.71⅞	.74⅝	.70⅝	.72½	.70½	.72	.70¼	.72	.70	.72¾	.70½	.74⅝	.72¼	.76⅛	.73⅜	.79	.76⅛	.81¾	.76¼	.81	.73½
1966–67	.81¼	.70½	.82⅞	.76¼	.87	.78⅛	.84⅜	.75½	.80	.76¼	.80⅞	.78¼	.80⅜	.76⅜	.78¾	.74¾	.75⅝	.69⅞	.75	.71½	.74⅞	.70	.72⅛	.69
1965–66	.73	.71⅝	.71½	.70⅛	.72	.67⅝	.69	.67¼	.68⅞	.67½	.70½	.68¾	.71¼	.68⅞	.73	.69¾	.72⅝	.70⅜	.70½	.68¼	.71	.68⅜	.71⅞	.67⅛
1964–65	.69¾	.66⅜	.68½	.65¾	.69¼	.66⅝	.70½	.68¾	.69¾	.67½	.71⅜	.68⅛	.71¾	.69⅝	.71¾	.70¼	.71¼	.66¼	.70¾	.67⅜	.74¼	.70⅛	.72½	.68
1963–64	.73¼	.70⅞	.75⅛	.68	.69⅞	.68	.75⅛	.69⅜	.74½	.71	.75	.70	.72½	.70⅞	.72⅜	.68½	.69	.65½	.67¼	.63½	.66⅛	.61½	.62½	.60
1962–63	.74	.71	.72¾	.68	.69½	.66¼	.69⅜	.64⅝	.72¼	.64⅛	.68¾	.65½	.70¾	.67⅜	.71¾	.68⅝	.71½	.67¾	.71¾	.69¼	.70¾	.68¾	.70⅜	.64
1961–62	.79	.74	.80	.75⅝	.78⅞	.75¼	.80½	.73	.75⅞	.71⅛	.74⅜	.71½	.74¾	.72¼	.75	.68½	.70	.63⅝	.70⅜	.66⅛	.71½	.67½	.74¼	.68⅜

July Delivery

	AUGUST		SEPTEMBER		OCTOBER		NOVEMBER		DECEMBER		JANUARY		FEBRUARY		MARCH		APRIL		MAY		JUNE		JULY	
	High	Low	High	Low	High	Low	High	Low	High	Low	High	Low	High	Low	High	Low	High	Low	High	Low	High	Low	High	Low
1970–71	.85	.75⅛	.77	.71⅜	.75¼	.71½	.77½	.72⅜	.75½	.70⅝	......	......	......	......	......	......	......	......	......	......	......	......	......	......
1969–70	.67¾	.65⅝	.68¼	.66⅜	.68⅞	.65¾	.68⅛	.64⅞	.67½	.64½	.67½	.63½	.64¼	.62¼	.64	.61½	.64½	.62¼	.65¾	.62⅝	.67	.62½	.67½	.62
1968–69	.61¼	.60¾	.62½	.60	.66	.60¾	.67⅜	.64¾	.66⅝	.63¾	.70¼	.65⅞	.69½	.63¾	.66½	.63⅛	.68¼	.64¼	.67	.62⅛	.63⅞	.59⅝	.64½	.60¾
1967–68	.71	.69⅝	.70½	.69¾	.71	.69½	.70¾	.69¼	.71¾	.69¾	.72⅞	.71	.73	.71	.75	.72⅝	.74	.69⅞	.72⅛	.66¼	.71½	.66⅜	.70¾	.64
1966–67	......	......	......	......	......	......	......	......	.76¾	.74¾	.76¾	.73⅛	.74⅜	.68½	.74½	.71⅝	.75⅞	.70½	.72½	.69½	.74½	.69½	.73	.68¾
1965–66	......	......	.65⅜	.65⅛	.66⅝	.65¼	.67¾	.66	.69⅛	.67⅛	.71	.67⅞	.71	.68½	.69⅛	.67⅜	.69⅛	.67⅛	.69	.66⅝	.76	.67⅞	.76¾	.72
1964–65	......	......	.68	.65⅛	.66	.63¾	.67	.64	.67⅜	.65½	.67⅞	.66⅝	.67½	.64⅛	.68⅝	.64⅞	.72½	.67⅜	.72	.66¼	.69⅛	.66¾	.71¼	.65⅞
1963–64	......	......	.72¼	.67⅛	.69⅞	.66⅛	.69	.66¼	.68¼	.67	.68	.66¼	.66¾	.64½	.67¼	.64⅞	.66⅞	.63	.63¾	.61¾	.63⅛	.59	.62¼	.59⅛
1962–63	......	......	.67⅞	.64	.69	.63⅝	.66¼	.63⅞	.68¾	.65⅜	.69½	.66½	.69¾	.67¼	.70¼	.68	.69¾	.67½	.68¼	.65	.68⅜	.65¾	.69½	.62¾
1961–62	......	......	.76¾	.72⅝	.75	.70¾	.74⅛	.71¾	.74	.72⅜	.74½	.68	.70⅛	.65½	.71¼	.67⅝	.72	.67¾	.71¾	.68	.68¾	.65⅛	.68	.61½

September Delivery

	OCTOBER		NOVEMBER		DECEMBER		JANUARY		FEBRUARY		MARCH		APRIL		MAY		JUNE		JULY		AUGUST		SEPTEMBER	
	High	Low	High	Low	High	Low	High	Low	High	Low	High	Low	High	Low	High	Low	High	Low	High	Low	High	Low	High	Low
1970–71	......	......	......	......	.73¼	.71	......	......	......	......	......	......	......	......	......	......	......	......	......	......	......	......	......	......
1969–70	.70½	.66⅝	.69½	.66½	.68½	.66½	.68	.63¾	.64½	.62½	.64¼	.62⅜	.64	.61½	.63⅜	.61½	.65¾	.60⅜	.66⅛	.62⅜	.83	.65	.84¾	.72¾
1968–69	.64	.63¼	.66⅞	.65	.66¾	.63	.68⅜	.64⅞	.68½	.63½	.66	.63⅛	.68⅜	.64⅜	.68	.62½	.64	.60¼	.63¼	.58⅜	.61⅜	.57⅞	.61⅜	.57⅛
1967–68	.71⅜	.68¼	.70⅞	.69⅝	.72½	.70⅝	.72⅜	.70⅞	.72¼	.70	.73¾	.71⅜	.73	.68¼	.69¾	.65⅞	.67⅝	.64¼	.66⅛	.60¼	.60⅜	.56	.61¾	.57⅜
1966–67	......	......	......	......	......	......	.76⅞	.74⅛	.74¾	.69⅜	.76	.72⅞	.76⅞	.71½	.73⅜	.70	.75	.69½	.70⅛	.67¾	.74	.68⅛	.71¼	.68⅝
1965–66	......	......	......	......	.68½	.68¼	.71	.68⅞	.70⅞	.69	.69⅝	.68¼	.69¼	.67⅝	.69⅞	.67¼	.76¾	.67⅞	.77	.71½	.78	.71½	.75¼	.70¾
1964–65	.67	66½	.67½	.67	.68⅝	.67	.68⅝	.67⅜	.68	.65¼	.68⅜	.66¼	.71¼	.67¾	.71½	.66¾	.69¼	.67⅜	.68⅜	.66⅜	.68⅝	.65⅛	.69⅛	.65¾
1963–64	......	......	......	......	......	......	.69¾	.67⅝	.68¼	.65⅞	.68⅞	.65⅞	.68¼	.64¾	.65¾	.63¾	.65⅛	.61¼	.63½	.60½	.65⅞	.62¾	.69⅜	.64⅜
1962–63	......	......	.67⅛	.66⅝	.69½	.66⅝	.69¼	.66¾	.69	.66⅞	.70¼	.67⅜	.69¾	.68¼	.68⅝	.66	.69⅛	.66⅜	.70⅞	.63¾	.65	.62⅜	.67⅜	.64⅛
1961–62	.75½	.73	.74¼	.72	.75	.72½	.75½	.69⅞	.71⅞	.67⅝	.72¾	.69⅜	.73¼	.69⅛	.72½	.66⅝	.68⅝	.66	.68¼	.61⅞	.64¼	.61⅛	.66	.63¾

December Delivery

	JANUARY		FEBRUARY		MARCH		APRIL		MAY		JUNE		JULY		AUGUST		SEPTEMBER		OCTOBER		NOVEMBER		DECEMBER	
	High	Low	High	Low	High	Low	High	Low	High	Low	High	Low	High	Low	High	Low	High	Low	High	Low	High	Low	High	Low
1970	......	......	.67½	.64½	.66¼	.65¼	.66⅜	.63⅝	.65⅝	.64¼	.70½	.63	.69¼	.65½	.86	.67	.84⅝	.76½	.82⅝	.75	.83¾	.77⅞	.85¾	.81
1969	.71	.69¼	.71	.66¼	.69	.65⅞	.70¼	.66⅝	.70⅛	.65	.66⅝	.63⅜	.66½	.61⅜	.65¼	.61⅜	.65¾	.62⅝	.64⅞	.60	.61⅛	.56¾	.61⅝	.56½
1968	.74⅝	.73	.74⅝	.72	.76¼	.73	.75¼	.71	.71¾	.68⅛	.69¼	.65¼	.67⅜	.61½	.62	.58½	.64½	.60¼	.67¾	.62⅜	.72¼	.66¾	.73½	.69
1967	.79⅜	.76	.77	.72¼	.78½	.75	.79½	.74½	.76¼	.72¾	.78½	.72	.72¼	.69¾	.72¾	.68½	.70¼	.69	.72⅝	.69⅜	.72¼	.70½	.76	.71¾
1966	.73¼	.70¾	.73	.71	.71½	.69¾	.71¼	.69⅝	.71⅞	.69¼	.79⅝	.70	.79⅛	.73¾	.82⅛	.74½	.80¼	.72	.77⅛	.73	.77⅜	.74½	.76½	.73¾
1965	.70½	.68½	.70	.67⅞	.70⅜	.68⅜	.73¾	.69⅞	.73½	.69	.71½	.69⅞	.70½	.68⅜	.70¾	.66¾	.69	.66	.67⅝	.66¼	.70	.67⅜	.74	.69⅞
1964	.72	.70	.70¼	.68¼	.71⅛	.68¾	.70¾	.67⅜	.68⅞	.66⅝	.68¼	.64¾	.66¼	.63⅜	.68⅜	.65⅛	.70¼	.67⅛	.68⅜	.65½	.68½	.66½	.72⅜	.66½
1963	......	......	.71¼	.69¼	.72⅜	.69¾	.72	.70⅜	.70⅞	.68¼	.71⅞	.69	.73¾	.66⅜	.67⅞	.66	.73⅜	.67½	.72⅞	.69¼	.72	.66⅜	.70	.67
1962	.74¼	.72	.74¼	.70	.75¾	.71¾	.76⅜	.72½	.75	.70¼	.71¾	.69⅜	.71	.65	.66⅝	.64¼	.67⅝	.63½	.69	.62⅜	.71	.64	.76	.69⅜
1961	.74	.73¼	.76¾	.72½	.73⅞	.67¼	.72⅝	.68¼	.74⅜	.71⅛	.75⅝	.70	.78½	.73⅛	.76¼	.72¼	.76¾	.68¾	.70¼	.65½	.68½	.65¾	.70½	.66¼

Source: Chicago Board of Trade, *Statistical Annual 1970.*

FIGURE 193
CHOICE STEERS
Monthly Range of Futures Prices
(dollars per 100 lbs.)
(Trading in New Choice Steer Contract to Begin March 1, 1971)

January Delivery

	FEB High	FEB Low	MAR High	MAR Low	APR High	APR Low	MAY High	MAY Low	JUN High	JUN Low	JUL High	JUL Low	AUG High	AUG Low	SEP High	SEP Low	OCT High	OCT Low	NOV High	NOV Low	DEC High	DEC Low	JAN High	JAN Low
1970-71																								
1969-70					30.00	28.70	30.62	29.50	30.45	29.60	28.35	27.30	27.90	27.45	28.10	27.95	29.00	28.30	29.10	28.80	29.75	29.10	29.65	29.00

February Delivery

	MAR High	MAR Low	APR High	APR Low	MAY High	MAY Low	JUN High	JUN Low	JUL High	JUL Low	AUG High	AUG Low	SEP High	SEP Low	OCT High	OCT Low	NOV High	NOV Low	DEC High	DEC Low	JAN High	JAN Low	FEB High	FEB Low
1970-71																								
1969-70	30.60	28.10	29.97	28.20	30.35	29.25	30.40	28.87	29.37	27.10	28.80	27.40	29.00	27.55	29.80	28.50	29.90	28.85	30.90	29.12	29.95	29.25	30.75	29.65
1968-69	27.00	26.50	26.67	26.37	26.50	26.35	26.75	26.32	27.05	26.10	26.22	25.50	26.25	25.65	26.80	25.80	27.95	26.30	28.57	27.60	29.42	27.85	29.60	28.90
1967-68	28.00	27.35	27.85	27.25	28.30	27.42	28.35	27.80	28.30	27.27	27.75	27.32	27.47	25.82	26.05	25.30	25.82	25.05	25.77	25.37	26.95	25.52	28.00	26.65
1966-67															27.30	26.15	27.05	25.55	26.67	25.72	26.45	24.75	25.50	24.65

April Delivery

	MAY High	MAY Low	JUN High	JUN Low	JUL High	JUL Low	AUG High	AUG Low	SEP High	SEP Low	OCT High	OCT Low	NOV High	NOV Low	DEC High	DEC Low	JAN High	JAN Low	FEB High	FEB Low	MAR High	MAR Low	APR High	APR Low
1970-71																								
1969-70			28.87	28.80	28.35	27.32	28.75	27.30	29.00	27.45	29.95	28.85	29.95	29.35	31.25	30.00	30.95	30.20	31.60	30.55	33.25	31.40	32.10	31.40
1968-69	26.65	26.45	26.75	26.37	27.00	26.10	26.12	25.62	26.25	25.62	26.35	25.77	27.47	25.90	27.75	27.15	28.32	26.90	29.10	27.87	31.40	29.05	31.40	30.25
1967-68	28.50	27.65	28.55	28.05	28.50	27.30	27.65	26.87	27.00	25.57	25.85	24.97	25.20	24.85	25.25	24.82	26.00	24.55	27.35	25.75	27.37	26.92	28.00	27.10
1966-67											27.80	26.67	27.95	26.30	27.62	26.77	27.67	25.30	25.77	25.00	25.80	25.00	25.15	24.50

June Delivery

	JUL High	JUL Low	AUG High	AUG Low	SEP High	SEP Low	OCT High	OCT Low	NOV High	NOV Low	DEC High	DEC Low	JAN High	JAN Low	FEB High	FEB Low	MAR High	MAR Low	APR High	APR Low	MAY High	MAY Low	JUN High	JUN Low
1970-71																								
1969-70					28.85	27.37	30.00	28.75	30.15	29.45	31.50	30.00	31.80	30.25	32.05	31.45	32.90	31.65	31.85	30.40	31.00	29.92	31.97	30.20
1968-69	26.90	26.80	25.87	25.55	26.15	25.62	26.07	25.77	27.20	26.07	27.37	26.87	27.62	26.65	28.70	27.37	31.82	28.65	31.60	29.20	34.10	31.15	35.15	33.50
1967-68	28.60	27.40	27.75	27.00	27.05	25.80	25.92	25.20	25.30	25.00	25.35	24.90	25.55	24.57	26.65	25.45	26.77	26.32	27.20	26.42	26.90	26.17	27.30	26.35
1966-67							28.70	27.25	28.80	27.10	28.40	27.60	28.45	26.20	26.60	25.50	26.37	25.50	26.10	25.30	26.55	25.25	26.37	25.95

August Delivery

	SEP High	SEP Low	OCT High	OCT Low	NOV High	NOV Low	DEC High	DEC Low	JAN High	JAN Low	FEB High	FEB Low	MAR High	MAR Low	APR High	APR Low	MAY High	MAY Low	JUN High	JUN Low	JUL High	JUL Low	AUG High	AUG Low
1970-71																								
1969-70			28.75	29.80	29.95	29.40	31.45	30.25	31.55	30.55	31.80	31.27	32.30	31.20	31.22	30.30	31.15	29.55	32.00	29.90	32.20	30.75	31.50	30.65
1968-69			26.40	25.87	27.20	25.90	27.30	26.90	27.75	26.75	28.80	27.40	31.72	28.80	31.25	29.12	32.80	30.57	33.20	31.20	32.17	28.72	32.05	30.07
1967-68	27.60	26.00	26.00	25.65	25.75	25.35	25.82	25.45	25.80	25.25	26.60	25.65	26.60	26.05	26.80	26.27	26.60	26.05	27.40	26.15	27.77	27.10	28.25	27.20
1966-67			28.80	27.70	28.90	27.60	28.65	27.95	29.00	26.95	27.45	26.10	26.87	26.15	26.65	26.15	27.50	26.17	27.45	26.92	27.47	26.60	27.80	26.60

October Delivery

	NOV High	NOV Low	DEC High	DEC Low	JAN High	JAN Low	FEB High	FEB Low	MAR High	MAR Low	APR High	APR Low	MAY High	MAY Low	JUN High	JUN Low	JUL High	JUL Low	AUG High	AUG Low	SEP High	SEP Low	OCT High	OCT Low
1970-71																								
1969-70	29.60	29.40	30.40	29.75	30.90	30.25	30.95	30.60	31.25	30.50	30.50	29.75	30.55	28.65	30.20	29.15	30.45	29.30	29.70	29.30	29.65	29.15	30.50	29.45
1968-69	26.80	26.20	27.30	26.85	27.67	26.70	28.75	27.42	31.27	28.45	30.57	28.60	31.47	29.75	31.77	29.30	30.50	27.10	29.70	27.75	28.80	27.80	29.35	28.35
1967-68	25.85	25.65	25.90	25.60	26.10	25.45	26.85	26.05	26.65	26.10	26.55	26.20	26.40	26.12	27.17	26.17	27.55	26.55	26.87	26.15	27.47	26.75	28.20	27.20
1966-67	29.25	28.10	28.80	28.32	29.35	27.50	27.80	26.30	27.40	26.65	27.15	26.60	27.85	26.65	27.80	27.35	28.10	27.15	28.35	27.22	28.37	26.70	27.12	26.50

December Delivery

	JAN High	JAN Low	FEB High	FEB Low	MAR High	MAR Low	APR High	APR Low	MAY High	MAY Low	JUN High	JUN Low	JUL High	JUL Low	AUG High	AUG Low	SEP High	SEP Low	OCT High	OCT Low	NOV High	NOV Low	DEC High	DEC Low
1970	30.85	30.25	30.60	30.50	31.10	30.70	30.05	29.60	30.05	28.25	29.70	29.00	29.60	28.90	29.45	28.90	29.65	29.05	29.30	29.00	28.70	28.00	28.25	27.20
1969	27.65	27.00	28.65	27.37	31.07	28.10	30.30	28.27	30.72	29.42	31.00	29.12	29.90	26.95	29.05	27.35	28.87	27.70	29.22	28.30	29.80	28.65	30.05	28.35
1968					27.00	26.52	26.95	26.32	26.65	26.12	26.35	26.05	26.72	26.20	27.15	26.20	26.37	25.50	26.65	25.95	27.77	27.30	29.80	28.50
1967	29.42	27.90	28.05	26.65	27.85	27.15	27.70	27.07	28.10	27.20	28.10	27.55	28.15	27.27	27.97	26.60	26.80	25.62	26.17	25.15	26.50	25.95		
1966																			29.15	27.95	29.25	28.20	28.95	28.47

Source: Chicago Board of Trade, *Statistical Annual 1970.*

FIGURE 194
ICED BROILERS
Monthly Range of Futures Prices
(dollars per 100 lbs.)

January Delivery

	FEBRUARY		MARCH		APRIL		MAY		JUNE		JULY		AUGUST		SEPTEMBER		OCTOBER		NOVEMBER		DECEMBER		JANUARY	
	High	Low	High	Low	High	Low	High	Low	High	Low	High	Low	High	Low	High	Low	High	Low	High	Low	High	Low	High	Low
1970–71	......	......									26.05	25.00	26.80	24.90	27.45	26.00	27.25	25.80	27.20	25.90	26.60	25.80	......	......
1969–70	......	......	26.32	25.55	26.20	25.40	26.40	26.00	26.82	25.95	27.50	25.80	27.80	26.05	26.32	25.32	27.07	25.57	27.85	26.30	28.50	26.30	28.12	27.10
1968–69	......	......									25.90	24.75	25.02	24.85	24.95	24.35	25.50	24.52	25.90	25.30	27.25	25.97

March Delivery

	APRIL		MAY		JUNE		JULY		AUGUST		SEPTEMBER		OCTOBER		NOVEMBER		DECEMBER		JANUARY		FEBRUARY		MARCH	
	High	Low	High	Low	High	Low	High	Low	High	Low	High	Low	High	Low	High	Low	High	Low	High	Low	High	Low	High	Low
1970–71	......	......					26.75	25.95	27.90	27.15	28.30	27.15	28.10	27.10	27.62	26.85								
1969–70	......	......	27.12	26.75	27.90	26.77	28.55	26.75	27.92	26.17	27.20	26.25	27.90	26.42	28.50	27.27	28.82	27.07	28.35	27.40	28.45	27.05	28.55	27.35
1968–69	......	......					26.50	25.30	25.67	25.55	25.67	25.25	25.75	25.35	26.85	25.72	27.30	26.30	27.62	26.55	29.00	27.42

April Delivery

	MAY		JUNE		JULY		AUGUST		SEPTEMBER		OCTOBER		NOVEMBER		DECEMBER		JANUARY		FEBRUARY		MARCH		APRIL	
	High	Low	High	Low	High	Low	High	Low	High	Low	High	Low	High	Low	High	Low	High	Low	High	Low	High	Low	High	Low
1970–71	......	......					27.80	27.50	28.40	27.37	28.25	27.30	28.20	27.37	27.90	27.27								

May Delivery

	JUNE		JULY		AUGUST		SEPTEMBER		OCTOBER		NOVEMBER		DECEMBER		JANUARY		FEBRUARY		MARCH		APRIL		MAY	
	High	Low	High	Low	High	Low	High	Low	High	Low	High	Low	High	Low	High	Low	High	Low	High	Low	High	Low	High	Low
1970–71	......	......					28.10	27.90	28.65	27.52	28.45	27.85	28.00	27.60										
1969–70	......	......	27.87	27.40	28.90	26.60	27.35	26.40	28.00	26.72	28.50	27.37	28.90	27.47	28.70	27.85	28.90	28.00	29.20	27.82	28.75	27.40	28.42	27.47
1968–69	......	......			27.00	25.80	25.97	25.85	25.95	25.40	26.05	25.60	26.62	25.90	26.75	26.00	26.87	26.32	28.12	26.50	28.20	26.85	30.40	28.00

June Delivery

	JULY		AUGUST		SEPTEMBER		OCTOBER		NOVEMBER		DECEMBER		JANUARY		FEBRUARY		MARCH		APRIL		MAY		JUNE	
	High	Low	High	Low	High	Low	High	Low	High	Low	High	Low	High	Low	High	Low	High	Low	High	Low	High	Low	High	Low
1970–71	......	......							28.60	28.15	28.25	27.97												
1970	......	......															29.10	28.25	29.22	27.95	28.67	26.80	28.25	26.65

July Delivery

	AUGUST		SEPTEMBER		OCTOBER		NOVEMBER		DECEMBER		JANUARY		FEBRUARY		MARCH		APRIL		MAY		JUNE		JULY	
	High	Low	High	Low	High	Low	High	Low	High	Low	High	Low	High	Low	High	Low	High	Low	High	Low	High	Low	High	Low
1970–71	......	......					28.50	28.30	28.70	28.35														
1969–70					28.80	27.95	28.92	28.07	29.10	27.95	29.00	28.22	29.27	28.60	29.92	28.70	29.50	28.35	29.10	27.32	28.35	26.07	26.90	24.35
1968–69	27.50	26.22	26.55	26.42	26.50	26.15	26.60	26.27	26.70	26.27	26.75	25.90	26.75	26.32	28.17	26.50	28.40	27.00	29.52	28.12	33.00	28.80	35.25	29.45

August Delivery

	SEPTEMBER		OCTOBER		NOVEMBER		DECEMBER		JANUARY		FEBRUARY		MARCH		APRIL		MAY		JUNE		JULY		AUGUST	
	High	Low	High	Low	High	Low	High	Low	High	Low	High	Low	High	Low	High	Low	High	Low	High	Low	High	Low	High	Low
1969–70																	27.77	27.20	27.55	25.87	26.27	23.90	26.20	24.20

FIGURE 194—*Continued*
ICED BROILERS
Monthly Range of Futures Prices
(dollars per 100 lbs.)

September Delivery

	OCTOBER		NOVEMBER		DECEMBER		JANUARY		FEBRUARY		MARCH		APRIL		MAY		JUNE		JULY		AUGUST		SEPTEMBER	
	High	Low	High	Low	High	Low	High	Low	High	Low	High	Low	High	Low	High	Low	High	Low	High	Low	High	Low	High	Low
1970–71																								
1969–70			27.85	27.60	27.60	26.40	27.50	26.70	27.30	26.80	27.55	26.62	27.27	26.12	27.05	26.15	26.82	25.07	25.82	24.00	25.25	23.80	27.40	24.00
1968–69			26.40	26.20	26.15	25.75	25.72	24.77	25.12	24.87	26.05	24.82	26.60	25.00	27.20	26.42	28.40	26.60	29.95	26.87	25.62	24.15	29.00	26.52

November Delivery

	DECEMBER		JANUARY		FEBRUARY		MARCH		APRIL		MAY		JUNE		JULY		AUGUST		SEPTEMBER		OCTOBER		NOVEMBER	
	High	Low	High	Low	High	Low	High	Low	High	Low	High	Low	High	Low	High	Low	High	Low	High	Low	High	Low	High	Low
1970–71																								
1969–70			26.20	26.00	26.20	25.70	26.10	25.55	25.87	25.17	25.70	25.07	25.35	24.15	24.70	23.65	24.95	23.50	25.77	24.20	25.75	24.02	25.77	24.00
1968–69			24.00	23.80	24.87	23.80	24.72	23.92	24.95	24.37	25.42	24.45	26.50	24.10			26.77	25.15	25.40	24.30	26.22	24.45	27.40	25.50
1967–68																	24.60	23.60	23.77	23.62	23.65	23.15	25.05	23.37

14

POSITION MANAGEMENT

In a well-discounted market, the trader's chances of guessing correctly are 50-50 and a program of buying and selling at random will break him at the rate at which he pays commissions. He must improve on a 50-50 proposition by the 2 percent to 6 percent that it costs him to play the game. This is done by simply not taking all the risks that are offered at random. The speculator must *choose his risks.* He can also improve on the proposition by *making more on winning positions than he loses on losing positions,* and *winning on more contracts than he loses on.* Any one of these methods of improving an even proposition can put the trader in a winning program. Two out of three of them are the result of proper position management.

One point is vital to the proper management of any commodity program. Margin equity is not money. Money can pay the rent, buy a car, or finance a trip to Bermuda. Commodity margin can only buy commodities. The stock market is often used as a place to store excess money and put it to work until it is needed for other purposes. Money cannot be stored in a commodity contract, and margin deposited with a broker must be either used to maintain a speculative position or left sterile in a noninterest-paying account. For this reason, money that will be needed later

ought to be placed in stocks or other such investment media. Money placed in a commodity account is best viewed as so many game tokens, allowing the trader to hold a position in the game and indicating how he is doing. Only if margin equity is viewed as game tokens, can the speculator attain the dispassion required for a skillful game.

The trader's primary objective the entire time he is playing commodities will be to stay in the game; any position that could knock him out of the game, if the worst possible thing happened, is simply too risky to be taken. Each play is best viewed as a single move in a series, with a sharp eye on what will happen to the margin account if the play goes wrong. A good commodity program will often cover a large number of plays based of "guesstimates" formed on many different inputs and carefully covered to avoid risking any more tokens than absolutely necessary to try the position. Even the best market analyst expects to be right no more than 40 percent of the time with his guesses and must be prepared to make his wins cover a larger number of losses and provide at least enough surplus to cover commissions. A typical winning commodities program sees something like 40 percent correct guesses leading to wins, 40 percent wrong guesses bringing a depletion of margin, and 20 percent plays that simply meander for no loss, no win, and a commission charge. If wins are to cover the losses and commissions, a program must be designed which will at least make theoretically possible a final outcome in the black.

PROGRAM (HAVE ONE)

The major part of any trading program is having it in the first place. A program should cover all possible contingencies that can happen to an open position. The trader should know before he opens a position on the commodities market exactly how much margin he is prepared to lose and set a stop-loss order to see that he does not lose more. He should know in advance when he wishes to add to his position and increase his profit. He should know in advance what indicates time to get out and let the market signal him when to do so. If each play is looked at as a tentative feeler put out to test the market, to be taken back if conditions are not comfortable, most of the rest of the rules normally applied to commodity programs become unnecessary.

Never answer a margin call is such a rule. A call from your broker asking for more money to maintain a position simply means that you have a position which is eating up all your game tokens. It has already depleted the margin set aside for the play and is eating into maintenance margin in your account or into money from outside the game altogether. If the position has depleted all its original margin allotment at the brokerage, it threatens to put you out of the game. If the margin call must be

met from money in a banking account, you are already out of the game.

A margin call is a sign you stayed around too long in a position that is not winning. Stop losses ought to always close positions before they degenerate to this extent.

Avoid thin markets. When a thin market takes off in his favor, a trader can make a great deal of money. When major news hits the market, however, it can send prices out of bounds like a croquet ball, with no possibility of closing the position. Thin markets are occasionally played by seasoned players "on a flyer." A trader who fully understands what he is doing and has his trading on a firm footing can afford a flyer, more for the sport than the winnings, but he knows what a flyer is, because he knows what proper playing is, and he will never risk his chances of staying around just for sport. He must have enough margin in his account to cover even the most drastic possible events.

Use stop losses to take you out of a losing market at a prearranged price. Mental stops simply don't work. A market slides gently against your position in what is nearly a horizontal course, making it difficult to get out. A margin call means the market is breaking you. It makes no difference that it is doing it slowly.

Let the market tell you what to do. A trader will often "guesstimate" how far a market can be expected to go and have a profit objective in mind before he opens a position. Closing the position, however, ought to be done when the market has shown itself to be out of steam. Closing positions manually will automatically ensure that the trader never takes a large profit. A market that has already coursed a long way can look precarious when really showing no signs of giving up. A trading program should detail in advance, before the heat of a large move, exactly what event will take the trader out of the market. Let the profits accumulate until the market has broken its trend by whatever system of trend measurement is used.

Never average down. Average down is a process carried over to commodities from the stock market where it is nearly as bad a practice. The trader who went long in potatoes at 2.80 cents finds himself in a losing position at 2.70 cents. The logic of averaging down is that the trader can buy potatoes at the lower price and average the two long positions for an average price of 2.75 cents. The market thus has only to come back half as far to return the lost money. No trading program set out in advance would ever call for instituting a long position in a sagging market which is what is being done in the attempt to average down. It is much easier to return profit on orange juice or pork bellies. Increasing a losing position increases the number of contracts that are returning a loss.

In attempting to average down, the trader is buying positions when the market is telling him to stay out or go short. The original loss of 0.10 cents can be taken with little more than a wince and once out of his long position, the trader has a much better chance of looking at the market objectively, choosing to stay out or, perhaps, go short. He can rationally decide what determines a change in the downtrend and set stop orders that will reinstate his position when the market shows signs of being more rewarding. By adding to a losing position, the trader is simply putting himself in a position to lose on more contracts if the price continues to drop than he would have won on had he been right in the first place.

Never straddle a loss. You will occasionally run into the trader who *knows* that wheat is worth $3 a bushel and is willing to do his part to hold up the market single-handedly if necessary. As the price drops out from under his long position, he posts margin but refuses to close out the position at his already substantial loss. He straddles, going short in another month for wheat, and using profits from the wise short sale to cover the margin losses he is sustaining on his long position. He cannot win. He has hedged in a loss which cannot be gotten rid of, no matter how admirably the market reacts. By taking the spread position, he takes pressure off his margin account, as margin requirements are considerably lower for straddled positions, but the loss is locked in. Losing positions must be closed. If the trader's original estimate of the market proves prophetic, he can easily reinstate himself when the price turns up at the cost of an extra commission.

Take the money and run. A commodity margin account is properly started with a sum of money that the player can afford to set aside for a game. Losing this sum should not affect his style of living. If the game is played well, this sum will grow and if it grows to the point that it is more money than he cares to use for a game, money ought to be taken out. There is no such thing in commodities or stocks as a paper profit.

Keep the margin account small enough so that it can be considered game tokens and when there is more, take it and run.

Winnings in commodities are often quite large in well-managed accounts, but fairly infrequent, punctuated with a large number of losses in the interim. If the tokens are to survive this attrition, losses must be kept minimal and losing positions closed immediately when the market moves against it. Adding to a losing position simply increases the size of the loss. Straddling simply locks it in. Moving a stop loss lets it grow beyond reasonable limits until it threatens the whole game.

STOP ORDERS

Stop orders are the most important part of a commodity program for any trader who closely manages his trades, and normally the vast majority of positions will be entered and closed through the use of stops. A stop order is any order which cannot be immediately filled by the pit trader but must go into his deck to be executed if the market reacts as specified in the order. The only orders which do not go into the pit trader's deck are those that can be filled immediately and those which specify that they are not to be held. "At market," "Fill or Kill," and time orders such as "At opening" or "At 11:00" which attempt to take advantage of technical market trends such as Friday sell-off, are the only frequently used orders which do not await placement.

Often a trader will determine in advance what constitutes the end of a resting period or trend and enter a stop order to be filled when conditions are met. A wheat trader faced with a resting, sidewise trending market may decide in advance that if the price hits $1.92, an upward trend is to be expected. He can leave an order with his broker, "Buy (March, May, July, September, or December) wheat at $1.92/stop." If wheat prices climb to his predetermined price, he will have purchased a contract at the best market price available. He will match this order with a stop loss, a second stop order below the first designed to take him out of the market if his prognosis of an upward trend proves to be wrong. Following the upward trend, the trader may decide at which levels he wishes to add contracts to his winning position and enter additional stop orders to see that they are bought only if the market continues to reward his long position. He may also decide what price behavior he considers indicative of the end of the trend and leave stop orders to take him out of the market. In this manner, he is sure to get all the profit offered without finding himself in the position of having to decide when the market has given him enough.

Stop orders are used to (1) enter positions if market price hits a predetermined level, (2) expand a position if the market continues its admirable move, (3) protect profits which have accrued or margin which has been committed on a new position, and (4) close out the position when market conditions are met which are considered indicative of the end of the trend. The process, of course, is the same for either uptrending or downtrending markets and long or short positions.

PLACING STOP ORDERS

Look at the chart of any commodity. How large a fluctuation can be simply called noise? (See Fig. 195 below.)

Noise is the insignificant random fluctuation that occurs within any formation. In the August soybean chart below, movements of 5 cents and less are common and indicate nothing about the course of prices to come. In this particular chart, a movement of less than 5 cents can be ignored and a stop-loss order would best be positioned 5 cents above any sell order and 5 cents below any purchase. In so doing, the trader is announcing in advance the amount of loss he is willing to take if he is wrong, in this case $250. (5 cents × 5,000 bushels in a soybean contract = $250.)

He knows at the onset of the trade that he stands to win as much as the market will give him, at the rate of $50 for each penny the market rises, but he has generally limited his loss to $250 plus a commission of $30. (It is possible, however, that his order may fill at a price above or below his stop price and his loss could, thereby, exceed the $250 estimate.)

Placing the stop-loss order closer than 5 cents to the opening of the position can limit loss even more but runs the very probable risk of being tripped by noise which does not indicate that the market is going against the trader. At all times, the stop loss ought to be as close as possible, limiting loss as tightly as it can be limited, without being tripped by noise.

FIGURE 195

Source: Commodity Research Bureau, Inc.

In most grains, commission runs about $30, ranging from $25 for oats to $30 for soybeans, which translate to about 0.5 cent per bushel over the full 5,000 bushels of the contract. In the event a trader is closed out of his position by a stop-loss order, but the market continues in the direction he forecast, he can reinstate himself at a loss of 0.5 cent lost by the repeated commission. Such being the case, it simply does not make sense for a trader to sit out a major move against his position. Rather than let the market sag, eating up margin as it goes,

the trader can simply stand aside until it rights itself and return to his original position. The market may sag 10 cents in the trader's absence and then he can return to his long position at a cost of 0.5 cent.

Never set a stop loss so far back it would be cheaper to leave the market and pay a commission to return at a later date. Never set a stop loss so close that it closes the position due to meaningless noise. A vertical line chart will give the impression at a glance that the trader could leave the market often at 0.5 cent losses and return often for his profits. In fact, prices vary up and down within the price range for a single day and a policy of setting a stop loss too close will generate many 0.5 cent losses in a single session. Scalping is best left to people physically in the pit.

Figure 196 opposite shows the price for February frozen pork bellies. In this particular chart, a range of 120 points would be sufficient to prevent activation of a stop loss by noise, and the stop loss would be set behind any purchase or sale by this amount. The trader is willing to take all that he is given, but hopefully can limit his loss to something near 1.2 cents on his position. [1.2¢ × 36,000 lbs. = $432.]

Emphasis has been placed on the phrase, *this particular chart*. The noise level of different times will vary, and setting stop-loss orders requires an inspection of the current chart for the commodity being traded. Pork bellies are often much quieter than in the above contract, and significant fluctuation would be less than the 1.20 cents found significant in this chart.

For February *frozen pork bellies*, a stop loss placed closer than 1.20 cents

FIGURE 196

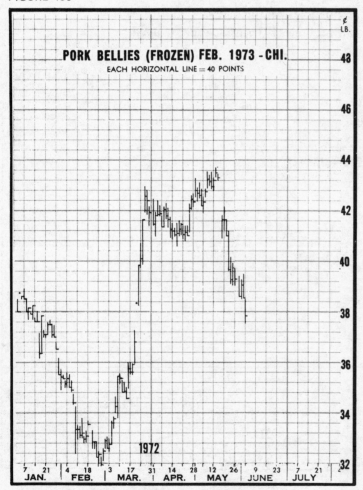

Source: Commodity Research Bureau, Inc.

runs the risk of closing the position when no indication has been made of the market's intention to move against the trader. Commission for a 36,000 pound contract of pork bellies is $45 which is equal to 13 points in price movement on a single pound of bacon. The trader has no reason to set his stop loss farther than 1.32 cents away from his opening purchase or sale price. To do so would not make sense as the trader could allow himself to be stopped out of the market when noise reached the significant level and reinstate himself for a loss of 1.20 cents + 0.12 cents in commission, when the market rights itself and heads in the direction originally predicted.

No trader would *plan* a program allowing a 4 cents loss in pork bellies when he could leave the market as soon as it began to move in the wrong direction by a significant amount and then reinstate himself when it corrected, for a total cost of only 1.32 cents. If the market does not right itself and return to the direction predicted, the trader has no position which is costing him margin, and can objectively judge the market, considering a short sale if that is called for, or leaving the market alone altogether.

Three things can happen to a protected position in any commodity. The market can go against the trader, taking him out at a roughly predictable loss—depending upon the volatility of the market. The market can trend sidewise until the trader simply closes for a loss of commission when his prediction no longer gives him reason to believe his original estimate was correct. Or the price can go with the open position, rewarding the trader as it goes. In the

case a profit is returned, the distance from the going price to the stop loss becomes larger than considered necessary on the basis of significance (noise level) and the stop loss is continually brought up (or moved down to cover a short position) so that it continues to provide protection as soon as the price reacts by more than noise. A stop order can be designed to continually trail the action and provide continued protection.

ALL MANNER OF STOPS

Tricky orders, like tricky systems, have a tendency to cause more confusion than they are worth, but, generally speaking, a speculator can enter just about any order his broker can understand and transmit to the pit in workable fashion. Some of the possible order restrictions have been mentioned in Chapter 5.

The most consistent trait of commodity markets is random fluctuation, and the trader can use stop orders as well to take advantage of noise as to filter it out. *Buy dips and sell bulges* is a commonly quoted axiom aiming at fractional profits to be made from noise. The trader might find wheat quoted at $1.92 and consider this price an indication of a new upward breakout in prices. He wishes to buy and could do so at market, but he can often do better with a M.I.T. order. "Buy March wheat at $1.91⅝ M.I.T." is an order with a good chance of being filled when prices dip at random. He can be pretty confident of a dip bringing price down the ⅜ cent that he is attempting to scalp, but takes the risk of not having his order filled at all.

Much of the time the trader will be waiting for a price that he considers significant. The trader who wished to buy if wheat ever went as high as $1.92 because he considered this even cent breakthrough to indicate higher wheat prices to come, could have left the stop order with his broker weeks in advance and been assured of being in the market when it performed as he'd hoped. Often an even cent breakthrough is considered significant as considerable friction may build up at this wholly psychological price. The trader might have left instructions with his broker to "STOP—BUY December Wheat at $1.91⅝ if December wheat hits $1.92." His order will not be filled unless the prior condition is met and December wheat crawls up to the significant price decided upon by the trader. If it does, his order will be filled at $1.91⅝ or any lower price that the pitman can get. The trader goes home and waits for a phone call telling him that his purchase has been made. This could be months hence, although the broker will normally confirm prior to making the purchase if the conditions begin to look plausible. The broker is under no compunction to call, but normally will if the relationship between him and his client is such that he feels free to do so.

An open position could be closed in a similar fashion when the market hits a price which the trader feels signifies the end of the trend, scalping an extra fraction after the key price has been hit.

Often a trader will closely watch one or two commodities and have game plans waiting for use on either side of the market, taking no position until the market indicates which direction it is headed. It is much easier to be calm and rational, taking advantage of every possible angle, before the battle begins and

before the excitement hits the boardroom. Before entering a position the trader can decide for himself on the basis of whatever plan or price levels he considered significant, how much loss he is willing to take, how he is going to add contracts to his position if he is right, how his stop loss is going to trail, and so on. When the excitement hits and he is no more clearheaded than the other doctors, lawyers, dentists, brokers, and assorted rabble that hang around a boardroom, his plan is rational, even if he is not.

Stop orders can be used to take advantage of other market conditions than fluctuation. The trader might wish to buy Kansas City wheat if Chicago wheat hits a certain price. He might buy December wheat if March wheat does a certain thing. Below are some of the orders that can be used to institute or close out a commodity position.

```
BUY / SELL   at 11:00
             at close
             at $1.90⅛
             at $1.90 if $1.91 hit
             at $1.90 if Kansas hits $1.87
             at market if Kansas hits $1.87
             at market if February hits $1.94
```

Market orders must be worked out with your broker.

ADDING TO A WINNING POSITION

A commodity program should never commit an entire planned position on the initial entry into the market. One or two contracts will suffice to keep the trader interested and take advantage of any correct guesses. If the price moves in his favor, he can add to the winning position according to a set schedule.

If the market rewards a trader's original two contracts, he can bring up his stop and add two more. He now has four contracts in a winning position with only two endangered by price reversal. If the move continues, orders are scaled in at even rates until the market indicates when to call it quits by turning and forcing a loss on the final two contracts. Eventually all markets turn; if they can they will do it at precisely the wrong time. A great number of new contracts near the turning point will cause a loss on a great many contracts, turning what might once have been a nice win into a disaster. *Never endanger your entire position* unless, of course, your entire position is one contract, which is hard to divide. By keeping the majority of any position below or above the stop loss, the trader will always have as many contracts as can safely be had on any profitable move, while standing to lose on only a few when the reversal finally comes. (See Fig. 197, p. 290.)

When the price reversal comes, such a trading program stands to lose on two contracts and to break even on two, if the stop loss is kept trailing at the same interval at which the new contracts are taken. In actual trading conditions, price will not move this smoothly but the principle of scaling will remain the same.

New contracts may be added more aggressively, say, at every 2 cents in price drop while the stop loss trails at 3 cents or even 4 cents. In such a case more contracts are endangered at any given time but the entire position will not be taken for a loss in a single reverse. By opening all 12 short contracts at the beginning, the trader would have made substantially more money on the last contracts to be scaled in on a scaling program, somewhat more on the middle contracts and the same amount

on the first contracts placed under scaling. Had the price gone against him, however, he stood to lose on all 12 contracts immediately. Very few commodities traders can easily sustain a loss on 12 contracts at one time. By placing all his contracts at once, the trader stands to lose on exactly as many contracts as he will win on if he is right, and foregoes one of the major position management tools.

A more conservative scaling schedule is open to traders who have the capital to open with larger positions. It is correspondingly safer and more likely to produce profitable results. This is to pyramid into price moves, with the base of the pyramid at the starting point, tapering into the price move.

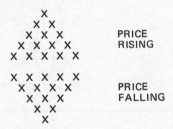

Such a schedule of scaling has the advantage that from the earliest point possible, the trader is guaranteed a profitable position. Having established five contracts which are showing a profit, he trails the stop-loss order to their level and opens four more contracts. He is now safe on five and risking four. If the move continues his way, he risks three more contracts, trailing his stop to the level at which he bought the second batch. He now has a guaranteed profit on five contracts, a break-even position on four and three in the fire. If the move continues in his favor, he has 12 contracts winning for him and can add more. When the reversal finally comes, he will lose on less than half his position, leaving him with at least some net gain, and maybe a very impressive profit. The stop-loss order, of course, offsets all contracts in the position, those close to the action and those bought or sold long ago, retaining large profits on the early ones to cover losses on the fewer that took a beating.

It is also possible to guarantee losing through pyramiding. By starting with two contracts and adding four more when the price goes with him, then eight, the trader guarantees that at least half his position will lose money when the reversal finally comes. Such a trading scheme has the advantage of being financed out of excess margin from the

FIGURE 197

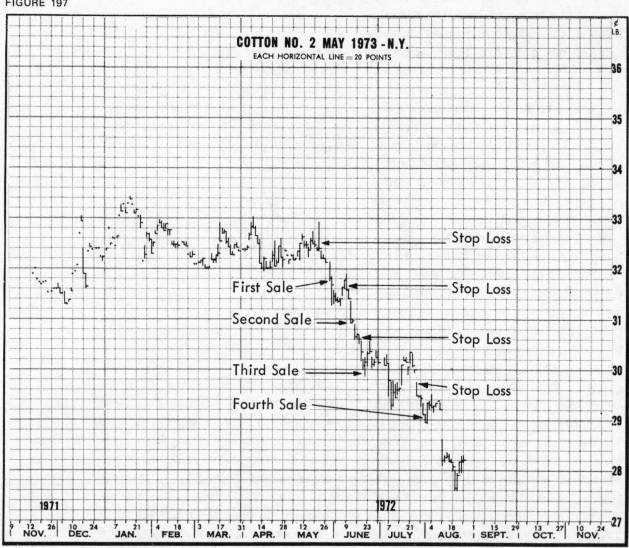

Orders are scaled in, adding to the position so long as the move continues profitable. With each addition, the stop loss is moved down to cover as much of the total position as possible. A single stop-loss level cancels the entire position.

Source: Commodity Research Bureau, Inc., with additions by author.

initial positions as winnings on the initial batch are used to finance the next batch, and so on, and extremely impressive accounts can be built up through such a system. Occasionally you will hear of the manager (who may be soliciting accounts) who has built $150,000 out of $10,000 in six months through such a system. Anybody who is making gigantic profits out of a risk situation is taking gigantic risks. Anybody can put $1,000 on the roulette wheel in Las Vegas and watch it grow to $2,000, $4,000, $8,000, $16,000, $32,000, and $64,000. In so doing, he is virtually guaranteed losing his original $1,000.

Improper scaling can only be profitable if the trader arbitrarily gets out of the market before the reversal in order to keep profits intact and so doing will assure him of missing out on any truly large moves. Any time a trader must choose to let himself out of a market, he is missing on the advantages he has to exploit. *Let the market decide.* If the player has more than half his position endangered, he must offset the position himself at his own discretion rather than letting the market indicate when it is tired. The temptation to close out a winning position and take small profits is great but must be overcome. Large price moves always look risky and get riskier looking the further they move from their original plateau. By taking profits out of a risky-looking market, the trader assures himself a string of small profits. He is going to lose more often than he wins and must pay commission; by keeping his profits as small as his losses, he will lose overall. Only the market knows how far it can go, and it doesn't know until it gets there.

PLACING A SPREAD

Spreading holds out a number of advantages to the commodity speculator. A spread is a position with one "leg" in one option month and a second "leg" in another, which may be a second trading month for the same commodity, a second commodity, or the same commodity on another exchange. Holding an equal number of long and short contracts in the spread, the trader is safe from major catastrophes except in the case of inversion, which simply requires that the trader not be short the near month on any spread when the near month comes to delivery. Because risk is lowered by spreading, margins are much lower, allowing the trader to hold positions for much less capital output and with much less risk.

The spreader is playing the price basis between options and is more interested in the basis amount than in absolute price levels. For this reason, timing is much less important in spreading than in single "naked positions." The position is placed on an order stipulating the premium or discount. "Buy five September eggs, sell five August eggs, September 6¢ over," is the normal manner of placing a spread and orders the spread made when the September option sells for 6 cents over the price of the August. Price level is not stipulated and the trader has little interest in it. So long as the spread between the two options remains at 6 cents the trader is in a break-even position. If the spread increases beyond 6 cents the trader takes his profit.

As in placing a naked position, the trader can often pick up fractional profits by playing noise levels. Basis will fluctuate as does single price levels, and can be picked up by the trader who sets his original order to be filled only at the best feasible spread amount. For this reason, stop orders, limit orders, and various other management tools are largely useless to the commodity spreader. He may watch the noise level for each option he is interested in spreading and so order his position that it can be filled only when the short side swings low and the long side peaks simultaneously. So long as he does not overstate his requirements, he has a good chance of filling his order while picking up as much as a half cent simply in the execution.

As the spreader has no interest in overall market movement, he has little use of chart reading devices and can best rely on historical highs and lows. "In the last 20 years, which option has advanced the most in the period from January 1st (when he will place his spread) to April 1st (when he will lift it), the March or May option?" The historical highs and lows table can provide this information, giving a set of odds for success in the spread. (See Fig. 198 opposite.)

"Which advances the most from February 1st to June 30th, pork bellies or live hogs?" If bellies advance further in 15 years out of 22, the spreader may go long bellies and short hogs.

Straddles provide one further advantage to the trader lucky enough to be interested in capital gains as a tax advantage. A long position which has shown a nice profit over a length of time can be held for the requisite six months while protecting it against deterioration through a straddle in the same commod-

ity for another delivery month. Spreads do not, however, always work out perfectly and a "tax straddle" might end up costing the trader more in commissions and losses than he saves on his income tax. They should be planned with real care and closely watched since the premiums and discounts between various futures can often fluctuate significantly. To avoid the consequences of such fluctuation (or to minimize it) a few tax straddles are placed in a "butterfly spread fashion"—that is, the trader goes long the nearby and most distant months and shorts two months in between, thereby hoping to minimize his risk of a deteriorating spread relationship.

COMPUTING PROFIT AND LOSS

Figuring profit and loss in commodity trading is simple but very important. As in any game, it is easy to forget small losses and remember large gains. Small profits and losses account for the majority of any trader's moves and it is important that they be remembered, for analyzing these will give the best picture of how a trader is doing; what he is doing right and what wrong. If a number of large losses is showing up over time, even though the trader is making money over all, the signal is to take a look at his stop losses and other management techniques.

Gross and net profit and loss are reported to the speculator by his brokerage at the closing of a position and the broker's confirmation slip makes an adequate record of trades past. Computing loss and profit during and before a trade, however, is often of more value and ought to be undertaken before any stops are placed. In the forms below, the value of a cent is simply 1 cent times the number of units in the contract. A point is 1/100 cent and is equal to 1 cent times the number of units in the contract divided by 100.

For figuring profit and loss, all commodities fit into one of three categories. (1) commodities which fluctuate in eighths of a cent; (2) commodities which trade in decimals, or points; (3) soybean meal. Soybean meal is a freak which trades in dollars per ton. In the case of lumber which is quoted in dollars per 1,000 board feet, and plywood which is quoted in dollars per 1,000 square feet, profit and loss can be computed by multiplying the points gained or lost on the position by the value per point and adding or subtracting the commission. (See Fig. 199, p. 294.)

FIGURE 198

HIGHEST & LOWEST PRICES OF MAY WHEAT FUTURES ON THE CHICAGO BOARD OF TRADE
IN CENTS PER BUSHEL

Year of Delivery		Year Prior to Delivery							Delivery Year					
		June	July	Aug.	Sept.	Oct.	Nov.	Dec.	Jan.	Feb.	Mar.	April	May	Range
1958	High	220½	220	224	223¼	221	226⅜	221⅛	214¼	218½	223½	221⅝	229⅜	229⅜
	Low	204¾	212⅞	215⅛	215	214¾	222¼	208⅝	210⅜	209	215¾	213⅝	215⅞	204¾
1959	High	197½	201⅞	197⅞	200	199⅞	199⅜	197⅝	195⅜	203¼	210¼	212⅜	195⅛	212⅜
	Low	191	192	193⅜	194⅛	195	196⅛	189⅜	191	194⅜	202¼	191⅞	183¼	183¼
1960	High	197¾	198⅝	200⅜	200⅜	202	202⅝	202⅛	203¾	202¼	208⅞	210¾	211	211
	Low	192⅝	195	196¾	196⅞	198½	198⅝	198½	200½	198½	199¼	205¼	193	192⅝
1961	High	196⅝	196⅝	198¼	198¼	202	203¾	205⅜	214½	215	212⅜	199⅝	191⅞	215
	Low	193¾	194⅛	194⅝	196⅜	197⅝	198⅞	201¼	205	207¾	197⅜	188¼	185⅛	185⅛
1962	High	209¾	211	214½	213⅞	212⅞	212⅜	212½	210¼	204¼	207⅞	213⅜	217	217
	Low	200½	206	209⅜	210½	208¾	209¾	209⅛	204¼	202⅞	203⅞	207⅜	212⅝	200½
1963	High	224	224	221⅜	218¼	215¼	211¼	210	212⅞	212⅛	208⅝	213⅜	228⅝	228⅝
	Low	213¾	218¾	214¼	202⅜	204⅞	206⅞	207⅜	205	204	200¼	206	200⅝	200¼
1964	High	192⅜	192¼	185	207	214½	215½	215⅜	219⅞	218	206¾	209½	210¼	219⅞
	Low	183	177¾	180¼	184	202⅛	204	210½	212¾	206	189¼	198½	194¼	177¾
1965	High	163¼	155	154¼	156	155¾	157⅞	155⅝	153	153	152½	151¾	148	163¼
	Low	151½	150⅛	148¾	151½	152¼	154⅜	148¾	147	149⅞	148	143½	142¾	142¾
1966	High	151⅜	154⅝	160	163¼	165½	167	173	172¼	170⅞	164¾	164¼	166¼	173
	Low	147	149	153½	157⅝	158¼	160	162¾	166⅝	162½	156½	156½	158¼	147
1967	High	202	202	203½	207	186½	189⅜	189¼	179⅝	180½	187	182¼	166¾	207
	Low	176¾	188	192	180½	174¼	174½	177⅜	163⅞	163⅝	172¼	160½	160	160
1968	High	187½	170⅝	169⅝	165½	163¾	161½	156¼	153½	152⅞	156	148	138⅛	187½
	Low	168	162	157⅜	157⅝	159¾	152½	150½	149⅜	149¼	146¾	133⅛	132⅝	132⅝
1969	High	153½	146	139¾	133⅞	139½	142¼	137⅞	139¼	137¼	134⅛	133⅛	135	153½
	Low	143¾	139¼	128⅞	127	129⅜	135⅜	132⅜	134¾	131¼	125⅛	125¾	128½	125⅛
1970	High	143⅜	141¾	137¾	139½	142¾	144	147	145½	149¾	148¼	153	151¾	153
	Low	138¾	130¼	131⅛	135¾	137¾	139¼	141	140⅛	140⅜	142⅞	144½	145¼	130¼
1971	High	153½	156	167⅞	174¾	175⅞	178¾	172⅞	170⅜	168	164⅛			
	Low	141¼	146¾	147⅝	162½	167⅛	168⅛	163¼	162	160¼	157¼			
1972	High													
	Low													

Source: Chicago Board of Trade

FIGURE 199

COMMODITIES WHICH FLUCTUATE IN EIGHTHS OF A CENT

Profitable plays		*Losing plays*	
Price sold at:	_____	Price bought at:	_____
Price bought at:	_____	Price sold at:	_____
Profit in cents:		Loss in cents:	
X value of cents X	_____	X value of cents X	_____
X value 1/8ths X	_____	X value 1/8ths X	_____
Gross profit $	_____	Trade loss $	_____
Deduct commission − $	_____	Add commission + $	_____
Net Profit $	_____	Net Loss $	_____

COMMODITIES WHICH TRADE IN POINTS

Profitable plays		*Losing plays*	
Price sold at:	_____	Price bought at:	_____
Price bought at:	_____	Price sold at:	_____
Profit in points	_____	Loss in points	_____
X value per point X	_____	X value per point X	_____
Gross profit $	_____	Trade loss $	_____
Deduct commission − $	_____	Add commission + $	_____
Net Profit $	_____	Net Loss $	_____

SOYBEAN MEAL

Profitable plays		*Losing plays*	
Price sold at:	_____	Price bought at:	_____
Price bought at:	_____	Price sold at:	_____
Profit in dollars $	_____	Loss in dollars $	_____
X 100	_____	X 100	_____
Gross profit $	_____	Trade loss $	_____
less commission − $	_____	plus commission + $	_____
Net Profit $	_____	Net Loss $	_____

15

THE GUESSTIMATOR

The commodity trader's problem is not one of gathering information. With very little exercise, he can easily swamp himself in far more data than he can possibly digest and the problem becomes one of sorting out the welter and coming to a single conclusion to buy or sell a commodity, which contract to choose, how to protect it, when to scale in more contracts, when to take a profit, and so forth. Information doesn't come in neat packages and decisions aren't made by nice rules, except possibly in books on how to do it, all of which helps produce such bastard words as "guesstimate." A little less than a science and a little more than a guess. As much as the decision-making process can be quantified, it probably looks something like this:

1. Your broker calls to tell you to "buy all the wheat futures you can handle" as there are rumors of a Russian wheat shortage and the September future is going to $1.75 by mid-August.
2. Keltner, in his market letter, recommends the purchase of wheat futures for a gradual postharvest rally to $1.65 by winter. Considers current cash market unduly depressed.
3. Merrill Lynch in its weekly commodity letter suggests leaving wheat alone except as a possible long-term capital

gain venture going into late spring.
4. Your own research indicates a surplus in wheat this year coupled with possible CCC dumping of excess stockpiles as farm lobbyists lose power in a Nixon sweep. Low prices seem likely to stay low with a possible decline by late September.
5. A study of world wheat conditions, including carryover and crops in Australia, Canada, South Africa, and the United States does indicate crop abundance. Members of the World International Wheat Agreement are well supplied. The Soviet Union, on the other hand, is expecting a bad year for the crop.
6. You have worked up a study comparing the relationship between the price of corn and wheat which indicates that wheat is relatively low priced and that to correct this imbalance, wheat prices will rise after harvest while corn prices continue to decline into harvest lows. Past history confirms that the wheat-corn ratio corrects itself with speed whenever an imbalance occurs.
7. On the suggestion of your broker, you checked out the supply of wheat in Chicago elevator stocks at this time of the year and find that when wheat stocks are under 5 million bushels by late July, the price of wheat stages a

15 cent rally after harvest in 15 out of the comparable 18 years. This suggests a rise to $1.57 by September.

8. Seasonal charts show a normal rise in wheat prices over the fall.

9. Vertical line charts indicate a resistance level at $1.50 and again at $1.55 and if price rises through these levels, an uptrend of good size may occur.

Also see Figure 200 below and Figures 201 and 202 on pages 297-99.

FIGURE 200

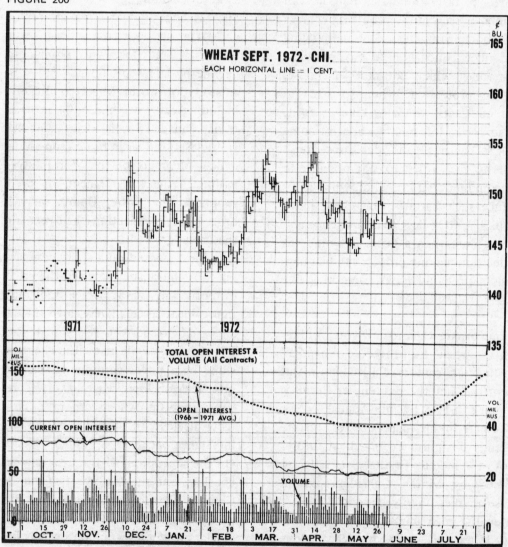

Source: Commodity Research Bureau, Inc.

FIGURE 201
THE GUESSTIMATOR

INPUTS

My broker says _WHEAT_   will (RISE) FALL to _1.75_ by _OCT_.
       (commodity)   (level)   (date)

Letter #1 says _WHEAT_   will (RISE) FALL to _1.65_ by _DEC_.

Letter #2 says _WHEAT_   will (RISE) FALL to _—_ by _SPRING_

Fundamental #1 _WHEAT_   will RISE (FALL) to _1.35_ by _SEPT_.

Fundamental #2 _WHEAT_   will RISE (FALL) to _—_ by _—_.

CORN says _WHEAT_   will (RISE) FALL to _—_ by _FALL_.

ELEVATOR says _WHEAT_   will (RISE) FALL to _1.57_ by _SEPT_.

CCC FLOOR/CEILING is at (level) $ _1.38_ .

ODDS FOR SUCCESS

I choose (month) _SEPT_ because _CASH AND_
FUTURES IMBALANCED — NEAR SHOULD RISE

I will BUY/SELL about (date) _1 JULY_ for covering about _1 SEPT_

General cash odds are .... _62_ % for success.
Specific cash odds are .... _72_ % for success.
General futures odds are .... _58_ % for success.
Specific futures odds are .... _83_ % for success.

REFINEMENTS

Charts confirm a breakout if price hits (level) _1.50 1/8_ .

Significant noise level appears to be (amount) _2 ¢_ .

I will set my stop-loss at (amount) _3 ¢_ .

Prior charts indicate a trailing stop-loss of (amount) _5 ¢_ .

Volume and Open Interest CONFIRM/DENY the breakout.

FIGURE 201—*Continued*

<u>THE PLAY</u>

I will BUY/SELL <u>SEPT</u> <u>WHEAT</u> at <u>MKT</u> on <u>—</u>
            (month) (commodity)   (price)   (date)

or when price hits <u>1.50⅛</u> for a possible move to <u>1.80</u>
                  (level)   (level)

by <u>SEPT 1</u>. I will set my stop-loss at <u>1.47⅛</u> and trail it
   (date)   (level)

by <u>5¢</u>. I will add contracts at <u>1.55⅛</u> and close my
   (amount)   (level)

position when <u>ANY 5¢ REACTION</u>.

I will open <u>3</u> contracts and commit $<u>3,000</u> on this
          (number)   (amount)

position and risk $<u>900</u>.
                 (amount)

<u>RECORD</u>

Position was opened on <u>7/2/72</u> at $ <u>1.50¼</u>
Position was increased on <u>7/18/72</u> at $ <u>1.55¼</u>
Position was closed on <u>9/1/72</u> at $ <u>1.80¼</u>
Gross PROFIT/LOSS was .... $ <u>8,250</u>
Minus Commission .... $ <u>180</u>
Net PROFIT/LOSS .... $ <u>8,070</u>

COMMENTS <u>LATER CONTRACT WOULD HAVE
BEEN BETTER - WHEAT FUTURES
SUBSEQUENTLY ROSE TO $3.00
PER BUSHEL.</u>

FIGURE 202

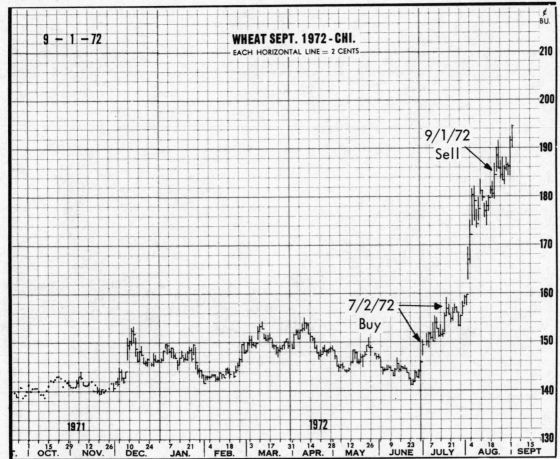

Source: Commodity Research Bureau, Inc., with additions by author.

Appendixes

Regional Offices, U. S. Department of Agriculture Commodity Exchange Authority

The Commodity Exchange Authority under the direction of Mr. Alex C. Caldwell supervises the commodity exchanges throughout the United States. Any trader who suspects any violation of federal law with regard to his commodity account should report this violation to the Commodity Exchange Authority director closest to the town where the violation occurred. The various regions and officers of the Commodity Exchange Authority are as follows:

UNITED STATES DEPARTMENT OF AGRICULTURE
Commodity Exchange Authority

Alex C. Caldwell, Administrator
Washington, D.C. 20250
Telephone: Area Code 202
388-4471

Regional Offices	*Markets Supervised*
EASTERN REGION T. Reed McMinn, Director 61 Broadway, Room 2101 New York, N.Y. 10006 Telephone: Area Code 212 264-1700	Citrus Associates of the New York Cotton Exchange, Inc. Commodity Exchange, Inc. International Commercial Exchange Memphis Board of Trade Clearing Association New York Cotton Exchange New York Mercantile Exchange New York Produce Exchange Wool Associates of the New York Cotton Exchange, Inc.
CENTRAL REGION Robert W. Clark, Director 141 West Jackson Blvd., Room A-1 Chicago, Illinois 60604 Telephone: Area Code 312 353-5990	Chicago Board of Trade Chicago Mercantile Exchange Chicago Open Board of Trade Milwaukee Grain Exchange
WESTERN REGION Samuel F. Gordon, Director 4800 Main Street, Room 356 Kansas City, Missouri 64112 Telephone: Area Code 816 931-5866 Suboffice 510 Grain Exchange Building Minneapolis, Minnesota 55415 Telephone: Area Code 612 725-2025	Duluth Board of Trade Kansas City Board of Trade Merchants' Exchange of St. Louis Minneapolis Grain Exchange New Orleans Cotton Exchange Northern California Grain Exchange Portland Grain Exchange Seattle Grain Exchange

Primary agricultural reports distributed free of charge by the U. S. Department of Agriculture

The U.S. Department of Agriculture, Washington, D.C. 20250, maintains a "computerized mailing list" which freely distributes the major agricultural reports to the public. For any interested person, and that includes most commodity traders, reports are available free for the asking. Simply write to the Department of Agriculture at the above address, identify the report (or reports) you wish to receive and your name will be added to the computerized mailing list.

The major agricultural reports which most commodity traders will be interested in are the following:

1. Prospective Plantings Report.
2. Production Reports.
3. Stocks in All Positions Report.
4. Annual summary of acreage, yield, and production.
5. The *Wheat Situation* Report.
6. *Grain Market News Weekly* (Feed Market News Weekly.)
7. Commitment of Traders in Commodity Futures Report.
8. *Feed Situation Report.*
9. Soybean and Flaxseed Stocks in All Positions Report.
10. Soybean Farm Stocks Report.
11. Soybean Acreage Report.
12. Monthly Soybean and Soybean Oil Crush Report.
13. Monthly Soybean Oil Factory Production Report.
14. Fats and Oils Situation Report.
15. Livestock and Meat Situation Reports.
16. The Hogs and Pigs Reports.
17. The Monthly Cold Storage Report.
18. The Livestock Commercial Slaughter and Meat Production Report.
19. Cattle and Calves Report.
20. Livestock and Poultry Inventory Report.
21. Meat Animals Annual Summary Report.
22. Shipments of Stocker and Feeder Cattle and Sheep Report.
23. Special Range Reports.
24. Cattle on Pastures Report.
25. Western Range and Livestock Report.
26. Special Wheat Pasture Report.
27. Sugar Reports.
28. Foreign Agricultural Circular on Sugar.
29. Sugar Crop Production Report.
30. The Census Bureau Monthly Report on Cocoa and Chocolate.
31. Cotton Production and Distribution Report.
32. Cottonseed and Cottonseed Products Report.
33. Poultry and Egg Production Report.

Fruit Situation Report

34. Weekly Butter Production Report.
35. Agricultural Prices Report.
36. Cotton Situation Report.
37. Poultry and Egg Situation Report.
38. World Agricultural Situation Report.

39. Demand and Price Situation Report.
40. Wool Situation Report.
41. Farm Income Situation Report.
42. Foreign Agricultural Bulletin.

Miscellaneous informative reports available to the commodity trader

In addition to the Department of Agriculture there are other sources of general and specific information for the commodity trader. Some of the more important source data which the commodity trader will wish to have access to or subscription of are as follows: (your broker can advise you how each may be secured or may secure them for you through his firm).

1. *The Wall Street Journal.*
2. *The New York Journal of Commerce.*
3. The annual report of the Chicago Board of Trade.
4. The annual report of the Chicago Mercantile Exchange.
5. The annual report of the Commodity Exchange Inc.
6. The annual report of the New York Coffee and Sugar Exchange.
7. The annual report of the New York Mercantile Exchange.
8. The annual report of the New York Cocoa Exchange.
9. The annual report of the New York Cotton Exchange.
10. The annual report of the Kansas City Board of Trade.
11. The annual report of the Minneapolis Grain Exchange.
12. *The Oil World Quarterly and Weekly.*
13. F. O. Licht's International Sugar Report.
14. *International Sugar Council Statistical Bulletin.*
15. *New York Coffee and Sugar Exchange Weekly Review.*
16. Ghana and Nigeria Cocoa Reports.
17. The Census Bureau Monthly Report.
18. *The Drover's Journal.*
19. *The National Provisioner.*
20. The Bureau of Mines *Minerals Yearbook.*
21. The Bureau of Mines Mineral Industry Surveys.
22. *The Engineering and Mining Journal.*
23. The New York Cotton Exchange Weekly Report.
24. Egg Producer's Price.
25. Dairy and Poultry News.
26. The Florida Canner's Association Reports.
27. State of Florida Crop Reporting Board.
28. The Winnipeg Grain Exchange Publications.
29. Sanford Evans Services, Ltd., Winnipeg.
30. Board of Grain Commissioners for Canada Publications.
31. *The Commodity Yearbook.*
32. The Commodity Exchange Authority has selected publications on specialized studies in the field of commodity trading.

The 23 commodity exchanges authorized by law to operate in the United States

Although not all are active it is theoretically possible to trade the following commodity futures on the following commodity exchanges.

1. *The Chicago Board of Trade* (organized April 3, 1848; 1,402 members; address: 141 W. Jackson Boulevard, Chicago, Illinois 60604).
   Wheat, corn, oats, rye, soybeans, soybean oil, soybean meal, grain sorghums, lard-drummed, lard-loose, steer carcass beef, live choice steers, iced broilers, plywood, silver, cotton, and currency futures.
   (The actively traded commodities are: wheat, corn, oats, soybeans, soybean oil, soybean meal, iced broilers, plywood, and silver.)

2. *The Chicago Mercantile Exchange* (organized as a branch of the Chicago Produce Exchange, 1898; changed to Chicago Mercantile Exchange, October 6, 1919; 500 members; address: 444 W. Jackson Boulevard, Chicago, Illinois 60606).
   International Monetary Market (division of Chicago Mercantile Exchange; chartered by State of Illinois, January 27, 1972; address: 444 W. Jackson Boulevard, Chicago, Illinois).
   Shell eggs, frozen eggs, potatoes, Idaho potatoes, onions, butter, pork bellies, skinned hams, chickens, hen turkeys, tom turkeys, frozen shrimp, live cattle (Midwest), live cattle (Western), dressed beef, live hogs, lumber, and currency futures.
   (The actively traded commodities are: eggs, Idaho potatoes, pork bellies, live cattle, live hogs, lumber, and currency futures.)

3. *Commodity Exchange Incorporated* (organized through the consolidation of the Rubber, National Silk, National Metal, and New York Hide Exchanges; trading began May 1, 1933; address: 81 Broad Street, New York, New York 10004).
   Copper, hides, lead, mercury, propane, rubber, silver, tin, zinc, burlap, and silk.
   (The actively traded commodities are: copper and silver.)

4. *New York Coffee and Sugar Exchange* (opened March 7, 1882: expanded to include sugar, December 16, 1914; present name adopted 1916; address: 79 Pine Street, New York, New York 10005).
   Coffee, sugar (world), sugar (domestic), molasses.
   (The actively traded commodity is world sugar.)

5. *The New York Mercantile Exchange* (formed in 1872; address: 6 Harrison Street, New York, New York 10013).
   Maine potatoes, Long Island pota-

toes, Idaho potatoes, onions, butter, eggs, rice, apples, aluminum, palladium, platinum, and plywood.
(The actively traded commodity is Maine potatoes.)

6. *The New York Cocoa Exchange* (trading began October 1, 1925; address: 127 John Street, New York, New York 10038).
Cocoa.

7. *The New York Cotton Exchange* (began trading 1870; address: 43 Exchange Place, New York, New York).
Cotton, wool, wool tops, frozen orange juice concentrate.
(The actively traded commodities are cotton and frozen orange juice.)

8. *The Kansas City Board of Trade* ("grain calls" began June 1876; organized in current form, January 2, 1895; address: 4800 Main Street, Kansas City, Missouri 64112).
Wheat, corn, grain sorghums, soybeans, bran, shorts, middlings, live feeder cattle.
(The actively traded commodity is wheat.)

9. *The Chicago Open Board of Trade* (address: 343 S. Dearborne, Chicago, Illinois 60604).
Wheat, corn, oats, rye, soybeans, and silver.
(All are traded in contracts of "job lots.")

10. *Minneapolis Grain Exchange* (address: 4th Street & 4th Avenue, Minneapolis, Minnesota 55402).
Wheat, corn, oats, rye, soybeans, barley, and flaxseed.
(The actively traded commodity is wheat.)

11. *The New York Produce Exchange:*
Cottonseed oil, soybean oil, tallow, pepper, fishmeal, and soybeans.
(The actively traded commodity is fishmeal, and it is not very active.)

12. *The West Coast Commodity Exchange* (organized October 15, 1970; address: 643 S. Olive Street, Los Angeles, California 90014).
Cocoa, silver, sugar, and copper.

13. *International Commercial Exchange* (formerly the New York Exchange, est. 1862; changed to current title, 1972; address: Two Broadway, New York, New York 10004).
International Commercial Paper.

14. *Winnipeg Commodity Exchange:*
Oats, rye, barley, flaxseed, rapeseed, cattle, and gold.

15. *Milwaukee Grain Exchange:*
Wheat, corn, oats, and rye.

16. *Seattle Grain Exchange:*
Wheat.

17. *St. Louis Mercantile Exchange:*
Millfeeds.

18. *Memphis Board of Trade Clearing Association:*
Cottonseed meal, soybean meal, soybeans.

19. *New Orleans Cotton Exchange:*
Cotton, cottonseed oil.

20. *The Pacific Coast Commodity Exchange* (incorporated, October 1970; organized for trading, October 1972; address: 315 Montgomery Street, San Francisco, California 94104).
Coconut oil.

21. *The Duluth Board of Trade:*
Wheat.

22. *Northern California Grain Exchange:*
Wheat.

23. *Portland Grain Exchange:*
Wheat.

Sample commodity orders as written by
commodity brokers and wired directly to the floor of
commodity exchanges to be filled on behalf
of the customer by a floor trader

FIGURE 203

TIME   ORDER PREPARATION MANUAL – COMMODITIES – ILLUSTRATION   1

USE FOR COMMODITIES ONLY

ADDRESS	C G B OF T KSC GRAINS	C G MERC	WPG	MPLS GRAINS	NY/LDN COMDYS	N Y COF & SUG	N Y CTN EXGE	COMEX N Y	OTHER	ORDER NUMBER	C.F.O. NUMBER
	☒ OBT/CX	☐ OME/CX	☐ OCG/CX	☐ OMP/CX	☐ OCC	☐ OCF/CC	☐ OCO/CC	☐ OCY/CC	☐ _____	CG 15	
										BY ORDER CLERK ONLY	BY ORDER CLERK ONLY

2 ☐ CXL ☐ BAS — BASIS COMMODITY MONTH PRICE ☐ STOP STP ☐ SPREAD ☐ SWITCH ☐ SCALE

3 ☐ CXL ☒ BUY QUANTITY **10** COMMODITY **MAY WHT** (MONTH) PRICE OR 'MKT' **MKT** OR BETTER ☐ OB STOP ☐ STP STOP LIMIT PRICE ___ LMT OR MARKET IF TOUCHED ☐ MIT LMT ON CLOSE ☐ CLO EOS / EDS ☐ WHEN DONE OR ☐ AND ☐

4 ☐ CXL ☐ SL QUANTITY COMMODITY MONTH PRICE OR 'MKT' ☐ P.T.S OR BETTER ☐ OB STOP ☐ STP STOP LIMIT PRICE ___ LMT OR MARKET IF TOUCHED ☐ MIT LMT ON CLOSE ☐ CLO PREM./DISCT. MONTH ☐ OVER ☐ UNDER

5 SPECIAL INSTRUCTIONS NOT HELD ☐ NH LEAVES ☐ LVS GOOD 'TIL CANCELLED ☐ GTC TODAY ONLY ☒ DAY GOOD THIS WEEK ☐ GTW IMMEDIATE FILL OR KILL ☐ FOK GOOD THIS MONTH ☐ GTM AT OPENING ONLY ☐ OPG GOOD THRU ☐ GT (DATE OR HOUR)

6 NO FORMER ORDER ☒ NFO CXL FORMER ORDER ☐ CXL REPLACEMENT CANCELLATION INSTRUCTIONS

7 ACCOUNT NUMBER **6 0 – 7 5 4 2 – 6 – 8 9** ☒ N NEW ☐ L LIQUIDATING NEW ACCOUNT ☒ NA ☒ T4

8 MISCELLANEOUS INFORMATION (28 CHAR. MAXIMUM) EXECUTED PRICE

9 GIVE UP ☐ GU FIRM'S SYMBOL (4 CHAR. MAX) BY TELETYPE CFN (QTY) OPERATOR ONLY

10 CUSTOMER'S NAME **ROBERT STEINBERG**

Reynolds & Co.

FORM 33-308

MARKET ORDER

TELETYPE IN-PUT

OBT/CX CG 15

BUY 10 MAY WHT MKT
DAY
NFO

60-7542-6-89 N NA T4
CFN 10

An order to BUY or SELL at the prevailing Bid-Asked price.

When entering orders in grains the quantity shall always be designated in units of 5,000 bushels per contract, written as 5 (one contract); 10 (2 contracts); etc. All other commodities (i.e., wool, cotton, etc.) are designated in contract units as 1, 2, 3, etc.

Note that "MKT" appears in the price field. Do *not* use a dash (–) in the price field when entering a market order. Exchange specifications require the use of "MKT", except in special cases which are described later.

Since this is a market order it has been designated as a "DAY" order on Line 5 (all market orders are "DAY" orders).

Also illustrated is the term "NA", on Line 7, which indicates that this is an order for a new account. Such notation is necessary only on the first day of activity of a new account.

FIGURE 204

ORDER PREPARATION MANUAL – COMMODITIES – ILLUSTRATION **2**

USE FOR COMMODITIES ONLY

ADDRESS										ORDER NUMBER	C.F.O. NUMBER
C G B OF T KSC GRAINS ☐ OBT/CX	C G MERC ☒ OME/CX	WPG ☐ OCG/CX	MPLS GRAINS ☐ OMP/CX	NY/LDN COMDYS ☐ OCC	N Y COF & SUG ☐ OCF/CC	N Y CTN EXGE ☐ OCO/CC	COMEX N Y ☐ OCY/CC	OTHER ☐ _____		HV 53 BY ORDER CLERK ONLY	BY ORDER CLERK ONLY

Line 2 — ☐ CXL BASIS ☐ BAS | COMMODITY | MONTH | PRICE | STOP ☐ STP | ☐ SPREAD ☐ SWITCH ☐ SCALE

Line 3 — ☐ CXL ☒ BUY QUANTITY **2** COMMODITY **DEC CATTLE** MONTH PRICE OR 'MKT' **2750** OR BETTER ☐ OB STOP ☐ STP STOP LIMIT PRICE ___ LMT OR MARKET IF TOUCHED ☐ MIT LMT ON CLOSE ☐ CLO EOS EDS ☐ WHEN DONE OR ☐ AND ☐

Line 4 — ☐ CXL ☐ SL QUANTITY COMMODITY MONTH PRICE OR 'MKT' ☐ PTS OR BETTER ☐ OB STOP ☐ STP STOP LIMIT PRICE ___ LMT OR MARKET IF TOUCHED ☐ MIT LMT ON CLOSE ☐ CLO PREM./DISCT. MONTH ☐ OVER ☐ UNDER

Line 5 — SPECIAL INSTRUCTIONS | NOT HELD ☐ NH | LEAVES ☐ LVS | GOOD 'TIL CANCELLED ☒ GTC TODAY ONLY ☐ DAY | GOOD THIS WEEK ☐ GTW IMMEDIATE FILL OR KILL ☐ FOK | GOOD THIS MONTH ☐ GTM AT OPENING ONLY ☐ OPG | GOOD THRU ☐ GT ___ (DATE OR HOUR)

Line 6 — NO FORMER ORDER ☒ NFO CXL FORMER ORDER ☐ CXL REPLACEMENT CANCELLATION INSTRUCTIONS

Line 7 — ACCOUNT NUMBER **4E - 3610 - 6 - 87** ☒ NEW N ☐ LIQUIDATING L ☐ NEW ACCOUNT NA ☒ T4

Line 8 — MISCELLANEOUS INFORMATION (28 CHAR. MAXIMUM) | EXECUTED PRICE

Line 9 — GIVE UP ☐ GU FIRM'S SYMBOL (4 CHAR. MAX) BY TELETYPE CFN (QTY) OPERATOR ONLY

Line 10 — CUSTOMER'S NAME **G. ADDAMS**

Reynolds & Co.
FORM 33-308

LIMIT ORDER

```
OME/CX HV 53

BUY 2 DEC CATTLE 2750
GTC
NFO

4E-3610-6-87 N T4
CFN 2
```

TELETYPE IN-PUT

An order to BUY or SELL at, or better than, the price shown on the order.

You will notice that the delivery month ("DEC") has been abbreviated. The correct abbreviations for the months can be found on Page 8.

The "N" checked on Line 7 indicates that the trade will be a new position. Check "L" if the trade is closing out a position.

"T4", on Line 7, *must* appear on all orders. (This is a CEA requirement.)

USE FOR COMMODITIES ONLY

ADDRESS	C G B OF T KSC GRAINS	C G MERC	WPG	MPLS GRAINS	NY/LDN COMDYS	N Y COF & SUG	N Y CTN EXGE	COMEX N Y	OTHER	ORDER NUMBER	C.F.O. NUMBER
	☐	☐	☐	☐	☐	☒	☐	☐	☐	NW 32	
	OBT/CX	OME/CX	OCG/CX	OMP/CX	OCC	OCF/CC	OCO/CC	OCY/CC ____		BY ORDER CLERK ONLY	BY ORDER CLERK ONLY

2 CXL ☐ | BAS ☒ | SEP   MONTH | No. 11 SUG   COMMODITY | PRICE 299 | ▨ | STOP ☐ STP | ☐ SPREAD   ☐ SWITCH   ☐ SCALE

3	QUANTITY	COMMODITY	PRICE OR 'MKT'	OR BETTER	STOP	STOP LIMIT PRICE		MARKET IF TOUCHED		ON CLOSE	EOS	WHEN DONE
CXL ☐ BUY ☐		MONTH		OB ☐	STP ☐	LMT ___	OR	MIT ☐	LMT	CLO ☐	EDS	OR ☐ AND ☐

4	QUANTITY	COMMODITY	PRICE OR 'MKT'	OR BETTER	STOP	STOP LIMIT PRICE		MARKET IF TOUCHED		ON CLOSE	PREM./DISCT.	OVER
CXL ☐ SL ☒	3 MCH MONTH	No.11 SUG	MKT ☐ P.T.S	OB ☐	STP ☐	LMT ___	OR	MIT ☐	LMT	CLO ☐	MONTH	UNDER

5	NOT HELD	LEAVES	GOOD 'TIL CANCELLED	GOOD THIS WEEK	GOOD THIS MONTH	GOOD THRU	(DATE OR HOUR)
	☐ NH	☐ LVS	☒ GTC / TODAY ONLY ☐ DAY	☐ GTW / IMMEDIATE FILL OR KILL ☐ FOK	☐ GTM / AT OPENING ONLY ☐ OPG	☐ GT ____	
SPECIAL INSTRUCTIONS							

6	NO FORMER ORDER	CXL FORMER ORDER	REPLACEMENT CANCELLATION INSTRUCTIONS
	☒ NFO	☐ CXL	

7 | ACCOUNT NUMBER | 4 0 – 5 0 6 1 – 7 – 5 4 | ☒ N NEW / ☐ L LIQUIDATING | ☐ NA NEW ACCOUNT / ☒ T 4

8	MISCELLANEOUS INFORMATION (28 CHAR. MAXIMUM)	EXECUTED PRICE

9	GIVE UP ☐ GU	FIRM'S SYMBOL (4 CHAR. MAX)	BY TELETYPE CFN (QTY) OPERATOR ONLY	

10 CUSTOMER'S NAME   **L. BAKER**

Reynolds & Co.

FORM 33-308

BASIS ORDERS

```
  OCF/CC NW 32

  BAS SEP NO 11 SUG 299
  SL 3 MCH NO 11 SUG MKT
  GTC
  NFO

  40-5061-7-54 N T4
  CFN 3
```

TELETYPE IN-PUT

Basis orders ("BAS") are used in situations where the client wants to buy or sell one delivery option of a commodity based on (or basis) the price of another delivery option of the same commodity.

Unlike contingent orders in which the execution of the customer's own order activated another of his own orders, the basis order is not contingent.

In basis orders, the basis section sets the conditions under which the order will be executed, but only one order is actually filled.

There are 3 types of BASIS orders:

(1) Market   (Illustration No. 3).
(2) Limit   (Illustration No. 4).
(3) Stop   (Illustration No. 5).

The market basis order is informing the broker to wait until September rises in price to 2.99¢ per pound and, at this level, to sell 3 contracts of March No. 11 Sugar (world sugar) at the market. However, the client only sells the March sugar . . . not the September, too.

FIGURE 206

ORDER PREPARATION MANUAL – COMMODITIES – ILLUSTRATION **4**

USE FOR COMMODITIES ONLY

ADDRESS									ORDER NUMBER	C.F.O. NUMBER
C G B OF T KSC GRAINS ☐ OBT/CX	C G MERC ☒ OME/CX	WPG ☐ OCG/CX	MPLS GRAINS ☐ OMP/CX	NY/LDN COMDYS ☐ OCC	NY COF & SUG ☐ OCF/CC	N Y CTN EXGE ☐ OCO/CC	COMEX NY ☐ OCY/CC	OTHER ☐ _____	**PG 78** BY ORDER CLERK ONLY	BY ORDER CLERK ONLY

② CXL ☐ BAS ☒ — BASIS **FEB** MONTH — COMMODITY **BLY** — PRICE **3020** — STOP ☐ STP — ☐ SPREAD   ☐ SWITCH   ☐ SCALE

③ CXL ☐ BUY ☒ — QUANTITY **7** — **AUG** MONTH — COMMODITY **BLY** — PRICE OR 'MKT' **3025** — OR BETTER ☐ OB — STOP ☐ STP — STOP LIMIT PRICE ___ LMT — OR — MARKET IF TOUCHED ☐ MIT — LMT — ON CLOSE ☐ CLO — EOS / EDS — ☐ WHEN DONE — OR ☐ AND ☐

④ CXL ☐ SL ☐ — QUANTITY — MONTH — COMMODITY — PRICE OR 'MKT' ☐ P.T.S — OR BETTER ☐ OB — STOP ☐ STP — STOP LIMIT PRICE ___ LMT — OR — MARKET IF TOUCHED ☐ MIT — LMT — ON CLOSE ☐ CLO — PREM./DISCT. MONTH — ☐ OVER ☐ UNDER

⑤ SPECIAL INSTRUCTIONS — NOT HELD ☐ NH — LEAVES ☐ LVS — GOOD 'TIL CANCELLED ☒ GTC — GOOD THIS WEEK ☐ GTW — GOOD THIS MONTH ☐ GTM — GOOD THRU ☐ GT — (DATE OR HOUR) — TODAY ONLY ☐ DAY — IMMEDIATE FILL OR KILL ☐ FOK — AT OPENING ONLY ☐ OPG

⑥ NO FORMER ORDER ☒ NFO — CXL FORMER ORDER ☐ CXL — REPLACEMENT CANCELLATION INSTRUCTIONS

⑦ ACCOUNT NUMBER **3 0 – 7 1 1 4 – 6 – 0 2** — NEW ☒ N LIQUIDATING ☐ L — NEW ACCOUNT ☐ NA ☒ T 4

⑧ MISCELLANEOUS INFORMATION (28 CHAR. MAXIMUM) — EXECUTED PRICE

⑨ GIVE UP ☐ GU — FIRM'S SYMBOL (4 CHAR. MAX) — BY TELETYPE CFN (QTY) OPERATOR ONLY

⑩ CUSTOMER'S NAME **CHAS. DEARBORN**

Reynolds & Co.
FORM 33-308

BASIS LIMIT ORDER

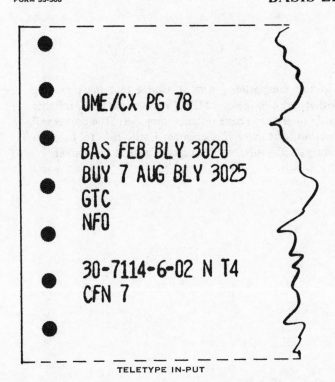

OME/CX PG 78

BAS FEB BLY 3020
BUY 7 AUG BLY 3025
GTC
NFO

30-7114-6-02 N T4
CFN 7

TELETYPE IN-PUT

In this case, February Pork Belly futures must decline to 30.20¢ per pound, and then the order to buy 7 contracts of August Pork Belly will be entered at its own limit of 30.25¢, and the conditions of a limit order prevail.

FIGURE 207

ORDER PREPARATION MANUAL – COMMODITIES – ILLUSTRATION   **5**

USE FOR COMMODITIES ONLY

ADDRESS	C G B OF T KSC GRAINS	C G MERC	WPG	MPLS GRAINS	NY/LDN COMDYS	N Y COF & SUG	N Y CTN EXGE	COMEX N Y	OTHER	ORDER NUMBER	C.F.D. NUMBER
	☐ OBT/CX	☒ OME/CX	☐ OCG/CX	☐ OMP/CX	☐ OCC	☐ OCF/CC	☐ OCO/CC	☐ OCY/CC	☐ _____	SY 9	BY ORDER CLERK ONLY

2 CXL — BASIS ☒ BAS — DEC CATTLE — PRICE 2250 — STOP ☒ STP — ☐ SPREAD — ☐ SWITCH — ☐ SCALE

3 CXL — ☒ BUY — QUANTITY 15 — AUG CATTLE — PRICE OR MKT MKT — OR BETTER ☐ OB — STOP ☐ STP — STOP LIMIT PRICE ☐ LMT — OR — MARKET IF TOUCHED ☐ MIT — LMT — ON CLOSE ☐ CLO — EOS — EDS — ☐ WHEN DONE — ☐ OR — ☐ AND

4 CXL — ☐ SL — QUANTITY — COMMODITY — PRICE OR MKT — OR BETTER ☐ OB — STOP ☐ STP — STOP LIMIT PRICE ☐ LMT — OR — MARKET IF TOUCHED ☐ MIT — LMT — ON CLOSE ☐ CLO — PREM./DISCT. — ☐ OVER — ☐ UNDER

5 SPECIAL INSTRUCTIONS — NOT HELD ☐ NH — LEAVES ☐ LVS — GOOD 'TIL CANCELLED ☒ GTC — GOOD THIS WEEK ☐ GTW — GOOD THIS MONTH ☐ GTM — GOOD THRU ☐ GT _____ (DATE OR HOUR) — TODAY ONLY ☐ DAY — IMMEDIATE FILL OR KILL ☐ FOK — AT OPENING ONLY ☐ OPG

6 NO FORMER ORDER ☒ NFO — CXL FORMER ORDER ☐ CXL — REPLACEMENT CANCELLATION INSTRUCTIONS

7 ACCOUNT NUMBER 3 6 – 0 8 4 9 – 6 – 1 5 — ☒ N NEW / ☐ L LIQUIDATING — ☐ NA NEW ACCOUNT / ☒ T4

8 MISCELLANEOUS INFORMATION (28 CHAR. MAXIMUM) — EXECUTED PRICE

9 GIVE UP ☐ GU — FIRM'S SYMBOL (4 CHAR. MAX) — BY TELETYPE CFN (QTY) — OPERATOR ONLY

10 CUSTOMER'S NAME — MICHAEL PATERNO

Reynolds & Co.
FORM 33-308

BASIS STOP ORDER

OME/CX SY 9

BAS DEC CATTLE 2250 STP
BUY 15 AUG CATTLE MKT
GTC
NFO

36-0849-6-15 N T4
CFN 15

In this illustration, we must assume that the prevailing market price is below 22.50¢ per pound for December Cattle or the stop basis order is improper. The broker will wait until the price of December Cattle rises to, or penetrates, 22.50¢, then buy 15 August Cattle at the market.

TELETYPE IN-PUT

FIGURE 208

ORDER PREPARATION MANUAL – COMMODITIES – ILLUSTRATION **6**

USE FOR COMMODITIES ONLY

ADDRESS

C G B O F T KSC GRAINS	C G MERC	WPG	MPLS GRAINS	NY/LDN COMDYS	N Y COF & SUG	N Y CTN EXGE	COMEX N Y	OTHER	ORDER NUMBER	C.F.O. NUMBER
☐	☐	☐	☒	☐	☐	☐	☐	☐	WS 49	
OBT/CX	OME/CX	OCG/CX	OMP/CX	OCC	OCF/CC	OCO/CC	OCY/CC		BY ORDER CLERK ONLY	BY ORDER CLERK ONLY

2

BASIS		COMMODITY	PRICE		STOP	☒ SPREAD
☐ CXL	☐ BAS	MONTH		▨	☐ STP	☐ SWITCH ☐ SCALE

3

		QUANTITY		COMMODITY	PRICE OR 'MKT'	OR BETTER	STOP	STOP LIMIT PRICE		MARKET IF TOUCHED		ON CLOSE	EOS		WHEN DONE
☐ CXL	☒ BUY	5	SEP	CG WHT		☐ OB	☐ STP	LMT	OR	☐ MIT	LMT	☐ CLO	EDS	☐ OR ☐ AND
			MONTH											

4

		QUANTITY		COMMODITY	PRICE OR 'MKT'	OR BETTER	STOP	STOP LIMIT PRICE		MARKET IF TOUCHED		ON CLOSE	PREM./DISCT.	
☐ CXL	☒ SL	5	DEC	MPLS WHT	2	☐ OB	☐ STP	LMT	OR	☐ MIT	LMT	☐ CLO	MPLS	☒ OVER ☐ UNDER
			MONTH		☒ P.T.S								MONTH	

5

	NOT HELD	LEAVES	GOOD 'TIL CANCELLED	GOOD THIS WEEK	GOOD THIS MONTH	GOOD THRU	(DATE OR HOUR)
	☐ NH	☐ LVS	☐ GTC	☐ GTW	☐ GTM	☐ GT	
			TODAY ONLY	IMMEDIATE FILL OR KILL	AT OPENING ONLY		
SPECIAL INSTRUCTIONS			☒ DAY	☐ FOK	☐ OPG		

6

NO FORMER ORDER	CXL FORMER ORDER	
☒ NFO	☐ CXL	REPLACEMENT CANCELLATION INSTRUCTIONS

7

ACCOUNT NUMBER			NEW	NEW ACCOUNT
7 0 — 5 0 4 2 — 6 — 3 6	☒ N	☐ L LIQUIDATING	☐ NA	☒ T 4

8

MISCELLANEOUS INFORMATION (28 CHAR. MAXIMUM)   EXECUTED PRICE

9

GIVE UP	FIRM'S SYMBOL	BY TELETYPE
☐ GU	(4 CHAR. MAX)	CFN (QTY) OPERATOR ONLY

10

CUSTOMER'S NAME   *THOMAS LOVELL*

Reynolds & Co.

FORM 33-308

SPREAD ORDER

- OMP/CX WS 49

- SPREAD
  BUY 5 SEP CG WHT
  SL 5 DEC MPLS WHT 2 PTS MPLS OVER
  DAY
  NFO

- 70-5042-6-36 N T4
  CFN 5 5

TELETYPE IN-PUT

Although these types of orders have the appearance of a switch order, they are used primarily when a client wants to assume new positions both ways. (In the switch order, Illustrations No. 7, one side is a liquidation of an old position.)

A spread order can be traded as: (1) same market, same commodity; (2) same market, related commodity; (3) * different market, same commodity, (illustrated above).

The "PREM/DISCT." and the "OVER" or "UNDER" designations are required on all spread orders (unless the price is "MKT") for clarity to the floor broker, *omitting either is likened to omitting the price.*

By making such orders spread, the Account Executive insures that his customer will receive the proper commission rates and margin rates, which are in some cases reduced amounts under regular rates, when applicable.

* *In doing orders between different markets, it is customary to send the order to the smaller of the two markets. Such orders are extremely difficult to execute, and may be accepted only without Firm responsibility, as it is physically impossible for our brokers to execute simultaneously in two separate markets.*

FIGURE 209

ORDER PREPARATION MANUAL – COMMODITIES – ILLUSTRATION 7

USE FOR COMMODITIES ONLY

	C G B O F T KSC GRAINS	C G MERC	WPG	MPLS GRAINS	NY/LDN COMDYS	N Y COF & SUG	N Y CTN EXGE	COMEX N Y	OTHER	ORDER NUMBER	C.F.O. NUMBER
ADDRESS	X ☐ OBT/CX	☐ OME/CX	☐ OCG/CX	☐ OMP/CX	☐ OCC	☐ OCF/CC	☐ OCO/CC	☐ OCY/CC	☐ _____	AV 26	
										BY ORDER CLERK ONLY	BY ORDER CLERK ONLY

	BASIS		COMMODITY	PRICE		STOP	
2	☐ CXL	☐ BAS	MONTH			☐ STP	☐ SPREAD X SWITCH ☐ SCALE

		QUANTITY	COMMODITY	PRICE OR 'MKT'	OR BETTER	STOP	STOP LIMIT PRICE		MARKET IF TOUCHED		ON CLOSE	EOS		WHEN DONE
3	☐ CXL X BUY	5	JLY WHT		☐ OB	☐ STP	LMT	OR	☐ MIT	LMT	☐ CLO	EDS	☐	OR ☐ AND ☐
		MONTH												

		QUANTITY	COMMODITY	PRICE OR 'MKT'	OR BETTER	STOP	STOP LIMIT PRICE		MARKET IF TOUCHED		ON CLOSE	PREM./DISCT.		
4	☐ CXL X SL	5	MAY WHT	2 X P.TS	☐ OB	☐ STP	LMT	OR	☐ MIT	LMT	☐ CLO	JLY MONTH	X OVER ☐ UNDER	

					NOT HELD	LEAVES	GOOD 'TIL CANCELLED	GOOD THIS WEEK	GOOD THIS MONTH	GOOD THRU	(DATE OR HOUR)
5					☐ NH	☐ LVS	X GTC TODAY ONLY ☐ DAY	☐ GTW IMMEDIATE FILL OR KILL ☐ FOK	☐ GTM AT OPENING ONLY ☐ OPG	☐ GT	_____
	SPECIAL INSTRUCTIONS										

	NO FORMER ORDER	CXL FORMER ORDER	REPLACEMENT CANCELLATION INSTRUCTIONS
6	X NFO	☐ CXL	

	ACCOUNT NUMBER			NEW ACCOUNT
7	7 2 – 3 5 1 6 – 6 – 4 2	X N LIQUIDATING X L	☐ NA X T 4	

	MISCELLANEOUS INFORMATION (28 CHAR. MAXIMUM)	EXECUTED PRICE
8		

	GIVE UP	FIRM'S SYMBOL	BY TELETYPE	
9	☐ GU	(4 CHAR. MAX)	CFN (QTY) OPERATOR ONLY	

	CUSTOMER'S NAME
10	FRANK O'REILLY

Reynolds & Co.

FORM 33-308

SWITCH ORDER

```
OBT/CX AV 26

SWITCH
BUY 5 JLY WHT
SL 5 MAY WHT 2 PTS JLY OVER
GTC
NFO

72-3516-6-42 N L T4
CFN 5 5
```

Customers with a position, either long or short, in a commodity may want to change to a nearer or distant option of the same commodity. The prime reason for this type of order is that the customer wants to avoid a delivery notice and move his position forward.

Usually, the customer would use the basic market switch order which is to BUY and SELL at the market, however, he may enter a "difference switch" order (as illustrated above). Note that, in this case, the prices of the two options are not specified. The broker is allowed to execute at any time he can do so, when July is selling at 2¢ (or less) above May.

TELETYPE IN-PUT

FIGURE 210
ORDER PREPARATION MANUAL – COMMODITIES – ILLUSTRATION **8**

USE FOR COMMODITIES ONLY

ORDER NUMBER: BR 83

Address section checkboxes: OBT/CX, OME/CX, OCG/CX, OMP/CX, OCC, OCF/CC, OCO/CC (checked), OCY/CC, OTHER

Line 2: CXL, BAS — SPREAD, SWITCH, SCALE (checked)

Line 3: CXL, BUY (checked) — **1 MCH Wool GR MKT** — AND (checked)

Line 4: CXL, SL

Line 5: **1 EA. 5 PTS. DOWN TOTAL 5** — NH, LVS, DAY (checked)

Line 6: NFO (checked), CXL

Line 7: **2 0 – 6 3 1 7 – 6 – 1 7** — N (checked), T4 (checked)

Line 10: CUSTOMER'S NAME **G. TELLER**

Reynolds & Co. FORM 33-306

SCALE ORDER

```
OCO/CC BR 83

SCALE
BUY 1 MCH WOOL GR MKT AND
1 EA 5 PTS DOWN TOTAL 5 DAY
NFO

20-6317-6-17 N T4
CFN 1
```

There are 4 types of SCALE orders:

(1) Market (Illustration No. 8).
(2) Limit (Illustration No. 9).
(3) Market if (Illustration No. 10).
(4) Stop (Illustration No. 11).

The activation of a scale order is contingent on the execution of a key market, limit, "MIT", or stop order which then causes a series of orders at different price levels to be put into the trading area by the floor broker.

The illustration above is that of a "market scale order", where the floor broker will immediately buy one contract of March Grease Wool at the prevailing price (since it is a market order). This execution will then set the limit for the other four contracts specified in the scale order, each of which is to be bought at a ½ cent (or 5 points) *below* the previous execution.

The total contracts to be bought (sold) **must** appear on Line 5, or your order will be challenged.

FIGURE 211

ORDER PREPARATION MANUAL – COMMODITIES – ILLUSTRATION   9

USE FOR COMMODITIES ONLY

ADDRESS	C G B OF T KSC GRAINS	C G MERC	WPG	MPLS GRAINS	NY/LDN COMDYS	N Y COF & SUG	N Y CTN EXGE	COMEX N Y	OTHER	ORDER NUMBER	C.F.O. NUMBER
	☐ OBT/CX	☐ OME/CX	☐ OCG/CX	☐ OMP/CX	☐ OCC	☐ OCF/CC	☒ OCO/CC	☐ OCY/CC ____	☐	DT 97 / BY ORDER CLERK ONLY	BY ORDER CLERK ONLY

2 — CXL ☐ / BAS ☐ — BASIS — COMMODITY — MONTH — PRICE — STOP ☐ / STP — ☐ SPREAD — ☐ SWITCH — ☒ SCALE

3 — CXL ☐ / BUY ☒ — QUANTITY **1** — COMMODITY **MCH WOOL GR** MONTH — PRICE OR 'MKT' **1250** — OR BETTER ☐ OB / STOP ☐ STP — STOP LIMIT PRICE ___ LMT — OR — MARKET IF TOUCHED ☐ MIT — ___ LMT — ON CLOSE ☐ CLO — EOS / EDS — ☐ WHEN DONE / OR ☐ / AND ☒

4 — CXL ☐ / SL ☐ — QUANTITY — COMMODITY — MONTH — PRICE OR 'MKT' ☐ P.T.A — OR BETTER ☐ OB / STOP ☐ STP — STOP LIMIT PRICE ___ LMT — OR — MARKET IF TOUCHED ☐ MIT — ___ LMT — ON CLOSE ☐ CLO — PREM./DISCT. MONTH — ☐ OVER / ☐ UNDER

5 — **1 EA. 5 PTS DOWN TOTAL 5** — SPECIAL INSTRUCTIONS — NOT HELD ☐ NH — LEAVES ☐ LVS — GOOD 'TIL CANCELLED ☐ GTC — GOOD THIS WEEK ☐ GTW — GOOD THIS MONTH ☐ GTM — GOOD THRU ☐ GT — (DATE OR HOUR) — TODAY ONLY ☒ DAY — IMMEDIATE FILL OR KILL ☐ FOK — AT OPENING ONLY ☐ OPG

6 — NO FORMER ORDER ☒ NFO — CXL FORMER ORDER ☐ CXL — REPLACEMENT CANCELLATION INSTRUCTIONS

7 — ACCOUNT NUMBER **0 3 – 5 5 0 8 – 6 – 7 1** — ☒ N NEW / ☐ L LIQUIDATING — ☐ NA NEW ACCOUNT / ☒ T 4

8 — MISCELLANEOUS INFORMATION (28 CHAR. MAXIMUM) — EXECUTED PRICE

9 — GIVE UP ☐ GU — FIRM'S SYMBOL (4 CHAR. MAX) — BY TELETYPE CFN _____ (QTY) — OPERATOR ONLY

10 — CUSTOMER'S NAME **AL JOHNSON**

Reynolds & Co.
FORM 33-308

SCALE LIMIT ORDER

OCO/CC DT 97

SCALE
BUY 1 MCH WOOL GR 1250 AND
1 EA 5 PTS DOWN TOTAL 5 DAY
NFO

03-5508-6-71 N T4
CFN 1

The only difference between this order and the market scale order (see previous illustration) is that the market would have to touch, or penetrate, the 1.250¢ price before the first contract can be bought and before the rest of the scale order is entered. There is a possibility, however, that if the market breaks, all or part of the remaining 4 contracts can be executed at the same price.

TELETYPE IN-PUT

FIGURE 212

ORDER PREPARATION MANUAL – COMMODITIES – ILLUSTRATION **10**

USE FOR COMMODITIES ONLY

ADDRESS	C G B O F T KSC GRAINS	C G MERC	WPG	MPLS GRAINS	NY/LDN COMDYS	NY COF & SUG	N Y CTN EXGE	COMEX N Y	OTHER	ORDER NUMBER	C.F.O. NUMBER
	☐	☐	☐	☐	☐	☒	☐	☐	☐	**LA 120**	
	OBT/CX	OME/CX	OCG/CX	OMP/CX	OCC	OCF/CC	OCO/CC	OCY/CC ____		BY ORDER CLERK ONLY	BY ORDER CLERK ONLY

2

	BASIS	COMMODITY	PRICE		STOP					
☐ **CXL**	☐ **BAS**	MONTH			☐ **STP**	☐ SPREAD				
						☐ SWITCH		☒ SCALE		

3

		QUANTITY	COMMODITY	PRICE OR 'MKT'	OR BETTER	STOP	STOP LIMIT PRICE		MARKET IF TOUCHED		ON CLOSE	EOS		WHEN DONE
☐ **CXL**	☒ **BUY**	**1** MCH No. 11 SUG	MONTH	**350**	☐ OB	☐ STP	___ LMT	OR	☒ MIT	LMT	☐ CLO	EDS	☐ OR ☒ AND	

4

		QUANTITY	COMMODITY	PRICE OR 'MKT'	OR BETTER	STOP	STOP LIMIT PRICE		MARKET IF TOUCHED		ON CLOSE	PREM./DISCT.		
☐ **CXL**	☐ **SL**	MONTH		☐ P.T.S	☐ OB	☐ STP	___ LMT	OR	☐ MIT	LMT	☐ CLO	MONTH	☐ OVER ☐ UNDER	

5

1 EA. 5 PTS DOWN MIT TOTAL 6	NOT HELD ☐ NH	LEAVES ☐ LVS	GOOD 'TIL CANCELLED ☒ GTC TODAY ONLY ☐ DAY	GOOD THIS WEEK ☐ GTW IMMEDIATE FILL OR KILL ☐ FOK	GOOD THIS MONTH ☐ GTM AT OPENING ONLY ☐ OPG	GOOD THRU ☐ GT	(DATE OR HOUR) ____

SPECIAL INSTRUCTIONS

6

NO FORMER ORDER ☒ NFO	CXL FORMER ORDER ☐ CXL	REPLACEMENT CANCELLATION INSTRUCTIONS

7

1 7 – 1 0 1 6 – 7 – 5 0	☒ NEW N ☐ L LIQUIDATING	☐ NEW ACCOUNT NA ☒ T4

ACCOUNT NUMBER

8

MISCELLANEOUS INFORMATION (28 CHAR. MAXIMUM) EXECUTED PRICE

9

GIVE UP ☐ GU	FIRM'S SYMBOL (4 CHAR. MAX)	BY TELETYPE CFN ___ (QTY) OPERATOR ONLY

10

CUSTOMER'S NAME **JOHN RODGERS**

Reynolds & Co. **SCALE MARKET IF TOUCHED ORDER ("MIT")**

FORM 33-308

```
OCF/CC LA 120

SCALE
BUY 1 MCH NO 11 SUG 350 MIT AND
1 EA 5 PTS DOWN MIT TOTAL 6 GTC
NFO

17-1016-7-50 N T4
CFN 1
```

The rule governing an "MIT" order (see Illustration No.19) must first take place *prior to any transaction*. That is, the limit price indicated must first be touched or penetrated, which will have the effect of making this a market scale order.

The floor broker would not buy the first contract until, and if, the market touches or penetrates the limit price of 3.50¢ at which point he would buy the first contract at the market. He would then buy on "MIT" the second contract 5 points *down*, and so on, until the six contracts (total specified) were bought.

TELETYPE IN-PUT

FIGURE 213
ORDER PREPARATION MANUAL – COMMODITIES – ILLUSTRATION 11

USE FOR COMMODITIES ONLY

										ORDER NUMBER	C.F.O. NUMBER
ADDRESS	C G B OF T KSC GRAINS ☐ OBT/CX	C G MERC ☐ OME/CX	WPG ☐ OCG/CX	MPLS GRAINS ☐ OMP/CX	NY/LDN COMDYS ☐ OCC	N Y COF & SUG ☒ OCF/CC	N Y CTN EXGE ☐ OCO/CC	COMEX N Y ☐ OCY/CC _____	OTHER ☐ _____	OD 68	
										BY ORDER CLERK ONLY	BY ORDER CLERK ONLY

Row 2: BASIS ☐ CXL ☐ BAS | COMMODITY (MONTH) | PRICE | STOP ☐ STP | ☐ SPREAD ☐ SWITCH ☒ SCALE

Row 3: ☐ CXL ☒ BUY | QUANTITY **1** | COMMODITY **MCH No.11 SUG** (MONTH) | PRICE OR 'MKT' **335** | OR BETTER ☐ OB | STOP ☒ STP | STOP LIMIT PRICE ___ LMT | OR | MARKET IF TOUCHED ☐ MIT | ___ LMT | ON CLOSE ☐ CLO | EOS / EDS | ☐ WHEN DONE / ☐ OR ☒ AND

Row 4: ☐ CXL ☐ SL | QUANTITY | COMMODITY (MONTH) | PRICE OR 'MKT' ☐ PTS | OR BETTER ☐ OB | STOP ☐ STP | STOP LIMIT PRICE ___ LMT | OR | MARKET IF TOUCHED ☐ MIT | ___ LMT | ON CLOSE ☐ CLO | PREM./DISCT. (MONTH) | ☐ OVER ☐ UNDER

Row 5: SPECIAL INSTRUCTIONS
1 EA. 5 PTS UP STP
TOTAL 5

NOT HELD ☐ NH | LEAVES ☐ LVS | GOOD 'TIL CANCELLED ☒ GTC | GOOD THIS WEEK ☐ GTW | GOOD THIS MONTH ☐ GTM | GOOD THRU ☐ GT (DATE or HOUR) _____ | TODAY ONLY ☐ DAY | IMMEDIATE FILL OR KILL ☐ FOK | AT OPENING ONLY ☐ OPG

Row 6: NO FORMER ORDER ☒ NFO | CXL FORMER ORDER ☐ CXL | REPLACEMENT CANCELLATION INSTRUCTIONS

Row 7: ACCOUNT NUMBER **5 6 – 0 3 7 1 – 7 – 1 2** | NEW ☒ N / LIQUIDATING ☐ L | NEW ACCOUNT ☐ NA / ☒ T 4

Row 8: MISCELLANEOUS INFORMATION (28 CHAR. MAXIMUM) | EXECUTED PRICE

Row 9: GIVE UP ☐ GU | FIRM'S SYMBOL (4 CHAR. MAX) | BY TELETYPE CFN (QTY) OPERATOR ONLY

Row 10: CUSTOMER'S NAME **HARRY KINGSLEY**

Reynolds & Co.
FORM 33-308

SCALE STOP ORDER

OCF/CC OD 68

SCALE
BUY 1 MCH NO 11 SUG 335 STP AND
1 EA 5 PTS UP STP TOTAL 5 GTC
NFO

56-0371-7-12 N T4
CFN 1

TELETYPE IN-PUT

Here the rules of the stop order come into play, and for this reason the stop scale order is for customers who want to *buy* on a set scale *up* (instead of on a scale *down* as in the 3 preceding illustrations), or for those who want to *sell* on a scale *down.*

The floor broker would not buy the first contract until, and if, the market touches or penetrates the limit price of 3.35¢, at which point he would buy the first contract at the market. He would then *buy on STOP* the second contract 5 points *up,* and so on, until the five contracts (total specified) were bought.

FIGURE 214

ORDER PREPARATION MANUAL – COMMODITIES – ILLUSTRATION **12**

USE FOR COMMODITIES ONLY

| ADDRESS | C G B OF T KSC GRAINS OBT/CX | C G MERC ☒ OME/CX | WPG OCG/CX | MPLS GRAINS OMP/CX | NY/LDN COMDYS OCC | N Y COF & SUG OCF/CC | N Y CTN EXGE OCO/CC | COMEX N Y OCY/CC | OTHER ☐ | ORDER NUMBER *RW 70* BY ORDER CLERK ONLY | C.F.O. NUMBER BY ORDER CLERK ONLY |

2	☐ CXL	BASIS ☐ BAS	COMMODITY MONTH	PRICE		STOP ☐ STP	☐ SPREAD ☐ SWITCH		☐ SCALE

| 3 | ☐ CXL | QUANTITY ☒ BUY | *5 MAY BLY* MONTH | PRICE OR 'MKT' *3250* | OR BETTER ☐ OB | STOP ☒ STP | STOP LIMIT PRICE ___ LMT | OR | MARKET IF TOUCHED ☐ MIT | ___ LMT | ON CLOSE ☐ CLO | EOS / EDS | ☐ WHEN DONE ☐ OR ☐ AND |

| 4 | ☐ CXL | QUANTITY ☐ SL | COMMODITY MONTH | PRICE OR 'MKT' ☐ PTS | OR BETTER ☐ OB | STOP ☐ STP | STOP LIMIT PRICE ___ LMT | OR | MARKET IF TOUCHED ☐ MIT | ___ LMT | ON CLOSE ☐ CLO | PREM./DISCT. MONTH | ☐ OVER ☐ UNDER |

| 5 | SPECIAL INSTRUCTIONS | NOT HELD ☐ NH | LEAVES ☐ LVS | GOOD 'TIL CANCELLED ☒ GTC / TODAY ONLY ☐ DAY | GOOD THIS WEEK ☐ GTW / IMMEDIATE FILL OR KILL ☐ FOK | GOOD THIS MONTH ☐ GTM / AT OPENING ONLY ☐ OPG | GOOD THRU ☐ GT | (DATE OR HOUR) |

| 6 | NO FORMER ORDER ☒ NFO | CXL FORMER ORDER ☐ CXL | REPLACEMENT CANCELLATION INSTRUCTIONS |

| 7 | ACCOUNT NUMBER *4 1 – 6 0 3 2 – 6 – 4 8* | ☒ NEW N ☐ L LIQUIDATING | ☐ NEW ACCOUNT NA ☒ T 4 |

| 8 | MISCELLANEOUS INFORMATION (28 CHAR. MAXIMUM) | EXECUTED PRICE |

| 9 | GIVE UP ☐ GU | FIRM'S SYMBOL (4 CHAR. MAX) | BY TELETYPE CFN (QTY) OPERATOR ONLY |

| 10 | CUSTOMER'S NAME *PAT LOGAN* |

Reynolds & Co.

FORM 33-308

STOP ORDER

OME/CX RW 70

BUY 5 MAY BLY 3250 STP
GTC
NFO

41-6032-6-48 N T4
CFN 5

A stop order to buy (sell) becomes a market order when a transaction occurs at or above (below) the stop price after the order is represented in the "PIT".

Note: Stop orders are not accepted in Orange Juice and Wool. A list of order restrictions appears on Page 8.

TELETYPE IN-PUT

FIGURE 215

ORDER PREPARATION MANUAL – COMMODITIES – ILLUSTRATION   **13**

USE FOR COMMODITIES ONLY

ADDRESS	C G B OF T KSC GRAINS	C G MERC	WPG	MPLS GRAINS	NY/LDN COMDYS	NY COF & SUG	NY CTN EXGE	COMEX NY	OTHER	ORDER NUMBER	C.F.O. NUMBER
	☐ OBT/CX	☒ OME/CX	☐ OCG/CX	☐ OMP/CX	☐ OCC	☐ OCF/CC	☐ OCO/CC	☐ OCY/CC	☐ _____	TM 51	
										BY ORDER CLERK ONLY	BY ORDER CLERK ONLY

2 ☐ CXL ☐ BAS BASIS | COMMODITY | MONTH | PRICE | [hatched] | STOP ☐ ☐ STP | ☐ SPREAD ☐ SWITCH ☐ SCALE

3 ☐ CXL ☐ BUY QUANTITY | MONTH | COMMODITY | PRICE OR 'MKT' | OR BETTER ☐ OB | STOP ☐ STP | STOP LIMIT PRICE ☐ LMT | OR | MARKET IF TOUCHED ☐ MIT | ☐ LMT | ON CLOSE ☐ CLO | EOS / EDS | ☐ WHEN DONE OR ☐ AND ☐

4 ☐ CXL ☒ SL QUANTITY **3** | MONTH **MAY** | COMMODITY **BLY** | PRICE OR 'MKT' **3250** ☐ P.T.B. | OR BETTER ☐ OB | STOP ☒ STP | STOP LIMIT PRICE **3240** ☐ LMT | OR | MARKET IF TOUCHED ☐ MIT | ☐ LMT | ON CLOSE ☐ CLO | PREM./DISCT. MONTH | ☐ OVER ☐ UNDER

5 SPECIAL INSTRUCTIONS | NOT HELD ☐ NH | LEAVES ☐ LVS | GOOD 'TIL CANCELLED ☒ GTC / TODAY ONLY ☐ DAY | GOOD THIS WEEK ☐ GTW / IMMEDIATE FILL OR KILL ☐ FOK | GOOD THIS MONTH ☐ GTM / AT OPENING ONLY ☐ OPG | GOOD THRU ☐ GT | (DATE OR HOUR) _____

6 NO FORMER ORDER ☒ NFO CXL FORMER ORDER ☐ CXL | REPLACEMENT CANCELLATION INSTRUCTIONS

7 ACCOUNT NUMBER **8 4 – 6 8 7 0 – 6 – 2 1** | NEW ☐ N LIQUIDATING ☒ L | NEW ACCOUNT ☐ NA ☒ T4 | EXECUTED PRICE

8 MISCELLANEOUS INFORMATION (28 CHAR. MAXIMUM) **V S   P U R C H   3 3 0 0   9/1 5**

9 GIVE UP ☐ GU | FIRM'S SYMBOL (4 CHAR. MAX) | BY TELETYPE CFN (QTY) OPERATOR ONLY

10 CUSTOMER'S NAME **CARL RICHARDS**

Reynolds & Co.

FORM 33-308

STOP LIMIT ORDER   (At Different Prices)

OME/CX TM 51

SL 3 MAY BLY 3250 STP 3240 LMT
GTC
NFO

84-6870-6-21 L T4
VS PURCH 3300 9/15
CFN 3

A stop limit order to buy (sell) becomes a limit order executable at the limit price, or at a better price, if obtainable, when a transaction occurs at or above (below) the stop price after the order is represented in the "PIT".

Note that the illustration has a limit price which differs from its stop price. This order will become a limit order of 32.40¢ when the commodity sells at 32.50¢ or less. It will then be executed at not less than 32.40¢, if obtainable in succeeding trades.

Stop limit orders are permissible in Orange Juice and Wool provided the stop price and the limit price are equal, as shown in Illustration No. 14.

FIGURE 216

ORDER PREPARATION MANUAL – COMMODITIES – ILLUSTRATION 14

USE FOR COMMODITIES ONLY

ADDRESS	C G B OF T KSC GRAINS	C G MERC	WPG	MPLS GRAINS	NY/LDN COMDYS	N Y COF & SUG	N Y CTN EXGE	COMEX N Y	OTHER	ORDER NUMBER	C.F.O. NUMBER
	☐	☐	☐	☐	☐	☐	☒	☐	☐	BE 74	
	OBT/CX	OME/CX	OCG/CX	OMP/CX	OCC	OCF/CC	OCO/CC	OCY/CC ___		BY ORDER CLERK ONLY	BY ORDER CLERK ONLY

2 — CXL ☐ | BAS ☐ | COMMODITY | MONTH | PRICE | STOP ☐ STP | ☐ SPREAD ☐ SWITCH | ☐ SCALE

3 — CXL ☐ | BUY ☐ | QUANTITY | COMMODITY | MONTH | PRICE OR 'MKT' | OR BETTER ☐ OB | STOP ☐ STP | STOP LIMIT PRICE ___ LMT | OR | MARKET IF TOUCHED ☐ MIT | ___ LMT | ON CLOSE ☐ CLO | EOS / EDS | ☐ WHEN DONE | OR ☐ AND ☐

4 — CXL ☐ | SL ☒ | QUANTITY **3** | **MAY** | COMMODITY **OJ** | MONTH | PRICE OR 'MKT' **2750** ☐ P.T.S. | OR BETTER ☐ OB | STOP ☒ STP | STOP LIMIT PRICE **2750** LMT | OR | MARKET IF TOUCHED ☐ MIT | ___ LMT | ON CLOSE ☐ CLO | PREM./DISCT. ___ MONTH | ☐ OVER ☐ UNDER

5 — SPECIAL INSTRUCTIONS | NOT HELD ☐ NH | LEAVES ☐ LVS | GOOD 'TIL CANCELLED ☒ GTC / TODAY ONLY ☐ DAY | GOOD THIS WEEK ☐ GTW / IMMEDIATE FILL OR KILL ☐ FOK | GOOD THIS MONTH ☐ GTM / AT OPENING ONLY ☐ OPG | GOOD THRU ☐ GT ___ (DATE OR HOUR)

6 — NO FORMER ORDER ☒ NFO | CXL FORMER ORDER ☐ CXL | REPLACEMENT CANCELLATION INSTRUCTIONS

7 — ACCOUNT NUMBER 1 5 – 1 6 4 2 – 6 – 0 3 | NEW ☐ N / LIQUIDATING ☒ L | NEW ACCOUNT ☐ NA / ☒ T4

8 — MISCELLANEOUS INFORMATION (28 CHAR. MAXIMUM) | EXECUTED PRICE

9 — GIVE UP ☐ GU | FIRM'S SYMBOL (4 CHAR. MAX) | BY TELETYPE CFN (QTY) OPERATOR ONLY

10 — CUSTOMER'S NAME **JOE MULLINS**

Reynolds & Co.
FORM 33-308

STOP LIMIT ORDER   (At Same Price)

TELETYPE IN-PUT

OCO/CC BE 74

SL 3 MAY OJ 2750 STP 2750 LMT
GTC
NFO

15-1642-6-03 L T4
CFN 3

This type of order is identical with the stop limit order in Illustration No. 13, except that the limit price, in this case, is the *same* as the stop price. Exchange specifications require that both the stop price and the limit price be entered, even though they are the same.

This is the only type of stop limit order acceptable in Orange Juice and Wool.

FIGURE 217

ORDER PREPARATION MANUAL – COMMODITIES – ILLUSTRATION   **15**

USE FOR COMMODITIES ONLY

ADDRESS	C G B OF T KSC GRAINS	C G MERC	WPG	MPLS GRAINS	NY/LDN COMDYS	N Y COF & SUG	N Y CTN EXGE	COMEX NY	OTHER	ORDER NUMBER	C.F.O. NUMBER
	☒ OBT/CX	☐ OME/CX	☐ OCG/CX	☐ OMP/CX	☐ OCC	☐ OCF/CC	☐ OCO/CC	☐ OCY/CC	☐	*CT 94/* **21**	
										BY ORDER CLERK ONLY	BY ORDER CLERK ONLY

Line 2 — BASIS | ☐ | ☐ BAS CXL | COMMODITY | MONTH | PRICE | ▨ | STOP ☐ STP | ☐ SPREAD ☐ SWITCH ☐ SCALE

Line 3 — ☒ CXL | ☒ BUY | QUANTITY *10 MAY* | COMMODITY *WHT* | PRICE OR 'MKT' *138* | OR BETTER ☐ OB | STOP ☐ STP | STOP LIMIT PRICE ☐ LMT | OR | MARKET IF TOUCHED ☐ MIT | ☐ LMT | ON CLOSE ☐ CLO | EOS / EDS | WHEN DONE ☐ / OR ☐ AND ☐

Line 4 — ☐ CXL | ☐ SL | QUANTITY | MONTH | COMMODITY | PRICE OR 'MKT' ☐ P.T.S | OR BETTER ☐ OB | STOP ☐ STP | STOP LIMIT PRICE ☐ LMT | OR | MARKET IF TOUCHED ☐ MIT | ☐ LMT | ON CLOSE ☐ CLO | PREM./DISCT. MONTH | ☐ OVER ☐ UNDER

Line 5 — SPECIAL INSTRUCTIONS | NOT HELD ☐ NH | LEAVES *5* ☒ LVS | GOOD 'TIL CANCELLED ☒ GTC / TODAY ONLY ☐ DAY | GOOD THIS WEEK ☐ GTW / IMMEDIATE FILL OR KILL ☐ FOK | GOOD THIS MONTH ☐ GTM / AT OPENING ONLY ☐ OPG | GOOD THRU ☐ GT | (DATE OR HOUR)

Line 6 — NO FORMER ORDER ☐ NFO | CXL FORMER ORDER ☐ CXL | REPLACEMENT CANCELLATION INSTRUCTIONS

Line 7 — *4 C – 6 3 7 1 – 6 – 1 1* ACCOUNT NUMBER | NEW ☐ N / ☒ L LIQUIDATING | NEW ACCOUNT ☐ NA / ☒ T 4

Line 8 — MISCELLANEOUS INFORMATION (28 CHAR. MAXIMUM) | EXECUTED PRICE

Line 9 — GIVE UP ☐ GU | FIRM'S SYMBOL (4 CHAR. MAX) | BY TELETYPE CFN (QTY) OPERATOR ONLY

Line 10 — CUSTOMER'S NAME *ROGER FARRELL*

Reynolds & Co.
FORM 33-308

CANCELLATIONS

There are 3 types of CANCELLATIONS:

(1) Simple Cancellations   (Illustration No. 15).
(2) Change of Price Only   (Illustration No. 16).
(3) Change other than Price (Illustration No. 17).

The basic rule is to describe the order being cancelled *exactly as it was originally entered.* However, when changing only the limit price, you may use an abbreviated format showing (in the gray area) only the price being cancelled (see next illustration).

In this illustration of a "simple" cancellation, note that the address (Line 1) is completed in addition to the gray area on Line 3 ("CXL"). The order to be cancelled is completely described on Line 3. Notice also, on Line 5, that this cancellation "LVS 5" (of the original 15). This partial cancellation procedure is preferred over complete cancellation and reinstatement.

It is the duty of the Order Clerk to enter the CFO number in the upper right corner. *Failure to enter a CFO number may cause the cancellation to be delayed.*

```
OBT/CX CT 94/21

CXL BUY 10 MAY WHT 138
LVS 5 GTC

4C-6371-6-11 L T4
CFN 10
```

TELETYPE IN-PUT

FIGURE 218

ORDER PREPARATION MANUAL – COMMODITIES – ILLUSTRATION **16**

USE FOR COMMODITIES ONLY

ADDRESS	C G B OF T KSC GRAINS	C G MERC	WPG	MPLS GRAINS	NY/LDN COMDYS	NY COF & SUG	N Y CTN EXGE	COMEX N Y	OTHER	ORDER NUMBER	C.F.O. NUMBER
	☐	☐	☐	☐	☐	☒	☐	☐	☐	AR 44 / 14	
	OBT/CX	OME/CX	OCG/CX	OMP/CX	OCC	OCF/CC	OCO/CC	OCY/CC ___		BY ORDER CLERK ONLY	BY ORDER CLERK ONLY

Line 2: CXL ☐ / BAS ☐ — BASIS / COMMODITY / PRICE / STOP ☐ STP / ☐ SPREAD / ☐ SWITCH / ☐ SCALE / MONTH

Line 3: CXL ☐ / BUY ☐ — QUANTITY / COMMODITY / PRICE OR 'MKT' / OR BETTER ☐ OB / STOP ☐ STP / STOP LIMIT PRICE ___ LMT / OR / MARKET IF TOUCHED ☐ MIT / LMT / ON CLOSE ☐ CLO / EOS / EDS / ☐ WHEN DONE / OR ☐ AND ☐ / MONTH

Line 4: CXL ☐ / SL ☒ — QUANTITY **5** / SEP **No 11 SUG** / **400** ☐ PTS / OR BETTER ☐ OB / STOP ☐ STP / STOP LIMIT PRICE ___ LMT / OR / MARKET IF TOUCHED ☐ MIT / LMT / ON CLOSE ☐ CLO / PREM./DISCT. / MONTH / ☐ OVER / ☐ UNDER / MONTH

Line 5: NOT HELD ☐ NH / LEAVES ☐ LVS / GOOD 'TIL CANCELLED ☐ GTC / GOOD THIS WEEK ☒ GTW / GOOD THIS MONTH ☐ GTM / GOOD THRU ☐ GT ___ (DATE OR HOUR) / TODAY ONLY ☐ DAY / IMMEDIATE FILL OR KILL ☐ FOK / AT OPENING ONLY ☐ OPG / SPECIAL INSTRUCTIONS

Line 6: NO FORMER ORDER ☐ NFO / CXL FORMER ORDER ☒ CXL **410** / REPLACEMENT CANCELLATION INSTRUCTIONS

Line 7: ACCOUNT NUMBER **43 – 5980 – 7 – 32** / NEW ☐ N / ☒ L LIQUIDATING / NEW ACCOUNT ☐ NA / ☒ T4

Line 8: MISCELLANEOUS INFORMATION (28 CHAR. MAXIMUM) / EXECUTED PRICE

Line 9: GIVE UP ☐ GU / FIRM'S SYMBOL (4 CHAR. MAX) / BY TELETYPE CFN ___ (QTY) / OPERATOR ONLY

Line 10: CUSTOMER'S NAME **SAM JACOBS**

Reynolds & Co.

FORM 33-308

CHANGE OF PRICE ONLY (Change of Limit)

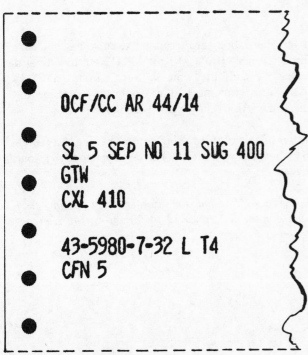

OCF/CC AR 44/14

SL 5 SEP NO 11 SUG 400
GTW
CXL 410

43-5980-7-32 L T4
CFN 5

TELETYPE IN-PUT

In this illustration, only the price of the former order is being cancelled (commonly referred to as a "change of limit"). The cancelled order (AR14) must have been originally entered as "GTW", otherwise the entire order (AR14) would have been described in the gray area (Line 6). (Compare with next illustration).

FIGURE 219

ORDER PREPARATION MANUAL – COMMODITIES – ILLUSTRATION   **17**

USE FOR COMMODITIES ONLY

	C G B OF T KSC GRAINS	C G MERC	WPG	MPLS GRAINS	NY/LDN COMDYS	N Y COF & SUG	N Y CTN EXGE	COMEX N Y	OTHER	ORDER NUMBER	C.F.O. NUMBER
ADDRESS	☐ OBT/CX	☐ OME/CX	☐ OCG/CX	☐ OMP/CX	☐ OCC	☒ OCF/CC	☐ OCO/CC	☐ OCY/CC ___	☐	AL 82 / 64 BY ORDER CLERK ONLY	BY ORDER CLERK ONLY

Line 2: ☐ CXL BASIS ☐ BAS COMMODITY MONTH PRICE STOP ☐ STP ☐ SPREAD ☐ SWITCH ☐ SCALE

Line 3: ☐ CXL QUANTITY ☐ BUY MONTH COMMODITY PRICE OR 'MKT' OR BETTER ☐ OB STOP ☐ STP STOP LIMIT PRICE ___ LMT OR MARKET IF TOUCHED ☐ MIT LMT ON CLOSE ☐ CLO EOS EDS ☐ WHEN DONE ☐ OR ☐ AND

Line 4: ☐ CXL QUANTITY ☒ SL **3 SEP No11 SUG MKT** MONTH ☐ P.T.A OR BETTER ☐ OB STOP ☐ STP STOP LIMIT PRICE ___ LMT OR MARKET IF TOUCHED ☐ MIT LMT ON CLOSE ☐ CLO PREM./DISCT. MONTH ☐ OVER ☐ UNDER

Line 5: SPECIAL INSTRUCTIONS NOT HELD ☐ NH LEAVES ☐ LVS GOOD 'TIL CANCELLED ☐ GTC GOOD THIS WEEK ☐ GTW GOOD THIS MONTH ☐ GTM GOOD THRU ☐ GT ___ (DATE OR HOUR) TODAY ONLY ☒ DAY IMMEDIATE FILL OR KILL ☐ FOK AT OPENING ONLY ☐ OPG

Line 6: NO FORMER ORDER ☐ NFO CXL FORMER ORDER ☒ CXL **SL 5 SEP No11 SUG 410 GTC** REPLACEMENT CANCELLATION INSTRUCTIONS

Line 7: ACCOUNT NUMBER **4 4 – 7 3 3 6 – 7 – 1 9** ☒ N NEW ☐ L LIQUIDATING NEW ACCOUNT ☐ NA ☒ T4

Line 8: MISCELLANEOUS INFORMATION (28 CHAR. MAXIMUM) EXECUTED PRICE

Line 9: GIVE UP ☐ GU FIRM'S SYMBOL (4 CHAR. MAX) BY TELETYPE CFN (QTY) OPERATOR ONLY

Line 10: CUSTOMER'S NAME **DENNIS MORAN**

Reynolds & Co.
FORM 33-308

CHANGE OTHER THAN PRICE

TELETYPE IN-PUT

- OCF/CC AL 82/64
- SL 3 SEP NO 11 SUG MKT DAY
- CXL SL 5 SEP NO 11 SUG 410 GTC
- 44-7336-7-19 N T4 CFN 3 5

In this illustration the Account Executive has not only changed the limit (from 410 to "MKT") but has changed the quantity and the "time in force" from "GTC" to "DAY", thus requiring that he completely describe the former order (AL 64) in the gray area on Line 6.

Entries of this type involving both an order and a cancellation, should always affect only one commodity on one exchange.

Teletypist – Note that the information in the gray field on line 6 must be converted to format on the teletypewriter input message.

FIGURE 220

PRICE ORDER PREPARATION MANUAL – COMMODITIES – ILLUSTRATION 18

USE FOR COMMODITIES ONLY

C G B O F T KSC GRAINS	C G MERC	WPG	MPLS GRAINS	NY/LDN COMDYS	N Y COF & SUG	N Y CTN EXGE	COMEX N Y	OTHER	ORDER NUMBER	C.F.O. NUMBER
☒ OBT/CX	☐ OME/CX	☐ OCG/CX	☐ OMP/CX	☐ OCC	☐ OCF/CC	☐ OCO/CC	☐ OCY/CC	☐ _____	SF 151 BY ORDER CLERK ONLY	BY ORDER CLERK ONLY

Line 2: ☐ CXL ☐ BAS | COMMODITY | PRICE | ☐ STP | ☐ SPREAD ☐ SWITCH ☐ SCALE

Line 3: ☐ CXL ☒ BUY | 10 MAY WHT 138 | ☒ OB ☐ STP | LMT OR MIT LMT ☐ CLO | EOS/EDS | ☐ WHEN DONE ☐ OR ☐ AND

Line 4: ☐ CXL ☐ SL | ☐ OB ☐ STP | LMT OR MIT LMT CLO | PREM./DISCT. | ☐ OVER ☐ UNDER

Line 5: NOT HELD ☐ NH | LEAVES ☐ LVS | ☐ GTC ☐ GTW ☐ GTM ☐ GT _____ | ☒ DAY ☐ FOK ☐ OPG

Line 6: ☒ NFO ☐ CXL — REPLACEMENT CANCELLATION INSTRUCTIONS

Line 7: ACCOUNT NUMBER 10-0954-6-50 ☐ N ☒ L | ☐ NA ☒ T4

Line 8: MISCELLANEOUS INFORMATION (28 CHAR. MAXIMUM) | EXECUTED PRICE

Line 9: ☐ GU | FIRM'S SYMBOL | CFN (QTY)

Line 10: CUSTOMER'S NAME — ED CARROLL

Reynolds & Co.
FORM 33-308

OR BETTER ORDER ("OB")

OBT/CX SF 151

BUY 10 MAY WHT 138 OB
DAY
NFO

10-0954-6-50 L T4
CFN 10

TELETYPE IN-PUT

In this illustration the Account Executive has checked "OB" on Line 3 to indicate that he knows the limit price of $1.38, for this "BUY" order, *exceeds the asked price at time of entry.*

If this were a "SELL" order, then "OB" would have been checked on Line 4. In that case, the Account Executive would then be indicating that he knows the limit price of $1.38 *is lower than the current bid price.*

Note: The term "Or Better" ("OB") is not accepted on stock orders. This term is, however, synonymous with the "BQ" (Beyond/Below Quote) definition which appears in the Order Preparation Manual for listed securities and corporate bonds.

FIGURE 221

ORDER PREPARATION MANUAL – COMMODITIES – ILLUSTRATION   **19**

USE FOR COMMODITIES ONLY

CG B OF T KSC GRAINS	C G MERC	WPG	MPLS GRAINS	NY/LDN COMDYS	NY COF & SUG	N Y CTN EXGE	COMEX N Y	OTHER	ORDER NUMBER	C.F.O. NUMBER
☐ OBT/CX	☐ OME/CX	☐ OCG/CX	☐ OMP/CX	☐ OCC	☒ OCF/CC	☐ OCO/CC	☐ OCY/CC	☐ _____	CR 82	

ADDRESS

2 ☐ CXL ☐ BAS (BASIS) | COMMODITY | MONTH | PRICE | | ☐ STP (STOP) | ☐ SPREAD ☐ SWITCH ☐ SCALE

3 ☐ CXL ☒ BUY | QUANTITY 2 | COMMODITY OCT No.11 SUG | MONTH | PRICE OR "MKT" 328 | OR BETTER ☐ OB | STOP ☐ STP | STOP LIMIT PRICE ☐ LMT | OR | MARKET IF TOUCHED ☒ MIT | ☐ LMT | ON CLOSE ☐ CLO | EOS / EDS | ☐ WHEN DONE ☐ OR ☐ AND

4 ☐ CXL ☐ SL | QUANTITY | COMMODITY | MONTH | PRICE OR "MKT" ☐ P.T.S | OR BETTER ☐ OB | STOP ☐ STP | STOP LIMIT PRICE ☐ LMT | OR | MARKET IF TOUCHED ☐ MIT | ☐ LMT | ON CLOSE ☐ CLO | PREM./DISCT. MONTH | ☐ OVER ☐ UNDER

5 SPECIAL INSTRUCTIONS | NOT HELD ☐ NH | LEAVES ☐ LVS | GOOD 'TIL CANCELLED ☐ GTC TODAY ONLY ☒ DAY | GOOD THIS WEEK ☐ GTW IMMEDIATE FILL OR KILL ☐ FOK | GOOD THIS MONTH ☐ GTM AT OPENING ONLY ☐ OPG | GOOD THRU ☐ GT | (DATE OR HOUR)

6 NO FORMER ORDER ☒ NFO | CXL FORMER ORDER ☐ CXL | REPLACEMENT CANCELLATION INSTRUCTIONS

7 ACCOUNT NUMBER 7 5 – 8 3 1 2 – 7 – 4 6 | NEW ☒ N LIQUIDATING ☐ L | NEW ACCOUNT ☐ NA ☒ T 4

8 MISCELLANEOUS INFORMATION (28 CHAR. MAXIMUM) | EXECUTED PRICE

9 GIVE UP ☐ GU | FIRM'S SYMBOL (4 CHAR. MAX) | BY TELETYPE CFN (QTY) OPERATOR ONLY

10 CUSTOMER'S NAME **LAWRENCE STANTON**

Reynolds & Co.

FORM 33-308

MARKET IF TOUCHED ORDER ("MIT")

TELETYPE IN-PUT

OCF/CC CR 82

BUY 2 OCT NO 11 SUG 328 MIT
DAY
NFO

75-8312-7-46 N T4
CFN 2

An "MIT" order to buy (sell) becomes a market order when a transaction occurs at or below (above) the "MIT" price after the order is represented in the "PIT".

"MIT" orders are entered on the opposite side of the market than are stop orders.

Compare with next illustration (No. 20).

FIGURE 222

ORDER PREPARATION MANUAL – COMMODITIES – ILLUSTRATION **20**

USE FOR COMMODITIES ONLY

ADDRESS										ORDER NUMBER	C.F.O. NUMBER
C G B OF T KSC GRAINS ☐ OBT/CX	C G MERC ☒ OME/CX	WPG ☐ OCG/CX	MPLS GRAINS ☐ OMP/CX	NY/LDN COMDYS ☐ OCC	N Y COF & SUG ☐ OCF/CC	N Y CTN EXGE ☐ OCO/CC	COMEX N Y ☐ OCY/CC ___	OTHER ☐		NC 24 / BY ORDER CLERK ONLY	BY ORDER CLERK ONLY

Row 2: **CXL** ☐ | BASIS ☐ **BAS** | COMMODITY | MONTH | PRICE | ▨ | STOP ☐ **STP** | ☐ SPREAD | ☐ SWITCH | ☐ SCALE

Row 3: **CXL** ☐ | ☐ **BUY** | QUANTITY | COMMODITY MONTH | PRICE OR 'MKT' | OR BETTER ☐ **OB** | STOP ☐ **STP** | STOP LIMIT PRICE ___ **LMT** | **OR** | MARKET IF TOUCHED ☐ **MIT** | ___ **LMT** | ON CLOSE ☐ **CLO** | EOS / EDS | ☐ WHEN DONE / OR ☐ AND ☐

Row 4: **CXL** ☐ | ☒ **SL** | QUANTITY **2** | **MAY BLY** MONTH | PRICE OR 'MKT' **3470** ☐ P.T.S | OR BETTER ☐ **OB** | STOP ☐ **STP** | STOP LIMIT PRICE ___ **LMT** | **OR** | MARKET IF TOUCHED ☒ **MIT** **3450** | **LMT** | ON CLOSE ☐ **CLO** | PREM./DISCT. MONTH | ☐ OVER ☐ UNDER

Row 5: SPECIAL INSTRUCTIONS | NOT HELD ☐ **NH** | LEAVES ☐ **LVS** | GOOD 'TIL CANCELLED ☐ GTC / TODAY ONLY ☒ DAY | GOOD THIS WEEK ☒ GTW / IMMEDIATE FILL OR KILL ☐ FOK | GOOD THIS MONTH ☐ GTM / AT OPENING ONLY ☐ OPG | GOOD THRU ☐ GT ___ (DATE OR HOUR)

Row 6: NO FORMER ORDER ☒ **NFO** | CXL FORMER ORDER ☐ **CXL** | REPLACEMENT CANCELLATION INSTRUCTIONS

Row 7: **2 5 – 0 6 7 2 – 6 – 0 4** ACCOUNT NUMBER | ☒ **N** NEW / ☐ **L** LIQUIDATING | NEW ACCOUNT ☐ **NA** / ☒ **T4**

Row 8: MISCELLANEOUS INFORMATION (28 CHAR. MAXIMUM) | EXECUTED PRICE

Row 9: GIVE UP ☐ **GU** | FIRM'S SYMBOL (4 CHAR. MAX) | BY TELETYPE **CFN** (QTY) OPERATOR ONLY

Row 10: CUSTOMER'S NAME **BRETT NATHANIEL**

Reynolds & Co.
FORM 33-308

MARKET IF TOUCHED ORDER ("MIT") — AT LIMIT

Teletype input:

```
OME/CX NC 24

SL 2 MAY BLY 3470 MIT 3450 LMT
DAY
NFO

25-0672-6-04 N T4
CFN 2
```

TELETYPE IN-PUT

An "MIT" limit order to buy (sell) becomes a limit order executable at the limit price, or at a better price, if obtainable, when a transaction occurs at or below (above) the "MIT" price after the order is represented in the "PIT".

Note that the illustration has a limit price which differs from its "MIT" price. This order will become a limit order at 34.50¢ when the commodity sells at 34.70¢ or more. It will then be executed at not less than 34.50¢, if obtainable in succeeding trades.

Compare with previous illustration (No. 19).

FIGURE 223

ORDER PREPARATION MANUAL – COMMODITIES – ILLUSTRATION   **21**

USE FOR COMMODITIES ONLY

ADDRESS	C G B O F T KSC GRAINS	C G MERC	WPG	MPLS GRAINS	NY/LDN COMDYS	N Y COF & SUG	N Y CTN EXGE	COMEX N Y	OTHER	ORDER NUMBER	C.F.O. NUMBER
	☐ OBT/CX	☒ OME/CX	☐ OCG/CX	☐ OMP/CX	☐ OCC	☐ OCF/CC	☐ OCO/CC	☐ OCY/CC ____	☐	**SZ 30** BY ORDER CLERK ONLY	BY ORDER CLERK ONLY

Form Rows:

② ☐ CXL ☐ BAS | BASIS | COMMODITY | MONTH | PRICE | STOP ☐ STP | ☐ SPREAD ☐ SWITCH ☐ SCALE

③ ☐ CXL ☒ BUY | QUANTITY **2** | COMMODITY **FEB BLY** MONTH | PRICE OR 'MKT' **3125** | OR BETTER ☐ OB | STOP ☐ STP | STOP LIMIT PRICE ___ LMT OR | MARKET IF TOUCHED ☐ MIT ___ LMT | ON CLOSE ☒ CLO | EOS / EDS | ☐ WHEN DONE ☐ OR ☐ AND

④ ☐ CXL ☐ SL | QUANTITY | COMMODITY MONTH | PRICE OR 'MKT' ☐ P.T.B | OR BETTER ☐ OB | STOP ☐ STP | STOP LIMIT PRICE ___ LMT OR | MARKET IF TOUCHED ☐ MIT ___ LMT | ON CLOSE ☐ CLO | PREM./DISCT. MONTH | ☐ OVER ☐ UNDER

⑤ | SPECIAL INSTRUCTIONS | NOT HELD ☐ NH | LEAVES ☐ LVS | GOOD 'TIL CANCELLED ☒ GTC / TODAY ONLY ☐ DAY | GOOD THIS WEEK ☐ GTW / IMMEDIATE FILL OR KILL ☐ FOK | GOOD THIS MONTH ☐ GTM / AT OPENING ONLY ☐ OPG | GOOD THRU ☐ GT | (DATE OR HOUR)

⑥ | NO FORMER ORDER ☒ NFO | CXL FORMER ORDER ☐ CXL | REPLACEMENT CANCELLATION INSTRUCTIONS

⑦ ACCOUNT NUMBER **1 8 – 2 3 4 1 – 6 – 8 0** | ☒ NEW N ☐ LIQUIDATING L | ☐ NEW ACCOUNT NA ☒ T4

⑧ MISCELLANEOUS INFORMATION (28 CHAR. MAXIMUM) | EXECUTED PRICE

⑨ GIVE UP ☐ GU | FIRM'S SYMBOL (4 CHAR. MAX) | BY TELETYPE CFN (QTY) OPERATOR ONLY

⑩ CUSTOMER'S NAME **Van Franco**

Reynolds & Co.

FORM 33-308

ON CLOSE ORDER ("CLO")

OME/CX SZ 30

BUY 2 FEB BLY 3125 CLO
GTC
NFO

18-2341-6-80 N T4
CFN 2

TELETYPE IN-PUT

A "CLO" order is an order which is to be executed at the close.

Unlike listed securities, a "CLO" order does *not* have to be a market order. It can be a limit, or even a stop order, if the customer so deems. Commodity "CLO" orders, with a limit specified, will be executed *only* on the close of the market, if possible.

Reynolds & Co. does not guaranty execution of any order received at the exchange 15 minutes prior to the close of the market.

USE FOR COMMODITIES ONLY

ADDRESS	C G B OF T KSC GRAINS	C G MERC	WPG	MPLS GRAINS	NY/LDN COMDYS	NY COF & SUG	N Y CTN EXGE	COMEX N Y	OTHER	ORDER NUMBER	C.F.O. NUMBER
	☐ OBT/CX	☒ OME/CX	☐ OCG/CX	☐ OMP/CX	☐ OCC	☐ OCF/CC	☐ OCO/CC	☐ OCY/CC	☐ _____	AN 127	
										BY ORDER CLERK ONLY	BY ORDER CLERK ONLY

Line 2:

	BASIS		COMMODITY	PRICE		STOP					
2	☐	☐			(hatched)	☐	☐ SPREAD				
	CXL	BAS	MONTH			STP	☐ SWITCH	☐ SCALE			

Line 3:

		QUANTITY	COMMODITY	PRICE OR 'MKT'	OR BETTER	STOP	STOP LIMIT PRICE		MARKET IF TOUCHED		ON CLOSE	EOS 3200	WHEN DONE
3	☐ ☒	5	MCH BLY	MKT	☐	☐		OR	☐		☐	EDS	☐
	CXL BUY		MONTH		OB	STP	LMT		MIT	LMT	CLO		OR AND ☐

Line 4:

		QUANTITY	COMMODITY	PRICE OR 'MKT'	OR BETTER	STOP	STOP LIMIT PRICE		MARKET IF TOUCHED		ON CLOSE	PREM./DISCT.	
4	☐ ☐		MONTH	☐ P.TS	☐	☐		OR	☐		☐	MONTH	☐ OVER
	CXL SL				OB	STP	LMT		MIT	LMT	CLO		☐ UNDER

Line 5:

		NOT HELD	LEAVES	GOOD 'TIL CANCELLED	GOOD THIS WEEK	GOOD THIS MONTH	GOOD THRU	(DATE OR HOUR)
5		☐ NH	☐ LVS	☐ GTC	☐ GTW	☐ GTM	☐ GT	_____
	SPECIAL INSTRUCTIONS			TODAY ONLY ☒ DAY	IMMEDIATE FILL OR KILL ☐ FOK	AT OPENING ONLY ☐ OPG		

Line 6:

	NO FORMER ORDER	CXL FORMER ORDER	REPLACEMENT CANCELLATION INSTRUCTIONS
6	☒ NFO	☐ CXL	

Line 7:

	ACCOUNT NUMBER		NEW	NEW ACCOUNT
7	3 A – 6 9 7 0 – 6 – 0 3		☒ N ☐ LIQUIDATING L	☐ NA ☒ T4

Line 8:

	MISCELLANEOUS INFORMATION (28 CHAR. MAXIMUM)	EXECUTED PRICE
8		

Line 9:

	GIVE UP	FIRM'S SYMBOL (4 CHAR. MAX)	BY TELETYPE CFN (QTY) OPERATOR ONLY
9	☐ GU		

Line 10:

	CUSTOMER'S NAME
10	ROGER HARRIS

Reynolds & Co.

FORM 33-308

ENTER OPEN STOP ORDER ("EOS")

```
OME/CX AN 127

BUY 5 MCH BLY MKT EOS 3200
DAY
NFO

3A-6970-6-03 N T4
CFN 5
```

TELETYPE IN-PUT

A contingent order to enter an open stop when the first portion of the order is executed. *The stop order will remain in open until it is "ticked off".*

These types of orders need not specify an exact price, but may be expressed in terms of cents or points (e.g., BUY 2 NOV EGGS MKT EOS 50 points). In this case the broker is instructed to buy 2 contracts of NOVEMBER EGGS at the prevailing price, and immediately place an open stop order to sell 50 points lower.

If the November Eggs were bought at 30.00¢ per dozen the open stop order to sell would be placed at 29.50¢.

When entering a sell order with an "EOS" (enter open stop to buy), the "EOS" must be written in the special instruction box on Line 5 (e.g., EOS 3210).

FIGURE 225

ORDER PREPARATION MANUAL — COMMODITIES — ILLUSTRATION   **23**

USE FOR COMMODITIES ONLY

ADDRESS	C G B OF T KSC GRAINS	C G MERC	WPG	MPLS GRAINS	NY/LDN COMDYS	N Y COF & SUG	N Y CTN EXGE	COMEX N Y	OTHER	ORDER NUMBER	C.F.O. NUMBER
	☐ OBT/CX	☒ OME/CX	☐ OCG/CX	☐ OMP/CX	☐ OCC	☐ OCF/CC	☐ OCO/CC	☐ OCY/CC ___	☐	DC 113	
										BY ORDER CLERK ONLY	BY ORDER CLERK ONLY

② CXL BAS — BASIS ☐ — COMMODITY ___ MONTH — PRICE — STOP ☐ STP — ☐ SPREAD — ☐ SWITCH — ☐ SCALE

③ CXL BUY ☒ — QUANTITY **3** — COMMODITY **DEC CATTLE** MONTH — PRICE OR 'MKT' **MKT** — OR BETTER ☐ OB — STOP ☐ STP — STOP LIMIT PRICE ___ LMT — OR — MARKET IF TOUCHED ☐ MIT — LMT — ON CLOSE ☐ CLO — EOS EDS **2750** — ☐ WHEN DONE — OR ☐ AND ☐

④ CXL SL ☐ — QUANTITY — COMMODITY — MONTH — PRICE OR 'MKT' ☐ PTS — OR BETTER ☐ OB — STOP ☐ STP — STOP LIMIT PRICE ___ LMT — OR — MARKET IF TOUCHED ☐ MIT — LMT — ON CLOSE ☐ CLO — PREM./DISCT. MONTH — ☐ OVER — ☐ UNDER

⑤ SPECIAL INSTRUCTIONS — NOT HELD ☐ **NH** — LEAVES ☐ **LVS** — GOOD 'TIL CANCELLED ☐ GTC — GOOD THIS WEEK ☐ GTW — GOOD THIS MONTH ☐ GTM — GOOD THRU ☐ GT ___ (DATE OR HOUR) — TODAY ONLY ☒ **DAY** — IMMEDIATE FILL OR KILL ☐ FOK — AT OPENING ONLY ☐ OPG

⑥ NO FORMER ORDER ☒ **NFO** — CXL FORMER ORDER ☐ **CXL** — REPLACEMENT CANCELLATION INSTRUCTIONS

⑦ ACCOUNT NUMBER **0 9 — 5 1 7 0 — 6 — 3 8** — ☒ N NEW ☐ L LIQUIDATING — NEW ACCOUNT ☐ NA ☒ T4

⑧ MISCELLANEOUS INFORMATION (28 CHAR. MAXIMUM) — EXECUTED PRICE

⑨ GIVE UP ☐ GU — FIRM'S SYMBOL (4 CHAR. MAX) — BY TELETYPE **CFN** (QTY) OPERATOR ONLY

⑩ CUSTOMER'S NAME **JAMES DONNELLY**

Reynolds & Co.
FORM 33-308

ENTER DAY STOP ORDER ("EDS")

```
OME/CX DC 113

BUY 3 DEC CATTLE MKT EDS 2750
DAY
NFO

09-5170-6-38 N T4
CFN 3
```

The only difference between this order and the preceding illustration ("EOS") is that, although the first portion of the order may be executed, the stop order, being a DAY order, if not executable the same day would expire at the close.

TELETYPE IN-PUT

FIGURE 226

ORDER PREPARATION MANUAL – COMMODITIES – ILLUSTRATION **24**

TENDERED

USE FOR COMMODITIES ONLY

ADDRESS										ORDER NUMBER	C.F.O. NUMBER
	C G B O F T KSC GRAINS	C G MERC	WPG	MPLS GRAINS	NY/LDN COMDYS	N Y COF & SUG	N Y CTN EXGE	COMEX N Y	OTHER ☐	**LR 62**	
	OBT/CX	OME/CX	OCG/CX	OMP/CX	☒ OCC	OCF/CC	OCO/CC	OCY/CC ___		BY ORDER CLERK ONLY	BY ORDER CLERK ONLY

Line 2: ☐ CXL ☐ BAS BASIS COMMODITY MONTH PRICE ☐ STOP ☐ STP ☐ SPREAD ☐ SWITCH ☐ SCALE

Line 3: ☐ CXL ☐ BUY QUANTITY COMMODITY MONTH PRICE OR 'MKT' OR BETTER ☐ OB STOP ☐ STP STOP LIMIT PRICE LMT OR MARKET IF TOUCHED ☐ MIT LMT ON CLOSE ☐ CLO EOS EDS ☐ WHEN DONE ☐ OR ☐ AND

Line 4: ☐ CXL ☒ SL QUANTITY **5** COMMODITY **AUG CATTLE** MONTH PRICE OR 'MKT' ☐ P.T.S. OR BETTER ☐ OB STOP ☐ STP STOP LIMIT PRICE LMT OR MARKET IF TOUCHED ☐ MIT LMT ON CLOSE ☐ CLO PREM./DISCT. MONTH ☐ OVER ☐ UNDER

Line 5: **MKT IF TENDERED AND REDELIVER** SPECIAL INSTRUCTIONS
NOT HELD ☐ NH LEAVES ☐ LVS GOOD 'TIL CANCELLED ☒ GTC TODAY ONLY ☐ DAY GOOD THIS WEEK ☐ GTW IMMEDIATE FILL OR KILL ☐ FOK GOOD THIS MONTH ☐ GTM AT OPENING ONLY ☐ OPG GOOD THRU ☐ GT (DATE OR HOUR)

Line 6: NO FORMER ORDER ☒ NFO CXL FORMER ORDER ☐ CXL REPLACEMENT CANCELLATION INSTRUCTIONS

Line 7: ACCOUNT NUMBER **47 – 6502 – 6 – 70** NEW ☒ N ☐ L LIQUIDATING ☐ NA NEW ACCOUNT ☒ T 4

Line 8: MISCELLANEOUS INFORMATION (28 CHAR. MAXIMUM) EXECUTED PRICE

Line 9: GIVE UP ☐ GU FIRM'S SYMBOL (4 CHAR. MAX) BY TELETYPE CFN (QTY) OPERATOR ONLY

Line 10: CUSTOMER'S NAME **MORRIS SCHWARTZ**

Reynolds & Co.

FORM 33-308

TENDERED ORDERS

There are 2 types of TENDERED orders:

(1) Market if tendered and redeliver (Illustration No. 24).
(2) Market and retender   (Illustration No. 25).

The customer, in order to protect himself from delivery of the commodity, may give instructions to sell his position immediately upon notice of delivery. This can be accomplished by entering an open order for the customer to sell his commodity at "MKT IF TENDERED AND REDELIVER" (illustrated above). Note that this term appears on Line 5, of the order, in the "SPECIAL INSTRUCTIONS" field. This is preferred over placing the term "MKT" in the price field, where the special instructions may be overlooked, causing the order to be erroneously executed.

All "if tendered" orders are addressed to OCC (New York Commodity Department), and will be acted upon *only* when the customer is "tendered" a delivery notice. If delivery notice is received after the market is closed, the sale will not be made until the following business day.

Compare this with the next illustration (No. 25).

```
OCC LR 62

SL 5 AUG CATTLE
MKT IF TENDERED AND REDELIVER GTC
NFO

47-6502-6-70 N T4
CFN 5
```

TELETYPE IN-PUT

FIGURE 227

ORDER PREPARATION MANUAL – COMMODITIES – ILLUSTRATION   **25**

USE FOR COMMODITIES ONLY

C G B OF T KSC GRAINS	C G MERC	WPG	MPLS GRAINS	NY/LDN COMDYS	N Y COF & SUG	N Y CTN EXGE	COMEX N Y	OTHER	ORDER NUMBER	C.F.O. NUMBER
☐ OBT/CX	☒ OME/CX	☐ OCG/CX	☐ OMP/CX	☐ OCC	☐ OCF/CC	☐ OCO/CC	☐ OCY/CC	☐ _____	**BS 33** / BY ORDER CLERK ONLY	BY ORDER CLERK ONLY

2 ☐ CXL ☐ BAS / BASIS | COMMODITY MONTH | PRICE | STOP ☐ STP | ☐ SPREAD ☐ SWITCH | ☐ SCALE

3 ☐ CXL ☐ BUY | QUANTITY MONTH | COMMODITY | PRICE OR 'MKT' | OR BETTER ☐ OB | STOP ☐ STP | STOP LIMIT PRICE LMT OR | MARKET IF TOUCHED ☐ MIT LMT | ON CLOSE ☐ CLO | EOS / EDS | WHEN DONE / OR AND

4 ☐ CXL ☒ SL | QUANTITY **5** MONTH | COMMODITY **AUG CATTLE** | PRICE OR 'MKT' **MKT** ☐ P.T.S | OR BETTER ☐ OB | STOP ☐ STP | STOP LIMIT PRICE LMT OR | MARKET IF TOUCHED ☐ MIT LMT | ON CLOSE ☐ CLO | PREM./DISCT. MONTH | ☐ OVER ☐ UNDER

5 **AND RETENDER**   SPECIAL INSTRUCTIONS | NOT HELD ☐ NH | LEAVES ☐ LVS | GOOD 'TIL CANCELLED ☐ GTC TODAY ONLY ☒ DAY | GOOD THIS WEEK ☐ GTW IMMEDIATE FILL OR KILL ☐ FOK | GOOD THIS MONTH ☐ GTM AT OPENING ONLY ☐ OPG | GOOD THRU ☐ GT | (DATE OR HOUR) _____

6 NO FORMER ORDER ☒ NFO | CXL FORMER ORDER ☐ CXL | REPLACEMENT CANCELLATION INSTRUCTIONS

7 ACCOUNT NUMBER **5 8 – 3 7 2 0 – 6 – 4 2** | ☒ N NEW ☐ L LIQUIDATING | NEW ACCOUNT ☐ NA ☒ T4

8 MISCELLANEOUS INFORMATION (28 CHAR. MAXIMUM) | EXECUTED PRICE

9 GIVE UP ☐ GU | FIRM'S SYMBOL (4 CHAR. MAX) | BY TELETYPE CFN (QTY) OPERATOR ONLY

10 CUSTOMER'S NAME **DOM MARINO**

Reynolds & Co.
FORM 33-308

MARKET AND RETENDER ORDER

OME/CX BS 33

SL 5 AUG CATTLE MKT
AND RETENDER DAY
NFO

58-3720-6-42 N T4
CFN 5

TELETYPE IN-PUT

This differs from the previous illustration in that the customer did not give instructions to sell prior to receiving actual delivery of the commodity, and he now wants to retender the commodity.

This order (as illustrated above) is directed to the exchange where the commodity is traded, as a straight market order. The instructions "AND RETENDER" must appear on Line 5, in the "SPECIAL INSTRUCTIONS" field.

FIGURE 228

ORDER PREPARATION MANUAL – COMMODITIES – ILLUSTRATION   **26**

USE FOR COMMODITIES ONLY

ADDRESS										ORDER NUMBER	C.F.O. NUMBEP
	C G B OF T KSC GRAINS ☐ OBT/CX	C G MERC ☐ OME/CX	WPG ☐ OCG/CX	MPLS GRAINS ☐ OMP/CX	NY/LDN COMDYS ☐ OCC	NY COF & SUG ☒ OCF/CC	N Y CTN EXGE ☐ OCO/CC	COMEX N Y ☐ OCY/CC ___	OTHER ☐	**FL 70** BY ORDER CLERK ONLY	BY ORDER CLERK ONLY

	BASIS	QUANTITY	COMMODITY	PRICE		STOP											
2 CXL	☐ ☐ BAS	MONTH	COMMODITY			☐ STP	☐ SPREAD ☐ SWITCH							☐ SCALE			

3 CXL BUY: ☐ ☒ | QUANTITY **5** | COMMODITY **MAY No.11 SUG** | PRICE OR 'MKT' **MKT** | OR BETTER ☐ OB | STOP ☐ STP | STOP LIMIT PRICE ___ LMT | OR | MARKET IF TOUCHED ☐ MIT | ___ LMT | ON CLOSE ☐ CLO | EOS / EDS | WHEN DONE ☐ OR ☐ AND ☐

4 CXL SL: ☐ ☐ | QUANTITY | COMMODITY | PRICE OR 'MKT' ☐ P.T.S | OR BETTER ☐ OB | STOP ☐ STP | STOP LIMIT PRICE ___ LMT | OR | MARKET IF TOUCHED ☐ MIT | ___ LMT | ON CLOSE ☐ CLO | PREM./DISC. MONTH | ☐ OVER ☐ UNDER

5 | SPECIAL INSTRUCTIONS | NOT HELD ☒ NH | LEAVES ☐ LVS | GOOD 'TIL CANCELLED ☐ GTC | GOOD THIS WEEK ☐ GTW | GOOD THIS MONTH ☐ GTM | GOOD THRU ☐ GT ___ | (DATE OR HOUR)
| | | | | TODAY ONLY ☒ DAY | IMMEDIATE FILL OR KILL ☐ FOK | AT OPENING ONLY ☐ OPG | |

6 | NO FORMER ORDER ☒ NFO | CXL FORMER ORDER ☐ CXL | REPLACEMENT CANCELLATION INSTRUCTIONS |

7 | ACCOUNT NUMBER 2 9 – 6 5 0 4 – 7 – 3 6 | NEW ☒ N ☐ L LIQUIDATING | NEW ACCOUNT ☐ NA ☒ T 4 |

8 | MISCELLANEOUS INFORMATION (28 CHAR. MAXIMUM) | EXECUTED PRICE |

9 | GIVE UP ☐ GU | FIRM'S SYMBOL (4 CHAR. MAX) | BY TELETYPE CFN (QTY) OPERATOR ONLY |

10 | CUSTOMER'S NAME **MATTHEW MICHAELS** |

Reynolds & Co.
FORM 33-308

NOT HELD ORDER   ("NH")

TELETYPE IN-PUT

```
OCF/CC FL 70

BUY 5 MAY NO 11 SUG MKT
NH DAY
NFO

29-6504-7-36 N T4
CFN 5
```

The "NOT HELD" order ("NH") is a market or limited price order in which the customer agrees that the Broker will not be held to sales appearing on the tape after the order is entered.

Such qualifying notations as "Disregard Tape" or "Take Time", which may have been used heretofore for the same purpose, are no longer recognized under the exchange nomenclature. While "NH" orders may be held over from day to day (provided they are entered as "GTC"), they are usually executed the same day. In this illustration the Account Executive has entered the order as a "DAY" order, it therefore cannot be held over to the following day.

FIGURE 229

ORDER PREPARATION MANUAL – COMMODITIES – ILLUSTRATION **27**

USE FOR COMMODITIES ONLY

ADDRESS	C G B OF T KSC GRAINS	C G MERC	WPG	MPLS GRAINS	NY/LDN COMDYS	N Y COF & SUG	N Y CTN EXGE	COMEX N Y	OTHER	ORDER NUMBER	C.F.O. NUMBER
	☐ OBT/CX	☐ OME/CX	☐ OCG/CX	☐ OMP/CX	☒ OCC	☐ OCF/CC	☐ OCO/CC	☐ OCY/CC	☐ _____	**PH 152** BY ORDER CLERK ONLY	BY ORDER CLERK ONLY

2 — ☐ CXL | BASIS ☐ BAS | COMMODITY | PRICE | | STOP ☐ STP | ☐ SPREAD / ☐ SWITCH / ☐ SCALE | MONTH

3 — ☐ CXL | ☒ BUY | QUANTITY **10** | COMMODITY **MAY COKE** | PRICE OR "MKT" **3315** | OR BETTER ☐ OB | STOP ☐ STP | STOP LIMIT PRICE ___ LMT | OR | MARKET IF TOUCHED ___ MIT | ___ LMT | ON CLOSE ☐ CLO | EOS / EDS | ☐ WHEN DONE / ☐ OR ☐ AND | MONTH

4 — ☐ CXL | ☐ SL | QUANTITY | COMMODITY | PRICE OR "MKT" ☐ P.T.S | OR BETTER ☐ OB | STOP ☐ STP | STOP LIMIT PRICE ___ LMT | OR | MARKET IF TOUCHED ___ MIT | ___ LMT | ON CLOSE ☐ CLO | PREM./DISCT. MONTH | ☐ OVER / ☐ UNDER

5 — SPECIAL INSTRUCTIONS

| NOT HELD ☐ NH | LEAVES ☐ LVS | GOOD 'TIL CANCELLED ☐ GTC / TODAY ONLY ☐ DAY | GOOD THIS WEEK ☐ GTW / IMMEDIATE FILL OR KILL ☐ FOK | GOOD THIS MONTH ☐ GTM / AT OPENING ONLY ☐ OPG | GOOD THRU ☒ GT **JULY 12** (DATE OR HOUR) |

6 — NO FORMER ORDER ☒ NFO | CXL FORMER ORDER ☐ CXL | REPLACEMENT CANCELLATION INSTRUCTIONS

7 — ACCOUNT NUMBER **5 0 – 4 3 7 1 – 7 – 6 2** | NEW ☐ N LIQUIDATING ☒ L | NEW ACCOUNT ☐ NA ☒ T 4

8 — MISCELLANEOUS INFORMATION (28 CHAR. MAXIMUM) | EXECUTED PRICE

9 — GIVE UP ☐ GU | FIRM'S SYMBOL (4 CHAR. MAX) | BY TELETYPE CFN (QTY) OPERATOR ONLY

10 — CUSTOMER'S NAME **PETER STOVINS**

Reynolds & Co.

FORM 33-308

"GOOD THRU" ORDER ("GT")

```
OCC PH 152

BUY 10 MAY COKE 3315
GT JULY 12
NFO

50-4371-7-62 L T4
CFN 10
```

TELETYPE IN-PUT

The order illustrated will expire at the close of business on July 12th. You also have the option of inserting the time of day in this field (e.g., GT 2:00 p.m. NYT). If the order is not executed by the specified time it will be cancelled.

All orders "GOOD THROUGH" a specified time must be written in New York time.

FIGURE 230

ORDER PREPARATION MANUAL – COMMODITIES – ILLUSTRATION **28**

USE FOR COMMODITIES ONLY

ADDRESS	C G B OF T KSC GRAINS	C G MERC	WPG	MPLS GRAINS	NY/LDN COMDYS	NY COF & SUG	N Y CTN EXGE	COMEX N Y	OTHER	ORDER NUMBER	C.F.O. NUMBER
	☐ OBT/CX	☐ OME/CX	☐ OCG/CX	☐ OMP/CX	☒ OCC	☐ OCF/CC	☐ OCO/CC	☐ OCY/CC _____	☐	PP 49 / BY ORDER CLERK ONLY	BY ORDER CLERK ONLY

Row 2:

| ② | CXL ☐ | BASIS BAS ☐ | COMMODITY | MONTH | PRICE | ///// | STOP ☐ STP | SPREAD ☐ | | SWITCH ☐ | SCALE ☐ |

Row 3:

| ③ | CXL ☐ | BUY ☒ | QUANTITY 10 | MAY MONTH | COMMODITY COKE | PRICE OR 'MKT' 3900 | OR BETTER ☐ OB | STOP ☐ STP | STOP LIMIT PRICE ☐ LMT | OR | MARKET IF TOUCHED ☐ MIT | ☐ LMT | ON CLOSE ☐ CLO | EOS ☐ / EDS ☐ | WHEN DONE ☐ / OR ☐ AND ☐ |

Row 4:

| ④ | CXL ☐ | SL ☐ | QUANTITY | MONTH | COMMODITY | PRICE OR 'MKT' ☐ P.T.B | OR BETTER ☐ OB | STOP ☐ STP | STOP LIMIT PRICE ☐ LMT | OR | MARKET IF TOUCHED ☐ MIT | ☐ LMT | ON CLOSE ☐ CLO | PREM./DISCT. MONTH | OVER ☐ / UNDER ☐ |

Row 5:

| ⑤ | SPECIAL INSTRUCTIONS | NOT HELD ☐ NH | LEAVES ☐ LVS | GOOD 'TIL CANCELLED ☐ GTC / TODAY ONLY ☐ DAY | GOOD THIS WEEK ☐ GTW / IMMEDIATE FILL OR KILL ☒ FOK | GOOD THIS MONTH ☐ GTM / AT OPENING ONLY ☐ OPG | GOOD THRU ☐ GT | (DATE OR HOUR) |

Row 6:

| ⑥ | NO FORMER ORDER ☒ NFO | CXL FORMER ORDER ☐ CXL | REPLACEMENT CANCELLATION INSTRUCTIONS |

Row 7:

| ⑦ | 3 H — 4 1 3 7 — 7 — 1 8 ACCOUNT NUMBER | NEW ☐ N LIQUIDATING ☒ L | NEW ACCOUNT ☐ NA ☒ T 4 |

Row 8:

| ⑧ | MISCELLANEOUS INFORMATION (28 CHAR. MAXIMUM) | EXECUTED PRICE |

Row 9:

| ⑨ | GIVE UP ☐ GU | FIRM'S SYMBOL (4 CHAR. MAX) | BY TELETYPE CFN (QTY) OPERATOR ONLY |

Row 10:

| ⑩ | CUSTOMER'S NAME M. A. BARBER |

Reynolds & Co.

FORM 33-308

FILL OR KILL ORDER ("FOK")

TELETYPE IN-PUT

- OCC PP 49

- BUY 10 MAY COKE 3900
  FOK
  NFO

- 3H-4137-7-18 L T4
  CFN 10

A "FILL OR KILL" order is a market or limited price order which is to be executed in whole, or in part, as soon as it is represented in the "PIT" and the portion not so executed is to be treated as cancelled.

Note that the definition for "FOK" in commodities differs from the definition for stock orders. The definition that is applied here is synonymous with the stock definition for an "Immediate or Cancel" ("OC") order. Nomenclature used in stocks, in many cases, is the same as commodities but their meanings may have significant variations. Careful attention should be given to every illustration and definition appearing in this manual and in the Order Preparation Manual, which deals mainly with listed securities.

FIGURE 231

ORDER PREPARATION MANUAL – COMMODITIES – ILLUSTRATION   **29**

USE FOR COMMODITIES ONLY

ADDRESS	C G B OF T KSC GRAINS	C G MERC	WPG	MPLS GRAINS	NY/LDN COMDYS	N Y COF & SUG	N Y CTN EXGE	COMEX N Y	OTHER	ORDER NUMBER	C.F.O. NUMBER
	☐	☒	☐	☐	☐	☐		☐	☐	**SB 12**	
	OBT/CX	OME/CX	OCG/CX	OMP/CX	OCC	OCF/CC	OCO/CC	OCY/CC ___		BY ORDER CLERK ONLY	BY ORDER CLERK ONLY

2 — ☐ CXL — ☐ BAS — BASIS — COMMODITY — MONTH — PRICE — ☐ STOP / ☐ STP — ☐ SPREAD — ☐ SWITCH — ☐ SCALE

3 — ☐ CXL — ☐ BUY — QUANTITY — COMMODITY — MONTH — PRICE OR 'MKT' — ☐ OB (OR BETTER) — ☐ STP (STOP) — STOP LIMIT PRICE ___ LMT — OR — MARKET IF TOUCHED ☐ MIT — LMT — ☐ CLO (ON CLOSE) — EOS / EDS — ☐ WHEN DONE — OR ☐ AND ☐

4 — ☐ CXL — ☒ SL — **2** — **FEB** **BLY** — MONTH — **MKT** — ☐ P.T.S — ☐ OB (OR BETTER) — ☐ STP (STOP) — STOP LIMIT PRICE ___ LMT — OR — MARKET IF TOUCHED ☐ MIT — LMT — ☐ CLO (ON CLOSE) — PREM./DISCT. ___ MONTH — ☐ OVER — ☐ UNDER

5 — SPECIAL INSTRUCTIONS — NOT HELD ☐ NH — LEAVES ☐ LVS — GOOD 'TIL CANCELLED ☐ GTC — GOOD THIS WEEK ☐ GTW — GOOD THIS MONTH ☐ GTM — GOOD THRU ☐ GT ___ (DATE OR HOUR) — TODAY ONLY ☐ DAY — IMMEDIATE FILL OR KILL ☐ FOK — AT OPENING ONLY ☒ OPG

6 — NO FORMER ORDER ☒ NFO — CXL FORMER ORDER ☐ CXL — REPLACEMENT CANCELLATION INSTRUCTIONS

7 — **1 6 – 3 5 6 0 – 6 – 6 7** — ACCOUNT NUMBER — ☐ N NEW / ☒ L LIQUIDATING — ☐ NA NEW ACCOUNT / ☒ T 4

8 — MISCELLANEOUS INFORMATION (28 CHAR. MAXIMUM) — EXECUTED PRICE

9 — GIVE UP ☐ GU — FIRM'S SYMBOL (4 CHAR. MAX) — BY TELETYPE CFN ___ (QTY) OPERATOR ONLY

10 — CUSTOMER'S NAME — **NICHOLAS DALTON**

Reynolds & Co.
FORM 33-S08

AT THE OPENING ONLY ORDER ("OPG")

```
OME/CX SB 12

SL 2 FEB BLY MKT
OPG
NFO

16-3560-6-67 L T4
CFN 2
```
TELETYPE IN-PUT

"At the Opening Only" ("OPG") is an order to be executed at the opening in the commodity or not at all, and any portion not so executed is to be treated as cancelled.

It is Reynolds & Co.'s policy that orders received at the exchange 15 minutes prior to the opening of the market will not be guaranteed to make the opening.

To be sure that you make the opening, enter your order as early as possible in the morning before the opening.

Orders received after the close of the Exchange will not be held over for the following morning unless the New York office, to meet emergency conditions, so specifies.

FIGURE 232

ORDER PREPARATION MANUAL – COMMODITIES – ILLUSTRATION **30**

USE FOR COMMODITIES ONLY

	C G B OF T KSC GRAINS	C G MERC	WPG	MPLS GRAINS	NY/LDN COMDYS	NY COF & SUG	N Y CTN EXGE	COMEX NY	OTHER	ORDER NUMBER	C.F.O. NUMBER
A D D R E S S	☐ OBT/CX	☐ OME/CX	☐ OCG/CX	☐ OMP/CX	☐ OCC	☒ OCF/CC	☐ OCO/CC	☐ OCY/CC	☐	**BM 28** BY ORDER CLERK ONLY	BY ORDER CLERK ONLY

2	CXL ☐	BASIS ☐ BAS		COMMODITY / MONTH	PRICE		STOP ☐ STP	☐ SPREAD				
								☐ SWITCH		☐ SCALE		

| **3** | CXL ☐ | BUY ☒ | QUANTITY **2** / MONTH | COMMODITY **MCH No.11 SUG** | PRICE OR 'MKT' **450** | OR BETTER ☐ OB | STOP ☐ STP | STOP LIMIT PRICE ☐ LMT | OR | MARKET IF TOUCHED ☐ MIT | ☐ LMT | ON CLOSE ☐ CLO | EOS ☐ / EDS ☐ | WHEN DONE ☐ / OR ☒ AND ☐ |

| **4** | CXL ☐ | SL ☒ | QUANTITY **2** / MONTH | COMMODITY **MCH No.11 SUG** | PRICE OR 'MKT' **470** ☐ P.T.S | OR BETTER ☐ OB | STOP ☐ STP | STOP LIMIT PRICE ☐ LMT | OR | MARKET IF TOUCHED ☐ MIT | ☐ LMT | ON CLOSE ☐ CLO | PREM./DISCT. MONTH | ☐ OVER / ☐ UNDER |

5	SPECIAL INSTRUCTIONS	NOT HELD ☐ NH	LEAVES ☐ LVS	GOOD 'TIL CANCELLED ☒ GTC / TODAY ONLY ☐ DAY	GOOD THIS WEEK ☐ GTW / IMMEDIATE FILL OR KILL ☐ FOK	GOOD THIS MONTH ☐ GTM / AT OPENING ONLY ☐ OPG	GOOD THRU ☐ GT	(DATE OR HOUR)

6	NO FORMER ORDER ☒ NFO	CXL FORMER ORDER ☐ CXL	REPLACEMENT CANCELLATION INSTRUCTIONS

7	ACCOUNT NUMBER **3 7 – 4 3 2 1 – 7 – 8 4**	NEW ☒ N / LIQUIDATING ☐ L	NEW ACCOUNT ☐ NA / ☒ T4

8	MISCELLANEOUS INFORMATION (28 CHAR. MAXIMUM)	EXECUTED PRICE

9	GIVE UP ☐ GU	FIRM'S SYMBOL (4 CHAR. MAX)	BY TELETYPE CFN (QTY) OPERATOR ONLY

10	CUSTOMER'S NAME **ARTHUR CHEMKOWSKI**

Reynolds & Co.
FORM 33-308

"OR" (ONE CANCELS OTHER) ORDERS

TELETYPE IN-PUT

```
OCF/CC BM 28

BUY 2 MCH NO 11 SUG 450 OR
SL 2 MCH NO 11 SUG 470
GTC
NFO

37-4321-7-84 N T4
CFN 2 2
```

An "OR" order instructs the broker to immediately cancel one side upon execution of the other side.

Two types of "OR" (one cancels other) orders are:

1. To BUY at a low limit or SELL at a high limit, *whichever occurs first.* Illustration No. 30.

2. To BUY (SELL) on STOP or BUY (SELL) at limit, *whichever occurs first.* Illustration No. 31.

In the order illustrated, the customer has instructed the broker to buy March Sugar when it drops to 4.50¢ or to sell March Sugar when it rises to 4.70¢, *whichever occurs first,* and to immediately cancel the untouched side upon execution of the other side. For example: If the buy side were executed at 4.50¢, the sell side will be automatically cancelled.

Compare with next illustration.

FIGURE 233

ORDER PREPARATION MANUAL – COMMODITIES – ILLUSTRATION   **31**

USE FOR COMMODITIES ONLY

| ADDRESS | C G B OF T KSC GRAINS ☐ OBT/CX | C G MERC ☐ OME/CX | WPG ☐ OCG/CX | MPLS GRAINS ☐ OMP/CX | NY/LDN COMDYS ☐ OCC | N Y COF & SUG ☒ OCF/CC | N Y CTN EXGE ☐ OCO/CC | COMEX N Y ☐ OCY/CC | OTHER ☐ _____ | ORDER NUMBER VI 42 / BY ORDER CLERK ONLY | C.F.O. NUMBER BY ORDER CLERK ONLY |

| 2 | CXL ☐   BASIS BAS ☐ | | COMMODITY   MONTH | PRICE | ///// | STOP ☐ STP | SPREAD ☐   SWITCH ☐ | | SCALE ☐ | |

| 3 | CXL ☐   BUY ☒ | QUANTITY 2   MONTH | COMMODITY MCH No.11 SUG | PRICE OR "MKT" 470 | OR BETTER ☐ OB | STOP ☒ STP | STOP LIMIT PRICE ___ LMT | OR 450 | MARKET IF TOUCHED ☐ MIT | ___ LMT | ON CLOSE ☐ CLO | EOS   EDS | WHEN DONE ☐   OR ☐ AND ☐ |

| 4 | CXL ☐   SL ☐ | QUANTITY   MONTH | COMMODITY | PRICE OR "MKT" ☐ P.T.S | OR BETTER ☐ OB | STOP ☐ STP | STOP LIMIT PRICE ___ LMT | OR | MARKET IF TOUCHED ☐ MIT | ___ LMT | ON CLOSE ☐ CLO | PREM./DISCT.   MONTH | OVER ☐   UNDER ☐ |

| 5 | SPECIAL INSTRUCTIONS | NOT HELD ☐ NH | LEAVES ☐ LVS | GOOD 'TIL CANCELLED ☒ GTC   TODAY ONLY ☐ DAY | GOOD THIS WEEK ☐ GTW   IMMEDIATE FILL OR KILL ☐ FOK | GOOD THIS MONTH ☐ GTM   AT OPENING ONLY ☐ OPG | GOOD THRU ☐ GT | (DATE OR HOUR) _____ |

| 6 | NO FORMER ORDER ☒ NFO | CXL FORMER ORDER ☐ CXL | REPLACEMENT CANCELLATION INSTRUCTIONS |

| 7 | ACCOUNT NUMBER   3 8 – 6 3 7 1 – 7 – 3 6 | NEW ☒ N LIQUIDATING ☐ L | NEW ACCOUNT ☐ NA ☒ T 4 |

| 8 | MISCELLANEOUS INFORMATION (28 CHAR. MAXIMUM) | EXECUTED PRICE |

| 9 | GIVE UP ☐ GU | FIRM'S SYMBOL (4 CHAR. MAX) | BY TELETYPE CFN   (QTY) OPERATOR ONLY |

| 10 | CUSTOMER'S NAME   ARCH JOHNSON |

Reynolds & Co.

FORM 33-308

"OR" (ONE CANCELS OTHER) ORDER – ON STOP

-
- OCF/CC VI 42
- BUY 2 MCH NO 11 SUG 470 STP OR 450 GTC
- NFO
- 38-6371-7-36 N T4 CFN 2
-
-

TELETYPE IN-PUT

In this illustration, the customer has shown that he wants to buy March Sugar, but not at its present level. He would want to pay 4.50¢, if it drops to that price, but to protect himself against a sudden upswing, and still be guaranteed an execution, he also enters a stop order at 4.70¢. This order, then, instructs the broker to buy March Sugar on stop if the market touches, or penetrates the 4.70¢ price or to buy it regular if the market drops to 4.50¢, and immediately cancel the side not executed.

See previous illustration for a variation of an "OR" order.

Glossary

Accumulate. Adding to a commodity position over a period of time during market fluctuations rather than all at one time and price.

Acreage allotment. That portion of a farmer's acreage which he may plant in crops and still receive the benefits of government price supports and financial assistance.

Acreage reserve. A program of the Department of Agriculture whereby the farmer receives payments from the government for not planting basic commodities on part or all of his acreage allotment.

Actuals. The physical commodity, such as corn, wheat, silver, as opposed to the futures contract which is merely a slip of paper.

Afloat. Commodities which are in transit or storage on ships or barges as opposed to being stored in land-based elevators and warehouses.

Arbitrage. The buying and selling of different futures contracts at the same time in order to profit from a discrepancy in price between the futures contracts.

Basis. (1) The spread between the actual cash commodity and the price of the future to which the cash purchase corresponds. (2) The locked-in price difference between the cash price for the commodity purchased and the

futures price for the commodity future sold.

Bear. A trader who believes that prices will decline in the near or long-term future.

Bid. An offering price to purchase a commodity or commodity future if the seller will sell at that price.

Break. A rapid decline in prices usually set off by an unexpected news or crop report which caught the commodity traders totally unprepared for such bearish news.

Board of Trade. The Chicago Board of Trade, 141 West Jackson Boulevard, Chicago, Illinois.

BOT. Symbol used by the brokerage profession to indicate the purchase of a commodity future by a customer.

Broker. An agent who on behalf of the customer is involved in the actual purchase and sale of the commodity future on the appropriate futures market exchange.

Brokerage. The fee charged by the firm which handles the customer's order for its services. This amount is set by the exchange where the transaction is executed.

Brokerage house. The firm, either a partnership or corporation, which handles for a fee various buy and sell orders for commodity clients.

Bucket shop. An illegal practice where-

341

by the brokerage house assuming that the customer will lose money on his futures transaction does not actually place the order, and when the customer would have suffered a loss by his position informs the customer that he did in fact suffer said loss, and then pockets the money for its own financial benefit.

Bulge. An advance in cash or futures commodity prices.

Bull. The opposite of a bear, a commodity trader who believes that prices will advance over the near or long term.

Bull market. A market where prices are in fact advancing.

Call. A period of time on certain commodity exchanges whereby an officer of that exchange supervises the price (and settles disputes over price) for the opening and closing of each futures month.

Calls and puts. Options whereby a trader for a specific amount of money buys or sells an option for commodity futures contracts which have the feature of limiting the loss for the investor to the amount of the purchase price but which set no limit on the profit for the trader. (Calls and puts are illegal on regulated commodities.)

Cargo. A load of a commodity, in the grain market usually 350,000 bushels.

Carload. A load of a commodity aboard a railroad car, usually from 1,800 to 2,000 bushels.

Carrying costs. The cost of storing and holding a commodity such as the cost of insurance, storage, inspection, and interest, which is passed onto the commodity futures trader who receives delivery on the cash commodity until he passes such delivery onto a third party.

Cash commodity. The actual physical commodity which can be seen, stored, eaten, consumed, or manufactured into a finished product.

Cash forward. The process whereby a cash dealer will sell cash commodities for delivery at a specified date in the future.

Cash price. The composite price for the actual cash commodity as set by the price at which that commodity is presently trading in the cash markets.

Cash transactions. The purchase and sale of commodities on the cash markets or commodities on the futures market for cash.

CCC. The Commodity Credit Corporation.

CEA. The Commodity Exchange Authority, a division of the Department of Agriculture responsible for supervision of and regulation of trading in various commodities as established by law.

C&F. The cost and freight required to ship actual commodities.

Certified stock. Stocks of a commodity which have passed the rigorous tests established by the various exchanges and certified as deliverable on the futures exchanges in connection with a short position in the futures market.

Chart. The process whereby price or other important data is transferred from mathematical figures to representation on a piece of paper for visual response.

Charter. The process whereby a ship or vessel is leased or engaged to deliver a product to a certain destination in exchange for a fee.

Chicago Board of Trade. The Chicago Board of Trade commodity futures exchange.

Chicago Mercantile Exchange. The Chicago Mercantile Exchange commodity futures exchange.

Chicago Open Board of Trade. The Chicago Open Board of Trade commodity futures exchange in such place where units of 1,000 bushels are traded as opposed to the Chicago Board of Trade where the smallest units of trade are 5,000 bushels.

Churning. A method whereby an unscrupulous broker will, over a period of time, make numerous purchase and sale transactions in the account of a customer in an unethical effort to provide a significant financial return for himself and his brokerage house in the form of trading commissions. In most cases of churning legal action can be taken against both the brokerage firm and the broker.

CIF. The cost, insurance, and freight required to ship actual commodities to a point of destination.

Clearinghouse. A separate corporation established by the various commodity futures exchanges through which all the transactions in the market during the day can be matched to their equal and opposite number to provide an orderly method of control over who owns what.

Clearing member. A member of the clearinghouse or association. Membership requirements for clearing members are higher than for exchange members since substantial financial net worth is required to be a clearing member and, therefore, not all exchange members are clearing members or allowed to clear their own trades and must work through individuals who are clearing members.

Clearing price. The closing price for the market for the day and the price at which all transactions are cleared at the clearinghouse for the purpose of margin requirements.

Close. The end of the trading session during which those traders who wish to liquidate do so and the last price of the commodities traded is known as the closing price.

Commission. The fee charged for trading in commodity futures by the brokerage house to the customer. All fees are identical and set by the exchanges but in the future a system of negotiated fees will be instituted whereby each brokerage house may negotiate with its customers for the fee it will charge.

Commission house. Same as a brokerage house, a firm which buys and sells commodity futures for the general public in exchange for a fee or commission.

Contract. A formal legal document between two parties whereby one party agrees to perform in a certain manner with respect to the other party and the other party agrees to perform in a certain manner with respect to the first party.

Contract grades. The grade of the actual cash commodity which may be delivered against a futures contract as set forth in the rules and regulations of the commodity futures exchange.

Controlled commodities. Those commodities which are controlled and regulated by the Commodity Exchange Authority as provided for by federal law.

Corner. To purchase or sell such a large position in the commodity markets, that in effect, the trader controls the market and can force prices to respond to his dominant position by moving in a direction which will return a substantial profit to the trader.

Country elevator. A storage facility in the country in which the actual cash commodity of the farmer is stored during a period when the owner wishes to hold the commodity prior to shipping it to the eventual user.

Country price. The price for the commodity which prevails in the actual country, usually quoted in terms of a premium or discount to the nearby futures contract and then converted into an actual cash price.

Cover. The buying of futures contracts in order to close out the previous selling of those same futures contracts.

Crop report. A report issued by the Department of Agriculture covering the current state of the actual commodity which is to be planted or is growing in the fields.

Crush. The method whereby the raw soybean is taken into a processing plant and crushed to yield the high-protein products of soybean meal and soybean oil.

Crush spread. A futures spreading position whereby a trader, believing that one is underpriced in relationship to the other, will buy futures contracts of soybeans and sell futures contracts of soybean meal and soybean oil, and in effect, thereby duplicating the operations of an actual processor of the cash products.

Day order. Orders that are good for one single day only and if they are not filled during that day are automatically canceled and must be entered again to be effective on the second day.

Day trader. A trader who enters and liquidates his positions during a single day holding no position overnight. This has the advantages of a reduced commission rate on some exchanges but is a very difficult process to make a financial profit on.

Deferred contracts. Those contracts on the futures exchange which are for months beyond the current closest trading month. A trader is often "long" the "nearby," and "short" the "deferred."

Delivery. The tendering of the physical commodity in the form of a warehouse or other receipt to the floor of the exchange during the delivery month in response to a short position held on the futures market. No actual delivery of the commodity is made, merely delivery of a piece of paper evidencing where the cash commodity can be located.

Delivery points. The various locations where the cash commodity may be stored and delivery made from so that the long trader who takes delivery will not have to travel outside of an area designated by the exchange to take receipt of the actual cash commodity.

Differentials. The price distinctions between various grades and locations of commodities.

Discretionary account. A commodity account whereby a third party, either the broker or another person, is given authority over the trading decisions in the account of the commodity customer on the belief that such third party is a more skilled trader than the customer who has the money to trade with. Such discretionary accounts are forbidden by many brokerage firms and are regulated with vigor by some exchanges. Check with your broker for the latest rules of his firm and the exchange.

Evening up. Terminating a futures position in advance of a significant crop report or other event so as not to be caught in a financially unsecure position, should an unexpected report be issued.

Ex-pit transactions. A procedure which is legal under certain circumstances whereby trades are executed outside of the actual futures pit whereby cash and futures are exchanged at a set price. Primarily used by those in the cash business who are capable of taking or making delivery of the cash product.

First notice day. The first day of the delivery period when notices may be given by the shorts to the longs of their intention to deliver on the contracts to which they are short and the precise amount they intend to deliver. First notice day varies with each commodity and each exchange.

Floor broker. A member of the exchange who stands in the actual pit and executes orders on behalf of his clients and himself.

F.O.B. Free on Board, Specifying that the commodity which is being shipped will be placed on the shipping vehicle at no cost to the purchaser but therefrom the purchaser will bear all costs associated with shipping that commodity.

FOK (Fill or Kill) order. A commodity order which has to be filled at the price specified immediately upon entering the pit where the futures are traded or it is no longer effective.

Foreign material. Objects foreign to the commodity which are discovered in the process of inspecting the commodity and which will result in the financial penalty to the seller unless such foreign material is removed from the commodity before it is sold or delivered.

Free supply. That quantity of a commodity which is not restricted by government ownership or control and therefore is readily available for the market should the price be high enough to induce the owners to part with it.

Fundamentalist. A trader who bases his market decisions upon an analysis of supply and demand statistics for the actual cash commodity rather than technical or chart considerations.

Futures. Contracts which relate to a cash commodity to be received and to be delivered at some specified time in the future under terms as set forth in a legally binding contract and subject to the rules and regulations of the future exchange where such contracts are traded.

G.T.C. (Good Till Canceled). A commodity market order which remains open and effective until either the price specified is reached and the order filled or the order is canceled by the customer who entered it. Another term for an "open order."

Hedger. A person in the cash commodity business, who in order to pass the risk along of owning, carrying, or using cash commodities, engaged in transactions on the futures exchange markets of an opposite character to his transactions on the cash market, so that his risks of the cash market can be passed along to the futures trader.

Initial margin. The amount of margin capital required by the brokerage firm to establish a position in the futures market. The minimum is set by the exchange itself; the amount required by the brokerage firm to protect its own financial interests may be higher, however.

Inspection. The process whereby a certified inspector examines cash commodities and grades and designates them as of a certain quality for purposes of the later sale or delivery of these commodities.

International Wheat Agreement. An agreement among the major wheat-consuming and producing nations of the world, regulating the sale and selling price of wheat by establishing a maximum and minimum price above or below, of which no member nation will sell or purchase wheat in world trade.

Inverted market. A futures market where the nearby contracts are selling at a price higher than the distant options due to a heavy near-term demand for the actual cash commodity.

Job lot. A trading unit consisting usually of 1,000 bushels as compared to the normal 5,000-bushel contracts and traded primarily on the Chicago Open Board of Trade and the Winnipeg Grain Exchange.

Key reversal day. A trading day in which the price range for a particular commodity option makes a higher high price than it did during the previous trading day and a lower low price than it did during the previous trading day and closes at a price below the close of the previous day. An indication for the "chart trader" that the near-term top of the market has been reached and that prices will decline in the near future.

Last trading day. The day when the futures trader must liquidate all his futures positions or make or receive delivery. After this day there will be no trading allowed in the futures options again for that particular option, month, and year.

Leverage. The financial power gained by risking only a small amount of money to control a large position in a commodity whereby a moderate price advance or decline in the commodity can return very substantial profits to the investor.

Life of contract. The period of time during which trading may take place in options for a particular commodity prior to the last trading day and expiration of trading in that option. Usually less than one year but in some cases up to 18 months.

Limit move. The maximum price at which a commodity may rise or decline from the previous day's closing price. Set by the commodity exchange itself, in an effort to regulate orderly trade, no transactions may be entered into outside of the range from the high limit to the low limit above or below the previous night's closing price.

Limit order. A price restriction placed on an order by the customer, indicating to the broker that the commodity future may be purchased or sold only at the price indicated or better, and may not be executed unless it can so be done at the limited price specified.

Limit position. The maximum number of contracts which a trader may hold as established by law and regulated by the Commodity Exchange Authority. This limit does not apply to bona fide hedging positions.

Liquidation. Taking a position in the futures market which closes out a previous position, normally selling contracts which the trader had previously bought but it may also apply to buying contracts back which the trader had previously sold.

Loan price. The amount of money which a cash commodity producer may borrow for his crop, provided his acreage is in compliance with government loan program provisions. Such loan may be defaulted whereby the grower receives for his crop the dollar value of the loan, or the crop may be redeemed and sold on the free market if prices rise above the loan value.

Loan program. A program of the Department of Agriculture whereby the government will loan money to farmers who have complied with specified acreage regulations at a set price for each unit of production produced. The farmer has the option of defaulting on the loan and thereby making the government the purchaser, or redeeming and selling on the free market.

Long. A trader who has bought futures contracts hoping for a price advance and has not liquidated his position is said to be "long" the market.

Long term. A period of time, usually lasting several months, during which the trader maintains his position hoping to earn a financial return for the same.

Low. The lowest price at which the cash or futures commodity traded for any particular period of time, day, week, month, year, or history.

Margin. The amount of money put up by commodity traders with their brokers as "good faith deposit" to assure they will perform on their long or short positions. Usually from 5 percent to 10 percent of the total value of the commodity contract. It is set by the exchanges and each member firm can go no lower than the minimum set by the exchange.

Margin call. A request by the brokerage firm that the customer add additional capital to his commodity account to cover a paper loss, which has occurred in his position, resulting in a paper deterioration of his original margin capital to the point where the firm no longer feels safe with the position.

Market order. An order given by a commodity customer to his broker to buy or sell commodity futures "at the market," meaning at any price at which the market is trading when his order reaches the trading pit.

Marketing quota. A restriction by the federal government on the amount of a commodity which a farmer may sell. Usually it is the quantity of wheat or cotton which the farmer is permitted to grow on his alloted acreage.

Maturity. The period of time during which shorts may deliver on their short positions to settle their commodity commitments. Usually this is the period between the "first notice day" and the "expiration date" of the commodity future.

Members' commission. The commission charged to a member of an exchange for the execution of a commodity order in the pits of that exchange. It is usually considerably less than the rate charged the general public and one of the reasons that a seat on a futures exchange can sell for from $1,000 to $100,000.

Moving average. A mathematical system used by technical commodity traders for averaging near-term prices relative to long-term prices to determine if the trend of prices is up or down and whether a purchase or sale should be made for the trader who wishes to follow the trend with his positions.

Nearby. The nearby futures contract, which is the month closest to the period of time during which one is asking the question, as opposed to the deferred futures contract which are all others except for the nearby.

Negotiable. Can be readily converted into cash by the party who is a holder in due course.

Net position. The commodity position held by a trader which is either the greater amount of the long position minus the short position or the short position minus the long position.

New crop. The supply of a commodity which will be available after harvest and which will then play a role in the marketplace.

Nominal price. An artificial price set by the reporter to give an idea of where commodity futures were traded to the general public even though there may have been no actual transactions at that price. It is usually the difference between the bid and the ask price at the close of the trading day.

Notice. A slip of paper by a short in the futures market advising the exchange and the members who are long of his intention to make an actual delivery

of the cash commodity in the form of a warehouse receipt.

Notice day. Any day during the month when the nearby contract is expiring when notices of intent to deliver may be made by those traders who are short in the futures market.

OCO (One Cancels the Other). A commodity order whereby the commodity trader, who does not know if the market will rise or decline, places orders on both sides of the trading range with the stipulation that whichever order fills first will thereby automatically cancel the other remaining open order.

Offer. A commitment on the part of a purchaser to buy commodities or commodity futures at a certain price, if the seller will sell at that price.

Offset. The liquidation of a futures position by buying back short positions or selling out long positions with the net result that the trader is out of the market altogether.

Old crop. The crop which has already been harvested and is presently in the pipelines of distribution throughout the country.

Omnibus account. A method whereby a commodity brokerage firm will carry one account where the funds are generally commingled with no knowledge of precisely who the true owners are or what portion of ownership each has. Illegal on some exchanges and forbidden by some brokerage houses.

On the close. An order given by a trader to his broker to buy or sell commodity futures within the closing minutes of the trading session usually referred to as "on the close."

On the open. An order given by a trader

to his broker to buy or sell commodity futures within the first five minutes of the trading session usually referred to as "on the open."

Open interest. The total of nonliquidated contracts which presently exist for any commodity future or commodity option (i.e., when one trader is long one contract and another trader is short one contract and neither have liquidated their position, the open interest is said to be "one"). The total number of parties involved would be two but the number of "open contracts" would only be one since a contract by its nature requires two parties.

Open order. An order which remains on the books of the commodity brokerage firm to be filled whenever the specified price is reached and is valid until either that price is reached or the order is canceled by the commodity trader.

Opening bell. The bell which opens the market in various commodity exchanges and signals the beginning of trading for that session.

Opening range. The range of prices at which commodity futures were traded during the opening moments of the trading session. Any buy or sell order given to the broker to be filled "at the open" will be filled within this price range.

Option. A term which is used in the trade to designate a particular commodity contract for a particular month. Actually, the term is incorrect since each contract is a legal contract and not an option. An option correctly is a put or a call which are illegal in regulated commodities.

Original margin. The amount of money originally required for each commodity contract which the trader wishes to buy or sell. The minimum amount is set by the exchange itself.

Overbought markets. A term used by people to describe a situation when they believe the market has advanced in price too far too fast, "it has been overbought," and therefore prices should decline when the buyers start to liquidate their position. The term is a carryover from the stock market where it has a validity due to the limited number of stocks available, but in the commodity market, where there is an independent cash market which sets the tone of the futures market, and where there is an unlimited supply of contracts which traders may enter into the meaning is less valid.

Oversold markets. The same as an overbought market except used to describe a situation where traders believe prices have declined too fast too soon and should therefore rebound to higher prices.

Paper losses. Losses which have occurred when one computes the cost of goods minus the current value of those goods if sold at today's prices.

Paper profits. Profits which have resulted when one computes the cost of goods sold minus the current value of those goods if sold at today's prices.

Paper trading. A system whereby a commodity trader makes simulated moves on "paper" rather than by taking actual commodity positions, in an effort to determine whether he would have made or lost money on his position without risking any actual capital in the marketplace.

Parity. An artificial price set by the government, which supposedly indicates an equal relationship between the value of commodities as received by the producer and the value of all other items which the producer must use in order to survive. Technically when "parity" is at 100, the money received by the farmer for his crops is exactly equal to the money he must spend for his farm and household supplies.

Pit. The actual ring on the exchange trading floor usually consisting of three or more levels where the trading of commodity futures takes place.

Point. The minimum amount that a commodity futures price may fluctuate, usually set by the exchange itself, and in the case of grain one eighth of a cent per bushel or $6.25 per contract.

Position. The holdings of a commodity trader, either long or short, is said to be his "position in the market."

Position limit. The limit set by federal law, which a commodity trader can hold in terms of futures contracts, unless he is a bona fide hedger and the positions he holds are bona fide hedging positions.

Position trader. A commodity trader who holds a naked long or short position hoping for the market to advance or decline in contrast to one who is not in the market, who day trades, or who trades spreads.

Premium. The price difference between one commodity futures contract and another or between various grades of cash commodities, the one with the highest value holding the "premium" over the other.

Price averaging. The procedure whereby a trader buys or sells commodity contracts over a period of time to arrive at an average price for his total inventory which he feels is reasonable under the conditions of the market.

Primary market. The central locations in the country where farmers who have raised commodities bring them for sale and distribution is said to be a "primary market."

Professional speculator. An individual who makes living in the process of speculating on various prices of various commodities and commodity futures.

Profit and loss statements. The statement sent by a brokerage house to its customers after they have effected a commodity transaction advising them as to the price they paid for their commodity contract, the price at which it was sold, and the resulting profit or loss suffered or earned on the trade.

Public elevators. Storage facilities located throughout the country which are available for use by any producer to store his crop at a fee charged by the owner of the elevator. As distinguished from private elevators which are owned and used by a private company and not available to the public.

Purchase agreement. The agreement whereby the government will buy from the farmer his commodities at a certain time for the loan value of those commodities.

Puts and calls. (See *Calls and Puts.*)

Pyramiding. Normally considered as the use of "paper profits" to buy or sell further commodity contracts.

Quickie. An order to be filled immediately upon its reaching of the trading floor at the price specified or it is to be canceled and no longer valid.

Range. The descriptive term for the trading activity of a commodity or commodity future, usually consisting of a quotation of the highest price and the lowest price for the trading session, and calling that price distinction as the "range" for the period.

Reaction. A market adjustment downward after prices have advanced substantially during any given period.

Realizing profits. Liquidating market positions in order to make actual profits out of which have up to that time been simply "paper profits."

Recovery. Opposite of a reaction, a market adjustment upward after prices have substantially declined during any given period.

Registered representative. The term chosen by the brokerage profession to describe the broker who solicits public business on behalf of that firm.

Regulated commodities. Those commodities which are regulated by federal law and come under the jurisdiction of the Commodity Exchange Authority as in the national interest to be regulated. Prices are not controlled but the federal government does take an active interest to see that no manipulation of free market forces occurs.

Resting order. An open order which is given to a broker by a customer to buy commodity futures at a price below the current market or sell commodity futures at a price above the current market.

Reversal. (See *Key Reversal Day.*) A trading session when the market closes at a lower price than it did during the previous session after making a higher high as compared to the previous day's range.

Ring. The actual trading pit where the futures contracts are traded by the members of the exchange on behalf of themselves and the general public.

Round lot. A full contract, usually 5,000 bushels, as opposed to the "job lot" or 1,000 bushel contracts traded on the Chicago Open Board of Trade and the Winnipeg Grain Exchange.

Round turn. The process of buying and then selling a commodity futures contract is said to be a "round turn" regardless of the order in which the buy or the sell occurred. When you have liquidated a position you have made a "round turn."

Rules. The rules and regulations set by the various exchanges and federal government for the purpose of maintaining fair play and an orderly market for the nation's commodities free from undue manipulation.

Sampling. The process whereby an inspector will take a portion of a commodity from a larger supply to determine the quality of the total supply for the purpose of grading it for sale to a purchaser.

Scalping. The attempt to make a financial profit by entering and exiting from a market in short periods of time after a very small profit has been made. Very difficult to achieve success at, if possible at all, due to the high commission schedule charged by the brokerage firms which handle public business.

Settlement price. The closing price of the day, or an average of the various closing prices of the day, for the purposes of clearing the transaction to determine what margin capital is owed by which firm to protect the net positions held on the books of that firm.

Short. A trader who has sold futures contracts is said to be "short" the market meaning that he has sold something he does not yet own and he must either buy the cash commodity and deliver it to fulfill his "short" position or else buy back his futures contract in the market and thereby liquidate his position.

Short hedge. The process whereby a cash dealer will buy cash commodities and rather than hold them unprotected will simultaneously sell the futures option which corresponds with his cash position for price protection.

Short squeeze. A term used to describe a situation when the traders who are short in the market are unable to buy the actual cash commodity to deliver and are, therefore, forced to go into the futures pit and buy futures contracts to liquidate their positions often at substantially higher prices than they may wish to pay for those contracts under normal conditions.

Soil bank. A program of the federal government to take land out of production and retire it from active use in order to maintain relatively limited production of agricultural crops and thereby high prices for farmers.

Speculation. The process of buying and selling in which the participant hopes to make a financial profit by his efforts.

Speculative investments. Investments which a trader makes with the understanding that by doing so he is undertaking a high degree of risk.

Spot commodity. The actual cash commodity traded in the cash markets. The same term as "actuals."

Spot price. The price at which the actual cash commodity is traded in the cash markets.

Spreads and straddles. A term used to describe a situation when a trader buys one commodity futures contract and sells another commodity futures contract (either of the same commodity or related commodities) in the hopes of making a financial profit from a widening of the relationship between these two commodity contracts or commodities.

Stop order (Stop-Loss Order). An open order given to a brokerage firm to liquidate your commodity position when a certain price has been reached in order to place a limit on the loss you wish to absorb from that position.

Switch. A term, also known as "rolling forward" used to describe the act whereby a holder of one commodity contract will liquidate his position in that contract and place it in another contract, such as the liquidation of March corn and the buying of May corn, in the hopes that May will rise in price at a greater rate than will March.

Tape trader. A commodity trader who closely watches the price ranges of the day and takes positions, usually short term, based upon his interpretation as to whether the market appears to be strong or weak.

Technical rally and technical decline. A situation when a market has made a very substantial price advance or decline in a very short period of time so that many traders have earned very significant profits. The market will often reverse itself for a few trading sessions merely to correct the rapid move and may be the result of those traders with profits realizing them.

Tender. The process whereby a party who is short in the futures market makes delivery upon his short position by tendering the actual commodity in the form of a warehouse receipt.

Terminal elevator. A major grain storage facility usually at key points in the United States where commodities come from wide points of distribution to be stored until ready for overseas shipment or processing domestically.

Ticker tape. The tape in the broker's office which describes the commodities which were traded during the day and the prices at which they were traded. It is usually compiled by Western Union and distributed throughout the United States moments after the actual trades occur.

Trading limit. A term used to describe either the limit on the trading range for a session or the limit on the number of contracts which a single commodity trader may hold.

Trading range. (See *Range.*)

Trading session. That period of time during a single day when commodity futures contracts are traded. The period of time from the opening of trading until the closing of trading.

Transfer notice. The same as delivery notice. The indication by a short in the futures market that he intends to make delivery on his contracts and indicating the time and place at which he intends to make such delivery.

Trend. The general price direction of the prices of a particular commodity, either up or down or sideways.

USDA. U.S. Department of Agriculture.

Variation margin. The term used to describe a situation where a paper loss has resulted in an original commodity position to such an extent that the brokerage firm no longer feels secure with the original margin and will require that the client put up additional "margin" to protect the house against the paper loss.

Variation margin call. The actual call by the brokerage house for more margin capital.

Visible supply. The amount of a commodity which can be located throughout the United States at the major known storage points. The actual commodity which can be counted and computed accurately.

Volume of trade. The number of contracts which are bought and sold during any trading period, day, week, month, year, and so on.

Warehouse receipt. A slip of paper tendered by a short in the futures market indicating that at a particular warehouse a certain amount of commodities are stored in the name of the seller and by tendering the negotiable warehouse receipt he is in effect tendering the actual commodity to whomever may be long in the futures market.

Wash sales. An illegal and fictitious transaction whereby certain persons will simultaneously buy and sell commodities to indicate an actual market and market price for the purpose of tax evasion.

Weak hands. A term commonly used by people who believe the market will decline further since the parties with long positions are not bona fide hedgers and will not accept delivery.

Index

Last trading day, 77
Leg, spreading, 142
Leverage, 7; *see also* Pyramiding
Limit order, 83
Limited risk; *see* Spreading and spreads *and* Stop orders
Limits, daily trading, 75-77, 80
Liquidation; *see* Orders
Liquidity, market, 42
Livestock and Meat Situation report, 124, 125
Loan program, 117
Loan rate, 118
Long the market, speculator as, 29, 74, 79
Losing position, 283
Losses, limit; *see* Stop orders
Losses, paper, 55
Lumber contract, 92, 96
Luck, effect of in trading, 23

M

Managed accounts, 68
Manipulation, as felony, 29, 80
Margins, commodity, 32, 57, 59, 60-62
  call, 57, 282
  maintenance, 57
  maximum formula, 62
  spread, 58
  stock versus commodity, 58, 61
Market analysis, 21, 107, 239-40
Market if tendered order, 84
Market if touched order, 83
Market order, 83
Mechanics of commodity trading, 71
Melamed, Leo, 46-47
Merrill Lynch, Pierce, Fenner & Smith, 51, 62, 66, 67
Metals, orders, 85
Minneapolis Grain Exchange, 142
Mix, trading, 53
Model, random walk, 231
Monthly statement, 64, 65
Moving averages, 249
Mutual funds, 68
Myths, commodity, 24

N

Naked positions, 58
Negative carrying charge; *see* Inversions
New Deal, 117
New Delhi, India, 102
New Orleans, 102, 103
New York Cocoa Exchange, 126
New York Coffee and Sugar Exchange, 72
New York Commodity Exchange, 113
New York Cotton Exchange, 26, 97
New York Journal of Commerce, 122
New York Mercantile Exchange, 88
New York Stock Exchange, 3, 14, 19, 64, 85
Newsletter, commodity, 69
Nigeria, cocoa market, 53
Nominal price, 155
Normal price relationship, 93-96
Notice, first day, 77

O

OCO order, 84
Oats market, 80, 141
Occupation of commodity traders, 36, 37, 42-44, 46
Odd lot trading, 64, 74

Odds, commodity, 261
Oils; *see* Soybean oil market
Onions, legislation, 150-52
Open interest, 32, 33, 48, 49, 98, 146-50, 250, 251
Opening order, 83
Orange juice market, 13, 20, 26, 80, 85, 126, 139, 195-200, 227
Orders
  execution, 85
  types of, 83, 309-40
Outsiders, 232

P

Pacific Coast Commodity Exchange, 6
Pacific Coast Stock Exchange, 85
Palladium market, 53, 56
Paper profits, 55
Parity, 117
Phones, direct to floor, 68
Pit traders, 35, 39, 86
Pit trading, 71, 73, 79
Planting intentions, 111, 117
Platinum market, 63, 82
Plywood market, 14, 15, 53
Poker playing, 32, 55
Pork belly market, 30, 74, 80, 88, 133, 140, 201-8, 259, 286
Portland, Oregon, 102
Position limits, 21, 23
Position management, 281-94
Potato market, 80, 88, 126, 151, 257
Poultry and Egg Situation report, 124
Power of attorney, 68
Premiums and discounts, 93, 96
Price averaging, 283
Price forecasting, 239
Price fluctuations, 75
Price support programs, 117, 119
Pricing, commodity, 107
Princeton University, investments, 54
Production; *see* Fundamentals in commodity analysis
Profit and loss calculation, 292-94
Profit and losses versus occupation of traders, 46
Profit potential, in commodities, 14
Propane market, 53, 85
Public speculator, 40
Pyramiding, effect of, 7, 13

R

Racetrack, speculation at, 32
Random price movements, 26, 227, 240
Random walk, 227-35, 240
Range, price and trading, 75, 239
Records, 64, 65
Recourse, 79
Regulated commodities, 80
Regulation; *see* Commodity Exchange Authority
Reporting levels, 22, 48, 76
Requirements for healthy markets, 50
Resistance levels, 244
Resting areas, 245
Resting orders; *see* Orders
Retail prices, 113
Reverse crush, 114
Risk assumption, 15, 54, 100, 132
Risk reward ratio, 14
Romania, 100
Rotterdam, 102